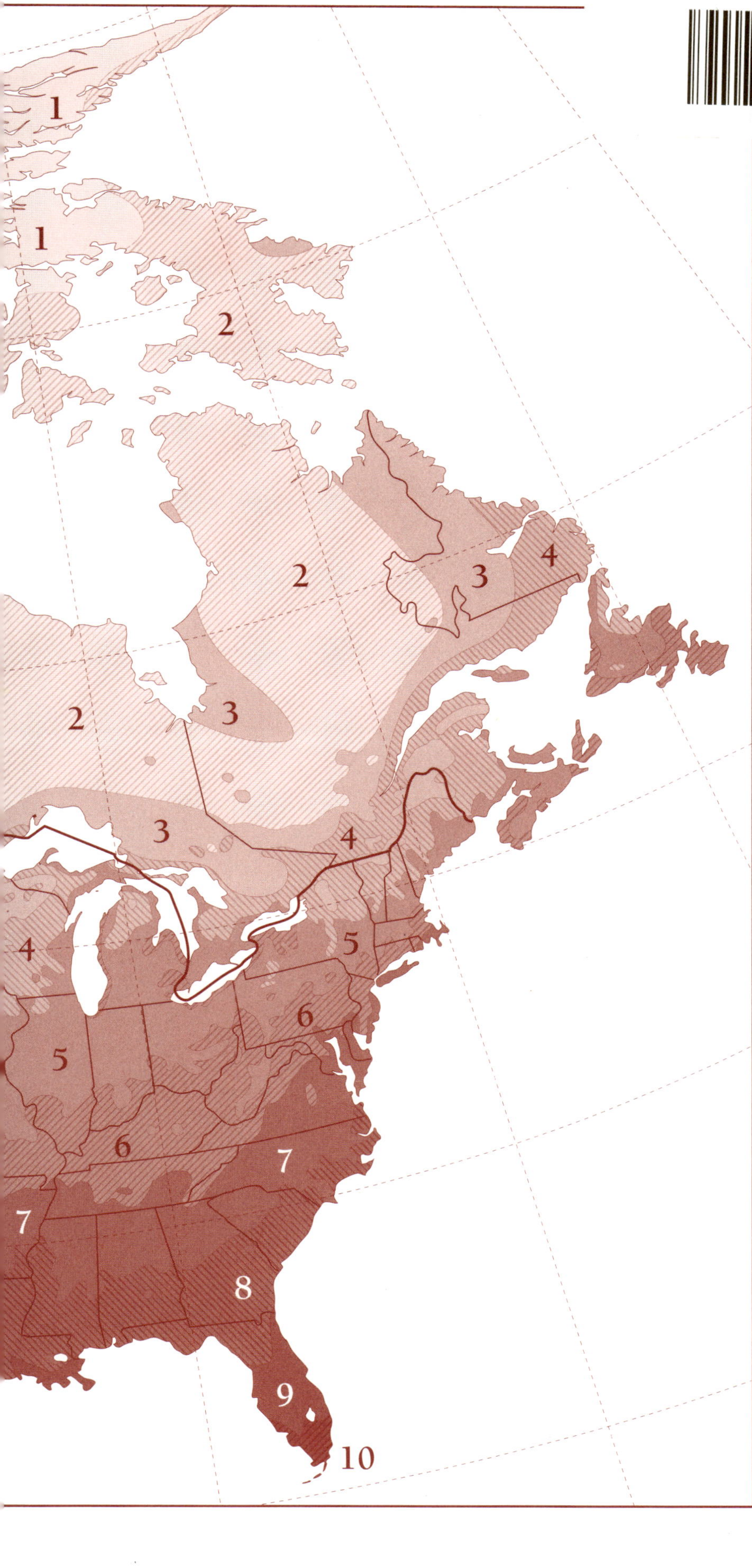

…cal
…l
…for
the years 1974 to 1986. The zone numbers accompanying the plants in this book indicate their lower limits of winter cold hardiness. Extreme summer heat and humidity also play a part in a plant's adaptability; many plants hardy in colder zones grow poorly in warmer, wetter ones.

Zone	Temperature
1	Below –50°F Below –46°C
2	–50° to –40°F –46° to –40°C
3	–40° to –30°F –40° to –34°C
4	–30° to –20°F –34° to –29°C
5	–20° to –10°F –29° to –23°C
6	–10° to 0°F –23° to –18°C
7	0° to 10°F –18° to –12°C
8	10° to 20°F –12° to –7°C
9	20° to 30°F –7° to –1°C
10	30° to 40°F –1° to 4°C
11	Above 40°F Above 4°C

READER'S DIGEST

PLANT PROPAGATION

READER'S DIGEST

PLANT PROPAGATION

ALAN TOOGOOD
Editor-in-chief

PETER ANDERSON
Photography

Reader's Digest

The Reader's Digest Association (Canada) Ltd.
MONTREAL

A DK PUBLISHING BOOK
www.dk.com

PROJECT EDITOR ANNELISE EVANS
PROJECT ART EDITOR CLARE SHEDDEN

US EDITOR RAY ROGERS

EDITORIAL ASSISTANT MARTHA SWIFT
DESIGN ASSISTANT FAY SINGER
DTP DESIGNER MATTHEW GREENFIELD

MANAGING EDITOR LOUISE ABBOTT
MANAGING ART EDITOR LEE GRIFFITHS

PRODUCTION PATRICIA HARRINGTON

ILLUSTRATIONS KAREN COCHRANE
CHAPTER OPENING MOTIFS SARAH YOUNG

SPECIAL THANKS TO THE STAFF AT
THE ROYAL HORTICULTURAL SOCIETY AND TO
DR. H. MARC CATHEY, AMERICAN HORTICULTURAL SOCIETY

Published in Canada in 1999 by
The Reader's Digest Association (Canada) Ltd.
1125 Stanley Street, Montreal, Quebec H3B 5H5

For information on this and other Reader's Digest products
or to request a catalogue, please call our 24-hour
Customer Service hotline at 1-800-465-0780

You can also visit us on the World Wide Web at
http://www.readersdigest.ca

Canadian Cataloguing in Publication Data
Main entry under title:
Plant propagation

Includes index.
ISBN 0-88850-673-2

1. Plant propagation. I. Anderson, Peter II. Toogood, Alan R.

SB119.P56 1999 635'.043 C98-901309-X

LEGAL NOTICE
Some named cultivars are protected under plant patent laws.
Gardeners are free to propagate such plants for their own purposes,
but it is illegal to propagate them for commercial gain. Protected
plants are usually indicated on the nursery tag or label.

Color reproduction by GRB Editrice, Verona, Italy
Printed and bound by Star Standard, Singapore
99 00 01 02 / 5 4 3 2 1

CONTENTS

HOW TO USE THIS BOOK

This book opens with a general introduction to plant propagation, explaining how practical techniques were, and continue to be, developed; how they relate to natural ways of plant reproduction; the influence of the climate and the propagation environment; how to use appropriate tools, equipment, and growing media; and common problems affecting propagated material.

The chapters that follow explain practical techniques and are arranged according to plant type: these adhere to botanical classification, so that each chapter discusses only true members of the type. For example, short-lived perennial plants grown as annuals may be found in the Perennials chapter. Woody climbing plants are included with shrubs, to which they are closely associated. Other climbers may be bulbous, annuals, or succulents and are discussed in relevant chapters. Fruits also fall into various plant groups, such as perennials, shrubs, and trees. The Bulbous Plants chapter covers corms, bulbs, and tubers; few rhizomes are true storage organs, so rhizomatous plants appear in the Perennials chapter. Alpine and water garden plants are artificial groupings based on their cultivation; since most such plants are perennials, they are featured in the Perennials chapter. Culinary herbs are included in the Vegetables chapter; other herbs are described where relevant.

Each practical chapter begins with basic techniques specific to the plant type in question and then details the finer points of propagation of many genera, plant by plant. Features on special-interest plants also appear in these chapters. Some popular genera with diverse habits (for example, some species may be trees, others shrubs) may have entries in more than one chapter.

PROPAGATION TECHNIQUE RATINGS

The rating system in the plant-by-plant A–Z dictionaries provides the reader with a quick reference to the relative ease or difficulty of each method of propagation that is listed for any particular genus. The ratings are as follows:

easy — moderate — challenging

BASIC TECHNIQUES

Each chapter has a detailed introduction explaining the basic principles and general techniques of propagation that may be broadly applied to the plant group covered by the chapter.

Methods in all or some of the following categories are covered according to their relevance to the plant group: sowing seeds, division, taking cuttings, layering, and grafting. Techniques particular to the plant group also are described.

The relative merits of different techniques are discussed, as well as gathering and preparation of propagation material, suitable growing media, practicalities of the technique, providing a favorable environment, factors that affect the success rate, and care of new plants up to the stage of planting out.

Standardized headings in each chapter cover basic categories of propagation

Photographic gallery illustrates range of features common to plants covered by chapter

Supplementary illustrations draw attention to additional points of interest

General principles of each technique as it applies to plants covered by chapter are explained

Reduced color indicates material to be discarded when preparing cuttings

Annotations highlight important details

Examples of commercial practice clarify methods that benefit gardeners

Text box discusses techniques or background information of particular interest

Step-by-step sequences explain how to carry out illustrated techniques

Tinted box indicates alternative to one or more of steps in technique illustrated

Photographic insets focus on details of each technique

Material is shown before and after preparation

FEATURES

Most chapters contain features on popular and botanically interesting plant groups. These are palms and cycads, conifers, heaths and heathers, roses, ferns, alpine plants, water garden plants, bromeliads, ornamental grasses, orchids, and culinary herbs.

Each feature focuses on modes of propagation that are peculiar to the featured plants, describing their characteristic ways of reproduction and how these are exploited in various techniques. The techniques are fully illustrated with step-by-step photographs and explanatory artworks. The plants' special needs are discussed, with tips on how to achieve success.

Further details of individual plants are given in A–Z listings in most features. Individual entries for conifers and alpine plants, both large and varied groups, are included in the main A–Z dictionaries of their chapters.

Tinted border indicates feature spread

Feature heading

Annotations highlight important details

Captions describe step by step exactly what to do

A–Z listing gives specific details on propagating popular or interesting plants in group covered by feature

Comparative illustrations show difference between good and bad propagation material

Text describes in detail special techniques and tips that particularly relate to the group of plants covered in each feature

Cross-section artworks illustrate how techniques take effect

A–Z DICTIONARIES

Practical chapters each include a plant-by-plant dictionary arranged alphabetically by botanical names and describing a range of genera in the plant group. These include genera that are commonly grown in various climates, are propagated in unusual ways, or need special care.

Entries are of varying lengths for different genera, according to the number and complexity of ways in which each is propagated. At the top of each entry, possible methods, when they may be undertaken, and easiness ratings are summarized for easy reference. Within each entry, guidance is given on the merits of each method covered to enable the reader to choose the most suitable. Where needed, individual species, hybrids, or cultivars are discussed.

Special methods not covered in the chapter's basic techniques are fully explained and illustrated in relevant entries. Cross-references are given to basic techniques or similar genera. Each spread also lists many additional genera, with concise details on how they are increased.

Vegetable chapter has index of common names

A–Z entries on specific genera in alphabetical order of botanical names; common names of the genus are given where relevant

Charts or tables in some chapters summarize important details such as when and how to sow seeds or which rootstock to use

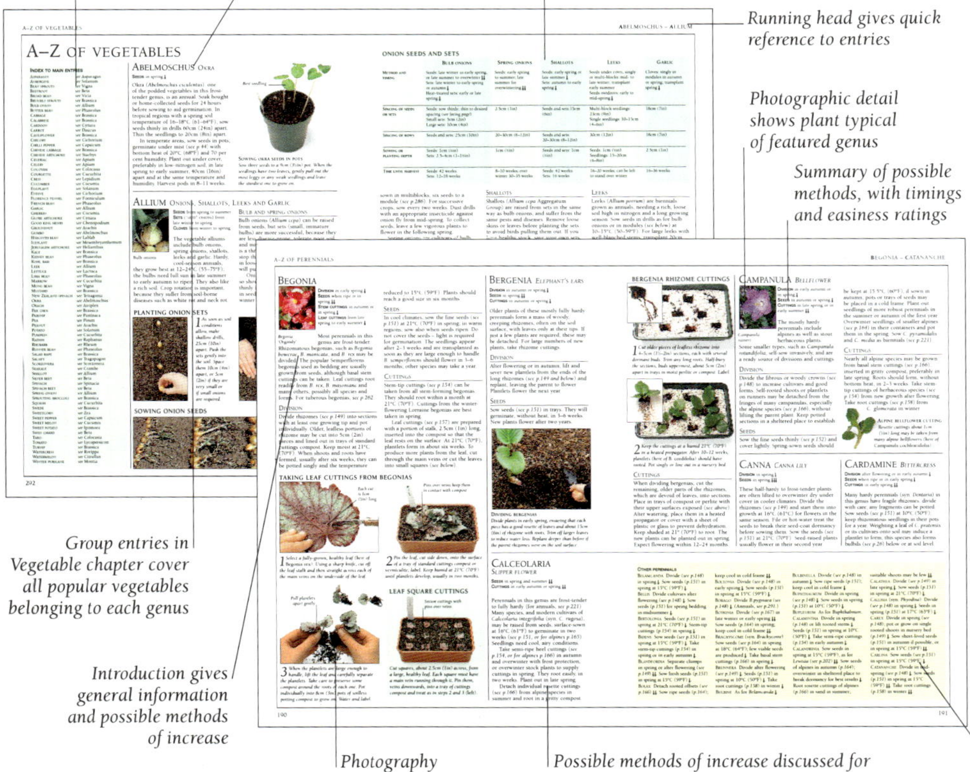

Running head gives quick reference to entries

Photographic detail shows plant typical of featured genus

Summary of possible methods, with timings and easiness ratings

Group entries in Vegetable chapter cover all popular vegetables belonging to each genus

Introduction gives general information and possible methods of increase

Photography illustrates techniques relevant to individual genus or species

Possible methods of increase discussed for each genus, cross-referenced to the relevant basic technique and including special tips on the genus or species within it

Listing gives concise details on propagating other genera

INTRODUCTION

An understanding of the ways in which plants grow and reproduce, and of the relevance and application of practical techniques, will allow the gardener to propagate plants with ease and confidence

The art of propagation is as old as civilization: from the beginning, farmers and gardeners have observed, learned, and adapted from nature to perfect ways of increasing plants in cultivation. The parallels between plant reproduction in the wild and long-established methods of propagation are here described, as well as the advances made with the help of modern technology that may influence the way we garden in the future.

The practice of propagation is always easier if based on a thorough understanding of how plants function. The mechanisms of both sexual reproduction (from seeds) and asexual or vegetative reproduction (such as layering) are explained and illustrated in detail to show how the techniques of propagation are applied, in what ways they improve on natural methods, and why they are successful.

The practicalities of propagation are also dealt with: suitable tools for the various tasks are illustrated, together with the range of containers that are used in propagation. The importance of the growing medium is recognized, with a survey of the types of ingredients, soil mixes, and other media that may be used, and their relative merits. Advice is also given on how to make suitable soil mixes at home.

Climate has a great influence on propagation, how it is done, what plants may be increased, and the likelihood of success. For instance, in colder climates, much propagation is carried out under cover, perhaps with artificial heat, whereas in warm or tropical regions, plants are easily raised in the open garden. The main types of climates and the consequent differences in propagation are summarized, with a full-color map.

Success in propagation usually depends on providing a supportive environment for the plant material and, later, for the new plants. Their special needs – and ways of supplying them, whether in the home, the open garden, or in a greenhouse – are discussed and amply illustrated. Finally, problems that are likely to affect plants at this stage are listed, together with ways to combat them.

REGAL FERN
The magnificent royal fern, Osmunda regalis, *may be raised from spores or propagated vegetatively. Spores must be sown quickly because they become nonviable after three days. Mature plants form clumps that may be divided.*

ANNUAL SEEDPOD
Like all annuals, Love-in-a-mist (Nigella damascena) *is raised from seeds. These are contained in attractive, inflated seed capsules. When the seeds ripen, each capsule splits open to scatter the seeds at the foot of the plant.*

LEARNING FROM NATURE

Plants have evolved a fascinating array of reproductive strategies in order to survive and increase and to colonize new ground. They have adapted to a wide range of adverse habitats, such as deserts (*see below*), high altitudes where winds damage foliage and discourage pollinating insects, and even water, where problems are completely different.

Since the dawn of civilization, the farmer and gardener have used their observations of plant reproduction in the wild to develop propagation methods in cultivation. All plant reproduction is by seeds (sexual reproduction) or by vegetative (asexual) methods.

REPRODUCTION FROM SEEDS

Sexual reproduction remains the most important method of increase for many plants (*see pp.16–21*). Genetic material from a male and female parent of one species (preferably on different plants) unites in the seed or spore. The seed embryo forms a new plant that often looks the same as the parents but has a different genetic makeup to either.

This capacity for evolution enables plants to adapt over a period of time to environmental changes or to colonize areas originally hostile to the species. Another advantage of producing seeds is that the plant embryos are able to lie dormant in hostile conditions, such as drought or winter, delaying the next stage of reproduction until favorable conditions occur.

Sexual reproduction can give rise to botanical subspecies or varieties, whose characteristics deviate to some degree from the parent species. This is most marked in mountainous areas where some plants become isolated on a valley floor or alpine peak from the more widespread species. The potential for variation is more dramatic where plants are isolated by water, creating colonies on separate islands. Geographical isolation can also result in endemism: a species limited to one locality (*see right*).

In contrast, where two species from the same genus grow in the same area, they may cross-breed to produce natural hybrids. *Arbutus* x *andrachnoides* grows wild in Greece and is a hybrid of two species, *Arbutus andrachne* and *A. unedo*.

In the wild, plants disperse hundreds or even millions of seeds in order that a few seedlings might survive to maturity. In cultivation, a high yield of good-quality seedlings may be obtained more quickly by providing them with as ideal an environment as possible (*see* The Propagation Environment, *pp.38–45*).

Humankind has also benefited from the genetic diversity of seeds, selecting forms that may have died out in the wild and developing from them plants with immense value in cultivation (*see* The Evolution of Bread Wheat, *facing page*). Seeds offer the potential to introduce an exciting range of plants with new forms of flower and leaf, hardiness, habit, adaptability for specific conditions, and resistance to pests and diseases.

However, seedlings may not be as suited to local conditions in the wild, or as garden-worthy in cultivation, as the parents. This risk can be reduced by the gardener, to some extent, by using seeds from known sources, where good-quality parents are selected and grown away from possible pollen contamination from inferior plants. Some seeds have a deep-seated or complex dormancy (*see p.19*), as in *Davidia involucrata*, where seeds do not always germinate in any quantity in

ENDEMIC PLANT *The desert rose (*Adenium obesum *subsp.* socotranum*) is found only on the small island of Socotra, off the northeast African coast. The isle has been isolated from the continent for 1.6 million years and has over 250 endemic species.*

▲ SAFETY IN NUMBERS Echium wildpretii *colonizes the stony, dry hills of the Canary Islands by producing huge quantities of seeds.*

► DESERT DENIZEN Welwitschia mirabilis *survives in the harsh deserts of southwestern Africa by collecting dew on its two leaves. The leaves are 6ft (2m) or more and channel dew into the ground above the plant's huge taproot. Each plant is either male or female so can only reproduce if a plant of the opposite sex is nearby.*

one season or may take several years to reproduce. Other species may fail to produce seeds at all or yield seeds with low viability, such as *Acer griseum*.

Vegetative reproduction

Nature has overcome the limitations of seeds by adopting asexual reproduction also, producing offspring (clones) that are genetically identical to the parent. Plants have many ways of increasing vegetatively from modified roots or stems. The simplest is by forming a mass, or crown, of shoots and buds, each capable of being a separate plant.

Some plants can regenerate shoots or roots from growth tissue to produce new plants (runners or layers). Others form specialized organs, including stem tubers (potatoes), corms (crocuses) and pseudobulbs (*Cymbidium* orchids), that store food (*see pp.25–7*). This enables a plant to survive unfavorable conditions and save energy for reproduction when favorable conditions occur.

Vegetative reproduction allows some plants to colonize an area more rapidly than by seeds, as any gardener who has encountered quack, or witch, grass (*Agropyron repens*) knows. It is also useful to plants at the fringes of their natural habitat, where flowering and seed production are difficult. Blackberries (*Rubus fruticosus*) rarely flower in dappled woodland, but they spread rapidly by tip layering (*see p.24*).

Gardeners have adapted natural vegetative, or clonal, reproduction to obtain plants that are always "true" to the parent (*see pp.22–27*). Methods such as division of herbaceous plants are even more reliable than seeds. Artificial ways of increase, such as by cuttings or air layering, have also been developed by exploiting plants' regenerative abilities.

Clonal propagation carries dangers, however. Genetically identical plants carry the same susceptibility to disease. The large UK population of English elms (*Ulmus procera*) was destroyed in the 1960–70s by Dutch elm disease. The trees usually reproduce by root suckers so were represented by just a few genetically different clones. If the elms had increased by seeds, they may have varied enough genetically for resistant trees to have occurred.

Learning from nature

Most plants have the capacity to increase sexually and asexually, which avoids disasters similar to that suffered by the English elm. This benefits gardeners, who can choose a propagation method to suit their needs and the capacity of each plant to reproduce in the local conditions.

The plant family can be a useful guide: plants in the same family often reproduce similarly. For example, most plants in the Gesneriaceae, such as African violets (*Saintpaulia*), *Columnea*, *Ramonda*, and *Streptocarpus* readily regenerate from leaf tissue. The Menthaceae, including coleus (*Solenostemon*), sage (*Salvia*), *Lamium*, and rosemary, root easily from stem cuttings – in the wild, stems close to moist soil produce roots.

Another factor is the plant's natural limit of distribution; often reproductive ability declines outside this area (*see pp.36–7*). This may be countered by providing controlled conditions (*see* The Propagation Environment, *pp.38–45*).

From the wild to the garden
Species can be increased selectively in cultivation to produce plants that bear little resemblance to wild species. Meadow tulips, such as Tulipa australis *(see far left), have been hybridized over many years to produce thousands of showy, large-bloomed cultivars, such as* Tulipa *'Estella Rijnveld' (left).*

Natural graft
In the wild, grafts can occur between woody plants of related, thin-barked species if they grow in close proximity. Two branches on one plant may grow together, as on this Parrotia. *Grafting has been copied in cultivation as a way of propagation, although it occurs in nature accidentally, not as a true mode of reproduction.*

THE EVOLUTION OF BREAD WHEAT

The turning point for agriculture in the Old World probably came in the Middle East in 8,000 BC. A wild goat grass crossed with wild wheat (*Triticum monococcum*) to form a rare, fertile hybrid with a larger ear. The hybrid, called emmer (*Triticum dicoccum*), was cultivated by the ancient Greeks and Romans because of its increased yields. In a second genetic accident, emmer crossed with another goat grass: the new fertile hybrid, with larger ears, was bread wheat. For two consequent hybrids to be fertile is an amazing coincidence.

The wild grasses, including emmer, had long, thin stalks which snapped easily and ears which broke up into grains attached to husks and were carried on the wind. This helped natural distribution of seeds, but made harvesting difficult.

Bread wheat had shorter, sturdier stalks and ears that did not disintegrate. The ears must be broken by thrashing, and the husks removed as chaff while the plump grains fall to the ground. Therefore bread wheat needs help for its distribution and man and plant have come together for mutual benefit.

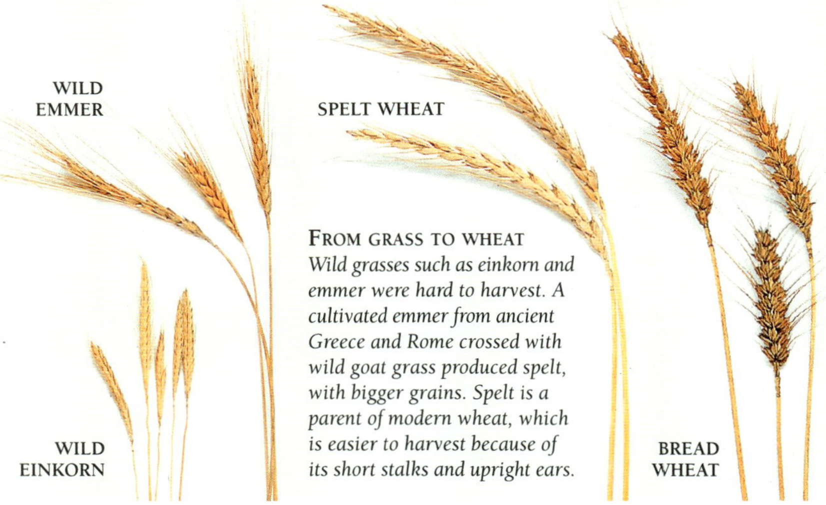

From grass to wheat
Wild grasses such as einkorn and emmer were hard to harvest. A cultivated emmer from ancient Greece and Rome crossed with wild goat grass produced spelt, with bigger grains. Spelt is a parent of modern wheat, which is easier to harvest because of its short stalks and upright ears.

Propagation in the Past

The cultivation and propagation of plants began when human tribes abandoned their nomadic, hunter-gatherer way of life to live in settled communities. This change occurred just after the last ice age and marked the beginning of modern civilization. It is often referred to as the "agricultural revolution" but appears to have been mainly the result of a remarkable genetic accident that led to the development of bread wheat (*see p.11*). This biological miracle took place in about 8,000 BC in the Middle East and was the trigger for the advent of farming.

Ancient civilizations throughout the world grew a wide range of food crops, including grains, from seeds, after noting how plants naturally dispersed seeds that later produced seedlings. In ancient Greek and Roman times, writers such as the poet Virgil recorded current methods of propagation in some detail. Olives, date palms, and cypresses were grown from seeds, as well as other food plants such as cabbages, turnips, lettuces, and herbs. To speed up germination, the Greeks soaked seeds in milk or honey. Seeds were also protected with thin sheets of mica or a form of bell glass.

Aaron's rod
Biblical references to propagating plants, such as Aaron's rod, abound. Moses placed staves from the 12 leaders of the Israelites in the tabernacle: "and behold, the rod of Aaron ... was budded, and brought forth buds, and bloomed blossoms and yielded almonds" (Numbers 17: 8), and so Aaron was chosen. This is probably one of the earliest recorded examples of a hardwood cutting.

Origins of vegetative propagation

Propagation from cuttings began when rooted shoots or suckers were detached and replanted. This led to propagation from unrooted cuttings. Romans dipped the bases of cuttings in ox manure to stimulate rooting. In the Middle East, settlers discovered how to propagate superior forms of grapes, olives, and figs to preserve their desirable characteristics by thrusting woody stems into the soil.

By 2,000 BC, grafting was fairly common in Greece, the Middle East, Egypt, and China. The earliest form of grafting was probably approach grafting, because it has a high success rate. The branch of one tree, while still attached to the parent tree, was securely attached to the branch of another tree after the bark of each branch had been wounded. This mimics natural grafting (*see p.11*) and illustrates how closely people were observing nature. Grafting was used to propagate plants that were difficult to root from cuttings and to encourage early fruiting.

The Romans were among the first to practise detached scion-grafting (*see also p.27*), where a piece of the chosen plant is removed and inserted into a cut in a rootstock, selected to provide vigor for the grafted plant. They used a variety of methods and may have even grafted a single rootstock with a number of different fruit cultivars, such as apples, to produce what is now known as a multiple tree (*see p.57*). The Romans and ancient Chinese also employed the technique of budding (*see p.27*).

Other natural vegetative reproduction methods were exploited by propagating from food-storage organs such as bulbs, tubers, and rhizomes (*see pp.25–27*). Plants increased in this way included onion and garlic (Mediterranean), sugar cane (tropical Africa), banana (India and Indonesia), potato and pineapple (South America), and bamboo (Asia).

Simple layering was adapted from natural layering of wild plants (*see p.24*). Records show that the Romans were layering grapes in the 1st century BC. Air layering (*see p.25*) probably began to be used 4,000 years ago in China; it is often still referred to as Chinese layering.

Toward the dawn of the first century AD, plant propagation practices were already well-established. Throughout the centuries that followed, these early propagation techniques were continually developed and improved.

Ancient Egyptian farming
This wall painting of Semedjem and his wife in the Valley of the Nobles, Thebes, shows that sowing grain seeds in drills was practiced in ancient Egypt. The mixed orchard of palms and olive trees (below) was probably grown from seeds or cuttings.

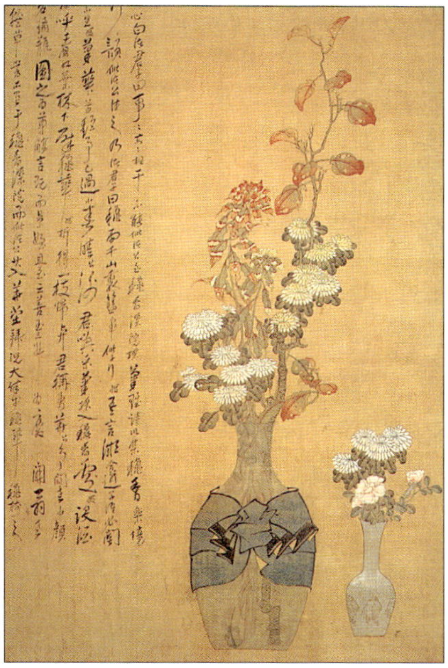

CHINESE CHRYSANTHEMUM
The ancient Chinese were expert gardeners, particularly in the art of hybridization. Hybrids of treasured plants such as the chrysanthemum were created for the delight of Emperors.

THE POWER OF MANURE

Providing bottom heat for propagation is easy today with the aid of electricity, but solid-fueled boilers and hot-water pipes were cumbersome and expensive in earlier times. One way of giving plants bottom heat, for propagation and forcing early crops, was the "hot bed," which came to prominence in the Victorian era. This ingenious but simple system relied on heat generated by microbial action on a mixture of equal parts fresh manure and deciduous leaves.

The hot bed consisted of a glazed frame placed in a pit, approximately 3ft (90cm) deep and 18in (45cm) longer and wider than the dimensions of the frame, filled with the manure mix. To activate the manure before filling the pit, the manure and leaves were thoroughly mixed, moistened, and left for about two weeks. The pile was turned three or four times during this period to ensure even heating. It was then placed in the pit, firmed, and watered. The frame was placed on top and soil added to a depth of 8in (20cm), to spread the heat. Pots and trays of cuttings or seeds were placed on the soil.

Hot beds are becoming popular again as gardeners realize the value of heat from decomposition. For anyone with access to manure, and the space for a large pit, they are practical, organic, and cheap (*see p.41*). A hot bed made in spring releases heat for up to eight weeks. Manure with high straw content releases less heat, but over a longer period.

HOT BED
Victorians gardeners often used hot beds like this restored one in Cornwall, England, for propagation and for raising tender vegetables or fruits (here pineapples) in winter.

VICTORIAN INFLUENCES

An explosion of plant-hunting took place in the western world in the 18th and 19th centuries. A wealth of new and exciting plants were discovered and traded between Europe and Japan, China, the East Indies, Australasia, Africa, North America, Mexico, and South America. New introductions arrived as seeds, bulbs, or even plants.

Enthusiasm for these new plants and the desire to grow and propagate them, coupled with the financial wealth of the plant collectors, was the inspiration for the golden age of the greenhouse (*see right*). Victorians were very inventive in both the construction and design. Their methods of controlling temperature and levels of light and humidity in the growing environment of the glasshouse were impressively complex.

The greenhouse enabled the creative use of propagation methods and the refinement of techniques. The role of "propagator" became important for any garden of note. Initially, trial and error must have been used when attempting to increase stocks of each unfamiliar plant. Propagators were proud of their new knowledge and often guarded it jealously to secure their reputations and future employment. This may be the origin of the mystique which often surrounds plant propagation even today.

The propagation equipment that was available to Victorian gardeners was fairly primitive compared to modern advances, yet their ideas still form the basis of what is done today. They used cold frames and hot beds (*see above*) to control temperature and humidity. Cold frames, sited to capture as much warmth as possible from the sun, especially in winter, were used for seeds, root cuttings, and easy stem cuttings.

Bell jars were used in great numbers. The bell-shaped glass jars, about 18in (45cm) tall, were placed over cuttings in prepared soil or in pots. Although difficult to control precisely, it was possible to maintain high humidity inside the bell jars. Warmth was provided by solar radiation. Bell jars were effective for raising small quantities of plants from seeds, stem or root cuttings, and even grafted plants. Today, bell jars have largely been replaced by more versatile cloches (*see p.39*).

Toward the end of the 19th century, gardeners split the base of a cutting and placed a wheat seed inside the cut stem before inserting the cutting in soil mix. As the wheat seed absorbed water and began to germinate, it released growth-promoting substances. These helped the cutting root more easily and with more vigor. The practice became obsolete after 1940, following the introduction of synthetic rooting hormones, or auxins (*see p.30*).

Gardeners also understood the need for seed treatments such as scarification; in the days of fob watches, pea seeds were carried in the vest pocket so they became scratched by the watch.

GLORIOUS GREENHOUSES
With the advent of the heated greenhouse in 18th-century Europe, temperature, light, and humidity could be controlled. This extended the range of plants that could be propagated, as in this tropical greenhouse, c. 1870.

MODERN PROPAGATION

Since the 1950s, modern technology and an increase in the exchange of information among professionals has led to the development of new propagation techniques for the first time in centuries. These new methods, together with modern equipment, make propagation much easier today. Continuing research regularly opens up more possibilities in propagation; these are first tested by professionals and, if they prove worthwhile, eventually benefit the gardener.

MIST PROPAGATION

The intermittent mist propagation system (*see below*) was designed in the 1950s for rooting stem cuttings, particularly of softwood and semi-ripe material. The unit provides bottom heat to stimulate rooting and constant, regulated humidity to keep the cuttings moist and cool. This advance allowed up to six batches of cuttings to be taken per bench per year, and many plants that had previously been grafted could be rooted, at a fraction of the cost.

Today, instead of a soil thermostat, digital sensors spaced evenly through the bed and linked to a central system are often used. Mist is provided when the mist-control sensor placed at the level of the cuttings indicates a fall in the moisture-film level on the cuttings. Mist propagation is widely used in commercial propagation and is useful for gardeners. If you cannot afford a dedicated unit (*see p.44*), create your own version with soil-warming cables and a misting system in a closed case.

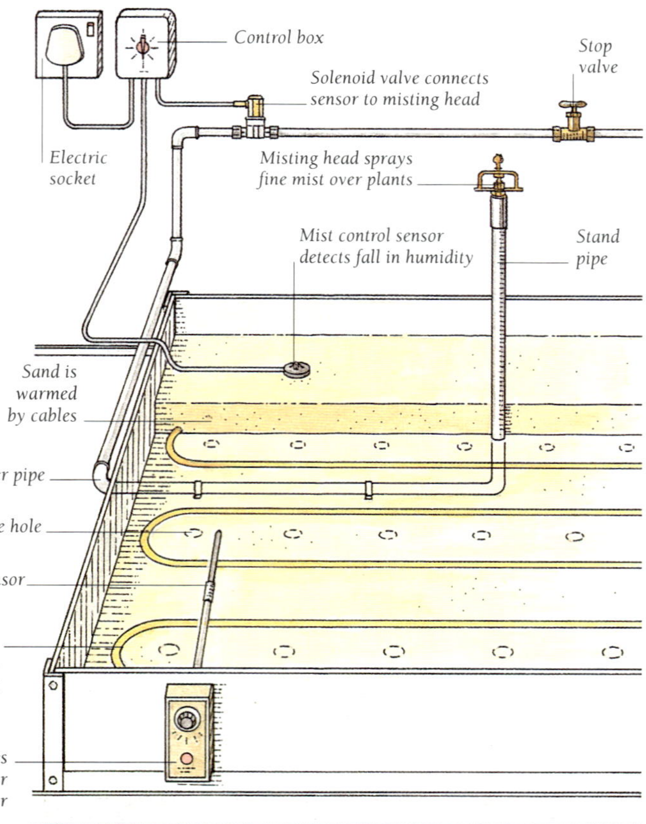

MIST PROPAGATION UNIT
This thermostatically controlled unit is self-contained and can be covered and insulated at the base and sides. It supplies bottom heat through an electrically heated bed of sand or soil mix. Bursts of fine water droplets maintain a constant film of water to prevent the cuttings from drying out.

PLASTIC FILM

Another development of the 1950s was plastic film. Cuttings are provided with bottom heat and the plastic film (a sheet of clear plastic) is draped over them in order to create a sealed environment, which maintains high humidity around the tops of the cuttings. This system is easily adopted by gardeners, although rotting can be a problem in cool temperatures. Plastic film can also be used with cold frames to warm soil before cuttings or seeds are inserted and then to cover new plants in the frame.

FOG PROPAGATION

The main development in the mid-1980s was fog propagation, which provides a much smaller water droplet than mist propagation, so that the air remains moist for a much longer period. It also avoids wetting the foliage, as in mist propagation, so is ideal for cuttings or seedlings that are prone to rot. In recent years, fog systems have been simplified and made more reliable (*see p.44*).

PREGERMINATED SEEDS
Pregerminated seeds (here of alfalfa, a cattle fodder crop) can be kept moist and supplied with nutrients by embedding them in beads of gel. The tiny seedlings grow unchecked before sowing.

SEED TREATMENTS

Seed priming exploits the natural ability of some seeds to halt development if soil conditions are unfavorable. It improves speed and uniformity of germination. Seeds are started into pregermination with a controlled amount of water and then redried just before the radicle (embryonic root) emerges. Timing of the treatment is critical. True germination does not occur until the seeds are sown.

In commerce, seeds are germinated, or chitted, until the radicle emerges, then packed, sometimes in gel (*see above*), and sent out for immediate sowing. Gardeners can also chit seeds; it is very useful for hard-coated seeds, especially of vegetables (*see p.282*).

Pelleted seeds are coated with an inert material, such as a polymer, that splits or softens on contact with water. The coating may contain fungicides, nutrients, and a fluorescent dye. The pellet makes sowing easier, particularly with small seeds, thus reducing losses.

MICROPROPAGATION

This technique, developed in the 1960s, is used to propagate huge numbers of plants from a small amount of material. It enables plants that are difficult to propagate by traditional means, new cultivars, and virus-free stocks of crop plants such as raspberries, to be made available to gardeners. To conserve plants in the wild, old and rare plants can be increased from existing stocks.

Micropropagation usually involves growing pieces of plant tissue *in vitro* (in glass) in sterile laboratory conditions (*see top of facing page*). This is possible because of the ability of most plants to regenerate from a single cell. Tissue from the shoot tip (meristem) is most often used, but root tips, calluses (which form on wounds), anthers, flower buds, leaves, seeds, or fruits may also provide suitable tissue. Temperature and levels

MICROPROPAGATING FROM PLANT CELLS

CULTURED PLANT TISSUE *Plant cells (here of tobacco) are grown on a nutrient gel until the cell mass produces embryo plants.*

CUTTING UP CULTURED TISSUE *The mass of plant tissue is cut into pieces, each with one embryo, then transferred to a rooting medium.*

ROOTING PLANTLETS *Hormones in the nutrient gel encourage the plantlets (here sundews) to produce roots and shoots like seedlings.*

YOUNG PLANTS *Plantlets (here orchids) are grown on in sealed, sterile flasks until they are large enough to transplant into pots.*

OTHER FORMS OF MICROPROPAGATION

The sterile conditions of micropropagation can be used to gain better yields and preserve disease-free stocks by adapting methods already used to increase plants. Plantlets are grown from tiny leaf cuttings; microtubers can be easily transported; orchid seeds have a much improved survival rate if protected from airborne bacteria.

AFRICAN VIOLET LEAF CUTTING

POTATO MICROTUBERS

ORCHID SEEDLINGS

of light, nutrients, and hormones are regulated in specially adapted growing rooms. The resulting plants are grown on in greenhouse conditions. Viruses and systemic disease rarely penetrate growing tips, so micropropagated plants are normally disease-free and may be safely introduced to other countries.

There are some disadvantages to micropropagation: it is costly; bacteria and viruses may not always be totally eradicated; plants may show genetic mutations; and plants may fail to adapt well to a normal growing environment.

THE FUTURE OF PROPAGATION

New scientific discoveries continue to affect plant propagation. The benefits of these techniques are not always yet available to gardeners but may be in the future. Recent innovations include genetic engineering – a controversial area – artificial seeds, and micrografting.

In genetic engineering, foreign genes with known, desirable characteristics are transferred into another plant cell (*see right*). It is possible to introduce a gene that is totally unrelated to the recipient plant – unlike natural hybridizing and traditional selective breeding, both of which also result in offspring that are genetically different to the parent plants. The technology, involving molecular biology, is very complex and not without problems. An average plant has 20,000 different genes, of which there may be five million copies in a single cell, so determining which gene is responsible for which characteristic can be difficult. The minute scale of the gene transfer operation demands special techniques. The finished cell is micropropagated to produce a stock plant for propagation.

Genetic engineering has immense potential to enhance the usefulness of existing plants and to create new ones. Current work is aimed at improving resistance of crops to disease, cold, and pests. Successes include potatoes that do not suffer cold damage and canola that yields more oil. There are concerns, however, about the consequences of introducing plants that could never occur in nature into the environment.

Naturally fertilized seeds contain genes from two parents; no two seeds are identical. It is now possible to create artificial seeds (somatic embryos) from vegetative tissue. This involves isolating embryos – grown in solution from single cells – and giving them a synthetic coating. Vast numbers of genetically uniform "seeds" can be produced, which give rise to genetically identical plants.

In micrografting, minute pieces of plant tissue are used to produce disease- and virus-free plants, especially fruit trees. First, seedling rootstocks are raised in sterile conditions. When a seedling reaches the first true leaf stage, it is micrografted with the tiny, virus-free tip (meristem) of the desired plant. After about six months, micrografts are ready for normal planting. Virus-free, micropropagated (clonal) rootstocks may also be used to avoid the variability that can occur with seedling rootstocks.

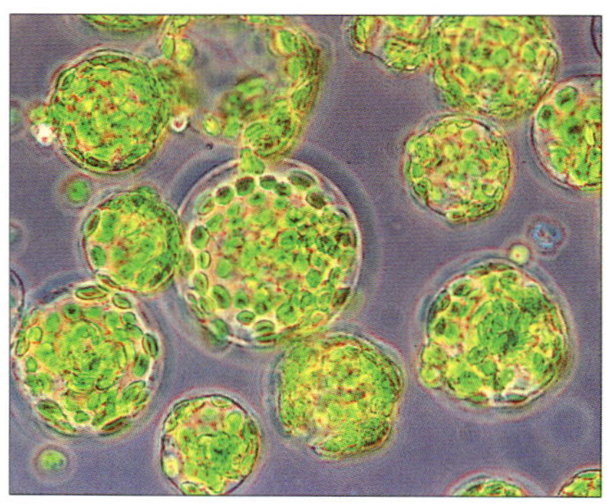

GENETIC ENGINEERING
Plant cells (here of tobacco) are chemically treated to remove their tough outer cell walls. Genes from other plant cells are then introduced into the cells, and the outer walls are regrown.

Sexual increase of plants

The seed is the basic biological unit for the reproduction of conifers (gymnosperms) and flowering plants (angiosperms). Each seed combines male and female genes in a plant embryo and gives rise to offspring that varies genetically from the parent plants. By this means, a species can preserve and perpetuate its identity yet constantly exchange genetic material within the species so that it can evolve and so adapt to changes in the environment.

Seeds also enable a plant to colonize a large area and can lie dormant until conditions are favorable, which greatly increases their chances of survival. Understanding how seeds are formed and dispersed and how they germinate is essential to successful propagation.

The structure of the flower

In angiosperms, the process of seed production begins with the flower: a structure that contains either male or female sex organs or both. Most flowers are composed of inner petals and outer sepals, collectively called tepals or perianth segments; they may show great diversity in shape and color.

The Talipot palm (*Corypha umbraculifera*) produces a massive cluster of thousands of flowers (inflorescence) at the apex of the palm. The plant is monocarpic: after flowering once, the palm dies. In contrast, the largest single flower in the world is produced by *Rafflesia*, a tropical parasite that has no leaves and blooms directly from the roots of the host plant. These flowers can measure 32in (80cm) across. Between these extremes are the flowers of more familiar garden plants such as irises and daisies.

Flower structure

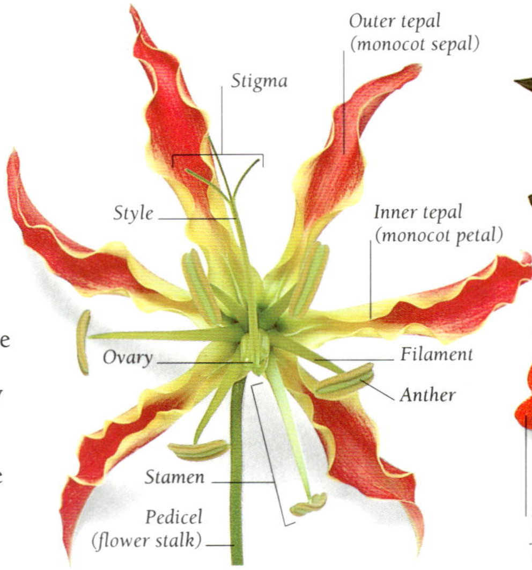

The female ovary in a monocot flower (here a gloriosa) gives rise to the seeds in a fruit. The style connects the ovary with the stigma, which receives pollen. Stamens form the male part of a flower; each is composed of a filament supporting an anther, which produces pollen.

The female reproductive part of the flower, which produces the seeds within some sort of fruit, is the ovary. The style, a slender stalk, connects the ovary with the stigma, which receives pollen. Ovary, style, and stigma form the carpel (or pistil). There may be one or several carpels, always at the center or apex of the flower. Surrounding the carpels in a bisexual flower (*see above*) are the stamens, the male part of the flower. Most stamens have a slender filament that supports the anther, where pollen is produced. Other flowers are single-sexed and have only stamens or carpels.

Sexuality of flowers

Some plants have bisexual flowers with stigmas and stamens. Other plants are monoecious, with separate male and female flowers, or dioecious, with flowers of only one sex borne on each plant.

Pollination

Before it can produce seeds, the flower must first be pollinated. Pollination is the transfer of (male) pollen from the anther to the (female) stigma. If a plant pollinates itself, instead of receiving pollen from another individual of the same species, genetic variation in the seed is reduced. The majority of plants, especially wild species, have systems to prevent self-pollination.

With some flowers, their anthers and stigmas ripen at different times, so that even if pollen drops onto the stigma of the same flower, it simply dies. Some (monoecious) species such as hazel (*Corylus*) and corn (*Zea mays*) have single-sex flowers of both sexes on the same plant. Sometimes they are on separate parts of the plant, as with corn, where the male flowers are grouped at the top of the plant to catch the wind. This favors cross-pollination, although self-pollination is still possible.

Other (dioecious) species separate male and female flowers by locating them on different individual plants. Examples include hollies (*Ilex*), poplars (*Populus*), willows (*Salix*), the shrub *Garrya elliptica*, and date palm (*Phoenix dactylifera*). Many dioecious plants are wind-pollinated. A danger of this method, in nature, is that an isolated plant may be unable to set seeds.

The disadvantage of dioecious plants for gardeners is that it may be at least five years before plants raised from

Pollinating agents

INSECTS *Many flowers, such as this loofah (*Luffa acutangula*), are large and brightly colored to attract insects such as beetles. Ripe pollen is sticky; it adheres to the beetle's carapace until it is carried to another flower.*

BATS *Several bats feed on nectar, especially in warm climates. Some cactus flowers bloom only at night and emit a powerful, foul-smelling scent especially to attract the bats. The pollen is then transported to other flowers on the bat's fur.*

seeds flower and may be sexed. Female (berrying) hollies cannot be selected for 7–20 years, for instance. In contrast, males of many willows (*Salix*) are more garden-worthy than the females because their catkins are larger and showier.

Pollinating agents

To ensure cross-pollination, plants have evolved a wide range of ingenious techniques. They often exploit insects or animals to transfer pollen from one flower to another (*see facing page*). The creatures are attracted by scent or by colored or large petals and rewarded with nectar, protein-rich pollen, or fleshy petals. Orchids have some of the most bizarre mechanisms, including flowers shaped or smelling like female insects to lure male insects into attempting to mate with the flowers. Bats, beetles, bees, butterflies, flies, small mammals, and moths are all agents of pollination.

Some plants have two or three kinds of flowers, which look similar. The prominence of stigmas and stamens differs, however, as with primroses (*Primula vulgaris*), so that an insect can pick up pollen only from the stamens of one flower or deposit pollen on the stigma of another flower.

Other plants use wind or water to transfer pollen, so the flowers are often less conspicuous because they need to offer no "bribe," but these methods are more wasteful and erratic.

Fertilization of a flower

For fertilization to occur, pollen must be compatible and alive. The stigma must also be receptive; usually it exudes a sugary solution and becomes sticky. This causes the pollen grains to stick; it also provides nutrients for the pollen grain to germinate. If the pollen is compatible, it will then grow and form a pollen tube. The tube burrows down the style so that male sex cells can enter the ovary and fertilize the female egg cell (ovule).

Both the male and female sex cells contain chromosomes (which hold genetic material) from each parent plant, but in only half the quantity of that in an adult plant. When a male sex cell fuses with the single egg nucleus, and the full set of chromosomes is effected, seeds begin to form.

The structure of seeds

Fully developed seeds usually consist of an embryo – a tiny plant with a shoot (plumule) and a root (radicle), together with seed leaves (cotyledons) – that is surrounded by a mass of food (endosperm).

In some plants, the seed's endosperm completely surrounds the embryo and forms the storage tissue of the mature embryo, as with onions (*Allium*). It may also act as a temporary food reserve within the seed leaves to nourish the embryo in the early stages just after germination, as with broad beans (*see above*) and sweet peas (*Lathyrus*).

In angiosperms, the endosperm develops before the embryo, but in most gymnosperms, the embryo forms first.

A hard outer layer – the seed coat or testa – protects the embryo and its food storage from attack by fungi, bacteria, insects, and animals, and from any environmental stress such as drought, flooding, and low and high temperatures. The maturing seed usually dries while on the plant to prepare it for a period of harsh conditions. Achieving the correct degree of dryness, or maximum dry weight, for the embryo at full maturity is thought to influence the seeds' capacity to germinate in most cases.

The amount and size of seeds varies immensely: some are as fine as dust, others as large as footballs. Generally the smaller the seeds, the more are produced. Seeds are usually enclosed. The protective casing and fertilized seeds form the fruit (*see left*).

Gymnosperms

Unlike angiosperms, the "naked" seeds of gymnosperms such as conifers are only partly enclosed by tissues of the parent plant. Conifer cones (*see also p.71*) are wind-pollinated, and seeds form on the scales of female cones. Other gymnosperms include cycads (*see also p.68*) and ginkgos (*see p.80*).

MONOCOTYLEDONS AND DICOTYLEDONS

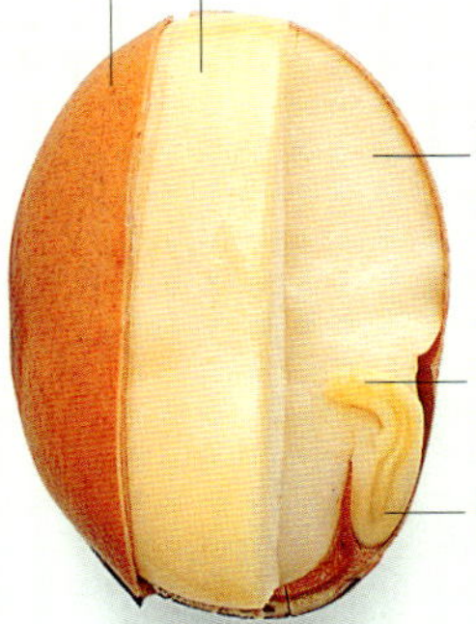

BROAD BEAN (*Vicia faba*)

Dicotyledonous seed *This germinating seed has two seed leaves, protected by a seed coat. The seed leaves make up the embryo, together with the tiny root and shoot at their base. Sometimes (as in this broad bean) the seed leaves contain food storage (endosperm).*

Flowering plants (angiosperms) are divided into two groups. Monocotyledons have one seed leaf (cotyledon), usually parallel veins on the leaves, indistinguishable petals and sepals in multiples of three, and nonwoody stems. Dicotyledons have two seed leaves, netlike veins on the leaves, often small green sepals, petals usually in multiples of four or five, and thicker stems that may have woody tissue, formed by the cambium.

MONOCOT LEAF

DICOT LEAF

HOW SEEDS DEVELOP

POLLINATED FLOWER

FADING BLOOM

UNRIPE FRUIT

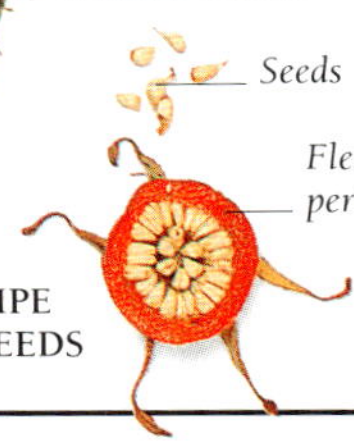

RIPE SEEDS

RIPE ROSEHIP

Once the flower has been fertilized, the petals begin to fade and then fall, and the ovary begins to swell. The stigma and stamens wither and die. The fertilized egg cells (ovules) within the ovary each develop a seed coat (testa) to protect their embryos, while the ovary wall forms a protective layer (pericarp) around the seeds.

Together the seeds and pericarp form the fruit. It may be succulent, when the middle layer of the pericarp becomes thick and fleshy as with the rosehip, or dry and hard or papery. As the seeds mature, the ripening fruit changes color. Fleshy fruits often ripen from green to a bright color.

Spore-bearing plants

Plants such as mosses, liverworts, ferns, club mosses, and horsetails reproduce by spores. A spore may look like a seed but is asexual and develops male and female sex organs independently from the plant that bore it. The consequent sexual stage of reproduction can occur only in the presence of water (*see also* Ferns, *p.159*).

Methods of seed dispersal

Once seeds have matured, they must be dispersed; if they all germinated close to the parent plant, they would compete for water, light, and nutrients. Plants have developed various strategies to ensure that their seeds are dispersed far and wide – one of the advantages of seeds over vegetative propagation.

The fruits or pods that contain the seeds have adapted to different dispersal methods. Some fruits are very simple and look like a big seed, such as the oak acorn (*Quercus*), which has a thick shell to protect the true, thin-coated seed inside. Acorns are resistant to physical damage and can survive rolling around the ground and being buried by animals.

Some seed coats develop into papery capsules or pods, as are produced by milkweeds and delphiniums; the pod dries unevenly as it ripens, causing tension in the pod walls that eventually splits it open to release large numbers of seeds. The seeds either drop to the ground or are carried off on the wind (*see below*).

Other seed pods, such as those of *Acanthus*, witch hazel (*Hamamelis*), and peas (*Pisum*), burst explosively to expel the seeds over quite some distance. The successful weed, hairy bittercress (*Cardamine hirsuta*), needs only to be touched or blown gently by the wind to cause its seed capsules to burst and eject seeds. The Mediterranean squirting cucumber (*Ecballium elaterium*) has a pod that fills with liquid as it ripens until the pressure bursts the pod from the stalk, expelling a stream of seeds and juice as it flies through the air.

Seeds of some plants, for example grasses and amaryllis (*Hippeastrum*), germinate as soon as they ripen, even while still on the parent plant if conditions are suitably wet. The germinating seeds then fall into the moist soil and grow immediately.

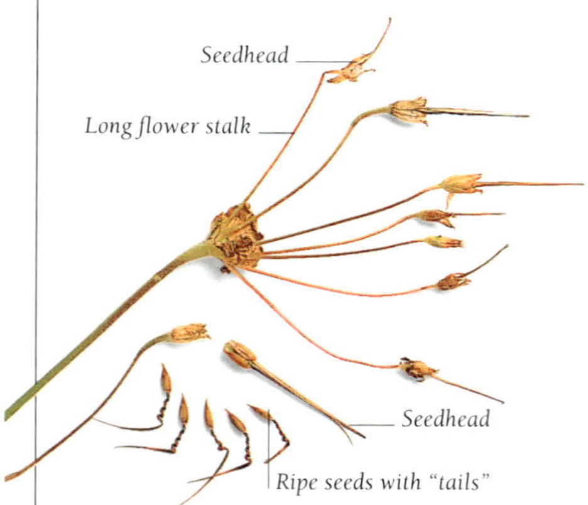

Heron's bill (*Erodium manescavii*) seeds
Each seedhead consists of five seeds with "tails." Ripe seedheads fall apart, and the seeds drop onto the warm soil. Each tail coils like a spring within ten minutes, enabling the seed to screw itself into the soil. The process can be triggered by placing a seed on the warm palm of the hand.

TYPES OF FRUIT

Seed dispersal by animals

Plants often have fleshy fruits to tempt animals to visit the plant and provide something for the animals to eat. The animals do not then need to digest the seeds, which often have more nutrients. The seeds pass unharmed through an animal's digestive system and are deposited in droppings (a ready-made seedbed) far away from the parent plant. Fleshy fruits include berries (grape, *Vitis*), drupes, or stone fruits, with single seeds (plum, *Prunus*), and pomes with several seeds (apple, *Malus*). Compound fleshy fruits include the pineapple (*Ananas*) and raspberry (*Rubus idaeus*), strictly collections of drupelets.

Many seeds and fruits have various appendages that are capable of latching onto animal hair or feathers, some very tenaciously. Such seedheads may be transported over a great distance before the unfortunate animal is able to dislodge them. The burrs of burdocks (*Arctium*) and cleavers (*Galium*) cling to fur and clothes tenaciously.

Wind dispersal of seeds

Many seeds are very small and carried by the wind. It is an economical method of transport because it demands less energy from the plant to produce a light, tiny seed than a large one with a fleshy fruit. Minute seeds are produced in great numbers to compensate for the reduced likelihood of landing on suitable soil.

Rhododendrons, and especially orchids, have extremely light seeds, which are carried on the wind. Other seeds have developed structures to keep them airborne. The seeds of willowherb (*Epilobium*) are plumed (*see facing page*); those of dandelions (*Taraxacum*) and lettuce have featherlike parachutes. *Ailanthus*, ash (*Fraxinus*), and maples (*Acer*) have prominent, papery wings that spin like helicopter blades (these winged seeds are known as samaras).

Seed dispersal by water

Plants that have adapted to growing in water or alongside watercourses produce seeds or fruits that are waterproof and buoyant. Seeds of the swamp cypress (*Taxodium distichum*) may be carried away by streams and rivers before they germinate. One of the most successful travelers on water is the coconut fruit (*Cocos nucifera*); it can survive a voyage across an entire ocean (*see facing page*).

METHODS OF SEED DISPERSAL

ON THE WIND *Some plants produce fluffy seedheads that contain small, light seeds with plumes, such as this rosebay willowherb* (Epilobium angustifolium). *The plumes enable the seeds to be carried over long distances on the wind. In this way, the plant can colonize very large areas.*

BY SEA *The coconut palm grows on the shore, so some fruits drop into the sea. Air trapped within the fibers of its outer husk makes a coconut very buoyant, allowing it to drift on ocean currents. It germinates when washed up on a distant shore.*

SEED DORMANCY

Seeds are regarded as being dormant if they fail to germinate when placed under conditions that are considered adequate for the species. The conditions include adequate temperature, moisture, air, and, in some cases, light. If these are present, nondormant seeds should soon germinate after absorbing water.

In areas where the seasons alternate between warm summers and cold winters, or where dry and wet seasons persist, dormancy prevents seeds from germinating as soon as they are ripe at the end of the growing season. The seedlings would be killed either through extreme cold or heat or from drought. Dormancy also results in staggered germination of seeds in the wild, thereby reducing competition between seedlings.

Seed dormancy is usually caused by a hard seed coat (pericarp), an immature embryo, or chemical inhibition of the embryo. According to the difficulty with which the dormancy is broken, it is also described as shallow, intermediate, or deep-seated dormancy.

Gardeners can overcome dormancy in several ways (*see below*). When dormant seeds have been primed for germination, they must be kept stable. Any change in conditions, such as increased heat, dryness, or lack of oxygen, will prompt the seeds to enter a secondary dormancy, which is extremely difficult to break.

SEED-COAT DORMANCY

Some seed coats contain waterproofing that is gradually broken down by low temperatures. Further decay of the seed coat is caused by bacteria and fungi in the soil. Until a seed absorbs moisture, it will not germinate. Drying of a seed coat as it ripens can also cause dormancy.

Physical degrading of the seed coat – scarification – allows moisture to reach the seed embryo. This can be achieved by rubbing seeds against an abrasive surface such as sandpaper. Large seeds can be chipped with a knife. Only a small area should be removed, and care must be taken not to damage the seeds. Crack large nuts carefully in a vise. Commercially, seeds are soaked in acid, but this is too dangerous for gardeners.

Collecting seeds as soon as they are fully developed, but early in the development of the seed coat, reduces the time needed to decompose the seed coat, so germination is more reliable.

Primula seeds germinate almost at once if sown while fully matured but before they dry. They are much slower to germinate once dry and released from the pod naturally. If hornbeam (*Carpinus betulus*) seeds are left on the tree until midwinter, the seed coats harden and delay germination for 2–3 years.

Seeds with a water-repellent covering on the seed coat, such as *Gleditsia* and *Fremontodendron*, may be soaked in hot water. This extracts the waterproofing, allowing the seeds to absorb water.

Subjecting the seeds to a temperature change – called stratification after the practice of chilling seeds in layers of sand – either before or after sowing is the simplest and often the most effective option, emulating in part the natural process. Seeds of alpine plants and many trees and shrubs respond well to this.

The period of chilling depends upon the severity of the dormancy. Seeds with shallow dormancy may need 3–4 weeks, those with intermediate dormancy need 4–8 weeks, and those with deep-seated dormancy between 8–20 weeks. Once 30 percent of seeds have embryo roots, they can all be sown.

EMBRYO DORMANCY

With some plants, such as orchids, holly (*Ilex*), and some *Viburnum*, the embryo is not fully developed when the seed is ripe. This results in complex dormancy. Seeds with rudimentary or immature embryos will not germinate after seed dispersal until the embryo develops further. This is normally achieved by subjecting seeds to warm temperatures for 60 days at 68°F (20°C), as is received during the first summer following the dispersal of ripe seeds in nature.

Once the embryo has fully matured germination may follow, but the seeds may also have seed coat or chemical dormancy, as with *Fraxinus excelsior* and peonies. These conditions can be relieved by natural or artificial chilling of 8–20 weeks at 34–36°F (1–2°C), for germination in the second spring.

CHEMICAL DORMANCY

Seeds borne in fleshy fruits, such as those of magnolias, roses, or *Sorbus*, are often inhibited from (*continued on p.20*)

VIABILITY OF SEEDS

Seeds, according to their habits in the wild and moisture content, have differing life spans. Some, especially fleshy seeds, die very quickly so need to be sown as soon as they ripen; others, particularly dry seeds, such as those of beans or tomatoes, can be kept for up to ten years. Correct storage, in dark, dry conditions below 39°F (4°C), can preserve viability, but exposure to higher temperatures or increased humidity may kill seeds or encourage premature germination. Plump, healthy seeds produce the most vigorous new plants.

BREAKING SEED DORMANCY

HEAT AND SMOKE *Plants native to areas that experience bush fires have seeds that often lie dormant until fire destroys competing plant life. The heat of bush fires makes the hard fruits of some plants, such as* Banksia, *pop open to release the seeds. Chemicals in smoke trigger germination in seeds of plants such as* Eriostemon.

ANIMALS *Some seeds, such as nuts, have very hard outer coats. These protect the seeds but also prevent moisture from reaching the seeds. Animals such as this squirrel eat some nuts but only damage the shells of others. Water can then pass through to the seeds and initiate germination.*

(*continued from p.19*) germinating by a chemical suppressant in the seed coat. It is normally degraded during passage through an animal's gut. To overcome this dormancy, the flesh should be cleaned off the seeds before they ripen.

Some seeds are triggered to germinate by chemicals in smoke. This happens in areas that experience bush fires, such as Australia and South Africa. Chemicals in the smoke prompt seeds to germinate when existing plants have been burned off, thus reducing competition for the seedlings. Previously, some seeds were treated by direct heat, which worked as long as smoke was generated. Now difficult-to-germinate seeds can be smoked in large numbers without heat or soaked in chemical solutions. Fire also acts to crack or damage the hard coats of seeds, such as those of the wattle (*Acacia*), facilitating germination.

CONDITIONS NEEDED FOR GERMINATION

Before a dried seed can begin to grow it must be rehydrated; water causes the seed coat to swell and burst. Most seeds double in size before germinating. Development of the seed embryo is a complex biochemical activity, and large amounts of oxygen are needed to unlock the seed's energy reserves. If the soil or soil mix is frozen, compacted, waterlogged, or baked hard, oxygen will not reach the seed embryo, and it will not be able to respire ("breathe").

Usually germination is prompted by temperatures typical of spring in the plant's natural habitat, allowing the seedlings time to become established before the following winter. Suitable temperatures vary considerably. *Fraxinus excelsior* germinates at 36°F (2°C) if its complex dormancy has been overcome. In contrast, seeds of zonal geraniums germinate best at 77°F (25°C).

A median temperature for flower and vegetable seeds from temperate climates is usually 46–64°F (8–18°C) or 59–75°F (15–24°C) for plants from warmer climates. Germination can be delayed in high temperatures. Supplying heat in excess of that needed for germination by artificial means is wasteful and costly and may cause a secondary dormancy.

Some seeds need light for germination, especially very fine seeds that have little or no food reserves to nourish the embryo. These include cress (*Lepidium sativum*), lettuce (*Lactuca*), and birch (*Betula*). Artificial light can be used (*see p.42*), but it should suffice to cover sown seeds lightly with soil mix or top-dress with vermiculite to expose them to natural light during spring and summer.

Nearly all seeds, if sown too deeply, either die in time or become dormant because they cannot recognize when the surface light is sufficient for growth. As a rule of thumb, seeds are best covered to no more than their own depth.

Some seeds can detect the levels of red in light to avoid germinating in shade, such as under trees, where the green leaves absorb red light waves.

HOW A SEED GERMINATES

There are two basic ways in which seeds germinate (*see below*). Plants such as the tomato (*Lycopersicon*) and beech (*Fagus*) emerge by elevating the seed leaves above the surface (epigeal germination) at the same time as the root radicle develops. If the shoot tip is frosted or killed, no further growth is possible.

Hypogeal germination occurs with plants such as the pea (*Pisum*), oak (*Quercus*), and some bulbs, when the seed leaves remain in the soil with the root. The growing shoot emerges only when the first true leaves form. If the seed is buried deep enough, it has a good chance of survival if the shoot tip is damaged and can produce a secondary shoot or shoots. Hypogeal germination causes difficulty for gardeners because it may be many months after germination before any sign of growth is visible.

Once germination begins, if the optimum levels of moisture, light, air, or warmth change, the seed will quickly die.

HOW A SEED GERMINATES

HYPOGEAL GERMINATION *Once the root emerges, the embryonic shoot (plumule) is pushed upward, leaving the seed leaves behind in the soil. The plumule then emerges above the soil and produces its first true leaves.*

EPIGEAL GERMINATION *The growth of the seed's root pushes the plumule and its protective seed leaves out of the soil. The seed leaves are borne at the tip of the growing shoot until the first true leaves are produced.*

HOME SEED GATHERING

As a general rule, if gathering seeds from the garden, they should be from a species, not a hybrid. Seedlings from a hybrid (unless stabilized to breed true to type) will be extremely variable; some may be as good or even better than the parent, but few will be the same. Ideally, gather seeds from a vigorous plant with typical characteristics that seeds prolifically. If the plant is isolated from similar species, the risk of natural hybridization is less and the seedlings should "come true," closely resembling the parents. The advantages of home-gathering seeds are various.

- Seeds with low viability have a better rate of germination if sown fresh.
- Gathering seeds at the point of ripeness can avoid seed-coat dormancy occurring. Early collection also enables presowing treatments that break complex dormancies to have effect before the most suitable sowing date for germination.
- A large number of plants may be obtained at little cost.
- Seeds from the garden often produce plants that are better adapted to local conditions. Home gathered vegetable seeds may be particularly adaptable. A hardy parent does not necessarily produce hardy offspring, but it is more likely.
- Increasing stocks of rare plants from gathered seeds helps conserve plants in the wild by reducing demand.
- Stocks of plants, especially vegetables, that are no longer available commercially may be preserved and genetic diversity within the genus promoted.

GATHERING SEEDS *Gather seedheads (here of hollyhocks,* Alcea*) as soon as they ripen, then clean the seeds for storing or sowing.*

HYBRIDIZATION

The exchange of maternal and paternal genetic material in plants by the sexual production of seeds, is fundamental to a plant's ability to adapt to environmental change, but it can be exploited to breed new plants (hybrids) with improved color, form, habit, disease resistance, or scent to suit the needs of gardeners.

A hybrid is a cross between two different plants. The differences may be minimal if the hybrid is between two selections of the same plant, or they may be more significant if the cross is between two species. Occasionally, the hybrid may be between two different genera. (A cultivar – short for cultivated variety – may be a hybrid but is not necessarily so. It may be a named form of a species, such as a variegated sport, that first arose in cultivation.)

If hybrids are produced from crossing two unrelated plants, the offspring often have great vigor, in the same manner as mongrel dogs are often very healthy. Conversely, if plants are self-pollinated for several generations, they tend to lose vigor, as in inbred pedigree dogs.

In commercial hybridizing, parent plants are screened over time to ensure that they are stable and will breed true. Two parents that each show some of the desired traits are selected. One parent is usually then chosen as the seed (female) parent and the other as the pollen (male) parent. Flowers on the seed parent have their stamens removed as soon as possible to avoid self-pollination and are hand-pollinated with pollen from the pollen parent to guarantee the parentage of each seed. The seed parent is also protected from contamination by insect pollinators by covering each flower with a bag or by keeping the plant under cover until seeds form.

The first hybrid (F1) generation is uniform (*see below*). If the F1 hybrids are crossed, the second (F2) generation will present the grower with a range of forms reflecting both parents, the F1 generation, and others. Often, the offspring are selected and hybridized with another plant to introduce further traits, or with siblings or one of the original parents to further reinforce desirable characteristics. F1 hybrids are frequently disease-resistant and offer a guarantee of performance, but they tend to flower at the same time and the seeds cost more than F2 seeds. For the vegetable grower, F1 seeds ensure a good crop. F2 or species seeds can give herbaceous flowering plants of good quality that flower successively.

HOW TO HYBRIDIZE A GARDEN PLANT

Breeding a commercially successful and stable hybrid is usually an expensive and laborious task, but the amateur gardener can have fun experimenting with this technique. Some genera, such as dahlias, irises, or roses, lend themselves to hybridizing on an amateur scale, often producing quite pleasing seedlings. Indeed, many hybrids that are now on the market were originally produced by amateur gardeners.

Home hybridizing is not very complicated but requires a methodical approach and a great deal of patience. It helps to concentrate on one species or genus. Have a specific aim, say to produce larger-flowered red-hot pokers that are hardy to -36°F (-20°C) or a range of double-flowered Oriental poppies. Do some research to find out if any characteristics that you are aiming for in the hybrid are evident within the species or genus. Then select parents that may be of interest and start hybridizing, crossing and backcrossing, selecting and reselecting the progeny.

Although plants differ in their flower forms, the hybridization procedure is basically the same (for details, *see* Roses, *pp.116–7*). Useful tools include small, fine paintbrushes for transferring pollen; a pair of strong tweezers and fine, sharp scissors; labels; fine net or muslin bags to place over pollinated flowers; and a notebook to record all the crosses.

HOW HYBRIDS ARE CREATED

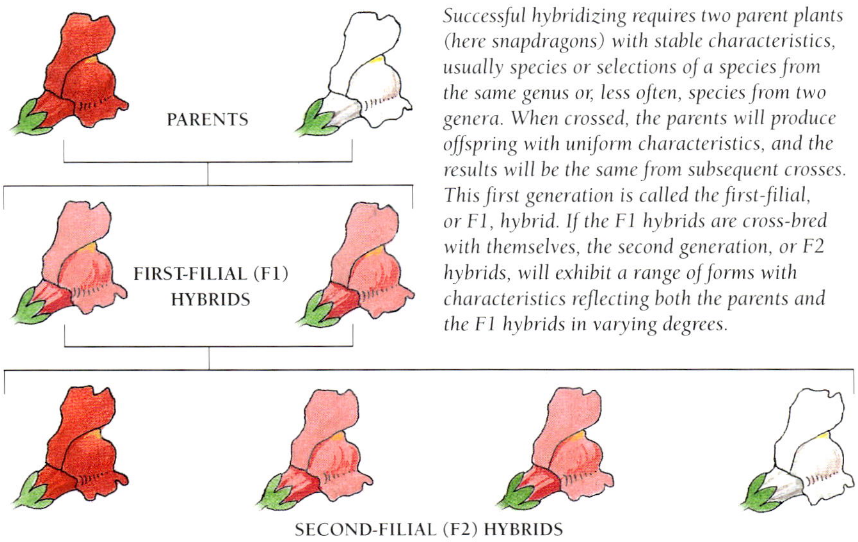

Successful hybridizing requires two parent plants (here snapdragons) with stable characteristics, usually species or selections of a species from the same genus or, less often, species from two genera. When crossed, the parents will produce offspring with uniform characteristics, and the results will be the same from subsequent crosses. This first generation is called the first-filial, or F1, hybrid. If the F1 hybrids are cross-bred with themselves, the second generation, or F2 hybrids, will exhibit a range of forms with characteristics reflecting both the parents and the F1 hybrids in varying degrees.

Vegetative propagation

In nature, some plants can reproduce asexually, or vegetatively, as well as sexually from seeds. The new plant is nearly always genetically identical to the parent (a clone), although minor mutations can occasionally occur. Vegetative propagation exploits this natural ability and extends it to involve the separation of vegetative parts of plant tissue such as roots, shoots, and leaves. Gardeners are able by these means to propagate from a single plant and to preserve characteristics such as variegation in the offspring. The various methods used include division, cuttings, layering, and grafting.

Division

Strictly, division is the separation of one plant into several self-supporting ones. It utilizes the habit of many plants that produce a mass of closely knit shoots or buds, forming a clump, or crown, of growth. The clump can be split into sections, each with at least one shoot or bud and its own roots. This is quick and easy but yields only a few new plants.

In temperate climates, division is often carried out when the plant starts into growth in spring. Water loss is minimized because of the lack of leaves, and roots grow quickly to reestablish the division. In tropical areas, divide plants whenever convenient; always trim the leaf area to reduce moisture loss, and provide shade and adequate water.

Naturally dividing alpines, such as *Campanula garganica*, *Raoulia australis*, and *Saxifraga paniculata* (*see below, left*), and herbaceous plants with fibrous roots, such as *Achillea, Aster* (*see below, center*), *Phlox*, and *Stokesia*, are simply pulled apart. Young crowns are easier to deal with than old, woody ones. Herbaceous plants with fleshy roots and buds, such as *Astilbe*, hellebores, and hostas (*see below, right*), are rather more difficult to divide without damage. Semi-woody herbaceous plants are usually evergreen; these include *Astelia*, pampas grass (*Cortaderia*), *Phormium*, and *Yucca filamentosa*. They produce swordlike leaves from ground level, crowded in dense terminal clusters, each with its own roots. Clumps are split with a sharp border spade or mattock. Young plants are easier to tackle.

A small number of woody shrubs and trees, including *Acer circinatum*, *Aesculus parviflora*, and *Aronia* x *prunifolia*, form clumps of growth from suckers below soil level; these can be removed to make new plants. Young parent plants may be lifted completely before dividing the clumps, but leave the central core intact.

The term "division" is also widely used to refer to processes similar to true division, for instance the separation from a parent plant of offsets of bulbs or cacti, of orchid pseudobulbs, and of rooted suckers and rooted runners.

Cuttings

Propagation from cuttings exploits the remarkable ability of a piece of plant tissue, from the stem, leaf, root, or bud, to regenerate into a fully developed plant, with roots and shoots. In this regenerative process, roots arising from stem, leaf, or bud tissue are known as adventitious roots.

To produce these, a group of growth (meristematic) cells, usually close to the central core of vascular (sap-carrying) tissue, changes, becoming root initials (root cells), which form root buds and then adventitious roots. These are also called "induced" or "wound" roots because, in most plants, they occur only after some type of wounding, such as cutting off a piece of bark.

In some plants, such as ivy (*Hedera*), poplars (*Populus*), and many in the mint family (rosemary and salvias), preformed root initials lie dormant in stems, so they root rapidly and easily from cuttings. A few plants, such as *Prunus* 'Colt', even form root buds, normally visible at the bases of shoots. Other, often hardy, woody plants are difficult to root: with these, callusing (*see facing page*) may hinder root formation, and it may be best to graft (*see p.27*).

Preparing cuttings

Most cuttings are taken from a plant stem; they may be severed between the leaf joints, or nodes, (internodal cutting) or just below a node (nodal cutting). Nodal cuttings expose the most vascular

Adventitious buds

A few, mostly succulent plants, for example this Kalanchoe daigremontiana, *can reproduce vegetatively by producing tiny plantlets, called adventitious buds, on the leaf margins. When fully formed, the plantlets drop to the ground and root into the soil. These provide a very easy means of propagation.*

Division of clump-forming plants

Naturally dividing alpine *Plants such as this* Saxifraga paniculata *produce new plantlets each year around the parent crown. Dividing the plant is a simple task: lift the plant and gently pull the plantlets apart for replanting.*

Fibrous-rooted herbaceous perennial *Clumps with fibrous roots (here of* Aster umbellatus*) are easily pulled or cut apart into pieces that will establish quickly. Clean off the soil to reveal the natural lines of division.*

Fleshy-rooted herbaceous perennial *Plants such as this hosta have a compacted crown that is difficult to divide without damaging the pronounced, fleshy buds and roots. Pull it apart into pieces with at least one bud and good roots.*

PREPARING CUTTINGS

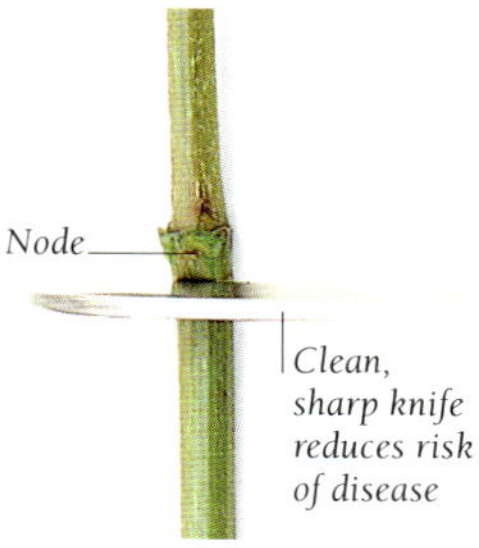

NODAL CUTTING *The cells involved in growth are most concentrated at the leaf joints, or nodes, so most cuttings are trimmed just below a node to optimize root formation.*

WOUNDING *A cutting from semi-ripe or hard wood often roots more readily if bark is cut away from the base of the stem. This exposes more of the growth cells in the cambium layer.*

HEEL CUTTING *Some cuttings, especially of semi-ripe wood, are taken by pulling away a small sideshoot so that it retains a "heel" of bark from the main shoot.*

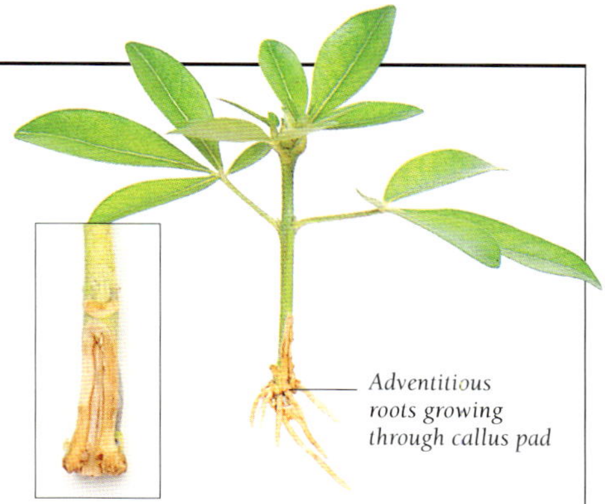

CALLUSING *When a stem is cut or wounded, it forms callus tissue (see inset) over the damaged cells. In difficult-to-root plants, or if the soil mix is too aerated or alkaline (high pH), the callus pad may thicken, preventing root growth. If this happens, pare away the excess with a scalpel.*

tissue, increasing the likelihood of root formation (*see above*). Other ways of encouraging rooting include wounding (*see above*), especially of woody plants, and the application of hormone rooting compound (*see p.30*). The growing tip may also be removed from a cutting to redistribute natural growth hormones (auxins) to the rest of the stem for root and shoot growth.

TYPES OF CUTTING

Cuttings are taken from stems, leaves, or roots (*see right*). There are several types.
SOFTWOOD CUTTINGS These are usually taken from the first flush of growth in spring. They have the highest rooting potential of stem cuttings but a low survival rate. They lose water and wilt quickly, as well as being vulnerable to bruising, which may expose the foliage and stem to attack from botrytis (rot).
GREENWOOD CUTTINGS The stems are still young but beginning to firm up. They are easier to handle than softwood cuttings and not so prone to wilting.
SEMI-RIPE CUTTINGS When stems are firmer and buds have developed, they are semi-ripe. Cuttings may be taken with a heel, especially from broadleaved evergreens and conifers.
HARDWOOD CUTTINGS These are from dormant wood. They are slower to root but robust and not prone to drying out.
LEAF-BUD CUTTINGS Often taken from shrubs, these provide an economical way of using semi-ripe stems.
LEAF CUTTINGS A few plants can regenerate new plants from a detached leaf or section of leaf tissue. These include members of the families Begoniaceae (*see p.190*), Crassulaceae (*see p.245*), and Gesneriaceae (*see p.207*). It is possible to root leaves of plants such as *Clematis, Hoya,* and *Mahonia,* but they cannot produce buds so can never develop into complete plants.
ROOT CUTTINGS A limited range of plants – ones that naturally produce shoots, or suckers, (*continued on p.24*)

TYPES OF CUTTING

SOFTWOOD *These are taken from new shoot tips (stem-tip cuttings) or basal shoots (basal stem cuttings) most often in spring, when they are almost fully developed but still soft.*

SEMI-RIPE *Once new growth has slowed and the shoots have started to become firm, which may be from midsummer to autumn, semi-ripe cuttings are taken from the stems.*

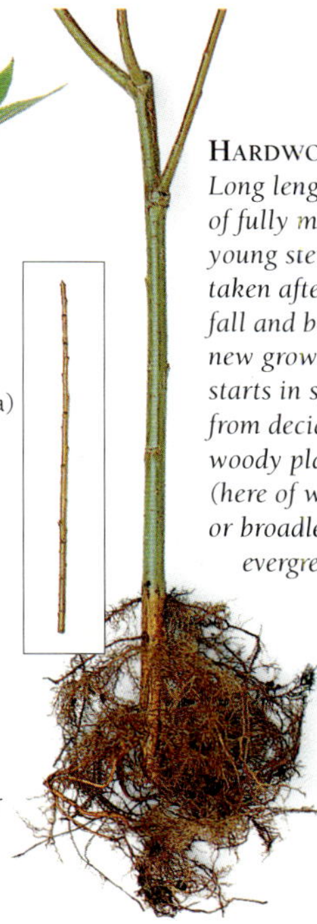

HARDWOOD *Long lengths of fully mature, young stems are taken after leaf fall and before new growth starts in spring from deciduous woody plants (here of willow) or broadleaved evergreens.*

WHOLE LEAF *Some plants have dormant buds at the leaf bases. These produce new plants when leaves are treated as cuttings.*

PART LEAF *A few plants regenerate from leaf tissue. Take leaf sections or wound leaves at any time in the growing season.*

LEAF-BUD *Semi-ripe cuttings with a short stem and one leaf can be taken from some plants to obtain more cuttings from one stem.*

ROOT *Lengths of healthy, strong root of pencil or medium thickness for the plant can be taken in the dormant season.*

(*continued from p.23*) from the roots, such as *Acanthus mollis* (*see p.158*) and *Rhus typhina* – can be propagated from root cuttings (*see p.23*). Their roots are usually thick and fleshy, in order to store the food that allows the root to survive as it produces shoots.

Success with cuttings

The process of taking cuttings is relatively simple, but success will depend on several factors. The inherent ability of the parent plant to produce adventitious roots will determine the degree of care needed to coax cuttings to root. Also, the condition of the parent influences the quality of the rooted cutting. Always choose a healthy plant; diseases or pests can be transmitted to a cutting. Material taken from young plants, especially when in active growth, is usually more likely to root. Water the parent plant thoroughly a few hours beforehand so that the tissue is fully turgid, especially for leafy cuttings.

Prepare and insert cuttings quickly to avoid losing moisture through transpiration. Hygiene is also essential to avoid introducing disease into a cutting through cuts or wounds. Keep surfaces and equipment clean (*see p.30*). The cutting tools should be sterile and as sharp as possible to avoid crushing plant cells along the cut.

In warm climates, cuttings of many plants may be rooted outdoors, directly inserted into prepared soil in shade at almost any time of year. In colder areas, a controlled environment is often vital; rooting may be unpredictable and slow. Bottom heat of 59–77°F (15–25°C) can promote rooting. The air should be much cooler to avoid encouraging growth of foliage instead of roots. The rooting medium (*see pp.32–5*) should be moist at all times and the air humid, especially with leafy cuttings. (*See* The Propagation Environment, *pp.38–45*.)

The time taken for a cutting to root depends upon the plant, the type of cutting, age of the stem, how it was prepared, and the rooting environment. Leafy cuttings root in about three weeks; woody cuttings take up to five months.

Layering

Some plants have a natural propensity to regenerate by self-layering – forming adventitious roots from the stems where they touch the soil (*see above, left*). Such plants include *Campsis*, *Hydrangea anomala* subsp. *petiolaris* (*see p.131*), and ivy (*Hedera*). Some form new plants by tip layering (*see above*).

These tendencies are exploited in layering, in which stems in active growth are induced to produce roots at the site of a wound (*see top of facing page*) while they are still attached to the parent plant. Once rooted, the stems, or layers, are severed from the parent plant and grown on individually. Layering is a good way of creating a small number of

NATURAL LAYERING

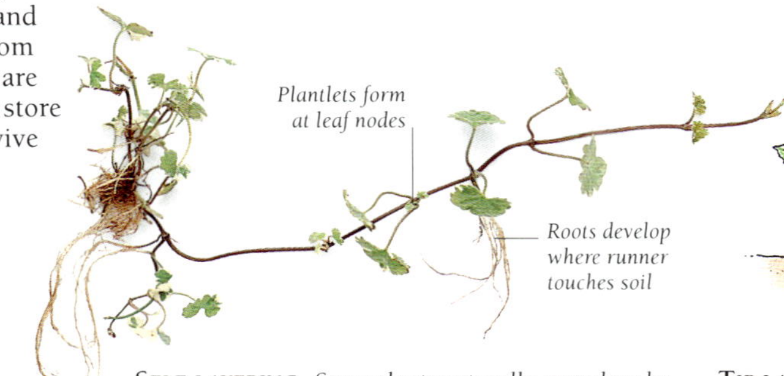

Self-layering *Some plants naturally reproduce by layering. Plants with runners, such as ground ivy (*Glechoma hederacea*), produce plantlets along their runners that are nourished by the parent until they root into the soil. Rooted stems are easily lifted and divided.*

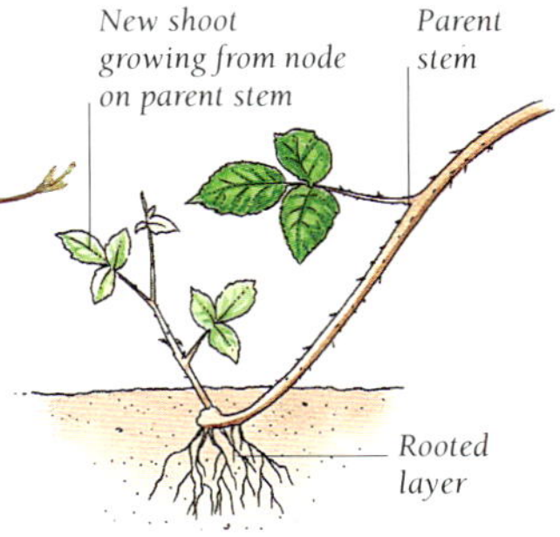

Tip layering *A few shrubs and climbers, notably brambles (*Rubus*), will root from the tips of their long, arching stems. Once the new shoot forms, the rooted tip can be detached.*

USING STOCK PLANTS FOR PROPAGATION

A stock plant is grown purely to provide cutting material. It can be encouraged to produce the best type of growth for cuttings while plants that are grown for garden display can be left untouched.

A stock plant should be healthy, mature, and vigorous, with compact, bushy growth and lots of young shoots. It should be a good example of its type; for instance, it should flower and fruit well. Cuttings from such plants root more easily and give better results. Avoid diseased plants, especially those infected by virus, because diseases can be passed on to cuttings. The age of a stock plant can affect its ability to root. New plant introductions, especially ones selected from seedlings, often show vastly improved rooting capacity over older plants of the same species.

There are several ways of conditioning a stock plant to improve its regenerative ability. High potassium levels and a pH appropriate to the plant in the growing medium, good light, and a restricted root run ensure high energy reserves for root and shoot development in cutting material. Hard pruning will produce strong basal shoots for cuttings. Subjecting the stock plant to 36°F (2°C) for two weeks, followed by forcing at 46–59°F (8–15°C), induces new shoots with enhanced rooting ability: this method suits certain deciduous plants such as some azaleas (*Rhododendron*), *Clematis*, and *Ceratostigma*. Keeping stems out of light for a time elongates the cell tissue, whitens the stem, and softens the skin (etiolation), helping difficult plants to root.

No more than 60 percent of the top-growth should be taken from a stock plant at any one time. After taking the cutting material, allow the plant to grow back.

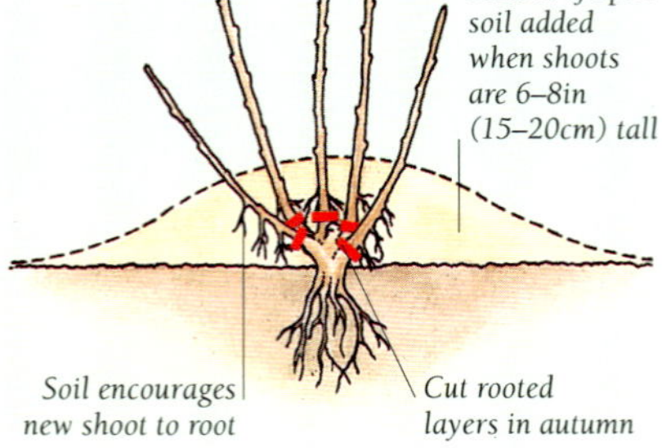

Traditional stooling *A young, strong stock shrub is cut hard back in late winter or early spring and new shoots are mounded with soil (see left) to produce rooted layers in the autumn, all of which are removed. The base (stool) will send up new shoots next year.*

Cuttings *A container-grown plant can be kept to supply cuttings repeatedly or just once before planting out. This Hebe yielded 84 semi-ripe stem-tip cuttings without appreciably altering its shape.*

INDUCING LAYERING

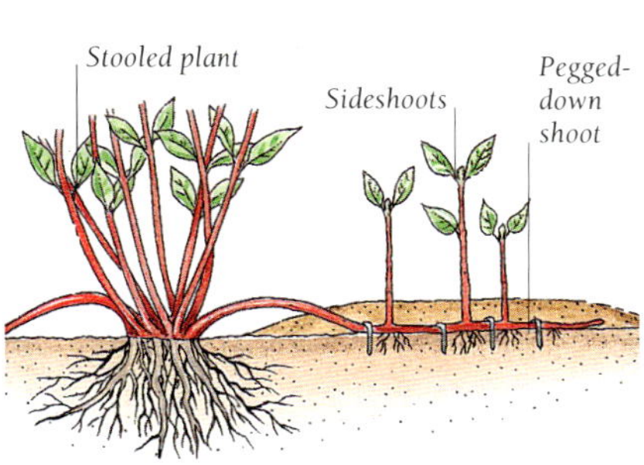

FRENCH LAYERING *In this form of stooling* (see facing page), *new shoots from the stool are pegged along the soil. Sideshoots are hilled up in stages to a depth of 6in (15cm). When these root, they are separated and grown on.*

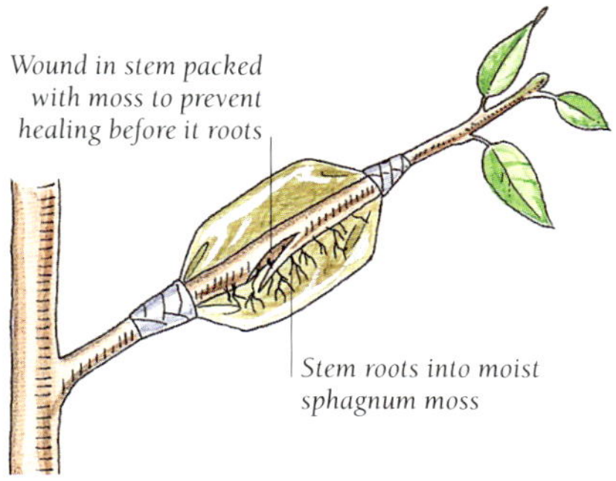

AIR LAYERING *This technique provides a way of layering an aerial shoot. The shoot is wounded with a shallow cut or by removing a ring of bark to stimulate rooting, and a plastic sleeve full of moss or soil mix is taped around the stem.*

WOUNDING A LAYERED STEM

Wounding prompts a layered stem to root. Do this by gently twisting the stem until the bark cracks (see above left), *scraping off a little bark, or by making a sloping cut into the stem to form a "tongue"* (above right).

new plants with relative certainty, since the new plant is nourished by its parent until rooted, but it is space-consuming.

Most layering involves pinning the stem to the ground, as in simple layering (*see p.106*) and serpentine layering (*see p.107*). With mounding (*see p.290*), stooling (*see box, facing page*), and the more complex French layering (*see above*), layered stems are also etiolated by hilling up, then pruned. This builds up nutrients and growth hormones needed for rooting at specific sites on the stems.

Air layering (*see above*) is used for stems that cannot be trained to reach soil level; instead, a rooting medium is packed around an aerial branch. Air layering works because removing the bark of the stem traps food that would normally go to the roots, thereby providing nutrients for rooting at the site of the wound on the stem.

STORAGE ORGANS

Some plants have natural food-storage organs that enable them to survive a period of dormancy until conditions are once again favorable for growth. They also provide energy for developing shoot systems during periods of growth. The storage organs may last for several years or be renewed annually. This natural vegetative process of regeneration can be exploited to produce many new plants. Many plants with storage organs are collectively known as bulbous plants, but only some of these are true bulbs.

BULBS are compressed stems with a basal plate from which roots grow. Each bulb contains a bud, with an embryonic shoot or a complete embryonic flower, which is enclosed by a series of fleshy leaves known as scales.

In bulbs such as those of daffodils, tulips, and onions, these scales are closely packed, completely encircling those within and not readily separated; this type of bulb is described as non-scaly (*see right*). The bulb is enclosed in a papery covering, or tunic, that protects it from surface damage and drying out. Others, such as fritillaries and lilies, produce narrower, modified scale leaves that are not protected by a tunic; these are known as scaly bulbs (*see below*) and are more susceptible to drying out.

Bulbs reproduce by producing offsets (*see below*) or sometimes bulblets and bulbils (*see p.26*). Detaching these and growing them on is the easiest and quickest means of propagating bulbs. Plants with bulbs can be increased in larger numbers by various, albeit slower and sometimes challenging, methods.

A bulb may be cut into segments, by chipping, or into pairs of scales, in twin-scaling, each retaining a piece of basal plate (*see below and p.259*). In suitable conditions, the chips or twin-scales can be induced to produce bulblets on their basal plates. Bulblets can then be grown on singly. When a scaly bulb is lifted from the ground, single scales may fall away and, if left in the soil, will form a new plant. In scaling (*see below and p.258*), the scale leaves are deliberately detached and induced to form bulblets as for chipping and twin-scaling.

For hyacinths mainly, scooping (*see p.270*) and scoring (*see below and p.270*) are effective. They involve wounding the basal plate: callus tissue then forms, encouraging bulblets to develop. In scooping, the center of the basal plate is removed, leaving the outer edge intact. When scoring a bulb, two shallow cuts are incised at right angles to each other into the basal plate (*continued on p.26*).

TYPES OF BULB

NONSCALY (DAFFODIL)

SCALY (LILY)

WAYS TO PROPAGATE FROM BULBS

OFFSETS

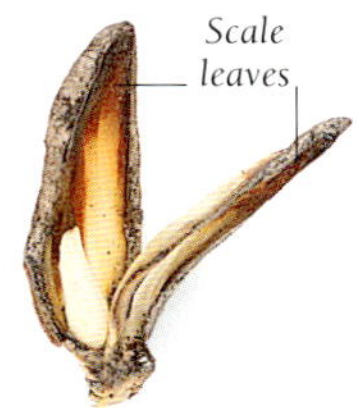

TWIN-SCALING

SCORING

SCALING

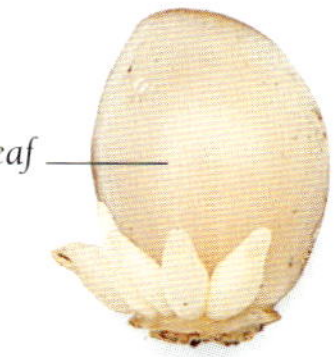

CHIPPING

BULBLETS

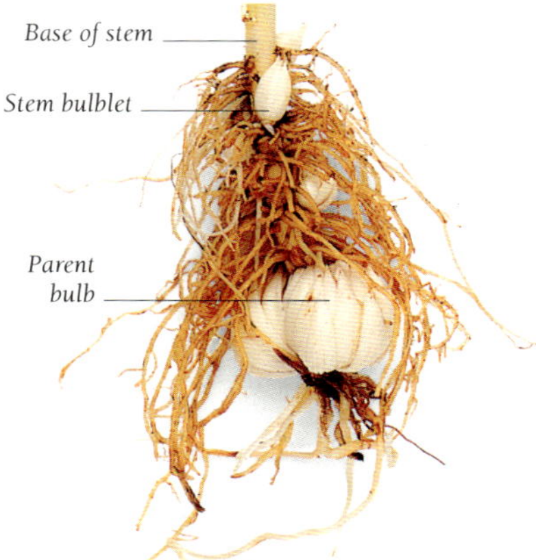

Tiny bulbs sometimes form naturally on the parent bulb or on rooting stems below ground (here on a lily). These may be detached and potted to develop into mature bulbs.

BULBILS

IN A FLOWERHEAD *Small bulblike structures form in the flowerheads of some bulbs, such as this tree onion. The bulbils weigh the stem down to the soil, into which the bulbils root* (see inset).

IN LEAF AXILS *Some plants (here a lily) form bulbils in leaf axils. Mature bulbils come away easily and can be grown like seeds* (see inset). *For more bulbils, cut back lilies before flowering.*

(*Continued from p.25.*) Some bulbous plants produce tiny bulbs (bulblets) or bulblike structures (bulbils), which in the wild root into the ground to form new plants (*see above*). These readily form new plants if detached.

CORMS are formed from the thickened underground base of a stem, usually within some overlapping, papery, scale-like leaves (*see below*). One or more buds arise on the upper surface. In most cases, the corm is renewed every year, forming at the base of the current season's stem, on top of the old corm. Tiny corms (cormels) may form around the parent and can be used for propagation.

RHIZOMES are usually swollen underground stems, either thick, as in bearded irises; thin, wide-spreading, and fast-growing, as in wild rye (*Elymus repens*); or in a crown, as in asparagus. Ferns produce a variety of rhizomatous structures (*see p.162*). As a rhizome grows, it often develops segments, each with buds that break into growth when conditions are favorable. The segments are cut apart to propagate them (*see below right*). Some rhizomes, such as those of mint, look like fleshy roots; treat these as root cuttings (*see p.288*).

ROOT TUBERS are swollen sections of root that are unable to form adventitious buds except at the crown (*see facing page*). Once the buds have produced shoots and the food storage is used up, the tubers die. New tubers form during the growing season. The plant can be increased by detaching a section of the crown with a bud.

STEM TUBERS are modified stems with the same function and life cycle as root tubers, but they possess more growth buds, over much of their surfaces. Many tubers may be produced by one plant, as in the potato (*Solanum tuberosum*). Tubers of perennials such as *Anemone coronaria* increase in size each growing season, producing leaf and flower shoots from the upper side and roots from either side, or both. To propagate stem tubers, take basal cuttings or cut into sections (*see facing page*).

PSEUDOBULBS are found only in sympodial orchids such as *Cymbidium*. They often resemble bulbs but are actually thickened stems arising from a rhizome. Pseudobulbs may be divided in various ways by cutting through the rhizome (*see p.179*).

OTHER STORAGE ORGANS Some plants, for example *Saxifraga granulata* and some kalanchoes, develop round, bulblike buds at the shoot axils. These can be propagated as for bulblets or cormels (*see above and below*). In some aquatic plants, for example frogbit (*Hydrocharis*) and *Hottonia*, these buds are relatively large and are known as turions. When mature, the buds drop off the parent plant and in spring rise to the surface to develop into new plants. Other plants produce tubercles (*see facing page*).

CORM AND CORMELS

A corm has one or more buds at the apex, from which a new corm grows each year. Usually, the old corm withers away. Tiny corms (cormels) may form between the old and new corm; they may be removed and grown on (see inset).

GRAFTING

Grafting and budding involve joining two separate plants so that they function as one, creating a strong, healthy plant that has only the best characteristics of its two parents. A root system is provided by one plant (the rootstock or stock) and the desired topgrowth by the other plant (the scion). Although the rootstock greatly influences the growth of the scion, both retain separate genetic identities, and there is no intermingling of cell tissue between the grafted parts. Shoots produced above and below the graft union will be characteristic of the rootstock or the scion, but not both.

Grafting and budding are labor-intensive, requiring skill in preparing the rootstock and scion and in caring for the graft to ensure that the parts unite. They are, however, useful ways of increase for woody and herbaceous plants that are difficult to root from cuttings and for cultivars, which rarely come true from seeds. They can be used to manipulate plants to grow in

RHIZOME

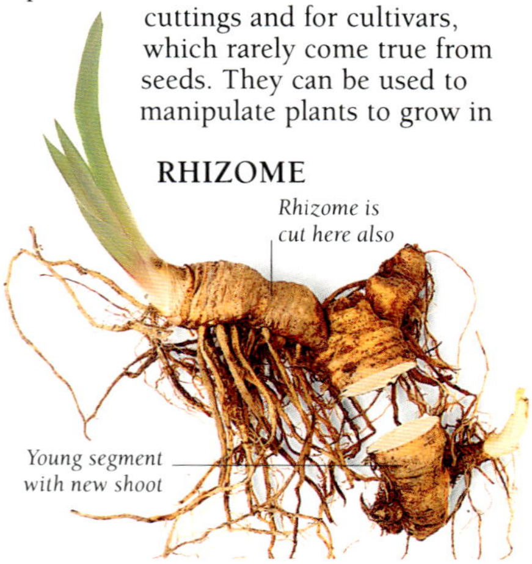

Rhizomes are sometimes swollen stems that usually grow horizontally below or on the soil. Mature rhizomes (here of iris) may be increased by cutting them into sections of young, healthy growth, each with at least one bud.

ROOT TUBER

Root tubers are swollen sections of root near the stem base (here of Senecio*). The buds are at the crown of the plant, which may be divided provided that each piece has a bud.*

STEM TUBER

DORMANT STEM TUBER *Stem tubers (here a* Cyclamen*) have the same storage function as root tubers, but because they are modified stems they produce more growth buds.*

BASAL CUTTING *One way of propagating stem tubers is to take basal cuttings (here of* Begonia*). These each consist of a new shoot with a piece of tuber at the base.*

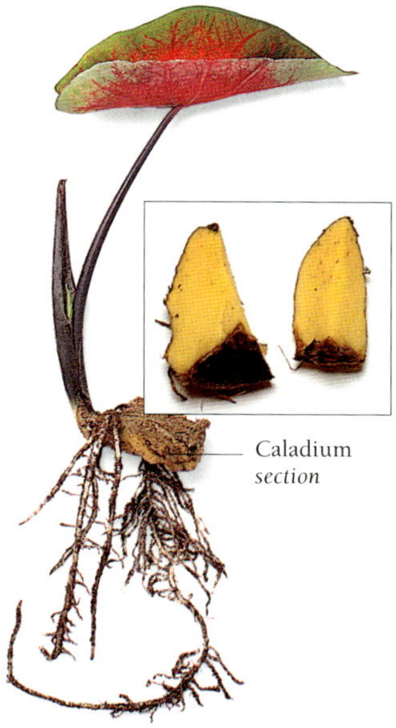

ROOTED SECTION *Many stem tubers may be cut into several wedge-shaped sections* (see inset)*, each with a bud. The bud should produce new roots and shoots.*

PROPAGATING FROM TUBERCLES

Tubercles are small, tuberlike structures that are actually fleshy, scaly rhizomes. They are most commonly produced below ground, as with Achimenes *(*see p.186*), but can also be formed from buds located in the leaf axils or in inflorescences toward the end of the growing season. They can be detached and grown on in the same way as bulbils (*see facing page*).*

a certain way or to adapt to specific conditions. Grafted plants often mature faster than those raised from cuttings. Rootstocks can confer disease- or pest-resistance or control the rate of scion growth; some produce dwarf or very vigorous fruit trees.

Plants must be closely related if a strong union is to form and remain strong throughout the life of the plant; those of the same species are normally compatible. Scion wood must be well-ripened and not pithy. As with cuttings, grafts should be prepared speedily so that the cut surfaces do not dry out. Use of strict hygiene and sharp knives are critical in preventing fungi and bacteria from contaminating the cut surfaces.

For the tissues to knit successfully, the cambium layers (*see right*) of scion and rootstock must be brought into firm contact. The cambium – a continuous, narrow band of thin-walled, regenerative cells just below the bark or rind – grows to form a bridge, or union, between the two parts in days. This consists of water- and food-conducting tissue, allowing the scion to benefit from the sap flowing from the stock. Tissue growth at the graft is enhanced by warm temperatures.

If the fibers of the rootstock and the scion fail to interlock, shoots may develop at the union. Corky tissue between the rootstock and scion may appear, making the union weak and prone to collapse at a later stage. Some rootstocks sucker from below the graft union, especially if roots are damaged. Ugly swellings at or near the union occur on trees if the growth rates of the scion and rootstock are very different.

TYPES OF GRAFTING

In approach grafting, the scion grows on its own roots until the graft union is made. It is rarely practiced today, except perhaps in the case of tomatoes (*see p.303*). Detached-scion grafting is used instead. This involves uniting a piece of the scion, the plant to be propagated, with the stock. The stock should be more advanced in growth than is the scion, ensuring that the union calluses well before the scion breaks into growth.

In apical grafting, the top of the stock is removed and replaced by a scion, end to end. Popular apical grafts are spliced side, whip, whip-and-tongue, and apical-wedge. In side grafting, such as a spliced side-veneer graft (*see p.73*), the scion is inserted without heading back the stock. (*See also pp.56–63 and pp.108–109.*) Budding is also a side graft, using a single bud (*see right*), often used for roses (*see p.114*), fruit trees, and some ornamental trees and shrubs, when scion material is limited. There are two types: chip-budding (*see p.60*) and T-budding (*see p.62*).

It is possible to graft three plants in line (double-working) to ensure root anchorage together with controlled vigor or to use the interstem (between the roots and the fruiting part of the tree) as a link between an incompatible rootstock and scion. Novelties such as weeping standards or multiple trees (*see p.57*) can be created by top-working.

THE GRAFT UNION

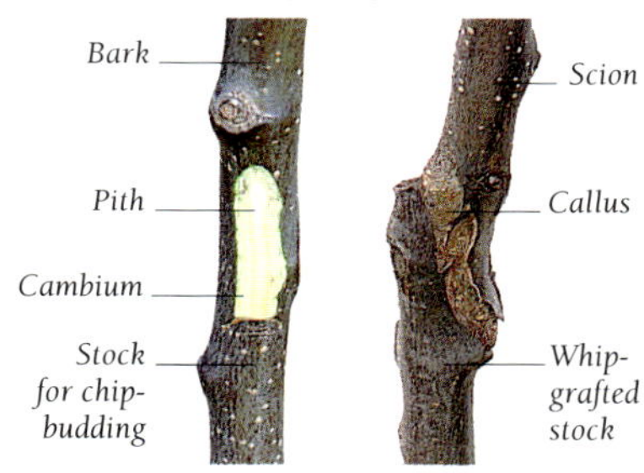

EXPOSED CAMBIUM CALLUSED UNION

Success in grafting depends on matching the cambiums of both rootstock (see above, left) *and scion. When in contact, these form a union between stock and scion and the wound seals itself with a corky layer or callus* (above right).

BASIC TYPES OF GRAFT

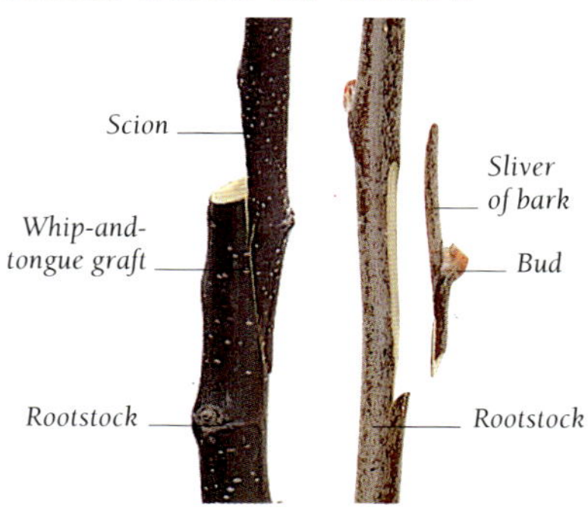

GRAFTING BUDDING

In detached-scion grafting, a prepared scion (shoot) is joined to the rootstock, which may or may not be cut back. In budding, the scion takes the form of a single bud; the rootstock is cut back when the bud begins to shoot.

Tools and Equipment

As well as general gardening tools, such as spades, forks for lifting plants, and rakes for preparing seedbeds, there are certain items that are essential or useful in preparation of propagation material. For details on larger items, such as greenhouse equipment, cloches, and shading, that are used once plant material has been prepared, see The Propagation Environment (*pp.38–45*).

A small, but essential, item is the label: always label propagated material to avoid confusion later. Note the name and include the date so you can judge when to expect growth. Many kinds, including plastic and copper (*see below*), are available. If storing seed packets in a refrigerator, use ballpoint pen on freezer-bag labels – it does not run.

Equipment for seeds and cuttings

Several items of equipment make sowing seeds or taking cuttings easier, such as dedicated seed sowers for large numbers of seeds (*see right*) and seed trays, pots, and other containers (*see p.30*). Also very useful are:

Sieves When sorting and cleaning home-gathered seeds, choose a clean sieve (*see below*) of a mesh size appropriate to the size of the seeds. When preparing soils or soil mixes, a metal or plastic soil sieve with $\frac{1}{8}$–$\frac{1}{2}$in (3–12mm) mesh is suitable to remove coarse material or lumps. Use one with a finer mesh to sift a covering of soil mix over seeds.

Dibbles and widgers These tools (*see bottom*) are used for making holes in soil or soil mix for seeds or cuttings and for lifting new plants after rooting or germination. Pencils, chopsticks, and old spoons also work well.

Garden line If sowing seeds in rows outdoors, use this (*see bottom, right*) as a guide to draw out the drills.

Seed Sowers

Hand-held sower *This seed sower has adjustable settings for different-sized seeds; it releases them one by one so they can be space-sown and will not need thinning.*

Wheeled sower *Use this seed sower to distribute seeds evenly along drills. It has a long handle, enabling the gardener to work without bending and making the task less tiring.*

Seed Sieves

FLOUR SIEVE — TEA STRAINER — SEED-SIEVING SET

Kitchen sieves (far left) can be used to sieve seeds but must not then be used for culinary purposes. Specialized seed sieves (left) are used in stacks. The chaff collects in the top coarse sieve and the seeds fall through to the middle or lower sieve, depending on their size. Dustlike chaff sifts through the lower, fine sieve into the metal bowl.

Plant Labels

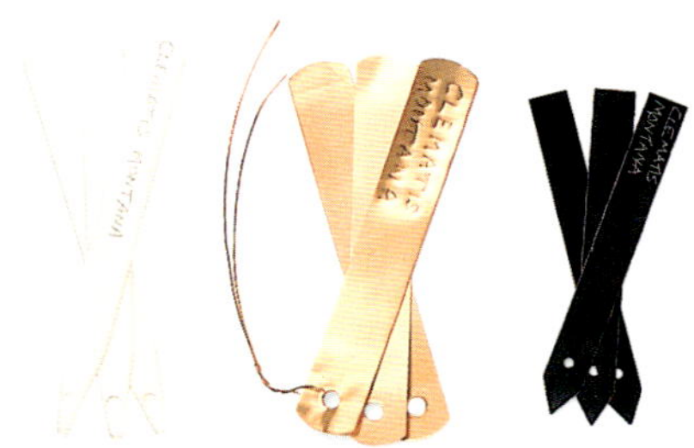

PLASTIC — COPPER — SCRATCH

Plastic labels may be written on in pencil so are reusable but fade and become brittle over time. Copper labels are permanent but cannot be reused and are expensive. Black scratch labels are permanent but are plastic and less durable.

Dibbles and Widgers

A dibble is a pencil-shaped tool, with or without a handle, used to make planting holes. Use a large dibble for sowing large seeds such as beans direct or for transplanting seedlings, especially those (such as leeks) that need a wide planting hole. A small dibble is ideal for sowing seeds or inserting cuttings in containers. Tray dibbles are fine for accurate space-sowing or for marking soil mix before dibbling. Widgers allow lifting of seedlings and cuttings with a minimum of disturbance to their new roots.

LARGE DIBBLE — MEASURING DIBBLE — STEEL WIDGER — PLASTIC WIDGER — SMALL DIBBLE — TRAY DIBBLE

Garden Line

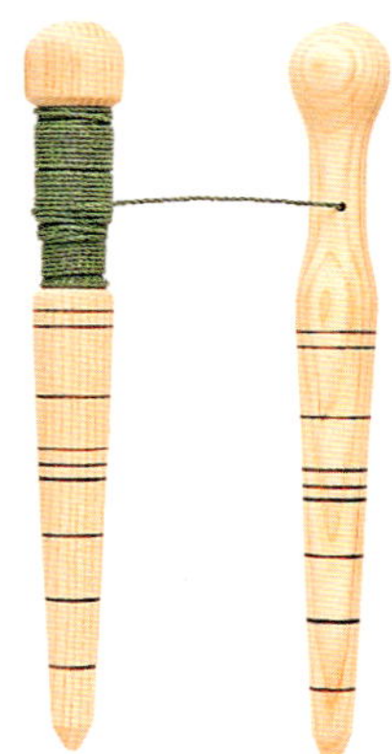

When marking out drills, use this tool as a guide. Plunge one stake into the soil and unfurl the line to the required length. Depth markings are scored into the stakes to keep the line level.

KNIVES AND CUTTERS

For propagation, it is important to use knives appropriate to the plant material and technique. Use a garden knife for standard cuttings but a scalpel for cutting soft tissue such as cacti.

GARDEN KNIFE GRAFTING KNIFE BUDDING KNIFE

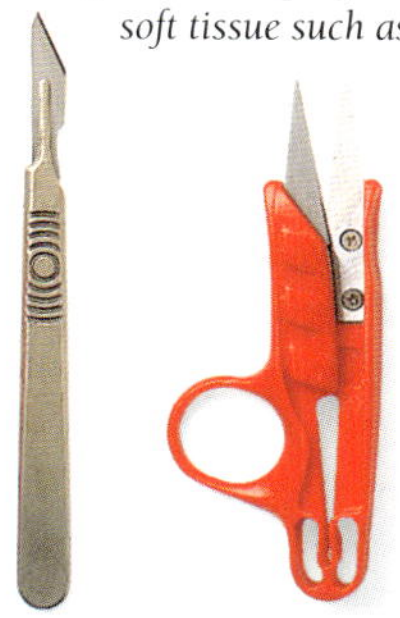

SCALPEL SNIPPERS

GRAFTING EQUIPMENT

Grafting tape, raffia, or rubber patches are used to hold together a graft while it is "taking." Sealants such as cold or hot grafting wax protect exposed wood around the graft from disease or drying out.

GRAFTING TAPE

RAFFIA

BUDDING PATCHES

GRAFTING WAX

Planting board A narrow board 10ft (3m) long and marked every 1in (2.5cm) allows you to stand on soil without compacting it and provides a straight edge to draw out drills and a rule to measure spacings.
Hoe Use a hoe to make seed drills (*see p.218*) and to weed between plants.
Knives and cutters A garden knife with a plastic or wooden handle is useful for taking and preparing cuttings (*see above*). Most have a carbon steel blade that is fixed or folds into the handle. Use snippers (*see above*) for very fine, soft stems. Pruners are good for taking woody cuttings; the scissor type makes a cleaner cut than anvil pruners Use a scalpel (*see above*) or fine-bladed craft knife for very small cuttings and for cutting very soft tissue, such as cacti. All blades used for propagation should be kept clean and very sharp.
Desiccant Silica gel crystals are useful for keeping stored seeds dry and may be reused. Place a layer of gel at the bottom of a container, and the seeds in labeled paper packets on top. Powdered milk can also be effective but is not reusable.
Paintbrush A small paintbrush with fine, soft bristles is useful for hand-pollinating flowers in order to improve seed set or in hybridizing.

POTTING BOX

A potting box, made from plastic or metal, provides a self-contained area for tasks that involve using soil mix, such as transplanting seedlings, sowing seeds, and potting cuttings. The potting box is easily cleaned and moved to a convenient spot.

Grafting equipment

Knives A grafting knife (*see above left*) has a strong, straight blade and is ideal for making accurate cuts in woody stems. A budding knife (*see above left*) has a spatula on the reverse of the blade, which is used for prying open the bark around the incision when budding. For intricate seedling grafts, safety-razor blades are more precise.
Binding materials As well as plastic grafting tape and raffia (*see above*), wide rubber bands or latex budding tape are used to bind a graft union until it calluses.
Budding patches Rubber patches (*see above*) are used to bind bud-grafts, especially of roses. The rubber rots away over two months as the union calluses.
Sealants For sealing grafts use wax, which may be applied cold (*see above*) or hot, or wound paint.

General propagation equipment

Other items that are particularly useful for propagation include the potting box (*see left*), which can be portable or built into greenhouse staging, and watering cans. Use a plastic or galvanized metal watering can (*see below*) with a fine rose. Begin watering seedlings and cuttings to the side (*continued on p.30*)

USING A WATERING CAN

Fine brass rose

Use a fine rose turned upward to water seedlings and cuttings (here of rosemary). This creates a fine, light spray and avoids disturbing the soil mix. Brass roses (see inset) give a finer spray than plastic.

THE IMPORTANCE OF HYGIENE

When propagating plants, it is essential to maintain high standards of hygiene to prevent any possibility of pests and diseases being transmitted through contamination. Sterilize tools and equipment before use, particularly blades of knives and pruners, either by heating them (*see right*) or wiping them in alcohol between each cut. It also helps to wear gloves (*see below*) or wash hands regularly, and keep work surfaces clean, especially when wounding plant material. Ideally, use new containers or sterile, preformed units such as rockwool plugs or compressed peat pellets (*see p.35*). Pots and other containers should always be scrubbed and sterilized (*see far right*).

LATEX GLOVES *These are close-fitting, with a more sensitive touch than gardening gloves, and sterile, so are ideal for use when preparing plant material such as cuttings or bulb sections. The gloves also protect against irritant sap.*

STERILIZING TOOLS *Keep knife, scalpel, or pruner blades sterile by heat-treating them. Dip a blade in alcohol and quickly pass it through a candle flame. Do not recontaminate the blade by touching it or wiping off any soot.*

CLEANING CONTAINERS *Dirty containers can harbor diseases and minute pests. Wear protective gloves and thoroughly scrub each pot with a stiff brush in dilute household disinfectant. Rinse and allow to dry before use.*

(*continued from p.29*) of the container, then move the spray over it to avoid drips disturbing the soil mix. A greenhouse watering can may have a long spout to reach the back of a bench.

MIST SPRAYERS These may be hand-held or pump-action and are useful for misting young plants that need a humid atmosphere. The nozzle can be adjusted to produce a fine spray.

PRESSER OR TAMPER Square or round wooden presses (*see top of facing page*) are easy to make and are useful for firming soil mix in pots. A firming board slightly smaller than a seed tray is also handy. You could also use an empty container of the same shape and size.

SHARPENING STONE Use this to keep blades of knives and pruners (*see p.29*) sharp. Always do this yourself, because everyone holds the knife at a different angle. A sharp blade will not crush the cells of the plant tissue along the cut, so there is less opportunity for disease to enter propagating material, improving the chances of success.

FUNGICIDE Before taking cuttings, apply a commercial fungicide to the parent plant to avoid contamination. Also dip prepared cuttings in a dilute fungicidal solution and dust cut surfaces, such as on fleshy roots or bulbs and tubers.

HORMONE ROOTING COMPOUND

This preparation contains synthetic hormones similar to those that occur naturally in plants and is used to encourage root growth, for example in cuttings and layered stems. It may also contain a fungicide to protect against rot. The compound is available in powder, gel, or liquid form. Gel adheres to a stem or wound better than powder and is less likely to coat the stem too thickly or to be wiped off as cuttings are inserted. These are generally available in three strengths: no.1, the weakest, is for softwood; no.2, of moderate strength, is for semi-ripe wood; and no.3, the strongest, is for hardwood – but often they are multipurpose.

When using hormone rooting compound, tip a small amount onto a lid or container and discard any unused compound when you are finished, so that the rest of the compound does not become contaminated. With powder, knock off any excess; too thick a layer may inhibit rooting. The compound lasts about a year in a refrigerator.

CONTAINERS

A wide range of containers, including the traditional pot and seed tray, are now available (*see below*). Plastic pots are more hygienic, lighter, and cheaper for propagation purposes than clay, or terracotta, pots. Plastic pots retain more moisture, but clay pots provide better aeration and drainage. Square pots take up less space and make more efficient use of bottom heat than round ones.

STANDARD AND HALF POTS Standard pots are as deep as they are broad. Half pots are one-half to two-thirds the depth of a standard pot. The pots are useful for small quantities of seeds or cuttings and for growing on young plants.

FLEXIBLE PLASTIC POTS AND SOFT PLASTIC POTS These are cheaper than rigid pots but are used only once and then discarded. They are good for raising summer bedding plants or vegetables and for growing on young plants.

POTS FOR PROPAGATION

PRESSER

Pressers are very useful for firming soil mix in containers. A small wooden presser with a handle is easily made; use a pot as a template. Firm the soil mix by pressing gently and evenly.

TRAYS AND INSERTS

As well as standard seed trays, many systems are available for seeds and cuttings. Strip and cell trays allow seedlings and rooted cuttings to be potted without much root disturbance. Those made of flexible plastic fit into a standard seed tray and do not last as long as the rigid forms. Drip, or watering, trays allow containers to be watered from below.

PANS These are one-third the depth of a standard pot (*see below*) so are good for shallow-rooting material that might rot in too great a depth of soil mix. Used for seeds, small cuttings, and bulbs.
DEEP POTS (LONG TOMS) These are used for direct sowing or transplanting deep-rooted plants, such as some trees and legumes, to avoid restricting the roots. They are also good for plants with long taproots, such as cycads, and other plants that might suffer a check in growth if the roots are disturbed.
ROOT-TRAINERS Each plastic pack of individual cells is hinged to allow root balls to be removed without disturbance. The sides are grooved vertically to train root growth. They are mainly used for deep-rooted trees and shrubs.
TUBE POTS Also known as sweet pea tubes, these are made of plastic or cardboard and can be planted out without disturbing the plant roots.
BIODEGRADABLE POTS These come singly or in strips and are usually made from compressed peat and other fibers. The roots grow through the pots into the soil when planted out. They are good for vegetables and summer bedding plants.
POT SAUCERS Saucers may be used for vegetable seeds, such as sprouts.
SEED TRAYS Standard or half seed trays (*see above, right*) may be used for sowing seeds, transplanting seedlings, and rooting small cuttings.
SEED TRAY INSERTS These allow strips or plugs of soil mix to be held in a seed tray (*see above, right*) to save space and avoid a stage of transplanting. Rigid inserts last longer than flexible ones.
DRIP TRAYS Drip trays (*see above right*) lined with capillary matting make watering easier. The matting holds a reservoir of moisture that is taken up into the soil mix as needed.
CELL TRAYS Cell, or module, trays in a range of sizes (*see right*) are now available for raising "plug" plants that are easy to transplant. Care is needed in watering, because they dry out quickly.

CELL TRAYS

Cell trays have been used commercially for a number of years and are now widely available to the amateur. The cells allow seedlings or cuttings to develop sturdy root systems before being potted up and to be handled without disturbing the roots or harming the stems. Fill a tray with soilless seed mix and sow seeds singly into the cells, or modules. When roots show at the base, allow them to dry out slightly, then push out of the cells with a pencil.

½IN-CELL TRAY
This is the smallest practical size of cell. Use this size to grow up to 576 small, fast-germinating seedlings.

¾IN-CELL TRAY
This tray allows up to 273 seedlings to develop several pairs of leaves.

1¼IN-CELL TRAY
Up to 135 seedlings may be grown in this tray. Pot plantlets into 2½in (6cm) pots.

1½IN-CELL TRAY
The larger trays hold up to 70 seedlings or small herbaceous cuttings.

ROCKWOOL TRAY
Trays of rockwool plugs can be used, but feed seedlings or cuttings with a dilute liquid fertilizer once they develop true leaves.

Soils and growing media

An appropriate growing medium is crucial to success in propagation. Soil beds outdoors are often used for growing on divisions and woody cuttings and direct sowing of seeds, especially of vegetables and annuals, but most methods involve soil mixes and inert media under cover to provide ideal conditions free from diseases and pests. Any propagation medium must be moisture-retentive but also porous to keep it aerated. It must be sufficiently free-draining so that the medium does not become waterlogged but not so much that the medium dries out.

SINGLE-DIGGING

Dig a trench 12in (30cm) wide and a spade's blade deep. Dig a second trench, placing the soil into the first. Continue, filling the last trench with the soil from the first.

STALE SEEDBED TECHNIQUE

1 This technique helps destroy as many weeds as possible before sowing seeds in a seedbed. Dig the soil lightly to disturb any weed seeds in the soil (see right of bed).

2 The weed seeds will germinate on the cultivated ground after a few weeks (see right of bed). Clear them by light hoeing or with a weedkiller, without disturbing the soil.

Soils

A healthy soil is vital for successful plant propagation. Soils consist of tiny particles of various weathered rocks and organic matter. Very fine particles impede drainage, so the soil becomes waterlogged and low in oxygen; large particles allow free drainage and air to reach roots but dry out quickly. The best soil has a mix of particle sizes. Fertile soil also includes trace minerals – such as boron, copper, iron, manganese, and zinc – needed for healthy growth. Loam soils have an ideal particle mix, with 8–25 percent clay, giving good drainage and water retention and high fertility. Soil is classified by its clay, silt, and sand content (*see chart below*); to identify a soil, rub a small amount of moist soil between your fingers. Soil preparation to achieve the ideal texture, fertility, and drainage for propagation is worthwhile.

The acidity of the soil should also be considered. This is determined by its pH level, on a scale of 1–14. To test your soil, use a commercial kit. A pH below 7 indicates acidic soil; if the soil has a pH over 7, it is alkaline. Regardless of the mature plant's preferred pH requirement, a low pH is best for cuttings, because any higher than 6.5 induces "hard" callus tissue to form and hinder root development (*see also p.23*). Maintaining a pH of 4.5–5 also helps prevent damping off (*see p.46*). Sulfur will increase acidity of alkaline soils.

BASIC SOIL TYPES AND HOW TO PREPARE THEM

Soil type	Soil characteristics	Preparing the soil
	Sandy *Dry, light, gritty, and very free-draining. A handful will not "ball" or stick together. Easy to work; warms up quickly in spring but not very fertile. Usually acidic (low pH).*	*Improve loose structure with small amounts of clay. Water and feed often. Add organic matter to hold moisture. Water-retentive crystals are useful on a small scale.*
	Alkaline *Pale, shallow, stony, free-draining, and low fertility. "Chalky," with pH of 7 or higher. May be deficient in minerals such as boron, manganese, and phosphorus.*	*"Hungry" soil that breaks down organic matter quickly; dress seed and nursery beds often with organic matter, preferably acidic, such as bark or well-rotted manure.*
	Peaty *Dark, crumbly, and rich in organic matter. Retains moisture well but can be too wet. Acidic (pH below 7). May lack phosphorus and contain too much manganese or aluminum.*	*Makes excellent soil if limed, drained, and fertilized. Add lime or mushroom compost to achieve best pH of 5.8. Add grit to improve drainage for seed and nursery beds.*
	Silty *Silky or soapy to the touch, with fine particles and a low amount of clay. Reasonably fertile and moisture-retentive but compacts easily, especially when dry.*	*Encourage crumbly structure by adding some clay or adding plenty of bulky organic matter. Ideal soil for propagation use, especially for early sowings.*
	Clay *Wet, sticky, heavy, and slow-draining. Rolls into malleable ball if pressed and goes shiny if smoothed. Usually very fertile. Slow to warm up in spring; bakes hard in hot weather.*	*Add lime to encourage fine particles to clump together; lay drainage channels of coarse sand or gravel. Add plenty of bulky organic matter and grit to open up soil texture.*

Outdoor beds

Special outdoor beds offer the best way to provide ideal conditions for seeds and for rooting new plants. Digging helps aerate the soil and break up compacted areas, as well as allowing organic matter and fertilizers to be added if necessary. For propagation, the important nutrients are potassium (for root growth) and nitrogen (for leaf and stem growth); phosphorus (for flowers and fruits) benefits established plants. Digging wet soil will cause compaction. Forking is less harmful to soil structure; it breaks up soil along existing natural lines.

Seeds require a fine "tilth" – level, moisture-retentive surface soil that consists of small, even particles. This ensures good contact between seeds and soil so that moisture can be absorbed for germination. Choose a sheltered site: if needed, erect a windbreak or shading.

About one month before sowing, single-dig the bed as shown (*see above, left*). Pile the soil from the first trench to one side and replace it in the last trench. Allow the bed to weather and break up naturally. Just before sowing, break up any remaining lumps with a rake, then level the ground by treading gently.

STERILIZING GARDEN SOIL

If you are planning to use garden soil in homemade soil mixes, it must first be sterilized to kill off harmful organisms that could adversely affect cuttings or seedlings during propagation. To do this, the soil must be sieved to remove stones and lumps, then heated to a minimum temperature either in a conventional oven or in a microwave (*see right*). It is also possible to obtain special soil-sterilizing units, but these are expensive.

IN THE OVEN *Sieve moist soil through a ¼in (5mm) sieve. Place a layer up to 3in (8cm) deep in a baking tray. Bake for 30 minutes at 400°F (200°C).*

IN A MICROWAVE OVEN *Sieve moist soil and place in a roasting bag. Seal it to stop soil from contaminating the oven. Pierce the bag; heat on full power for ten minutes.*

Rake the surface with progressively finer rakes in different directions to obtain a fine tilth. Stale seedbeds (*see facing page*) avoid problems with weeds.

Sometimes fertilizers are also needed to improve the soil's fertility. Add leaf mold for seeds or cuttings of woody plants: it contains mycorrhizae, tiny fungi that benefit root and shoot growth. Before sowing in cold climates, the soil may be warmed by covering it with plastic sheeting. Hardier plants need a minimum soil temperature of 50°F (10°C); tender plants prefer a minimum of 59°F (15°C).

Nursery beds are prepared in much the same way as seedbeds but do not need such a fine surface tilth.

Raised or deep beds avoid the need to walk on and compact the soil and are free-draining, providing a useful option for gardens with heavy soils. They are especially effective for vegetables (*see p.283*) or long-term propagation.

SOIL MIXES

When propagating plants under cover, soil mix is usually preferred to soil, because it is relatively free from pests and diseases and is light and well-aerated. Like the best soil (*see facing page*), it should have a mix of particle sizes and be acidic. There is a wide range of commercial soil mixes available for use in propagation.

SEED SOIL MIX Specifically made seed soil mix is moisture-retentive, fine-textured, and low in nutrients (because mineral salts can harm seedlings). Seed soil mix frequently contains sterilized soil, peat or peat substitute, and sand, or it may be soilless (without garden soil). The texture allows good contact between fine seeds and the moist soil mix, aiding germination.

ROOTING MEDIUM Mixes intended for rooting cuttings need to be free-draining because they are used in high-humidity environments. A standard rooting medium typically contains equal parts of sand and peat (or peat substitute). It may also be based on bark or perlite or a high proportion of coarse sand (river sand). Since these mixes are low in nutrients, they may or may not contain a slow-release fertilizer. If not, the cuttings will need feeding once rooted; alternatively, for cuttings that will be in the pot for some time, such as those of woody plants, add a little fertilizer to the bottom of the pot so that the new roots are not scorched.

BASIC SOIL MIX This is not often used at the propagation stage, except in the case of woody plants or root cuttings. Such mixes may be soilless or soil-based; both types are free-draining. The soil-based potting mixes provide a steady supply of nutrients to the propagated material. Soilless types are moisture-retentive and well-aerated but quickly lose nutrients so are suitable only for short-term use, such as growing on seedlings and sowing large seeds.

SPECIALIZED SOIL MIXES Commercial mixes formulated for the special growing needs of particular plant groups are also available. These include orchid mix, often based on porous bark for high aeration and open drainage; alpine and cactus soil mixes, which are gritty and very free-draining (*continued on p.34*)

COMMON INGREDIENTS FOR SOIL MIXES

SOIL *High-quality, sterilized garden soil with good nutrient supply, drainage, aeration, and moisture retention. For substantial, soil-based mixes.*

GRIT *Used in very fine (right) or fine (left) to coarse grades. Substantially improves drainage, especially for alpine and cactus mixes.*

PEAT *Stable, long-lasting, well-aerated, and moisture-retentive, but low in nutrients. Hard to rewet once dry. For lightweight, short-term mixes.*

PERLITE *Expanded volcanic rock granules. Sterile, inert, and light; retains moisture but drains freely. Medium/coarse grades aid aeration/drainage.*

FINE BARK *Fine grades of chipped bark used as peat substitute or for very free-draining, acidic mixes, especially for orchids or palms.*

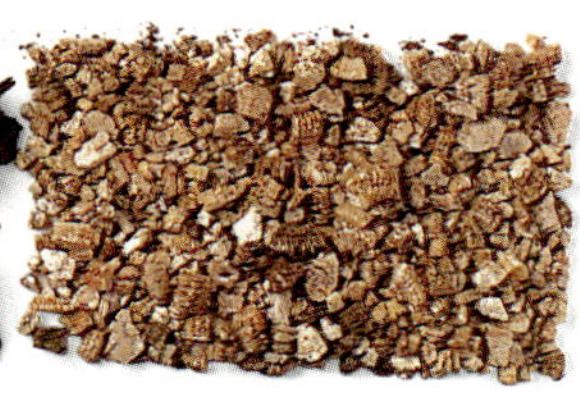

VERMICULITE *Expanded and air-blown mica. Acts similarly to perlite but holds more water and less air. Fine grade aids drainage and aeration.*

COIR *Fiber from coconut husks, used as peat substitute. Dries out less quickly than peat but needs more feeding. Good base for soilless mixes.*

SAND *Fine sand (left) helps drainage and aeration in seed soil mixes; coarse sand (right) gives more open texture to rooting media.*

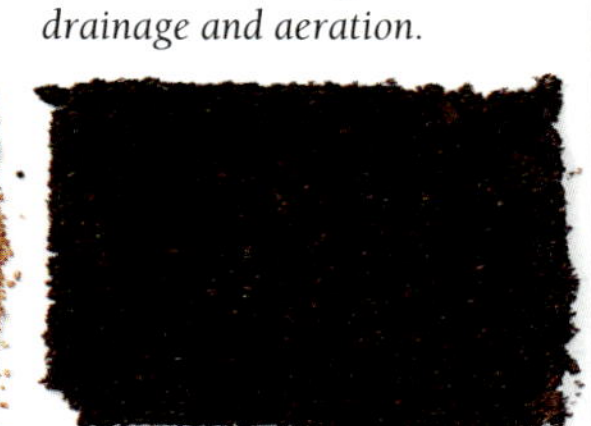

LEAF MOLD *Well-rotted, sieved leaves. May harbor pests or disease. Coarse texture best in rooting media or potting mixes.*

MAKING SOIL MIX

Some useful soil-mix recipes for use in general propagation are listed below. Recommendations for soil mixes are generally expressed in parts, indicating the relative proportions by volume of each ingredient. Parts may also be expressed as a formula, for example 3:1:1. Here (*see right*), a seed soil mix is made up from peat (or peat substitute), fine bark, and perlite, with a pinch of slow-release fertilizer.

Soil-based seed mix
2 parts soil
1 part peat (or peat substitute)
1 part sand
To each 8 gallons (36 liters), add 1½oz (42g) superphosfate and ¾oz (21g) ground limestone
For an ericaceous (acidic) mix, use an acidic soil and omit the limestone

Soilless seed mix
3 parts peat (or peat substitute)
1 part fine bark
1 part perlite
To each 8 gallons (36 liters), add 1¼oz (36g) of slow-release fertilizer and 1¼oz (36g) of dolomitic limestone

Soilless rooting media
1 part peat (or peat substitute)
1 part sand (or perlite or vermiculite)

OR

1 part peat
1 part bark (⅛–½in/3–15mm particle size)
To each 8 gallons (36 liters), add 1¼oz (36g) of slow-release fertilizer

OR

1 part peat
1 part bark (⅛–½in/3–15mm particle size)
1 part perlite
To each 8 gallons (36 liters), add 1¼oz (36g) of slow-release fertilizer

Soil-based potting mix
7 parts soil
3 parts peat (or peat substitute)
2 parts sand
To each 8 gallons (36 liters), add 4oz (113g) of general-purpose fertilizer and ¾oz (21g) ground limestone
For richer mixes, double or triple the quantities of fertilizer and limestone
For an ericaceous (acidic) mix, use an acidic soil and omit the limestone
A suitable formula for fertilizer to be mixed at home is:
2 parts bonemeal
2 parts superphosfate
1 part potassium sulfate
(*parts by weight*)

Soilless potting mix
3 parts peat (or peat substitute)
1 part sand (or perlite)
To each 8 gallons (36 liters) add:
½oz (14g) ammonium nitrate
1oz (28g) potassium nitrate
2oz (56g) superphosfate
3oz (85g) ground limestone
3oz (85g) dolomitic limestone
½oz (14g) prepared horticultural trace elements
For an ericaceous (acidic) mix, omit the limestone

In all formulas, parts are by volume unless otherwise stated

(*continued from p.33*) but low in nutrients; or aquatic soil mix, based on soil for anchorage but low in nutrients to avoid excessive algal growth.

Making your own soil mixes

You can make your own soil mixes to obtain the ideal medium for individual plants. Propagation mixes can be made up from various ingredients (*see p.33*). Most mixes are based on soil, peat, or peat substitutes, combined with other ingredients that have different properties. Inert substances such as perlite, vermiculite, and rockwool fiber (*see facing page*) are useful, since each has been processed in extremely high temperatures and is therefore sterile. Perlite also does not compact easily, so it retains air but not water.

Peat is highly acidic and therefore is suitably sterile. Peat substitutes, such as coir (coconut fiber), pine bark, animal waste products, or straw, have been composted and heat-treated. Washed and graded horticultural sands and grits are also safe. Leaf mold is not sterile so is best for potting mixes. Organic materials such as ground crab shells promote microorganisms that combat damping off (*see p.46*) so may be added as a biological control. For long-term propagation, add slow-release fertilizers.

When mixing composts, strict hygiene should be observed to avoid contamination with bacteria and minute pests. Tools, work surfaces, and soil-mix bins should always be kept clean and rendered sterile (*see p.30*) before each new batch of soil mix is made. If the mix is not used immediately, it should be stored in sealed plastic bags to avoid the risk of cross-contamination.

Maintaining soil-mix quality

Ideally, 25–30 percent of the growing medium should consist of air. Excessive compaction of soil mix causes poor air penetration, waterlogging at the base of the container, and very low levels of oxygen. This results in the rotting of water-soaked bases of cuttings or death of root hairs and root tips of seedlings. When using mixes, care must be taken to firm appropriately (*see right*).

It is also difficult to keep mixes aerated because of natural compaction through watering and decomposition of organic matter. This can be prevented by using 3in (8cm) or more deep, well-drained containers (*see pp.30–31*) and placing them on a drained base, such as sand or pea gravel, where excess water may accumulate. The extra volume of mix acts as a buffer zone, compensating for overwatering by keeping the bases of cuttings clear of any wet zone at the bottom of the container.

Do not use a very fine sieve for seed soil mix, since it may cause a crust to form (capping), which hinders seedling growth. Sieve mix through your fingers or a coarse sieve.

Compressed peat blocks

These small, biodegradable blocks of peat, enclosed by a fine mesh, contain a special fertilizer. Once soaked in water, they swell to form individual planting

FIRMING SOIL MIX

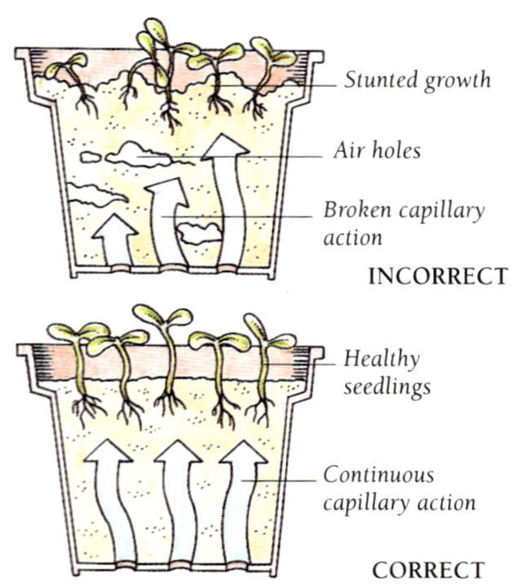

Water is drawn up through soil mix by capillary action, but air pockets interfere with the water columns essential for capillary rise. Lightly firm soilless mixes, especially at the edges of a container. Soil-based mixes can be firmed slightly more than soilless mixtures.

COMPRESSED PEAT BLOCKS
These more than double in size when soaked in a tray of water for 10–20 minutes. A plastic mesh holds the peat together. Once wetted, a seed or cutting can be inserted into the hollow at the top of each block.

units (*see above*). Make sure that the blocks do not dry out, and when the new roots begin to show through the mesh, treat as rockwool plugs (*see below*).

INERT GROWING MEDIA

There are a number of sterile, inert media now available to gardeners, all of which avoid the problem of harboring diseases or pests associated with soils and soil mixes. Pure sands, grits, and rockwool also discourage the pathogens that cause damping off. Propagating with inert media utilizes the principle of hydroculture, literally "growing in water." Seeds or cuttings have access to an unlimited supply of water and of nutrients, which are added directly to the water in the form of liquid fertilizer. There is also unlimited oxygen, because the plant roots are in almost direct contact with the air. Some of the inert media in use today include rockwool, clay granules, florist's foam, perlite, gel, sand, pumice, and grit.

ROCKWOOL

This material is made from fibers spun from molten mineral rock. Its porous structure provides the precise water: air ratio needed for healthy growth of seeds and cuttings. Do not confuse it with the water-repellent rockwool that is used for construction. Rockwool comes in different forms (*see below*): fibers may be used for aeration in soil mixes or in trays for root cuttings (*see p.158*); loose fibers are best for slow-rooting cuttings to increase aeration. Insert seeds or cuttings singly in preformed plugs.

To use plugs, soak them first in tepid water for 20–60 minutes, after which they will have absorbed a good deal of water. Drain thoroughly – never let rockwool stand in water, because it will become waterlogged, reducing aeration. Insert one or two seeds (*see also p.222*) or a cutting in each plug. Monitor water levels daily to ensure the rockwool does not dry out. To check a plug, gently squeeze one corner. If water comes to the surface, then no more moisture is required; otherwise, stand it in tepid water, for a few minutes only, and allow to drain.

As soon as roots appear, seedlings or cuttings should be transplanted, each with its rockwool cube, into soil mix to grow on, thereby avoiding disturbing the roots. Alternatively, the plugs may be inserted in larger planting blocks and grown on, and fed with liquid fertilizer, before planting out. Plugs should be well covered by the soil or soil mix so that they do not act as wicks and dry out the roots. In soil or soil mix, rockwool disintegrates over time.

OTHER INERT MEDIA

Florist's foam (*see left*) may be used like rockwool, especially for easily rooted herbaceous cuttings. Cuttings may be rooted in granular media as in rooting medium, but nutrients need to be added in the form of liquid fertilizer. A mixture of two parts medium-grade perlite to one part fine-grade vermiculite is less costly than rockwool, although results are not always as good. Sand, clay pellets, and grits are cleaner than soil and give better aeration and drainage.

Water-retentive gel (*see left*) can be used for rooting woody cuttings, such as yew (*Taxus*); add a liquid fertilizer to the water used to hydrate the crystals, insert the cuttings, and keep in a sealed container until they root. Easily rooted herbaceous cuttings root even in water (*see p.156*).

WATER-RETENTIVE GEL

This gel is commonly used in container soil mixes to conserve water. The dry crystals absorb water, increasing in volume to form a granular jelly. Some cuttings can be rooted in the gel.

FLORIST'S FOAM

Because of its water-retentive capacity and light, open texture, florist's foam is used to root cuttings of some plants, such as fuchsias. It is available in block or round form.

PROPAGATING WITH ROCKWOOL

There are various forms of rockwool. Loose fibers enhance aeration in soil mixes; greenmix's blend of water-retentive and resistant fibers makes a good peat substitute. Plugs are good for cuttings and seeds; once rooted, they can be "potted on" into planting blocks. Hormone rooting gel and liquid fertilizer can improve results.

HYDROCULTURE

Cuttings or seedlings started in inert, sterile media, such as this Anthemis *cutting rooted in water-retentive gel, are usually potted on into soil mix. In hydroculture, the new plants are potted on into other inert media, such as clay granules (see inset). A liquid fertilizer added to a water reservoir supplies nutrients.*

PROPAGATION IN DIFFERENT CLIMATES

Propagation, and gardening generally, is easier if plants are suited to the climate and can be grown outdoors all year round. Plants that are grown outside their natural habitats generally require artificially enhanced conditions under cover, such as heat and humidity, for propagation. Some plants simply refuse to thrive in unsuitable climates: for example, high-altitude species may not survive at lower levels with warmer conditions, and cool-temperate plants are not suited to the tropics.

Climate has an important influence on propagation methods and types of material used. For example, in some regions, a shrub is best rooted from cuttings, while in other climates it is better to layer it (*see* bilberry, *right*). In warm regions, much propagation is carried out in open ground, but in cool climates the same plants must be raised under cover (*see Bougainvillea, below*).

Indeed, in warm zones many plants, including various cool-climate subjects, increase so successfully that they have become noxious weeds; in some areas of Australia *Ailanthus altissima*, *Lantana camara*, *Tradescantia fluminensis*, and some *Opuntia* (*see facing page*) are weeds.

Climate also affects the timing of propagation. In warm regions, suitable seasons may be advanced or extended beyond those advised in this book, while in cold climates with long winters and late springs, the gardener may need to delay propagation such as outdoor seed sowing. If the growing season is short, propagation needs to be accelerated or the season must be extended artificially.

In choosing the best method, season, and plant material for propagation, it is therefore vital to consider the local climate and the conditions required by each method as described in the A–Z entries of each chapter. It may then be necessary to take steps to improve the conditions for propagation (see The Propagation Environment, *pp.38–45*).

BILBERRY
*In the wild, the bilberry (*Vaccinium myrtillus*) is a native of shady, damp woodland. In climates that have long, hot summers, they can be successfully grown from hardwood cuttings because the new shoots will be fully matured by the autumn. In cooler regions, however, better results may be had from layering.*

BOUGAINVILLEA 'SCARLET LADY'
In humid equatorial regions, hardwood cuttings of Bougainvillea *root speedily in open ground, but in temperate climates, soft- or greenwood heel cuttings need more care and still root slowly.*

EXTREME CLIMATES

Extreme climates have a narrow range of natural vegetation that is frequently modified for survival. For example, arid and semi-arid regions are home to many drought-tolerant plants, typically many succulents in Mexican deserts and dry-area acacias in Australia. Spiny shrubs, annuals, and grasses predominate in arid regions; bulbous plants in cold deserts.

All propagation can be done outdoors during the long, warm seasons in arid and semi-arid climates, but shade and wind structures are essential, as is water conservation. Propagation is still often easier in containers rather than in the open ground, which may also be low in nutrients. It is best to stick to plants that are adapted; cuttings of plants such as succulents should root readily and seeds germinate freely, given adequate water.

At the other extreme are high-altitude and subpolar climates, which are very cold. In the Himalayas, rhododendrons are the main high-altitude plants, while mountains around the globe give rise to a diverse range of alpine plants. These include dwarf and prostrate perennials and shrubs and dwarf bulbous plants. Subpolar plants are also low-growing; many are in the heath family, Ericaceae, including dwarf rhododendrons.

Again for propagation, it is best to choose native plants that, for example, need cool conditions to germinate their seeds. The short growing season may need to be extended by artificial means. Outdoor propagation is generally out of the question in winter; under cover, it demands artificial heat and, in subpolar regions, extra lighting. New plants need protection from severe cold, such as a well-insulated, frost-free greenhouse, and are best planted out in spring.

COOL AND MILD TEMPERATE ZONES

Maritime and continental climates in cool temperate zones are noted for their wide range of hardy trees, conifers, and perennials. Generally ideal for plant growth, a vast range of plants from all over the world can be grown. Winter cold and frost governs propagation. In maritime areas, spring often starts early,

TYPES OF CLIMATE

ARID Very hot, dry desert with cold seasons; unpredictable and sparse rainfall.
SEMI-ARID Edges of true deserts (semi-desert). Hot, but not so extreme as arid, with more vegetation and rainfall.
HUMID EQUATORIAL Hot, wet, and humid all year round. Very high rainfall; tropical monsoon seasons.
SEASONAL TROPICAL Summers hot, wet, and humid; winters warm and dry.
HUMID Subtropical and warm temperate climates with rainfall all year, especially in summer when hot or warm, causing humidity. Winters mild, sometimes cold.
MEDITERRANEAN Warm temperate climate. Hot or warm summers with little or no rain. Cool, wet winters. Drought-prone.
MARITIME In cool to mild climates, wet, windy, with year-round rainfall and cloudy, dull weather. Mild springs and autumns. Winter frosts in cool climates.
COOL CONTINENTAL Cool temperate areas. Winters long and cold; sometimes severe cold and snow. Warm, short springs, summers long, warm, or very hot, autumns short. Rainfall all year, often in summer.
HIGH ALTITUDE Short summers; long, cold winters with heavy snow. Permanent snow at very high altitudes. High light intensity
SUBPOLAR AND ICE CAP Subpolar climates have short summers, long, snowy winters, low light intensity. Ice cap has permanent snow and ice.

OPUNTIA
Climate affects the way in which this plant is grown. In cold climates, it is a popular houseplant; in arid North Africa, the prickly pear is widely used as a hedging plant and fruit crop; but in Australia, it has become a pernicious weed.

so propagation times, particularly for outdoor seed sowing, can be advanced; in other areas, spring is delayed and so is propagation. Spring and autumn are often mild and ideal for propagation. Greenhouses with artificial heat, cold frames, and cloches are used extensively.

Continental climates often have long, cold winters that delay outdoor propagation and establishment of new plants before the following winter. Artificial heat is vital for propagation to extend the season and overwinter new plants. Summers may be too hot for seeds of plants to germinate, when shading for young plants is the priority.

Warm temperate and subtropical areas

In the Mediterranean, native plants include olives (*Olea europea*), *Cistus*, lavender, and many bulbous plants. Humid climates support a diverse and vast range of plants, from bulbs and camellias to palms, fuchsias, and pines.

In warm temperate regions, seeds of cool-climate plants may fail to germinate in excessive heat, but propagation can be delayed until autumn, winter, or very early spring. Shade is vital in summer, as is adequate water and humidity. Seeds germinate and cuttings root readily in the natural warmth, so artificial heat is not needed, except sometimes in winter.

Subtropical climates are similar but often there is adequate natural humidity.

Tropical regions

Humid equatorial climates are noted for tropical rainforests with abundant trees, shrubs, and perennials such as bromeliads and orchids. Forests packed with plants also occur in seasonal tropical climates. With constant warmth, propagation may depend more on rainfall, but take local conditions into account. Shelter and shade are vital. Plants are often started in containers. In seasonal tropical areas, winter may be better for propagation. All propagation can be done outdoors in both climates – cuttings and offsets of plants root freely in open ground.

Australia and New Zealand

Propagation times in this book are primarily for cool temperate climates and may differ in warmer climates of Australia and New Zealand, and regions such as southern California, where there are warm summers and mild winters, because the growing season is longer. Gardeners should use timings given as guidelines only and take account of local conditions.

In general, such climates allow much propagation to be undertaken earlier or later in the year, or outdoors rather than under cover. Check local advice on sowing times for purchased or home-gathered seeds.

Some cool-climate plants do not thrive in warm to subtropical areas in the heat and without a cool, dormant period. Some seeds and bulbs require a cold period in a refrigerator before germination or growth can occur.

CLIMATIC ZONES OF THE WORLD

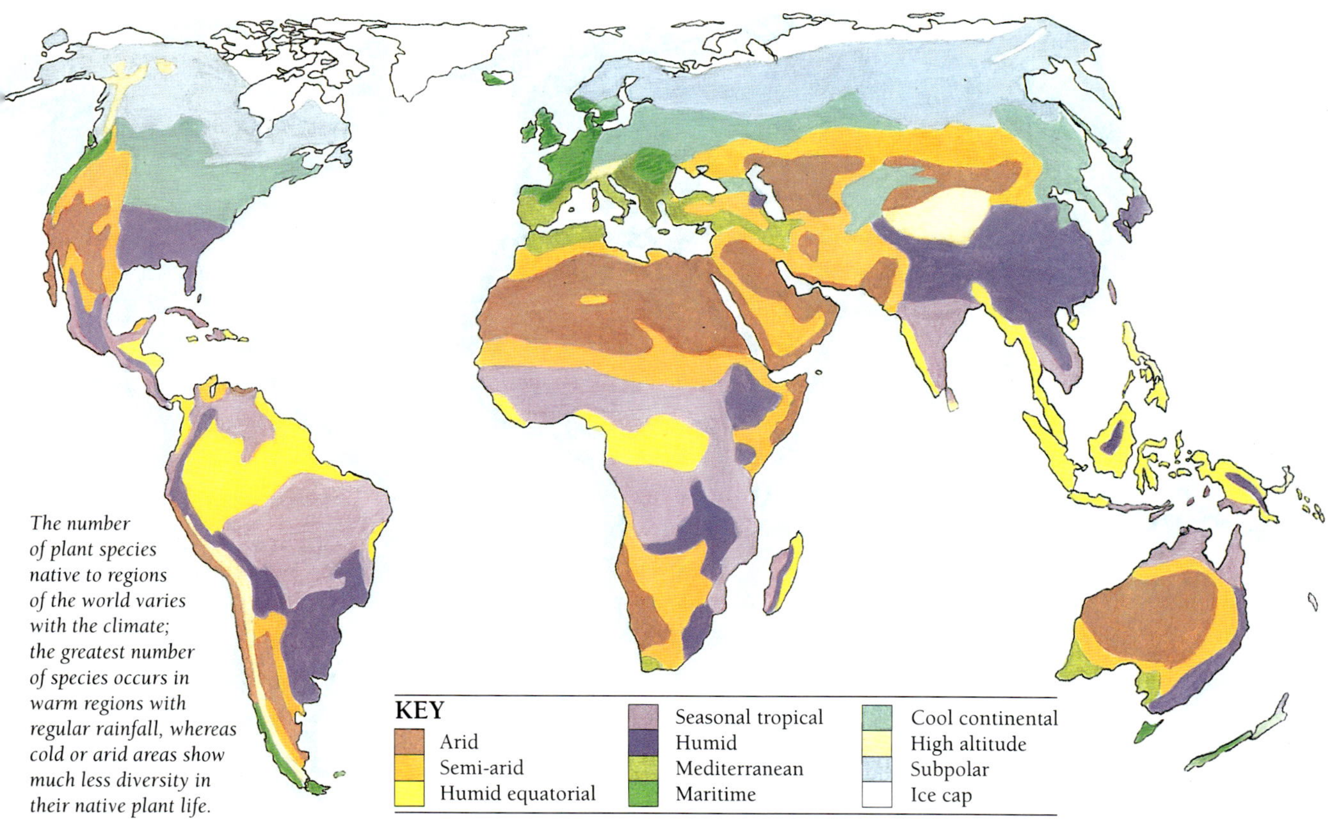

The number of plant species native to regions of the world varies with the climate; the greatest number of species occurs in warm regions with regular rainfall, whereas cold or arid areas show much less diversity in their native plant life.

THE PROPAGATION ENVIRONMENT

Once any plant material has been correctly prepared for propagation and inserted into a suitable growing medium (*see pp.32–35*), it is important to provide conditions that will enable the propagated material to survive and establish as a young plant. With a simple process such as division, all that is often required is to replant the divided sections in soil appropriate to the plant's needs or perhaps to grow them on in pots out of drying wind and sun.

Propagation involving regenerative processes, such as the formation of new roots, shoots, or bulblets, immediately demands some form of environmental support until the new plants become independent. This also applies to grafts and much seed propagation.

The degree of care needed depends on the species of plant and the mode of propagation used. Easily rooted plants, for example those propagated by hardwood cuttings outdoors in winter, require minimal care, in contrast with leafy cuttings taken in summer from a difficult-to-root plant – these will need a closely regulated environment.

In colder climates, favorable conditions can often only be achieved under cover, whether it be in the home, conservatory, or greenhouse, to extend the growing season or increase tender plants. For outdoor propagation, cold frames, cloches, or nursery beds offer a degree of shelter. In warmer regions, windbreaks, shading structures, and irrigation systems may be required.

Propagating plants away from their natural or adapted habitat makes them vulnerable to attacks from pests and diseases (*see p.46*), so the propagation area should be kept as clean as possible.

Generally, seeds require water, warmth, air (oxygen), and sometimes light to germinate; seedlings and vegetative material need water, warmth, air (oxygen, carbon dioxide), light, and sometimes nutrients to grow.

THE AERIAL ENVIRONMENT

The humidity of the air affects the rate at which plants transpire, allowing water to evaporate from leaf pores. The more humid the air, the less the plants transpire. This is a critical issue for unrooted leafy cuttings which in spring and summer need an atmosphere of 98–100 percent humidity, and about 90 percent in winter, to prevent wilting. Wilting cuttings have a reduced ability to regenerate, form callus tissue at the base, or subsequently develop roots.

Cuttings absorb moisture through their cut bases more quickly than through leaves, but once callus tissue forms (in 3–7 days) water can be taken in only by the leaves. The reduced transpiration can stress cuttings, resulting in leaf drop, so humidity is essential for the survival of the cuttings.

Leafy cuttings obtain energy for rooting by photosynthesis; for this to occur, light, water, and carbon dioxide are needed. Long summer days assist with this process, but intense light in summer overheats the air, which in turn causes excessive transpiration and stress to cuttings. Shading (*see p.47*) to create indirect light aids rooting in a wide range of plants. Photosynthesis is then restricted but can be maximized by ventilating the propagation area to ensure a normal atmospheric balance. Ventilation must be regulated to avoid excessive loss of humidity. Plants are

ELEMENTS TO CONTROL IN THE ENVIRONMENT

There are two factors to be considered in propagation: the aerial environment and growing medium. Elements in each must be balanced to encourage growth.

AERIAL ENVIRONMENT
- Humidity: to prevent moisture loss by transpiration
- Light: to allow photosynthesis without scorching
- Temperature: appropriate to plant
- Air quality: oxygen for respiration and carbon dioxide for photosynthesis

GROWING MEDIUM
- Moisture level: to encourage roots and for photosynthesis
- Temperature: to encourage growth
- Aeration: sufficient oxygen for growth and to avoid diseases
- pH (acidity and alkalinity): usually acidic, but appropriate to the plant
- Nutrient level: low until roots establish, then increased for steady growth

MAINTAINING HUMIDITY ON A SMALL SCALE

TENTING *The easiest way to cover a single pot is to create a tent over the propagated material with a clean, transparent plastic bag. Hold the bag clear of the plant material with a wire hoop or a few split stakes. Alternatively, put the pot in the bag, inflate the bag, and seal it.*

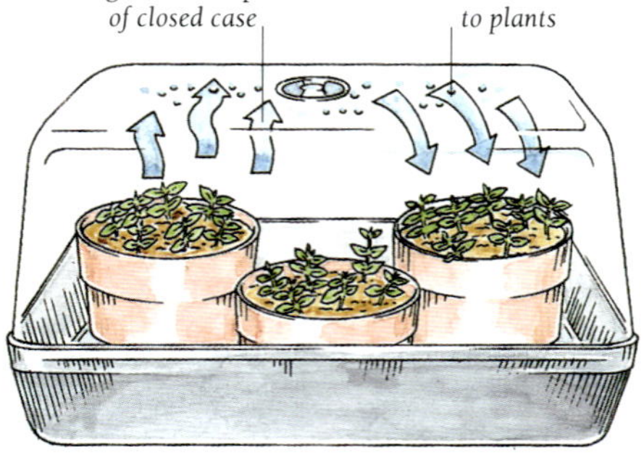

◄ MOVEMENT OF MOISTURE *Propagated material such as leafy cuttings or seeds often must be kept in a contained space to keep the air humid. The cover stops moisture in the atmosphere from evaporating, and the vent allows excess humidity to be controlled.*

▼ WINDOWSILL CLOSED CASE *Portable closed cases can be used indoors to maintain the high humidity needed to root leafy cuttings or germinate seeds. Some are fitted with electric heating elements to provide bottom heat and modular inserts to make efficient use of the available space.*

COMMON TYPES OF CLOCHE

BOTTLE CLOCHE *Make an individual cloche by cutting the bottom off a clear plastic bottle. Leave the bottle cap on and use it as a vent.*

BELL CLOCHE *Much used in the nineteenth century, these were made of glass and were easy to move from one spot to another, particularly in the kitchen garden. The curved walls ensure that condensation trickles to the ground instead of falling onto the young plants, which might cause damage. Bell cloches are now available in glass or less costly plastic.*

RIGID PLASTIC TUNNEL CLOCHE *This can be any length and is held in position by a metal or plastic frame that anchors it to the soil.*

PLASTIC BARN CLOCHE *The extra height of the sloping top makes this a versatile cloche. Many designs are available in plastic or glass; large cloches will straddle a deep bed, as here.*

PLASTIC-FILM TUNNEL CLOCHE *Sturdy wire hoops are covered by plastic film, which allows easy accessibility but needs careful pegging down. A long cloche can be divided into sections.*

FLOATING CLOCHE *Made of perforated plastic film or woven polypropylene fleece, this inexpensive cloche "floats" up as young plants grow. It also allows air and moisture through.*

temperature-dependent and grow best in warmth, so a minimum temperature appropriate to the plant must also be maintained. All these factors demand a fine balance of environmental control.

Other propagation material requires varying degrees of control in the aerial environment (*see relevant chapters*). Seeds, grafts, and bulbous material all need good ventilation, some humidity, and warmth. Bromeliads and orchids need more humidity, and alpines and succulents less, than most plants.

PROPAGATION IN THE HOME

The simplest propagation environment can be created by keeping individual containers on a bright windowsill or bay window or in a glassed-in porch. The location provides warmth and light; humidity is maintained by covering the container. For a seed tray, use plastic wrap or a sheet of glass or plastic; for a pot of cuttings, use a plastic bag (*see far left*) or a bottle cloche (*see top, left*).

CLOSED CASES

Closed cases provide the high humidity needed to germinate seeds or root leafy cuttings. Small windowsill closed cases (*see facing page*) work better indoors rather than in a greenhouse. Larger, heated closed cases are useful in a greenhouse in cooler climates to create higher temperatures and humidity.

The closed case's heating element should be capable of providing a minimum soil-mix temperature of 59°F (15°C) – or 75°F (24°C) for tropical plant material – in winter and early spring, when outside temperatures may be below freezing. An adjustable thermostat will allow greater control of the temperature.

Rigid plastic lids retain heat better than thin plastic covers. Adjustable vents in the lids allow moisture to escape and stop the atmosphere from becoming too humid, encouraging rot. Vents should be kept closed until seeds have germinated and cuttings rooted.

CLOCHES

In the open garden in cooler climates, cloches may be used to warm the soil and air, increase local humidity, and give shelter from drying winds and some protection from pests. They can give seedlings, especially of vegetables, an early start, provide a suitable rooting environment for a wide range of easily rooted cuttings, and be used as a temporary shelter to harden off (*see p.45*) or overwinter new plants.

A wide range of designs and materials is available (*see above*). The best are glass or plastic; plastic allows less light penetration and retains less heat. A minimum thickness of 150 gauge will suffice, but 300, 600 or 800 gauge offers much greater protection. Single-thickness plastic film does not retain heat as well as glass or rigid plastic but is cheaper. Plastic film and rigid polypropylene lasts five years or more; rigid, twin-walled polycarbonate lasts for at least ten years (*continued on p.40*).

COLD FRAMES

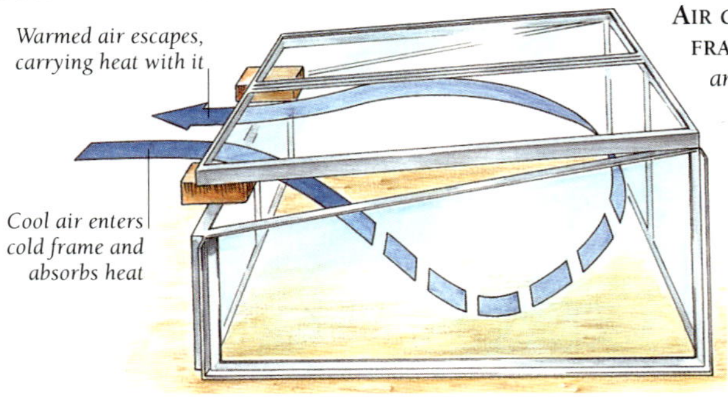

AIR CIRCULATION IN A COLD FRAME *Cold air expands and rises as it heats up on a warm day. Open the panes of the cold frame in warm weather to allow some warm air to escape and the temperature inside the cold frame to remain reasonably cool. This will reduce the risk of new plants suffering scorch.*

MOVEABLE COLD FRAME *Glass or plastic frames with lightweight aluminum frames may be placed over prepared soil in the garden to form a nursery bed. Use a sheet mulch to suppress weeds; plant through slits in the mulch.*

PERMANENT COLD FRAME *A fixed frame can provide a nursery bed for seedlings and cuttings. Line the base with a thick layer of drainage material, such as broken pots or coarse gravel. Add 6in (15cm) of well-drained soil mix..*

(*Continued from p.39.*) Well-fitting end pieces are essential to stop the cloche from becoming a wind tunnel. In sunny weather, shading (*see p.45*) may be needed to prevent scorching.

Rigid cloches are more costly but easier to move about, making watering and transplanting easier. Some are self-watering, with permeable coverings that allow rainwater to trickle through or a tubular system connected to a hose. Floating cloches of woven fleece protect against light frost.

COLD FRAMES

More permanent structures than cloches, cold frames provide a halfway house between the greenhouse and the open garden in cool climates, providing propagation material and new plants with higher soil and air temperatures, reduced temperature fluctuation, shelter from winds, and adequate light levels.

Cold frames may be used to raise seedlings early in the season, propagate leafless and leafy cuttings, overwinter seedlings and rooted cuttings, protect grafts, and harden off new plants. They may also be used to expose hardy seeds, such as those of alpines and many trees, to a period of winter cold. Cold frames also suit plant material, such as that of gray-foliaged Mediterranean plants or hardwood cuttings, that do not like the humidity of a closed case.

A good number of pots or trays can be accommodated in a cold frame. Cuttings or seedlings can also be inserted directly to root in a nursery bed in the frame (*see above*). Soil-warming cables (*see facing page*) may be used in the bed.

Cold frames with metal frameworks let in most light and can be moved around the garden to follow the best light at different times of year, but they do not retain heat or exclude drafts as well as wooden and brick frames. Permanent frames must be sited in a sheltered position, where maximum light is received in winter and spring.

Cold frames overheat in sun unless they are ventilated (*see left*) and shaded well. Hinged panes (covers) can be wedged open to stop overheating but may admit strong winds. Sliding panes can be removed entirely, but this leaves plants unprotected in hard rain.

If the temperature falls below 23°F (–5°C), insulate the frame to avoid cold damage. Wrap the outside with thick layers of burlap or polyester blankets, line the inside with styrofoam, or, in daytime, use bubble plastic so that light can still pass through.

KEEPING OUT WORMS

In the open garden, worms are great aerators of the soil and are the gardener's friends, but in a container in a cold frame, they are menaces. The worms are forced to go around and around, compacting the soil mix instead of aerating it. To stop most worms, line the frame with water-permeable fabric or line the bases of pots with window screening. A drench of a very dilute solution of potassium permanganate will bring any worms to the surface.

OUTDOOR NURSERY BEDS

Large numbers of new plants and seedlings in containers can be grown on in an outdoor nursery bed. The beds suppress weeds, isolate young plants from soil-borne diseases, and enable containers to drain freely while giving plants access to water through capillary action. Sand beds require the least watering. Level a site, enclose it with 3in (8cm) high wooden boards, then line it with fabric or sand (*see below*).

OUTDOOR NURSERY BEDS

WATER-PERMEABLE FABRIC BED *If the soil is uneven or badly drained, cover it with sand first. Line the soil and edging boards with black plastic, woven fabric, or geotextile. The lining allows soil moisture to reach the pots.*

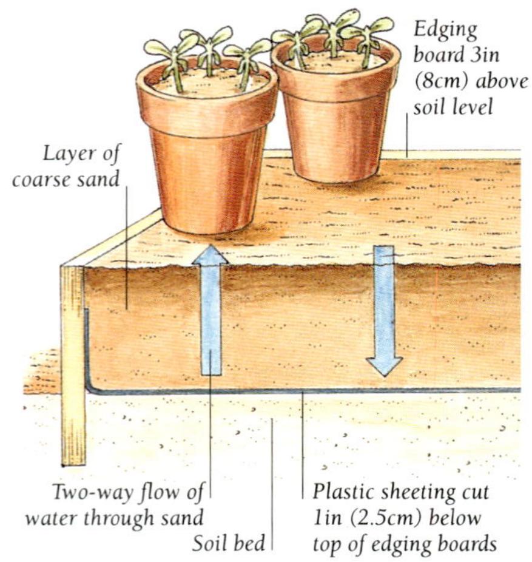

SAND BED *Line the bed with a double plastic sheet. Cover with sand to within 1in (2.5cm) of the top. Trim the plastic sheet; fill to the top with sand; level. The sand is a water reservoir; excess water drains away between the board and lining.*

THE GROWING-MEDIUM ENVIRONMENT
The choice of growing medium should provide the propagated material with the appropriate pH level and amount of oxygen and nutrients (*see pp.32–5*), but correct watering and temperature control of the medium is needed for the various growth processes, such as root initiation or seed germination, to occur.

The growing medium must be kept moist, but not waterlogged, which will deprive the roots or seeds of oxygen and promote rot. Initially, if the propagated material is covered, the moisture level in the growing medium will remain fairly constant, but once growth begins, the growing medium should be watered when needed to keep it moist (*see p.44*).

The temperature of the growing medium can affect certain biological processes that indirectly affect plant growth, such as the release of fertilizer nutrients into soil mix.

For most propagation under cover, the growing medium should be heated separately – if not, its temperature will normally fall below that of the air. The reasons for this are the transfer of heat into cooler areas beneath the medium; evaporation cooling the surface; any watering or misting with cool water; and loss of radiant heat at night.

To counteract these effects, a system providing thermostatically controlled bottom, or basal, heat can be used to ensure that the growing medium is of a higher temperature than the air – hence the old adage "warm bottoms, cold tops." This enables unrooted leafy cuttings in particular to avoid moisture stress during root formation, especially during high summer.

Bottom heat that is as high as 77–86°F (25–30°C) can cause a decline in root growth. The optimum temperature for root formation, at minimum cost, is within 59–77°F (15–25°C) for most material; 64°F (18°C) is a good average.

There are various ways of supplying bottom heat (*see below*). The simplest is in a heated closed case. Soil-warming cables are sold in varying lengths and wattages that are designed to heat given areas, such as a bench or closed case. For mist propagation (*see p.44*), use twice the standard amount of cable. Use a cable with a wired-in thermostat connected to a grounded socket with a circuit breaker. If using a propagating blanket, place a plastic hood over seed trays to maintain humidity. An organic hot bed is a fairly inexpensive option, but it cannot be precisely regulated.

PROVIDING BOTTOM HEAT

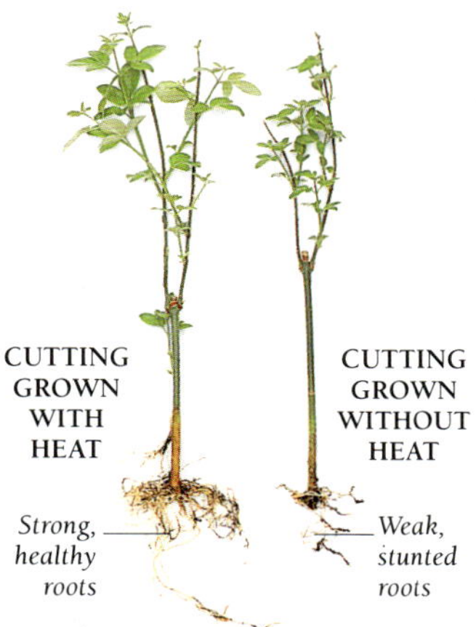

EFFECTS OF BOTTOM HEAT *If the temperature of the rooting medium is warmer than the air, cuttings usually root more quickly and strongly. Seeds may also germinate more successfully.*

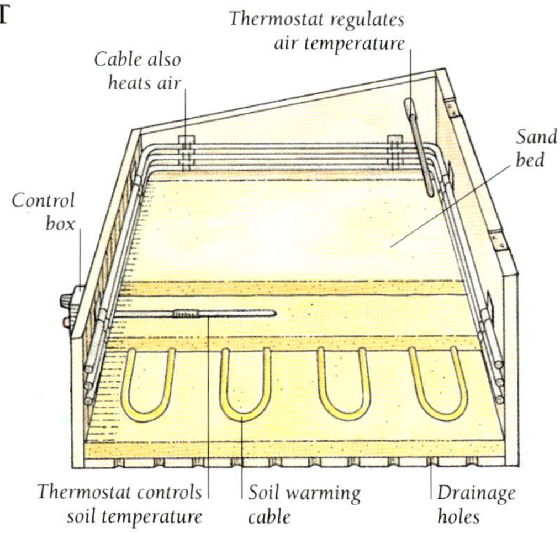

SOIL-WARMING CABLE *Lay the cable, used here in a propagating case, in a series of "S" bends in a bed of moist sand at a depth of 2–3in (5–8cm), making sure that the loops do not touch. Cables can also be used to warm air in enclosed spaces, as in this instance.*

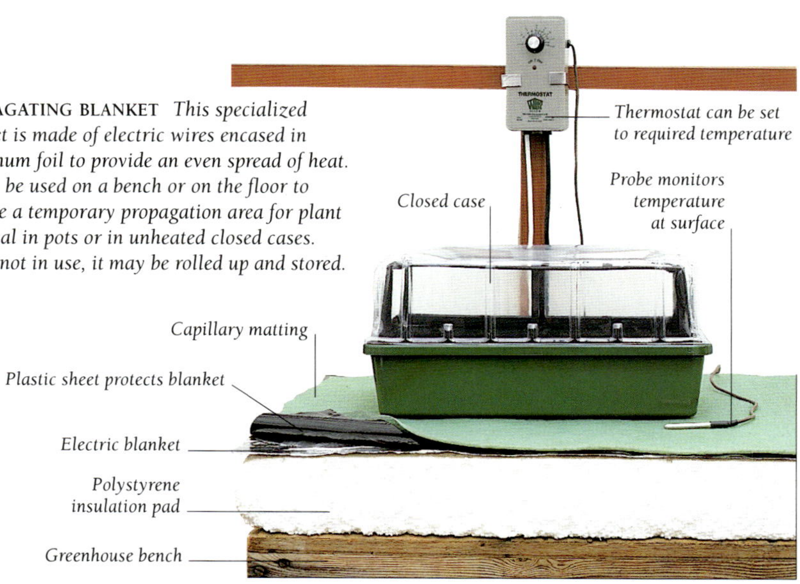

PROPAGATING BLANKET *This specialized blanket is made of electric wires encased in aluminum foil to provide an even spread of heat. It may be used on a bench or on the floor to provide a temporary propagation area for plant material in pots or in unheated closed cases. When not in use, it may be rolled up and stored.*

MAKING A HOT BED

1 *Fork over the soil in a greenhouse border. Cover with a 9in (23cm) layer of fresh, strawy horse manure and 2in (5cm) of soil. Dust with lime to neutralize the acidity.*

2 *Build up the bed with two more layers of manure, soil, and lime, finishing with a firm, level layer of soil. Leave for a day or so for the bed to start heating up before use.*

The greenhouse

For those interested in propagating plants in cold climates, a greenhouse is a valuable asset, allowing a sophisticated degree of environmental regulation. There are many different styles available. Some models are designed for maximum light penetration, heat conservation, or ventilation, while others make the most economical use of space.

A lean-to or mini-greenhouse benefits from the warmth and insulation of the house wall, but extreme temperature changes are more common. Plastic tunnels are mostly used for raising crops at soil level. They offer some protection from cold and winds but not the warm conditions of a traditional greenhouse. Ventilation may be a problem.

The minimum temperature in the greenhouse will determine the range of plants that can be propagated. There are four categories of greenhouse: cold, cool, temperate and warm.

A cold greenhouse is not heated at all and may be useful for propagating alpines and cuttings, overwintering plants, and raising summer crops and hardy seedlings.

A cool greenhouse is heated just enough to keep it above freezing, with minimum daytime temperatures of 41–50°F (5–10°C) and a nighttime minimum of 36°F (2°C). It is good for overwintering tender rooted cuttings and raising early bedding plants. A closed case must be used to germinate seeds or to root cuttings.

A temperate greenhouse has minimum daytime temperatures of 50–55°F (10–13°C) and a nighttime minimum of 45°F (7°C). Additional warmth may be needed for propagation in spring. It is used mainly for hardy to slightly tender material, such as many bedding or vegetable crops.

A warm greenhouse has high humidity and a daytime temperature of at least 55–64°F (13–18°C), with a nighttime minimum of 55°F (13°C). A wide range of plants can be propagated, including tropical and subtropical plants – many without special propagation equipment.

Regulating the atmosphere

During the growing season, relative humidity in the greenhouse of 40–75 percent is beneficial. In winter, lower humidity is needed, at an appropriate level for the plants. Wet and dry bulb thermometers, used with hygrometric tables, or hygrometers, may be used to measure relative humidity. The level of humidity is somewhat dependent on the air temperature, since warm air holds more water than cold. Humidity may be increased by splashing water on the floor or staging ("damping down"), mist-spraying automatically or by hand, or allowing water in a tray to evaporate. Humidity is decreased by ventilation.

A minimum temperature may be maintained by use of electric, gas, or kerosene heaters. Electric ones are most efficient and reliable and usually have a thermostat, which means that no heat is wasted. Electric fan heaters are the most useful, ensuring good air circulation. Kerosene heaters are least efficient, since they are not controlled by a thermostat and produce plant-toxic fumes and water vapor. If the heater has no thermostat, use a maximum/minimum thermometer to monitor nighttime temperatures. In cold regions, a cold alarm is useful.

Adequate ventilation is essential to control air temperature and humidity. The area covered by ventilators should be equal to one-sixth of the greenhouse floor. Use air vents, louver windows, extractor fans, or automatic systems (*see facing page*) to avoid a buildup of overheated air in warm weather, of stuffy, damp air in cold conditions, or of fumes from gas or kerosene heaters.

Louver ventilators are usually below the staging and are useful for controlling air flow through the greenhouse in winter, when roof ventilators may allow too much heat to escape. Vents must close tightly to exclude drafts. Use a household extractor fan that is powerful enough for the size of the greenhouse, and install it at the opposite end of the greenhouse to a door or louver window to replace stale air with fresh.

In hot weather, external shading helps control the air temperature and protect propagated material from stress and scorching sunlight; use specially formulated shading washes (*see p.45*), blinds (*see facing page*), flexible mesh, or fabric or rigid polycarbonate sheets. A shading wash should be applied to reduce the bright sunlight of summer then washed off with a cleaning solution. Shading fabric may be hung on wire runners across or along the length of the propagating bench or greenhouse.

Blinds are used mainly externally and are more versatile than washes, since they may be rolled up or down or used in only one section of the greenhouse, as necessary. Flexible shading meshes can be used externally or internally, and although they are less adaptable than blinds, they can be cut to length and placed in position for a season.

Grow lamp *Special lamps are used to extend daylength and promote early germination or rooting or improve growth of new plants, especially in winter or spring. They may be metal halide (closest to natural light), mercury vapor, or fluorescent, and have reflectors that direct light onto plants and fixtures insulated against humid air.*

ALTERNATIVE TYPES OF GREENHOUSE

Plastic tunnel greenhouse *This is a low-cost structure, made of a large, tunnel-shaped frame covered with heavy-duty, transparent plastic. The plastic is good only for a year or so; it becomes opaque, reducing light penetration.*

Mini-greenhouse *Usually aluminum-framed, this is a useful propagating area if space is limited. Place against a wall or fence, facing south (Northern Hemisphere) or north (Southern Hemisphere) for maximum heat and light.*

Winter insulation can supplement and reduce the cost of heating but may also diminish light levels. Bubble plastic, which consists of double or triple skins of transparent plastic with air cells in-between, can be cut to size and is very efficient. A single layer of plastic sheeting may also be used – it is less expensive and cuts out less light.

Thermal screens are good for conserving heat at night. They consist of sheets of clear plastic or translucent fabric hung on wires between the eaves and drawn horizontally across the greenhouse in the evening. A high-humidity area for tropical plants or a warmer area for early seedlings may be created at one end of the greenhouse with a vertical screen.

Greenhouse staging

For propagation, it is most useful to have staging, whether permanent or freestanding, around the three sides of the greenhouse. There should be a good-sized gap between the back of the staging and the greenhouse walls to allow for air circulation. Slatted or mesh benches permit a (*continued on p.44*)

THE PROPAGATOR'S GREENHOUSE

A greenhouse provides the gardener with the opportunity to create a number of separate, controlled environments. This greenhouse is equipped with all the elements necessary to propagate and raise a wide range of plants. Some of the equipment, such as the closed propagating case, may be purchased as a unit or be specially built. Elements such as insulation or heating may not be necessary in warm climates.

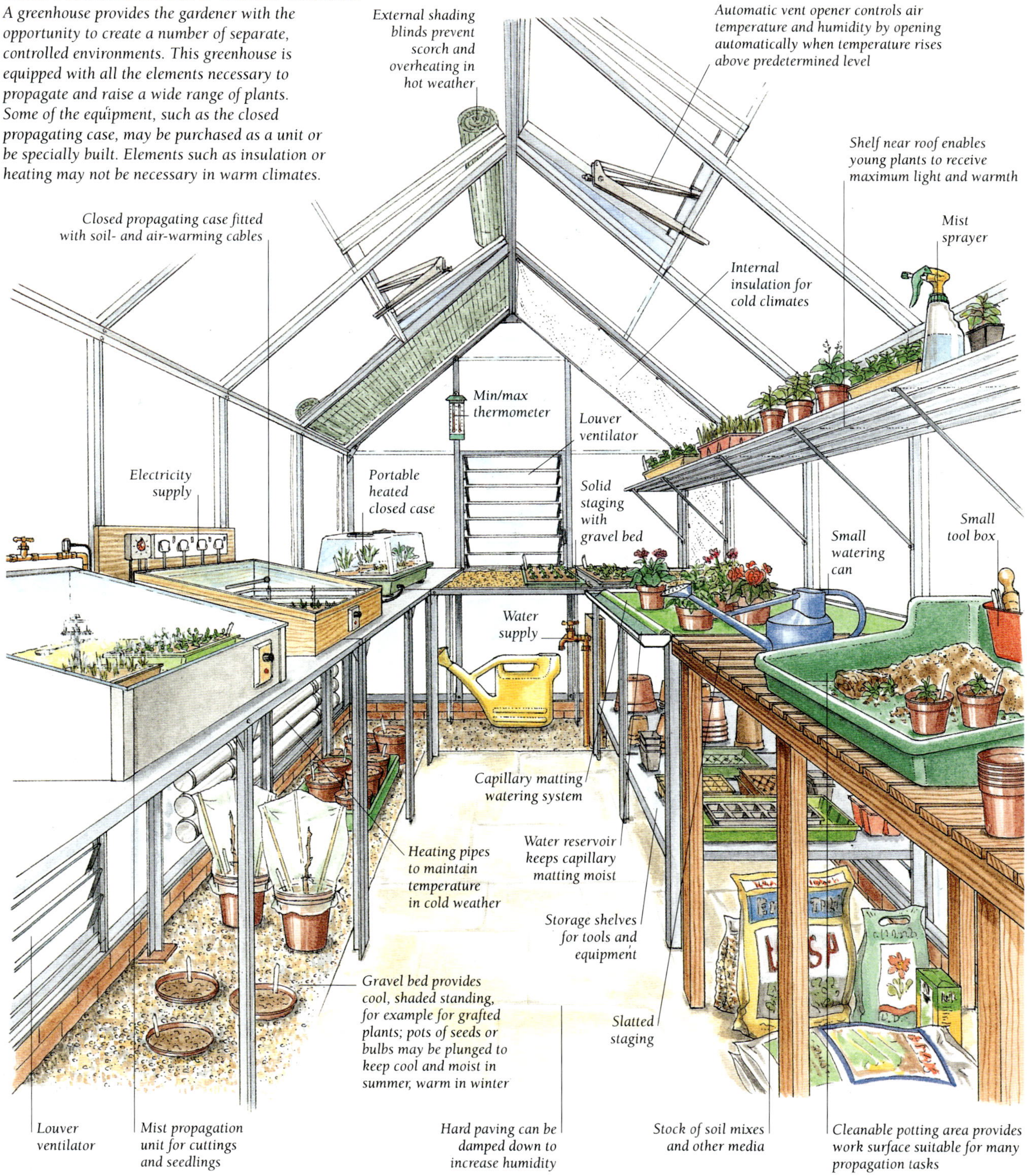

PLASTIC-FILM TENT *This way of covering a heated bench is used widely in plant nurseries to keep the air humid until cuttings root. Tie 4ft (1.2m) stakes to the legs of the bench or staging. Make hoops of strong wire and insert the ends into the tops of the stakes. Drape a sheet of opaque plastic over the hoops so that it completely encloses the top of the bench.*

(*continued from p.43*) freer flow of air than solid staging; they are useful for raising plants in pots, such as alpines or cacti and succulents that need very free-draining growing media. Solid surface staging can be fitted with a capillary (*see p.43*) or a trickle-hose watering system.

To convert solid surface staging into a propagating bench, choose a bench that is at least 4in (10cm) deep. Line the base with a 1in (2.5cm) layer of small gravel or clay pellets, then 1in (2.5cm) of coarse horticultural sand. Lay soil-warming cables (*see p.41*) and cover with another 1in (2.5cm) of sand. Fill it with soil mix for direct rooting of cuttings or more sand to provide bottom heat for containers. Alternatively, use a propagating blanket (*see p.41*). The bench may also be covered with plastic film for extra humidity (*see above*).

GREENHOUSE WATERING SYSTEMS

A watering can fitted with a fine rose is the most efficient way to water a mixed collection of new plants, especially in colder weather. In spring, delicate new plants can be damaged by cold water. Always fill a watering can and allow it to stand, or keep a water tank under the staging, so that the water is the same temperature as in the greenhouse.

In very warm conditions, automatic systems save time. A capillary system consists of a ¾–2in (2–5cm) deep sand bed or layer of capillary matting that is kept constantly wet by water from a reservoir (*see p.43*). The water seeps into the sand or matting and then into pots or seed trays by capillary action. Plastic pots usually allow good contact with the capillary layer, but clay pots may need a wick of capillary matting to be placed in each drainage hole. These systems are too wet for winter use.

Trickle irrigation systems employ a network of narrow-gauge tubing that carries water from a reservoir to individual containers. The reservoir is refilled regularly or fed by the water supply. Nozzles on each tube release water drop by drop and can be adjusted to suit the needs of each container of plants.

Seep hoses, widely used in the open garden, are perforated so that water seeps out along the length of the hoses, but these may not be able to supply a sufficient amount of water in a very warm greenhouse.

PLASTIC-FILM PROPAGATION

Used for a wide range of plants, including subtropical and tropical ones, plastic-film propagation involves laying a sheet of clear or opaque plastic directly onto pots or trays of cuttings after watering them in. This is an inexpensive way of creating high humidity and warmth around the cuttings, but it needs careful management. The cuttings must be ventilated to avoid excess condensation, but without loss of humidity. The plastic film should be removed at least once a week for about 30 minutes.

This technique is also used in plastic tunnels to create extra warmth. Some cuttings, especially those with hairy leaves, are better left uncovered. In an enclosed environment, the hairs trap water droplets, which can lead to rot. Cuttings with waxy or succulent leaves are also prone to rot if covered.

SPECIALIZED PROPAGATION UNITS

Leafy cuttings may be rooted in mist- and fog-propagation units more rapidly and in larger numbers than by other, more conventional means. These automatic systems are based on those in use in commercial nurseries (*see below and p.14*). They provide a constantly warm and humid environment, so avoiding the need to water and reducing heat loss by evaporation and moisture loss by transpiration. The cuttings are less prone to fungal diseases, since spores are washed out of the air and from leaves before they can infect plant tissues.

Mist propagation covers cuttings with a film of water; fog propagation avoids this by creating a finer vapor so is best for cuttings that are susceptible to rot. Mist units are not generally covered, but this can create too humid an atmosphere for other plants in the greenhouse.

GRAFTED PLANTS UNDER COVER

Grafted plants already possess roots and shoots but need warmth and humidity at the union of the rootstock and scion to encourage it to callus over ("heal," *see p.27*). This may be achieved by tenting each graft in a plastic bag (*see p.38*), using plastic film (*see above*), or placing the graft union in a special hot-air pipe (*see p.109*). Too much warmth at the

SPECIALIZED PROPAGATION UNITS

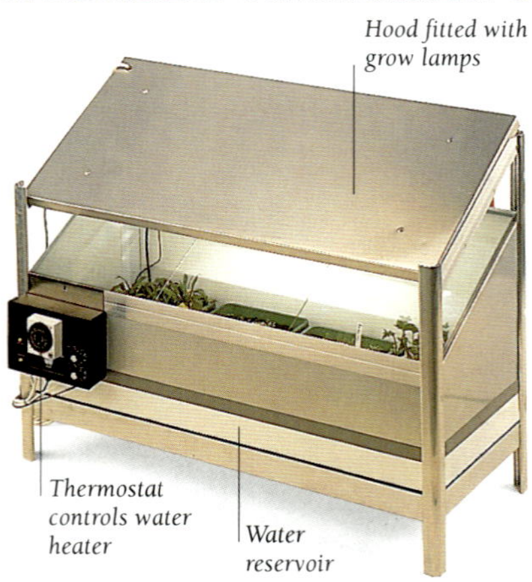

FOG PROPAGATION UNIT *This unit pumps fresh air through a water reservoir, creating a warm "fog" around the propagated material without wetting the leaves. Vapor condenses on the sides and runs back into the reservoir.*

MIST PROPAGATION UNIT *The misting head automatically delivers an intermittent spray of fine droplets over the propagated plants. The heated bench aids rooting, while the mist cools the topgrowth and prevents moisture loss.*

USING SHADING TO PROTECT NEW PLANTS

Shading should protect plant material from being scorched by direct sun while still allowing sufficient light for good growth to pass through it. Some shading materials are used for the greenhouse (*see p.42*), for example shading washes, but others can be used on smaller structures, such as flexible meshes (*see below*) and newpaper. In warmer climates, shade houses are useful. These are constructed from wooden slats, brushwood, or woven shadecloth; slats are best because they create dappled light.

FLEXIBLE MESH *Plastic mesh can be cut to size and used as internal or exterior shading. The amount of shade given depends on the mesh size.*

SHADING WASH *Washes make very effective shading because they reduce the heat from the sun significantly while allowing enough light through for good plant growth. Apply the wash externally.*

SUN TUNNELS *In climates with hot sun, tunnel cloches of white woven material stretched over wire hoops may be constructed to any length. They filter the sunlight but do not reduce the heat much.*

roots or shoots encourages early root and bud growth before the graft union has formed.

WEANING PROPAGATED PLANTS

Once the propagated plants have fully functioning root and shoot systems that are adequate for independent survival, the process of weaning the new plants from the propagation environment into a growing environment should take place. The amount of care needed for this process depends on the species, mode of propagation, time of year, and type of propagation environment.

Leafy cuttings that have been rooted in summer in mist or fog propagation units or under plastic film are most vulnerable during weaning. It may take 2–3 weeks for the plants to fully acclimatize. First, bottom heat is turned off, allowing it to fall naturally to the air temperature. The humidity level is then gradually reduced. Plastic film is removed for a longer period each day; after 3–7 days, the covers should not be replaced at night. A similar program is followed for mist and fog propagation units: the duration and frequency of the mist or fog bursts are reduced, then the units are switched off at night.

Other propagated plants that are in covered or special environments within the greenhouse, such as closed cases, covered benches, or high-humidity tents, should be gradually exposed to the open greenhouse atmosphere over 1–3 weeks. Once weaned, new plants can be placed in well-ventilated areas at temperatures appropriate to the species. They should be shaded because direct sunlight heats the air, causing stress in young plants and scorching tender new foliage.

At this stage, excessive growth should be discouraged to avoid shoots developing at a faster rate than can be supported by the new roots. This can be achieved by keeping the growing medium slightly drier than before.

If new plants are to be overwintered under cover, a frost-free environment is sufficient for hardy plants. More tender subjects should be kept at a minimum temperature appropriate to their needs.

Some commercial growers have an automatic system to brush the tops of seedlings, especially of vegetables, for 1–2 minutes per day: this mimics the effects of wind and rain, making growth sturdier and more robust. Gardeners can do the same, lightly brushing seedlings with hands or a piece of cardboard.

HARDENING OFF

Before planting out, young plants must be hardened off – acclimatized to the temperatures outdoors. This may take 1–3 weeks and must not be rushed because, over a period of days, the natural waxes coating the leaves must undergo changes in form and thickness to reduce water loss. Stomatal pores on the leaf also need to adapt to the less favorable conditions.

Transferring young plants to a cold frame is ideal – it can be ventilated increasingly, as conditions permit, until the covers are fully open at night as well as by day. A cloche may also be used but does not give as much cold protection as a cold frame. Alternatively, place the containers near a wall or hedge and cover at night, and by day in poor conditions, with newspaper, plastic sheeting, or shade netting.

PROTECTING OUTDOOR BEDS

Outdoor seedbeds and nursery beds do not have the controlled environment found under cover but may need some form of protection. Drying winds can stress plant material by increasing moisture loss: erect windbreaks on the side of the prevailing winds or use cloches. In warm climates or seasons, beds may need irrigation: seep hoses (*see facing page*) are useful; lay them along the feet of the new plants.

Barriers can be erected to protect the beds against pests; for example, yarn can be strung across seedbeds to deter birds, and barriers of mesh or fleece put up to stop rodents or carrot root maggot.

HARDENING OFF NEW PLANTS
In cold climates, a cold frame provides a good halfway house between the greenhouse and the open garden. Keep new plants in the cold frame for 1–3 weeks before planting out.

PROTECTION AGAINST PESTS
Birds and rodents can devastate seedbeds. Bend wire netting that has a mesh no bigger than 1in (2.5cm) to form a cage and peg it firmly into the soil. The mesh also serves as a plant support.

PLANT PROBLEMS

In nature, plants adapt to share specific environments with a wide range of both beneficial and hostile organisms, such as animals, insects, bacteria, and viruses, forming a complex structure of relationships that allow the plants to thrive. Propagated plants are usually removed and isolated from this natural balance in a type of monoculture that leaves them vulnerable to attack from harmful pests and diseases.

The use of bottom heat, frequent watering, and high humidity that are so often essential in propagation also encourage the proliferation of a range of debilitating fungi. These are often introduced through poor hygiene in preparation of the plant material or in contaminated soil mixes and include species of *Phytophthora*, *Pythium*, and *Rhizoctonia*, which cause damping off (*see below*) and seedling blight.

It is best to try to prevent plant problems occurring at all and, if this fails, to recognize and treat them at an early stage. The pictures below and the chart opposite describe some diseases, pests, and disorders affecting new plants.

PREVENTING PROBLEMS

The first principle of propagation is to take material from healthy, strong plants; pests and diseases can be transmitted from the parent. This can be a particular problem with viruses (*see below*) and pests that are not easily discernable such as nematodes (*see right*); plants prone to such problems, such as *Phlox*, are best raised from seeds or root cuttings.

To avoid introducing pests or diseases when preparing material, especially if any wounding is involved, it is wise to observe good hygiene (*see p.30*) and to use sterile growing media (*see p.32*). Providing the best possible conditions for the propagated material (*see* The Propagation Environment, *pp.38–45*) ensures it is less vulnerable to attack.

Certain pests can be troublesome if they gain a hold in the propagation environment. Spider mites, for instance, hibernate during winter in nooks and crannies in the greenhouse. To avoid an infestation during the growing season, scrub the propagation area annually with a solution of disinfectant. This also helps control whiteflies, mildew, and the various fungi that cause damping off or blackleg (*see below*). Outdoors, use barriers (*see p.45*) against pests, such as mice (*see below*), birds, and rabbits, which damage seedlings and new plants.

CONTROLLING PROBLEMS

Regularly check new plants and control any problems as soon as they arise; for example, discard any cuttings that show signs of rot, viruses, or cold damage (*see below*). If using organic or chemical controls, choose the most appropriate product available in your area.

COMMON PROBLEMS AFFECTING PROPAGATED MATERIAL

VIRUSES *Leaves and stems are stunted or distorted and usually develop yellow streaks, mottling, or spots. There are many viruses that are often transmitted from infected parents or by sap-feeding insects, such as aphids. Destroy affected plants promptly and clean hands and tools thoroughly after handling.*

APHIDS *These sap-feeding insects cause stunted growth and distorted leaves and excrete sugary honeydew on which sooty mold grows, especially in high humidity. Organic insecticides include pyrethrum, derris, and insecticidal soaps; if you choose to use a stronger chemical control, exercise caution.*

BLACKLEG *Before or as roots form, the base of a cutting darkens and atrophies; the upper parts then discolor and die. This is caused by soil- or water-borne fungi being introduced through dirty containers, tools, unsterilized soil mix, or water. Always observe strict hygiene and use a fungicidal rooting compound and clean water.*

DAMPING OFF *Seedlings flop over, often with a brown shrunken ring at the stem base, and white fungus appears. The water- and soil-borne fungi spread rapidly in wet soil mix, humid warmth, poor light, and dense sowings. When sowing, observe good hygiene and sow thinly. Treat with a fungicide.*

COLD DAMAGE *The upper parts of leaves on cuttings or seedlings turn brown or black or appear pale green or brown as if scorched and may wilt, wither, or die back. Nip off affected leaves or discard severely damaged plants. Prevent cold damage by ensuring a warm environment, such as in a heated closed case.*

MOUSE DAMAGE *Seeds, especially pea, bean, and corn seeds, and crocus corms outdoors are eaten, leaving the shoots lying on the surface. Firm the soil over crocus corms to stop mice from discovering them. Cover a newly sown seedbed with wire netting, set mouse traps nearby, or sow the seeds indoors.*

OTHER COMMON PROBLEMS AFFECTING PROPAGATED MATERIAL

PROBLEM	CAUSE	CONTROL
DOWNY MILDEW Yellow or discolored areas on upper leaf surfaces, corresponding to fuzzy, grayish white or purplish fungal growth beneath, common on young plants. Infection may spread and seedlings can be killed or their growth badly checked.	Several different fungi, in particular species of *Peronospora*, *Bremia*, and *Plasmopara*, which are encouraged by humid conditions.	Remove infected leaves as soon as seen. Improve air circulation around plants by extra spacing and weed control. In greenhouse, increase ventilation; avoid overhead watering and crowding of pots or trays. Spray infected plants with suitable fungicide.
ETIOLATION Plant looks pale, with poor leaf development and widely spaced nodes.	Inadequate light supply, causing extended growth toward light source and abnormal chlorophyll development.	Move plants to a bright, airy location. Provide adequate light for newly germinated seedlings.
FOOT AND ROOT ROTS Deterioration of tissues around the stem base, causing upper parts of plant to wilt, discolor, and die. Roots may turn black and break or rot.	A range of soil- and water-borne fungi that flourish where growing conditions are not adequately hygienic. Tomatoes, cucumbers, and melons are sometimes affected, especially in greenhouses. If unchecked, fungi build up in the soil.	No cure available. To avoid spread of fungi, discard infected plants promptly, together with the soil or soil mix around the roots. Good hygiene prevents introduction and spread. Replant resistant plants.
FUNGUS GNAT Grayish-brown flies, ⅙in (3–4mm) long, fly or run over soil mix. Seedlings and cuttings fail to grow. Translucent white larvae may be seen.	Black-headed larvae, up to ¼in (5mm) long, of flies (such as *Bradysia*) feed mainly on decaying organic matter but also roots of seedlings and cuttings. They may bore into the bases of stems of cuttings.	Maintain good hygiene and avoid overwatering. Introduce a predatory mite (*Hypoaspis miles*) or nematode (*Heterorhabditis*) to feed on grubs. Drench soil mix with spray-strength permethrin.
GRAY MOLD (BOTRYTIS) Gray, occasionally off-white or gray-brown, fuzzy, fungal growth develops on infected areas and may attack all parts above ground. Usually gains entry via wounds or points of damage.	A common fungus, *Botrytis cinerea*, that thrives in damp conditions. Its spores are almost always present in the air and are spread by rain or water splash and air currents. Spores may persist year to year as hard, black sclerotia (dormant spores) in soil or on infected plant debris.	Remove dead or injured plant parts before they are infected, cutting back into healthy growth. Do not leave plant debris lying around. Improve air circulation and reduce humidity. Spray with a suitable fungicide.
NEMATODES These sap-feeding pests leave no visible holes in the leaves but release a toxic saliva that results in leaf distortion and discoloration. Soil-dwelling nematodes can kill roots and spread virus diseases.	Microscopic, wormlike animals that feed in host plant, such as narcissus nematode, or live in soil and attack root hairs (*Pratylenchus*, *Longidorus*, *Trichodorus*, *Xiphinema* species). Main pests on flowering plants in greenhouses are leaf nematodes (*Aphelenchoides* species).	Do not replant parts of gardens from which infected plants have been removed with the same types of plant. Strict hygiene is essential; discard all infested leaves and plants. No effective chemical control for nematodes.
POWDERY MILDEW White, powdery, fungal growth on upper leaf surfaces, and then on all parts above ground. Affected parts, especially young foliage, may yellow and become distorted. Growth may be poor, in extreme cases causing dieback and death.	Various fungi, in particular many species of *Oidium*, *Microsphaera*, *Podosphaera*, *Uncinula*, *Erysiphe*, and *Phyllactinea*, which thrive on plants growing in dry soil. Some only infect a single genus or closely related host plants; other attack widely. Spores are spread by wind and rain splash; the fungi may overwinter on plant surfaces.	Avoid dry sites and mulch as necessary. Keep plants adequately watered, but avoid overhead watering. Remove infected leaves immediately. Spray with a suitable fungicide.
RUSTS Patches of spores, either as masses or pustules, usually bright orange or dark brown, develop on the lower leaf surface, with yellow discoloration above.	Various fungi, most often *Puccinia* and *Melampsora* species, which thrive in humid conditions. The spores are spread by water splash and air currents.	Remove infected leaves, improve air circulation, and discourage lush growth. Spray plants with a suitable fungicide.
SCORCH Leaves wilt, turn yellow or brown, become dry and crisp, and may die; margins are affected first. Stems may die back.	Excessively high temperatures, especially in a greenhouse, bright but not necessarily hot sunlight, or wind drying out the leaves.	Try to prevent it from occurring by improving ventilation, providing shade, and damping down the greenhouse floor or giving shelter from wind.
SLUGS AND SNAILS Irregular holes appear in foliage of seedlings and cuttings, and stems are damaged at soil level. Slimy mucilage may leave a distinctive silvery deposit.	Slugs (such as *Milax*, *Arion*, and *Deroceras* species) and snails (such as *Helix aspersa*); these are slimy-bodied mollusks that feed on soft plant material, mainly at night or after rain.	Protect vulnerable plants, especially in wet weather. Remove by hand after dark or during overcast days; use beer traps or barriers such as diatomaceous earth. Scatter poisoned baits among plants.
SPIDER MITES Leaves develop a fine pale mottling on the upper surface; foliage becomes dull green, then yellowish white. Leaves fall prematurely, and a fine silk webbing may cover the plant.	Sap-feeding mites, *Tetranychus urticae*, that attack a wide range of indoor and greenhouse plants and those outdoors in warm, dry sites. Mites are less than 1⁄16in (1mm) long and have four pairs of legs. They breed rapidly in warm, dry conditions; some have resistance to miticides.	Maintain high humidity. Under cover, introduce the predatory mite *Phytoseiulus persimilis* before a heavy infestation develops. Plants may be sprayed with an insecticidal soap or other pesticide.
THRIPS A fine, silver-white discoloration, mottled with tiny black dots, appears on the upper surface of the leaves.	There are many different species of thrips – narrow-bodied, elongate, brownish black insects to ⅛in (2mm) long, sometimes crossed with pale bands, that feed by sucking sap. They thrive in hot, dry conditions.	Water plants regularly, improve air circulation and lower temperature. Spray with a suitable pesticide when signs of damage are seen.
VINE WEEVIL LARVAE Plants grow slowly, wilt, and may die. Outer tissues of seedlings of woody plants and cuttings may be gnawed from the stems below ground.	Plump, creamy white, legless grubs of the beetle *Otiorhynchus sulcatus*, up to ½in (1cm) long, with brown heads and slightly curved bodies that live in soil and feed on roots. Long-term, container-grown plants, such as cuttings and seedlings of woody plants, are most at risk.	Good hygiene avoids providing shelters for adults. Water a pathogenic nematode (*Heterorhabditis* or *Steinernema* species) into the soil or soil mix in late summer before the grubs become too large.
WIREWORMS Stems of seedlings are bitten through just below soil level.	Slender, stiff-bodied, orange-brown larvae of click beetles (such as *Agriotes* species), to 1in (2.5cm) long, that live in soil. They are most numerous in newly dug grassland, but gradually decline if land is cultivated regularly.	Where damage is seen, lure worms to gather under bits of wood, then destroy them. Regularly cultivate and weed the soil. Protect seedlings by dusting seed rows with insecticide.

GARDEN TREES

With their distinctive silhouettes and longevity, trees provide continuity and structure in the garden. They are expensive to buy but not especially hard to propagate and, once established, will give pleasure for generations to come.

Trees may provide the framework or focal point of a garden and may link the garden with the landscape beyond. They are woody perennials with a crown of branches, usually at the top of a single stem or trunk, and include conifers, or cone-bearing trees. Palms and cycads are also mostly treelike in form. Valued for their shape, which provides year-round interest, many trees also offer seasonal displays of handsome foliage and bark, showy flowers, and brilliant berries. While some are purely ornamental, other trees also bear edible crops.

Since they are slow-growing compared with herbaceous plants, trees tend to be expensive, so it may be worth growing your own, especially if a number of plants are needed for hedges, orchards, woodland gardens, or screening. Propagating trees also makes it possible to obtain more unusual species, replace declining trees, or determine the size and shape of the tree.

Taking cuttings is commonly used to increase many ornamental trees because it is fairly simple and provides new plants quite quickly. Trees naturally reproduce from seeds, so this is an easy way to raise species. Hybrids and cultivars rarely come true to type, but natural seedling variation may yield a new variety. Seed-raised trees usually take at least twice as long to reach flowering size than do those that have been propagated by vegetative techniques.

Grafting and budding are the principal ways of propagating fruit trees, joining fruiting cultivars with specifically bred rootstocks to restrict their growth or provide disease resistance. The new plants also establish quickly. Much used by commercial growers, grafting and budding are often shrouded in mystery, but some of the techniques are well within the capabilities of the avid gardener. Grafting and budding also may be used for ornamental trees that are difficult or slow to propagate by other means. Layering, whether simple layering that occurs naturally with some trees or air layering, is another option when only one or two new plants are required.

AUTUMN HARVEST
The horse chestnut (Aesculus hippocastanum) *often produces a prolific crop of fruits. These are best gathered as soon as they fall and, once the spiny husks are removed, sown fresh in pots or in nursery beds of fertile soil.*

PAULOWNIA TOMENTOSA 'LILACINA'
This tree thrives in climates with long, hot summers and is usually grown from seeds or root cuttings. Clusters of flowers at the shoot tips appear before the leaves, followed by large, woody seedpods that split open when ripe to release flat seeds.

Taking cuttings

Selecting hardwood cutting material *Choose strong, straight stems with healthy buds (left). Avoid those that appear old, spindly, or damaged (far left), or that have soft green growth (center).*

Taking cuttings is one of the most common propagation methods for trees: it is usually fairly simple and provides new plants relatively quickly, although care is needed when selecting cuttings material. Most hardwood cuttings will yield a sapling ready for planting out in one year; other types of cutting need to be grown on for 2–3 years. A few species, such as some conifers, take up to five years.

Hardwood cuttings

This is one of the easiest and least costly ways of raising many deciduous trees; it requires no special skill other than knowing which trees are suitable, when to take the cuttings, and how to provide basic conditions for rooting and growth.

The time to take the cuttings is during a tree's dormant period, usually from mid- to late autumn and in late winter, the best times being immediately after leaf-fall or just before bud break. Look for healthy, vigorous shoots, avoiding weak or very spindly growth (*see above*). In most cases, cut off each shoot at the union of the one- and two-year-old wood (*see below*). With very vigorous plants such as poplars (*Populus*) or willows (*Salix*) that root readily, take material from well-ripened wood of the current season's growth. The length of prepared cuttings varies enormously: they are commonly about 8in (20cm) but may be as long as 6ft (2m) in some instances, as for certain willows. The diameter also varies, depending on the length of the shoot, from pencil thickness to about 3in (8cm).

For plants that root easily, the simplest way to root hardwood cuttings is in open ground. For this purpose, it is best to use a patch that has been cultivated, with a soil that is open and friable. You can then easily insert the cuttings into the soil. If the soil is at all heavy, however, insert the cuttings in a slit trench, as shown below. The planting depth depends on whether you are raising single- or multistemmed trees (*see box, bottom left*). Check each row after winter because frost may have caused the trench to open, in which case the cuttings should be refirmed.

For trees that are slow to root, such as *Metasequoia* (dawn redwood) or *Laburnum*, overwinter bundles of cuttings in sand (*see facing page*). Each bundle should have no more than ten cuttings; otherwise, the ones in the middle will dry out. Sand will allow the cuttings to undergo a period of cold but will protect them from wide fluctuations in temperature. Use sharp sand with no soil in it so that the surface does not "cap over," or form a crust. Make sure it is moist, and periodically check moisture levels.

Leave the cuttings in the sand until just before bud break in early spring, then line them out in a nursery bed or pot individually in containers. In the following autumn, if the saplings are large enough, plant them out in their permanent positions. Otherwise, lift

Fast-rooting hardwood cuttings

1 In autumn, make a narrow trench 6–10in (15–25cm) deep by pushing the spade into the soil and pressing it slightly forward. To improve drainage, sprinkle some sharp sand into the trench bottom.

2 Select a well-ripened shoot at least 12in (30cm) long from the current season's growth (here of a fig tree, Ficus americana*). Make the cut so that it is flush with the main stem, or just above a bud.*

3 Remove any leaves and the soft growth from the tip of each cutting. Trim the cutting to a length of 8–9in (20–23cm), making an angled cut above the top bud and a straight cut below the bottom bud.

4 Space the cuttings in the trench about 4–6in (10–15cm) apart at the appropriate depth (see box, below)*. Firm the soil well, label, and water. Space additional rows 12–15in (30–38cm) apart.*

5 After several months, the cuttings should begin to root; by the end of the following growing season, sturdy new topgrowth should have developed.

6 Lift the rooted cuttings after leaf-fall in autumn, wrapping the roots in plastic to prevent drying out. Transplant the cuttings or pot them singly to grow on.

Planting depths

Multistemmed ornamental and fruit trees *Insert each cutting with the top one-third or 1–1¼in (2.5–3cm) showing above the surface of the soil.*

Single-stemmed ornamental trees *Cuttings should be buried so that the top bud of each cutting sits just below the surface of the soil.*

the cuttings and replant them, spaced 12in (30cm) apart in rows 18in (45cm) apart, to grow on for another year.

Another option is to root cuttings in containers. Insert three to five cuttings per pot into rooting medium (*see p.34*) after dipping the bases in hormone rooting compound. Label, water, and leave in a sheltered place, such as a cold frame. They should root by spring; pot them individually or in groups into larger containers.

Heel cuttings

Cuttings from woody plants were taken traditionally by pulling an appropriately sized shoot away from the main stem, retaining a small sliver of bark, or heel, at the base. The heel contains high levels of growth hormones (auxins). These cuttings are still useful, especially for plants that have pithy stems, such as elder (*Sambucus*), or plants that are old or in less than peak condition. They are not so effective with broadleaved trees. Heel cuttings may be taken from all types of wood, from hard- to softwood.

Semi-ripe cuttings

This technique is suitable for rooting certain broadleaved evergreens, for example *Magnolia grandiflora*, *Prunus lusitanica*, and hollies (*Ilex*), as well as many conifers (*see p.70*). The best time of year is usually late summer to early autumn, although cuttings may be taken in early summer or late autumn.

Select material from the current season's growth that has partly ripened or hardened to take stem-tip cuttings as shown (*right*). If the semi-ripe shoot is long enough, several cuttings may be taken; take the lower cuttings with the basal cut just below a node and the top cut above a node. Alternatively, take heel cuttings (*see above*). If the leaves are large, cut them down. After treating them with hormone rooting compound, insert the cuttings into pots, deep seed trays, or cell packs.

For the soil mix, use a free-draining medium such as a peat and bark mixture or other soilless mix (*see p.34*). Alternatively, use rockwool plugs or a bench bed of rooting medium in the greenhouse. Keep the cuttings humid and frost-free in a closed case or a cold frame, or under plastic. Bottom heat of 64–70°F (18–21°C) will aid rooting.

Periodically check the cuttings to ensure that the medium is sufficiently moist and the temperature is correct, as well as removing any dead leaves, which are potential sources of fungal infection. Maintain high humidity by spraying the cuttings before covering them again. Rooting usually occurs during autumn or winter; the cuttings may then be potted individually in spring.

SLOW-ROOTING HARDWOOD CUTTINGS OF TREES

1 For tree species that do not root easily, tie the cuttings (here of Metasequoia*) using garden twine into small bundles of up to ten cuttings. Dip the base of the cuttings in a small dish of hormone rooting powder or gel.*

2 Insert the bundles into a sand box or bed in a sheltered place or cold frame over winter. By spring, they should have rooted. Lift the bundles and insert the cuttings singly in a prepared trench (see facing page).

SEMI-RIPE CUTTINGS OF TREES

1 Select a healthy shoot from the current season's growth that is soft at the tip but firm at the base (here of a magnolia). Using pruners, cut straight above a node to obtain a cutting 4–6in (10–15cm) in length.

2 Remove all except the top two leaves, then cut these two in half with a clean, sharp knife to reduce moisture loss. To stimulate rooting, wound the base of the stem by slicing off a 1¼in (3cm) sliver of bark from one side.

3 Put a small amount of hormone rooting powder (or gel) into a saucer and dip the wounded stem into it. Tap the stem gently to remove any excess powder (see inset)*. Discard any remaining rooting compound from the dish when all the cuttings have been prepared.*

4 Fill 3in (8cm) pots with a mixture of equal parts peat and fine bark. Make a hole of 3–4in (8–10cm) in depth in each pot. Insert each cutting just deep enough for it to be able to stand upright. Firm the soil around the stem. Label and water the cuttings.

Softwood cuttings

Although less commonly used than hardwood or semi-ripe cuttings, this technique is suitable for raising various (primarily deciduous) trees, including some ornamental cherries (*Prunus*) as well as certain maples (*Acer*), birches (*Betula*), and elms (*Ulmus*). Softwood cuttings are usually taken in late spring from the fast-growing tips of new shoots, and they typically root very easily. The shoots must be turgid, so the best time to take cuttings (*see right*) is early in the morning. They do dry out and wilt rapidly, however, so it is vital to prepare and insert them as quickly as possible after taking them from the parent plant.

To save time, prepare the cells or pots before taking the cuttings. Use a free-draining rooting medium, such as equal parts fine bark or peat mixed with perlite or coarse sand. Firm the medium to just below the rim and water it. If using plug trays of rockwool (*see p.35*), soak them beforehand.

Take the cuttings by removing new, soft growth of the correct length at the junction of the new and old wood. Trim the stub from the parent shoot to avoid dieback. Even a small loss of moisture at this stage will hinder rooting, so put the cuttings in a partially inflated plastic bag (to minimize bruising) as you take them and seal, or immerse the cuttings in water. If any cutting is longer than 4in (10cm), remove the growing tip; this diverts growth hormones to the base and aids rooting. Place at once in a closed case, plastic-film tent, or mist bench (*see pp.38–44*) to minimize moisture loss, with bottom heat of 64–75°F (18–24°C).

Check the cuttings regularly, remove any dead or diseased leaves, and spray with fungicide once a week. Rooting should occur in 6–10 weeks. Feed the cuttings regularly to ensure strong new topgrowth. Pot in the following spring and plant out after 2–3 years.

TAKING SOFTWOOD CUTTINGS

1 Remove 2–3in (5–8cm) long, soft shoot tips (here of Betula utilis *var.* jacquemontii*). Cut straight across the union of the old and new wood. Keep the cuttings in a closed plastic bag. Trim the bottom two leaves from each shoot.*

2 Dip the cuttings in a fungicidal solution, and then dip the base of the stems in hormone rooting compound. Insert in cell packs in equal parts peat and perlite. Water (see inset) and label.

Greenwood cuttings

These cuttings are taken when the stems are slightly firmer and darker than for softwood cuttings. Take the cuttings between late spring and midsummer, although cuttings in warm climates may root at other times of year. Prepare them as shown (*see below*) and keep under mist or in a high-humidity tent. Once rooted, feed the cuttings regularly during the growing season, then pot them the following spring.

TAKING GREENWOOD CUTTINGS

1 In early summer, cut across the union of old and new wood to take cuttings of 10–12in (25–30cm) in length from the current season's growth (here of Liquidambar*).*

2 To prepare each cutting, trim off the soft wood at the tip of the shoot, just above a node. Take off the bottom leaf and wound the base of the stem. A prepared cutting should be 3–4in (8–10cm) long, with three nodes.

3 Dip the base of each cutting in hormone rooting compound. Fill a cell pack with equal parts peat and perlite. Insert each cutting just deep enough to stand upright. Water them in well and label.

Sowing seeds

Raising trees from seeds is generally straightforward and inexpensive and is useful for producing large numbers of plants, or rootstocks for subsequent grafting. Seedlings often establish well and are unlikely to carry viruses from the parent plant. Seed-raised plants take 2–5 times as long as cuttings to attain flowering size, however, and may vary in appearance, hardiness, and growth. It is impossible to predict the sex of new plants (vital for species that have foul-smelling fruits, such as *Ginkgo biloba*, or in which only female plants have fruits, for example *Ilex*).

Success with tree seeds depends as much on the treatment of seeds before sowing as on the sowing method. Many seeds germinate more successfully if sown as soon as they ripen, but purchased seeds are adequate if stored correctly. Some seeds, especially those of the northern temperate regions, must be treated to break their natural dormancy before sowing.

FRUITS AND SEEDPODS

Trees develop different fruiting bodies, which protect unfertilized seeds and aid dispersal of ripe seeds. Most trees have fleshy fruits to tempt animals to eat them, dry seedheads to scatter seeds on the wind, or hard-shelled nuts to stop animals from eating them. Cones do not enclose the seeds, unlike other seedheads.

STONE FRUIT
Peach (*Prunus*)

BERRIES
Mountain ash (*Sorbus*)

PODS
Laburnum

CATKIN
Birch (*Betula*)

CONE
Pine (*Pinus*)

WINGED SEED
Maple (*Acer*)

CAPSULE
Horse chestnut (*Aesculus*)

Collecting and cleaning seeds

Both dry and fleshy fruits may be picked by hand (taking care not to damage the parent plant). Preparation depends on the type of seeds. Those that ripen in spring or summer, such as poplar (*Populus*) and willow (*Salix*), require little cleaning other than teasing apart the seedhead.

Pods Spread out pods of trees such as *Cercis*, *Laburnum*, or *Robinia* in a warm room in a paper bag or with newspaper over them. The pods will split open after a few days and shed the seeds.

Winged seeds The wings of seeds such as of ash (*Fraxinus*) or maples (*Acer*) may be left on the seeds or cut or rubbed off for ease of handling.

Nuts Remove the outer husks from nuts such as those of beech (*Fagus*), hazel (*Corylus*), and chestnut (*Castanea*), but preserve the shells.

Catkins Collect catkins from trees such as alder (*Alnus*) while still green before they ripen and keep in paper bags for a week or two until they disintegrate.

Fleshy fruits With large fruits such as apples (*Malus*) and pears (*Pyrus*), cut open the fruits and remove the seeds. Pulp smaller fruits and leave in warm water for up to four days to separate out the seeds (*see below*), which should sink to the bottom. Dish detergent added to the water may assist separation. Once the seeds are clean, pat them dry.

Cones Dry ripe cones in a warm place to release the seeds (*see* Conifers, *p.71*).

Storing tree seeds

It is important to store seeds correctly to preserve their viability until you can sow them. Remove damaged or shriveled seeds before storing – they are liable to be diseased. Tree seeds are usually stored at 37°F (3°C) in a refrigerator (not a freezer). Most are refrigerated dry, to avoid the risk of fungal disease or rot, in sealed and labeled plastic bags. Seeds from fleshy fruits are only surface-dried. Large seeds, such as walnuts (*Juglans*) and oaks (*Quercus*), and oily seeds, such as magnolias, cannot take up water once they dry out and so will not germinate. Store these seeds in a plastic bag of moist vermiculite or sand or in a mix of moist peat and sand (*see below*).

Overcoming seed dormancy

In nature, dormancy ensures that seeds do not germinate before the onset of spring, but it can inhibit germination even in good conditions. There are various ways to overcome dormancy: the first is scarification (*continued on p.54*).

EXTRACTING SEEDS FROM FLESHY FRUITS

1 Put the fruits (here Sorbus*) in a sieve and hold under running water. Squash them with your thumb until they are well mashed.*

2 Put the fruit pulp in a jar and fill with water. Allow to settle. Drain the contents through a sieve. Viable seeds should stay in the jar.

STORING TREE SEEDS

Certain seeds must not be allowed to dry out. Store mixed with moist peat and coarse sand in a clear plastic bag in the refrigerator.

SCARIFYING SEEDS

Scarify seeds with an impermeable coating to speed germination. Abrade part of the seed coat to allow moisture to get in.

(*Continued from p.53.*) Tree seeds such as *Acacia* and *Robinia* with very hard seed coats must be abraded or scarified to let water into the seed. Use sandpaper (*see p.53*) or a file, gently crack the seed coat using a nutcracker, or nick it with a sharp knife. You can also carefully burn a small hole in the seed with a soldering iron.

Soften hard seed coats by soaking in hot (not boiling) water for up to 48 hours, depending on the size of the seeds. Sow seeds directly after soaking; if allowed to dry out again, they will die.

Some trees, for example hawthorns (*Crataegus*), lindens (*Tilia*), and mountain ashes (*Sorbus*), develop germination inhibitors in the seeds as they ripen. Gather seeds when they are mature but not fully ripe, before the inhibitors develop, to ensure good germination. Clean and store the seeds as usual and sow them in spring.

Other tree seeds have a physiological (or embryo) dormancy, sensitive to certain levels of cold and heat. Such seeds are treated by stratification, of which there are two types.

COLD MOIST STRATIFICATION This is the most common technique, especially for hardy trees, and involves chilling seeds to mimic the passing of winter; they also must be kept moist so that the seeds can start to respire. Traditionally, seeds in cold climates were sown in autumn to overwinter in containers in a cold frame or in an open seedbed. Germination varied depending on local conditions, with a low success rate following a mild winter. Chilling seeds in a refrigerator at 34–41°F(1–5°C), usually at 37°F (3°C), has the advantage that you can provide a cold period at any time of year and expect a more even germination.

To chill small numbers of seeds, soak them in water for 48 hours, allow to drain, then refrigerate in a labeled and sealed plastic bag for 4–20 weeks before sowing. Twelve weeks is the average, but it depends on the species (*see* A–Z of Garden Trees, *pp.74–91*).

For large quantities, store the seeds in a plastic bag filled with peat or a mixture of equal parts peat and coarse sand or vermiculite. This should be moist, not wet. Periodically turn the bag to circulate air and avoid a buildup of warmth or carbon dioxide released by the seeds. If the seeds germinate in the bag prematurely, sow them at once.

WARM MOIST STRATIFICATION Some seeds, such as ash (*Fraxinus*) or *Davidia*, are doubly dormant and germinate naturally after 18 months, or in the second spring, after ripening, with only a few seeds germinating in the first spring. If freshly collected seeds are exposed to a spell of warmth to simulate summer ripening, followed by a cold period, they should all germinate during the first spring. Place the seeds in a plastic bag, as for cold stratification, and keep them warm for up to 12 weeks at 64–75°F (18–24°C), then cold stratify them in the refrigerator. Alternatively, sow the ripe seeds in containers, then keep them warm at

SOWING TREE SEEDS IN CONTAINERS

1 Fill a 3in (8cm) pot with seed soil mix, and firm it gently to about ½in (1cm) below the rim of the pot. Sow larger seeds (here of Betula*) singly, spacing them evenly over the surface. Broadcast-sow fine seeds.*

2 For large seeds, sieve seed soil mix over the seeds until they are just covered to their own depth with mix. Cover fine seeds with a very light dusting of mix or a thin layer of fine grit or fine-grade vermiculite.

3 Cover the soil mix with a ¼in (5mm) layer of small gravel. Label and water well, using a fine-rosed watering can. Leave the pot in a sheltered place – usually in a cold frame, closed case, or heated greenhouse.

4 Keep temperate species at 54–59°F (12–15°C) and warm-temperate and tropical species at 70°F (21°C). The seeds should germinate and the seedlings grow to 1–2in (2.5–5cm) in height within 6–8 weeks.

5 Knock the seedlings out of their pot. The soil mix should break up, making it easier to tease out the roots. Always hold the seedlings by their leaves, since their roots and stems are very fragile and are easily damaged.

6 Transplant each seedling individually in a 3in (8cm) pot filled with soilless potting mix. Firm gently around the seedling, label, and water. Grow on in the same place as before. Harden them off gradually after 3–4 weeks.

SOWING LARGE SEEDS

1 Sow large tree seeds, or those that produce seedlings with long taproots (here of oak), individually in 4in (10cm) deep pots. Press each seed into unfirmed, soil-based seed mix. Cover the seed to its own depth with more mix to ¼in (5mm) below the pot rim.

2 After sowing, water and label the pot. Place in a sheltered place such as a cold frame or in a closed case under cover. By using a deep pot for such seedlings, the taproot can develop without any restriction (see inset).

the same temperature in a heated closed case before exposing them to a period of winter cold outdoors.

Sowing tree seeds in containers

This is the most widely practiced means of seed-raising because it allows more control over environmental conditions and pests than when sowing direct outdoors and generally gives a higher success rate in raising healthy seedlings.

There are many suitable containers, including standard pots, seed trays for large numbers of seeds, and specialized containers such as root-trainers or deep pots (*see above*) for taprooted trees such as oaks (*Quercus*) and *Eucalyptus*.

In general, a free-draining, mildly acidic, soilless mix is used (*see p.34*). For lime-hating trees such as *Arbutus menziesii*, use an acidic seed soil mix. Seeds that germinate slowly (12 months or more) are best sown in a heavier, soil-based seed mix. Sow the seeds as shown (*see facing page*). Usually the seeds are covered with fine grit or small gravel to prevent "capping," or a crust forming on the surface, and to avoid growth of mosses or liverworts, but if germination is likely to be very rapid, use vermiculite instead.

Place the containers in a sheltered place at an appropriate temperature (*see facing page*). A night minimum of 50°F (10°C) is generally sufficient under cover. For some tender species, however, 59–68°F (15–20°C) is preferable. Always keep seeds for at least a year if they do not germinate in the first year – they may come up during the second spring.

Once germination occurs, transplant the seedlings as soon as they are large enough to handle by the leaves, then return them to where they were before. After hardening off the seedlings (*see p.45*), pot them on or line them out in a nursery bed. Seedlings raised in root-trainers (because they dislike root disturbance) should be planted into their final locations as soon as possible.

Sowing tree seeds in a seedbed

If there are no facilities under cover or if it is difficult to provide full aftercare for seedlings, you may choose to sow direct outdoors. Protect the site from wind, if possible, with a hedge or artificial windbreak. The seedbed must be free of weeds; prepare the soil in the preceding spring and summer so that you can hoe off any weed seedlings. Incorporating well-rotted leaf mold at this stage also helps; it usually contains mycorrhizae, soil-borne fungi that help seedling growth and improve soil structure. Cultivate the bed to one spit (spade's blade) deep. Raise the seedbed as shown below, by boarding around the margins or hilling up the soil. This creates as even-textured and as well-drained a soil structure as possible to aid germination.

Before sowing (in early to midspring or, in cold climates for seeds that require a cold period, in mid- to late autumn), rake over the soil surface, remove any large stones, and tread evenly over the bed to firm the soil.

Many tree seeds are fairly large and can be space-sown, either in drills (*see below*) or in individual holes. Small seeds are sown in drills. Always sow seeds at the correct depth: aim to cover the seeds by roughly twice their own diameter. Large seeds should be sown at least 2–3in (5–8cm) deep.

Make drills using a draw hoe, the tip of a stake, or by pressing a board into the soil. To reduce the risk of fungal attack, sow small seeds thinly, directly from the packet or by taking a pinch of seeds and running it along the drill. Cover the seeds as shown. If necessary, thin the seedlings to 2in (5cm) apart. Transplant into a nursery bed after a year to grow on, and keep them fed and well watered.

SOWING TREE SEEDS IN A SEEDBED

1 Prepare a raised seedbed, 4–8in (10–20cm) deep and 3ft (1m) wide. Make drills 4–6in (10–15cm) apart with a hoe. Space-sow the seeds 1¼–3in (3–8cm) apart, keeping one type of seed in each drill. Label each drill.

2 Cover the seeds lightly with soil by drawing it over with the back of a rake. Rake a ¾in (2cm) deep layer of fine gravel over the entire bed. Allow the seedlings to grow on for up to a year until they are ready to transplant.

Grafting and Budding

Grafting has acquired an undeserved mystique, probably because it is largely used by commercial growers, but there is no reason for home gardeners not to try it. Once you understand the basic principles, and with a little practice and confidence with specific techniques, you should be able to graft successfully.

Grafting involves uniting parts of two separate plants to combine some of the benefits of each: the root system, or rootstock, of one, and a portion of stem from the plant to be propagated, known as the scion, which forms the plant's topgrowth. Grafted plants, unlike cuttings, have the advantage of an already-formed root system, so they establish relatively quickly and are usually ready for planting out in 2–3 years.

In some cases, the rootstock confers a valuable quality such as disease resistance or restricted size (useful for fruit trees, which otherwise grow too tall to harvest easily). Certain trees, for example apples (*Malus*) and fruiting and ornamental cherries (*Prunus*), grow less well and produce smaller crops when grown on their own roots than when they are grafted. Stocks and scions must be compatible, usually of the same genus and often derived from the same species.

Obtaining rootstocks for grafting

Good-quality rootstocks are essential to produce good-quality trees. You may be able to buy stocks, usually from speciality nurseries, but it is better to raise your own – you can then use as many stocks as you need and can be sure of them being the correct size. If buying fruit stocks, try to obtain virus-free certified stocks wherever possible, and make sure that you obtain the correct stock for the type and size of tree you want to grow (*see* A–Z of Garden Trees *for details, pp.74–91*).

Rootstocks should be well-rooted and straight, of medium thickness for the plant and about 18in (45cm) tall. Plant them while dormant in well-prepared soil: this should be free-draining, enriched with well-rotted manure, and free from perennial weeds. Add a general slow-release fertilizer at a rate according to the manufacturer's instructions.

Ornamental stocks are usually raised from seeds, such as Norway maple (*Acer platanoides*), bird cherry (*Prunus avium*), hawthorn (*Crataegus monogyna*), black locust (*Robinia pseudocacacia*), European beech (*Fagus sylvatica*), and mountain ash (*Sorbus aucuparia*). Fruit-tree stocks, flowering crabapples, certain ornamental plums, and hazels (*Corylus*) are better obtained by stooling (*see below*) or trench layering (*see facing page*); these are called clonal rootstocks because they are identical to the parent.

Rootstocks from stooling

The principal technique in this form of layering, shown below, involves hilling up an easily rooted, usually two-year-old parent plant to stimulate rooting at the base of the stems. The parent plant is cut back hard (*see box, below*) before hilling up to obtain as many new shoots as possible.

Growing rootstocks by stooling

1 Select a healthy 1–2-year-old stock plant (here, apple) with plenty of shoots. Hill up the base of the stems in stages from spring to late summer. Each time, firm lightly and water.

2 Throughout the growing season, keep the soil around the stock plant moist to encourage rooting from the lower stems. In late autumn, carefully rake away the soil mound.

3 With a hand fork, carefully tease out the soil from around the roots to expose the new roots growing from the bases of the hilled-up stems. Take care not to damage the roots.

4 Remove rooted shoots from the stock plant. Use sharp pruners to make a straight cut just above the neck of the parent plant. Re-cover the roots of the plant with 2in (5cm) of soil.

5 Dig a straight-backed trench in a nursery bed and line out the rooted layers 9in (23cm) deep and 12–18in (30–45cm) apart. Label and water well. Grow on to use as rootstocks.

Stooling a stock plant

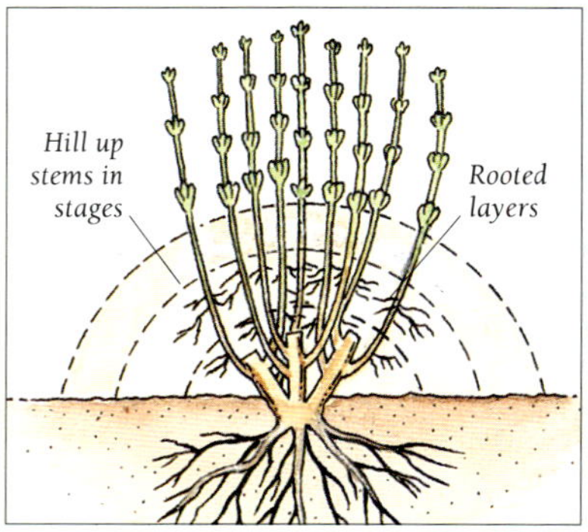

To obtain lots of young shoots, cut back the stock plant to 3in (8cm) in late winter or early spring. Begin hilling up (see step 1) when the new shoots are 6in (15cm) long.

TRENCH LAYERING

1 In the dormant season, plant the parent stock at an angle in a nursery bed. The next winter, dig a trench along the row. Peg each shoot to the trench base. Cover with friable soil. Hill up new sideshoots in stages as they grow, over spring and summer.

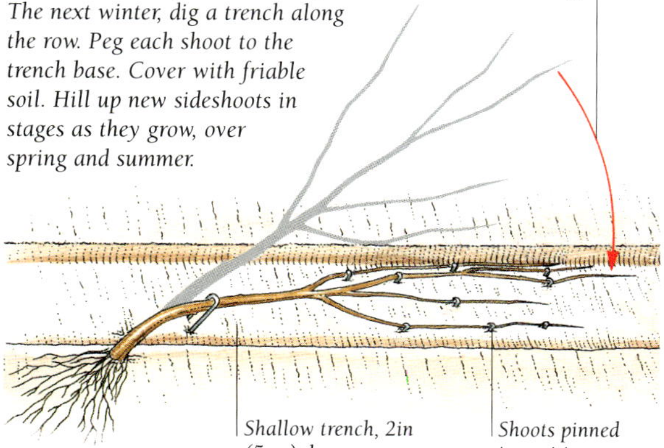

2 The following winter, carefully remove the hilled-up soil to reveal the adventitious roots at the base of each sideshoot, or layer.

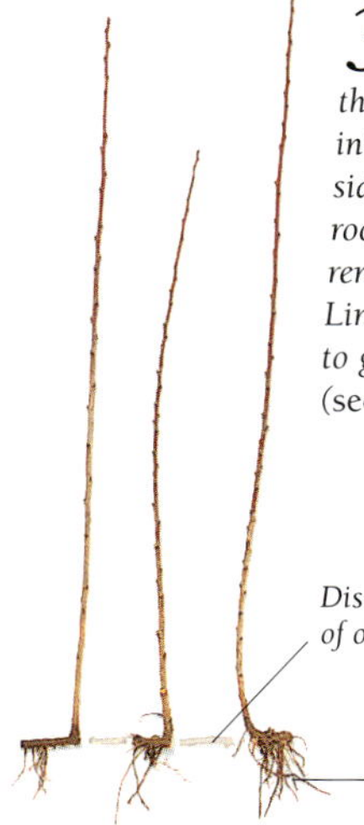

3 Cut off the layered stems at the base of the plant. Cut each stem into sections, each with a sideshoot and a developing root system. Discard the remainder of the stem. Line out the rooted layers to grow on, as for stooling (see facing page).

Once rooted, these shoots, or layers, may be cut off the parent and lined out in a trench to grow on (*see step 5, facing page*), ready for subsequent grafting. It is important to plant the layers quite deeply in the trench so that the young rootstocks produce shoots that are as straight as possible as well as have good root systems. Firm well after planting. If growing a large number of stocks, space the rows 3ft (90cm) apart and orient them north to south to minimize shade.

After planting, lightly prune any weak growth and remove any sideshoots below about 12in (30cm) flush with the stem, in order to leave a clean stem for budding and grafting (*see pp.58–63*). During summer, rub out any sideshoots that appear below about 12in (30cm).

The young stocks must make active growth for budding and grafting to succeed, so good irrigation is important; the most effective and economical method is to lay a drip line or a seep hose (*see p.44*) along each row of stocks.

Rootstocks from trench layering

This method (also known as "etiolation" layering) is used for fruit trees including apples (*Malus*), pears (*Pyrus*), cherries and peaches (*Prunus*), walnuts (*Juglans*), mulberries (*Morus*), and quinces (*Cydonia oblonga*). The technique works on the principle that shoots produce roots more easily when they are pale and drawn (etiolated). Two-year-old parent plants are planted at an angle (*see above*) in autumn; they should be spaced in rows 5ft (1.5m) apart at 2ft (60cm) intervals to allow room for hilling up.

In the following late winter, make a shallow trench along the row of plants, then peg down the young shoots, using wooden pegs or staples of heavy wire, into the bottom of the trench. Cut back weak sideshoots, but leave strong ones unpruned or just lightly tip them back. All the sideshoots must be pegged down flat or removed entirely. Fill in the trench with friable soil or compost.

As new sideshoots push through the soil in spring, they become etiolated. Once they appear, hill up the shoots with another 1in (2.5cm) layer of soil; use fresh soil or compost to reduce the risk of disease. Repeat this process twice or three times more in the early part of the growing season, and as needed throughout the season, until the plants are hilled up to a height of 6–8in (15–20cm). Take care to keep the soil moist during this time to encourage the shoots to root into the soil.

In the following late winter, uncover and sever rooted shoots (*see above*). Select new shoots near the base of the plant. Repeat the process as required.

Pest and disease control

In general, rootstocks are susceptible to the same pests and diseases as the scion cultivars, although some have a degree of resistance – for example, one of the main stocks for grafting citrus trees, the Japanese bitter orange (*Poncirus trifoliata*), resists phytophthora root disease. It is vital to keep stocks well fed and watered to increase their resistance and to control any problems, ensuring active growth of the stock and reducing the risk of infection to the scion cultivar.

Apple and quince stocks are usually susceptible to apple powdery mildew, particularly if they are not well watered. Check for and control aphids, especially on stone-fruit stocks, because the insects transmit virus diseases.

GRAFTING MULTIPLE SCIONS

In some cases, you may want to graft more than one scion onto a stock. For fruit trees, creating a multiple tree using scions from two or three different cultivars provides a choice of fruit on a single tree (for example, both cooking and eating apples, or peaches and nectarines, as below) or may be done to aid cross-fertilization. For ornamental trees, using multiple scions helps create a more balanced crown. It is especially valuable for a weeping tree, using scions of naturally pendent forms grafted onto a tall stem.

Multiple tree *Fruit-tree rootstocks can have scions from two or more related cultivars grafted onto them. Here, cultivars of a nectarine (left-hand side) and a peach (right-hand side) are budded onto a* Prunus *stock.*

Top-working *Two scions of* Salix caprea *'Kilmarnock' have been whip-and-tongue grafted (see inset and p.59) onto a rootstock of* S. x stipularis *to produce a more balanced canopy than would be achieved with only one scion.*

SPLICED SIDE GRAFTING

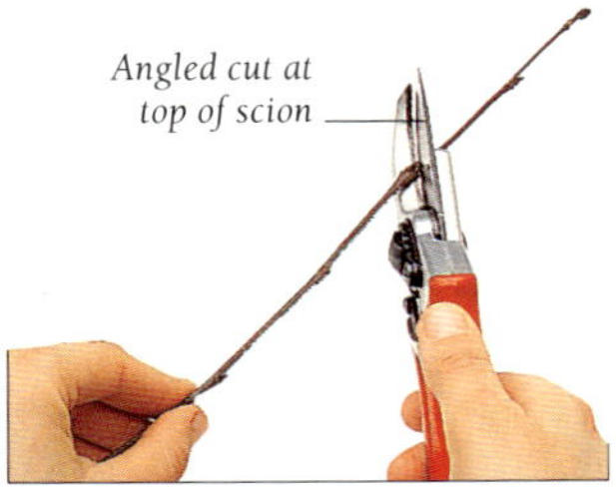

1 For the scions, gather strong, one-year-old stems and trim each one down to 6–10in (15–25cm), cutting just above a bud or pair of buds. Refrigerate in a plastic bag until ready to graft.

2 To graft, make a short, downward nick about 1in (2.5cm) below the top of each stock. Then, starting near the top of the stock, make a sloping, downward cut to meet the inner point of the first cut.

3 Remove the sliver of wood. Make the final cut by cutting straight up from the inner corner of the first cut. This creates a flat-sided stem (see inset) with a "shoulder" at the base.

4 To prepare the scion, make a shallow, sloping cut about 1in (2.5cm) long down to the base. Then make a short, angled cut at the base of the scion from the opposite side (see inset).

5 Immediately fit the base of the scion into the cut in the stock (see inset), so that the cambiums meet. Bind the graft with some grafting tape (or raffia) until it is completely covered.

6 To prevent the graft from losing moisture and failing, brush a layer of wound sealant or grafting wax over all the external cut surfaces on both the stock and the scion.

7 A successful graft should "take" within a few weeks, when the buds of the scion will show signs of growth. If any suckers appear on the stock, remove them, or they will divert growth away from the scion.

Grafting techniques

The principles of grafting are largely the same, regardless of method, but different techniques are used according to the plant being grafted and the relative sizes of rootstock and scion (*for details of specific plants, see* A–Z of Garden Trees, *pp.74–91*). Most grafting is done in late winter to early spring or in mid- to late summer. Ornamentals are often grafted onto containerized stocks under cover (bench grafting) where it is easier to control conditions, whereas fruit trees are usually budded or grafted outdoors (field budding or grafting) onto stocks or trees in open ground.

For a graft to succeed, it is vital that the cambiums (thin regenerative layers just below the bark) of stock and scion are in close contact and that the graft does not dry out or become infected before it "takes" and calluses. The cuts therefore must be as precise as possible: practice first on willow stems. Make one graft at a time; use a clean, sharp knife; and work as quickly as possible to prevent the cuts from drying out. Avoid touching the cut surfaces, and ensure the cambiums align before sealing the graft.

In warm, humid climates, scions may be taken up to 12in (30cm) in length; they will take and mature more quickly.

Spliced side grafting

This is usually carried out just before bud break in late winter or early spring and is useful if the stock is thicker than the scion. Two-year-old, seed-raised stocks are most often used; it is essential that they have straight stems and a good root system in an 3–4in (8–10cm) pot. A potbound plant cannot support a graft. Bring the stocks into a cool greenhouse with a nighttime minimum of 45–50°F (7–10°C) 2–3 weeks before grafting. Keep on the dry side to avoid excessive sap flow, which hinders union of a graft.

Collect scions from the tree to be propagated, choosing healthy, vigorous, one-year-old shoots. Remove them by cutting into the two-year-old wood to retain the union between new and old wood (scions graft more successfully if they have older wood at the base). Keep the scions fresh in a plastic bag in a refrigerator until you are ready to graft.

Head back the stock to 3–4in (8–10cm) above the base; cut as shown above. Take a scion, trim the base at the union of the new and old wood, then remove the top buds so that the scion is 6–10in (15–25cm) long. Cut the base of the scion to match the cut on the stock, ensuring that a dormant bud is retained opposite the cut. Position the base of the scion in the cut on the stock and secure with grafting tape or raffia. Seal any exposed cut surfaces and label the plant.

Whip grafting

This is used if the stock and scion are exactly the same diameter, as for spliced side grafting, but with a simpler cut. This slanting, downward cut, 1–2in (2.5–5cm) long, starts at one side of the top of the stock and ends on the opposite side of the stem. Cut the scion to match and proceed as for spliced side grafting.

Apical-wedge grafting

This is similar to spliced side grafting, but the scions are only 6in (15cm) long. Cut down into the stock across the center to a depth of 1–2in (2.5–5cm). Trim the base of the scion into a V-shape, making a 2in (5cm) slanting cut on each side. Push the base of the scion into the stock. The top, or "church window," of both cuts on the scion should be visible above the stock. Treat thereafter as for spliced side grafting.

Spliced side-veneer grafting

With trees that are difficult to unite with a stock or have thin bark, such as Japanese maples (*Acer*), the stock is headed back only once the graft has taken. Conifers are also grafted in this way. This graft is done just before bud break or in mid- to late summer. If the latter, collect scions early in the morning from ripe wood of the current season's growth, cutting into old wood as before. Prepare the scion otherwise as for a spliced side graft. Trim off leaves from the bottom 6in (15cm) of the stock, then graft as for conifers (*see p.73*).

Once the graft has taken, the top of the stock above the union is gradually headed back. How quickly you do this depends on the plant being grafted (*see* A–Z of Garden Trees, *pp.74–91*). In the first 12 months after grafting, the stock is used as a support for the scion, which is loosely tied to it. By the second spring after grafting, the stock should have been headed back completely.

Caring for bench-grafted plants

For grafts carried out in late winter or early spring, in cold climates, line out the plants on the bench in a cool greenhouse with a nighttime minimum of 50°F (10°C). If possible, apply bottom heat of 59–64°F (15–18°C) to encourage the rootstock into growth before the scion. Alternatively, place the grafts in a hot pipe to encourage them to callus (*see p.109*). Remove any suckers as soon as they appear on the rootstock. Pot the plants in late spring or early summer.

In warm climates or with summer-grafted plants that may lose moisture through their leaves, keep them in high humidity, in a closed case or plastic-film tent, at a nighttime minimum of 59°F (15°C). Each day, check for fungal disease and mist-spray to keep up the humidity. Keep the rootstocks on the dry side until callusing of the graft and shoot growth is evident, then wean the plants off the humidity 6–8 weeks later. Keep them cool but frost-free for the first winter, then pot on in spring.

Whip-and-tongue grafting

This is a very common method of field grafting, widely used for fruit trees and for some ornamentals, where the larger root system of the rootstock results in a superior tree. It may also be used on plants where budding (*see pp.60–62*) has failed: the plant is grafted in spring following the attempted budding to obtain a tree in the same length of time. This graft is most suitable when stock and scion are of a similar diameter, not more than 1in (2.5cm), for a neat union. Use established rootstocks (usually planted at least 12 months in advance).

Gather scions, as shown below, of roughly pencil thickness from dormant trees, when the growth hormones are concentrated at the buds. Heel them in (*see below*) or keep in a dry plastic bag in a refrigerator. In early spring, prepare the stocks and scions with matching cuts, then fit together. If the cut on the stock is much wider than that on the scion, place the scion off center so there is good cambial contact on at least one side. If the cut is large, cover it, as well as the "church window" on the scion, with grafting wax to prevent moisture loss and to keep water from entering the graft, which may make it fail. The graft should callus after six weeks or so.

One or all three buds on the scion should grow out. Choose one to grow on to form the tree (usually the topmost one); you will probably need to tie it to a stake to ensure that it grows straight. Cut back any others once they have three or four leaves. Remove any sideshoots from below the graft union once they are 3–4in (8–10cm) long (they are useful to feed the stock until then).

WHIP-AND-TONGUE GRAFTING

1 Select healthy, vigorous hardwood shoots of the previous season's growth from the scion tree in late winter. Use pruners to take lengths of about 9in (23cm), cutting obliquely just above a bud.

2 Make bundles of five or six scions. Prepare a sheltered, free-draining site and heel them in, leaving 2–3in (5–8cm) above the soil surface. This will keep them moist but dormant until grafting.

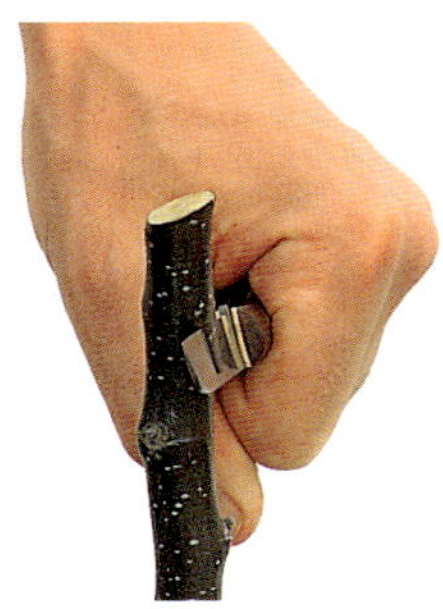

3 Prepare each stock just before bud break in early spring. Cut off the top, about 6–12in (15–30cm) above ground level. Trim off any sideshoots. Make a 1½in (3.5cm) upward-sloping cut on one side.

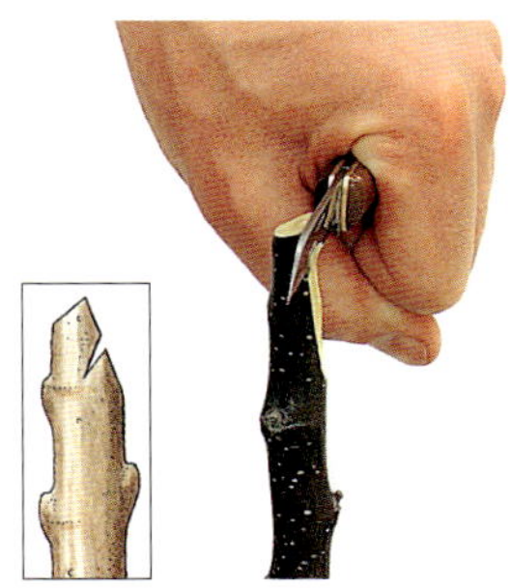

4 Make a shallow incision, about ¼in (5mm) deep, approximately one-third of the way down the exposed cambium layer of the stock. This forms a tongue (see inset) *to link into a similar one on the scion.*

5 Lift the scion. Cut off any soft growth at the tip. Trim to three or four buds. Choose a bud 1½in (3.5cm) from the base; remove a slice of wood on the opposite side, cutting from the bud to the base.

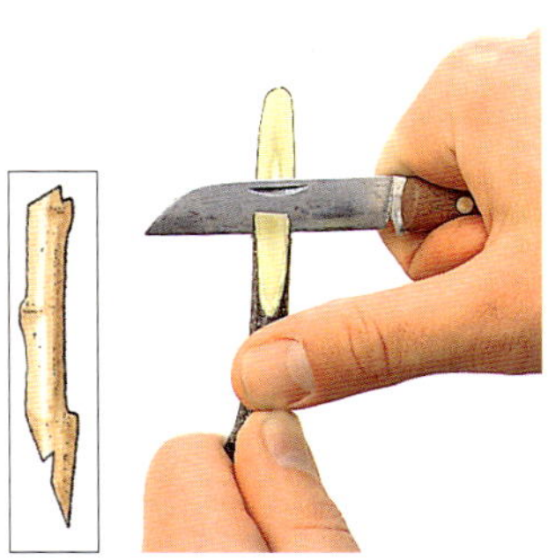

6 Match the tongue on the stock by making a similar slit into the cambium layer on the scion (see inset). *Take care not to touch and contaminate any of the cut surfaces with your hands.*

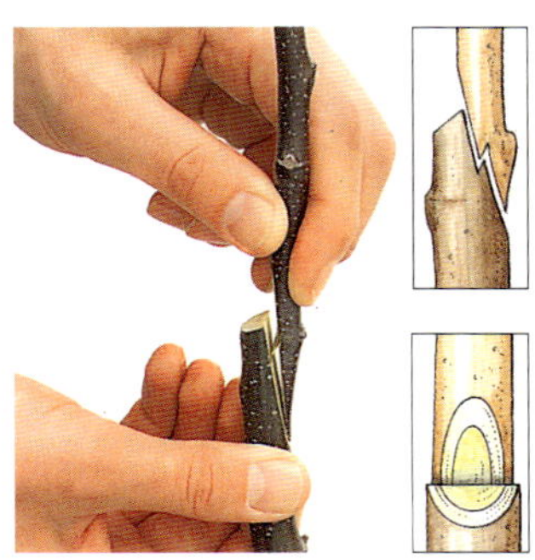

7 Fit the tongue of the scion into that on the stock (top inset). *Use the arches of the cambium layer* (see bottom inset) *to guide you and adjust the scion until the cambiums fit well together.*

8 When the two cambium layers are in close contact, bind the scion and stock firmly together with grafting tape or raffia. Remove the tape when a callus forms around the graft union (see inset).

CHIP-BUDDING: PREPARING THE SCION

1 In midsummer, select a vigorous, ripened shoot (here of apple) of the current season's wood. The shoot, or budstick, should be of pencil thickness and have well-developed buds.

2 Use a clean, sharp knife to trim off all the leaves from the budstick, leaving a ⅛in (3–4mm) stub of each leaf stalk (petiole). Remove the soft tip from the top of the shoot.

ORNAMENTAL TREES

For container-grown ornamental trees, when removing the leaves from the budstick (here of a magnolia), cut through each leaf stalk to leave a ¾–1in (2–2.5cm) stub. Remove each bud chip as shown in steps 3–5, below.

3 Select the first bud at the base of the budstick. Cut into the stem about ¾in (2cm) below the bud to a depth of ¼in (5mm), angling the knife blade downward at an angle of 30°.

4 Make another incision about 1½in (4cm) above the first. Slice downward behind the bud toward the first cut. The bud chip should then come away from the budstick (see inset).

5 The bud chip (see ornamental bud chip, inset) consists of a dormant bud, trimmed leaf stalk, and slice of wood. Holding the bud chip by the leaf stalk, put it in a plastic bag.

BUDDING TREES

Budding, also known as bud-grafting, employs similar principles to grafting (*see p.58*), except that the scion consists of a single growth bud rather than a length of stem. There are two main techniques: chip-budding (*see above*) and T-budding, or shield budding (*see p.62*). Both are extensively used by commercial growers, especially for fruit trees, but they are also well within the capabilities of the avid gardener. Any tree that may be whip-and-tongue grafted (*see p.59*) may be budded (*see also* A–Z of Garden Trees, *pp.74–91*).

CHIP-BUDDING FRUIT TREES

This is the most successful technique for grafting fruit trees. Although a very old method, it has only in recent years become widely used. It has an advantage over T-budding in that it can be carried out over a longer period of the year, although it is usually done between midsummer and early autumn.

For best results, use healthy, virus-free rootstocks and virus-free scion wood if possible (usually available for only a few cultivars that are mainly grown commercially). For the scion material, or budsticks, select pencil-thick shoots of well-ripened new growth where the base of the shoot is starting to turn brown and woody. It is best to take shoots from the periphery of the tree, usually on the sunny side. Avoid weak, green, etiolated shoots. The shoots must not dry out, so place them in a bucket of water immediately.

Prepare a budstick by removing the leaf blades, as shown above, to leave short leaf stalks (petioles). Also remove the stipules (leaflike structures at the bases of leaf stalks) to minimize any water loss, and any immature, unripe growth toward the tip of the shoot.

If budding a large number of plants and preparing several budsticks, keep them wrapped in a damp cloth until ready to use, and graft one bud at a time. Work from the base of the budstick to select the first bud. Avoid any large, prominent buds that may be fruit buds. With stone fruits such as cherries or peaches, check that the buds are small, pointed leaf buds, not large, round fruit buds. Holding the budstick firmly, make a cut below the bud at an angle of about 30° (*see above*). Make another incision above the first and slice downward behind the bud toward the first incision. Remove the bud chip, holding it carefully by the leaf stalk so as not to touch and contaminate the exposed cambium layer.

Prepare each rootstock by removing sideshoots and leaves from the lower main stem (*see facing page*). Select an area of clean, smooth stem at a height of 6–12in (15–30cm) above ground level (preferably on the shady side of the stock). Remove a piece of wood from the stock. Make the first cut just above a node to prevent the knife from slipping, then tailor the cut as closely to the size and shape of the bud chip as possible to ensure a close match of the cambiums.

Position the bud chip on the stock, making sure that the cambiums meet; place it off center if necessary to ensure good cambial contact on at least one side. Bind the bud chip to the stock with grafting tape or 1in (2.5cm) budding tape. Tuck in one end of the tape below the bud, then bind around and over the bud to avoid the wind drying it (or around the bud, only if it is very large).

Once the bud unites with the stock, you should notice a callus forming around the edges. If the bud has taken successfully, the leaf stalk will look plump and healthy and should drop off at or before leaf fall; if so, you may then remove the tape. If the bud has not taken, however, the leaf stalk will wither and turn brown and will not fall off. If the bud fails, leave the stock until the following early spring, cut back the stock to below the failed bud, and whip-and-tongue graft it instead (*see p.59*).

Care of chip-budded fruit trees

In the following late winter or early spring, when the buds of the rootstock start into growth, cut back the stock to just above the bud, (*see below*).

As the bud shoot develops and grows out, shoots should also grow out from the stock below the bud. Remove these when they are about 3–4in (8–10cm) long and the bud shoot is growing strongly (before this they are needed to feed the stock). If the bud shoot does not grow straight, tie it to a stake to support it, but leave it unsupported otherwise. Any flowers produced by the bud should be removed, so that all the nutrients go into the developing shoot.

During the following autumn, the tree should be ready to plant out in its final position or, if required, transplanted for further training into a nursery bed.

Chip-budding ornamental trees

Some ornamental trees, including crab-apples (*Malus*), hawthorns (*Crataegus*), *Laburnum*, magnolias, and *Sorbus*, as well as ornamental cherries (*Prunus*) and pears (*Pyrus*), may be propagated successfully by chip-budding. For those that are field-budded, the procedures are identical to those used for fruit trees.

Some ornamental trees (*see* A–Z of Garden Trees, *pp.74–91*) may be budded in a cool greenhouse using container-grown stocks. The technique is similar to field-budding and is carried out in mid- to late summer. The budsticks are prepared in a slightly different way, however (*see box, facing page*); budding is carried out at about 2in (5cm) above the base of the stem. The bud and leaf stalk are also left exposed (*see box, below*) because they do not need to be covered with grafting tape to stop them from drying out, as in field budding.

In 10–14 days, the leaf stalk should fall off if the bud has taken successfully. Leave the grafting tape in place until the bud is growing strongly, then cut back the stock to just above the developing bud to channel energy into the bud. By the end of autumn, some shoot growth should be evident. Keep the plants frost-free over the winter. Pot them on in spring and cut back again to promote bushy growth. The budded trees should be ready to plant in their permanent positions in 6–12 months.

CHIP-BUDDING: UNITING THE SCION AND STOCK

1 To prepare the rootstock, stand astride the plant. Remove all the sideshoots and leaves from the bottom 12in (30cm) of the stem, using a clean, sharp knife.

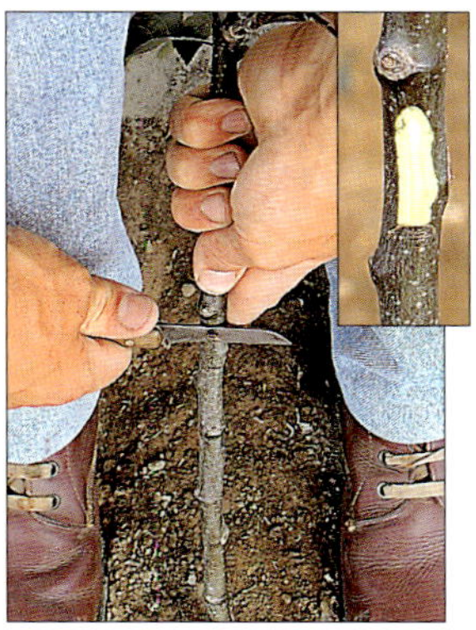

2 Select an area of clean, smooth stem. Make a shallow cut just above a node. Remove a sliver of bark to reveal the cambium (see inset) *and leave a lip at the base.*

ORNAMENTAL TREES

Preparing the stock
Prepare a container-grown rootstock by removing all the leaves from the bottom 10–12in (25–30cm) of the stem, using a sharp knife.

3 Place the bud chip in position on the stock (see inset). *If the cut on the stock is wider than the bud chip, place the chip to one side so that the cambium layers meet.*

4 Bind the bud chip to the stock using grafting tape. Bind around and over the bud. Carefully remove the tape once the bud chip unites with the stock (usually in 6–8 weeks).

Binding the bud chip
Bind the bud chip securely to the stock, but leave both the bud and the leaf stalk exposed. The leaf stalk will drop off in 10–14 days if the bud takes.

Pruning a chip-budded tree
In the following late winter or early spring, remove the top of the stock. Use pruners to cut just above the grafted bud, using an angled cut (see inset). *During the spring and summer, a shoot from the grafted bud will develop* (above).

T-BUDDING TREES

1 *Take a ripened shoot from current season's growth on the scion plant and strip off the leaves. Cut a healthy bud from the scion, with a strip of bark extending roughly 1in (2.5cm) above and below the bud. Remove the sliver of wood behind the bark.*

2 *About 6–12in (15–30cm) above ground level, make a T-shaped cut in the bark of the stock. With the reverse blade of the knife, carefully peel back the flaps of bark to expose the pith. The bark should lift away smoothly if the technique is to be successful.*

3 *Hold the bud by its leaf stalk and carefully slide it in behind the flaps of bark on the stock. Trim away any exposed "tail" so that it is level with the horizontal cut on the stock. Cut back the leaf stalk. Bind the entire bud with clear plastic grafting tape.*

T-BUDDING TREES

This is the most widely used technique worldwide for grafting fruit trees, as well as for some ornamentals, for example magnolias, and may also be used to create a standard tree. Although it is effective, its popularity may soon be overtaken by chip-budding (which has proved to be easier and more successful and is now more widely practiced, *see p.60*). Its name derives from the T-shaped cut that is made on the rootstock into which the bud is inserted. It is also known as shield budding because the bud is taken with a piece of bark, like a small shield.

The principal drawback of T-budding is that it can be carried out only when the bark of the stock lifts easily away from the wood, usually in summer. Drought impedes this, so in dry weather prepare the stocks by keeping them well watered for up to two weeks before T-budding. The T-bud is more fragile than a chip bud because the wood is not retained. In addition, there is a greater risk of infection by airborne fungal diseases, particularly apple canker, which can be inoculated below the bark on the bud shield.

However, T-budding is a well-proven technique, and some people find it easier than chip-budding. (*See* A–Z of Garden Trees, *pp.74–91, for suitable trees.*)

As with chip-budding and whip-and-tongue grafting (*see p.59*), use healthy, virus-free rootstocks whenever possible and, if available, virus-free scion wood. As for chip-budding, the stocks should be at least two years old and planted out in the autumn before T-budding.

PREPARING THE STOCK AND SCION

Collect the scion material from the plant you wish to propagate in the same way as for chip-budding (*see p.60*), selecting ripened shoots from the current season's growth. The preparation of the budstick is slightly different, however. Strip off the leaves, but leave a fairly long leaf stalk (petiole) of about ¼–½in (5–10mm) to act as a handle. It is best to use a specialized budding knife because it has a flattened part on the reverse of the blade or the handle designed specifically for lifting the bark on the rootstock.

Hold the budstick by the top end and select the first good bud. Insert the knife ¾–1in (2–2.5cm) below the bud. Make a shallow cut beneath the bud toward the top of the budstick, then lift the blade of the knife to remove the bud with a "tail" (*see above*). Keep buds clean and moist in a dish of water or wrapped in a damp cloth while you quickly prepare the rootstocks.

At a height of 6–12in (15–30cm) from the ground, make a T-shaped cut into the bark of the stock. The top cut needs to be only about ½in (1cm) across, while the vertical, downward cut should be 1–1½in (2.5–4cm) long. Press with the knife firmly to cut through the bark, but take care not to score too deeply and cut into the pith. Using the spatula, lift the two bark flaps (*see above*).

Hold the bud by its leaf stalk and gently insert it into the T-cut on the stock, sliding it down between the bark and the pith beneath so that it is well below the horizontal cut. Do not push in the bud too hard, or it may be damaged. Sever the remaining tail of the bud by cutting into the bark again at the horizontal cut (*see above*). Then secure the bud in place with plastic tape or raffia in the same way as for a chip-budded ornamental tree (*see box, p.61*), leaving the bud uncovered to avoid exerting too much pressure on it.

PRUNING A FRUIT TREE FOR RIND GRAFTING

As new growth begins, the sap riser draws the sap toward the grafts, promoting swift healing and helping to reduce the number of new shoots that may form around the pruning cuts.

In spring, head back most of the main branches of the stock tree to within 24–30in (60–75cm) of the main branch fork. Leave one or two smaller branches to act as sap risers.

About six weeks after budding, the T-cut should have callused, so you can remove the tape or raffia. Thereafter, treat the budded plant in the same way as for a chip-budded tree (*see pp.60–61*).

Inverted T-budding

In some cases, such as in a wet climate, an inverted T-cut is made on the stock to prevent water from entering the graft and causing rot. This method is also frequently used for grafting cultivars of citrus (*see* Citrus, *p.78*). The technique is largely as for conventional T-budding, except that the bud is pushed upward beneath the bark flaps.

Rind grafting

Sometimes it may be desirable to change a mature fruit tree (usually an apple or pear) from one cultivar to another, often to introduce a new pollinator for nearby trees and so improve cropping or simply to try a new cultivar. The newly grafted cultivar should bear fruit fairly quickly because it benefits from having a mature root and main branch system. This practice is known as grafting over and may be carried out by top-working a pruned-back tree.

Rind grafting is often used for top-working and is usually the best way of inserting grafts into a large branch. It takes its name from the process of inserting scions under the bark (known as rind by commercial fruit growers). Ornamental trees are not rind-grafted; it tends to create unsightly graft unions.

Rind grafting using dormant scions is carried out when the sap is rising in the stock tree so that the bark will lift easily, usually in midspring.

To prepare a tree for rind grafting, you first need to cut back most of the main branches (*see facing page and below*). One or two branches are left intact to draw the sap toward the grafts, which speeds healing and callusing. Take scions from pencil-thick ripened shoots of the previous season's growth.

Graft one branch at a time: cut the bark of the branch so that you can insert the scions. Make a long, straight cut through the bark, down the branch as shown below. Make 2–4 evenly spaced cuts, depending on the branch circumference, then lift the bark.

Prepare the scions as shown below, then insert one scion into each cut in the bark. Make sure that the tapering side of the base of each scion lies inward so that it is in contact with the cambial layer of the stock branch. Bind them with grafting tape and seal the graft with grafting wax. The graft should unite and grow rapidly, so remove the tape after about six weeks to prevent constriction.

Only one scion will be needed to form the new branch, but leave them all in place during the first growing season and remove all but the most vigorous one in the following winter. If any shoots develop on the stem around and below the grafts, remove them when they are 3–4in (8–10cm) long.

RIND GRAFTING A FRUIT TREE

*1 Head back all but one or two of the main branches on the rootstock, leaving a sap riser (*see facing page*). Trim the bark around the cuts, if necessary, so that the pruned surface has no snags.*

2 With a clean, sharp grafting knife, score a cut in the bark that extends downward about 2in (5cm) from the pruned end of the branch. Make up to four equally spaced cuts around the branch.

3 With the reverse edge of the grafting knife, or with a thin spatula, lift the bark to one side of each cut and carefully ease it away to expose the cambium layer of the branch beneath.

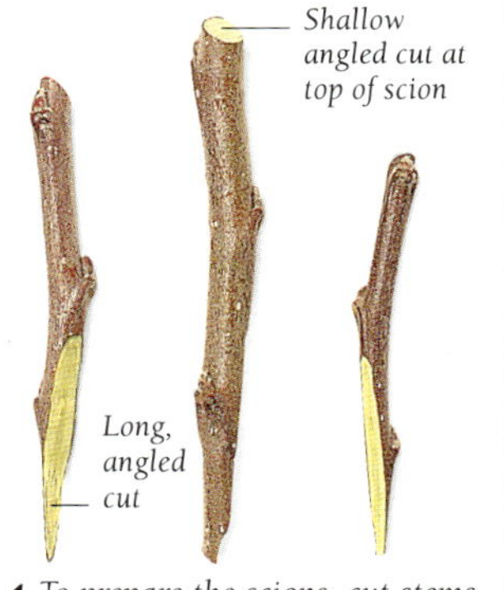

4 To prepare the scions, cut stems into sections each with three nodes. Make a cut just above, and angled away from, the upper bud. Trim a 1½in (4cm) sliver of wood from the base, opposite a bud.

5 Carefully slide a prepared scion beneath each cut in the bark on the stock. Make sure that the cut surface at the base of each scion is in close contact with the stock's cambium layer.

6 Bind the graft union with plastic grafting tape, making sure that each turn overlaps the previous one. Bind from the top of the branch to about 1in (2.5cm) below the cuts and tie off the tape.

7 Seal the cut surface of each branch with a wound paint or grafting wax to prevent entry of water. Avoid coating the edge near the scions, so that the buds have room to swell and grow.

*8 In the following winter, remove all but the strongest scion from each branch, cutting flush with the pruned surface of the branch. The scions will grow on to form the new branches (*see above*).*

Layering

This process may occur naturally in some trees, when one or more low-growing stems root into the ground; this ability can be exploited in simple layering to obtain a small number of new plants. Air layering also induces adventitious roots to form on a stem, but it is carried out above ground and is useful for trees with an upright habit.

Simple layering a tree

Carry out layering from midautumn to early spring, ideally in mid- to late autumn for deciduous trees and in early spring for evergreens.

Thoroughly cultivate the ground where the selected shoot will be layered. Select a strong, healthy shoot, preferably of the previous season's growth; they are more pliable and most likely to root in the first season. Wound the shoot (*see right*) or twist it until the bark splits to concentrate the sap at the rooting point. Peg down the shoot and stake the tip – tie it loosely to allow for new growth. Fill in around the shoot with soil mixed with rooting medium. Firm well to prevent natural settling of soil exposing new roots, then water. Keep the layers watered during the summer. Check for rooting in the following autumn: once rooted, layers of deciduous trees should be lifted in mid- to late autumn and those of evergreens in early spring.

Cut each layer from the parent just below the new roots, then grow on in a nursery bed or pot singly. Trim back the parent shoot either to the main stem or an appropriate sideshoot. Most layers should be ready for planting out in 2–3 years, but some may take five years.

Air layering a tree

Air layer a shoot outdoors in early spring, or whenever the shoot is ripe, as shown below. Wound the stem by removing a ½–1in (1–2.5cm) wide ring of bark or cutting a tongue. Opaque plastic bags make the best sleeves because they retain moisture and reflect light, so the rooting medium does not become too hot. Once the layer has rooted and been potted, grow it on under mist or in a closed case as for rooted cuttings (*see pp.50–52*), and plant out two years later.

Simple layering a tree

1 Wound the shoot 12in (30cm) from the tip, on the underside of the stem opposite a bud. Cut off a 1–2in (2.5–5cm) sliver of bark, or cut a tongue and open with a matchstick.

2 Dust the wound with hormone rooting powder. Mix some rooting medium into the soil beneath and peg down the shoot each side of the wound, at a depth of 3–6in (8–15cm). Tie in the exposed shoot tip to a stake. Fill in, firm, water, and label.

Air layering a tree

1 Trim the leaves (here of Ficus elastica*) from a straight length of stem. Make a sleeve by cutting the base of a plastic bag; slide it over the stem. Secure the lower end with tape.*

2 Make a sloping, upward cut ¼in (5mm) deep and 1in (2.5cm) long (see inset). Dust under the tongue with hormone rooting powder, then push in a little moist sphagnum moss.

3 Roll the sleeve into place around the wound. Pack the sleeve evenly with more moss so it covers the wound completely. Seal the upper end of the sleeve to the stem with tape.

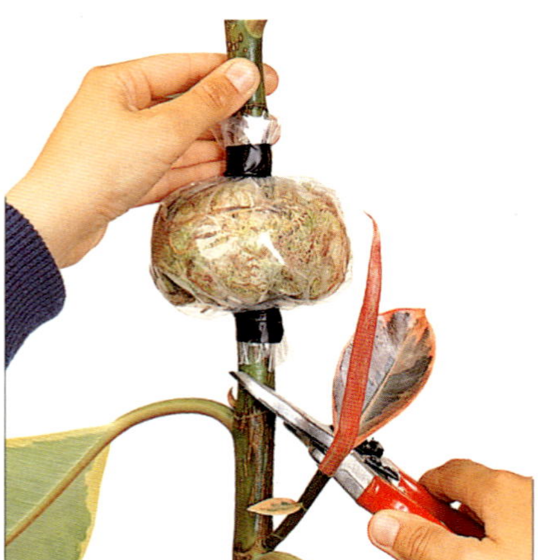

4 Wait until new roots show through the sleeve or, if using an opaque sleeve, open it to check for roots after 2–3 months. (If the stem is slow to root, leave it until the following spring.) Remove the rooted layer, cutting through the stem at an angle just above a node on the parent plant with pruners. Remove the plastic sleeve.

5 Gently tease out the moss from the roots. Pot the layer into a pot about 2in (5cm) larger than the root ball. Fill with a potting mix suited to the plant. Firm gently to avoid damaging the roots. Cut back vigorous topgrowth to ensure the roots can sustain the new plant. Water, label, and treat as a rooted cutting.

Palms

Palms are evergreen and are grown outdoors in tropical and subtropical climates. They need moist, well-drained soil in full sun to deep shade, depending on the species. Some palms, such as *Phoenix* species and the palmettos (*Sabal*), come from sunny regions and can tolerate sun as young plants, while palms native to rainforests, such as *Chamaedorea*, prefer shade even when mature. Many need shelter from strong winds. Cold winds can stunt or damage new leaves, while hot winds increase moisture loss.

In warm climates, palms are grown outdoors, but elsewhere they must be cultivated under cover or as houseplants, or outdoors in summer. A few tolerate some cold, however, such as *Butia capitata* and *Trachycarpus fortunei*. When propagating, the best way to mimic natural growing conditions for many palms is with a mist propagation unit (*see p.44 and right*) in a sunny greenhouse. This is a tent or case over a heated bench, which helps keep the soil mix moist and the air humid. It should be ventilated regularly to reduce the risk of rot attacking young plants.

Palms can be propagated in two ways, from seeds or by division. Most are best grown from seeds, which are relatively easy to obtain, but some palms produce suckers or offsets and can be more quickly increased by division.

Palms from seeds

Palms have inflorescences made of many small flowers; some flower repeatedly, while a few, such as *Caryota rumphiana* var. *albertii*, flower once and die. The fruits have moist flesh, as with the date palm (*Phoenix dactylifera*), or dry flesh, as in the coconut palm (*Cocos nucifera*).

Seeds are collected when the fruits ripen and change color (*see below*). Clean off all the pulp to prevent rot, then wrap the seeds in damp tissue paper or peat moss. To remove dry flesh, soak the fruits in warm water for 1–2 days until soft, then scrape off to reveal the seeds. The hard-coated seeds are best sown fresh. Germinated seedlings can be held for several months in a container without fertilizer. When you want the plants to begin growing actively, transfer to another pot, water, and fertilize: they will grow rapidly.

Purchased seeds may be supplied dry; if so, soak them in warm water for at least 24 hours and up to two weeks, then sow at once. File (*see p.53*) or crack them carefully in a vise or nutcracker to enable moisture to reach the seeds for germination.

Mist propagation tent

A mist propagation tent in a greenhouse allows in plenty of diffuse light. Heating cables provide bottom heat of 77–82°F (25–28°C), and humidity is kept close to 100 percent with fine water sprays from overhead pipes.

Gathering palm seeds

1 *As soon as the berries (here of* Coccothrinax fragrans*) ripen and change color, usually from green to red or purple, cut off a bunch.*

2 *Peel off the flesh and sow at once. Seeds may be stored briefly in damp tissue paper in a plastic bag at 68°F (20°C).*

A–Z of palms

Borassus Seeds as for large taprooted seeds (*see p.66*); germination 2–4 months. *Butia* Sow seeds in spring; file or crack woody coats. Seeds of Jelly palm (*B. capitata*, syn. *Cocos capitata*) are difficult to germinate (in 6–8 weeks); soak in warm water for up to 48 hours. Slow-growing. *Caryota* Fishtail palm Sow fresh seeds spring to summer. Germination in 3–6 weeks; handle toxic seeds with care. Divide suckering species such as *C. mitis* in spring. *Chamaedorea* Seeds in spring; germination in 6–8 weeks. *Cocos nucifera* Coconut Sow seeds in spring as for large seeds (*see p.66*) at 81–86°F (27–30°C); germination in 5–6 months; growth is rapid. *Dypsis* (syn. *Neodypsis*) Divide basal offsets. *Howea* Sentry palm Sow seeds spring to summer. Slow and erratic germination in 1–2 years or more. Grow seedlings in well-drained, rich soil in bright, indirect light and mild, humid conditions; lightly fertilize in the growing season. *Jubaea* Chilean wine palm Sow seeds in spring; germination in 3–6 months. *Latania* Latan palm Sow seeds in spring. *Livistona* Fan palm Sow seeds in spring at 73°F (23°C). Germination in two months. Grows best in semishade with deep, fertile soil. Only female of cabbage palm (*L. australis*) needed to set seeds, which tolerate some drying out but then take longer to germinate. *Lodoicea* Coco-de-mer, double coconut Sow seeds as for large seeds (*see p.66*). Has 3ft (1m) taproot. *Phoenix* Sow seeds spring to summer; germination in 1–2 months. Protect from direct sun for 2–3 years. Divide suckers; slow-rooting offsets need humidity at 86°F (30°C) until roots form; seedlings need 64–68°F (18–20°C). *Rhapis* Lady palm Sow seeds in summer; germination in 4–6 weeks. Divide basal offsets. *Roystonea* Royal palm Sow seeds in spring; germination in 2–3 months. *Sabal* Palmetto Sow seeds in spring; germination two months. Division of basal offsets. Tolerates wide range of soils. *Trachycarpus* Sow kidney-shaped seeds in spring. File or nick woody seed coats to allow moisture to penetrate and begin germination, in up to two months. Needs sun. *Washingtonia* Sow seeds spring to summer; germination in 4–6 weeks. Protect from strong sunlight until one year old.

SOWING PALM SEEDS

1 Sow about ten seeds (here of Caryota) in a deep 6in (15cm) pot; space them evenly and not too close to the rim where they may dry out. Cover with their own depth of soil mix.

2 Keep the pot in a warm, bright, humid position. Once their first leaves have formed, usually about two months after sowing, pot the seedlings. The roots of each seedling should be well developed (see inset).

3 Pot each seedling individually into a pot that is just larger than its root system. Label, water, and grow on in humid, shady conditions. Boost the young plant with a foliar fertilizer while it is in active growth.

Sowing palm seeds

Palm seeds are best sown in pots. Deep clay pots are preferable; they prevent waterlogging and accomodate their long taproots. Fill each pot with a suitable seed soil mix, such as equal parts of peat and fine grit, water it well, then allow to drain. Sow the seeds evenly (*see above*). An air temperature of 86–97°F (30–35°C) and high humidity are essential for a good rate of germination. Never allow the seeds to dry out; otherwise, they will die. Germination can take from three weeks to 18 months. Don't expect more than two-thirds of the seeds to germinate.

Seeds sown in warm climates usually germinate up to a week earlier than in colder climates. Protect pots of seeds from harsh sunlight by placing them in a shade house (*see p.45*) with 30–45 percent shade, depending on the region.

In colder climates, place a heated closed case supplying bottom heat of 77–82°F (25–28°C) in a sunny spot in the greenhouse to provide maximum heat and light. Maintain the humidity by watering regularly and lightly spraying over the pots. Alternatively, use a mist propagation unit (*see pp.44 and 65*). Overheating can cause the seeds to rot, so ventilate the unit regularly.

For large quantities of palms, sow seeds in drills in a raised seed bed (*see p.55*) in moist, light, free-draining soil or soil mix to minimize damage to the roots when transplanting seedlings.

Pregerminating palm seeds

If space is limited, palm seeds may be pregerminated in a bag (*see above right*) of soilless mix or damp peat moss, kept under a greenhouse bench or in a warm cupboard. Seeds treated in this way germinate earlier – usually in four to eight weeks, depending on the species. The seeds should be checked daily for signs of sprouting, then potted before they become too large. Seeds produce roots first, then shoots, but they can be potted as soon as they have roots.

To reduce the risk of rot, pot the seedlings into pots just larger than their roots. A potting mix of equal parts coarse bark, soil, fine grit, and peat, or one of equal parts loose rockwool, soil-based mix and perlite, with a little slow-release fertilizer, is suitable. Keep the seedlings in humid, bright shade for four to six weeks after potting until they are established.

Large palm seeds

A few palms have giant seeds that send out long taproots, or "sinkers," such as the double coconut (*Lodoicea maldivica*) or the toddy palm (*Borassus flabellifer*). These are best direct sown individually in a deep container (*see right*). A large seed may be sown in an outdoor bed, but the conditions may not be ideal for

PREGERMINATING PALM SEEDS

1 Mix the seeds (here of Caryota mitis) with moist peat in a clear plastic bag. Seal and label the bag, then keep it in light shade at about 66°F (19°C). When the roots are about 2in (5cm) long (see inset), pot the seedlings.

2 Handle each seedling by the seed case to avoid damaging the new roots and any shoot. Pot singly in 2–3in (5–8cm) pots of a suitable potting mix, covering each seed to its own depth. Water and label the pots. Grow the seedlings on in humid, bright shade.

LARGE PALM SEEDS

For coconuts and other palms that produce large seeds, choose a deep pot to allow the taproot to develop. Half-bury each seed in a suitable potting mix. After germination, grow on the seedling in the same container; the seed husk will gradually disintegrate as the shoot develops.

germination, and the sinker will be open to attack from insects and other creatures. The seed should be only half buried, leaving the top exposed so the seedling can emerge directly into light.

Care of seedlings

Seedling palms need protection from hot sun for two to three years; rainforest palms are particularly vulnerable to harsh light. They tolerate much more sun if they are well watered than those allowed to dry out between waterings. Moving any palm seedling from shade into very bright sun can severely scorch the leaves. If planting positions are in full sun, keep the seedlings first in filtered sunlight, and keep well watered.

Summer watering is essential: water frequently and thoroughly, and mulch the seedbeds. A light foliar feed may be applied during the growing season.

Dividing palms

Some palms, such as *Chrysalidocarpus* species, lady palms (*Rhapis*), *Phoenix*, and some *Chamaedorea*, readily produce offsets, or suckers, at the base of the plant. These may be removed, usually in spring, and then potted or planted out, depending on the climate (*see below*). Division is a fairly simple technique, but care will be needed to prevent rot from entering the wounded tissue, in which case the division will fail.

If the base of the offset is below soil level, carefully scrape away the soil with a hand fork or remove the plant from its pot to expose the roots. Cut off the offset, retaining as many of the roots as possible to enable the offset to establish. Gently ease it free, avoiding any damage to the parent plant, which will leave it vulnerable to rot. If needed, dust any wounds to the parent's roots with a fungicide before replacing the soil or repotting. Trim the offset's roots, treat with fungicide, then plant out or pot.

A good potting mix can be made from equal parts peat, fine bark, fine grit, soil, and coarse sand. Pot the offset in a clay pot just large enough for the roots. The young plant must be shaded from hot sun at a minimum air temperature of 66°F (19°C) and kept well watered until established.

If planting an offset outdoors (*see below*), choose a shady site with moist soil, sheltered from the wind if possible. Make sure that the planting hole allows the roots to spread out naturally.

Rootless offsets

Some palms have very few roots, so extra care is necessary with these. A rootless offset is still obtaining nutrients from the parent plant. Root growth can be stimulated by cutting a notch, or slice, at the base of the offset. Dust the wound with fungicide, re-cover it with soil, and keep the offset well watered. Remove any leaves to enable the offset to conserve moisture.

Alternatively, remove the rootless offset and seal it in a clean plastic bag. Leave it in deep shade at a minimum temperature of 66°F (19°C), in a greenhouse if necessary. In this case, there is no need to remove any leaves, because the sealed bag preserves a humid atmosphere. Ventilate the bag by opening it for an hour or two each day.

After a few months, roots should form: open the bag to harden off the offset for a few days, then pot or plant out. Plant the offset slightly deeper than before to encourage root growth, and remove some of its leaves to reduce water loss. Keep the offset well watered, and do not allow it to dry out.

Dividing and potting a palm offset

1 *Ease the palm (here a lady palm) from its pot. Select an offset with 3–6 pairs of leaves and a good root system. Gently tease out the offset's roots with a hand fork.*

2 *Use pruners to sever the offset from the main stem, cutting straight across the root as close to the parent plant as possible. Return the parent plant to its pot.*

3 *The offset should have a vigorous, healthy root system that is in proportion to the topgrowth. Trim off any damaged or diseased roots with a clean, sharp knife.*

4 *Protect the cut root of the offset from rot by dipping it in a small quantity of fungicidal powder, such as sulfur dust. Shake off any excess powder: if it is too thick, it may hinder rooting.*

5 *Place the offset in a pot just large enough for the roots, then backfill with a suitable soil mix, keeping the offset at the same depth as it was before. Grow on in warm shade with high humidity.*

Planting an offset into a bed

To divide a palm growing in open ground, first select an offset from the parent plant (here a lady palm). Detach and prepare the offset (see steps 1 to 4, left), taking care to avoid damaging the rootball. Restore the soil around the parent's rootball.

Prepare a planting hole in open, well-drained, moist soil. Make the hole sufficiently large to spread out the roots of the offset naturally. Locate the soil mark on the stem and plant at the same depth. Firm in gently, water in, and label.

Cycads

Cycads resemble palms, being evergreen trees or shrubs, but are botanically unrelated. They are primitive plants, reproducing by means of seeds produced by unisexual conelike structures, which bear either ovules or pollen sacs. The ovules develop into seeds. Some cycads produce suckers, or offsets, which can be detached and grown on. Propagation is very similar to palms (*see pp.65–67*), therefore, but it is more challenging.

Cycads from seeds

When raising cycads from seeds, the gardener can expect a success rate of no more than 50 percent. To achieve the best possible rate of germination, the seeds should be tested for viability and then prepared before sowing.

A mature male and female cycad are needed to produce viable seeds. Gather the seeds when the "cones" fall to the ground. The nutlike seeds are up to 3in (8cm) long, with a woody casing covered by a thin red, yellow, or orange pulp. This fleshy outer coat contains an inhibitor that delays germination and so must be removed: peel or scrape off the flesh, then wash the seeds in water.

Many cycad seeds may be infertile or dead, so it is worth sorting them before sowing. A quick way to test viability is to shake them: any that rattle are not viable. Another method is the flotation test. Drop the seeds into water. If they float, they are not ripe; if they sink, they should germinate. This test is not totally accurate; seeds of some *Cycas* species float to be dispersed by the sea.

To allow moisture to penetrate the seed and initiate germination, make a shallow cut in the hard seed coat at one end of each seed, using a sharp knife or file (*see below*). Take care not to cut too deep, which will damage the embryo.

In warm climates, if the seeds are more than two weeks old, they should then be soaked in warm water for up to 24 hours to improve the rate of germination. In cool climates, soak the seeds for two or three days.

Sowing cycad seeds

A good seed soil mix for cycads can be made from equal parts compost or peat, and three parts coarse grit. This mix provides good aeration and moisture retention. Cycad seedlings have long taproots, so it is best to sow them singly in deep clay pots. Sowing in a raised seedbed is not recommended, because the roots are very sensitive and root disturbance will either kill the plants or check their growth.

For best results, the seeds may be germinated before sowing (*see below left*), but seeds may also be sown direct into pots (*see below*). The seeds should be half exposed and should be kept well watered and misted.

To germinate, cycad seeds require a minimum air temperature of 70–86°F (21–30°C) and 60–70 percent relative humidity. In cold regions, these conditions can be provided in a heated closed case or a mist propagation unit (*see pp.44 and 65*). Cycad seeds usually take much longer – from four to 15 months – to germinate than those of palms. Fresh seeds take a week or two less to germinate in warm climates.

Sowing pregerminated seeds

1 Half fill a clear plastic bag with moist peat. Put in a dozen seeds (here of Macrozamia moorei*, see inset); seal and label. Keep in light shade with bottom heat of 77–82°F (25–28°C) until seeds germinate.*

2 When the roots emerge, sow the seeds in a suitable seed soil mix in deep pots, which will allow the taproot to develop. Make sure that the root is covered, but leave the seed case half exposed. Water well and label.

3 Grow on the seedling in high humidity in light shade. Provide bottom heat to ensure a minimum air temperature of 66°F (19°C). Keep well watered until the shoot emerges, and pot when it has two or three leaves.

Sowing seeds in pots

With a sharp knife, nick the seed coat, cutting no deeper than ⅛in (1–2mm) (see inset) to avoid damaging the embryo. Soak for 1–2 days. Prepare deep clay pots with a suitable seed soil mix and press each seed horizontally into the surface to half its depth. Water and label, then grow on in warm shade with high humidity.

CARE OF CYCAD SEEDLINGS

Once the taproot is well established and the shoot has two or three leaves, pot each seedling. Take care, because the young root is very brittle. Use a potting mix of equal parts of coarse bark, coarse grit, shredded rockwool or medium-grade perlite, soil, and peat – or of equal parts soil-based potting mix, rockwool, and perlite. Add a little slow-release fertilizer.

Place the seedlings in a shade house (*see p.45*) or greenhouse with 40 percent shade and high humidity. Keep them well watered. A twice-monthly application of half-strength liquid fertilizer during the growing season is beneficial.

Some cycads tolerate hot sun from an early stage, but others, such as those that originate from rainforests (for example, some *Zamia* species) need gentler treatment. The seedling leaves are very sensitive, and hot, bright sun will scorch them. Most new plants need a period of hardening off. Keep them in shade for at least three to four months, and gradually bring them into full sun over a period of one year.

Sun-hardened cycads are generally quite tolerant of wind, but rainforest species may suffer. Cold winds may damage new growth, while hot winds may desicate leaves. Plant out seedlings when they have developed good roots and a few leaves; this is generally after 2–5 years, depending on the species.

CYCAS REVOLUTA WITH OFFSETS

DIVIDING CYCADS

Cycads may be propagated from the offsets, or suckers, that are produced on the trunk or at the base of some plants. The offsets must be removed and handled with care until well established.

To detach a basal offset (*see right*), remove the soil or soil mix to expose the base where it is attached to the parent plant, and cut it off. Trim the wounds and treat with fungicide to stop rot from entering the damaged tissues. If the offset has much topgrowth, remove the lower leaves to reduce moisture loss and treat the entire offset with fungicide.

Hang the offset in a cool, dry place until the wounds heal. Prepare a large clay pot with a soil mix made of equal parts peat and coarse sand or grit, or of equal parts soil-based potting mix, perlite, and rockwool. Pot the offset and, if necessary, stake it to protect the fronds.

Divided offsets need very similar conditions to seedlings (*see above*) to establish successfully; generally this will take 1–3 years, depending on the species. In colder climates, root growth is greatly improved in a mist propagation unit (*see pp.44 and 65*).

Some cycads, particularly *Cycas*, may produce offsets from their trunks when mature. Although much smaller than basal offsets, they still yield vigorous plants. The offsets begin as small swellings on the trunk, often caused by damage, which then produce leaves. Once the growth is developed, detach it as for basal offsets (*see above*).

DIVISION OF CYCAD OFFSETS

1 To expose the offsets, tilt the pot and scrape away the top layer of soil mix with a trowel. Slice off an offset from the base of the trunk with a clean, sharp knife or with a pruning saw.

2 To prevent the trunk of the parent plant from rotting, trim the wound, if necessary, to leave a smooth surface and dust the cut with fungicide such as sulfur dust.

Mature plants sucker freely

3 Trim the wound on the offset to produce a clean surface free of any snags. Dust the wound with fungicide (see inset) to protect it from rot. Take care not to touch the wound with your hands to avoid contaminating it.

4 Place the offset in an open-meshed bag that allows free air circulation. Hang in shade for 1–3 days to allow the wound to callus over.

5 Pot in a 6–8in (15–20cm) pot at the same depth as it was before and support with a stake. Grow on in light shade at a minimum of 70°F (21°C).

A–Z OF CYCADS

BOWENIA Sow fresh seeds; germination takes up to one year.
CYCAS FERN PALM, SAGO PALM Sow seeds at 43–54°F (6–12°C). Seeds of Zamia palm (*C. media*) germinate in 6–8 months. Seeds of Japanese sago palm (*C. revoluta*) germinate in 3–4 months. Division of basal offsets; 6–8 months to rooting.
DIOON Sow short-lived seeds fresh; germination in 6–18 months; seedlings are fast growing.
ENCEPHALARTOS Sow seeds in spring; germination in 2–6 months; seedlings grow fast in favorable conditions.
LEPIDOZAMIA Sow short-lived, toxic seeds fresh after removing outer seed coat; up to two years to germinate, then fast-growing.
MACROZAMIA Sow seeds in spring. *M. moorei* germinates at 50–59°F (10–15°C).
ZAMIA Sow seeds in spring; germination in 2–4 months.

Conifers

Most conifers, whether trees or shrubs, can be raised in a variety of ways, the principal methods being cuttings, seeds, and grafting. Taking cuttings is the easiest method for many types, suitable for selected cultivars and clones, and yields a number of identical plants – ideal for an avenue or hedge. Species are most often raised from seeds (cultivars may not come true), but this may be slow. Grafting is usually used if seeds are unavailable or for cultivars that do not root well from cuttings.

Taking cuttings

Conifers are usually propagated from the current year's growth, using semi-ripe or ripewood (fully ripe or woody) cuttings. The basic principles are similar to those for other trees and shrubs, but there are some key differences. The main one is that many conifers make new growth from specialized buds; the way a shoot develops is determined by where it is located on the parent plant. In coniferous trees, leading or main shoots grow more or less straight upward, while sideshoots grow outward. With most conifers, it is very difficult to make a cutting taken from a sideshoot form a leading shoot (although with pines and deciduous types, there is no problem); with some, such as monkey puzzles (*Araucaria*), it is almost impossible.

Even with cypresses, which generally form leading shoots quite readily, there are several cultivariants. These are forms created by taking cuttings from different parts of the same parent: each part has different genes "switched on," so that the various cuttings produce cultivars that are genetically the same but different in their form or growth pattern (such as a naturally dwarf form). The differences in form remain fixed in the cuttings, as in cultivars of Lawson's cypress, for example *Chamaecyparis lawsoniana* 'Ellwoodii' and 'Fletcheri').

Cuttings taken from young (juvenile) growth usually root best. Such growth persists into the mature plant with the cypress family, including *Cupressus*, *Chamaecyparis*, and junipers. In spruces (such as *Picea*), however, the juvenile factor fades (often after only five or six years), and cuttings from older trees are less likely to root. It is also essential to take cuttings from growth that is vigorous, not weak or sickly (*see right*).

Taking cuttings material

Select strong leading shoots with young foliage at the tips (these have the best growing points). Take 2–6in (5–15cm) long cuttings of the semi-ripe or ripe wood, cutting just below a node.

When to take cuttings

Take cuttings from summer until just before growth resumes in spring, ideally in early to midautumn or in midwinter, peak times for rooting ability. Easily rooting conifers root well throughout this period, but the more difficult ones tend to root poorly, except during one or

Taking conifer cuttings

1 Prepare a pot, adding a pinch of slow-release fertilizer at the bottom (to avoid burning the new roots). Take young shoots, not adult ones with fruits (see inset, left).

2 If needed, strip off the sideshoots or needles from the bottom third of each stem (here of Chamaecyparis *'Chilworth Silver'). The small wounds left on the stems encourage rooting.*

3 Dip the base of each cutting in hormone rooting compound (here powder). Insert easily rooted cuttings singly in 3in (8cm) pots: make a hole, insert a cutting, firm, and water.

4 Insert 6–7 cuttings of slow-rooting conifers (here Juniperus conferta*) to a 6in (15cm) pot, in case some do not take. Label all cuttings.*

5 Spray the cuttings with a fungicide to prevent rot. Place them in a heated closed case or in a cold frame. Check weekly and water lightly if needed, but do not saturate the medium. Shade the cuttings from hot sun to avoid scorch. They should root in three months.

other (or both) peak times. (*See* A–Z of Garden Trees, *pp.74–91 for details of specific plants.*) Different clones of the same species often show markedly differing rooting ability. If you take cuttings in early spring, they are starting to make new growth, even if it is not apparent, so they are unlikely to have sufficient reserves to make roots as well. In late spring and early summer, the growth is too soft and will rot.

Preparing conifer cuttings

The rooting medium should be well-aerated (oxygen around the bases of the cuttings aids rooting and helps to prevent rot) and able to retain moisture. You could use peat, perlite, conifer bark, or vermiculite, or mixtures of these with coarse sand, in equal parts (*see pp.33–4*). If the cuttings are to be under mist, use a higher proportion (3:1) of sand, perlite, or vermiculite. Do not firm the medium in the pots.

Cuttings are usually prepared as shown (*see facing page*), from one-year-old growth. This tends to determine the size of the cutting, but it should be no longer than 6in (15cm). With scale-leaved conifers such as cypresses, remove sideshoots from the base of the cuttings. Retain the needlelike leaves of cuttings from conifers such as spruces – they may aid aeration at the base.

Caring for the cuttings

Root cuttings under plastic film on a heated bench (*see p.44*), under mist, or in a sheltered site such as a heated cold frame (cuttings in the open outdoors will not tolerate freezing temperatures). If using a heated bench or mist, take the cuttings in autumn or late winter. Late winter is best if using bottom heat (*see p.41*), which should be at about 68°F (20°C), because less heat is needed. Make sure that the bottom heat does not dry out the bases of the cuttings; this is less of a problem with mist. If using a cold frame, take cuttings in autumn and shade them from direct sun while letting in as much light as possible. Rooting with heat speeds the process by a few weeks.

Although there will be little or no sign of any rooting activity in cuttings taken in autumn, they will form root initials over the winter and will probably root only as new growth is made in the following early summer.

Once the cuttings are well rooted, pot in a soil-based potting mix (*see p.34*), with slow-release fertilizer to encourage vigorous growth. Provide partial shade for a few days until they settle in their roots, then place in bright light to stimulate growth. Control vine weevils with an insecticidal or nematode drench in midsummer and autumn.

SELECTING RIPE CONES

UNRIPE Scots pine | RIPENING Scots pine | MATURE Scots pine

RIPE *Pinus coulteri* | OPEN *Pinus coulteri*

Many cones change color as they ripen, usually in the late summer or autumn. Pinus sylvestris, *the Scots pine* (see above), *turns from green to brown. When gathering cones for seeds, take them just after they change color, but before they start to open (dehisce).*

UNRIPE *Tsuga chinensis* | OPEN *Tsuga chinensis*

Conifers from seeds

Raising conifers from seeds is the most economical way to raise a large number of plants, but some species are slow to germinate or grow. Conifers produce seeds in cones (modified from leaves), hence their common name. Nearly all conifers are gymnosperms, which means "naked seeds"; unlike other plants, the seeds are not enclosed in a fruit or a capsule and develop while exposed to the air (*see also p.16*). Conifer seeds may be sown in the same way as other tree seeds (*see pp.53–55*), but they are unique in the way they are collected.

Gathering the cones

Conifer fruits usually ripen (*see above*) in autumn, changing color in the process. They may ripen after one, two, or three summers, depending on the species; it is important to know which, because immature cones may look very similar to ripe ones, but unripe seeds will not germinate. This is particularly important for genera such as *Juniperus*, where in some species the only visible difference is a change in the fruits from green to blackish purple or blue, or in *Cupressus*, where one-year-old cones look mature. (*See* A–Z of Garden Trees, *pp.74–91 for details of specific plants.*)

The first necessity is to find a tree that is fruiting well. Conifers are wind-pollinated, and little pollen is carried more than 300ft (90m) or so. Although conifers can self-pollinate, the number of seeds fertilized, or set, is usually quite low unless there are several plants to ensure adequate cross-pollination. Also, if there are few cones, it is likely that conditions were unfavorable for pollen production, so expect few viable seeds.

Gathering cones from tall conifers may be difficult, but wind and animals often detach cones, and usually some may be found on the ground. Avoid any with signs of insect damage, indicating that a cone-eating insect has beaten you to it. Take care to collect only female, seed-bearing cones (*see box, below*).

If necessary, it is worth gathering cones that are nearly ripe, because the seeds are often viable (albeit at a lower percentage) a couple of months before the cones ripen fully. Some conifers retain seeds in the cones for a long time. These are mainly certain pines (*Pinus*) whose cones open in the wild only after a forest fire (which removes competing vegetation and leaves a natural seedbed). A few viable seeds may persist in the old cones of most (*continued on p.72*)

AVOIDING PITFALLS

When collecting seeds, take care to select only the female cones, which contain the seeds. Beware of galls or male cones that may look similar to female cones.

Male or female? *All conifers have separate male and female flowers. Some trees are either male or female. This male flower from a cedar* (Cedrus) *looks like a cone, but it sheds yellow pollen.*

Pineapple gall *Certain spruces* (Picea) *may develop conelike galls, caused by aphidlike adelgids. A gall (here at the base of a shoot) is identified by needles sticking out of them.*

EXTRACTING THE SEEDS

1 *Put just-ripe cones in a paper-lined cardboard box, and label. Leave the box in a warm closet or over a radiator until the scales open.*

2 *When the cones are fully open, tip out the winged seeds. Use tweezers to pull out any seeds that are lodged between the scales. With these conifer cones, the dark seeds are more likely to be viable than the pale ones.*

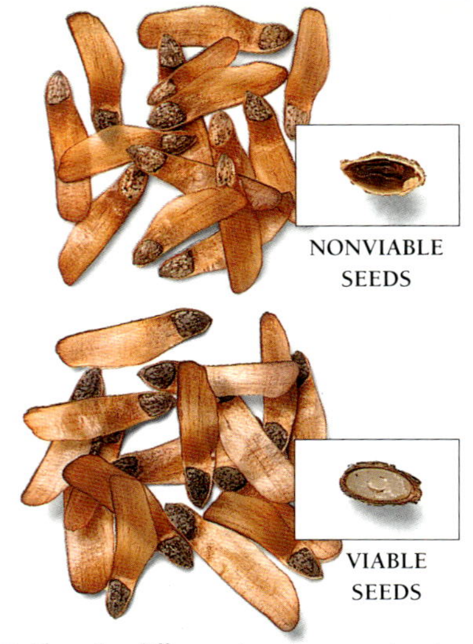

3 *If a color difference is not apparent, cut some seeds in half (see insets) to gauge which proportion is viable. Nonviable seeds will be shriveled; viable seeds will be fat.*

CEDAR CONES

Female cones of the cedar (*Cedrus*) take three or four years to ripen (*see right*). The young cone may only be 1in (2.5cm) long by the first autumn. In the second year, although the cone is much bigger, it is green and still unripe. By the third autumn, the cone begins ripening and changing color but remains unopened. This long process can be accelerated by picking brown closed cones and alternately soaking and drying them to prompt dehiscence. Soak in tepid water for 12 hours, then dry in gentle heat for 24 hours.

Cedar cones have a circular arrangement of flattened scales, to which the seeds are attached. The scales loosen as the cone ripens and fall off, layer by layer until only the central rachis, or stalk, remains attached to the tree.

members of the Pinaceae, except for the firs (*Abies*).

After handling cones or seeds, your fingers will be covered in resin, which is hard to remove with soap or commercial cleaners. The simplest solution is to rub a little butter into the resin, then use soap or detergent to remove the butter.

Extracting the seeds

Extraction is usually a matter of letting the cones open to release the seeds. With a few exceptions, they have no fleshy coat or hard covering to be removed. Any surface moisture should be dried off (at which stage they can be stored), but do not try to force open the cones. Instead, lay them out on a tray or in an open box and let them dry naturally at room temperature at first, especially if they are still slightly green. Once they are fully ripe and dry, the scales should part naturally and start to release the seeds.

If they fail to open, provide some heat, up to 104–113°F (40–45°C); one way is to place them in a cooling oven. Most seeds will fall out (*see above*), but some will remain lodged in the cones. Pick them out with tweezers, shake the cones vigorously in a large plastic bag, or tap the cone tip on a hard surface.

Many conifer seeds, for example the noble fir (*Abies procera*), have a wing to aid dispersal; you may remove or retain it without affecting germination. In some genera, especially firs, cedars, and bald cypresses (*Taxodium*), the cones break apart on maturity, then the seeds and scales fall off (*see box, above*). With these conifers, soak the cones for several days before drying them. Once dry, separate the seeds from the scales.

In a few of the soft pines, the cones fall intact and do not open; break them open manually – this may be difficult. The seeds of junipers, yews (*Taxus*), and some other conifers have a fleshy coat. It is not essential to clean this off because it should break down naturally, but removing it may hasten germination.

Storing conifer seeds

The seeds of nearly all conifers may be stored for five to 20 years or more in a refrigerator at 34–39°F (1–4°C), or for even longer in a freezer at 8°F (-18°C). First dry the seeds in a warm, airy place before putting them into clean, labeled plastic bags or small containers.

Testing seeds for viability

A high proportion of conifer seeds are usually dead or infertile. There are two methods of testing the seeds before sowing. Place large seeds such as those of pines (*Pinus*) in water. Viable seeds will sink, while any insect-infested and empty seeds will float. This will not work with seeds of some conifers, such as firs, however.

The alternative test involves cutting a sample of the seeds in half (*see above*). Nonviable seeds are hollow or have only a little resin; viable seeds have a fat, usually white, embryo.

Breaking seed dormancy

Some conifer seeds are dormant and need to be treated before sowing (*see p.54*), while others germinate easily. Many seeds germinate more quickly and evenly if stratified for a short period in a refrigerator. Mix the seeds with moist peat or sand and chill at 34–39°F (1–4°C) for about three weeks, then sow immediately (if the seeds germinate in the refrigerator, sow them at once).

Some seeds are doubly dormant and do not germinate for several years, such as juniper seeds. Speed the process by mixing them with damp peat or sand and giving them a warm period of about 20 weeks at 59–68°F (15–20°C), for instance in a heated closet, then a cold period of 12 weeks in the bottom of a refrigerator. You may prefer to wait; it takes less effort and is more reliable.

Grafting

As for other plants, grafting conifers involves uniting a scion of the plant you wish to propagate onto a rootstock. It is used where seeds are not available (as with cultivars) or are inappropriate and with conifers that are difficult to root or grow poorly from cuttings, such as blue spruces (*Picea pungens*).

With conifers, the rootstock acts mainly to provide roots rather than to control the growth of the crown (such as with fruit trees, *see p.56*), so it is desirable for the scion to root as well.

There are two principal seasons for grafting: late winter, which is suitable for all conifers, and late summer, in which mainly blue spruces are grafted.

Selecting rootstocks and scions

The rootstock is usually a two-year-old plant and should be a species that is compatible with the scion; ideally, use one as closely related as possible. Grafts involving different genera are possible – larch (*Larix*) and *Pseudotsuga* can be grafted onto each other – if necessary. In addition, the stock must have a similar growth rate to the scion; otherwise, there will be an imbalance at the union and graft incompatibility may result. Graft incompatibility may occur at any stage.

For best results, pot the stocks some months before grafting so that they are well rooted (but not potbound). With plants grafted in late winter, bring the stocks under cover in midwinter, then prompt them to make root growth by keeping them at 50–59°F (10–15°C). It is also possible to use bare-root stocks for winter grafts.

The selection of scion material is very important, because of the tendency of sideshoots to grow only sideways (*see* "Taking cuttings," *p.70*). Take healthy leading shoots of the previous or the current year's growth, 3–6in (8–15cm) long, preferably from the outer, upper crown. Weaker shoots of cypresses and pines will also grow well.

For winter grafting, collect scions from fully dormant conifers in early to midwinter. Store in plastic bags in the refrigerator at or below 39°F (4°C). For summer grafting, collect scions in the morning and keep them in plastic bags in cool shade to avoid moisture loss.

SPLICED SIDE-VENEER GRAFTING

1 Near the rootstock's base (here Pinus sylvestris*), cut downward obliquely, a quarter of the way into the stem.*

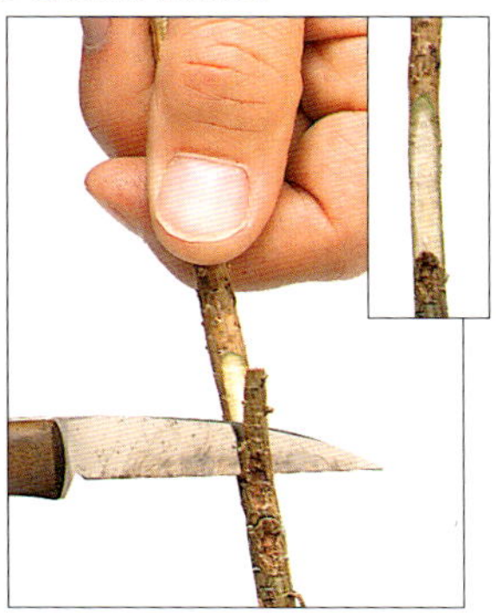

*2 Make a 1¼in (3cm) long, flat cut down the stem to finish at the first cut. Remove the sliver of wood (*see inset*).*

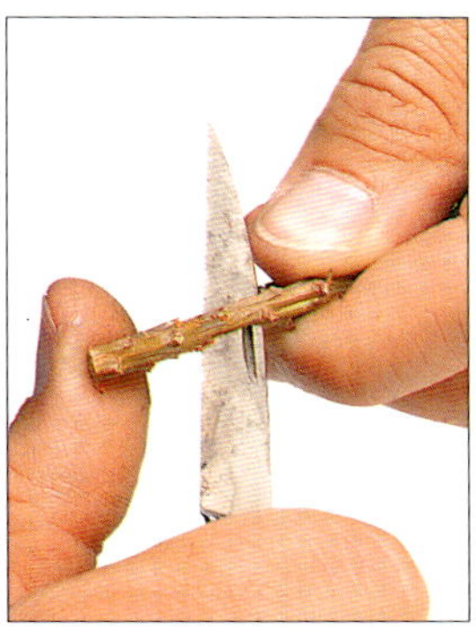

3 Strip off the leaves from the bottom 2in (5cm) of the scion. Cut it to match the stock. Do not cut into the pith.

*4 Align the prepared scion (*see inset*) so that it fits snugly into the cut on the stock. It is important that the cambiums meet exactly.*

*5 Bind the stock and scion firmly, but not too tightly, with grafting tape or a ⅓in (1cm) wide rubber band. Bind the entire cut (*see inset*).*

6 Plunge in a pot of moist peat to cover the graft. Label; put in a plastic-film tent or covered bench until a callus (inset) forms.

Grafting a conifer

The technique used is the spliced side-veneer graft, as shown below. For each graft, a rootstock and scion of similar diameter is best. Trim off any sideshoots and pinch off any needles from the base of the stock but do not cut it back; this is essential to draw the sap upward and promote healing of the graft.

Working as near the base as possible, cut a piece of wood from the stock (*see below*) so it can receive the scion. Strip the leaves from the lower stem of the scion. Make matching cuts to shape the scion so it fits the cut on the stock. Do not cut into the scion to the pith – this will hinder its ability to callus over.

For a successful graft, it is imperative that the cambiums (the thin layer of regenerative cells, usually green, just beneath the bark) of both stock and scion meet. If the stock cut is broader than that on the scion, align the cambiums on one side only. Be careful, since there could be a difference in bark thickness. The best union will often form at the pointed end of the scion (and if scion rooting occurs, the roots usually come from the base of the scion on one or both sides).

Bind the graft as shown, but do not apply too much tension. The purpose is to hold the cambiums together so that the graft union can develop; the scion just above the top of the cut and the shoulder at the base of the cut are both susceptible to being crushed.

Caring for grafted conifers

The grafts must be kept moist and warm: plunge pot-grown stocks in moist peat or lay bare-root stocks in a tray of moist peat; leave the foliage free. Place the plants in a plastic-film tent or covered case in full light, but not in direct sun. Bottom heat of 64–68°F (18-20°C) or a hot pipe (*see p.109*) in late winter will hasten union of the graft but is not necessary in summer.

After 5–6 weeks, the graft should start to unite and form a callus. Admit air gradually over the next month or so to harden off the plants. After about three months, they may be taken out of the humid environment. If bare-root, the grafted plants may be potted or lined out in a nursery bed to grow on.

Start removing the topgrowth of the stock in one or two stages once the scion has made ½–1in (1–2.5cm) of new growth. With *Abies* and related conifers, head back the stock slowly, pinching out new shoots rather than cutting back the stock, until the scion has grown actively for about a year. The stock's foliage is essential both to feed the roots and to draw sap from the roots to the graft. Removing it too quickly risks starving both roots and graft.

A–Z OF GARDEN TREES

ABIES FIR

Abies koreana

CUTTINGS in mid- to late winter
SEEDS in spring
GRAFTING in mid- to late winter or late summer

Female cones of these conifers are usually erect; male cones are pendent. Hardwood cuttings root only if taken from younger trees. Seeds are reliable but slow. Rare plants are best grafted.

CUTTINGS

Treat hardwood cuttings (*see p.50*) from ripened current season's growth with hormone rooting compound. Root in a plastic-film tent with bottom heat of 59–68°F (15–20°C). Rooting is usually slow. After bud break in spring, feed the cuttings to encourage strong growth.

SEEDS

Ripe cones break up, as for cedars (*see p.72*). Soak in water for 30 hours, then cold stratify the seeds for 4–6 weeks before sowing (*see p.54*). The seedlings should appear after 3–4 weeks; they do best at 50–59°F (10–15°C). Transplant them in the second year.

GRAFTING

For rootstocks, use any *Abies* of similar thickness to the scions; the best are *A. alba*, *A. nordmanniana*, and *A. grandis*. Use a spliced side-veneer graft (*see p.73*), and set the base of the scion below soil mix level to encourage rooting from both sides. Place in a plastic-film tent at 64–68°F (18–20°C) to callus. Head back the rootstock gradually over two years; otherwise, the scion and roots may die.

SELECTING SCION MATERIAL
To ensure a grafted plant (here Abies koreana*) has a treelike habit, take scions from shoots, with leaves arranged radially, that grow directly from the trunk (epicormic). Alternatively, take strong shoots with a whorl of 4–5 buds (*see top inset*) from the outer upper crown.*

ACACIA MIMOSA, WATTLE

Acacia baileyana

GREENWOOD CUTTINGS in early to midsummer
ROOT CUTTINGS in early to midwinter
SEEDS in early spring

Most of the many fast-growing trees in this genus are rather tender. Seeds are the only natural, and most effective, means of increase. Cuttings give limited results. Young *Acacia* resent root disturbance, so raise seeds and cuttings in individual containers and plant out after 1–2 years for flowers in the third year.

Take greenwood cuttings (*see p.52*) with a heel, rather than a wound, and insert into cells of soil mix or rockwool. Some species, such as *A. melanoxylon*, can be raised from root cuttings from mature trees. Remove roots about ¼in (5mm) thick, wash them, and cut into 1–2in (2.5–5cm) lengths. Press horizontally into pots of seed soil mix, cover with more mix, and top with vermiculite.

The seeds have hard coats: abrade them with sandpaper or soak in very hot water, then cool for 24 hours before sowing (*p.54*) at a minimum of 59°F (15°C). Transplant into root-trainers.

ACER MAPLE

CUTTINGS in midspring to early summer
SEEDS in mid- to late autumn or spring
GRAFTING in late winter or mid- to late summer
LAYERING in mid- to late autumn or early spring

There are deciduous and evergreen species in this large genus. Snakebark species, *Acer cappadocicum*, and vigorous *A. palmatum* cultivars such as 'Osakazuki' may be raised from cuttings, and species maples from seeds. Layering is simplest if only a few plants are needed; grafting is useful for difficult-to-root cultivars.

CUTTINGS

Take softwood cuttings in early summer (*see p.52*). Alternatively, lift a stock plant, bring it into early growth under cover, and take cuttings in midspring to ensure they put on enough growth in the first year to grow well in the spring.

SEEDS

Some species, such as *A. griseum*, do not set viable seeds unless several plants are nearby. If the winged seeds dry out, soak for 48 hours before storing or sowing. Sow fresh seeds in a seedbed (*see p.55*) or in pots in a cold frame, or store in a refrigerator (*see p.53*) and sow in spring. Seeds germinate at 50–59°F (10–15°C), but often not until the second spring.

GRAFTING

Spliced side-veneer graft cultivars of *A. palmatum* and *A. japonicum* in winter or summer (*see p.58*). Chip- or T-bud *A. platanoides* and *A. pseudoplatanus* (*see pp.60–62*) in the field in midsummer. Moderate success may be achieved if the scion and rootstock are from the same genus, usually the same species. Rare species such as *A. mono* may be grafted onto common stocks such as *A. platanoides*. Weak-growing cultivars of *A. palmatum* thrive only when grafted.

LAYERING

Many species and cultivars may be simple layered (*see p.64*), depending on suitable ground conditions.

AESCULUS HORSE CHESTNUT, BUCKEYE

CUTTINGS in early to midwinter
SEEDS in midautumn
BUDDING in mid- to late summer

There are mostly trees in this genus. Root cuttings may be taken from a few species. Take 2–3in (5–8cm) long pieces of root, then treat as for *Ailanthus* root cuttings (*see facing page*). Gather and sow the conkers as they ripen (*see right*). Germination occurs at 50–59°F (10–15°C). You may also space-sow seeds in a raised bed (*see p.55*).

Increase *A. hippocastanum* cultivars by chip-budding them onto seedling stocks 6in (15cm) above soil level (*see p.60*). *A.* x *carnea* seedlings make better stocks than *A. hippocastanum*, which is too vigorous and forms a poor union, except with its own cultivars.

GATHERING SEEDS
Gather ripe fruits (here of Aesculus hippocastanum*) when they fall to the ground. Remove the husks; sow at once. Alternatively, store in moist peat at 37°F (3°C), then sow individually in pots in late winter.*

AILANTHUS *TREE OF HEAVEN*

CUTTINGS in early winter
SEEDS from late summer to early autumn
SUCKERS from late autumn to spring

Only one species, *Ailanthus altissima*, is sometimes intentionally cultivated. The winged seeds germinate readily if sown as soon as they are ripe, or cold stratify for 60 days at 41°F (5°C). Female trees, which in some individuals form clusters of attractive red fruits, need to be pollinated by a male plant, which has foul-smelling flowers. Taking root cuttings from an existing female plant is the best method: take and prepare them as shown below. They should root in 3–4 months. Line out the rooted cuttings in a nursery bed (or pot them) in late spring and plant out after the second winter. *A. altissima* often produces suckers; these should be severed from the tree. If a sucker has a good set of roots, replant it elsewhere.

TAKING ROOT CUTTINGS OF AILANTHUS

1 Choose a tree that is healthy and growing vigorously. Carefully uncover some of the roots (see left) by loosening the topsoil with a fork. Look for roots that are about ½in (1cm) in diameter. Dig out the soil below the root.

2 Using pruners or long-handled loppers, remove a section of root at least 12in (30cm) long, making a clean, straight cut. Shake off the excess soil, but do not wash the root.

3 Cut the root into 2in (5cm) lengths (see below), with the top ends straight and the bottom ends angled so that you know which way up to insert the cuttings. Push each cutting, angled end downward, vertically into rooting medium so that the flat end is covered, just below the surface (see left). Water and label the cuttings, then place in a cool place to root.

OTHER GARDEN TREES

ACMENA Take semi-ripe cuttings in late summer as for *Metrosideros* (*see p.84*). Sow fleshy seeds as for *Dracaena* (*p.79*) when ripe or in spring.
ADANSONIA Remove seeds from outer coating when fruits are ripe; sow singly at once or in spring in containers (*see p.54*) in free-draining soil mix at 70°F (21°C).
AGATHIS (syn. *Dammara*) Sow seeds at 50–55°F (10–13°C) in early spring.
AGONIS Sow seeds in spring as for *Grevillea* (*see p.80*). Whip or side-veneer graft (*p.58*) *A. flexuosa* 'Variegata' onto *A. flexuosa* seedlings.
ALLOCASUARINA Sow seeds (*see p.54*) in spring at 59°F (15°C).
AMELANCHIER Take greenwood cuttings (*see p.52*) of cultivars. Sow fleshy-coated seeds as for *Sorbus* (*see p.90*). (*See also p.118.*)
AMHERSTIA NOBILIS Seeds often infertile; sow singly (*see p.54*) at 70°F (21°C) in spring.
ANACARDIUM Sow fleshy seeds as for *Dracaena* (*see p.79*) in spring.
ANGOPHORA Sow seeds in early spring as *Eucalyptus* (*see p.80*).
ANNONA (syn. *Cherimoya*) Sow seeds fresh (*see p.54*) in spring or dry in spring at 70°F (21°C) in very fertile soil mix.

AMELANCHIER ASIATICA

ALBIZIA *MIMOSA*

CUTTINGS in early to midsummer
SEEDS in early spring

Most of the trees in this genus (syn. *Paraserianthes*) are quite tender, but the silk tree (*Albizia julibrissin*) is much hardier (to Zone 6). Saplings flower in three years.

Greenwood cuttings (*see p.52*) yield variable results. Take them with a heel, treat with hormone rooting compound, and insert into rockwool plugs for the best results.

In the wild, the hard seed coats withstand long periods of dessication. Gather the seeds from pealike pods and soften their coats in very hot water before sowing; allow to cool for 24 hours. Sow into containers (*see p.54*) at a night-time minimum of 59°F (15°C). Soon after germination, transplant into root-trainers to avoid disturbing taproots.

ALNUS *ALDER*

CUTTINGS in late spring
SEEDS in autumn or late winter
GRAFTING in late winter

Vigorous species, such as *Alnus glutinosa*, *A. rubra* (syn. *A. oregona*), *A.* × *spaethii*, and their cultivars, can be increased from softwood cuttings (*see p.52*).

Gather the seeds in midautumn (*see below*). Store them at 37°F (3°C) in sealed plastic bags for 180 days, then sow (*see p.54*) in containers to germinate at 50–59°F (10–15°C). Alternatively, sow fresh seeds in a raised bed (*see p.55*). Avoid windy days for outdoor sowing, because the seeds are very light and can blow away easily.

Whip graft or spliced side-veneer graft (*see p.58*) cultivars of *A. glutinosa* or *A. incana* onto *A. glutinosa* rootstocks in 3½ or 5in (9 or 13cm) pots. Take scions from the previous year's growth. If the stock girth is much greater than that of the scion, an apical-wedge graft (*see Laburnum, p.82*) is suitable.

ALDER FRUITS
Alders bear male and female catkins on one tree. Female catkins develop into woody, conelike fruits (here of Alnus incana). Gather these when they turn brown in autumn. Keep the fruits in a warm, dry place until they release the seeds.

ARAUCARIA

SEEDS in early autumn

These are curious-looking large trees, including the monkey puzzle tree (*Araucaria araucana*, syn. *A. imbricata*). Male trees have large, conical pollen cones, and females have smaller, round cones that disintegrate after 1–2 years to scatter the seeds. These will not germinate if they dry out.

Chill fresh, ripe seeds in a bag of slightly damp peat or sand at 34–39°F (1–4°C) for 3–12 weeks. When the seeds begin to germinate, sow in pots (*see p.54*). Keep in a bright, frost-free place at about 59°F (15°C). The seed leaves of most species remain below ground as the shoot of adult foliage emerges (hypogeal germination, *p.20*).

BRACHYCHITON *BOTTLETREE, KURRAJONG*

SEMI-RIPE CUTTINGS in summer
HARDWOOD CUTTINGS in early autumn
SEEDS in spring

These are evergreen or deciduous trees. Both types of cuttings need humidity and bottom heat to root successfully. Sow seeds fresh at 61–64°F (16–18°C), singly into root-trainers or transplant seedlings as soon as possible.

ARBUTUS *STRAWBERRY TREE, MANZANITA*

CUTTINGS in late summer to early autumn
SEEDS in late winter to early spring

Most are tree species, including *Arbutus andrachne*, *A. menziesii*, and *A. unedo*. *A.* × *andrachnoides* rarely produces fruits in cooler climates, so try semi-ripe cuttings (*see p.51*). They need high humidity and bottom heat of 64–70°F (18–21°C) to root. Use acidic soil mix.

Gather the fruits of other species and soak them for several days in warm water to remove the pulp. Store cleaned seeds in moist sand in the refrigerator for 60 days (*see p.53*).

Sow into containers (*see p.54*) and keep them at 60–70°F (15–21°C). If the seeds fail to germinate, chill for two months or leave outdoors in autumn to germinate the next spring.

ARBUTUS UNEDO
The strawberrylike fruits follow the white flowers in autumn and take a year to ripen to red. Gather and clean them as soon as they change color.

CALOCEDRUS *INCENSE CEDAR*

CUTTINGS in late summer to midautumn
SEEDS in spring

There are three species in this genus. Take 4in (10cm) semi-ripe cuttings (*see p.70*), with or without a heel, for best results. They may be set outdoors, but bottom heat of about 64°F (18°C) in a closed case improves rooting, which may take until early summer. Gather ripe, yellow-brown cones in autumn. Store the seeds (*see p.72*) until spring; sow in containers (*see p.54*). Keep at 59°F (15°C) to speed germination, but delay transplanting until the following spring.

BETULA *BIRCH*

CUTTINGS in midspring to early summer
SEEDS in midsummer or late winter
GRAFTING in late winter to early spring

Only seeds from species of trees in this genus come true, so birches are most often rooted from cuttings or are grafted, but care must be taken with the choice of rootstocks.

CUTTINGS

Take softwood cuttings (*see p.52*), and feed regularly once they have rooted to ensure they put on sufficient growth in the first season; otherwise, they may fail to grow the following spring.

SEEDS

Gather the seeds (*see below*), dry, and store them in a refrigerator (*see p.53*), then sow in containers (*see p.54*) to germinate at 50–59°F (10–15°C). Fresh seeds may also be sown in a raised seedbed (*see p.55*). The seeds are very light, so avoid sowing on a windy day.

GRAFTING

Most birches are grafted onto *Betula pendula*, but incompatibility may be a problem. If possible, use seedling stocks of *B. nigra* for ornamental species such as *B. albosinensis*, *B. ermanii*, and *B. utilis*.

Whip graft or spliced side graft the plant (*see p.58*). To avoid sap bleeding at the union, keep the soil mix on the dry side until the scion buds break. Pot on once the graft takes so that the scion grows well in the first season.

GATHERING BIRCH SEEDS
In midsummer, break a ripe catkin into a plastic bag. Place the seeds and chaff on a tray and gently blow off the chaff to leave the seeds behind.

SELF-SOWN BIRCH SEEDLING
Birches self-sow readily, so look for seedlings in late spring. Transplant when the seedling (here of Betula pendula*) has 2–4 leaves.*

AFTERCARE OF GRAFTED BIRCH TREES
Encourage callusing of grafted plants (here Betula utilis *var.* jacquemontii*) by placing them in a "hot pipe" (see p.109).*

CARICA *PAPAYA*

SEEDS in spring

This is really an arborescent herb. Both a male and female plant, or a bisexual plant, are needed for the commonly grown species, *Carica papaya*, to fruit. Sow the seeds fresh (*see p.54*) or in spring in a seedbed or in tube pots to avoid disturbing the roots; they should germinate readily at 64°F (18°C). Root suckers may be detached in early spring or early autumn.

CATALPA *INDIAN BEAN TREE*

GREENWOOD CUTTINGS in early to midsummer
ROOT CUTTINGS in early to midwinter
SEEDS in early to midspring or in autumn
BUDDING in midsummer

Greenwood cuttings (*see p.52*) of these trees have limited success; take them with a heel and root in rockwool plugs. Root cuttings are best taken only from species, as for *Ailanthus* (*see p.75*). Gather the seeds (*see below*) and store dry in sealed plastic bags at room temperature. Sow (*see p.54*) at 59–70°F (15–21°C).

Chip-bud (*see p.60*) *C. bignonioides* and *C.* x *erubescens* cultivars 6in (15cm) above soil level onto pot- or field-grown stocks of *C. bignonioides*. *C. bignonioides* 'Aurea' may be top-worked, budding 2–3 buds onto a 6ft (2m) stem to create a standard.

CATALPA SEEDPODS
Gather the green pods as they ripen to brown, before they split and shed their seeds. They may split when dry, or you can cut them open to extract the seeds.

CEDRUS *CEDAR*

SEEDS in spring
GRAFTING in late summer or mid- to late winter

The species may be grown from seeds gathered from three-year-old cones (*see pp.71–2*). Break the wings off the seeds before storing (*see p.72*); cold moist stratify (*see p.54*) for two weeks before sowing in pots (*see p.54*) at a temperature of about 59°F (15°C).

Graft cultivars, especially *C. libani* 'Glauca', onto two-year-old seedlings such as *C. deodara*. Keep the stock in active growth until midsummer; spliced side-veneer graft (*see p.73*) a scion from vigorous shoots of the new growth.

CERCIS *REDBUD*

Cercis siliquastrum 'Bodnant'

CUTTINGS in early to midsummer
SEEDS in midwinter
GRAFTING in midwinter

The trees in this genus are not easy to propagate. Try taking greenwood cuttings as for *Acacia* (*see p.74*). Gather seeds from mid- to late autumn and soak (*see right*). Sow in containers (*see p.54*) and germinate at 59–70°F (15–21°C). It is possible to apical-wedge graft scions onto one-year-old pot-grown seedlings of *C. siliquastrum*, but these may be difficult to obtain. Bring them under cover a few weeks before grafting as for *Laburnum* (*see p.82*).

CERCIS SEEDPODS
These trees belong to the pea family and produce flattened seedpods (here of Cercis siliquastrum*) and very hard-coated seeds. Soak the seeds in very hot water and cool for 24 hours. Stratify in the refrigerator for 8–12 weeks, then sow.*

OTHER GARDEN TREES

ARDISIA Take semi-ripe cuttings (*see p.51*) in late summer. Sow fleshy seeds as for *Dracaena* (*p.79*) in spring.
ARTOCARPUS Take semi-ripe cuttings (*see p.51*) with bottom heat of 70°F (21°C) in late spring.
ATHROTAXIS Semi-ripe cuttings (*see p.70*) in summer. Sow seeds (*pp.54–5*) in seedbed or pots in late winter or early spring.
AUSTROCEDRUS CHILENSIS (syn. *Libocedrus chilensis*). Semi-ripe cuttings (*see p.70*) in summer. Sow seeds (*pp.54–5*) in seedbed or in pots in late winter or early spring.
BACKHOUSIA As for *Eucalyptus* (*see p.80*).
BANKSIA *See p.119.*
BARKLYA Sow seeds fresh in autumn or scarify to sow in spring (*see p.54*); takes 8–10 years to flower. Take semi-ripe cuttings (*p.51*) in late summer to autumn. Air layer (*p.64*) any time.
BAUHINIA Sow seeds as for *Acacia* (*see p.74*) in spring. Whip graft (*p.58*) or spliced side-veneer graft (*p.58*) in spring.
BERTHOLLETIA EXCELSA Remove seeds (Brazil nuts) from husk; sow singly in free-draining soil mix at 70°F (21°C) in spring. Whip graft (*see p.58*) or spliced side-veneer graft (*p.58*) in early spring.
BIXA ORELLANA Sow seeds as for *Acacia* (*see p.74*), but at 70°F (21°C). Spliced side-veneer graft (*p.58*) or whip graft (*p.58*) scions taken from flowering trees in spring to obtain flowering plants more quickly – in 1–2 years, instead of five.
BOLUSANTHUS SPECIOSUS Sow seeds as for *Acacia* (*see p.74*), but at 70°F (21°C).
BOMBAX Remove seeds from husk; sow singly in pots (*see p.54*) in free-draining soil mix at 70°F (21°C) as soon as ripe.
BROUSSONETIA Take greenwood cuttings as for *Magnolia* (*see p.83*) from early to midsummer. Sow seeds as for *Cornus* (*p.78*) in spring. Spliced side-veneer graft (*p.58*) or whip graft (*p.58*) *B. papyrifera* cultivars.
BROWNEA Take 6ft (2m) hardwood cuttings as for *Salix* (*see p.89*). Sow seeds as for *Acacia* (*p.74*), but at 70°F (21°C).
CAESALPINIA Seeds as for *Acacia* (*see p.74*). Take softwood cuttings (*p.52*) in spring. Spliced side-veneer graft (*p.58*) or whip graft (*p.58*) in spring.
CALLITRIS Sow seeds (*see p.54*) at 55–64°F (13–18°C) in spring.
CALODENDRUM Take semi-ripe cuttings (*see p.51*) in late summer or early autumn. Sow seeds as soon as ripe (*p.54*) at 70°F (21°C); takes quite a few years to flower.
CALPURNIA Seeds as for *Acacia* (*see p.74*).
CARPINUS Take greenwood cuttings (*see p.52*) in early summer. Sow seeds in seedbed (*p.55*) in autumn. Whip graft (*p.58*) in winter; top-work *C. betulus* for a weeping standard.
CARYA Sow seeds as for *Juglans* (*see p.81*). Whip-and-tongue graft as for *Juglans*.
CASSIA Sow seeds as for *Acacia* (*see p.74*).
CASTANEA Sow seeds as for *Aesculus* (*see p.74*). Graft as for *Malus* (*p.84*). Chip-bud as for *Malus*.
CASUARINA Take semi-ripe cuttings as for *Metrosideros* (*see p.84*). Sow seeds as for *Acacia* (*p.74*).
CEIBA Tease seeds from silky fiber (kapok) of seedheads; sow singly in containers (*see p.54*) in free-draining soil mix at 70°F (21°C) in spring.
CELTIS Sow seeds as for *Zelkova* (*see p.91*). Whip graft as for *Betula* (*see facing page*) onto seed-raised stocks of *C. occidentalis*.
CERATONIA Sow seeds as for *Acacia* (*see p.74*). Bud cultivars as for *Citrus* (*p.78*) in spring or midsummer.
CERCIDIPHYLLUM JAPONICUM Sow seeds as for *Acer* (*see p.74*). Graft form a *pendulum* as for *Corylus avellana* 'Pendula' (*p.78*), onto seed-raised stock. Simple layer as for *Magnolia* (*p.83*).

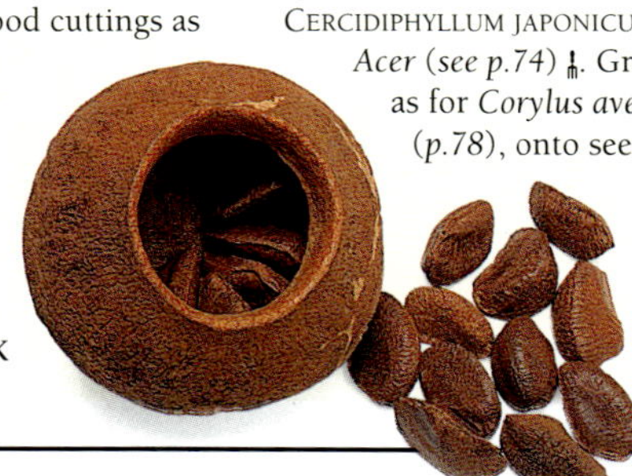

BERTHOLLETIA EXCELSA
SEEDS AND HUSK

CHAMAECYPARIS *CYPRESS*

Chamaecyparis nootkatensis 'Pendula'

CUTTINGS in late summer to midautumn ⋔
SEEDS in spring ⋔
GRAFTING in late winter ⋔⋔

Propagate species of these trees from seeds or cuttings. Some dwarf or slow-growing cultivars do not root freely, so they must be grafted.

CUTTINGS

Cuttings root at almost any time, but 4–6in (10–15cm) semi-ripe cuttings (*see p.51*) are best, provided the base is not too woody. Insert into rooting medium and keep humid on a mist- or covered bench or under plastic film (*see p.44*) with bottom heat of about 68°F (20°C), but no higher, to promote rooting. This may take 6–9 months.

SEEDS

Extract seeds in autumn from one-year-old cones; store in the refrigerator for 60 days at 41°F (5°C) until sowing (*see p.72*) with bottom heat of 59°F (15°C). Transplant the seedlings in midsummer.

GRAFTING

Spliced side-veneer graft cultivars such as *C. lawsoniana* 'Lutea' and *C. obtusa* 'Crippsii' onto slightly thicker two-year-old seedlings of *C. lawsoniana* (*see p.73*). With bottom heat of 68°F (20°C), the graft should callus after several weeks.

CITRUS

CUTTINGS in summer ⋔⋔
SEEDS in summer ⋔⋔
GRAFTING in late summer or early autumn ⋔⋔⋔

Citrus cultivars are grafted onto rootstocks for vigor, disease resistance, and early crops. Cuttings or seeds are worth a try, but these may be prone to phytophthora root diseases.

CUTTINGS

Some citrus, for example lemons (*Citrus limon*), root more easily than others from semi-ripe cuttings (*see p.51*).

SEEDS

Unusually, citrus produce seeds with several embryos, some of which are asexually derived (apomictic), so the seedlings are clones of the parent. Sow seeds in pots (*see p.54*); weed out puny or very vigorous sexual seedlings. The plants should flower in seven years.

GRAFTING

Citrus is often grafted onto a Japanese bitter orange seedling (*Poncirus trifoliata*). Take a chip-bud (*see p.60*) and put under the bark as in T-budding (*see p.62*).

LEMONS (*CITRUS LIMON*)
As well as lemons, Citrus *includes grapefruits, limes, tangerines, oranges, kumquats, and their hybrids; they are all quite tender.*

CORNUS *DOGWOOD*

CUTTINGS in late spring or early summer ⋔⋔
SEEDS in late winter or early spring ⋔⋔
GRAFTING in late winter ⋔⋔

There are small, deciduous or evergreen trees in this genus. Those with variegated foliage are best taken from softwood cuttings, as for maples (*Acer*) (*see p.74*) or for quicker results, grafted. Use seed-raised *Cornus florida* or *C. kousa* as rootstocks with whip (*see p.58*) or spliced side-veneer graft (*see p.58*). Raise *C. mas* and *C. nuttallii* from seeds (*see below*).

CORNUS FRUITS
Dogwoods have small, round fruits; some are edible and strawberrylike, such as those of Cornus *'Porlock' (above). Gather the ripe fruits and treat the seeds as for* Arbutus *(see p.76).*

CORYLUS *HAZELNUT*

CUTTINGS in early and midsummer ⋔⋔
SEEDS in late winter ⋔
GRAFTING in late winter ⋔⋔
LAYERING in mid- and late autumn ⋔

Trees in this genus include the nut-bearing *Corylus avellana* and *C. maxima*, which may be raised from seeds (*see p.54*). Most of their cultivars are usually propagated by greenwood cuttings (*see p.52*). They can also be simple layered (*see p.64*) from stock plants; cut back the stock plants hard in early spring of the previous year to obtain vigorous shoots for layering.

Most hazels may be grafted onto two-year-old *C. avellana* seedlings or cuttings by whip (*see p.58*) or spliced side-veneer techniques (*see p.58*). *C. avellana* 'Contorta' and 'Pendula' must always be grafted; whip or apical-wedge graft (*see p.58*) the scion onto a 6ft (2m) stem of *C. maxima* or *C. avellana*. Cut out any suckers from the stock as they appear.

HAZELNUTS
Gather the nuts as soon as they fall, store in moist peat at 37°F (3°C) for 2–6 months, and sow into individual containers.

CRATAEGUS *HAWTHORN*

SEEDS in midautumn or late winter ⋔
BUDDING in mid- to late summer ⋔⋔

Gather fruits of the many trees in the genus in midautumn; the best time is while they are still green and before any germination inhibitors develop. Soak them in warm water for several days to clean the flesh off the seeds. Sow into containers (*see p.54*) and place in a sheltered site, or store in a refrigerator (*see p.53*) and sow in late winter. Germination occurs at 50–59°F (10–15°C) but is erratic, so keep the seeds until the second spring.

It is quicker to graft if only one or two plants are required. Several species make good seed-raised stocks at two or three years old, such as *Crataegus crus-galli*, *C. laevigata* (syn. *C. oxyacantha*), or *C. monogyna*. Chip-bud in the field 6in (15cm) from soil level (*see p.60*).

CRYPTOMERIA
JAPANESE CEDAR

CUTTINGS in late summer to early autumn ⋔
SEEDS in spring ⋔
GRAFTING in late winter ⋔⋔⋔

Root 3–5in (8–13cm) semi-ripe cuttings of this single species as for *Chamaecyparis* (*see above*). This is an unusual conifer in being able to grow new shoots from the base if cut down (coppiced); the shoots will root readily as cuttings.

The solitary female cones ripen to brown; gather the seeds in autumn (*see p.71*). Store dry, then stratify in damp peat in the refrigerator for three weeks before sowing (*see p.54*). Bottom heat of 59–68°F (15–20°C) aids germination.

Some dwarf forms do not have sufficient cuttings material; spliced side-veneer graft (*see p.73*) scions onto pot-grown rootstocks. Keep at 68°F (20°C) for a few weeks until the graft calluses.

x CUPRESSOCYPARIS

CUTTINGS in mid- to late summer

Most commonly cultivated are cultivars of the Leyland cypress (x *Cupressocyparis leylandii*, syn. *Cupressus leylandii*). For best results, take 6in (15cm) semi-ripe cuttings (*see p.70*) from slightly shaded basal shoots; treat as for *Chamaecyparis* (*see facing page*).

DAVIDIA *HANDKERCHIEF TREE*

SEEDS in spring

Davidia involucrata is also called the dove or ghost tree. Clean ripe fruits; sow (*see p.54*) at once, singly; keep at 70°F (21°C) for three months, then move outdoors. Seeds are doubly dormant and may not germinate for two winters. Flowers in ten years.

CUPRESSUS *CYPRESS*

CUTTINGS in late winter or late summer
SEEDS in late winter or spring
GRAFTING in late winter

Most of the cultivars of these trees may be rooted from cuttings (*see p.70*). For best results, take 3–4in (8–10cm) green shoots in late winter and root under mist with bottom heat of 68°F (20°C). Cuttings may also be rooted under cover in summer.

Ripe, two-year-old cones are difficult to identify. Look for a branch bearing three sizes of cone and choose the largest, or find cones borne on shoots well back from the growing tips. Seeds (*see p.54*) germinate best at 59°F (15°C).

Certain cultivars do not root easily from cuttings, such as *C. macrocarpa* 'Goldcrest'; these may be better spliced side-veneer grafted (*see p.73*).

OTHER GARDEN TREES

CHRYSOPHYLLUM Root hardwood cuttings (*see p.50*) of well-ripened shoots in high heat and humidity in late summer to autumn. Sow seeds (*p.54*) in spring.
CINNAMOMUM Take semi-ripe cuttings (*see p.51*) at any time. Extract seeds from fleshy fruits in spring; sow immediately (*p.54*) at 55–64°F (13–18°C).
CITHAREXYLUM Take semi-ripe cuttings (*see p.51*) at any time. Sow seeds as for *Cinnamomum*.
CLADRASTIS Take root cuttings as for *Acacia* (*see p.74*). Seeds as for *Cercis* (*p.77*).
CLETHRA Take semi-ripe cuttings of evergreens as for *Arbutus* (*see p.76*). Take greenwood cuttings of deciduous species (*p.52*) in early summer. Sow seeds as for *Rhododendron* (*p.138*). Layer as for *Magnolia* (*p.83*).
COCCOLOBA Extract seeds from ripe fleshy fruits; sow at once (*see p.54*) at 70°F (21°C). Simple layer ripe stems at any time (*p.64*).
COLVILLEA RACEMOSA Seeds often infertile; sow (*see p.54*) as soon as ripe, singly in containers at 70°F (21°C).
CORDIA Take semi-ripe cuttings (*see p.51*) at any time. Sow seeds (*p.54*) when ripe.
CORDYLINE. As for *Dracaena* (*see right*).
CORYNOCARPUS Sow seeds as for *Dracaena* (*see right*). Semi-ripe cuttings, primarily of variegated forms, as for *Arbutus* (*p.76*).
+ CRATAEGOMESPILUS Whip-and-tongue graft as for *Malus* (*see p.84*). Chip-bud as for *Crataegus* (*facing page*).
CRINODENDRON Take semi-ripe cuttings as for *Ilex* (*see p.81*) in late summer.
CYDONIA Whip-and-tongue graft, chip-bud, or T-bud onto clonal cydonia rootstocks as for *Pyrus* (*see p.88*).
CYPHOMANDRA Take softwood cuttings (*see p.52*) in spring. Sow seeds as for *Dracaena* (*right*) in spring.
DACRYDIUM Take semi-ripe cuttings (*see p.70*) from mid- to late summer. Sow seeds (*p.54*) in mid- to late summer.
DELONIX Sow seeds as for *Acacia* (*see p.74*), but at 70°F (21°C).
DILLENIA Extract seeds from fleshy fruits when ripe; sow (*see p.54*) at 70°F (21°C).
DIOSPYROS Male and female persimmons needed for seeds; sow as soon as ripe after removing seed coats (*see p.54*). Whip-and-tongue graft (*p.59*), chip-bud (*p.60*) or T-bud (*p.62*) cultivars onto seedling stocks mid-to late summer.
DOMBEYA Take semi-ripe cuttings (*see p.51*) in late summer. Sow seeds as soon as ripe in spring (*p.54*) at 70°F (21°C).
ELAEOCARPUS Take semi-ripe cuttings (*see p.51*) in late summer. Sow seeds as for *Dracaena* (*right*) in spring.
ELEUTHEROCOCCUS (syn. *Acanthopanax*) Take softwood cuttings (*see p.52*) in late spring. Take root cuttings as for *Ailanthus* (*p.75*). Sow seeds as for *Sorbus* (*p.90*).
EMBOTHRIUM Take root cuttings as for *Robinia* (*see p.89*). Sow seeds as for *Grevillea* (*p.80*). Separate suckers as for *Populus* (*p.86*); pot suckers at 50°F (10°C).
ERIOBOTRYA Sow loquat seeds fresh (*see p.54*) in late spring. Chip-bud (*p.60*) or T-bud (*p.62*) onto clonal cydonia rootstock in mid- to late summer.

CYDONIA OBLONGA

DRACAENA

Dracaena marginata 'Tricolor'

CUTTINGS any time
SEEDS in early spring

The treelike species of this genus are grown for their foliage. Variegated cultivars must be increased from cuttings to retain the variegation. It takes three to five years to obtain a good-sized plant.

CUTTINGS

Take stem cuttings from healthy, strong sideshoots and split, as shown below, for the optimum number of new plants. Alternatively, insert whole sections of stem vertically. Leaf-bud cuttings also root well (*see below*). Instead of sharp sand, you may use a free-draining soil mix or rockwool. Cuttings root within 8–12 weeks.

SEEDS

Extract the seeds from the berries (*see p.53*) and sow in containers (*see p.54*) at 68–80°F (20–25°C). Germination should take 4–6 weeks. Transplant the seedlings into individual pots; once settled, grow on at 59°F (15°C).

LEAF-BUD CUTTING
Take a 2–3in (5–8cm) section of stem, with one leaf, cutting just above a node. Fill a pan with moist, sharp sand, then insert the stem vertically so that it is half-buried. Trim the leaf by half its length to avoid moisture loss. Water, label, and keep in bright shade at 64–70°F (18–21°C) until rooted.

Use a half pot or pan: too great a depth of soil mix or sand may lead to rot

STEM CUTTINGS
Remove sections of a healthy stem, each with one or two nodes. Slice each section in two lengthwise with a sharp knife. If the pith is moist, root in moist, sharp sand to avoid rot; if it is dry, use a free-draining rooting medium. Lay the cuttings wounded sides down. Label, then treat as leaf-bud cuttings.

EUCALYPTUS *GUM*

SEEDS in early spring ⚲

The fast-growing trees in the genus are suitable for Zones 9–10. In the wild, the woody seed capsules persist on the tree, so they can be gathered any time. If they do not split easily, the seeds may be immature. *Eucalyptus* seeds benefit from a cold period at 37–41°F (3–5°C) for two months (*see p.54*). They dislike root disturbance, so transplant or sow into root-trainers (*see below*). Seeds germinate quickly at 59–68°F (15–20°C). Plant out seedlings in 12–15 months.

EXTRACTING SEEDS
Leave ripe woody seed capsules (here of Eucalyptus pauciflora *subsp.* niphophila*) in a warm, dry place for 1–2 weeks until they split open to release seeds and fine brown chaff.*

SOWING SEEDS IN ROOT-TRAINERS
Fill the root-trainers with soilless seed mix. Sow a pinch of seeds into each cell. Lightly cover with sieved mix and a thin layer of fine grit. Water and label. Thin each cell to one seedling.

FAGUS *BEECH*

SEEDS from late summer to late autumn or in late winter ⚲
GRAFTING in late winter or early spring ⚲⚲

The simplest way to grow these large-growing trees is from seeds. Gather the nuts when ripe and sow at once outdoors (*see p.55*), or store in the refrigerator for six weeks before sowing in late winter (*see p.54*) to avoid losing seeds to rodents. Germination is at 50°F (10°C).

Two- or three-year-old seedlings of the European beech, *Fagus sylvatica*, are often used as rootstocks for whip or spliced side grafting (*see p.58*). Beeches have thin bark, so spliced side-veneer grafting (*see p.58*) is also suitable. Graft at soil level for a neat graft union – a top-worked graft on a tall stem may look ugly. Tie the growing scion into a split stake so that it grows straight. Stake weeping forms with a sturdy stake of the desired length of the mature stem.

FICUS *FIG*

Ficus elastica 'Doescheri'

HARDWOOD CUTTINGS in late autumn or late winter ⚲
SEMI-RIPE CUTTINGS all year round ⚲
LEAF-BUD CUTTINGS all year round ⚲
AIR LAYERING in late autumn or spring ⚲

A few of the tree species are fairly hardy, such as the edible fig (*Ficus carica*), but most are tender. Figs may be increased from the appropriate type of cutting, but air layering is easy if only one or two plants are required.

CUTTINGS

Take hardwood cuttings of *F. carica*, tie into bundles (*see p.51*), and keep in frost-free conditions in autumn; large cuttings up to 3ft (90cm) long may be rooted direct. In winter, root standard cuttings in pots at 50–59°F (10–15°C). Semi-ripe cuttings (*see p.51*) of tender evergreens can be taken all year. Species with thick stems, such as the Indian rubber plant, *F. elastica*, may be grown from leaf-bud cuttings (*see below*). Rolling the leaf reduces moisture loss. It should produce a decent-sized pot plant in two years.

AIR LAYERING

This can be done on a mature plant if conditions are conducive to rooting – that is, in controlled humidity at 59–68°F (15–20°C). Layer a stem (*see p.64*); after three months, if it shows signs of drying out, mist-spray the root ball.

LEAF-BUD CUTTING
Using a sharp knife or pruners, cut straight across a stem just above a node and 1in (2.5cm) below the node. Keeping the waxy side outermost, roll the leaf to form a cylinder, secure with a rubber band, and pot into soilless potting mix. The leaf node should sit on the soil mix surface. Support the cutting with a split stake through the rolled leaf. Keep humid at 68°F (20°C) until rooted.

FRAXINUS *ASH*

SEEDS in mid- to late autumn ⚲
GRAFTING in late winter or early spring ⚲⚲⚲

Seeds of these trees are doubly dormant, so they need a period of warm moist stratification (see *p.54*).

Line out one-year-old seedlings of *Fraxinus excelsior* in a nursery bed and use as rootstocks for whip-and-tongue grafting (see *p.59*) after another 1–2 years. Graft close to the soil just before the buds break in spring. Top-work 'Pendula' at the desired height onto four-year-old stocks. Alternatively, whip graft (see *p.58*) onto pot-grown stocks.

GINKGO *MAIDENHAIR TREE*

CUTTINGS in late spring to early summer ⚲⚲⚲
SEEDS in late winter ⚲
GRAFTING in late winter ⚲⚲

There is a single species, *Ginkgo biloba*; a male and female tree are needed to produce seeds. The plumlike fruits of the female tree have an unpleasant smell when ripe. Gather these in mid-autumn and clean off the pulp. Wash the nutlike seeds with a mild detergent to remove germination inhibitors, then store in the refrigerator for 30–60 days before sowing outdoors (*see p.54*). Plants may be raised from softwood cuttings (as for *Betula*, *p.76*) or by grafting, using a whip-and-tongue (*see p.59*) or spliced side-veneer graft (*see p.58*).

GLEDITSIA *HONEYLOCUST*

SEEDS in late autumn ⚲
GRAFTING in late winter to early spring ⚲⚲⚲

Young plants of these trees are prone to cold damage. Scarify the seeds (*see below*) before sowing (*see p.54*) to germinate at 50–59°F (10–15°C). Whip-and-tongue graft cultivars outdoors as for *Fraxinus* (*see left*) or use a spliced side graft (*see p.58*).

PREPARING GLEDITSIA SEEDS FOR SOWING
Soak seeds in warm water for 48 hours. Mix with an equal volume of moist sand in a plastic bag and chill at 37°F (3°C) for 2–3 months.

GREVILLEA *SILKY OAK*

SEEDS in late winter ⚲

Only *Grevillea robusta* germinates readily; scarify or soak the seeds (*see p.54*) of other species for 48 hours before sowing, or stratify for 30 days at 41°F (5°C). Sow the seeds in containers and cover thinly with vermiculite. Germination occurs at 50–59°F (10–15°C); the seedlings grow quickly.

ILEX *Holly*

Ilex x altaclerensis 'Balearica'

HARDWOOD CUTTINGS in autumn to midwinter
SEMI-RIPE CUTTINGS in late summer to autumn
SEEDS in early spring
GRAFTING in spring, late summer or early autumn
LAYERING in spring

There are many useful trees (and shrubs) in this genus. Most root readily from cuttings. If only a few plants are needed, try layering. Hollies self-sow freely in the wild and will germinate just as readily, if slowly (sometimes taking three years), in cultivation. Grafting is feasible, but is useful only for creating a standard.

CUTTINGS

Take semi-ripe (*see p.51*) or hardwood (*see p.50*) stem cuttings around 3in (8cm) long, with the top two leaves intact and a ¾in (2cm) basal wound to stimulate rooting. This may take up to three months.

Semi-ripe cuttings of easily rooting *Ilex aquifolium* can be taken a little early, but remove the soft tips. For deciduous species, such as *I. verticillata*, take cuttings in early or midsummer and do not wound the cuttings; they should root in 6–8 weeks. Provide bottom heat for hardwood cuttings taken in winter. Cuttings of evergreens may suffer leaf drop, caused by wet soil mix raising the humidity under cover. If this happens, discard the cuttings.

SEEDS

Hollies are usually unisexual; for seeds, you need a berry-bearing female and a male nearby to ensure pollination. Gather the berries in winter, clean off the flesh (*see p.53*), and sow at once. Alternatively, store the seeds in a warm, moist place to allow the embryos to mature. Then chill the seeds in moist soil mix in the refrigerator (*see p.53*) to break their dormancy before sowing outdoors in a seedbed (*see p.55*).

GRAFTING

Chip-bud (*see pp.60–1*) three buds of the scion plant onto *I. aquifolium* at the desired height for a standard plant.

LAYERING

Chose a flexible, vigorous young shoot that is close to the ground, then simple layer it (*see p.64*).

SELECTING HOLLY SHOOTS FOR CUTTINGS
Holly shoots darken as they ripen, so avoid softwood shoots with lighter green leaves. Look for a terminal bud that has stopped growing; if the bud is pale green, the growth hormones are still concentrated at the tip rather than in the stem where they would help the cutting to root.

JUGLANS *Walnut*

SEEDS in mid- to late autumn
GRAFTING in early spring

Ornamental walnuts are raised from seeds. Gather the ripe fruits, clean off the green, fibrous husks, and sow the "nuts" immediately, or stratify for 120–190 days at 41°F (5°C). Sow in a seedbed (see p.55) or into root-trainers, covering the seeds with 1in (2.5cm) of soil mix and ⅛in (3mm) grit. Germinate at 50°F (10°C). Plant out seedlings in 3–5 years.

Cultivars of *Juglans regia* and *J. nigra*, grown for their edible nuts, are usually whip-and-tongue grafted (see p.55). Use 2–3-year-old pot-grown stocks of *J. regia* or *J. nigra*; keep cool and dormant until 7–10 days before grafting to avoid sap rising too quickly. Use a slightly narrower scion than the stock so the thinner scion bark will align with the stock's cambium more easily.

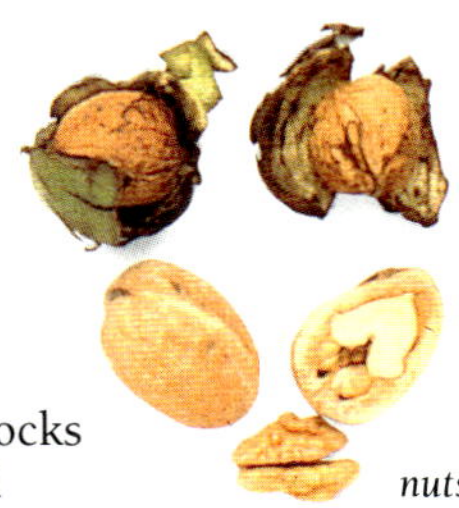

RIPE WALNUTS
Walnuts are stone fruits, not true nuts. The husks blacken and disintegrate on the tree to release the ripe "nuts." Gather the fruits while still green and remove the husks.

OTHER GARDEN TREES

EUCOMMIA Take softwood cuttings as for *Acer* (*see p.74*). Seeds as for *Ulmus* (*p.91*).
EUCRYPHIA Take softwood cuttings as for *Stewartia* (*see p.90*). Take semi-ripe cuttings as for *Arbutus* (*p.76*). Sow seeds as for *Stewartia* (*p.90*).
EUPTELEA Sow seeds as for *Stewartia* (*see p.90*). Layer as for *Magnolia* (*p.83*).
FIRMIANA Remove seeds when ripe from outer coating; sow singly (*see p.54*) in free-draining soil mix at 70°F (21°C).
FRANKLINIA ALATAMAHA Take softwood cuttings as for *Acer* (*see p.74*). Sow seeds as for *Stewartia* (*p.90*).
GEIJERA Scarify fresh seeds and sow in autumn (*see pp.53–4*).
GORDONIA Semi-ripe cuttings as for *Arbutus* (*see p.76*). Sow seeds as for *Stewartia* (*p.90*).
GYMNOCLADUS Take root cuttings as *Acacia* (*see p.74*). Sow seeds as for *Acacia*.
HAKEA Sow seeds as for most *Grevilleas* (*see facing page*); avoid disturbing roots.
HALESIA Take softwood cuttings as for *Magnolia* (*see p.83*). Sow seeds as for *Davidia* (*p.79*).
HOHERIA Take greenwood cuttings (*see p.52*) of deciduous trees in early to midsummer. Take semi-ripe cuttings (*p.51*) of evergreens in late summer or early autumn. All cuttings need mist and bottom heat of 70°F (21°C). Sow seeds as for *Grevillea robusta* (*facing page*).
HOVENIA Abrade fresh seeds, then soak in water for 48 hours before sowing outdoors (*see p.55*) in autumn in cool climates, or refrigerate moist for 90 days, then sow at 50°F (10°C) in spring.
HYMENOSPORUM FLAVUM Take semi-ripe cuttings as *Hoheria*. Sow seeds as for *Grevillea robusta* (*see facing page*).
JACARANDA Take greenwood cuttings as *Acacia* (*see p.74*). Sow seeds as for *Acacia*.

JUNIPERUS *JUNIPER*

Juniperus recurva

CUTTINGS in late summer, autumn or in late winter
SEEDS at any time

There are shrub and tree species in this genus (syn. *Sabina*). To succeed, cuttings must be taken from suitable shoots. Raising junipers from seeds is slow, but it yields plants of both sexes.

CUTTINGS

Choose strong, juvenile shoots that are still green at the base; juvenile leaves are needlelike. Treat as semi-ripe cuttings (*see p.70*) to root by the next summer. In late winter, root cuttings in humidity with bottom heat of about 68°F (20°C).

SEEDS

Junipers of both sexes are needed to produce female cones with viable seeds; these are berrylike when ripe and often blackish purple or blue. *J. recurva* and most juniper cones ripen in two years, *J. virginiana* cones in the first autumn, and *J. communis* cones after three years. Clean off any fleshy coating, then sow seeds in pots (*see p.54*). Germination takes 2–5 years. Expose the seeds to cold in winter and heat in summer, but keep the soil mix moist. Pot the slow-growing seedlings in their second year.

LABURNUM *GOLDEN CHAIN TREE*

Laburnum alpinum

CUTTINGS in late autumn
SEEDS in early spring
GRAFTING in early spring
BUDDING in midsummer

Hardwood cuttings of these trees can be very successful. Seeds are also useful for raising the two species. For a tree that will flower in three years, try grafting or budding.

CUTTINGS

Take 8–12in (20–30cm) hardwood cuttings (*see p.50*) with a heel or at the union of the current and last season's growth. Cutting into the pithy tissue of new growth hinders rooting. Root in a slit trench with coarse grit in the base, or in bundles in a cold frame (*see p.51*), then pot in spring.

SEEDS

Gather the pealike seeds from ripe pods and treat as for *Robinia* (*see p.89*).

GRAFTING

Grow on two-year-old *Laburnum anagyroides* in a nursery bed for a year to use as rootstocks for chip-budding (*see p.60*). Insert the buds 3–4in (8–10cm) above soil level. Train the new growth up a stake, then stop it at the desired height (according to whether it is to be a multi- or single-stemmed tree) to allow it to branch. It is faster to top-work three buds of the pendulous form at 5–6ft (1.5–2m) onto three- or four-year-old stocks (*see box, p.57*).

Apical-wedge grafting (*see p.58*) is often more successful than budding. Cut down a two-year-old stock to just above a bud at soil level to draw the sap up the stem, or graft pendulous forms onto 5–6ft (1.5–2m) tall stocks. Protect newly grafted plants from cold, if necessary.

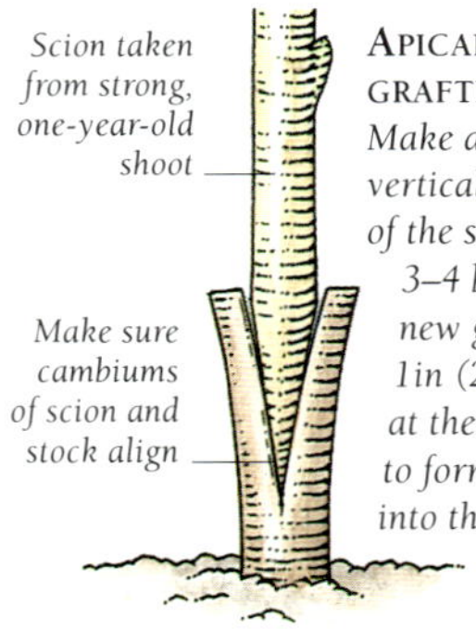

APICAL-WEDGE GRAFTING LABURNUM *Make a 1in (2.5cm) vertical cut into the center of the stock. Take a scion 3–4 buds long from the new growth; make two 1in (2.5cm) sloping cuts at the base of the scion to form a wedge. Insert into the cut in the stock.*

LARIX *LARCH*

CUTTINGS in midsummer
SEEDS in late winter to spring
GRAFTING in late winter or late summer

Female, usually purple, cones of these trees ripen in the first year to brown, but old cones may have a few viable seeds (*see p.71*). No stratification is required; bottom heat of about 59°F (15°C) aids germination. Seedlings grow fast and at two years may be used as stock plants for softwood cuttings (*see p.52*); they root readily if kept humid.

Cultivars and rarer species that do not set seeds are best spliced side-veneer grafted (*see p.73*). For stocks, pot two-year-old seedlings in spring; keep warm and dry in winter for three weeks so they start into growth without forming too much sap. Most shoots may be taken as scions while fully dormant in mid- to late winter; store them in a plastic bag in a refrigerator. Keep the grafted plant rather dry at 64–68°F (18–20°C) until a callus forms and the buds break.

LIQUIDAMBAR *SWEET GUM*

CUTTINGS in midsummer
SEEDS in late autumn or late winter
GRAFTING in late winter to early spring
LAYERING in late autumn

Seedlings of these trees vary greatly, hence the wide range of cultivars. Extract seeds from the spiky, round fruit clusters and sow them outdoors (*see p.55*) or store in moist vermiculite (*see p.53*) for two months before sowing and keep in a bright spot with a night temperature of 59–68°F (15–20°C) for germination in six weeks.

Most cultivars root well from greenwood cuttings (*see p.52*), but for large, vigorous trees, especially of variegated forms, it is better to whip or spliced side graft them (*see p.58*). For rootstocks, use two-year-old pot-grown species. Plant out grafted trees after five years. A low branch may be simple layered (*see p.64*).

LIRIODENDRON

TULIP TREE, YELLOW POPLAR

Liriodendron tulipifera

CUTTINGS in midsummer
SEEDS in late autumn or late winter
GRAFTING in late winter

Sowing seeds is the simplest way to raise the two species in this genus, but seed viability is quite low. Gather the winged nutlike fruits in midautumn, break open, and sow the seeds outdoors (*see p.55*) or store in the refrigerator (*see p.53*) for 60–90 days, then sow and germinate at 59–68°F (15–20°C) in six weeks.

Take greenwood cuttings (*see p.52*) from vigorous shoots. To propagate a cultivar, such as *Liriodendron tulipifera* 'Fastigiatum', whip or spliced side graft (*see p.58*) onto a pot-grown two-year-old seedling. Plant out in 3–5 years.

MACLURA *OSAGE ORANGE*

HARDWOOD CUTTINGS in late autumn or in late winter
ROOT CUTTINGS in early to midwinter
SEEDS in mid- to late autumn

Only *Maclura pomifera* is commonly grown. Extract the seeds from the fleshy fruits; soak in water for 48 hours and keep moist for eight weeks in the refrigerator before sowing (*see p.54*). Cuttings are slow to root. If taking hardwood cuttings immediately after leaf fall, store in bundles in sand (*see p.51*) until late winter, then insert into individual pots and supply bottom heat of 59–68°F (15–20°C). Take root cuttings as for *Acacia* (*see p.74*).

MAGNOLIA

SEMI-RIPE CUTTINGS in early to midautumn
SOFTWOOD CUTTINGS in late spring to early summer
GREENWOOD CUTTINGS in early to midsummer
SEEDS in mid- to late autumn
GRAFTING in late winter to early spring
BUDDING in mid- to late summer
LAYERING in late autumn to early spring

There are mostly trees in this genus, plus a few shrubs. Cuttings may be taken from plants with suitable shoots. Grafting is often the best option if only a single plant is needed and for trees that do not root readily. Seeds and layering are easier, but slower.

CUTTINGS

Take soft- and greenwood cuttings (*see p.52*) from 3–5in (8–13cm) new shoots of vigorous, deciduous magnolias.

Commercially, stock plants are grown under cover for softwood cuttings in late spring. This allows time (8–12 weeks) for cuttings to root and put on some growth before winter in colder climates. A stock plant bought in spring from a garden center is as good because it will probably have been grown under cover. Take nodal stem-tip cuttings (*see above*), and root in humid shade: young leaves scorch easily. Bottom heat of 64–70°F (18–21°C) helps. Liquid-feed rooted cuttings (so they are ripened by autumn and more likely to grow away in spring) and overwinter in a frost-free place.

Take semi-ripe cuttings (*see p.51*) of evergreen species and cultivars such as *Magnolia grandiflora*. Remove any decaying leaves to avoid risk of rot.

SEEDS

Before sowing seeds (*see p.55*) fresh, clean them (*see right*). If you cannot thoroughly clean them, use a fungicide to prevent rot or damping off. If only a few germinate, transplant the seedlings in midsummer and return the pot to a cold frame for a second winter.

SOFTWOOD CUTTINGS FROM A STOCK PLANT

1 A stock plant (here Magnolia 'Spectrum'), kept under cover in colder regions, gives plenty of new sideshoots for early softwood cuttings. Take 4in (10cm) long cuttings, cutting straight across the stem above a node.

2 Trim all but the top two leaves off each cutting. Cut the lower leaf in half to reduce moisture loss. Nip out any leading bud.

Alternatively, stratify the seeds for 3–6 months at 41°F (5°C), then sow under cover in spring, with 68°F (20°C) bottom heat, to germinate evenly in 5–6 weeks. Seed-raised hybrids flower in 3–10 years, but species may take much longer (up to 30 years for *M. campbellii*).

GRAFTING

Chip-bud (*see p.60*) deciduous magnolias that are difficult to root (for example *M. campbellii*, *M. macrophylla*, and large trees). Rootstocks and scions are usually compatible, but match growth habits as closely as possible. Keep the plants frost-free until spring, then pot them before they start into growth and plant out when 15 months old. Use two-year-old, pot-grown seedlings of *M. campbellii* var. *mollicomata* as stocks for *M. campbellii* and cultivars and keep in cool shade. Whip or spliced side grafting (*see p.58*) may be used if budding fails.

LAYERING

Simple layer (*see p.64*) deciduous trees any time between late autumn or early spring and evergreens in early spring.

EXTRACTING MAGNOLIA SEEDS

1 Gather the ripe cone (see inset); dry until the fleshy fruits come away freely. Soak these in warm water with some liquid detergent for 1–2 days to remove the waterproof coating. Once the flesh has softened, drain off the water.

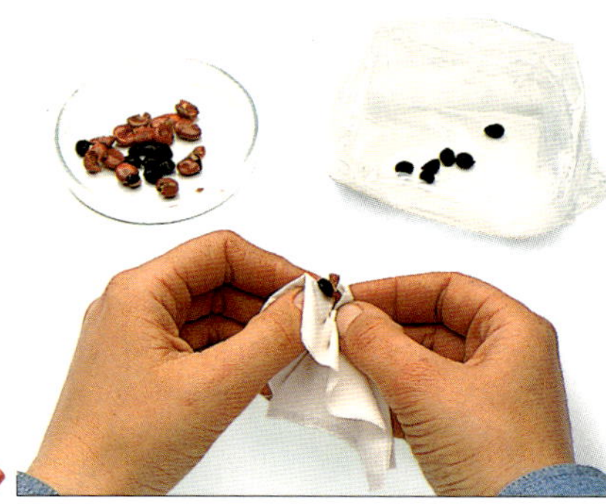

2 Remove any flesh, then dry the seeds with tissue. Either sow the seeds fresh and overwinter in a cold frame, or mix with moist peat, vermiculite, or sand, place in a plastic bag, and refrigerate for two months before sowing.

OTHER GARDEN TREES

KALOPANAX Sow seeds as for *Davidia* (*see p.79*).
KNIGHTIA Sow seeds as for *Grevillea robusta* (*see p.80*).
KOELREUTERIA Take root cuttings as for *Acacia* (*see p.74*). Sow seeds as for *Hovenia* (*p.81*). Apical-wedge graft as for *Laburnum* (*see facing page*).
LAGERSTROEMIA Take softwood cuttings as for *Stewartia* (*see p.90*). Seeds are plentiful; sow as for *Stewartia*.
LAGUNARIA Sow seeds in spring (*see p.54*) at 77°F (25°C); hairs on seed capsules may irritate.
LAURELIA Take semi-ripe cuttings as for *Metrosideros* (*see p.84*). Sow seeds as for *Grevillea robusta* (*p.80*).
LAURUS Take semi-ripe cuttings, sow seeds, and layer as for *Ilex* (*see p.81*).
LEUCADENDRON Sow seeds as for *Grevillea robusta* (*see p.80*).
LIBOCEDRUS Take semi-ripe cuttings (*see p.70*) in summer. Sow seeds (*p.72*) in spring.
LINDERA Semi-ripe cuttings (*see p.51*) in late summer. Seeds as for *Davidia* (*p.79*); female and male trees needed for fruits.
LITCHI Hardwood cuttings (*see p.50*) from two-year-old wood in late summer to early autumn. Air layer in late winter (*p.64*).
LITHOCARPUS Sow acorns as for *Quercus* (*see p.88*). Spliced side-veneer graft onto pot-grown stocks (*p.58*); use freely seeding species as understocks for any that are shy to fruit.
LOMATIA Take softwood cuttings (*see p.52*) in late spring and semi-ripe cuttings (*p.51*) in late summer. Sow seeds as for *Grevillea robusta* (*p.80*).
LOPHOMYRTUS Semi-ripe cuttings as for *Metrosideros* (*see p.84*). Sow seeds as for *Sorbus* (*p.90*).
LOPHOSTEMON Take semi-ripe cuttings and sow seeds as for *Metrosideros* (*see p.84*).
MAACKIA Take root cuttings as for *Acacia* (*see p.74*). Sow seeds as for *Acacia*.
MACADAMIA Soak seeds in warm water as soon as ripe for 12–24 hours; sow singly in containers (*see p.55*) at 70°F (21°C).

MALUS *APPLE, CRABAPPLE*

Malus 'John Downie'

SEEDS in late autumn or late winter
GRAFTING in late winter
BUDDING in mid- to late summer

Most ornamental crabapples in this genus are self-sterile, but *Malus baccata, M. florentina, M. hupehensis, M. sikkimensis,* and *M. toringoides* come true to type. Clean the ripe fruits (*see p.53*) in autumn and sow outdoors (*see p.55*). Alternatively, store the seeds in a refrigerator (*see p.53*); in early winter, soak the seeds for 48 hours, drain, and refrigerate for 3–6 months before sowing.

Most ornamental and fruiting trees are grafted. Suitable seed-raised rootstocks (*see chart below*) may be available from speciality nurseries: plant them out in a nursery bed in the winter before chip-budding (*see p.60*). It is usual to bud near soil level, but a few pendulous forms may be budded onto a 5–6ft (1.5–2m) stem. Alternatively, whip-and-tongue graft scions (*see p.59*) onto a rootstock obtained by stooling or trench layering (*see pp.56–7*).

APPLE ROOTSTOCKS
Most cultivars may be grafted onto any of the stocks listed below; choose a stock to determine the size of the grafted tree and according to availability. Dwarfing stocks are best for garden fruit trees. Use MM111 and M25 for large ornamental trees.

NAME OF ROOTSTOCK	HEIGHT AND SPREAD OF GRAFTED TREE
M27 Very dwarfing	4–6ft (1.2–2m)
M9 Dwarfing	6–10ft (2–3m)
M26 Semi-dwarfing	8–12ft (2.4–3.6m)
MM106 Semi-dwarfing, resists woolly aphid	12–18ft (3.6–5.5m)
MM111 Semi-vigorous, resists woolly aphid	15–20ft (4.5–6m)
M25 Vigorous	20–25ft (6–7.6m)
Mark Dwarfing, very hardy	6–10ft (2–3m)
Budagovski 9 (Bud 9) Dwarfing, very hardy	6–10ft (2–3m)
'Northern Spy' Semi-dwarfing, resists woolly aphid	12–15ft (3.6–5m)
MM104 Vigorous, drought resistant in dry areas	15–25ft (5–8m)
Ottawa 3 Vigorous, Canadian series	8–10ft (2.4–3m)

METASEQUOIA *DAWN REDWOOD*

SOFTWOOD CUTTINGS in summer
HARDWOOD CUTTINGS in late winter
SEEDS in spring

This tree, *Metasequoia glyptostroboides*, is a living fossil. Softwood cuttings (*see p.52*) root well if taken from persistent shoots, which shed only their leaves; cuttings from deciduous shoots without buds (which are shed entire) may root but inevitably die. Unusually for conifers, hardwood cuttings may be successful, although slow (*see right and p.51*). Bottom heat of 64–68°F (18–20°C) ensures rooting in 10–12 weeks; without heat, useful numbers should root, albeit after several months. If raising cuttings in a cold frame, pot them on in autumn.

Ovoid female cones are frequently produced, but male flowers form only after hot summers, so in some areas it may be necessary to import viable seeds. After sowing (*see pp.54–5*), shade from strong sun and keep moist at 59°F (15°C) to hasten germination.

HARDWOOD CUTTING
Take 5in (13cm) cuttings from the current season's growth when it is dormant. Do not remove any buds; tears in the bark may admit disease. Store in sand until late winter; treat with hormone rooting compound and insert in equal parts peat and fine bark to a depth of 2in (5cm).

METROSIDEROS

CUTTINGS in late summer to midautumn
SEEDS in late winter to early spring

Some of the trees in this genus are known as pohutakawas. Root semi-ripe cuttings (*see p.51*) in a closed case with bottom heat of 64–70°F (18–21°C). Store seeds dry over winter, then surface-sow in pots (*see p.54*) to germinate at 55–59°F (13–15°C). Seedlings and cuttings may be planted out or potted after 2–3 years.

MORUS *MULBERRY*

Morus nigra

CUTTINGS in late autumn
BUDDING in late summer

Trees in this genus are sometimes grown for their fruit. Take standard hardwood cuttings (*see p.50*), or thick pieces of two- to four-year-old wood (truncheons), and root them outdoors. Chip- or T-bud (*see pp.60–2*) scions of fruit trees onto two-year-old seedling rootstocks.

NOTHOFAGUS *SOUTHERN BEECH*

CUTTINGS in early to midautumn
SEEDS in autumn or in mid- to late winter

Trees in this genus are usually grown from seeds (*see pp.54–5*), although garden seedlings may be hybrids. Sow seeds from the nutlike fruits fresh or store dry over winter at 37–41°F (3–5°C). Seedlings may not be ready to plant out for four years. Take semi-ripe cuttings of evergreens such as *Nothofagus betuloides* and *N. dombeyi* (*see p.51*). Root in rockwool or peat and sand in humidity, with bottom heat of 64–70°F (18–21°C). Plant in three years.

NYSSA *TUPELO, BLACK GUM*

SEEDS in late autumn or in late winter
GRAFTING in late winter
LAYERING in late autumn or in early spring

Tupelos are traditionally raised from seeds. Gather the blue fruits before the birds eat them, clean off the flesh, and sow outdoors (*see p.55*). Alternatively, stratify for six months at 41°F (5°C) (*see p.53*), then, eight weeks before sowing, soak in water for 48 hours, drain, and refrigerate again. Germination occurs with a minimum nighttime temperature of 50°F (10°C).

Selected forms can be spliced side or whip grafted (*see p.58*) onto a two- or three-year-old seed-raised rootstock. Layer a mature plant with suitable shoots as for *Tilia* (*see p.91*). Saplings may be planted out after 3–4 years.

OSTRYA *HOP HORNBEAM*

Ostrya virginiana

SEEDS in mid- to late autumn or in late winter
GRAFTING in late winter or in early spring

The small female catkins of these trees develop into hoplike clusters of fruits. Seeds do not germinate reliably, but the yield can be improved by stratifying the seeds (*see p.54*). Sow fresh, slightly green, cleaned seeds outdoors (*see p.55*). Alternatively, soak for 48 hours; drain; refrigerate for four months; sow in pots, covered with ⅛in (3mm) of grit; and germinate with a nighttime minimum of 50°F (10°C). Keep for at least a year to allow as many seedlings as possible to germinate.

"Nurse" graft *Ostrya* onto two- or three-year-old *Carpinus betulus* seedlings, as for *Parrotia* (*see facing page*), for a good-sized tree in 5–6 years.

PARROTIA

SEEDS in autumn or late winter
GRAFTING in late winter
LAYERING in early summer or midautumn

Parrotia persica is most often raised from seeds. Sow fresh seeds outdoors in autumn, or soak for 48 hours, drain, and chill for ten weeks before sowing (*see p.54*). Germination and growth rates tend to be variable; a second flush of seedlings may appear in the second spring. Ironwoods can be layered, as for lindens (*see* Tilia, *p.91*).

Cultivar scions can be spliced side or whip grafted (*see p.58*) onto two- or three-year-old seedlings of *Hamamelis virginiana* or *H. vernalis*. To overcome incompatibility, graft low on the stock. When potting the grafted plant, cover the graft union with soil mix to promote rooting of the scion. This is a "nurse graft"; cut away the stock when the scion has large enough roots of its own. Saplings attain a good size in five years.

OTHER GARDEN TREES

MANGIFERA Take semi-ripe cuttings (*see p.51*) in late summer with bottom heat of 70°F (21°C). Remove mango flesh and tough outer seed coat; sow large seeds (*p.55*) fresh at 68–77°F (20–25°C).
MANGLIETIA Sow seeds and layer as for *Magnolia* (*see p.83*). Chip-bud as for *Magnolia*.
MELALEUCA Semi-ripe cuttings and seeds as for *Metrosideros* (*see facing page*).
MELICYTUS (syn. *Hymenanthera*) Softwood cuttings as for *Stewartia* (*see p.90*). Sow seeds as for *Dracaena* (*p.79*).
MELIOSMA Take root cuttings as for *Acacia* (*see p.74*). Sow seeds of evergreens as for *Dracaena* (*p.79*) and deciduous species as for *Sorbus* (*p.90*).
MESPILUS Chip- or T-bud (*see pp.60–62*) or whip-and-tongue graft (*p.59*) medlar scion onto *Cydonia* or *Crataegus* stocks.
MICHELIA Take semi-ripe cuttings (*see p.51*). Sow seeds as for *Magnolia* (*p.83*).
OLEA Take semi-ripe cuttings in summer (*see p.51*). Crack the hard seed coats; sow in spring (*p.54*) to germinate in 4–5 months.
PANDANUS Take cuttings as for *Dracaena* (*see p.79*). Clean flesh off seeds; soak for 24 hours; sow singly (*p.55*) at 70°F (21°C) in spring. Divide suckers in spring as for *Yucca* (*p.145*).
PAULOWNIA Take root cuttings as *Acacia* (*see p.74*). *P. spiralis* may form roots on upper stems; remove entire shoot in spring and plant. Seeds as for *Stewartia* (*p.90*).
PELTOPHORUM Sow seeds as for *Acacia* (*see p.74*), but at 70°F (21°C).
PHELLODENDRON Root cuttings as for *Acacia* (*see p.74*). Seeds as for *Sorbus* (*p.90*).

PERSEA *AVOCADO*

SEEDS when ripe or in spring
GRAFTING in early spring

Persea americana is usually raised from seeds (*see below*) because it comes virtually true to type. Soak seeds to avoid avocado root rot. Germination occurs at 68–77°F (20–25°C). Grow on the seedlings until they are 12–16in (30–40cm) tall before planting out.

Graft cultivars, for disease resistance and reliable fruiting, onto one- or two-year-old seedling rootstocks of Mexican species, using an apical wedge graft (*see p.58*) or a side-wedge or saddle graft (*see right*). The saddle graft unites large areas of cambium, resulting in a strong union, but it requires skill to match the cuts.

GRAFTING AN AVOCADO

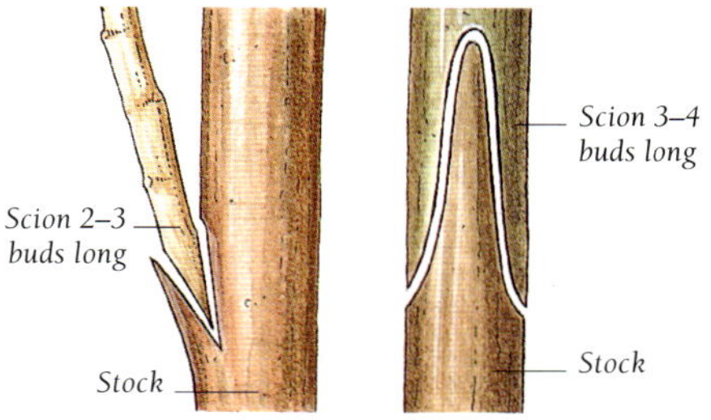

SIDE-WEDGE GRAFT SADDLE GRAFT

To side-wedge graft, make two angled cuts, one slightly longer than the other, at the base of the scion, and one downward cut into the rootstock. To saddle graft, cut deep into the scion wood on two sides, twisting sharply into the center. Cut the stock to match.

GROWING AVOCADOS FROM SEEDS

1 Soak healthy, undamaged seeds in hot water at 106–130°F (40–52°C) for 30 minutes. Trim about ½in (1cm) off the pointed end with a clean, sharp knife. Dip the wound in fungicide.

2 Place each seed in a 6in (15cm) pot of moist seed soil mix so that the cut top of the seed lies just above the mix surface (above). *It should germinate in about four weeks* (right).

PICEA *SPRUCE*

Picea morrisonicola

CUTTINGS in midsummer or late winter
SEEDS in spring
GRAFTING in late summer or late winter

Cuttings of these conifers are best taken from young plants or dwarf forms. Sow seeds, if available. *Picea breweriana* is very slow from seeds and is best grafted, as are cultivars of trees.

CUTTINGS

Take cuttings from trees that are less than 5–6 years old if possible. Choose nearly ripe shoots (*see p.70*); they should be firm but not woody at the base. If taking cuttings in midwinter, provide bottom heat of 59–68°F (15–20°C) to aid rooting. The cuttings should root, and the buds break, by early summer.

SEEDS

Gather pendent female cones, which ripen in a season from green or red to purple or brown in autumn; male cones are yellow to reddish purple and are pendent in spring. Extract the seeds (*see p.72*) and store in a refrigerator until spring, then sow in containers or in a seedbed (*see pp.53–4*). Transplant slow-growing seedlings in the second spring: those of vigorous species, for example *P. abies* and *P. sitchensis*, may be transplanted when 2in (5cm) tall.

GRAFTING

Select vigorous shoots with at least three side buds at the tip as scions to obtain a well-formed tree. One-year-old shoots are best, but two-year-old shoots may be used. Pot the rootstocks (usually two-year-old seedlings of *P. abies*) in winter so they may establish before summer grafting. Keep on the dry side to prevent the sap rising and pinch out the current season's growth just prior to grafting.

Use a spliced side-veneer graft (*see p.73*) and plunge the plant into moist peat with bottom heat of 70–73°F (21–23°C) until the graft calluses. For winter grafting, use a plastic-film tent with bottom heat of 59–64°F (15–18°C). Failed rootstocks from summer grafting can be recycled for winter grafting. If the base of the scion roots, this results in a more robust, own-root plant.

PINUS *Pine*

SEEDS in spring
GRAFTING in late winter or early spring

Pines form the largest genus of conifers. Species are raised from seeds; cultivars are grafted.

SEEDS

Cones ripen over two years (three years in *Pinus pinea*) to brown; either in late winter to spring, such as those of *Pinus sylvestris*, or in autumn. Extract the seeds (*see p.72*); some cones, such as those of *P. radiata* (syn. *P. insignis*), open in the wild only after a forest fire; flame them for a few minutes, allow them to cool, and moisten, then dry them.

Refrigerate seeds (*see p.72*) for three to seven weeks to improve germination. Sow into containers (*see p.54*) and provide bottom heat of about 59°F (15°C). Protect seedlings from frost and slugs, and transplant when they are 2in (5cm) tall and woody at the base. They have juvenile leaves for the first 2–3 years.

GRAFTING

Pot two-year-old seedling rootstocks in spring. Bring under cover in late winter. Spliced side-veneer graft (*see p.73*) and plunge in moist peat with bottom heat of 64°F (18°C) to callus in six weeks.

PLATANUS *Sycamore, Plane*

CUTTINGS in late autumn
SEEDS in late autumn or in late winter

The London plane (*Platanus* x *hispanica*, syn. *P.* x *acerifolia*) is actually a complex group of hybrids. The best forms are increased by hardwood cuttings (*see p.50*). Take material from vigorous shoots of the current season's wood, directly after leaf fall. Rooted cuttings can be planted out after 12 months.

Seeds produce interesting variations. Gather the seeds (*see below*) in autumn and sow them immediately in a seedbed (*see p.55*) Alternatively, store the seeds dry in the refrigerator: five weeks before sowing in late winter, soak the seeds for 48 hours, allow to drain, and return to the refrigerator. Seedlings will be ready for planting in 2–3 years.

SYCAMORE SEEDHEADS *These tightly packed seed clusters turn brown when ripe. Pick them off the tree in early winter and pry the seeds apart.*

POPULUS *Poplar, Aspen, Cottonwood*

Populus maximowiczii

CUTTINGS in late autumn to late winter
SEEDS in midsummer
GRAFTING in late winter
SUCKERS in early to late winter

Hardwood cuttings provide the simplest way of propagating most of these fast-growing trees, apart from thick-stemmed species such as *Populus wilsonii*. They are much larger than standard cuttings and so produce a mature plant more quickly. Take the cuttings after leaf fall (*see below*).

Male and female trees are needed to produce the fluffy seedheads, which have copious amounts of seeds. Spread the down on pots of soil mix (*see p.54*); cover with ⅛in (3mm) of very fine grit. Keep in a closed case with a nighttime minimum of 50°F (10°C), ideally under mist. Germination should be quite rapid; transplant seedlings as soon as you can handle them. Plant out 18 months later.

Cuttings of some species, such as *P. szechuanica* and *P. wilsonii*, do not root readily. Instead, whip or spliced side graft them (*see p.58*) onto two-year-old seedling rootstocks of *P. lasiocarpa*.

A number of poplars sucker freely, for example *P. alba* and *P. tremula*. While the tree is dormant, sever a sucker below its roots and replant or pot to grow on.

TAKING HARDWOOD CUTTINGS OF POPLAR

1 *Select vigorous, straight shoots (here of* Populus x interamericana*) up to 6ft (2m) long from the current season's growth. Cut straight across the union with the main branch.*

2 *Remove the tip of each shoot, if it is still soft, cutting back to the ripened hard wood. Trim off any sideshoots. The cuttings are best rooted where they are to mature. Make individual planting holes for the cuttings by driving a wooden stake or metal rod into the ground to a depth of about 3ft (90cm).*

3 *Drop the cuttings into the holes and firm in. Here, the cuttings have been spaced 6ft (2m) apart in two staggered rows. When rooted and into growth in the following years, they will be pruned regularly to form a hedge.*

OTHER GARDEN TREES

PISTACIA Take softwood cuttings (*see p.52*) in midsummer. Refrigerate moist seeds for two months; sow (*p.54*) in spring at 50–59°F (10–15°C). Chip-bud onto field-grown stocks of *P. atlantica* or *P. terebinthus*, as for *Robinia* (*p.89*).
PLATYCARYA STROBILACEA Sow seeds from conelike fruits as for *Fagus* (*see p.80*). Whip-and-tongue graft as for *Fagus*.
PLUMERIA Take hardwood cuttings (*see p.50*) when dormant; if white latex is still flowing, dry cuttings in cool, dark place for few days before inserting in free-draining soil mix at 70°F (21°C). Sow seeds (*p.54*) as soon as seedpod splits in summer at 70°F (21°C).
PODOCARPUS Semi-ripe cuttings (*see p.70*) in late summer. Seeds from single-seeded fruits (*pp.54–5*) in autumn or spring.
PSEUDOLARIX AMABILIS (syn. *P. kaempferi*) Take greenwood cuttings (*see p.52*) in early summer. Sow seeds (*p.55*) from ripe, brown, scaly cones in pots in spring.

PRUNUS *CHERRY, PEACH, PLUM, APRICOT, ALMOND*

Prunus 'Yae-murasaki'

HARDWOOD CUTTINGS in late autumn
SEMI-RIPE CUTTINGS in early to midautumn
SEEDS in midautumn or late winter
GRAFTING in late winter or early spring
BUDDING in mid- to late summer

Of the many trees in this genus (syn. *Amygdalus*), the orchard trees, such as almonds, apricots, cherries, damsons, peaches, and plums, are best grafted: those grown on their own roots tend to be too vigorous and slow to bear fruit. Hardwood cuttings are used to propagate some ornamentals, as well as certain rootstocks; evergreen trees may be increased from semi-ripe cuttings. Species may be grown from seeds, but the seedlings tend to vary widely.

CUTTINGS

Strong shoots of the ornamentals *Prunus avium*, *P. cerasifera*, and *P. pseudocerasus* form aerial, or adventitious, root buds. These enable hardwood cuttings to root easily, albeit slowly. Take cuttings in autumn and overwinter in bundles (*see p.51*). Hardwood cuttings can also be taken from stock plants to use as rootstocks, such as *P. cerasifera* 'Myrobalan', 'Pixy', and 'Colt'. The latter has aerial root buds and roots from large cuttings (*see below*)

Semi-ripe cuttings of evergreens such as *P. lusitanica* (*see p.51*) root best with basal heat of 68°F (20°C).

SEEDS

Seeds should be gathered, cleaned, and stratified as for *Pyrus* (*see p.88*), to ensure a good rate of germination.

GRAFTING

When grafting *Prunus*, it is important to use a compatible rootstock (*see chart, below*). Seed-raised stocks are no longer used, except of the wild cherry, *P. avium*, for scions of the Japanese ornamental cherries. Otherwise, two-year-old stocks raised from layers (*see pp.56–7*) or from cuttings are best. Stocks are generally lined out in open ground to grow on before grafting. Chip- or T-bud (*see pp.60–2*) or whip-and-tongue graft (*see p.59*) at ground level on a short stem. For weeping trees, you may top-work onto a 5–6ft (1.5–2m) stem of a four- or five-year-old stock (*see p.57*) for quick results, but the union may be unsightly. If the stock is too broad for the scion, use an apical-wedge graft (*see p.58*).

GATHERING ALMOND SEEDS
*Almonds (*Prunus dulcis*) are stone fruits, not nuts: gather them in autumn as they fall. Peel off the soft husks and chill before sowing in spring.*

RAISING PRUNUS 'COLT' ROOTSTOCKS

1 *To raise rootstocks from a* Prunus *'Colt' stock plant, in late autumn take ripe shoots with good numbers of roots breaking at the base of current season's growth. Cut across each stem.*

2 *Cut each shoot down to about 18–24in (45–60cm) long and trim off all the leaves. Tie the cuttings into bundles of ten or so, using garden twine.*

3 *Dig a 14–18in (40–50cm) deep trench in a shaded nursery bed. Drop in the bundles, rooting ends down. Make sure that they do not touch. Hill them up so they are about three-quarters buried. Alternatively, line out the cuttings singly in a slit trench, about 12in (30cm) apart.*

4 *The following spring, lift the bundles and plant the cuttings at 12in (30cm) intervals. The following summer, they will be ready to be used as rootstocks for budding* (see above).

PRUNUS ROOTSTOCKS

Prunus cultivars may be grafted onto the principal rootstocks listed below; choose a stock to determine the size of the grafted tree and according to local availability.

PLUMS, GAGES, CHERRY PLUMS (*P. CERASIFERA*), DAMSONS, AND BULLACES
'Pixy' Semi-dwarfing (Europe)
'St. Julien A' Semi-vigorous (Europe and USA)
'Brompton' Vigorous (Europe and USA)
'Marianna 2624' Semi-vigorous, resistant to oak root fungus, root knot nematodes, and tomato ring spot virus (Australia)
'Myrobalan' Vigorous (Europe, USA, and Australia)

PEACHES, NECTARINES, APRICOTS, ALMONDS
'St. Julien A' *as above*
'Brompton' *as above*
'Elberta' Vigorous (Australia), for peaches and nectarines
'Marianna 2624' *as above*, for apricots and sometimes almonds
'Nemaguard' Semi-vigorous (Australia), for almonds and peaches
'Golden Queen' Vigorous (Australia), for almonds, nectarines, and peaches

JAPANESE APRICOT (*P. MUME*)
P. cerasifera Vigorous (Europe)

CHERRIES, ORNAMENTAL PRUNUS
'Colt' Semi-dwarfing (Europe)
'Mazard'/'Malling F12/1' Very vigorous, resists nematodes and canker (Europe, USA, and Australia)

PSEUDOTSUGA *DOUGLAS FIR*

SEEDS in spring

The female cones of these trees have protruding, trident-shaped bracts. Collect them in the first autumn and extract the seeds (*see p.72*). It is not essential to remove the wings. Store the seeds in a refrigerator and sow in spring in containers (*see p.54*), covering them with no more than their own depth of soil mix or fine grit. Bottom heat of 59–64°F (15–18°C) is not needed, although it will hasten germination.

PYRUS *PEAR*

Pyrus calleryana 'Chanticleer'

SEEDS in mid- to late autumn or in late winter
GRAFTING in early spring
BUDDING in mid- to late summer

Grafting is the best way to propagate all of the cultivated fruit trees and most ornamental pears in this genus. They do not root easily from cuttings and tend to form trees that are too vigorous and slow to fruit if grown on their own roots. Ornamental pears may be raised from seeds, but the seedlings will vary.

SEEDS

Clean seeds and sow directly (*see pp.53–5*) or stratify for 90 days at 41°F (5°C). Six weeks before sowing, add enough water to cover the seeds in their bag, chill for 48 hours, drain, and return to the refrigerator. Some of the seeds may have germinated when you come to sow them; if so, surface-sow them and cover with ⅛in (3mm) of fine-grade vermiculite. Transplant singly as soon as possible, then pot on in the following spring or line out in open ground.

ROOTSTOCKS FOR FRUITING PEARS
Use stocks according to local availability and the size of tree required.
Quince C Semi-dwarfing
Quince A Semi-vigorous
Quince BA29 Slightly more vigorous than Quince A
Adams 332 Semi-dwarfing, slightly more vigorous than Quince C
OHF 33 (Brokmal) Slightly more vigorous than Quince A; good fireblight resistance
***P. calleryana* D6** Vigorous (Australia)

CULTIVARS INCOMPATIBLE WITH QUINCE
'Belle Julie', 'Beurré Clairgeau', 'Bristol Cross', 'Clapp's Favourite', 'Docteur Jules Guyot', 'Doyenné d'Eté', 'Forelle', 'Jargonelle', 'Marguérite Marillat', 'Marie-Louise', 'Merton Pride', 'Packham's Triumph', 'Souvenir du Congrès', and most clones of 'Williams' Bon Chrétien'

INTERSTOCKS FOR DOUBLE-WORKING
'Beurré Hardy', 'Doyenné du Comice', 'Improved Fertility'

GRAFTING

For ornamental pears, chip-bud (*see p.60*) fairly close to the ground onto two- or three-year-old stocks of *Pyrus communis*. In some regions, *P. calleryana* is preferred because it is resistant to fireblight and is good for cultivars such as 'Bradford' or 'Chanticleer', which are not compatible with *P. communis*. A budded plant is usually ready for planting after two years. Graft three evenly spaced buds of the weeping pear, *P. salicifolia* 'Pendula', onto a 5–6ft (1.5–2m) stock for a balanced canopy (*see p.57*).

If the bud fails to take, use the whip-and-tongue graft (*see p.59*) instead. In early spring, head back the rootstock to remove the failed buds, then graft the scion onto the stock and wax over the cut surfaces to prevent drying out.

Graft fruit trees using the whip-and-tongue method or chip- or T-budding (*see pp.60–2*). The principal stocks (*see chart, below*) for fruit trees are clonal quinces (*Cydonia oblonga*). They are easier to propagate than clonal stocks of *P. communis*, are more dwarfing, and generally bear better quality fruit earlier.

Some fruit cultivars (*see chart, below*) are not compatible with quince stocks. These need to be "double-worked" using a cultivar that is compatible as an interstock (a "bridging" scion compatible with both the stock and the cultivar to be propagated). If you do not know if a cultivar is compatible with the stock, it is best to double-work it (*see below*).

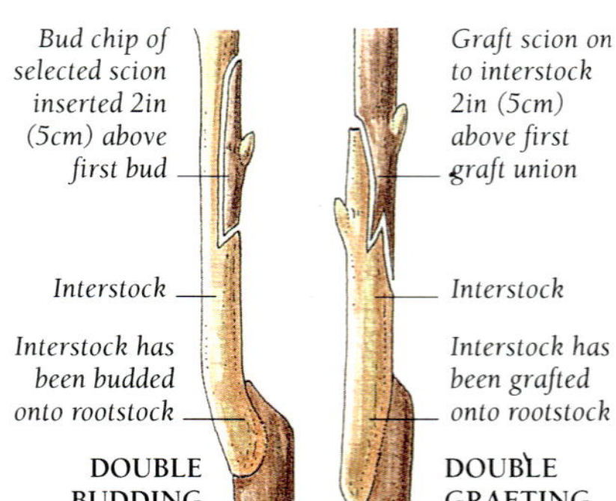

DOUBLE-WORKING FRUITING PEARS
Chip-bud or whip-and-tongue graft an interstock onto the stock in the first year. The next year, bud or graft a scion onto the interstock on the opposite side. Cut back the interstock to above the second bud once it begins to shoot.

QUERCUS *OAK*

Quercus macranthera

CUTTINGS in early to mid-autumn
SEEDS in mid- to late autumn or in early spring
GRAFTING in late winter

The best way to raise these trees is from seeds, if they are produced. Evergreen oaks can be increased by cuttings, but only a low percentage root and growth is slow. Evergreens, as well as rare deciduous species and cultivars, may also be grafted.

CUTTINGS

Insert semi-ripe cuttings (*see p.51*) in rockwool or equal parts peat and perlite. Root with bottom heat of 64–68°F (18–20°C).

SEEDS

Once mature, a large tree can produce thousands of acorns and thus self-sows readily (*see below*). Gather fresh acorns that have no weevil holes and sow immediately (*see pp.53–5*), either singly into deep pots or root-trainers or in seedbeds protected from rodents. If rodents are a problem, store moist acorns in the refrigerator and sow in early spring. Transplant seedlings once or twice before planting out (*see below*).

GRAFTING

Oaks fall into botanically related groups such as the red, Turkey, or white oaks. Always graft a scion onto a rootstock from the same group to avoid problems with incompatibility. Whip or spliced side graft (*see p.58*) rare deciduous oaks onto suitable stocks. Spliced side-veneer graft evergreens (*see p.58*) onto three- or four-year-old pot-grown seedlings. Grafts should unite in 5–6 weeks. Do not head back the stock fully until growth begins in the second year. Plant out grafted oaks 3–4 years later.

SELF-SOWN OAK SEEDLING
In spring, as soon as they have two or three leaves, transplant self-sown seedlings into a nursery bed. Transplant again before planting out to encourage growth of a fibrous root system. This enables the sapling to establish more easily.

ROBINIA *Locust*

Robinia 'Idaho'

CUTTINGS in late autumn to early winter
SEEDS in late winter
BUDDING in early spring
DIVISION in late winter to early spring

Root cuttings are best taken from young trees in this genus. Most may be grown from seeds. Cultivars of *Robinia pseudoacacia* must be increased by grafting; the suckering habit of some species can be exploited.

CUTTINGS

Take 3–6in (8–15cm) root cuttings as for *Ailanthus* (*see p.75*). In cold areas, store them vertically in a box of sand in a frost-free place. Then in early spring, insert them ½in (1cm) deep in free-draining soil mix to root at 50°F (10°C). Plant when 2–3ft (60–90cm) tall.

SEEDS

Break down the impermeable seed coats by abrading them (*see p.53*), or place in hot water and leave for 48 hours. Sow in pots (*see p.54*); keep in a sheltered place with a nighttime minimum of 50–59°F (10–15°C) to germinate in three months.

GRAFTING

Chip- or T-bud *R. pseudoacacia* cultivars onto two-year-old *R. pseudoacacia* stocks (*see pp.60–2*). *R. pseudoacacia* 'Umbraculifera' has a dense, umbrella-like canopy: top-work two buds at a height of 5–6ft (1.5–2m) onto three- or four-year-old stocks. An apical-wedge graft (*see p.58*) is less easy and the graft union is not as neat.

DIVISION

Remove suckers of *R. pseudoacacia* before the tree starts into growth and replant to grow on. The tree will sucker more freely if cut back hard in spring: do this to raise *R. pseudoacacia* stocks.

SALIX *Willow*

CUTTINGS in late autumn to early spring
SEEDS in late spring to midsummer
GRAFTING from mid- to late winter

The many species of tree willows are most easily grown from cuttings, but they can be grafted to create an attractive weeping standard. Seeds, if produced on female trees, must be sown fresh.

CUTTINGS

Hardwood cuttings of vigorous willows may be as long as 6ft (2m) and planted out immediately to mature faster than standard 8in (20cm) cuttings (*see p.50*). Take cuttings in late autumn from new, fully hardened wood that does not need to be very woody. Line them out in open ground, pot them, or place them in bundles in a frost-free sandbed to root. Select those in active growth in spring to pot. *Salix fargesii* and *S. moupinensis* do not root very readily in open ground. Cuttings may also be taken of green or semi-ripe wood (*see pp.51–2*).

SEEDS

Seeds must be sown fresh. Collect the seedheads as soon as they are ripe and fluffy. Tease apart the down, sow it (*see p.54*), and cover with ⅛in (3mm) of fine grit. Place under mist or in a closed case to germinate in a day or so.

STOCK PLANT OF WILLOW
Willows can be cut down almost to the ground (coppiced) each year to produce new long shoots for cuttings. The shoots can also be hilled up to encourage them to root (stooling, see p.56).

GRAFTING

Whip-and-tongue graft (*see p.59*) two or three scions of *S. caprea* 'Kilmarnock' or *S. caprea* var. *pendula* onto hardwood cuttings of *S.* x *smithiana* or *S. viminalis* as shown below. Seal the grafted area with wax to prevent drying out and keep moist and frost-free to callus. Graft a half-standard of *S. integra* 'Hakuro-nishiki' onto 30–36in (75–90cm) stems of *S.* x *smithiana* or *S. caprea*.

CREATING A STANDARD WEEPING WILLOW

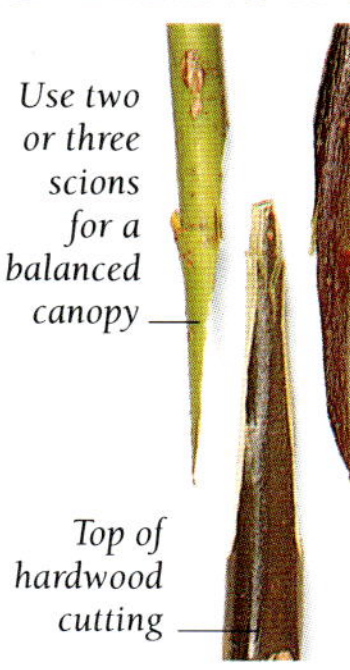

GRAFTING A PLANT
Prepare a 6ft (2m) hardwood cutting to use as a rootstock (here Salix *'Bowles' Hybrid'). Insert it into a pot of soil-based potting mix. Whip-and-tongue graft two or more scions of* S. caprea *'Kilmarnock' onto the top of the cutting.*

GRAFTED PLANT
The cutting will root and the graft callus and shoot simultaneously, within 12 weeks. Once new growth begins, feed and water. Rub out any sideshoots as they appear on the stem. Plant out after two years.

OTHER GARDEN TREES

PTELEA Softwood cuttings (*see p.52*) in late spring. Take root cuttings as for *Acacia* (*p.74*). Sow seeds as for *Sorbus* (*p.90*).
PTEROCARYA Root cuttings as for *Acacia* (*see p.74*). Sow seeds as for *Fagus* (*p.80*). Simple layer (*p.64*) in late autumn to spring. Remove suckers as for *Robinia*.
PTEROCELTIS TATARINOWII Sow seeds as for *Zelkova* (*see p.91*).
RADERMACHERA Take semi-ripe cuttings (*see p.51*) in summer. Sow seeds as soon as ripe (*p.54*) at 70°F (21°C) in late summer.
RAVENALA MADAGASCARIENSIS Sow seeds (*see p.54*) at 70°F (21°C) when ripe; scarify. Remove rooted suckers in spring.
REHDERODENDRON Softwood cuttings as *Stewartia* (*see p.90*). Seeds as *Davidia* (*p.79*).
ROTHMANNIA Take semi-ripe cuttings (*see p.51*) in summer. Sow seeds as soon as ripe after soaking for 24 hours (*p.54*).
SAPINDUS Semi-ripe cuttings (*see p.51*) from midsummer to early autumn. Remove fleshy seed coats; sow at 70°F (21°C) in soil-based mix in spring.
SAPIUM Sow seeds of temperate and hardy species as *Magnolia* (*see p.83*) and of tropical species as for *Coccoloba* (*p.79*). Whip graft (*p.58*) cultivars in late winter.
SASSAFRAS Take root cuttings as for *Acacia* (*see p.74*). Sow seeds as for *Sorbus* (*p.90*), but cold moist stratify (*p.54*) for 3–4 months before sowing.
SCHEFFLERA (syn. *Brassaia*) Take semi-ripe cuttings, leaf-bud cuttings and air layer as for *Ficus* (*see p.80*). Extract seeds from fleshy fruits when ripe; sow at once (*p.54*) at 70°F (21°C).
SCHINUS Take semi-ripe cuttings as for *Grevillea* (*see p.80*). Sow seeds as for *Acacia* (*p.74*).
SCHOTIA Seeds as *Acacia* (*p.74*).
SCIADOPITYS VERTICILLATA Semi-ripe cuttings (*see p.70*) in late summer. Cones ripe in second year; sow seeds (*p.54*) in spring.

SEQUOIADENDRON *GIANT REDWOOD*

CUTTINGS from spring to late autumn
SEEDS in spring

This single species, *Sequoiadendron giganteum*, is closely related to *Sequoia*, the coast redwood. Best results are likely from 4in (10cm) cuttings taken in late summer from the green shoot tips. Treat as for greenwood cuttings (*see p.52*); bottom heat of 68°F (20°C) is beneficial.

Extract the seeds (*see p.71*), store in a refrigerator and sow in containers (*see p.54*), covering them with only their own depth of soil mix or fine grit. Bottom heat of 59°F (15°C) should hasten germination.

The fast-growing seedlings are prone to damping off (*see p.46*). Transplant the seedlings when they are 2–3in (5–8cm) tall.

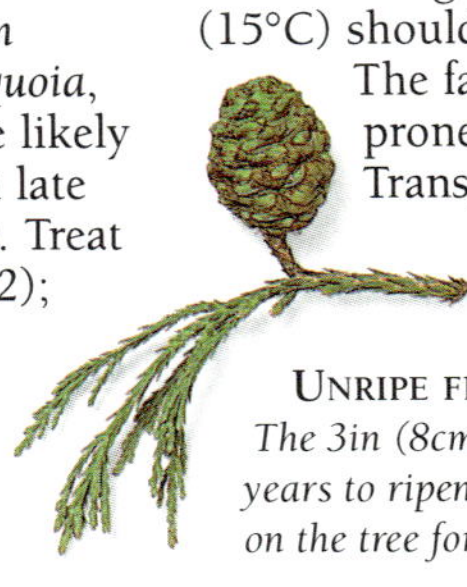

UNRIPE FEMALE CONE
The 3in (8cm) long, ovoid cones take two years to ripen from green to brown but remain on the tree for many years.

SOPHORA

CUTTINGS from midsummer to early autumn
SEEDS in midwinter
GRAFTING in late winter
BUDDING in mid- to late summer

There are both trees and shrubs in this genus. Evergreen species such as *Sophora microphylla* (syn. *Edwardsia microphylla*) and *S. tetraptera* may be raised from semi-ripe cuttings (*see p.51*).

Treat the hard, pealike seeds as for *Robinia* (*see p.89*); plant the seedlings out in the third growing season. The pendulous form of the Japanese pagoda tree (*S. japonica* 'Pendula') sets seeds fairly freely, but only in long, hot summers; only a small percentage of seedlings will come true.

Whip or spliced side graft (*see p.58*) cultivars of deciduous species such as *S. japonica* onto two- or three-year-old pot-grown seedlings or chip-bud (*see p.60*) outdoors. *S. japonica* 'Pendula' can also be top-worked onto four- or five-year-old seedlings: spliced side-veneer graft (*see p.58*) two scions or chip-bud two buds at 5–6ft (1.5–2m) on the stem.

SORBUS *MOUNTAIN ASH*

Sorbus commixta

SEEDS in early autumn to late winter
GRAFTING in late winter to early spring
BUDDING in mid- to late summer

Not all the trees in this genus come true from seeds, but many, including *Sorbus cashmiriana*, *S. hupehensis* (syn. *S. glabrescens*), and *S. forrestii*, are apomictic; that is, viable seeds develop without being fertilized and produce seedlings identical to the parent. Mountain ashes may also be grafted, but care must be taken to use compatible rootstocks.

SEEDS

Sow seeds from berries gathered just after ripening in the autumn before germination inhibitors develop. Otherwise, cold stratify the seeds for two months at 41°F (5°C), or as shown right, before sowing. The seeds usually germinate readily; transplant singly in late spring; plant in the next autumn.

GRAFTING

Botanically, *Sorbus* is divided into three groups: Aria (whitebeams), Aucuparia (mountain ashes) and Micromeles. The Aucuparia cultivars can be chip-budded (*see p.60*) onto *S. aucuparia*, and Aria onto *S. aria* or sometimes *S. latifolia*. Budded plants may be planted out in 15 months.

Trees in the Micromeles group (such as *S. folgneri* and *S. megalocarpa*) are spliced side or whip grafted (*see p.58*), as are rare species such as *S. harrowiana*. *S. alnifolia* is used as a rootstock for *S. megalocarpa* and *S. aucuparia* as a stock for *S. harrowiana*. If the graft unions are waxed, keep the plants at 50°F (10°C). If unwaxed, they may be placed in a high-humidity tent.

STRATIFYING SORBUS SEEDS
Place the seeds on moist blotting paper in a saucer, then refrigerate for two months before sowing. Check regularly and remoisten the paper, if necessary. If the seeds start to germinate, sow them immediately.

STEWARTIA

Stewartia monadelpha

CUTTINGS in early summer
SEEDS in late autumn or in late winter

There are deciduous and evergreen trees in this genus (syn. *Stuartia*). Root softwood cuttings (*see p.52*) with bottom heat of 65–70°F (19–21°C). Feed rooted cuttings well so they make enough root growth to grow well in spring. Seeds are not easy to obtain from trees or suppliers. They need chilling (*see p.54*) and a nighttime minimum of 50°F (10°C). If they do not germinate in three months, leave outdoors for a year. Plant out seedlings in the third year.

TAXUS *YEW*

CUTTINGS in autumn
GRAFTING in late summer or late winter
SEEDS at any time of year

Female trees in this genus do not have cones but single-seeded fruits in fleshy red cups, or arils. Raising yews from seeds is a slow process. Cuttings are quicker but must be taken from suitable shoots. Some cultivars are reluctant to root so therefore must be grafted.

CUTTINGS

Take 4–6in (10–15cm) cuttings (*see p.70*) from one- to three-year-old shoots that are strongly upright and nearly ripe, but green at the base. Hormone rooting compound helps. Cuttings root by early summer outdoors, and earlier under mist with bottom heat of 68°F (20°C).

SEEDS

The arils turn red as the seeds ripen in autumn. The hard seed coats are usually broken down in the gut of a bird or mammal and germinate after a period of cold. Speed germination by mixing the seeds with damp peat or sand (*see p.53*) and keeping them at about 68°F (20°C), for example in a warm closet, for 4–5 months, then chilling them for three months at around 34°F (1°C). However, seeds that germinate in late summer will have too little time to put on growth before winter. It may be more practical to store the seeds, sow them in spring in pots (*see p.54*), and keep them outdoors for 1–2 years until they germinate.

GRAFTING

In spring, pot pencil-thick three-year-old seedlings; grow on until late summer. Spliced side-veneer graft onto these rootstocks, as for *Picea* (*see p.85*). Extra heat is not needed, but shading may be. The union should callus in six weeks.

TILIA *LINDEN*

SEEDS in mid- to late autumn or mid- to late winter
BUDDING in mid- to late summer
LAYERING in late autumn or early spring

Seeds of these trees are not always available or easy to germinate but may be used to raise rare species. Chip-budding is the accepted method of propagating many lindens, but care must be taken to use a compatible rootstock. The European linden (*Tilia* x *europaea*) may also be layered.

SEEDS

Linden seeds have dormant embryos and impermeable seed coats, so they germinate erratically. Gather seeds when just ripe, before germination inhibitors develop, or soak in warm water for 48 hours, drain, store until midwinter, sow (*see p.54*) and keep at about 50°F (10°C). If they do not germinate in three months, give the seeds a second period of cold.

BUDDING

T. americana, *T. cordata*, *T.* x *euchlora*, and, more extensively, *T. platyphyllos* are used as rootstocks for chip-budding (*see p.60*). Grafts should take in 4–6 weeks.

LAYERING

If large numbers of plants are needed, stool a young tree (*see p.56*) to obtain plenty of strong, new shoots in alternate years. In the following year, simple layer each shoot (*see p.64*) after preparing the ground with a mixture of peat and sand. Remove rooted shoots in the following autumn at leaf fall or in the following spring. Head back the stooled plant to one or two buds to repeat the process.

If only one or two plants are needed, simple layer a low branch. The point of contact with the soil, and of wounding, may be on second- or third-year wood. If the wound is on older wood, it may not root in the first season; tease away the soil in autumn to inspect the new roots and, if needed, leave for a year.

LINDEN FRUITS
Gather the nutlike fruits (here of Tilia oliveri*) before they fall. Remove the outer husks. Sow the seeds immediately outdoors in cold climates, or chill before sowing* (see pp.54–5).

ULMUS *ELM*

CUTTINGS in midsummer
SEEDS in autumn or mid- to late winter
BUDDING in mid- to late summer

Seeds from species of these trees, such as *U. americana*, *U. glabra*, *U. parvifolia*, and *U. pumila* germinate well. *U. americana*, *U.* x *hollandica*, and *U. parvifolia* may be propagated from cuttings. Chip-bud *U.* x *hollandica* 'Jacqueline Hillier' and cultivars of *U. glabra*, such as 'Lutescens' and 'Crispa'.

CUTTINGS

Rooted soft- or greenwood cuttings (*see p.52*) need to make good growth to survive the winter. Keep frost-free and pot before growth commences in spring.

SEEDS

As soon as they ripen in mid- to late autumn, sow the winged seeds thinly in seed trays (*see p.54*) and overwinter outdoors. Alternatively, store the seeds dry at 37°F (3°C) and sow in late winter.

BUDDING

Chip-bud cultivars (*see p.60*) onto two- or three-year-old *U. glabra* seedlings that have been grown on in a nursery bed. *U. glabra* 'Camperdownii' is usually top-worked to create a standard: chip-bud three buds at a height of 5–6ft (1.5–2m) onto five- or six-year-old stocks that have been trained into a straight stem. The buds should take in 4–6 weeks.

ZELKOVA

SEEDS in mid- to late autumn
GRAFTING in late winter or in early spring

The seeds of these trees need a period of cold before sowing (*see p.54*) and a nighttime minimum of 50°F (10°C) to germinate within 8–10 weeks. Protect the seedlings from frost and transplant in midsummer or early in the next spring. Grow on for three years.

Whip or spliced side graft (*see p.58*) cultivars such as *Zelkova serrata* 'Village Green' or *Z.* x *verschaffeltii* onto two- or three-year-old pot-grown seedlings of *Zelkova*, *Ulmus parviflora*, or *U. pumila*. Keep the stocks watered sparingly at 50–55°F (10–12°C) for a few weeks before grafting. Prepare 4–6in (10–15cm) scions from vigorous, new or two-year-old wood, and seal each graft with wax to prevent drying out. Keep the plants on the open bench with an air temperature of 50°F (10°C) and bottom heat of 65°F (18°C) and regularly mist-spray. Grafts should take in six weeks.

OTHER GARDEN TREES

SEQUOIA As for *Sequoiadendron* (*see p.90*).
SESBANIA (syn. *Daubentonia*) Take greenwood cuttings as for *Acacia* (*see p.74*). Sow seeds as for *Acacia*.
SPATHODEA CAMPANULATA Semi-ripe cuttings as *Magnolia* (*see p.83*). Remove seeds from outer coating; sow singly (*p.54*) in free-draining soil mix at 70°F (21°C) in spring.
STENOCARPUS Semi-ripe cuttings as for *Ilex* (*see p.81*). Sow fresh seeds (*p.54*) in spring or summer at 59–68°F (15–20°C).
STYRAX Take softwood cuttings as for *Stewartia* (*see p.90*). Seeds are thought to be doubly dormant, but low yields may be gained by sowing seeds as for *Stewartia*.
SYZYGIUM Take semi-ripe cuttings (*see p.51*) in summer. Sow seeds (*p.54*) from fleshy fruits when ripe at 70°F (21°C).
TABEBUIA Take semi-ripe cuttings (*see p.51*) of evergreens in late spring and softwood cuttings of deciduous species as for *Acer* (*p.74*). Sow seeds as soon as ripe (*p.54*) at 70°F (21°C).
TAMARINDUS Take greenwood cuttings as for *Acacia* (*see p.74*). Sow seeds as *Acacia*.
TAXODIUM Take hardwood cuttings (*see p.50*) in late winter or softwood cuttings (*p.52*) in summer from persistent shoots with buds; root under mist with bottom heat of 64–68°F (18–20°C). Sow seeds (*p.53*) from single brown cones in spring.

SYZYGIUM AROMATICUM

TECOMA Take greenwood and root cuttings as for *Catalpa* (*see p.77*). Sow seeds as for *Catalpa*.
TERMINALIA Sow seeds as for *Spathodea*.
THEVETIA Take semi-ripe cuttings (*see p.51*) of cultivars in mid- to late summer. Sow seeds as for *Syzygium*.
THUJA (syn. *Platycladus*) Take semi-ripe cuttings (*see p.70*) with a heel from late summer to midautumn; supply humidity and bottom heat of 64°F (18°C). Erect female cones have hinged scales; sow seeds (*p.54*) in spring at 59°F (15°C).
TOONA Take root cuttings as for *Acacia* (*see p.74*). Sow cleaned seeds (*p.54*) as soon as ripe at 50°F (10°C) in autumn.
TSUGA Take semi-ripe cuttings (*see p.70*) in autumn; give bottom heat of 64°F (18°C). Seeds from pendent female cones are viable for years if stored correctly; chill for three weeks before sowing (*p.54*) in spring.

SHRUBS AND CLIMBING PLANTS

Shrubs and woody climbers form the backbone of any garden planting but vary enormously in habit, form, and productive lifespan; they can be propagated by an equally wide range of techniques

Shrubs and climbing plants represent an invaluable and long-lasting source of shape, texture, and color in the garden. They encompass a wide spectrum of sizes and habits, from fast-growing climbers (that provide almost instant cover for unsightly buildings or walls) and ground-cover plants to slow-maturing woody shrubs that will grace a border over a period of many years.

A shrub is a deciduous or evergreen perennial with multiple woody stems or branches, generally originating from or near its base. Subshrubs are woody-based plants with soft-wooded stems. Climbers are plants that climb or cling by means of modified stems, roots, leaves, or leaf stalks, using other plants or objects as support. Woody-stemmed climbers are covered here.

The rooting of cuttings, in their many variations, is by far the most widely used method of propagating shrubs and climbers, especially when a large number of new plants is required. Many may also be raised in numbers from seeds, although, as with other plants, only species will come true to type.

The natural propensity of some shrubs and climbers to produce suckers or rooted layers can be exploited as an easy and reliable method of propagation where only a few new plants are needed, especially for shrubs that are difficult to propagate by other means, such as some camellias, magnolias, and rhododendrons. Heaths and heathers respond particularly well to layering.

Cultivars that are difficult to propagate (or that require a rootstock to control growth and flowering, as in the case of roses), are best grafted or budded. This requires a little more care but, if successful, rewards the gardener with a fast-growing and vigorous plant.

FATSIA CUTTING
The evergreen shrub Fatsia japonica *and its variegated cultivar are grown for their striking foliage and architectural value. Both forms can be easily increased from semi-ripe cuttings taken throughout the year.*

CLEMATIS 'BILL MACKENZIE'
This particular clematis is prized for its yellow lantern-shaped flowers and its silvery seedheads. It is thought to be a hybrid of Clematis tangutica *and* C. orientalis, *of which there are many forms in cultivation.*

TAKING CUTTINGS

Raising new plants from cuttings is frequently a very straightforward process, and it is the most popular technique for propagating the majority of shrubs and climbers. Choosing the type of cutting and the ripeness of the wood best suited to a particular plant is very important to the success of the process (*see pp.118–45* for information on individual plants).

It is important to select cutting material very carefully, avoiding any shoots where pests or diseases may be present and discarding any damaged material, since this will be vulnerable to fungal attack. Use typical, horizontal shoots, with nodes that are normally spaced, rather than atypical, very upright, stretched-out shoots. Never propagate from a variegated plant that is showing signs of reverting to its all-green form.

Some plants produce juvenile foliage, which turns into adult foliage after a number of years. This often coincides with a slowing down of the annual rate of growth of the plant, as it turns its attention to flowering. An example of this is the English ivy (*Hedera helix*). Unless you specifically require the adult foliage form of a plant, always remember

HOW SHOOTS RIPEN

This Pyracantha *shoot shows the different stages of woodiness. The softwood at the tip is still green, soft, and sappy, while the greenwood in the middle is less flexible. The base of the shoot is semi-ripe, becoming woody and dark.*

TRIMMING A CUTTING

NODAL CUTTING *Ribes*

INTERNODAL CUTTING *Buddleja*

Cuttings are usually trimmed just below a node, where the growth hormones accumulate (see left). Easily rooted plants can be cut between the nodes (see right), to create more cuttings quickly.

TYPES OF CUTTING

Taking cuttings is one of the easiest ways of propagating many shrubs and climbers, with a wide variety of types that can be used. They can be collected from early summer (softwood) to winter (hardwood).

SOFTWOOD CUTTING *Cotoneaster*

HEEL CUTTING *Ceanothus*

SEMI-RIPE CUTTING *Abelia*

LEAF-BUD CUTTING *Clematis*

HARDWOOD CUTTING *Salix*

to take cuttings from stems that have juvenile foliage, because these will root much more readily.

Cuttings root most easily when the parent plant is young and producing good lengths of new growth each year. Juvenility can often be restored to a plant by pruning back hard into old wood. The best material is usually the new growth that is neither very thin and weak, nor very vigorous; the latter is often hollow and prone to rot. Choose instead the material in between these two extremes, which has the normal pattern of internodal growth between two leaves or two sets of leaves.

Most cuttings will be from wood of the current season's growth. Some shrubs, such as deciduous azaleas and magnolias, root best if the material is forced under protection early in the year. In some regions, by the time growth occurs in the garden it may be too late to root cuttings with confidence. Alternatively, use plants bought from the local garden center, which invariably will have been grown under protection, as stock plants (*see p.24*).

NODAL AND INTERNODAL CUTTINGS

With most shrubs and climbers, "nodal" cuttings, trimmed just below a node (*see left*), root well. Some plants, however, also root very readily when the base of the cutting is made some way below the node. Such a cutting is described as "internodal," because the cut is made at a point between the nodes rather than just below them.

People often think that one stem yields only a single cutting from the stem tip. On the contrary, several nodal cuttings or many more internodal cuttings can be obtained from one length (*see right*) of stem. This applies to greenwood, semi-ripe, and hardwood cuttings. Make sure that the stem cuttings are uniform in size, because then they will root at a similar speed, which aids handling later on.

PREPARING CUTTINGS

Collect material early in the day, when the plant is fully turgid, before the sun diminishes the plant's vital water reserves that have been built up overnight. Store fresh cuttings in a clean plastic bag and label them correctly. Note both the name and details of propagation. You can either prepare the cuttings immediately or store them in a cool place, out of direct sunlight, for a couple of hours at most. If you are unable to continue on the same day, place the plastic bags containing the material in a refrigerator, where the cuttings will

STEM CUTTINGS

SOFTWOOD *Verbena*

GREENWOOD *Philadelphus*

SEMI-RIPE *Lonicera*

HARDWOOD *Deutzia*

One stem-tip and several stem cuttings can be taken from one stem, increasing the yield of cuttings from fewer shoots. Keep the cuttings the same size.

remain fresh and in good condition for a number of days. When preparing cuttings, keep tools, equipment, and surfaces sterile (*see p.30*).

Almost all cuttings respond to artificial rooting hormones, available as powders, liquids, and gels (*see p.29*). On difficult subjects, they can mean the difference between success and failure.

Wounding a cutting, by removing a sliver of bark at the base of its stem, exposes the area where most cell division takes place and so increases the uptake of water and rooting hormone. On some shrubs, such as rhododendrons, wounding is essential; otherwise, roots often fail to break through the tough outer layers of cells. Take care not to create too deep a wound and expose the pith, however, since this may lead to rot and failure.

Rooting cuttings

For shrub and climbers, a good rooting medium is one of equal parts peat and bark with a particle size of $\frac{1}{8}$–$\frac{1}{2}$in (3–12mm), or peat and perlite. For a free-draining medium, use equal parts of peat, medium-grade perlite, and bark. Rockwool (or florist's foam) is a good alternative: with easily rooted material, watering is easier, whereas cuttings that are difficult to root have a better rate of success, provided that the medium is kept moist but not wet. (*See also pp.32–5 for suitable mixes and media.*)

All cuttings, before being inserted in the rooting medium, benefit from a heavy fungicidal spray, or "sprench," a compromise between spraying and drenching. Gray mold, or botrytis, is the most common disease affecting cuttings; use a fungicide every two weeks while cuttings are rooting.

After inserting the cuttings, water the medium thoroughly, and then make sure that it does not dry out at any time. If under cover, air the cuttings at least twice a week, for ten minutes at a time, removing any dead material or fallen foliage. If in a greenhouse, when it is hot provide additional shading and damp down at least three times a day. Keep containers out of direct sunlight.

Slow-release fertilizer improves the vigor of a rooted cutting: add a teaspoon to each quart of medium in summer, and a half teaspoon in winter. Liquid feeding with a balanced fertilizer at the package's recommended rate throughout the entire growing season is an equally beneficial alternative to slow-release fertilizer.

Semi-ripe cuttings

This type of cutting involves material of the current season's growth that has begun to firm; the base of the cutting should be quite hard, while the tip of the cutting should (*continued on p.96*)

SELECTING SEMI-RIPE CUTTINGS

To take semi-ripe cuttings (here from a shrubby honeysuckle, Lonicera*), select lengths of healthy new wood that has not fully hardened* (see right)*. Do not choose shoots that have become too woody or those that are still soft and sappy* (see far right)*.*

TAKING SEMI-RIPE CUTTINGS

1 *In mid- to late summer, select a healthy shoot of the current season's growth (here from a Japanese laurel,* Aucuba*). Use clean, sharp pruners to sever the cutting just above a node.*

2 *If not prepared immediately, put the shoot in a clear plastic bag and label. Store in a cool place out of direct sunlight for a couple of hours or in a refrigerator for a few days.*

3 *Remove the sideshoots from the main stem. Trim each sideshoot to 4–6in (10–15cm) long, cutting just below a node. Remove the lowest pair of leaves and the soft tip.*

4 *Make a shallow wound on one side of the stem by carefully cutting away a piece of bark $\frac{1}{2}$–$\frac{3}{4}$in (1–2cm) long from the base of the stem. This will help stimulate rooting.*

5 *Dip the base of the cutting, including the entire wound, into some hormone rooting compound (here in powder form). Make sure that the wound has an even, but thin, coating.*

6 *Insert the cuttings in rooting medium in a nursery bed outdoors (or under mist), spacing them 3–4in (8–10cm) apart. Water well. Cover to keep humid until rooted.*

still be actively growing and therefore still soft. The list of shrubs and climbers for which this method is suitable covers a very wide range of plants, including both evergreen and deciduous species, from *Cotoneaster* and *Mahonia* to some lavenders. Semi-ripe cuttings are good for obtaining large numbers of plants to produce a hedge of boxwood or *Pyracantha*, for example. Many commercial nurseries keep stock plants of shrubs such as boxwood as hedges because the clippings make ideal and plentiful cuttings.

The best time to take semi-ripe cuttings is from mid- to late summer, or even in early autumn. In warm climates, growth may be semi-ripe in early summer. The length of the cutting is dependent on the growth habit of the plant being propagated, but between 2½–4in (6–10cm) is suitable for cuttings of most shrubs and climbers. Choose a healthy-looking stem (*see p.95*), remove any sideshoots, and trim the cutting. Wound the stem and apply a generous coating of hormone rooting compound, shaking off any excess if using powder.

Semi-ripe cuttings may be rooted in a variety of situations. To prepare an outdoor nursery bed, mix some soilless potting mix into the soil to a depth of 6–8in (15–20cm) and insert the cuttings directly into it. Cover the bed to keep the soil mix moist (*see below*) and shade if necessary to protect the cuttings from being scorched. The cuttings may also be inserted in rooting medium in containers, in cells in soil mix, or in rockwool. Place the containers in a cold frame, a plastic tunnel, or on a heated bench under a plastic tent (*see p.44*), according to the conditions required (*see pp.118–45* for individual plant needs).

Although semi-ripe cuttings are less prone to wilting than softwood cuttings, a humid environment is essential so that the rooting process can take place with the minimum of stress. Gray-leaved plants need a slightly drier environment to prevent the cuttings from rotting, which will occur if their foliage is constantly damp. Regularly air such cuttings in a plastic tent. They also root well in a frost-free cold frame or similar structure rather than in the more humid atmosphere of a greenhouse.

During winter, inspect the cuttings regularly and remove any fallen leaves. Water if the medium shows any signs of drying out. The cuttings will normally require a further growing season before rooting satisfactorily and should be gradually hardened off (*see p.45*) during spring and summer before the new plants are potted or planted out.

Direct rooting of cuttings in pots

For easily rooted plants with a very high success rate, space out 2–3 semi-ripe cuttings in a 3–4in (8–10cm) pot. This extra space produces cuttings ready to be planted into the garden without the need for any intermediate stage of potting, and in some cases advancing planting by an entire growing season. Incorporate fertilizer into the rooting medium or apply a liquid feed once the cuttings have rooted, because they will be in the same soil mix longer than usual. If specimen plants are required, pot the cuttings singly into larger containers when needed. This technique is demanding on propagation space, so do not attempt it unless the plant is suited to this method (*see pp.118–45*).

Heel and mallet cuttings

For plants that are difficult to root, it is a good idea to take heel cuttings (*see above*). The heel forms an area where the natural rooting hormones of the plant build up, creating better chances of success in rooting the cutting. It also provides a hard end-point to the cutting, which is consequently less prone to fungal attack. It is possible to root many *Ceanothus* species in this way. Some *Berberis* species and their cultivars root best from mallet cuttings (*see p.119*).

Outdoor nursery beds

If rooting cuttings in any quantity, an outdoor nursery bed provides the best conditions in which to grow on new plants in containers once hardened off. There are two types: sand beds and water-permeable fabric beds (*see p.40*).

Water-permeable fabric suppresses weeds, helps protect plants from soil-borne diseases, and allows containers to drain freely while giving plants access to water through capillary action. Sand beds need less watering than fabric beds, because they provide a water reservoir. Excess water drains away, but the soil mix in the pots does not dry out.

HEEL CUTTINGS

1 *Carefully pull away a healthy sideshoot of the current season's growth (here of a Ceanothus), so that it comes away with a sliver, or "heel," of bark from the parent shoot. The sideshoot should be about 4in(10cm) long.*

2 *Trim off the "tail" of the heel with a clean, sharp knife. The heel contains growth hormones that will encourage rooting. Depending on the maturity of the stem, follow the technique for greenwood, semi-ripe, or hardwood cuttings.*

SEMI-RIPE CUTTINGS UNDER COVER

You can root cuttings under a large cloche or plastic tunnel. Prepare an outdoor nursery bed by mixing rooting medium into the soil. Insert the cuttings direct. Keep the medium moist. Shade the cloche with netting to protect the cuttings from strong sunlight.

Leaf-bud cuttings

This method makes economical use of semi-ripe material from the parent plant, producing many cuttings from one vigorous shoot. A leaf-bud cutting (*see right*) requires only a short piece of semi-ripe stem to provide food reserves, since it also manufactures some food through its leaf or leaves. Leaf-bud cuttings can be internodal, which usually works well with clematis and honeysuckle (*Lonicera*), or nodal, which is more suitable for plants with hollow stems or ones that are susceptible to rot, such as camellias.

In late summer or early autumn, using pruners or a sharp knife, remove a strong shoot (*see below*), severing it between the nodes to create a number of internodal cuttings, each with 1–2 leaves. You should end up with several from one stem. Alternatively, if more appropriate for the individual plant (*see pp.118–45*), divide it into nodal cuttings by cutting just below a node at the base of each cutting and just above the node at the top. When preparing leaf-bud cuttings, always take care to retain the growth buds in the leaf axil at the tip: they are all too easily nipped out by mistake. With some species, the buds are quite long; in this case, the cutting should be cut back to just above the top pair of leaves, so as not to damage the buds. With smaller buds, cut back to just above the top leaves.

If the plant from which you are taking cuttings has large leaves, it is a good idea to trim them by cutting across the leaf (*see* Lonicera *cutting, above*). Wounding the cutting is not necessary, but may be a good idea for plants that have very woody stems. Apply a good coating of hormone rooting compound to the base of each cutting, shaking off the excess if using powder. Insert the cuttings into a pot filled with rooting medium. After watering in and labeling, keep the cuttings humid by placing them in a closed case or under plastic. Some less hardy plants may require bottom heat to aid rooting.

When the cuttings have rooted, usually about eight weeks later, pot the young plants into individual containers in soil mix and grow them on until established.

LEAF-BUD CUTTINGS

Leaf-bud cuttings are made up of a single leaf or a pair of leaves containing a growth bud and a short piece of stem. They can be either nodal or internodal. Semi-ripe leaf-bud cuttings are taken in late summer or early autumn.

TAKING LEAF-BUD CUTTINGS FROM SHRUBS AND CLIMBING PLANTS

1 *Select a healthy shoot of the current season's growth (here of ivy,* Hedera*). Take the length required (you will produce as many cuttings as there are nodes), cutting just above a node. Put in a plastic bag to keep the shoot from drying out.*

2 *Use clean pruners or a garden knife to cut up the shoot. Cut the stem just above every node to create internodal cuttings with one or two leaves (see above). Prepare nodal cuttings by trimming each cutting below a node at the base and above the node at the top.*

3 *Dip each prepared cutting (see inset) in some hormone rooting compound such as gel. Fill a pot with rooting medium and make holes for the cuttings. Insert each cutting into the medium so that the leaves are held just above the surface and do not touch.*

4 *Firm and water in the cuttings and label the pots. Place them under cover and keep the environment humid by misting if needed. Bottom heat is not required for ivies. The cuttings should take about eight weeks to root.*

5 *Pot the rooted cuttings individually in soilless potting mix, into pots about ½in (1cm) larger than the root ball of each cutting (see inset). Water in each cutting thoroughly and label.*

Hardwood cuttings

Typical examples of plants propagated from hardwood cuttings are shrubby dogwoods (*Cornus*) and willows (*Salix*), but there is a vast range of material that can be increased in this way, including both evergreen and deciduous species. These include grapes and the climbing *Polygonum* (syn. *Fallopia*), deciduous shrubs including *Forsythia* and *Tamarix*, and the evergreen *Prunus laurocerasus* and *Elaeagnus*. Deciduous and evergreen hardwood cuttings require quite different handling.

Deciduous plants are propagated from late autumn to midwinter, once the current season's growth has completely matured. Usually, the cuttings are leafless; those taken in late autumn may retain some leaves in temperate climates, but these will soon fall. Evergreen cuttings are taken at a similar time, when the leading growth bud is resting and the new growth has fully matured.

Hardwood cuttings are normally much bigger than softwood or semi-ripe ones, since they are much slower to root and need additional food reserves in order to survive the winter. A standard cutting should be about 8in (20cm) long – the length of a pair of pruners. This will help ensure uniformity, which is important if you want all the cuttings to root and develop at a similar rate. Using your pruners, make a horizontal cut just below a node and a sloping cut away from the bud at the top – this enables you to consistently insert the cuttings the right way up.

Several cuttings can usually be taken from one length of ripened, current season's growth, especially with the long stems of climbers. Always discard the thin growth at the tip and the thick growth at the base, because these are more likely either to rot or take longer to root. Take cuttings of medium thickness for the individual plant.

Deciduous hardwood cuttings

Dip prepared cuttings in hormone rooting compound. (If the plant is not easily rooted, wound each cutting by taking a ½–¾in (1–2cm) sliver of bark from the base.) Insert the cuttings in an appropriate rooting medium, in an outdoor trench or nursery bed, or in pots in a cold frame. A slit trench (*see below*) is suitable for most deciduous shrubs and climbers. Choose a sheltered site, because winds can very quickly desiccate the cuttings, and remove all perennial weeds from the soil.

Well-drained soil is essential, because waterlogged soil will kill the cuttings. Improve drainage and aeration if needed, especially in heavy soils, by running sand along the base of the trench. Insert the cuttings so that only the top quarter is exposed; less of the cutting will be vulnerable to drying out by any cold winter or spring winds, and a much larger root system will develop. Firm in the cuttings after filling in the trench to make sure that there is good contact between each cutting and the soil. Check the cuttings periodically, since frost will lift the plants, which will need firming in again.

Hardwood cuttings root slowly, and they may come into leaf in the following spring before they have developed a substantial root system. At this point, it is critical that you do not allow them to dry out. Water them throughout the growing season and keep them free of weeds in order to maximize growth. Lift the new plants in autumn, when they should be large enough to plant out.

Where only a few new plants are wanted, insert the cuttings into 6in (15cm) pots (*see below right*). In colder climates, place the pots in a cold frame or, to speed up the process, on a heated bench in a frost-free greenhouse. The added protection can bring the cuttings into early growth, which often leads to the foliage being scorched and the subsequent death of the cutting. If

DECIDUOUS HARDWOOD CUTTINGS

1 From late autumn to early winter, take well-ripened shoots of deciduous shrubs or climbers (here Forsythia*). Cut each shoot at the base of the current season's growth. Cuttings taken in autumn may still have a few leaves; trim these off.*

2 Trim off the tip of each shoot if it has not ripened. Cut the shoots into 8in (20cm) sections (about the length of a pair of pruners). Make a horizontal cut just below a node at the base of each cutting and a cut sloping away from a bud at the top.

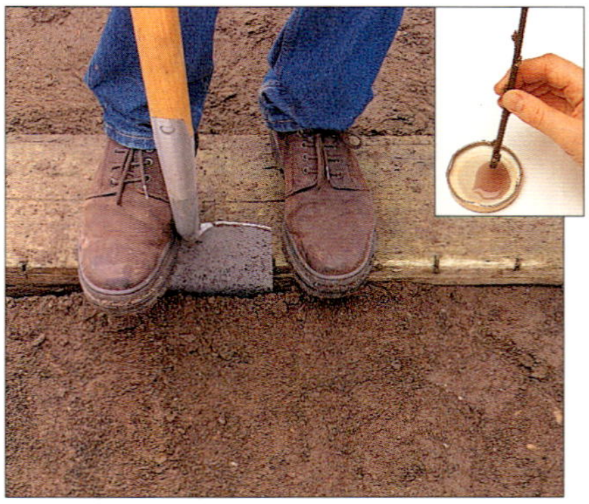

3 Prepare a slit trench in free-draining soil: push the spade into the soil about 6in (15cm) down and press the blade forward to open out the trench. Dip the base of each cutting in hormone rooting compound (see inset).

4 Insert the cuttings about 2in (5cm) apart so that about a quarter of each is visible. Rows of cuttings should be 12in (30cm) apart. Backfill the trench and firm the soil around the cuttings. Label, then water if the soil is dry.

CUTTINGS IN POTS

If only a few cuttings are required, insert the cuttings, as in step 4, into 6in (15cm) pots of soil-based rooting medium – about four per pot. Label, then place in a cold frame.

EVERGREEN CUTTINGS

1 To prepare evergreen hardwood cuttings (here of Escallonia*), cut the shoots into sections 8–10in (20–25cm) in length. Trim each cutting just below a node at the base and just above a node at the top. Strip the leaves and any side-shoots from the bottom half of each cutting to reduce the risk of rot.*

2 Insert 5–8 cuttings in a deep 6in (15cm) pot, so that the foliage sits just above the surface. Bottom heat will speed rooting, which normally takes 6–10 weeks. Placing the pots in a plastic tent to keep the cuttings humid is also beneficial.

SPACE-SAVING HARDWOOD CUTTINGS

▲ **IN A ROLL** *Cut a strip of black plastic about 2in (5cm) wider than the height of the cuttings. Cover it with a ½in (1cm) layer of peat and fine bark. Space the cuttings about 3in (8cm) apart on the medium. Roll up carefully, secure with raffia, label, and water well.*

◄ **IN BUNDLES** *Prepared cuttings may be bundled up and overwintered in 6–8in (15–20cm) of fine grit in a sheltered place to callus; many, here dogwood (*Cornus*) and willow (*Salix*) cuttings, will root. In spring, separate the bundles and line out in a bed.*

rooting has already started, cover the pot with fleece to avoid scorch; otherwise, remove it to a cold frame or cloche to slow down new growth. Indeed, often the best way is to place the pots on a heated bench for a couple of weeks to speed callusing and then to remove them to a cold frame to continue the rooting process. This principle is followed in large-scale commercial production of fruit tree rootstocks.

For easily rooted subjects, such as willows and flowering currants (*Ribes*), where large numbers of cuttings are needed, insert cuttings in large, prepared nursery beds (*see right*). To improve drainage, either use a raised bed or pour sharp sand into the bottom of each hole before inserting the cutting. As with trenches, place the cuttings 2in (5cm) apart, in rows 12in (30cm) apart. It is best to stand on a wooden board when planting to prevent compacting the soil. The width of the board also acts as a spacing guide between rows. After inserting them, treat the cuttings as for those in slit trenches (*see facing page*).

EVERGREEN HARDWOOD CUTTINGS

Although evergreen cuttings will root in a sheltered place outdoors, such as in a cold frame, they respond well to the additional humidity provided by a plastic tent, either in a greenhouse or outside in a tunnel cloche. This is because they are susceptible, unlike deciduous hardwood cuttings, to losing moisture through their foliage. Small numbers of evergreen hardwood cuttings may be rooted in pots in a greenhouse (*see above*). Bottom heat is not usually required but speeds rooting, which is normally rapid and prodigious.

Rooted hardwood cuttings of many evergreens, such as *Prunus lusitanica* and x *Cupressocyparis leylandii*, may be used for hedging. Take cuttings up to 20in (50cm) long for growing on in large pots; new plants can reach 3ft (90cm) by autumn. Reduce foliage on large-leaved subjects by up to a half to lessen the risk of botrytis and for easier handling.

USING A COVERED NURSERY BED

Hardwood cuttings root well in a covered nursery bed, such as in a cold frame; this is useful in colder climates for propagating some less hardy species. First mix perlite or peat and grit into the soil for a more free-draining rooting medium. Late winter into spring is the critical time, because the cuttings may not yet have many roots but the buds may come into growth early, owing to the protected environment. The secret of success is the hardening-off process.

Do this gradually, first putting just a crack of air on the cuttings, and then working toward removing the cold frame's panes. Fleece is very useful for shading cuttings to reduce moisture loss on bright days before the cuttings are fully hardened. On sunny days, open the frame to prevent warm air from encouraging the buds to break early.

It may be necessary to water the nursery bed a few times in autumn and (very occasionally) during the winter. If inserting cuttings in autumn, remember to provide some form of shading. Lift and pot or plant out the rooted cuttings in the following spring or autumn, depending on their rate of growth.

SAVING SPACE

If you are short of space, there are other ways of rooting large numbers of easily rooted hardwood cuttings (*see above*). Wrap them in a plastic roll and pot when they have rooted after 12–20 weeks. Store bundles of cuttings in a box of fine grit in a frost-free place to callus, and sometimes root, over winter. Then plant out the cuttings in spring.

LARGE NURSERY BED
*Large numbers of hardwood cuttings, here of willows (*Salix*), are best lined out in nursery beds, grown on for a year, then planted out.*

SOFTWOOD CUTTINGS

1 In early spring to early summer, cut off nonflowering, vigorous shoots (here of Hydrangea macrophylla*) with 2–3 pairs of leaves. Use pruners to cut just below a node.*

2 To prepare each cutting, remove the soft tip from the shoot just above the node and then remove the lowest pair of leaves. The stem of the cutting should be about 1½–2in (4–5cm) in length.

3 Fill 5in (13cm) pots with rooting medium and space the cuttings around the edge. The leaves should be just above the surface of the medium and should not touch each other.

4 Water the cuttings with a fungicidal solution, label, and place under cover. Leave in a shaded place. Bottom heat of 59°F (15°C) will speed the rooting process.

5 Once the cuttings have rooted, harden them off. Gently tease apart and pot individually into 3½in (9cm) pots. Pinch out the growing tips to encourage bushy growth (see inset).

SOFTWOOD CUTTINGS

Softwood cuttings are taken from the plant in spring and early summer, before the new growth has begun to firm. This method is suitable for most deciduous shrubs and climbers. Softwood cuttings should usually be 1½–2in (4–5cm) long, with two or three pairs of leaves retained at the top (*see above*). Keep the cuttings in a clean plastic bag, until required, to prevent them from wilting.

Remove the soft tip from each cutting, because it is vulnerable to both rotting and scorch. This also ensures that, once rooted, the cutting does not immediately grow upward from the tip alone, thus ensuring a bushy plant from the start. If the tip is removed, some growth hormones also become redistributed to build up at the base of the cutting, which will assist rooting. Remove the lowest pair of leaves to make it easier to insert the cutting into the medium. On delicate material, this should be done cleanly with a sharp knife or pruners; where there is no risk of damaging the stem with more robust plants, pinch off the foliage between thumb and forefinger. Take care to leave no snags, which may encourage rot.

Inserting the cuttings correctly is important. With softwood cuttings, it is best to make a hole in the medium with a stick or pencil so the soft material is able to enter the medium with minimal resistance, thus reducing the risk of damage. Insert each cutting to just below the first pair of leaves, then firm gently around each stem. Water in the cuttings thoroughly with a fungicidal solution so that the medium is moist right to the container bottom.

The cuttings will benefit from a warm, protected environment, such as a closed case. To speed rooting, provide bottom heat at a temperature of about

GREENWOOD CUTTINGS

In late spring, take greenwood cuttings from vigorous shoots (here of Philadelphus*) that are firm and slightly woody at the base. Prepare as for softwood cuttings (see above).*

GROWN-ON CUTTINGS
*Many deciduous shrub cuttings produce significant growth in one year. These 2–3ft (60–90cm) dogwoods (*Cornus*) were raised from stem-tip cuttings taken in midsummer, kept under cover over winter, planted in early summer in nursery beds, and grown on until late summer.*

59°F (15°C). When the cuttings root, knock them out of the container and gently pull them apart. Pot singly in 3½in (9cm) pots. Pinch out the growing tips of new plants to encourage bushy growth. Grow on in a sheltered site.

GREENWOOD CUTTINGS

Greenwood cuttings are similar to softwood cuttings but are taken when the new growth is just beginning to firm. This material is easier to handle because it does not wilt quite so readily; however, it is treated in the same way.

Usually, there is no discernible difference in stem color, and therefore distinguishing between the two types of cutting is more a question of the feel of the material. In reality, many cuttings intended to be softwood end up as greenwood cuttings – it is all a matter of timing. For most deciduous plants and some evergreens, if you miss the softwood season, greenwood cuttings root just as well, but there are a few exceptions (*see pp.118–45*).

STEM-TIP CUTTINGS

Stem-tip cuttings, in which the soft tip is retained, are taken when the material has ripened more than for softwood or greenwood cuttings but the plant is in active growth, usually around mid-summer. The soft tip is then less likely to rot. This method, which can produce excellent rapid growth (*see above*), is suitable for most common deciduous shrubs, such as *Fuchsia, Potentilla, Weigela,* lilacs, and mock orange, and some evergreens, such as camellias, heliotrope, and *Hibiscus rosa-sinensis*.

Nodal cuttings are more likely to succeed, since some plants will not root internodally. Prepare each cutting from new growth, up to 4in (10cm) long, by making a clean cut just below a node. Continue as for softwood cuttings.

DIVISION

This is a propagation technique that is associated mainly with herbaceous perennials (*see pp.148–50*), but it is also appropriate for a number of suckering shrubs. Where only a few new plants are needed, this method of propagation is very quick and easy. Division can be used for deciduous and evergreen genera, such as *Gaultheria, Kerria, Ruscus,* and sweet box (*Sarcococca*).

Timing is not absolutely critical, but in order to ensure success, division of suckers is best carried out when the plant is not actively growing or is dormant. Early spring is ideal; the plant quickly recovers from the stress of the division because the ground is usually moist, and, although the soil is warming up, the air temperature is not yet too high. Summer is best avoided because the new plants will be prone to wilting and scorch in the hot sun.

Most shrubs produce suckers on long underground stems (stolons); a few, such as roses (*see p.113*), sucker from the main stem just above the roots. When separating suckers from the parent plant (*see below*), use a fork to lift the underground stem that runs between the suckering shoots and the parent plant. If the sucker has fibrous roots at the base, it may be propagated: sever the stem close to the parent plant and prepare each sucker as shown below.

Replant the rooted suckers directly into soil that has been prepared with well-rotted manure or compost. Firm and water in each sucker. Alternatively, pot the suckers in potting mix in 2–3in (5–8cm) pots. Water the suckers regularly until the new plants are well established. With plants such as snowberries (*Symphoricarpos*) that are usually prone to legginess, cut back suckers to 12–18in (30–45cm) to ensure bushy regrowth.

Shrubs that have a clumping habit may be divided in a similar way to herbaceous plants (*see p.148*). Lift the entire clump, divide into good-sized pieces with healthy roots and top-growth using a spade or sharp knife, and discard the rest. Division of this sort may also be used to rejuvenate a mature shrub that has grown beyond its designated area; a common example of this is *Sorbaria sorbifolia*. Prepare and grow on the divisions as for suckers.

DIVISION OF SUCKERING SHRUBS

1 *In early spring, lift an underground stem with suckers on it, without disturbing the parent plant (here a* Gaultheria shallon*). Check that there are fibrous roots at the base of the suckers.*

2 *Using a sharp pair of pruners, remove the long, suckering stem by cutting it off close to the parent plant. Firm back the soil well around the base of the parent plant.*

3 *Cut the main stem back to the fibrous roots, then divide the suckers so that each has its own roots. Cut back the topgrowth by about half to reduce moisture loss.*

4 *Replant the suckers in open ground or in 2–3in (5–8cm) pots. Firm the soil well around the suckers, water in, and label. Water regularly while the suckers are establishing.*

SOWING SEEDS

There are many shrubs and climbers that can be grown from seeds, with always the chance of creating something new. The sense of excitement as germination takes place and seedlings appear is the same however long it takes, be it a *Daphne* requiring a winter's chill or an *Abutilon* that needs only a warm, moist soil mix in spring. Remember that only species "come true" from seeds; a plant grown from seeds gathered from your favorite *Caryopteris* cultivar is unlikely to have exactly the same characteristics as its parent.

Shrubs and climbers have three basic types of seedhead: nuts or nutlike fruit containing often short-lived seeds with a high water content (such as *Corylus*); capsules or pods that enclose smaller, drier seeds (such as *Cytisus*); and fleshy fruits and berries (such as *Viburnum*). The first consideration when gathering seeds is that the plant from which you propose to gather must be healthy and vigorous. Plants showing a lack of vigor will often be harboring viruses, which can be transferred by seeds.

NUTS AND NUTLIKE FRUITS

Nuts and nutlike fruits generally ripen in autumn; they should be gathered when they would naturally fall, or just immediately before. Gather them by hand-picking; alternatively, if the plant is large enough, place a sheet of cloth or plastic around its base and shake the branches until the nuts fall onto the sheet. Remove the nuts from the outer casings, clean, and sow at once in deep pots. Discard any nuts that show the slightest imperfections.

Alternatively, store the cleaned seeds in moist peat in a bag hung up in a garage or shed and out of reach of rodents (or in a refrigerator), and sow them in late winter to spring. This is advisable in areas where the soil is poorly drained and there are usually above-average levels of winter rainfall.

GATHERING SEEDS FROM RIPE BERRIES

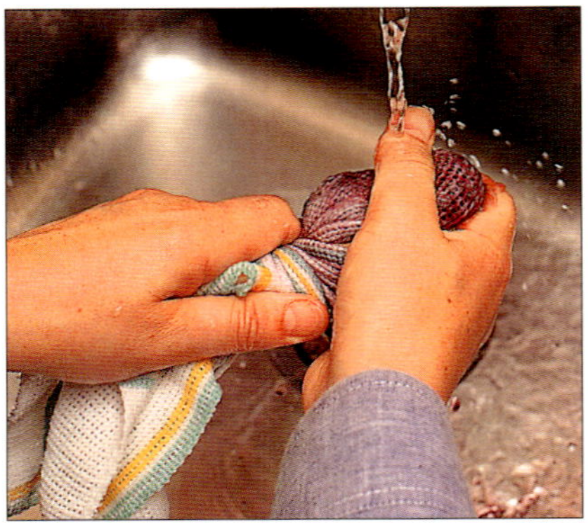

1 *For berries with large seeds (here* Mahonia*), put a handful into cheesecloth or muslin, twist to secure, and hold under cold running water. Squeeze until no more juice runs out.*

2 *Open out the cloth carefully and pick out the seeds from the mashed pulp. Allow them to dry on some paper towels or blotting paper in an airy place for a couple of days.*

PODS AND CAPSULES

Dry seeds that have been collected from pods or capsules are easier to handle than the moist seeds found in nuts and nutlike fruits; if stored correctly, they will retain their viability for many years. Check suitable seedpods daily as they begin to ripen; they are usually ready for gathering once the pod starts to turn from green to brown.

Always gather pods or capsules when the weather is dry, since moisture will increase the likelihood of fungal attack. Before gathering medium-sized or large seeds, open one or two of the seedpods to see if there is in fact a developed seed inside. Ripe, viable seeds are plump, healthy, and usually still green.

Place the pods in a paper bag and seal it tightly. Alternatively, spread the pods on newspaper in a tray and cover them with fleece or more newspaper – pods often "explode" to shed their seeds in all directions.

Some subshrubs that produce flower spikes may be treated as if they were herbaceous perennials; cut off a complete spike of seed capsules and hang it upside down in a paper bag. After a few days, shake the drying seeds free. Do not be tempted to extract seeds that remain in the capsules, since these are likely to be unripe and nonviable.

After extracting the seeds, clean off any chaff attached to them, since such material is likely to rot, increasing the likelihood of damping off (*see p.46*). Remove the worst of the debris by hand; alternatively, run the seeds through a series of sieves (*see p.28*) until only clean seeds remain.

Store dry seeds in a refrigerator. Place them in a clearly labeled paper bag or envelope inside a plastic box or cookie tin. To maintain a dry atmosphere, first place silica gel in the bottom of the tin.

SCARIFYING SEEDS OF SHRUBS AND CLIMBING PLANTS

USING A KNIFE *Nick the hard coat of very large seeds (here of* Paeonia delavayi *var.* lutea*) with a sharp knife (see inset). Take care not to damage the "eye" of the seed or to cut too deeply.*

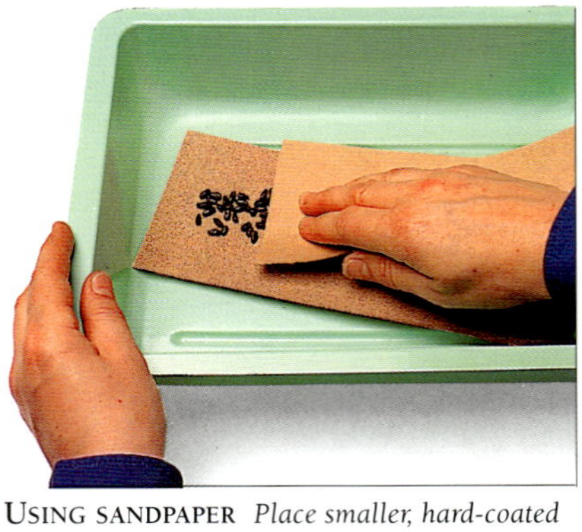

USING SANDPAPER *Place smaller, hard-coated seeds (here of* Caragana brevispina*) between two sheets of sandpaper in a seed tray and rub them to scratch and weaken their surfaces.*

USING HOT WATER *To soften the seedcoats of smaller seeds (here of* Sophora davidii*), place in a bowl and pour boiling water over them. Allow to soak for 24 hours, then sow at once.*

SOWING SEEDS IN CONTAINERS

1 *Fill a tray with seed soil mix. Firm gently, water, and allow to drain. Sow the seeds evenly over the surface by tapping them from a folded piece of paper.*

2 *Cover the seeds with a fine layer of soil mix, then add a ¼in (5mm) layer of grit. Label and cover with wire netting to protect the seedlings. Place in a cold frame.*

3 *Once the germinated seedlings are large enough to handle, lift them carefully, using a knife or similar implement. Always hold the seedlings by their leaves.*

4 *Insert the seedlings singly into 2½–3½in (6–9cm) pots, or in rows into trays, in soilless potting mix. Gently firm around the base of each seedling. Label; water.*

COLD STRATIFICATION OF SEEDS

BEFORE SOWING *Seeds that are stored before sowing (here of* Aronia melanocarpa*) can be chilled in a refrigerator. Put them in some moist vermiculite or peat in a clear plastic bag, label, and store for 1–3 months.*

AFTER SOWING *Seeds that are sown fresh, such as clematis, can be plunged in a sandbed or cold frame outdoors over winter. Sow seeds thinly in pans of gritty seed soil mix, then cover with a fine layer of mix and one of grit.*

FLESHY FRUITS AND BERRIES

These are usually hard and green and, as they ripen, soften and change color, often from yellow to red. The important thing is to watch out for the turn. If you leave it too late, the soft, succulent fruit may be taken by birds. Gather fruits by hand-picking or shaking the plant.

Removing the seeds from fruits or berries can be achieved in many ways. Squeeze berries in cloth (*see facing page*), gently mash them through a sieve, then wash off the pulp. Alternatively, put fruit in water to rot, then mash the pulp and place in clean water. The pulp and dead seeds should rise to the top while viable, heavy seeds settle on the bottom. Whichever method you choose, dry the seeds on paper towels for a couple of days before storing them.

With members of the rose family (Rosaceae), it is frequently best to layer whole fruits in coarse sand in a tray or in a large pot and leave them outside for the winter. Keep the sand moist. This provides the period of chilling needed before many of this family germinate. In late winter or early spring, remove the decomposed fruits from the sand.

SCARIFICATION OF SEEDS

Many shrubs and climbers, especially members of the pea and bean family (Fabaceae), have hard seed coats that prevent germination until the coat is broken down to admit moisture to the seed within. There are several ways to deal with this problem; these are known as scarification and involve nicking or abrading the seeds or soaking them in hot water (*see facing page*).

Nature softens hard seed coats by subjecting the seeds to warm, moist conditions in spring, when bacterial activity is at its height. This can be mimicked by storing the seeds in moist soil mix and hanging them up in a shed during the summer. In commerce, for roses particularly, compost activators may be added to speed up the process.

Some impermeable seeds have chemical germination inhibitors on the seed coats: remove these just before sowing by soaking the seeds in hot water, mild detergent, or alcohol. Wash the seeds thoroughly afterward.

Some seeds need several treatments for multiple dormancies; scarify them first to allow other treatments to take effect. A safer option is to sow the seeds outdoors and let nature take its course.

STRATIFICATION OF SEEDS

Some seeds are prompted to germinate by temperature changes. Many woody plants native to temperate climates exhibit cold-temperature dormancy, where seeds require a winter's chilling before germinating in spring. This can be overcome by storing the seeds in a refrigerator at 41°F (5°C) before sowing, or by sowing in autumn and over-wintering outdoors (*see left*). Even seeds that do not need winter chilling may germinate more quickly and uniformly after a short period of cold stratification.

Some hard-coated seeds require a period of warm stratification. Place the seeds in a plastic bag in an equal volume of sand and leaf mold, or an equal volume of peat and sand, and store for 4–12 weeks at 68–77°F (20–25°C). This is usually followed by cold stratification before sowing.

SMOKE TREATMENT OF SEEDS

In nature, some seeds germinate only after a bush fire. The flames scarify the seed coat, and chemicals in the smoke stimulate germination. To simulate this, sow a tray of seeds, cover with 2½–4in (6–10cm) of dry leaves, burn them, and water in the ash. Kits, smoke paper, and smoke water containing chemicals found in smoke may also be available.

SOWING SEEDS IN CONTAINERS

Most seeds of shrubs and climbing plants are best sown in containers (*see above*), so that the conditions they need can be easily provided. Seeds that need a period of chilling or take more than a year to germinate, such as *Daphne*, can be sown in autumn (*continued on p.104*)

COVERING SEEDS SOWN IN CONTAINERS

VERMICULITE *Use a ½in (1cm) layer of vermiculite to cover fast-germinating seeds, usually of climbers or tender shrubs. Vermiculite allows air and light to reach the seeds and keeps them moist.*

GRIT *Cover slow-germinating seeds, mostly of hardy species, with fine grit or coarse sand to allow seedlings to grow healthily* (see right). *If soil mix is exposed for a long while, it is susceptible to growth of moss and liverworts, which competes with seedlings* (see left).

(*continued from p.103*) and overwintered in cool climates in a sheltered place, such as a sandbed or cold frame. (In areas without cold winters, such seeds should be stratified in a refrigerator, *see p.103*.) Other seeds germinate readily from a spring sowing; these are treated in the same way as bedding plants or easy herbaceous perennials, and the seedlings are suited to the controlled atmosphere of a greenhouse. *Abutilon*, for example, responds well to this treatment.

SOWING THE SEEDS

Fill seed trays, seed pans, or pots with a good-quality, gritty seed soil mix (*see p.34*), containing only a little fertilizer – too much can kill seedlings. Thoroughly water the mix before sowing.

For small or medium-sized seeds, firm the soil mix to leave a ⅛in (3mm) gap between the mix and the rim. For large seeds, the gap may be ½–⅝in (10–15mm). Sow the seeds and cover with a fine layer of mix. Then add ¼in (5mm) of coarse sand or fine grit (*see above right*) for autumn-sown seeds. For spring sowings, instead of grit use a ½in (1cm) layer of vermiculite (*see above left*): fine-grade for small or medium-sized seeds, medium-grade for large seeds.

Some seeds, such as rhododendron seeds, are so fine that they do not have sufficient food reserves to push through the soil mix, or they require light in order to germinate. Sow such seeds on the surface of mix that has been sieved: tiny seeds can easily fall between cracks of a coarse surface. To give the seedlings as much light as possible, leave only a fraction of an inch between the soil mix and the rim. Mix the seeds with a small amount of fine sand, then gently tap the mixture onto the soil mix to sow evenly.

AUTUMN-SOWN SEEDS

After sowing, label the containers and cover with wire netting to protect the seedlings from birds or animals. Place in a sheltered place (*see below*) to overwinter at 14–28°F (-10 to -2°C) and subsequently germinate. Check them regularly and water if necessary.

When the seedlings are large enough to handle, they should be transplanted individually into cells, trays, or small pots (*see p.103*). Take care not to disturb their roots. This may be in the first spring after sowing, or up to a year after germination. If then grown on under protection as before, the new plants should make rapid growth.

SPRING-SOWN SEEDS

A temperature of 59–68°F (15–20°C) is required for germination, unless otherwise stated (*see* A–Z of Shrubs and Climbing Plants, *pp.118–45*). The surface of the soil mix must also remain moist at all times; either place the container in a closed case, under a plastic tent, on a mist bench, or cover it with a sheet of glass. Some seeds require bottom heat for successful germination; for these, a propagating blanket (*see p.41*) covered with capillary matting works well.

Fine seeds that lose viability at temperatures above 68°F (20°C) respond well to being placed on a mist bench, but seeds requiring temperatures higher than this often struggle to germinate, owing to the cooling effect of the mist.

Inspect the soil mix regularly to check that it has not dried out, and water as necessary. Never water a container from above once fine seed is surface-sown; place it in a shallow dish of water for a short time. Spray the seedlings occasionally with fungicide.

When the seedlings are large enough to handle, transplant into trays or pots in low-nutrient potting mix, as for autumn-sown seeds. Place out of direct sunlight until established. Harden off young plants by gradually exposing them to outdoor conditions.

SOWING IN RAISED SEEDBEDS

Seeds of some shrubs and climbers, especially those native to your area, can be sown outside in raised seedbeds.

Select a sheltered site and raise the soil level by 8in (20cm) to improve the drainage. Remove perennial weeds and dig the soil thoroughly. Large seeds can be sown in rows in autumn; smaller ones can be left until late winter. Cover with ¾–1¼in (2–3cm) of pea gravel. Do not allow germinating seeds to dry out; cover with fleece or loose leaves to reduce frost heaving. (*See also* Garden Trees, *p.55*.)

SEEDLINGS IN A COLD FRAME

Some seeds, especially of hardy shrubs or climbers, require a period of winter chilling before they will germinate. In colder climates, place containers of seeds in a cold frame after autumn sowing. The cold frame allows exposure to cold while protecting the seeds from disturbance by birds, animals, or the elements. Once the seeds germinate, the seedlings can remain in the cold frame for up to a year before being transplanted.

Layering

In nature, many plants reproduce by layering, a process where roots form at the point at which a plant's stem touches the soil. Some plants have shoots that trail along the ground, such as snowberries (*Symphoricarpos*) or heathers (*see p.111*); others with an upright habit may suffer storm damage that causes a branch to fall to the ground while remaining partly attached to the plant.

Layering is like rooting cuttings that are still attached to, and are protected by, the parent plant, and consequently does not require as controlled an environment to succeed (unless layering a tropical plant in a cool climate). Many shrubs that are difficult to root from cuttings, such as smoke bush (*Cotinus*) and hazels (*Corylus*), respond well to layering. Layering requires less skill and aftercare than grafting, which is often used for plants that are difficult to root.

If only one or two plants are wanted, air or simple layering can be used to propagate many shrubs or climbers quickly. Other forms of layering produce greater numbers of new plants, or layers.

Air layering

Air layering is normally used when it is not possible to lower a branch down to ground level. It can be successful in a wide range of shrubs and climbers, from the tender rubber plant (*Ficus elastica* 'Decora') and philodendrons to many hardy species. This technique can produce a *Daphne* large enough to be planted straight into the garden within 12 months. Plants are best air layered in spring for replanting in the autumn or the following spring.

Layers may be made on wood of any age, but material that is 1–2 years old produces roots more readily (*see below*). Select a straight branch and trim off any leaves and sideshoots to leave about 12in (30cm) of clear stem. Wound the stem by making a sloping cut into the center of the stem to create a "tongue." Alternatively, remove a band of bark ¼–½in (5–12mm) wide by scoring two shallow, parallel cuts around the stem and peeling off the bark. Apply hormone rooting compound to the wound to encourage rooting.

Tuck some moist sphagnum moss into the sloping cut of the wound to keep it open, using the reverse of a knife blade. Enclose the wound in a black plastic sleeve, secured below the wound, to keep out moisture and prevent growth of algae. Pack the sleeve with sphagnum moss, then secure it above the wound. Alternatively, use clear plastic wrap for the sleeve and cover it with black plastic or aluminum foil.

Leave the layer in place, occasionally removing the plastic sleeve to check for rooting, which should occur within a year. When roots have developed, sever the new plant below the wound and pot or replant it. Water in well at planting time, and again throughout the first summer until it is well established. In colder climates, in the first few weeks cover the plant with fleece to protect it from the elements.

For tender plants that are grown under cover in cooler regions, the technique is identical, but rooting takes place more quickly; new plants can be ready for potting within 2–3 months.

Air layering shrubs and climbers

1 In spring, choose a 1–2-year-old shoot that is straight, healthy, and vigorous (here of a rhododendron). Trim off sideshoots and leaves for about 12in (30cm). Do not leave any snags.

2 Wound the stem, making a 1¼in (3cm) angled cut toward the shoot tip (see inset). Apply hormone rooting compound to the wound. Pack it with a little moist sphagnum moss.

3 Wrap the stem loosely with black plastic. Seal it around the stem and below the wound with tape. Pack the sleeve with moss to cover the wound.

4 Seal the upper end of the sleeve around the stem with more tape. Black plastic retains moisture without encouraging growth of algae. Leave the layer in place for up to a year. Check it occasionally for signs of rooting.

5 When strong new roots have formed, carefully remove the plastic sleeve. Cut through the stem just below the root ball. Tease out the roots, but do not try to remove all the moss. For rhododendrons, prune back new growth to one bud above the old wood. Pot the layer in soilless potting mix or plant out in prepared soil. Water well and label.

Simple layering

When you want only a couple of new plants, simple layering is a good way of propagating a wide range of shrubs and climbers quickly. You can do this at any time of the year, but the best times are autumn and early spring. The pliant shoots of most climbers can be simply pegged onto the surface of the soil to root, while the stiffer stems of many shrubs require a trench.

For most climbing plants, choose a shoot no more than two years old and 2–3ft (60–90cm) long that is growing horizontally and close to the ground and is supple enough to be pinned down and then bent upward at a right angle. Avoid very thin stems and thick watershoots. If no suitable material is available, prune the plant back hard to encourage more vigorous new shoots.

Before securing the layer, prepare the ground next to the parent plant where the shoot reaches the surface by digging it over and incorporating into it some free-draining rooting medium to a depth of 12in (30cm). Make sure that the medium is mixed thoroughly into the soil; rooting medium quickly dries out if exposed to the air.

Trim off any leaves and sideshoots from the layer for 12in (30cm) behind the growing tip (*see below*). Wound the underside of the stem of the layer about halfway along its length, or through a node, by making a slanting cut through to the middle of the stem, to form a "tongue." Alternatively, twist the stem to damage the bark or remove a 1in (2.5cm) sliver of bark from the underside of the stem. Treat the wound with hormone rooting compound.

Remove some of the enriched soil from underneath the layer before pinning it down securely with several long, galvanized-wire, U-shaped pins or staples on each side of the wound. Ideally, you should pin the layer down at the point where one-year-old wood joins older wood. In practice, this is not always possible since the branch may not be long enough. Mound up soil over the layer to a depth of 3in (8cm) and firm – otherwise as the soil settles it will leave the stem exposed. Bend the tip of the shoot so that it is as close to vertical as possible, and attach it to a stake. The angle created by bending the shoot aids rooting by concentrating the growth hormones at the rooting site instead of the growing tip. As the shoot grows, continue to tie it in loosely. Water the layer well, and check it weekly during the summer to ensure that it does not dry out. Keep the area free of weeds.

Some plants root quickly, but most take at least a year. Do not be too anxious to separate the layer from its parent, since it is crucial for the young plant to establish a good root system. When well rooted, sever the new plant, and either pot up or plant out directly.

When layering a shrub (*see below*), select a pliant shoot and prepare the stem as for climbers. Use a stake to mark where the stem touches the ground. Dig a sloping trench, 3in (8cm) deep, and peg the shoot into the bottom. Bend the shoot to as near vertical as it will go, and tie the stem tip to the stake. Backfill the hole, firm, and water in.

SIMPLE LAYERING OF A CLIMBER

1 *In autumn, select a young, low-growing shoot (here of* Akebia quinata*). Remove leaves and sideshoots from at least 12in (30cm) of the stem behind the shoot tip.*

2 *Make a slanting cut up to 1in (2.5cm) long, on the underside of the shoot, in the middle of the clear length of stem, to make a "tongue."*

3 *Use a brush to dust the wound with hormone rooting compound, here powder (see inset). Shake off any excess.*

4 *Peg the clean length of stem, wounded side down, into the soil with wire staples. Mound up the soil to a depth of 3in (8cm) over the shoot. Stake the tip of the shoot to keep it upright.*

5 *Once it has rooted, usually in the following autumn, sever the layer close to the parent plant and lift the layer with a hand fork. Cut away the old stem on the layer back to the new roots.*

6 *Pot the new plant into soilless potting mix, water well, and label. Plant it out when well established. Alternatively, you can plant it directly into its permanent growing position.*

SIMPLE LAYERING OF A SHRUB

1 *Mark the position where the stem touches the soil with a stake. Dig a sloping trench about 3in (8cm) deep leading from the stake toward the shrub.*

2 *Peg the prepared stem into the base of the trench with wire staples. Bend up the stem tip and tie it to the stake. Fill in the hole, lightly firm, and water.*

SELF-LAYERING A CLIMBER

1 *Where a shoot (here of an ivy, Hedera) has rooted into the ground and is producing healthy, new growth, carefully lift it, using a hand fork. With pruners, sever the self-layered stem from the parent plant, cutting straight across the stem just above a node.*

2 *Cut the rooted stem into sections, making sure each has a good root system and strong new growth. Remove the lower leaves from each section, cutting close to the main stem. Sections with just one or two leaves (*see top right*) can be used but will take longer to establish.*

3 *Pot each layer individually using soilless potting mix. Water well and label. Grow on in a sheltered spot outdoors until the new plants become established. Sections that are already well rooted can be planted directly into their final positions.*

Self-layering

Some plants, such as ivies (*Hedera*) and some of the smaller-leaved, low-growing cotoneasters, naturally layer themselves, their sprawling stems rooting into the ground as they grow. To propagate them, lift a rooted shoot with a hand fork, sever it with pruners, cut into rooted sections, and pot singly (*see above*).

Alternatively, remove a rooted sideshoot, or layer, by cutting through the main stem on either side with a spade. Well-rooted layers may be planted out; this is best done in early spring, when the layers will establish quickly in the warming soil. When planting, prepare the ground thoroughly and water in well. In colder climates, protect the new plants with fleece for a few days while they establish.

Serpentine layering

This is useful for plants that produce long shoots of new growth each year, including many climbers such as clematis, golden hops, grapes, and wisteria. In effect, it adapts the process of self-layering and makes it possible to obtain quite a few layers from one shoot. In early spring, prepare the ground as for simple layering (*see facing page*), take one of the previous year's shoots, and bring it to ground level. If the stem is very thin, there is no need to wound it, but wounding speeds the process.

Wound the stem between the nodes and "snake" the shoot in and out of the soil (*see above right*), pinning the wounds below the soil with wire staples so that at least one bud remains above ground between the layers. Alternatively, wound just behind a node, or even through it, and "snake" the shoot along the soil surface, pinning the stem over the wounds. Often layers root by autumn, but some take until spring. When the layers are well rooted, treat them as for self-layering (*see above*).

SERPENTINE LAYERING OF A CLIMBER

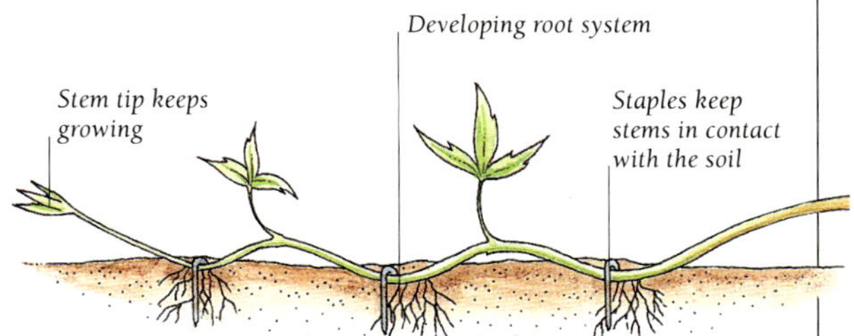

To layer a shoot *Choose a healthy, trailing shoot and trim off the leaves and sideshoots. Wound the stem between each node* (see above) *or just behind the growth buds* (see left)*. Apply hormone rooting powder to encourage rooting, then pin the stem to the ground, over the wound, with wire staples.*

How layers develop *Once the stem is in contact with the ground, the wounds stimulate rooting. Nutrients for this process are provided by the parent plant as the growing tip of the shoot draws sap along the layered stem* (see above)*. The layers, each with roots and a shoot, can be severed when rooted.*

FRENCH LAYERING A SHRUB

French layering of ornamental shrubs is not often undertaken commercially because of the length of time it takes, but it is worthwhile for the gardener: it is very reliable, especially for shrubs that are difficult to root. It involves cutting back a vigorous, young stock plant to 2in (5cm) in spring to encourage formation of long, new shoots, a process called stooling (*see p.24*).

The following early spring, trim the growing tips and pin the shoots down on prepared soil so they radiate from the parent plant like spokes on a wheel. As sideshoots grow, mound them with soil (*see below*). Water and weed the layers regularly. In autumn, lift and sever the rooted layers from the parent for potting or planting. The shoots at the center can be layered next year.

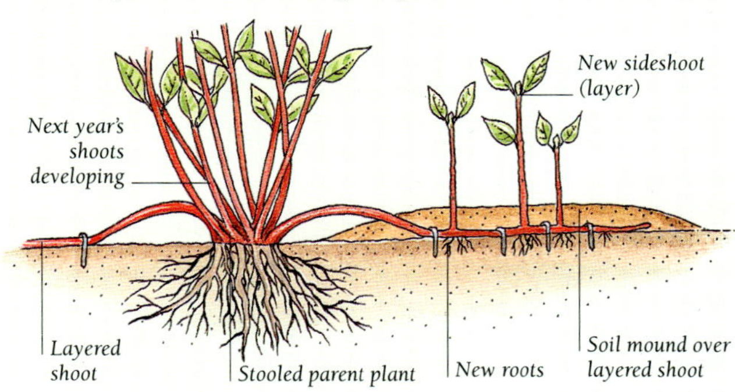

Rooting layers *Pin down each shoot of the previous season's growth. When the sideshoots are 2½–3in (6–8cm) tall, mound soil over them, leaving the tips exposed. Mound again later in the summer to a depth of 6in (15cm).*

Grafting

Grafting is often used for cultivars that are difficult to propagate by other means or to produce a plant more quickly. There are many different types of graft. For most shrubs and climbers, the best choice is apical-wedge grafting (*see below*). This graft provides consistently good results and is one of the easiest to perform. Other grafts suitable for shrubs and climbers include whip grafting and spliced side-veneer grafting (*see facing page*).

The first requirement is a good-quality rootstock, that is, a plant of a species compatible with the cultivar to be grafted. Usually this is a one or two-year-old seedling, but with magnolias and rhododendrons, stocks can also be raised from cuttings. For summer grafting, stocks must be container-grown; for winter grafting, they can be either container-grown or bare-root.

If raising only a few rootstocks, transplant seedlings into deep, square 3½in (9cm) pots, to provide space for the all-important root system to develop. With some plants, the seedling will have grown sufficiently to graft in the first summer or winter. Normally, the stock is ready when its girth measures ¼–½in (6–10mm), but it is more important that the stock girth matches that of the scion (*see p.27*). Particularly in summer, stock and scion should be at a similar stage of growth. Keep the soil mix of container-grown stocks just moist for two weeks before grafting so that the union is not flooded by an overactive flow of sap, which will stop it uniting with the scion.

Always take scions from cultivars that are true to type, free of pests and diseases, and still producing good levels of extension growth (new shoots that increase the plant's size) annually. The length of the scion depends on what is available, but 3–5in (8–12cm), with two to four healthy buds, is usually best. There is no strict rule as to the girth, but anything less than ⅜in (8mm) is difficult to work with. Where new growth is limited, try smaller scions, but a good union is less assured. If new growth is poor, use two-year-old wood; this produces very acceptable results with *Hibiscus* and some other genera.

It is vital not to let the scion material dry out, so unless it is used immediately, store it in a plastic bag in a refrigerator, where it will stay fresh for up to a week. Making accurate grafting cuts is crucial to success, so practice making the cuts on other shoots, such as willow, first.

Apical-wedge grafting

When preparing a scion (*see below*), imagine you are making a sharpened spear. Make an angled cut at the base, normally starting just above a bud and exiting at the center of the stem base. Move the knife slowly through the stem to perfect an evenly slanting cut. Repeat on the other side of the stem to create a symmetrical wedge.

The cambium layer, a band of thin-walled cells between the bark and the wood and essential to the success of the graft, should now be exposed. Remove any weak or unripe terminal buds at the top of the scion. With some material, such as wisteria, it is possible to create several scions from one length of wood.

To prepare a rootstock, clean and dry the stem, then head it back to just above the roots; cut straight across the stem and leave just enough for easy handling. If the cut is at all uneven, slice off a thin layer to neaten the surface. Make a vertical slit in the newly cut surface of the stock to a depth ⅛in (2–3mm) shorter than the scion's wedge. Where the stock and scion are of a similar girth, make the cut on the stock in the middle so that the cambium layers match up exactly; if the scion is smaller, cut the stock off-center

APICAL-WEDGE GRAFTING

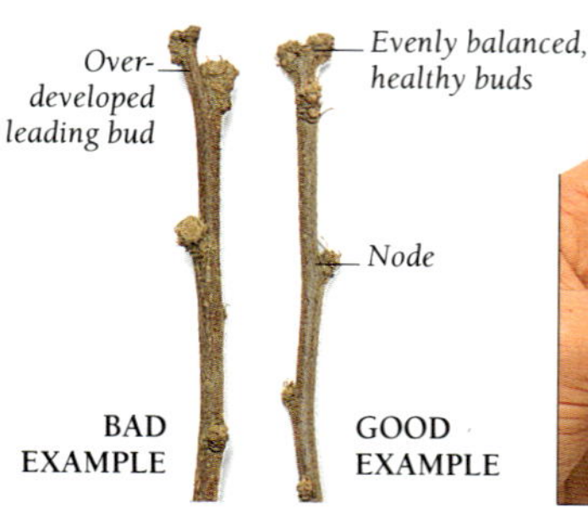

1 Take scions from ripe, healthy shoots of the current season's growth, with good buds at the tips and closely spaced nodes.

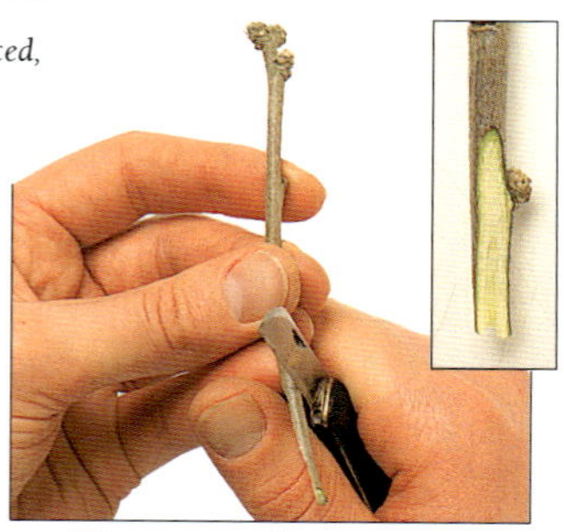

2 Trim a scion shoot to 4–6in (10–15cm) with 4–6 nodes. Make two slanting cuts, ¾–1¼in (2–3cm) long, at the base (inset).

3 Head back a bare-root stock plant (here Hibiscus syriacus*) to 1in (2.5cm) above the roots. Cut ¾–1¼in (2–3cm) into the stem.*

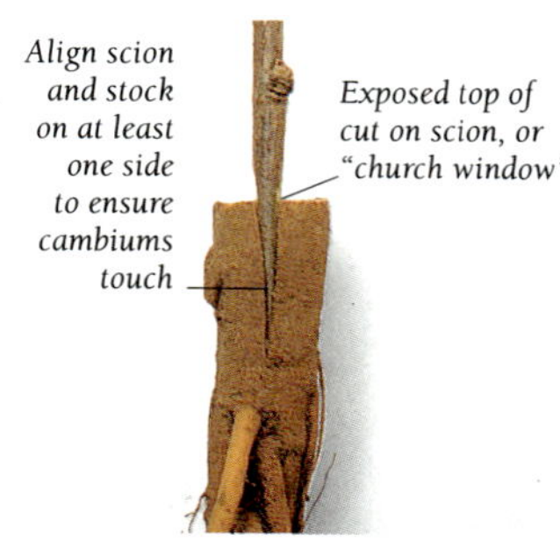

4 Push the wedge-shaped base of the scion carefully into the cut on the stock. Make sure that the cambiums of stock and scion meet.

5 Bind the graft with a narrow rubber band, cut to form a strip. Wrap it from the top of the stock to just below the graft. If the scion bud is large, bind around it. Tuck in the end of the rubber band to secure it.

6 Seal the "church window" of the scion and the cut surface of the stock with wax or wound sealant to prevent any moisture loss. If using wax, melt a little in a jar stood in a bowl of boiling water, and apply with a clean plant label or small paintbrush.

7 Lay the grafted plant in a seed tray, with the scion resting on the rim. Cover the roots and graft with moist soil mix. Label.

COMMON TYPES OF GRAFT

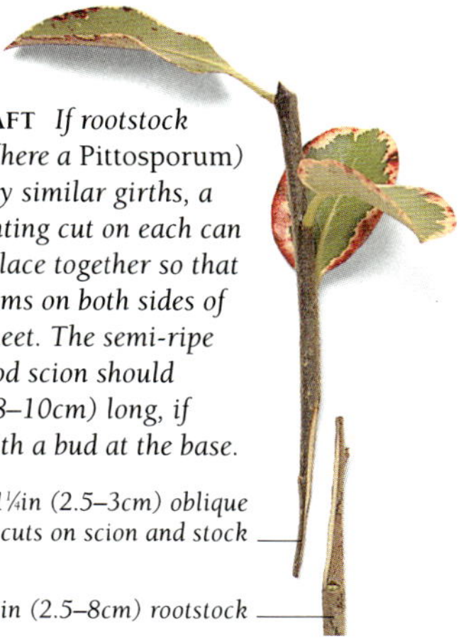

WHIP GRAFT *If rootstock and scion (here a* Pittosporum*) have closely similar girths, a simple slanting cut on each can be made. Place together so that the cambiums on both sides of the graft meet. The semi-ripe or hardwood scion should be 3–4in (8–10cm) long, if possible with a bud at the base.*

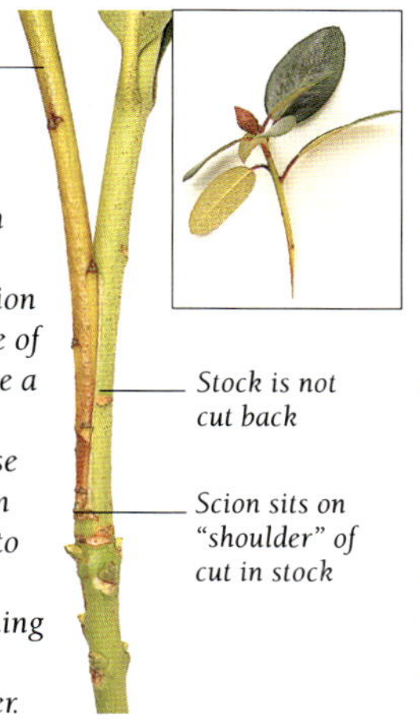

SPLICED SIDE-VENEER GRAFT *Trim any leaves from the lower stems of a 4–5in (10–13cm) scion and a rootstock (here of rhododendron). Make a downward nick 1in (2.5cm) from the base of the stock and a 1in (2.5cm) sloping cut to meet it. Remove the wood. Make a matching cut on the scion (see inset) and fit together.*

to make a narrower incision and ensure the cambiums match on both sides. Another option is to match cambiums on one side only (*see facing page*). Push the scion gently into the slit in the stock, all the way to the bottom; this should leave a little of the cut surface of the scion exposed – the "church window" – to let excess sap escape.

Strips of elastic bands are ideal for holding the graft together while the union calluses. Apply even pressure as you wrap the band around the stem and take care not to misalign the cambiums. Normally, only sufficient pressure is applied to hold the graft in place, but if the graft is poor, pull in the stock to make improved contact with the scion.

Apply a commercial grafting wax or wound sealant to the union and to the top of the scion if it has been cut. You can also tie in the graft with plastic grafting tape, making the use of wax unnecessary.

OTHER TYPES OF GRAFT

Where stocks and scions have similar girths, whip grafting and spliced side-veneer grafting are good alternative methods (*see above*). The principles of grafting are the same, but the carpentry involved in fitting together stock and scion may differ (*see pp.118–45 for individual plant requirements and p.27*).

AFTERCARE OF GRAFTED PLANTS

This is crucial to success. The graft is sensitive to drying out, but watering the pot could flood the union and cause rot, so house the graft in a closed case or tent it under plastic to provide a warm, humid environment. Maintain a temperature of 64–68°F (18–20°C), which in winter usually means placing the grafts on a heated bench (*see p.41*). Water the sand or capillary matting well before placing the grafts on the bench. In summer, shading is essential to prevent scorch.

To prevent fungal disease, air the plastic tent or propagating case first thing every day for 5–10 minutes, drying off any surface moisture that has condensed on the rootstock. Take care: too much ventilation too early on will dry out the union.

Callusing is the first sign of a successful graft union and usually begins after 3–4 weeks. Soft white tissue appears around the edge of the union on and around the church window, and also along the length of the cut in the stock. At this stage, the graft should be hardened off in preparation for moving onto the open bench. Open the case a fraction of an inch overnight, and increase the exposure by degrees over a period of up to four weeks. During this time, the callus will turn from white to yellow and brown, hardening as it changes.

Never move the grafts on a warm, bright day. When they are taken out, shading may be needed and the surfaces around the graft should be damped down for the first few days. Begin watering very sparingly. Pot bare-root grafts only when they are clearly successful, each in a container a little larger than the root ball. Growth is often prodigious, especially in protected conditions; a grafted plant is usually large enough to plant out the following autumn or spring.

HOT-PIPE CALLUSING OF GRAFTS

This process, used commercially on a large scale, applies hot air to the graft while the rootstock and scion are kept frost-free and cool and therefore less liable to dry out. This enables the callus to form quickly, giving flexibility to the commercial grower and making it easier for the gardener to achieve success with difficult subjects, such as dogwoods (*Cornus*) and hazels (*Corylus*). All types of graft respond well, whether on bare-rooted or container-grown stocks.

A small-scale hot pipe may be made in a cold greenhouse or a shed. You need a length of 3in (8cm) plastic drainpipe, soil-warming cable that is twice the length of the pipe with a thermostat and control box, and an electricity supply. Cut 1in (2.5cm) wide sections to half the depth of the drainpipe to create slots at the spacings shown below. Double up the cable inside the pipe and tape it to the bottom. Raise the pipe up slightly on wooden blocks.

Melt some grafting wax until it is just warm to the touch; dip each graft and all of the scion in the wax to seal it and prevent desiccation. Place the grafted plants in the hot pipe, as shown below. Set the thermostat to maintain a temperature of 68–77°F (20–25°C) within the pipe. Successful grafts should callus within three weeks.

1 Cut 1in (2.5cm) wide slots in the pipe: 1in (2.5cm) apart for bare-root, or 3in (8cm) apart for pot-grown, rootstocks. Place each plant with its grafted area inside a slot.

2 Cover bare roots with moist soil to prevent drying out. Lay some capillary matting over the slots and secure with insulating tape.

Heaths and heathers

There are three principal genera of these shrubby evergreens: *Calluna*, a heather with only one species but many cultivars, flowering from midsummer to late autumn; *Daboecia*, a heather with two summer-flowering species, of which only *D. cantabrica* is grown in gardens; and *Erica*, a heath that includes many winter- and summer-flowering species and cultivars. Heaths and heathers range from groundcover plants to tree heaths up to 20ft (7m) tall. The majority need moist, acidic soil and full sun or an exposed site. Propagation of cultivars is vegetative, by layering or cuttings, because the seeds do not come true.

Taking cuttings

Of all the heathers, cuttings from *Daboecia* and *Erica* root most readily and are least prone to disease. Take semi-ripe cuttings (*see below*) from healthy, vigorous, nonflowering shoots. Some heaths are rarely out of flower, so it may be necessary to take cuttings of flowering shoots (*see below right*). Cuttings of the Australasian native heath (*Epacris*) are taken in early summer, as well as after a flowering flush.

Commerical nurseries do not remove leaves from cuttings, but it is a useful precaution against rot. Do not bother stripping off the tiny leaves of calluna shoots. Insert the cuttings in a well-drained and aerated medium. Rooting hormone is not needed. Do not use nitrogenous fertilizer in the medium: heaths and heathers are sensitive to the salts that these preparations contain. Species and cultivars root at differing rates, so insert the cuttings individually in cells, or several of one species or cultivar to a 5in (13cm) pot. For best results, root the cuttings in an enclosed space at 59–70°F (15–21°C). Heaths and heathers are prone to rot, so spray or water in a general fungicide and remember to ventilate the cuttings daily.

Pot up rooted cuttings singly before hardening them in spring (*see facing page*). Water the cuttings from below only when the medium has almost dried out to avoid problems with algae, liverworts, and mosses growing on the surface of the medium.

Alternatively, root the cuttings in a prepared bed in a sheltered place, such as in a cold frame; site the frame in the shade to avoid extreme variations of temperature affecting the cuttings. After 4–6 months, grow them on in a nursery bed with free-draining soil, or pot them singly. Leave in a sunny position until autumn, when they may be planted out.

Heaths and heathers are susceptible to vine weevils: apply a nematode drench in midsummer to the young plants and again in early autumn if they have not yet been planted out.

Semi-ripe cuttings

1 From late summer to autumn, select a strong, healthy, nonflowering sideshoot (here of Calluna vulgaris *'Robert Chapman'). Remove it with clean pruners, cutting straight across the stem about 4in (10cm) below the stem tip.*

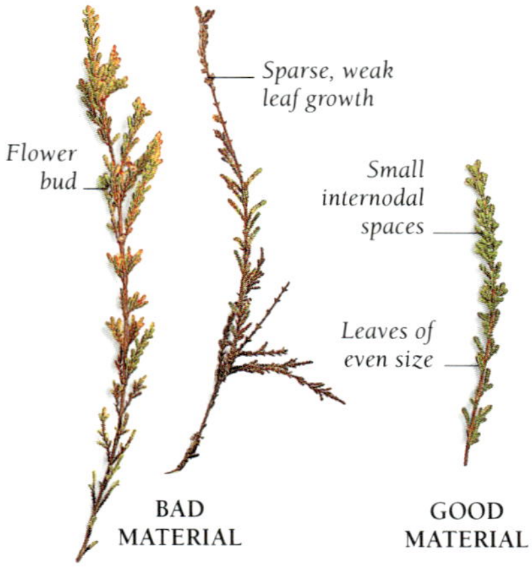

2 The cutting on the right, with its compact, even growth, should make a good plant. The two cuttings on the left are unlikely to be successful. They are weak and spindly, and the presence of flower buds will inhibit rooting.

Flowering shoots

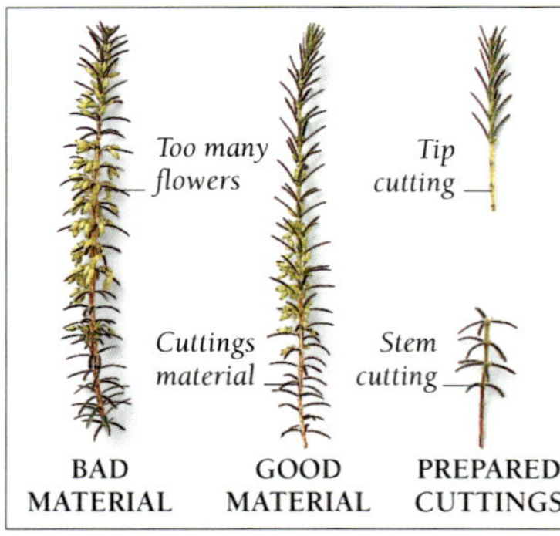

Choose a shoot of Erica carnea *that has only a few flower buds concentrated on one part of the stem, and take 2in (5cm) cuttings, one at the base and one from the tip. Prepare the cuttings* (see steps 3 and 4 below).

3 Trim each stem to a length of about 1½–2in (4–5cm). Holding the base of the cutting firm with your finger, cut straight across the stem at the appropriate point with a clean, sharp knife.

4 Strip leaves from Erica *and* Daboecia *cuttings: lightly hold each stem about one third from the base and quickly pull it through finger and thumb. Pinch out the tips of all cuttings* (see inset).

5 Fill cells or pots with a mixture of equal parts moist leaf mold and peat, or equal parts fine bark and peat. Insert the cuttings so that the lowest leaves are just resting on the surface. Do not firm in the cuttings.

6 Water in the cuttings with a general-purpose fungicide, using a watering can with a fine rose. Label the cuttings, then place them in a closed case – a heated one speeds rooting. Allow to root in a place out of direct sunlight.

GROWING ON SEMI-RIPE CUTTINGS

1 The cuttings should root after 8–12 weeks. To keep them growing vigorously, begin feeding them regularly once a week with a low-nitrogen fertilizer such as for tomatoes. Pinch out the growing tips regularly to encourage formation of bushy new growth.

2 After 4–6 months, when the plants are well developed, pot them individually into 3in (8cm) pots of soilless potting mix, using an acidic formula for lime-hating heathers. Grow on outdoors, protecting from severe cold if needed to prevent young shoots from dying back.

3 From late summer onward, plant out the heaths and heathers in their final positions. For the best effect, plant them in irregular groups, spacing them 8–10in (20–25cm) apart. They should rapidly grow into one another to form large clumps.

Layering

In the wild, sandy soil drifts over heaths and heathers, which then root readily from the stems, so layering these plants is even easier than cuttings. Layered plants are not always as uniformly bushy as plants grown from cuttings, however.

Mix in a little sharp sand and peat into the soil in a shallow trench around the parent plant to provide a good, well-drained rooting medium. In early to midautumn or spring, bend down healthy, strong sideshoots and cover with a little of the prepared soil. Peg down the shoots with wire staples or weigh them down with small stones. There is no need to cut or wound the stems. One year later, cut off the rooted stems; grow on in a nursery bed or in pots for six months before planting out.

If only one or two rooted layers are required, simply prepare the soil beneath the chosen shoots (*see right*).

Alternatively, to layer a large number of shoots, lift the plant in midspring, dig out the hole, and replant, leaving one-third of the shoots exposed. This type of layering is "dropping" (*see right*).

Fill in between the shoots as shown. Other options, which make it easier to weed around the plant if the shoots are few, is to arrange them into a row or, if the shoots are not brittle, to press them around the edge of the hole to form a circle. Firm the soil to encourage the shoots to root into it.

Keep the plant well watered until autumn. Clear away the soil and remove the rooted cuttings, cutting just below the new roots on each stem. Discard the old plant. Pot the rooted layers and grow on as for cuttings (*see above*).

Sowing seeds

Raise species such as *Erica terminalis* and *Calluna vulgaris* from seeds. Sow in winter to early spring as for rhododendrons (*see p.138*). *Epacris* germinates better if treated with smoke (*see p.103*).

LAYERING

In spring, select a healthy shoot from around the edge of the plant. Work a little leaf mold or peat and grit or coarse sand into the soil below the shoot to promote drainage.

Bury the shoot in the prepared area of soil and place a stone over it to keep it in place. The following spring, lift the rooted layer, sever from the parent, and plant out.

DROPPING HEATHERS

1 In spring, lift a mature plant. Dig a hole deep enough to two-thirds bury the plant. "Drop" the plant into the hole and fill in with soil around the roots.

2 Work a mixture of equal parts grit and peat between the shoots up to soil level. Firm in gently and label.

3 Water the plant during dry spells. By autumn, the buried sections of the stems should have formed roots. Lift the whole plant and sever the rooted shoots from the parent plant. Pot them singly to grow on or plant them out in a sheltered spot.

Roses

Contrary to common belief, all roses, whether species roses, old garden roses, or modern cultivars, are easily increased, even by gardeners with only limited space.

Roses are propagated in basically three ways. Cuttings are easiest for the gardener, although they are not recommended for producing high-quality plants from most modern hybrid tea or floribunda roses. Grafting or T-budding roses, methods favored by commercial growers, require some planning and rootstocks that have been grown on in advance, but they usually produce more vigorous plants.

Raising roses from seeds can be challenging and is usually most reliable with species roses. However, the rose is a classic candidate for hybridization, and some amateur rose growers have produced worthwhile cultivars.

HARDWOOD CUTTINGS

Selecting suitable stems *In late summer or autumn, take well-ripened, healthy, woody shoots from the current season's growth, approximately 12–24 in (30–60cm) long.*

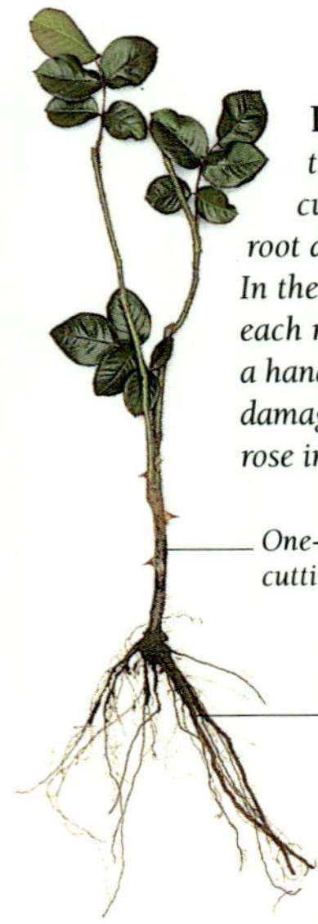

Rooted cutting *By the following spring, the cuttings should start to root and produce new shoots. In the following autumn, lift each rooted cutting (left) with a hand fork, taking care not to damage the roots. Plant the new rose in its permanent position.*

Taking cuttings

Hardwood cuttings are most successful from miniature, groundcover, and species roses, as well as some older *Rosa wichurana* (syn. *R. wichuraiana*) ramblers; they are taken in much the same way as for other shrubs (*see p.100*).

Although a controlled environment and a little care are required, increasing roses from softwood cuttings has proved very effective for some of the more difficult species and cultivars such as *R. banksiae* and *R.* 'Mermaid', as well as for mass-production of pot roses.

Hardwood cuttings of roses

First prepare a slit trench in semi-shade, about 8in (20cm) deep, and sprinkle some sharp sand along the bottom to improve the drainage. Gather suitable shoots (*see above*), cutting each at an angle just above an outward-facing bud. Place the shoots in damp newspaper or moss to prevent them from drying out before they can be prepared. Divide the stems into 9in (23cm) lengths, removing all but the top two leaves and cutting through a bud at the base of each cutting. There is no need to leave a heel.

Dip the base of the cuttings first in water, then in hormone rooting powder, and place in the trench 4–6in (10–15cm) apart. Fill in the trench and hill it up so that the leaves are at soil level. Firm and water in well. In dry conditions, protect the cuttings with a black plastic mulch. Rooted cuttings may be planted out in a year (*see above*). Quicker results may be obtained by rooting 3in (8cm) cuttings in rooting medium in 3in (8cm) pots under cover, supplying bottom heat of approximately 21°C (70°F) in a closed case or on a propagating blanket (*see p.41*). The rooted cuttings should be ready for planting out by the following spring. This works particularly well for most groundcover and miniature roses.

Softwood cuttings of roses

Cuttings should be taken from plants that have been encouraged to produce young wood by pruning them hard in early spring, preferably in a protected environment such as a greenhouse. The first new shoots from garden plants may also be used as cuttings, if they have not

TAKING SOFTWOOD CUTTINGS OF ROSES

1 In early to midsummer, choose healthy shoots (here of Rosa banksiae*) of the current season's growth. Remove each by cutting just above a node with pruners. Immediately place the cuttings in a plastic bag to keep them fresh.*

2 Cut each shoot into sections, cutting above each node along the stem, so that each internodal cutting retains one leaf at the top. Discard the growing tip: it is too soft to root. Trim the leaflets to reduce moisture loss.

3 Immerse each cutting in fungicidal solution, then dip its base in hormone rooting powder. Insert the cuttings in 1in (2.5cm) deep holes in large plugs of rockwool, or space them 2in (5cm) apart in seed soil mix in deep seed trays.

been exposed to herbicides. This simple technique does not work for hybrid teas and grandifloras, however.

Early to midspring is the best time to take softwood stem-tip cuttings, when new shoots are only 1½–2in (4–5cm) long and need no trimming. Internodal stem cuttings from longer soft shoots may be taken in summer (*see facing page*). Treat all cuttings with systemic fungicide to prevent rot and hormone rooting compound to aid rooting. When inserting the cuttings into the medium or rockwool, ensure they do not touch.

Maintain high humidity around the cuttings by tenting them in a plastic bag or placing them in a closed case or mist unit (*see p.44*). Provide bottom heat of about 81°F (27°C) at first, then after four weeks or so, reduce it to 64–70°F (18–21°C). Harden off the rooted cuttings by gradually reducing the time they are covered. Pot them singly into 3in (8cm) pots in a soilless mix.

A reasonably sized plant can be produced in this way in two months or so. Cut back the young plants by about 50 percent to ensure bushy growth. The prunings provide very good material for further propagation – this is a common practice in commercial nurseries.

Dividing rose suckers

Some roses, particularly rugosas and the Scotch rose (*R. pimpinellifolia*) cultivars, are often grown from hardwood cuttings on their own roots, rather than grafted onto different rootstocks. Suckers, freely produced by these roses, are therefore true to type and can be removed and planted out. This is particularly useful if many plants are desired, perhaps for a hedge. Lift suckers when not in active growth with a reasonable length of root (*see below*), and replant immediately.

DIVIDING A ROSE SUCKER

In late autumn or early spring, select a well-developed sucker and, using pruners, sever it from the rootstock, retaining as many roots as possible. Prepare a hole wide and deep enough for the roots. Plant immediately, water, and firm.

Grafting

Standard grafting and T-budding (*see pp.114–15*) involve uniting material from two different roses to combine the virtues of both. A scion or bud from the topgrowth of the rose to be propagated is united with a rootstock selected for its vigor and hardiness. Grafting roses requires a warm, humid environment under cover but allows large quantities of new plants to be produced in the same growing season. Budding is done in the open garden, but it takes much longer.

Grafting roses

Grafting is most appropriate for miniature roses and some groundcover kinds; it is used extensively to produce plants for the cut-flower industry.

Conventional seedling rootstocks, such as *R. laxa* or *R. chinensis* 'Major', are used for commercial grafting and may be obtainable by the gardener from specialized nurseries. They are graded according to the diameter of the stem, or "neck": roughly 3/16–1/5in or 1/3–1/2in (5–8mm or 8–12mm).

The rootstocks are brought into the greenhouse early in the year, and must be heeled in into a 7in (18cm) deep peat bed, supplied with bottom heat of 64°F (18°C) to encourage growth.

The type of graft used is similar to that used to rind graft fruit trees (*see p.63*). Take semi-ripe shoots as they develop in spring for use as scions. Cut the shoots into short lengths, each with a bud and one leaf (*see above*). Trim the base of each stem into a wedge by removing a sliver from one side of the stem. Lift the rootstocks, then remove the topgrowth with a straight cut at the top of each "neck" just below the branches. Slit the bark, insert a prepared scion under the flaps (*see above*), and secure with thin thread or grafting tape.

Pot each grafted rootstock in seed soil mix and place in a closed case or mist unit at a temperature of 59–75°F (15–24°C). Leave for about four weeks until the graft calluses and the scion begins to grow. Pot on into 5in (13cm) pot. Harden off over six weeks, then plant in final positions in late spring.

GRAFTING ROSES

1 Select a semi-ripe shoot of the current season's growth. Take a stem cutting with one leaf stalk. Make an angled cut above the top node and cut the bottom 1in (2.5cm) of the stem into a wedge shape.

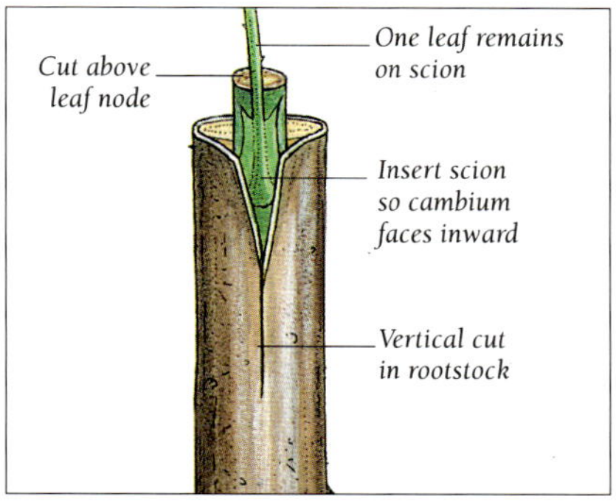

2 Cut straight across the top of the "neck" of the rootstock, using pruners. From the top, make a vertical cut in the bark, 1in (2.5cm) in length, and gently open up the bark flaps. Slide the scion into the cut and bind securely.

How to propagate each type of rose

Hybrid Tea (Large-flowered bush) roses Grafting, T-budding, hybridizing.
Floribunda (Cluster-flowered bush) roses Grafting, T-budding, hybridizing.
Miniature roses Hardwood and softwood cuttings, grafting for container-grown plants, T-budding, hybridizing.
Groundcover roses Hardwood cuttings, grafting, T-budding, hybridizing.
Climbing and rambler roses Hardwood cuttings for some of the older *Rosa wichurana* ramblers, softwood cuttings for difficult subjects such as *Rosa banksiae* cultivars and *Rosa* 'Mermaid', T-budding, hybridizing.
Modern shrub roses Hardwood cuttings, T-budding, hybridizing.
Old garden roses Hardwood cuttings, division, T-budding.
Species roses Hardwood cuttings, division, T-budding, seeds.

HIPS OF *ROSA* 'FRU DAGMAR HASTRUP'

T-BUDDING ROSES

Until the advent of hybrid tea (large-flowered bush) roses, all roses were grown from cuttings. As breeding progressed, many cultivars lost the ability to develop a satisfactory root system. Budding onto a more vigorous rootstock had long been used for other plants, and by the mid-nineteenth century it was adopted as the principal method of propagation for all types of rose in commercial nurseries. Although slow and a little more challenging for the gardener, it is still the best way of producing high-quality plants from garden cultivars.

Stocks for budding roses may be available during winter from specialized nurseries. They are graded according to the "neck" size, roughly 3/16–1/3in or 1/3–1/2in (5–8mm or 8–12mm), and various stocks are available in different regions (*see box, right*), but most are compatible with any cultivar. If the soil is frozen or too wet, the stocks should be heeled in until they can be planted in early spring. The planting site should be weed-free and prepared well beforehand by digging in compost or well-rotted manure.

Commercial growers plant stocks 8in (20cm) apart in rows 3ft (90cm) apart. Small quantities may be planted singly in holes made with a stick or in a slit trench (*see below*). If they are not already trimmed, cut back the topgrowth to 9in (23cm) and the roots to 6in (15cm). The neck should be covered with soil up to, but not above, the branches to keep the bark moist and supple at the point where the bud is to be inserted. Firm the soil well. Water only in very dry conditions, and control weeds to prevent competition. Budwood for use in budding is taken from the roses to be propagated at the beginning of the summer, after the stems have ripened, or hardened, and have begun to flower. A good test of whether the wood is ready is to break off some thorns: with the majority of cultivars they should come away cleanly.

Gather the budsticks (*see below right*) and store in damp moss or newspaper in a cool place until needed, labeling them carefully. Never stand them in water;

SEED-RAISED ROOTSTOCKS

ROSA LAXA Popular stock; universally produces high-quality plants, almost free from suckers. Tends to go dry (reduced sap flow) in midsummer, thus early budding is essential. Rust disease was a problem but is now easily controlled with suitable rose fungicide. Principal stock available to gardeners in UK.

R. CANINA 'INERMIS' Almost as popular as *R. laxa*, particularly in Mediterranean areas.

R. 'DR. HUEY' Popular stock in southern California, Arizona, and southeastern Australia; tolerates dry, alkaline soils.

R. x FORTUNEANA Deep-rooted rose, good for sandy soils in warm climates, such as Western Australia.

ROOTSTOCKS GROWN FROM CUTTINGS

R. MULTIFLORA Roots very easily; in warm climates can be T-budded eight weeks after rooting. Common in eastern Australia and New Zealand. Good for weeping forms.

R. CANINA cultivars.

R. 'DR. HUEY'

R. CHINENSIS 'MAJOR' Used widely in hot climates; tolerates dry, alkaline soils.

ROOTSTOCKS FOR STANDARD ROSES

R. CANINA (Wild dog rose) Traditional standard stock.

R. MULTIFLORA, R. POLMERIANA, R. RUGOSA and cultivars.

Local advice on the most suitable stocks may be obtained from any large rose nursery.

T-BUDDING: PLANTING THE ROOTSTOCK

1 In early spring, dig a V-shaped trench with a spade, deep enough for the roots of the rootstock (here Rosa laxa*) to be accommodated. Place the stock in the trench.*

2 Fill in the trench and firm in the soil gently, then hill up around the neck of the stock as far as the base of the branches. Label and water in well.

T-BUDDING: PREPARING THE BUDSTICK

1 In early summer, cut off lengths of vigorous, ripening, flowering shoots, about 12in (30cm) long. Make an angled cut at the base of each shoot just above a bud.

2 Remove the soft topgrowth and leaves from each budstick. Cut each leaf stalk about 1/4in (5mm) from the stem to leave a handle. Label and keep moist.

T-BUDDING: PREPARING THE ROOTSTOCK

1 In midsummer, uncover the "neck" of the rootstock by gently easing the soil away with a hand fork. This should be done just before preparing the bud, so that the neck of the stock does not dry out.

2 Clean the bark of the stem gently using a soft, dry cloth. This will remove any soil or grit, which could blunt the blade of the budding knife.

3 Make a 1/4in (5mm) horizontal cut into the bark, about 1in (2.5cm) below the topgrowth. Then make a vertical cut upward to join the horizontal cut so that they form a T-shaped incision.

4 Using the reverse blade of the knife, gently pry open the flaps of bark created by the two cuts. The thin, green cambium will be revealed underneath. The stock is now ready to receive the bud.

T-BUDDING: PREPARING THE BUD

1 *Hold a budstick so that the buds point upward. Snap off the thorns from the stick, making sure that no snags remain.*

2 *Insert the knife about ¼in (5mm) away from a leaf stalk. With a straight, scooping action, cut out the stalk and the bud, together with a 1in (2.5cm) long "tail."*

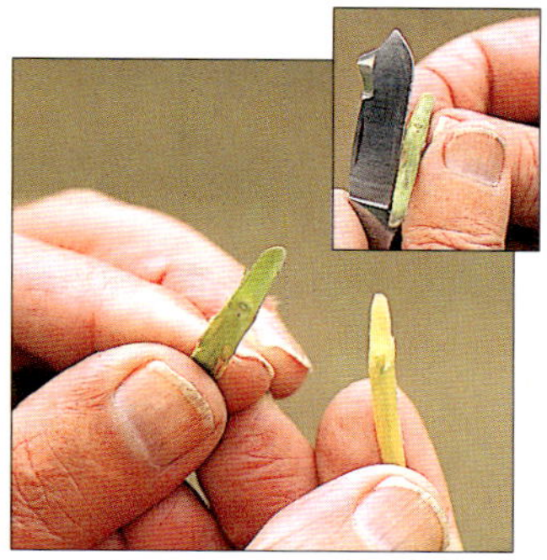

3 *Hold the bud by its tail and peel away the wood from the green bark. Discard the wood. Trim off the tail (see inset) to leave a scion that is about ½in (1cm) long.*

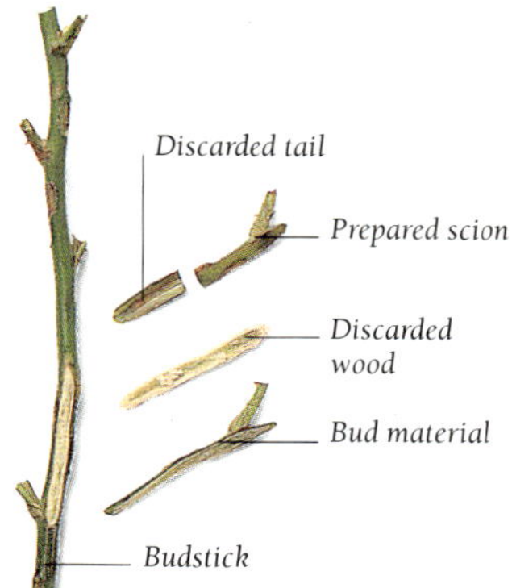

BUDSTICK MATERIAL *Each stage in the preparation of the bud or scion involves discarding different parts of the budstick (see above).*

T-BUDDING: UNITING THE GRAFT

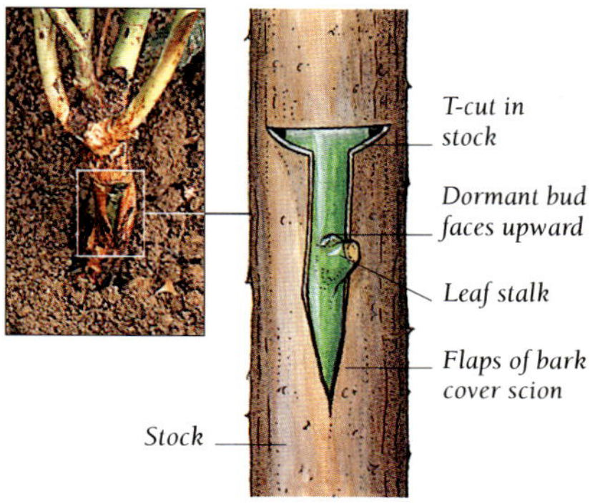

1 *Hold the scion by the leaf stalk and slip the tapered end under the bark flaps in the rootstock (see above left). Sit the bud neatly under the flaps; if needed, trim the scion across the top so it fits in the T-cut (see above right).*

2 *To ensure close contact between the scion and stock, secure a rubber grafting patch (see inset) around the graft, pinning it on the side opposite the bud. As the stock heals and calluses over, the rubber patch will rot off.*

THE FOLLOWING SPRING *In early spring, cut off the top of the stock with pruners, just above the dormant bud. For a stronger, multistemmed plant, cut back the shoot emerging from the bud (see inset) to 3in (8cm) or more in late spring.*

T-BUDDING ONTO A STANDARD ROOTSTOCK

USING MULTIPLE BUDS *Insert two or three buds, 3in (8cm) apart, around the stock stem, at a height of 3½–4ft (1.1–1.2m) from the ground. Secure each with a rubber patch.*

CUTTING BACK IN SPRING *In spring, cut back the stock just above the new shoots that are developing from the grafted buds.*

they will rot at the base. Budsticks may be kept until midsummer, which is the most suitable time for budding. In warm climates, buds taken in late summer should shoot in the following spring.

Newcomers to budding should get in plenty of practice at cutting, using young willow sticks, before attempting to bud the roses. The actual process should be carried out quickly to prevent the bud or neck from drying out.

When ready for budding, remove the soil from around the stock stem. Prepare the neck to receive the bud by making a T-shaped cut in the bark (*see facing page*). Cut out a bud on a shield-shaped sliver of bark from a budstick and then remove the wood (*see top*); the prepared bud is known as the scion. Insert the scion into the T-cut and secure with a budding patch (*see above*).

The graft should heal in 3–4 weeks. In cold climates, the rootstock should be hilled up for the winter to protect it, but this is not necessary in milder climates. If it has been hilled up, uncover the budded stock in early spring. Cut back the stock to just above the dormant bud, using very sharp pruners. As the season progresses, the bud should begin to grow. It is a good idea to prune back the new shoot (*see above*) to encourage a bushy plant. If a vigorous climber has been budded, it will need staking as it develops. By early autumn, the rose will mature sufficiently to transplant to its permanent position.

T-BUDDING STANDARD ROSES

The method of budding is the same as for bush roses, but usually two or three buds are inserted around the stem to obtain a balanced head (*see left*). The height of the buds above soil level determines the type of standard: 2ft (60cm) produces a half standard; 3ft (90cm) gives a full standard; 4ft (1.2m) yields a shrub or weeping standard.

In theory, all roses can be grown as standard plants, but many will look ugly simply because of their upright habit. The best results can be obtained from cultivars of miniature and floribunda roses, groundcover roses, some lax-growing shrub roses, and the older *wichurana* ramblers that will grow into weeping standards. Standard stems require staking to avoid wind damage.

Roses from seeds

All species or wild roses can be grown from seeds to obtain seedlings identical to their parents. The greatest problem is germinating the seeds, which can take as long as two seasons. In order to overcome their dormancy, the seeds need to be stratified or chilled before sowing (*see p.103*). Rosehips ripen in mid- to late autumn; many cultivar hips are green when ripe, not red like those of species. Seeds may be stratified before or after extracting them from the hips.

Seeds extracted from freshly collected hips (*see right*) should be placed either in a plastic bag or in a seed tray in moist peat, vermiculite, or sand. Label and keep the seeds at about 70°F (21°C) until late winter, then chill the seeds by placing the bag or tray in the refrigerator at just above freezing (35°F/2°C) for 3–4 weeks.

The seeds can then be sown in cells (*see right*) and left in a cool, sheltered place such as a cold frame. They may take a year to germinate. Pot the seedlings when they have their first true leaves, then grow on until they are established. Harden off the seedlings (*see p.45*), and pot on as necessary until they are large enough to be planted out.

In cold climates, the hips may be layered 2in (5cm) deep in a container in moist peat, vermiculite, or coarse sand and left outdoors for 12–15 months in a cool, shady place. This allows the seedcoats to break down naturally. In the early spring of the second year, remove and clean the stratified seeds (*see above*), then sow them in an outdoor seedbed. Prepare the seedbed with 4in (10cm) of a soil-based seed mix.

Sow the seeds 1–2in (2.5–5cm) apart and cover them with ½in (1cm) of seed soil mix or fine soil and ½in (1cm) of fine gravel. Germination can take as long as two months. Transplant the seedling roses into a nursery bed in the following autumn and plant them out in the garden 2–3 years later.

Hybridizing roses

The production of new cultivars by crossing two different roses and then selecting the best of the seedlings is a time-consuming, but exciting, exercise for commercial growers; it is also enjoyed by many home gardeners.

Expert breeders consider the parents' chromosomal makeup and employ a strategy of using genes in the parents, not necessarily commercial cultivars, which have been selected for their desirable features. For the first-time hybridizer, it is more practical to use as parents modern cultivars that are fertile and are known to yield a good harvest of hips. Select roses whose characteristics you wish to perpetuate, such as disease resistance, habit, flower form, scent, or color. In practice, two popular named cultivars, when crossed, will rarely produce anything of commercial significance.

Many species crossed with a cultivar will produce sterile progeny. If a repeat-flowering, or remontant, rose is crossed with a nonremontant rose, it will probably yield nonremontant seedlings.

Growing species roses from seeds

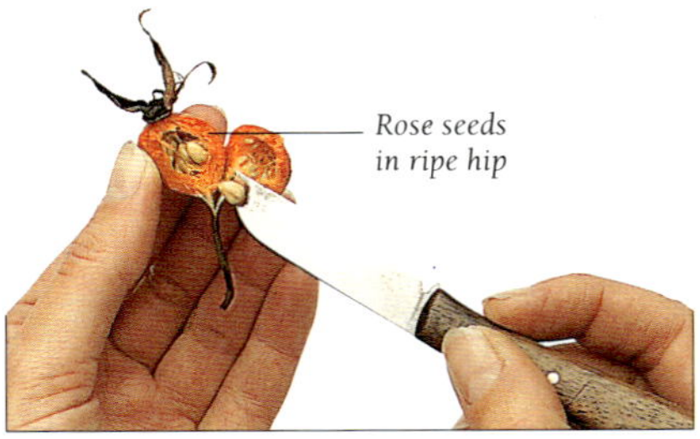

1 In autumn, cut open a ripe hip taken from the parent plant with a clean, sharp knife. Use the reverse of the knife blade to flick out the individual seeds.

2 Put the seeds into a clear plastic bag containing peat, and keep it at about 70°F (21°C) for 2–3 months. Then place the bag in a refrigerator for 3–4 weeks.

3 Fill a cell tray with a mix of one part sand to one part peat substitute (or peat). Sow the seeds singly and cover to their own depth with grit. Label. Place in a cold frame.

4 When the seedlings have their first pairs of true leaves, transplant them singly into 2in (5cm) pots filled with a soil-based potting mix. Put the pots back into the cold frame.

Hybridizing: preparing the pollen parent

1 To collect pollen for immediate use, take a partly open flower, cutting just above a node, and keep it indoors in water.

2 Once the flower is fully open and the anthers have split to reveal the pollen (usually after 24 hours), gently pull off all the flower petals. The anthers should be left intact.

3 The exposed anthers are now ready to release their pollen. Brush a clean camel-hair brush over the anthers to collect the pollen.

Storing rose pollen

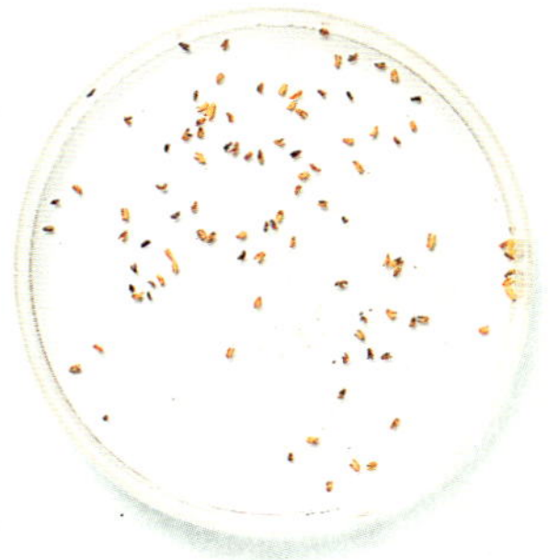

Anthers may be gathered up to one month before hybridizing and stored in a clean dish. When ripe, the pollen looks fluffy.

HYBRIDIZING: PREPARING THE SEED PARENT

1 Choose a healthy flower that is not fully open and not yet pollinated on the seed parent.

2 Pull off the petals with a quick twist, working inward, to reveal the immature anthers.

3 Carefully pluck out the anthers with tweezers. Do not damage the stigmas. Leave for 24–48 hours.

4 Transfer the ripe pollen onto the now sticky stigmas using a camel-hair brush or a clean finger.

5 Label the pollinated flower with the name of the pollen parent and allow to ripen. Flowers on the same seed parent may be fertilized with pollen from different roses.

Hybridized seedlings
Rose seedlings grown from hybridized seeds should be raised to flowering size in a nursery bed in a cool greenhouse or frost-free place.

A selection can then be made based on foliage and flower color. This can vary enormously among seedlings from the same parents (see left). Many will be pink or vermilion.

The best results in hybridizing roses are achieved in a controlled environment free from insect pollinators. A well-ventilated greenhouse is ideal, but an elaborate heating system is not needed except in very cold climates. A large greenhouse also provides more even temperatures. Hygiene is of greater importance, and in early autumn the greenhouse must be thoroughly washed down and disinfected (*see p.38*). Allow sufficient time for the greenhouse to air and dry out before bringing in plants.

Of the two roses selected for hybridizing, one acts as a pollen (male) parent, providing ripe pollen, and one as the seed (female) parent, producing hips and seeds. Many-petaled roses do not produce much pollen, while some roses may not form well-developed hips. Weather also exerts an influence.

Pot the chosen parents in rich potting mix in large containers and leave outdoors in early autumn. Bring into the greenhouse in midwinter at a minimum of 40°F (4.5°C), where they can develop. Prune bush roses lightly after a month inside. On sunny days provide good ventilation and water lightly, but do not feed them. By midspring, young shoots should be developing.

Pollinating the seed parent

Prepare the pollen parent first (*see facing page*) to gather the pollen: ripe pollen looks floury or fluffy in texture. Pollen can be gathered up to a month before the seed parent is ready if necessary, but it must be kept very dry.

The flower of the seed parent must be well developed but not fully open; the anthers will still be immature and will not yet have pollinated the flower. Remove the petals and anthers of the seed parent (*see above*), making sure that no fragments are left, because these may allow rot fungi to attack the plant. Within 24–48 hours, the stigmas will be ripe and sticky and ready to receive pollen from the male flower. Once it is pollinated, label the seed parent with the names of both parents. If using pollen from different parents for different flowers, clean the brush thoroughly between applications.

If successful, the hip should develop and ripen by midautumn. Remove any new buds or shoots as they appear, keep watering to a minimum, and do not feed the rose to keep new growth to a minimum. Do, however, provide ample ventilation. If the pollination was unsuccessful, the hip will rot or shrivel.

Care of hybridized seedlings

In autumn, extract and stratify seeds in sand from successful hips, as for species roses (*see facing page*). Sow the seeds in a prepared seedbed under cover, such as in a cool greenhouse. Water as required, but avoid excessive watering. Rose seedlings can sometimes be subject to dieback or rot, usually as a result of overwatering or extreme temperatures. Strict hygiene, using a complete rose fungicide, is the only answer.

Expect to see germination within two months and growth of 9–18in (23–45cm) in the first year, when most of the new plants will bear small blooms. Since the parentage is known, the color and form of the blooms will provide clues to the eventual plant. A lack of blooms indicates that the seedlings are only summer-flowering: select more reliable repeat-blooming parents next time.

In midsummer, choose the best three or four seedlings and T-bud them onto rootstocks outdoors (*see p.114*). In the following year, the full results of the hybridization will become evident. The hybridizer should build up a stock of the most promising cultivars throughout the following seasons, disposing of the less choice hybrids along the way.

A–Z OF SHRUBS AND CLIMBING PLANTS

ABELIA

SOFTWOOD CUTTINGS in spring
GREENWOOD CUTTINGS from late spring
SEMI-RIPE CUTTINGS from early to late summer

Cuttings of these deciduous and evergreen shrubs root very readily in a closed case or mist bench. Softwood cuttings (*see p.100*) from the first flush of growth root in 2–4 weeks. In colder regions, do not pot greenwood cuttings (*see p.101*) taken after midsummer; prune cuttings for a bushy habit, but allow new growth time to ripen – if not well established, they overwinter badly. Keep semi-ripe cuttings (*see p.95*) taken in late summer frost-free. Plants flower in 1–2 years.

ALLAMANDA

Allamanda cathartica

CUTTINGS throughout summer
DIVISION in spring

The evergreen shrubs and scrambling climbers in this genus root readily from greenwood nodal stem cuttings (*see p.101*). Take 2–3in (5–8cm) cuttings and root in humidity with bottom heat of 59°F (15°C). Cuttings should root in 6–8 weeks and flower in 2–3 years.

Alternatively, for instant new plants, divide clumps of mature specimens (*see p.101*), cut back hard, and replant.

AMELANCHIER *JUNEBERRY, SHADBUSH*

CUTTINGS in late spring
DIVISION in early spring
SEEDS in autumn or spring
LAYERING at any time

Many shrubby species in this genus produce suckers and are easily divided. They also hybridize readily, so seeds may not come true. New plants flower in 2–3 years.

CUTTINGS

For best results, take softwood cuttings (*see p.100*) once the new growth is no more than 4in (10cm) long.

DIVISION

Divide clump-forming species (*see p.101*); lift and replant rooted suckers (*see p.101*) of *Amelanchier canadensis*.

SEEDS

Gather seeds from ripe, black fruits and sow fresh in summer or autumn (*see p.103*). If stored, dry seeds have hard coats: sow in spring (*see p.104*) to germinate the next spring; or, before sowing, warm and then cold stratify (*see p.103*) the seeds to hasten germination.

LAYERING

The technique of simple layering (*see p.106*) is effective for all species in this genus, especially *A. lamarckii*.

ABUTILON *FLOWERING MAPLE, INDIAN MALLOW, PARLOR MAPLE*

SOFTWOOD, GREENWOOD AND SEMI-RIPE CUTTINGS at any time
HARDWOOD CUTTINGS in autumn
SEEDS in early spring

Most of the evergreen and deciduous flowering shrubs in this genus can be increased from soft- or greenwood cuttings (*see pp.100–101*) at any time. If using the cuttings for summer bedding, take them as nodal stem-tip cuttings in late summer. Root as for *Abelia* (*see above*), pot, and provide a minimum winter temperature of 41°F (5°C). For *Abutilon megapotamicum*, *A. pictum* 'Thompsonii', and their related cultivars, use semi-ripe stem cuttings (*see p.95*). Hardwood cuttings (*see p.98*) of both *A.* x *suntense* and *A. vitifolium* root well; keep them frost-free.

Sow seeds (*see pp.103–4*), gathered from dry seedpods. Germination is rapid under cover, but watch for whitefly and spider mite (*see p.47*). It usually takes two years for new plants to flower.

ACTINIDIA *KIWI FRUIT, CHINESE GOOSEBERRY, SILVER VINE*

GREENWOOD OR SEMI-RIPE CUTTINGS in early summer
HARDWOOD CUTTINGS in late autumn to midwinter
SEEDS in spring or autumn
LAYERING in autumn
GRAFTING in late winter

Cuttings are the easiest way to increase most of these mainly deciduous climbers. Greenwood is best for *Actinidia deliciosa* (syn. *A. chinensis*) and *A. kolomikta*; semi-ripe or hardwood for *A. arguta*; hardwood for *A. deliciosa*. Seed-raised species grow rapidly. New plants flower and fruit in 2–3 years.

CUTTINGS

For greenwood cuttings (*see p.101*), use hormone rooting compound and reduce *A. deliciosa* leaves to 2in (5cm). Take shoots for semi-ripe and hardwood cuttings (*see p.95 and p.98*) that are not too vigorous and prone to rot.

SEEDS

A male and female plant are needed for fruits (*see right*). Seeds germinate at once if sown fresh; spring sowings need a three-month cold period (*see p.103*).

LAYERING

If only one or two plants are needed, simple layering (*see p.106*) works well for all forms.

GRAFTING

For named cultivars, use a whip-and-tongue graft with seedling rootstocks (*see p.59*). Grafted plants tend to be more vigorous than cuttings.

EXTRACTING ACTINIDIA SEEDS FROM FRUITS
Slice a ripe fruit (here of A. deliciosa*) in half. Flick out the seeds with the tip of a knife. Place the seeds into a fine-meshed sieve and wash off the pulp under running water before drying and storing the seeds. Alternatively, sow seeds fresh in a container without washing them.*

AUCUBA *JAPANESE LAUREL*

CUTTINGS from late summer
SEEDS in autumn
LAYERING in spring and autumn

Of these evergreen shrubs, only *Aucuba japonica* is commonly grown. Semi-ripe cuttings can be easily rooted in a sheltered nursery bed, such as in a cold frame (*see p.95*) If preferred, reduce the foliage for ease of handling; bottom heat at 70°F (21°C) speeds rooting, in 6–8 weeks. Leave the cuttings until spring before potting. New plants mature in 3–4 years.

Gather seeds from ripe berries (*see below*); sow fresh in autumn (*see p.103*). Germination may take 18 months.

Simple layering (*see p.106*) works well; layers can be planted out in 12 months.

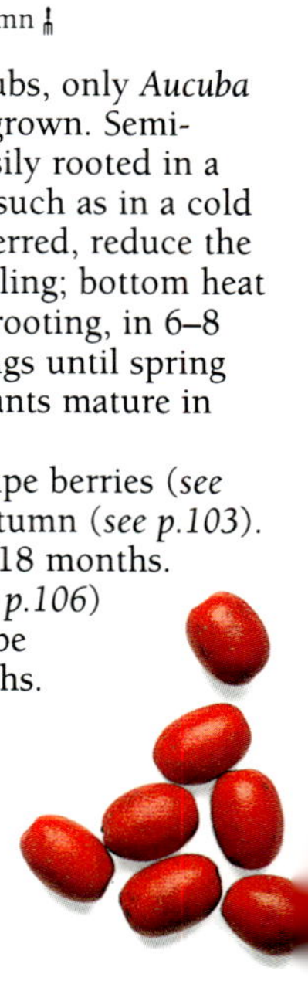

AUCUBA BERRIES
Rub the berries in a rough cloth to remove the flesh from the large seeds.

BERBERIS *BARBERRY*

SEMI-RIPE CUTTINGS from midsummer
MALLET CUTTINGS in early summer or autumn
HARDWOOD CUTTINGS from late autumn to midwinter
DIVISION at any time
SEEDS in late winter or early spring
GRAFTING in late winter

These are deciduous and evergreen, thorny shrubs. Cuttings can be tricky, so divide mound-forming species or graft less ready-rooting cultivars. New plants usually take at least two years to flower.

Cuttings from semi-ripe wood (*see p.95*) root most quickly, especially in rockwool plugs (*see p.35*). Mallet cuttings (*see below*) are best for *Berberis* x *lologensis* and its cultivars. Both types respond to hormone rooting compound. Protect semi-ripe and evergreen hardwood cuttings (*see p.99*) with a cold frame or cloche in colder climates.

Mound-forming species such as *B. buxifolia* can be divided (*see p.101*) in any season, but spring and autumn division gives the best results.

Seeds gathered from ripe fruits need a short period of chilling to break their dormancy. Layer the berries in sand (*see p.103*), or sow outside or in pots (*see p.104*) to germinate by summer.

Propagate *B.* x *lologensis, B. linearifolia,* and their cultivars by spliced side grafts (*see p.109*) onto cutting-raised, one-year-old rootstocks of *B.* x *ottawensis*.

TAKING MALLET CUTTINGS

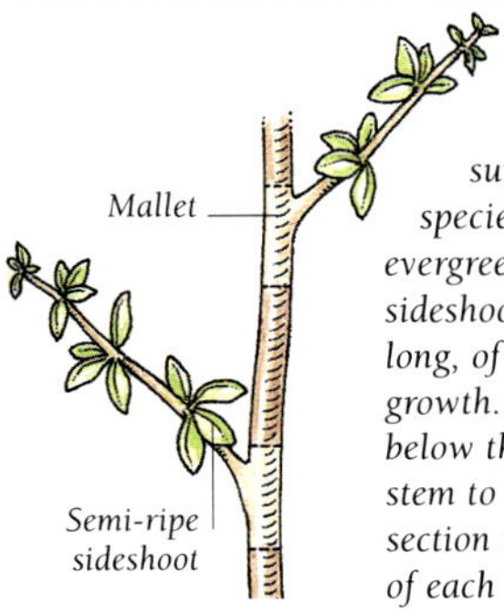

1 Take mallet cuttings from last year's stems, in early summer for deciduous species or autumn for evergreens. Choose short sideshoots, about 4in (10cm) long, of the current season's growth. Cut just above and below the joint on the main stem to leave a ½in (1cm) section (mallet) at the base of each cutting.

2 Remove the lower leaves and soft tip of each sideshoot. Slit the mallet lengthwise if its diameter is more than ¼in (5mm). Then treat the cuttings as semi-ripe cuttings. This method gives thin-stemmed cuttings a more substantial base from which to produce roots.

BOUGAINVILLEA

Bougainvillea glabra 'Variegata'

SOFTWOOD OR SEMI-RIPE CUTTINGS in summer
HARDWOOD CUTTINGS in winter
LAYERING in late winter and early spring

Layering is usually a more effective method than cuttings in colder climates for propagating the deciduous and evergreen, scrambling climbers in this genus. New plants generally flower in 2–3 years.

CUTTINGS

Softwood or semi-ripe cuttings (*see pp.100 and 95*), 2–3in (5–8cm) long, taken with a heel or a piece of last year's growth (*see p.96*), will root in 4–6 weeks if kept humid. Bottom heat of 59°F (15°C) speeds the process.

Root hardwood cuttings (*see p.98*) in deep pots on a heated bench at 70°F (21°C) in colder climates. In warm, humid climates they may be rooted outdoors; they take up to three months to root but form sturdy plants.

LAYERING

Use either simple or serpentine layering (*see pp.106–7*); container-grown plants may be layered into pots and separated.

OTHER SHRUBS AND CLIMBING PLANTS

ABELIOPHYLLUM Take softwood to semi-ripe cuttings (*see pp. 100–101 and 95*). Simple layer in spring (*see p.106*). Sow seeds in autumn (*see p.104*).
ACACIA Take semi-ripe cuttings (*see p.95*). Soak seeds in hot water (*see p.103*); sow in spring at 70–77°F (21–25°C).
ACALYPHA Root softwood or stem-tip cuttings (*see p.100–01*) at 70–81°F (21–27°C). Divide clumps (*see p.101*) in spring.
ACCA Root semi-ripe cuttings (*see p.95*) in a frost-free place or under protection with bottom heat. Sow seeds as for *Fatsia* (*see p.128*).
AESCULUS Sow fresh seeds outside in autumn (*see p.103*). Divide suckers (*see p.101*).
AKEBIA Take greenwood cuttings (*see p.101*) in late spring to midsummer. Sow seeds in spring after a short period of cold stratification (*see pp.103–4*). Serpentine layering (*see p.107*) gives best results.
ALOYSIA Take softwood to semi-ripe cuttings from spring to midsummer as for *Caryopteris* (*see p.121*).
ALYOGYNE Root semi-ripe cuttings (*see p.95*) with gentle bottom heat. Sow seeds in spring (*see p.104*).
AMPELOPSIS Take softwood to greenwood cuttings as for *Parthenocissus* (*see p.136*). Sow seeds in autumn (*see p.103*).
APHELANDRA Take greenwood cuttings (*see p.101*); use 68–77°F (20–25°C) bottom heat.
ARALIA Take root cuttings of species as for *Celastrus* (*see p.122*). Divide suckers as for *Amelanchier* (*see p.118*). Sow fresh seeds in autumn (*see p.103*). Spliced side graft variegated forms (*see p.109*).
ARCTOSTAPHYLOS Take semi-ripe cuttings (*see p.95*) in autumn. Soak seeds in hot water; sow in autumn (*see pp.103–4*).
ARDISIA Take softwood to semi-ripe cuttings in summer as for *Hibiscus rosa-sinensis* (*see p.131*). Sow seeds as for *Passiflora* (*see p.136*).
ARGYRANTHEMUM Take softwood to semi-ripe, nodal stem-tip cuttings (*see pp.101 and 95*).
ARISTOLOCHIA Take softwood cuttings (*see p.100*) of tender species in spring; for hardier ones, take greenwood cuttings (*see p.101*) until midsummer. Sow seeds in spring (*see p.104*).
ARONIA Root softwood to greenwood cuttings in early summer (*see pp.100–01*). Divide suckers (*see p.101*) in late winter. Sow seeds in autumn (*see p.103*).
ARTEMISIA Insert greenwood stem-tip cuttings (*see p.101*) in spring in a free-draining medium under plastic. Take semi-ripe stem-tip cuttings as for *Phlomis* (*see p.137*).
ASIMINA Take root cuttings in winter as for *Celastrus* (*see p.122*). Sow seeds in autumn (*see p.103*).
BANKSIA Root semi-ripe stem-tip cuttings (*see p.101*) in late summer in rockwool plugs or free-draining medium. Space-sow seeds in spring after giving smoke treatment (*see pp.103–4*).
BAUERA Root semi-ripe cuttings (*see p.95*) in midsummer in a free-draining medium. Sow seeds in spring (*see p.104*) at 68–77°F (20–25°C).
BORONIA Root semi-ripe cuttings as for *Phlomis* (*see p.137*). Sow seeds in spring (*see p.104*) and keep them cool.
BRUCKENTHALIA Take greenwood cuttings as for evergreen azaleas (*see Rhododendron, p.138*). Sow seeds as for *Rhododendron* (*see p.138*).
BRUGMANSIA Root softwood to semi-ripe cuttings (*see pp.100–01 and 95*) in spring and summer in a free-draining medium or rockwool plugs. Sow seeds in spring (*see p.104*) at 68–77°F (20–25°C).
BRUNFELSIA Take softwood and greenwood cuttings (*see pp.100–01*) in spring and summer.

BANKSIA ATTENUATA

BUDDLEJA *BUTTERFLY BUSH, BUDDLEIA*

Buddleja davidii 'Empire Blue'

SOFTWOOD OR GREENWOOD CUTTINGS in spring and summer
SEMI-RIPE CUTTINGS from midsummer
HARDWOOD CUTTINGS from autumn to midwinter
SEEDS in spring

The shrubs in this genus root readily from softwood and greenwood nodal stem-tip or internodal cuttings (*see pp.100–01*) and from semi-ripe cuttings (*see p.95*). Reduce foliage by half on *Buddleja davidii* cultivars. With *B. globosa*, avoid material affected by leaf and bud nematodes. Keep hardwood cuttings (*see p.98*) frost-free.

Sow seeds outdoors (*see pp.103–04*) where they are to flower in 6–12 months when the soil reaches 50°F (10°C).

BUXUS *BOXWOOD*

GREENWOOD CUTTINGS from early to midsummer
SEMI-RIPE CUTTINGS from late summer to late autumn
DIVISION in spring
SEEDS in early spring

Use a free-draining medium to root cuttings of the evergreen shrubs in this genus. Take nodal stem-tip cuttings from greenwood (*see p.101*). Semi-ripe cuttings (*see below*) root in 6–8 weeks outdoors, or under cover in cold climates. They root more quickly if placed under plastic and given bottom heat.

Buxus sempervirens and its cultivars can be divided using a spade (*see p.101*). Sow seeds after a short period of cold (*see pp.103–04*) for more even germination. Boxwood is slow-growing, more so from seeds, so it may take 4–5 years to obtain a plant ready for planting out.

BOXWOOD CUTTINGS

1 *Root large numbers of 4in (10cm) semi-ripe cuttings (here of* Buxus sempervirens*) in cells or soil mix plugs (see inset). The following spring, pot the cuttings singly into 3in (8cm) pots.*

2 *Grow on the cuttings, pinching out the tips regularly. In the autumn, plant them out into a well-prepared nursery bed, spacing them 12–18in (30–45cm) and grow on for 3–4 years.*

CALLICARPA *BEAUTYBERRY*

SOFTWOOD CUTTINGS in early summer
SEMI-RIPE CUTTINGS from early summer
HARDWOOD CUTTINGS in late autumn to midwinter
SEEDS in autumn or spring

Softwood and semi-ripe cuttings (*see pp.100 and 95*) of the shrubs in the genus root best with hormone rooting compound. For *Callicarpa japonica*, try hardwood cuttings (*see p.98*). Sow seeds from the fruits fresh or dried (*see pp.103–04*).

CAMPSIS *TRUMPET VINE*

SEMI-RIPE CUTTINGS in summer
HARDWOOD CUTTINGS from autumn to midwinter
ROOT CUTTINGS in winter
SEEDS in spring
LAYERING in summer or winter

The roots of these vigorous, deciduous climbers, if taken as cuttings while the plant is dormant (*see Celastrus, p.122*), produce strong plants that are more easily overwintered than those from other cuttings. A flowering plant may be raised in three years.

Take more semi-ripe cuttings (*see p.95*) than you need in colder climates, since rooted cuttings do not always overwinter well. When taking hardwood cuttings (*see p.98*), check that the wood is living (green below the bark) – many of the new shoots may die back. They root easily if kept cool and humid.

Seeds gathered in autumn from dry capsules and sown in spring (*see p.104*) germinate readily. *Campsis radicans* climbs by means of aerial roots and is a good plant for self-layering (*see p.107*).

CAMELLIA

SEMI-RIPE CUTTINGS from midsummer to early autumn
HARDWOOD CUTTINGS from autumn to late winter
SEEDS in autumn or spring
LAYERING in spring
GRAFTING in mid- to late winter

Most of the evergreen shrubs in this genus root from semi-ripe cuttings (*see p.95*). They need care and free-draining medium in colder climates but are easy in warmer regions. Cuttings may be internodal or nodal (*see below*), with ⅝in (1.5cm) wounds, but nodal tip cuttings produce a flowering plant quickly, in 3–4 years. Apply hormone rooting compound sparingly on single-node cuttings. With hardwood cuttings (*see p.98*), pinch out flower buds and give bottom heat of 54–68°F (12–20°C); rooting takes 6–12 weeks.

Gather seeds as soon as the fleshy fruits split. Sow fresh, or soak the hard seed coats in hot water before sowing in spring (*see pp.103–4*). Camellias make good subjects for hybridizing (*see p.21*).

HYBRIDIZING CAMELLIAS
To prepare a camellia for pollination, select a bloom that has not fully opened (see inset) and carefully remove all the petals and stamens with a pair of tweezers to expose the stigmas.

Simple layer (*see p.106*) low-growing shoots of no more than ½in (12mm) diameter. Allow up to two years for the layer to root before lifting.

Camellia reticulata and its cultivars are more successful if grafted than when taken as cuttings. Apical-wedge (*see p.108*), whip (*see p.109*) or cleft graft (*see right*) onto two-year-old seedlings or cuttings of *C. japonica*, *C. saluenensis*, or *C. reticulata* to flower in 2–3 years.

TYPES OF SEMI-RIPE CUTTING

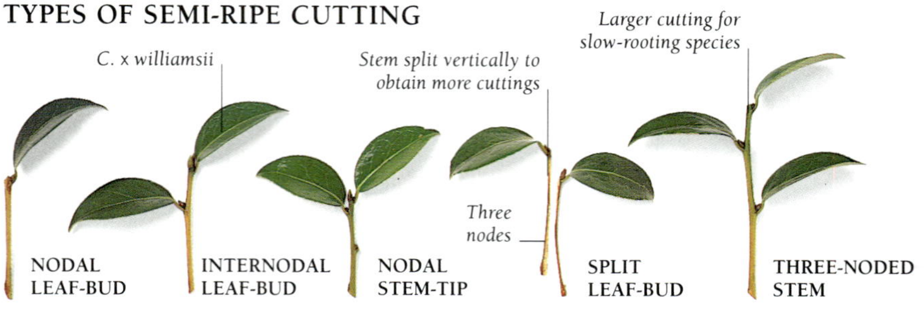

CARYOPTERIS
BLUEMIST SHRUB

SOFTWOOD CUTTINGS from spring to midsummer
GREENWOOD CUTTINGS from late spring to midsummer
SEMI-RIPE CUTTINGS from mid- to late summer
HARDWOOD CUTTINGS from late autumn to midwinter
SEEDS in spring

The deciduous subshrubs in this genus root readily from softwood and greenwood cuttings (*see pp.100–01*) and are prime candidates for rooting directly in a 3½in (9cm) pot (*see p.96*). Rooting occurs within three weeks in a warm, humid environment. Treat semi-ripe cuttings (*see p.95*) as above, or root in a cold frame or cloche. Hardwood cuttings (*see p.98*) also root well in frost-free sites outdoors or in containers on a heated bench in a frost-free greenhouse.

Seeds gathered from dry fruits in autumn, dried, then sown in spring (*see pp.103–4*) germinate readily. New plants flower in 2–3 years.

CLEFT GRAFTING CAMELLIA

1 Prepare two scions: take semi-ripe shoots with 3–4 buds. Trim off the lower leaves and any flower buds. Cut two 1in (2.5cm) slivers of bark from the base of each to form a wedge that has no bark on one side and some bark and the lowest bud on the other (see inset).

2 Cut the rootstock down to 3in (8cm) and make a 1in (2.5cm) vertical cut into the top. Slide one of the scions into each end of the cut, so that the bark of the scion is flush with that of the stock (see inset). *Seal the union with grafting wax and allow to callus.*

CEANOTHUS *CALIFORNIA LILAC*

SOFTWOOD CUTTINGS from late spring to midsummer
SEMI-RIPE CUTTINGS from midsummer to late autumn
HARDWOOD CUTTINGS from late autumn to late winter
ROOT CUTTINGS in autumn
SEEDS in late winter

These are evergreen and deciduous shrubs. Evergreens are best grown from semi-ripe or hardwood cuttings, and deciduous shrubs from softwood cuttings, to flower in 2–3 years. All species may be seed-raised.

CUTTINGS

Nodal stem-tip softwood cuttings (*see pp.100–01*), 3in (8cm) long, of deciduous and semi-deciduous cultivars root in 4–6 weeks in a free-draining medium with hormone rooting compound. Take semi-ripe cuttings of evergreen cultivars with a heel (*see pp.95–6*) if possible. Bottom heat of 54–59°F (12–15°C) will speed rooting.

Hardwood cuttings (*see p.98*) of small-leaved species such as *Ceanothus impressus* and their cultivars need a dry rooting medium to prevent rot; they root well in rockwool plugs. Take root cuttings as for *Celastrus* (*see p.122*).

SEEDS

Soak the hard seeds in hot water before sowing (*see pp.103–4*). Some species need three months' chilling; others respond to smoke treatment.

CEANOTHUS 'PIN CUSHION'
Cuttings of this and other evergreen Ceanothus *are best taken with a heel, if possible, from semi-ripe wood to encourage rooting.*

OTHER SHRUBS AND CLIMBING PLANTS

BUPLEURUM Semi-ripe cuttings (*see p.100*) in summer. Sow seeds in spring (*see p.104*).
CAESALPINIA Root softwood and greenwood cuttings (*see pp.100–01*) in spring and summer in a free-draining medium. Sow seeds as for *Clianthus* (*see p.124*); tender species require 68–77°F (20–25°C).
CALCEOLARIA Take softwood cuttings (*see p.100*) in spring and early summer. Bottom heat is not needed; cuttings will rot if the environment is too damp. Sow seeds in spring (*see p.104*); no heat is needed.
CALLIANDRA Take semi-ripe cuttings (*see p.95*) in summer. Simple layer (*see p.106*) in spring. Sow seeds in spring (*see p.104*) at 61–64°F (16–18°C) after treating with smoke (*see p.103*).
CALLISTEMON Root greenwood to semi-ripe cuttings in summer and autumn as for *Olearia* (*see p.135*). Surface-sow seeds in spring (*see p.104*).
CALLUNA *See pp.110–11.*
CALOCHONE Take semi-ripe cuttings (*see p.95*) in summer.
CALOTHAMNUS Root greenwood to semi-ripe cuttings in summer and autumn as for *Olearia* (*see p.135*). Surface-sow seeds in spring (*see p.104*).
CALYCANTHUS Root greenwood and semi-ripe cuttings (*see pp.101 and 95*) in summer in a free-draining medium with bottom heat. Sow seeds in autumn (*see p.103*).
CALYTRIX Root greenwood to semi-ripe cuttings in summer and autumn as for *Olearia* (*see p.135*).
CANTUA Root greenwood and semi-ripe cuttings (*see pp.101 and 95*) throughout summer with gentle bottom heat. Sow seeds in spring (*see p.104*).
CARAGANA Take cuttings in summer as for deciduous *Viburnum* (*see p.143*). Treat seeds as for *Clianthus* (*see p.124*). Topwork weeping forms onto *C. arborescens* as for *Salix caprea* var. *pendula* (*see p.89*).
CARISSA Take semi-ripe cuttings (*see p.95*) in summer. Sow seeds in autumn or spring (*see pp.103–04*) at 64–70°F (18–21°C).
CARMICHAELIA Root semi-ripe cuttings from midsummer to autumn as for *Olearia* (*see p.135*). Seeds as for *Clianthus* (*see p.124*).
CARPENTERIA Often micropropagated; take greenwood cuttings (*see p.101*) from micropropagated stock to obtain better rooting. Sow seeds in spring (*see p.104*) at 77°F (25°C).
CASSINIA Root cuttings as for *Lavandula* (*see p.132*); cuttings can rot off.
CASSIOPE Take greenwood cuttings as for evergreen azaleas (*see Rhododendron, p.138*). Sow seeds and layer as for *Erica* (*see pp.110–11*).
CASTANOPSIS Sow seeds in autumn (*see p.103*).

CALLISTEMON CITRINUS 'FIREBRAND'

CELASTRUS *BITTERSWEET*

Celastrus orbiculatus

SOFTWOOD OR GREENWOOD CUTTINGS in early summer
ROOT CUTTINGS in winter

For this genus of mainly deciduous climbers, nodal softwood or greenwood cuttings (*see pp.100–01*) may be taken from the stem-tips and will root well. Several cuttings may also be taken from one shoot. Prune growth on new plants by about 50 percent to ensure a well-branched plant. New plants from cuttings reach maturity in 3–4 years.

One length of root provides several cuttings, without any special care or facilities. Trim root cuttings (*see below*) to size using a sharp knife or pruners. Discard thin roots, and ensure only undamaged material is used.

In colder climates, cuttings will root and produce shoots in a cold frame but respond more quickly in a frost-free greenhouse. If they are slow to shoot, place them on a heated bench for a couple of weeks. They should be ready for potting in spring. Alternatively, insert two cuttings directly in a 3½in (9cm) pot to avoid any root disturbance.

TAKING BITTERSWEET ROOT CUTTINGS

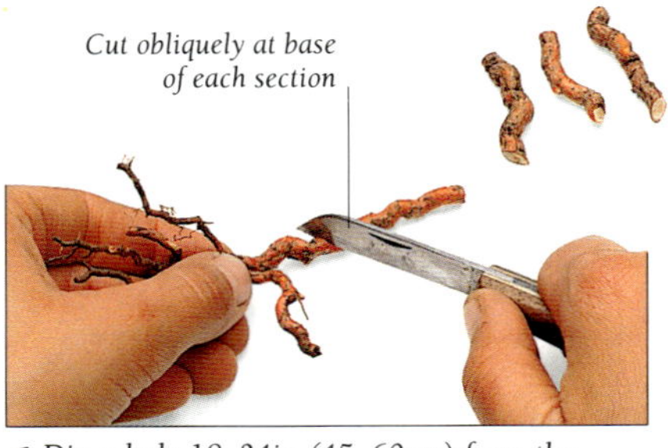

1 Dig a hole 18–24in (45–60cm) from the base of the parent plant to expose the roots. Remove lengths of root at least 4in (10cm) long that are between the thickness of pencil and a finger, cutting straight across at the top of each root. Wash off the soil and divide the roots into 1½–2in (4–5cm) sections (see inset).

2 Dust the cuttings with fungicide. Fill a pot with a free-draining soilless potting mix and firm. Press the cuttings vertically into the mix so that the flat-cut ends are slightly above the surface. Space them 2–3in (5–8cm) apart. Cover with a ½in (1cm) layer of sharp sand. Water, label, and keep in a frost-free place.

CHAENOMELES *FLOWERING OR JAPANESE QUINCE, JAPONICA*

SOFTWOOD OR GREENWOOD CUTTINGS in late spring to early summer
HARDWOOD CUTTINGS from autumn to midwinter
ROOT CUTTINGS from autumn to midwinter
SEEDS in autumn or spring
LAYERING in late winter

Hardwood cuttings of these deciduous shrubs produce a large plant more quickly than other methods, usually in 2–3 years. Spreading forms are easy to layer.

CUTTINGS

Nodal stem-tip softwood or greenwood cuttings (*see pp.100–01*) are best taken with a heel (*see p.96*) and respond to hormone rooting compound. Humidity of 100 percent prevents scorch. Rooting takes about four weeks. Hardwood cuttings (*see p.98*) with a wound root easily if treated with hormone rooting compound and kept cool and humid.

Root cuttings should be ⅜in (8mm) in diameter and 3in (8cm) long; treat as for *Celastrus* (*see above*), but place horizontally on the surface and lightly cover. You can also root cuttings in nursery beds (*see p.96*).

SEEDS

Gather seeds from ripe fruits (*see below*) and sow fresh in autumn (*see p.103*). Alternatively, sow seeds in spring after providing a three-month period of cold stratification (*see pp.103–4*).

LAYERING

Simple layering (*see p.106*) is very effective. Layers should be ready to lift in spring.

COLLECTING FLOWERING QUINCE SEEDS
Wait until the fruits have turned yellow and come easily off the branch in autumn. Using a sharp knife, cut through the outer flesh carefully by scoring around the fruit once. Twist open the fruit so as not to damage any seeds. Pick out the seeds with a blunt knife or plant label.

CISSUS

CUTTINGS at any time

This large genus includes a range of shrubs and vines that can be easily increased from cuttings. New plants will flower in two years. Softwood and semi-ripe nodal or internodal cuttings (*see pp.100 and 95*), 2½–3in (6–8cm) in length, will root readily. If the cuttings are kept warm at 68–77°F (20–25°C) and humid, rooting usually takes 3–6 weeks.

CISTUS *SUN ROSE, ROCK ROSE*

SOFTWOOD CUTTINGS from late spring to early summer
SEMI-RIPE CUTTINGS from midsummer to late winter
SEEDS in spring

Cuttings of these small to medium-sized evergreen shrubs must be protected against rot. Seeds may be sown as for bedding plants to obtain flowering plants in two years.

CUTTINGS

Softwood cuttings (*see p.100*) root readily. *Cistus* produce many sideshoots, and it is important to select material carefully (*see below*). Rooting takes up to four weeks. You can also root directly in pots (*see p.96*).

Semi-ripe cuttings (*see p.95*) do well in a cold frame over winter. Material taken in late winter from stock plants (grown under cover in colder climates) before new growth commences roots quickly. Watch out for powdery mildew, particularly on *C.* x *purpureus* and its cultivars; this reduces rooting potential. If present, the foliage will be weak, with yellow and brown blotches. Spray the plant with a fungicide before taking cuttings from it.

SEEDS

Seeds from dry capsules germinate readily. Sow them (*see pp.103–04*) in a sheltered sunny site, where they are to flower, or in a seedbed.

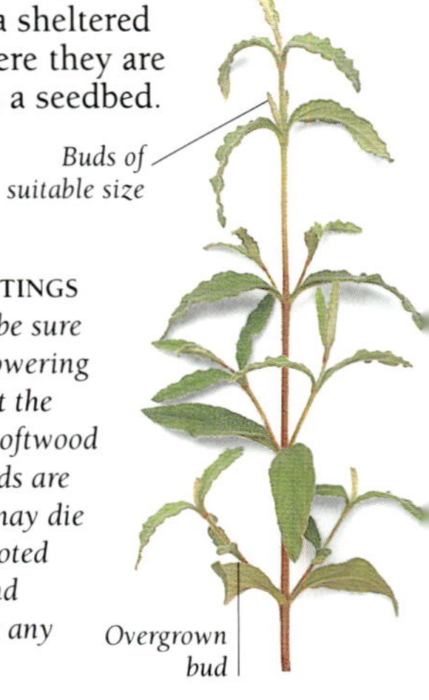

SOFTWOOD CUTTINGS
In early summer, be sure to choose a nonflowering shoot with buds at the correct stage for softwood cuttings. If the buds are overgrown, they may die off, leaving the rooted cutting "blind" and unable to produce any new shoots.

CLEMATIS *OLD MAN'S BEARD, TRAVELER'S JOY, VIRGIN'S BOWER*

CUTTINGS from spring to late summer
SEEDS in autumn
LAYERING in late winter to spring
GRAFTING in late winter

Of the deciduous and evergreen climbers in the genus, deciduous cultivars are often grown from softwood cuttings and species from semi-ripe cuttings. Layering (*see p.107*) is most suited to *Clematis montana* and its cultivars. Grafting larger-flowered hybrids ensures more vigorous plants. Sow seeds of species. It usually takes 2–3 years for new plants to flower.

CUTTINGS

Leaf-bud cuttings (*see p.97*) can be taken from softwood and semi-ripe shoots. They are prepared in the same way (*see below*), but cuttings of softwood are taken from spring to midsummer and of semi-ripe wood from mid- to late summer. They all root well, but semi-ripe cuttings need less humidity. For large-leaved softwood cuttings, for example in some of the *Clematis montana* cultivars, reduce the cutting to a single leaf to avoid overcrowding and botrytis.

COLLECTING AND SOWING CLEMATIS SEEDS

1 *Choose a dry day and pull away the ripe, fluffy seedheads. There is no need to remove the plumes from the seeds.*

2 *Sow the seeds thinly in a prepared pan of free-draining soil mix. Cover with a thin layer of mix and top-dress with grit. Label.*

Pot rooted semi-ripe cuttings (*see p.95*) in spring. *C. armandii* and its cultivars root well from semi-ripe or hardwood cuttings (*see p.98*) taken in midwinter 4–6 weeks before new growth starts and inserted in rockwool plugs. Each cutting must have a well-formed bud. Apply hormone rooting compound and keep humid with 54–59°F (12–15°C) bottom heat. Once rooted, pot and grow on the cuttings in a moist atmosphere.

PREPARED CUTTING

STRONG BUDS

WEAK BUDS

LEAF-BUD CUTTINGS
Take internodal leaf-bud cuttings about 2in (5cm) long from the current season's growth. Look for well-formed buds in the leaf axils; weak buds may not produce new shoots. Larger-leaved cultivars, such as this Clematis armandii, *should be trimmed to only one leaf, rather than two. If necessary, cut the leaflets in half to reduce moisture loss.*

SEEDS

Gather and sow seeds fresh in autumn (*see above*). They need a period of cold stratification (*see p.103*) to ensure even germination in spring.

LAYERING

Serpentine layer (*see p.107*) shoots of the previous season's growth. The layers should root by the following summer.

GRAFTING

Use one- or two-year-old *C. vitalba* seedlings as rootstocks. Take 1⅜in (3.5cm) scions from the current season's growth of the cultivar, cut just above a bud. Apical-wedge graft (*see p.108*) the scions onto 3in (8cm) long and ⅛in (3mm) thick roots. Pot singly so that the buds are level with the soil mix surface. Each root will sustain its scion until the scion produces its own roots and is self-supporting (this is called a nurse graft).

CLERODENDRUM *GLORY BOWER*

SOFTWOOD CUTTINGS in late spring to early summer
SEMI-RIPE CUTTINGS in summer
ROOT CUTTINGS in autumn to midwinter
SEEDS in spring
DIVISION from late winter to spring

The evergreen and deciduous shrubs and climbers in this genus root readily from softwood and semi-ripe cuttings (*see pp.100 and 95*) in 3–6 weeks. Take root cuttings as for *Celastrus* (*see p.122*), but insert singly in 3½in (9cm) pots for flowers in 2–3 years. Gather seeds from the fruits, then provide a three-month period of cold stratification before sowing in spring (*see pp.103–04*).

Take advantage of natural suckers of *Clerodendrum bungei* by separating them (*see right*) in spring. Mature plants of clump-forming species can be divided from late winter to spring (*see p.101*). Suckers will flower in the same year.

DIVIDING *CLERODENDRUM BUNGEI*
Select a healthy sucker (left in picture) with its own fibrous roots. Remove the soil carefully from between the parent and the sucker to expose the underground stems (stolons) linking them. Slice through the stolons with the blade of a spade. Lift the sucker, trim any damaged or overlong roots, and plant out in prepared soil.

OTHER SHRUBS AND CLIMBING PLANTS

CEPHALANTHUS Take semi-ripe cuttings in summer, or hardwood in winter (*see pp.95 and 98*). Sow seeds in autumn (*see p.103*).
CERATOSTIGMA Take softwood cuttings in early summer as for *Fuchsia* (*see p.128*).
CESTRUM Take softwood to semi-ripe cuttings (*see pp.100–01 and 95*).
CHIMONANTHUS Take softwood cuttings with a heel (*see pp.100 and 96*) in late spring. Simple layer (*see p.106*). Sow seeds in autumn (*see p.103*).
CHIONANTHUS Sow seeds in autumn (*see p.103*) to germinate after two winters.
CHOISYA Root greenwood to hardwood cuttings as for *Escallonia* (*see p.127*).
x CITROFORTUNELLA Root semi-ripe cuttings in summer (*see p.95*). Air layer in spring (*see p.105*).
CLETHRA Take cuttings as for evergreen azaleas (*see Rhododendron, p.138*). Sow seeds as for *Rhododendron* (*see p.138*).

CLIANTHUS *GLORY PEA*

CUTTINGS from late spring to early autumn
SEEDS in spring
GRAFTING in spring

These evergreen to semi-evergreen climbing shrubs root readily from softwood and semi-ripe cuttings (*see pp.100 and 95*). Take stem cuttings from new growth, trimming just below a node, and reduce the compound leaf by up to half. Rooting takes about four weeks; pot early-rooted cuttings into 3½in (9cm) pots. Water sparingly over winter, and pinch out tips for bushy plants. Slug damage can be severe.

Gather the hard seeds from the long, hairy pods, then scarify by abrading or soaking (*see p.102*) prior to sowing to ensure good germination, in 10–14 days.

The desert pea, *Clianthus formosus*, recently renamed *Swainsona formosa*, is very short-lived unless grafted (*see right*) onto seedlings of *C. puniceus* or *Colutea arborescens*. Use stock seedlings that have been germinated ten days earlier than the scion seedlings. Work as quickly as possible to prevent the cuts from drying; keep the stock in a plastic bag while preparing the scion. Grafted plants flower in 1–3 years.

GRAFTING A *CLIANTHUS FORMOSUS* SEEDLING

*1 When it has two seed leaves, carefully lift the rootstock seedling (*Colutea arborescens*). With a sterilized razor blade, slit the top ⅝in (1.5cm) of the stem, starting between the leaves.*

*2 Lift a *Clianthus formosus* seedling, also at the two-leaf stage. Cut off the roots, making an angled cut on each side of the stem to form a wedge at the base (*see inset*).*

3 Gently insert the scion into the cut stem of the stock seedling, as far as it will go. Bind the graft with soft knitting yarn. Pot the grafted seedling in soilless seed mix in a 2in (5cm) pot. Set the graft just above soil level.

*4 Place in a humid case at a minimum of 64°F (18°C). Once the graft has taken (*see inset*) and the seedling is in active growth, remove the yarn. Cut it away carefully with a scalpel; hold the seedling steady with tweezers.*

CODIAEUM *CROTON*

Codiaeum 'Flamingo'

CUTTINGS at any time
LAYERING at any time

If several plants are required, cuttings are easily taken from the evergreen shrubs in this small genus. Take softwood and greenwood nodal stem-tip cuttings (*see pp.100–01*), and dip the cut stems in powdered charcoal to staunch the sap before inserting them in the medium. Supply 68–77°F (20–25°C) bottom heat. Cuttings should root in 4–6 weeks. New plants should mature in two years.

If only one or two new plants are required, crotons can be air layered (*see p.105*) for a good-sized plant in a year.

CORNUS *DOGWOOD*

SOFTWOOD CUTTINGS in late spring or early summer
HARDWOOD CUTTINGS from late autumn to midwinter
DIVISION from late winter to early spring
SEEDS in autumn
GRAFTING in late winter

The deciduous shrubs in this genus are usually easy to propagate. *Cornus alba* and *C. stolonifera* and their cultivars do not root readily from softwood: take nodal cuttings at the correct stage (*see right and p.100*), no more than 2¾in (7cm) long, from the new stem tips. Use a free-draining medium and a weak hormone rooting compound. Rooting takes about four weeks.

The best way to increase dogwoods grown for their colorful winter stems is to root hardwood cuttings (*see p.98*) in a sheltered site. Sow seeds gathered from ripe fruits fresh in autumn (*see p.103*) before they become dormant, or cold stratify (*see p.102*) seeds to be sown in spring. Lift and grow on rooted suckers of *C. stolonifera* (*see p.101*). Spliced side graft (*see p.58*) hard-to-root cultivars of *C. florida* such as 'Rubra'.

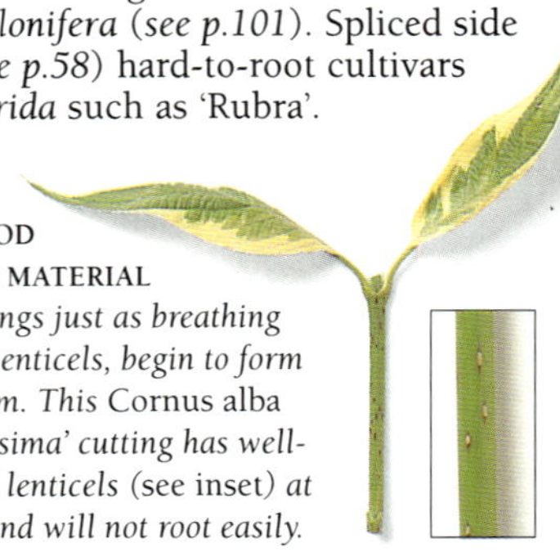

SOFTWOOD CUTTING MATERIAL
Take cuttings just as breathing pores, or lenticels, begin to form on the stem. This Cornus alba 'Elegantissima' cutting has well-developed lenticels (see inset) at the base and will not root easily.

OTHER SHRUBS AND CLIMBING PLANTS

COBAEA Sow seeds in spring (*see p.104*).
COLLETIA Root semi-ripe cuttings (*see p.95*) in autumn in open medium with gentle heat.
COLUTEA Take softwood cuttings (*see p.100*). Treat seeds as for *Clianthus* (*see above*).
CONVOLVULUS Take semi-ripe cuttings (*see p.95*) in summer and autumn; keep dryish.
COPROSMA Take semi-ripe cuttings as for *Pittosporum* (*see p.137*). Sow seeds in spring without extra heat (*see p.104*).
COROKIA Softwood cuttings (*see p.100*) in summer. Semi-ripe cuttings (*see p.95*) in summer and autumn; keep dryish.
CORONILLA Take greenwood stem-tip cuttings (*see p.101*) in early summer. Sow seeds as for *Clianthus* (*see above*).
CORYLOPSIS Softwood cuttings as for *Syringa* (*see p.142*). Seeds sown outside in spring (*see p.104*) take two years to germinate. Simple or French layer in spring or autumn (*see p.106*).
CUPHEA Root softwood to semi-ripe cuttings (*see pp.100–01 and 95*) from spring to autumn. Sow seeds in spring (*see p.104*).
CYRILLA Root semi-ripe cuttings (*see p.95*) from midsummer in a free-draining medium. Take root cuttings as for *Celastrus* (*see p.122*). Sow seeds in spring (*see p.104*).
DABOECIA *See pp.110–11*.

CORYLUS *Filbert, hazel*

CUTTINGS in late spring to early summer
SEEDS in autumn
LAYERING in late winter and spring
GRAFTING in late winter

Some of these shrubs tend to sucker, especially grafted plants. Avoid this with purple-leaved *Corylus maxima* cultivars by taking softwood nodal stem-tip cuttings (*see p.100*), no more than 3–4in (8–10cm) long with the tip and one juvenile leaf retained. They will root in rockwool plugs in 4–8 weeks. Lightly wound the bottom ¾in (2cm) of the stem of each cutting and apply some hormone rooting compound.

Seeds gathered and sown fresh (*see p.103*) germinate well if subjected to a period of winter cold.

C. avellana and *C. maxima* cultivars are often French layered (*see p.107*). They can also be stooled (*see p.56*); to improve results, wound young shoots and treat with hormone rooting compound before hilling up.

Whip graft (*see p.109*) named cultivars onto *C. avellana* rootstocks for good-sized plants in 2–3 years.

COTONEASTER

Cotoneaster salicifolius 'Gnom'

SOFTWOOD OR GREENWOOD CUTTINGS from spring to midsummer
SEMI-RIPE CUTTINGS from midsummer to autumn
SEEDS in spring
LAYERING in early spring
GRAFTING in late winter

This large genus includes a wide range of deciduous and evergreen shrubs, which all root well from cuttings. The prostrate forms lend themselves to layering, and grafting may be used to create a standard plant. New plants usually mature within 2–3 years.

CUTTINGS

All cotoneasters root readily from softwood and greenwood cuttings (*see pp.100–01*); take stem cuttings of species with long shoots, such as *Cotoneaster dammeri*. Cotoneasters are good candidates for rooting directly in pots (*see p.96*). *C. integrifolius* roots best when the growing tip is retained.

In colder areas, semi-ripe cuttings (*see p.95*) can be rooted in a cold frame. If rooting cuttings under plastic or in a closed case, rooting occurs more rapidly with bottom heat.

SEEDS

Extract the hard-coated seeds from ripe fruits (*see p.102*) in autumn and provide periods of first warm and then cold stratification before sowing in spring (*see pp.103–4*). They should germinate in the following year. Cotoneasters hybridize freely and they do not generally come true.

LAYERING

Simple layering (*see p.106*) works well if only one or two plants are required. Plants may also self-layer (*see p.107*).

GRAFTING

Whip graft (*see p.101*) scions of *C.* 'Hybridus Pendulus' onto a tall, straight-stemmed rootstock to produce a weeping shrub or a small tree. This is known as top-working (*see Hedera, p.130*). Use a two-year-old pot-grown *C. bullatus* or *C. frigidus* as a rootstock.

COTINUS *Smoke bush*

CUTTINGS in spring
SEEDS in late summer to early autumn or spring
LAYERING in late winter or early spring

Increasing the large, deciduous shrubs in this genus from cuttings or seeds can be tricky. Simple layering is the easiest way to obtain one or two new plants, but using a stock plant for French layering will yield many more. A good-sized plant may be obtained in 2–3 years.

CUTTINGS

Insert thin softwood nodal stem-tip cuttings (*see pp.100–01*), 1½–2½in (4–6cm) long with 2–3 young leaves, in free-draining medium. Hormone rooting compound and a moist atmosphere aid rooting, which takes up to six weeks. In cooler areas, encourage rooted cuttings to put as much growth on as possible before autumn, since they often fail to overwinter if too small.

SEEDS

Seeds gathered as they ripen (*see below*) and sown fresh (*see p.103*) germinate well in spring. Stored seeds develop hard coats so must be scarified and cold stratified (*see p.103*) for spring sowing.

LAYERING

Simple layer (*see p.106*) in late winter for rooted layers by autumn. If French layered (*see p.107*) in spring, a bush sends up a host of new shoots that will also be well rooted by autumn.

EXTRACTING SMOKE BUSH SEEDS

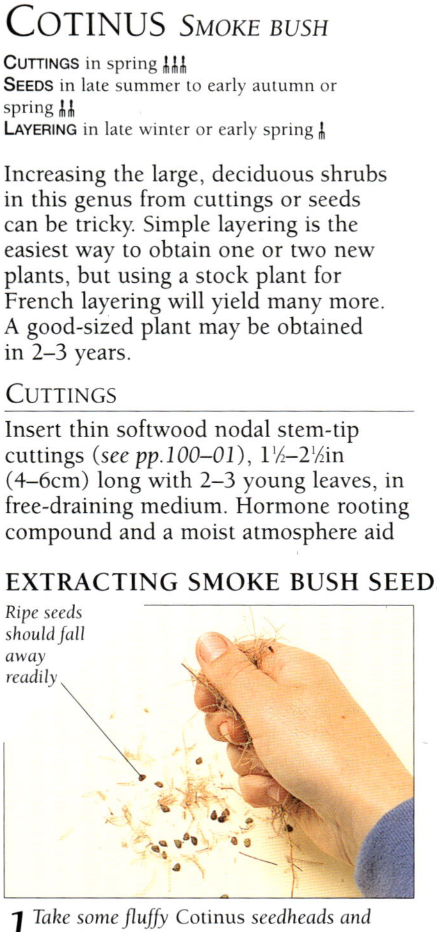

1 Take some fluffy Cotinus *seedheads and "scrunch" them over a sheet of paper to separate the black seeds from their plumes.*

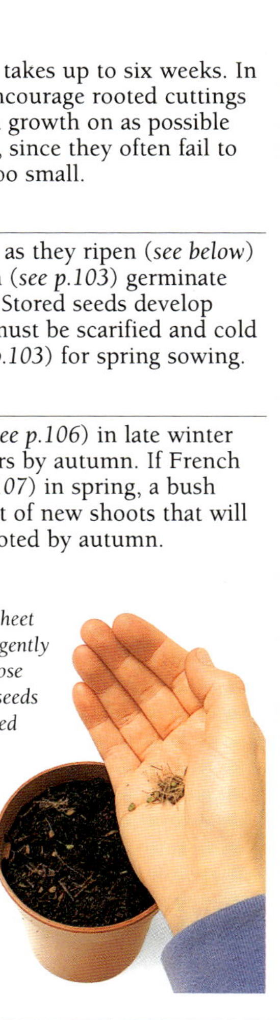

2 Hold up the sheet of paper and gently blow away the loose plumes. Sow the seeds in a small pot filled with soilless seed mix. (Do not worry if any chaff falls on the mix.) Cover with a fine layer of mix, water, and label.

CYTISUS *Broom*

Cytisus x *praecox* 'Allgold'

SEMI-RIPE CUTTINGS in late summer or early autumn
HARDWOOD CUTTINGS in midwinter
SEEDS in autumn or spring

New plants of these deciduous and evergreen shrubs usually flower within two years. Root semi-ripe cuttings with or without a heel (*see pp.95–6*) in a very free-draining medium or rockwool plugs. Overwatering leads to basal rot. Humidity, bottom heat of 54–59°F (12–15°C), and hormone rooting compound speed rooting, but it still takes 2–6 months. For *Cytisus* x *praecox* and its cultivars, well-ripened hardwood cuttings of strong, juvenile stems (*see p.98*) root best with humidity and bottom heat. Spray every two weeks with a fungicide and ventilate weekly.

All species grow readily from seeds, but hard seed coats can be a problem. Sow freshly gathered seeds outdoors in autumn (*see p.103*) to germinate in spring. Transplant pot-sown seedlings at the seed-leaf stage into 3½in (9cm) pots for planting the following autumn. Soak spring-sown seeds in hot water (*see pp.103–4*) before sowing. Seedlings of *Cytisus battandieri* (syn. *Argyrocytisus battandieri*), the pineapple broom, may need a second growing season before planting out. Protect young plants from mice and rabbits.

Daphne

Daphne cneorum

Greenwood cuttings in spring to early summer
Semi-ripe cuttings in summer
Root cuttings in autumn and winter
Seeds in midsummer or autumn
Layering in late spring to early summer
Grafting in winter

These deciduous and evergreen shrubs hate drying out, so however they are propagated, keep new plants moist. Daphnes are fickle rooters because of the presence of virus in most plants; *Daphne* x *burkwoodii*, *D. cneorum*, *D. odora*, and their cultivars are easiest to root. Root cuttings of *Daphne mezereum* and *D. genkwa* work well. Daphnes do not tolerate root disturbance.

D. mezereum is often raised from seeds. Species with prostrate or spreading growth, such as *D. blagayana* and *D. cneorum*, are best layered. The more difficult species and hybrids are grafted; it can be tricky with small alpines but is usually successful. New plants flower in 2–3 years.

Cuttings

Take nodal stem-tip greenwood and semi-ripe cuttings (*see pp.101 and 95*), 2–4in (5–10cm) long, just as the base begins to firm up. Hormone rooting compound, a free-draining medium, and bottom heat of 59°F (15°C) will improve rooting. For alpines, take ⅝–2¾in (1.5–7cm) cuttings and use a mix of 2–3 parts coarse sand to one of peat. In cold climates, cuttings can be rooted in a cold frame. Cuttings with virus often drop their leaves; destroy them. Healthy cuttings take 6–10 weeks to root. Take root cuttings as for *Celastrus* (*see p.122*).

Seeds

Harvest the ripe fruits (*see p.103*) and remove the pulp, but there is no need to clean the seeds completely. Sow at once in containers (*see p.104*) in gritty seed soil mix and place in a frost-free place. Most germinate in spring after a winter's chilling. Leave for another year to germinate all the seeds. For alpines, stratify fresh seeds in layers of moist peat or sand in pots outdoors or in a refrigerator for six weeks (*see p.103*). Dried seeds germinate less successfully.

Layering

Simple-layered (*see p.106*) shoots take a year to become well rooted. Daphnes may also be air layered (*see p.105*).

Grafting

Water the rootstocks well in their pots prior to grafting (*see below*). For scions, use strong, healthy cuttings of the previous year's growth – about 1–2in (2.5–5cm) long for alpines, and standard length for other daphnes.

TYPES OF GRAFT USED FOR DAPHNES

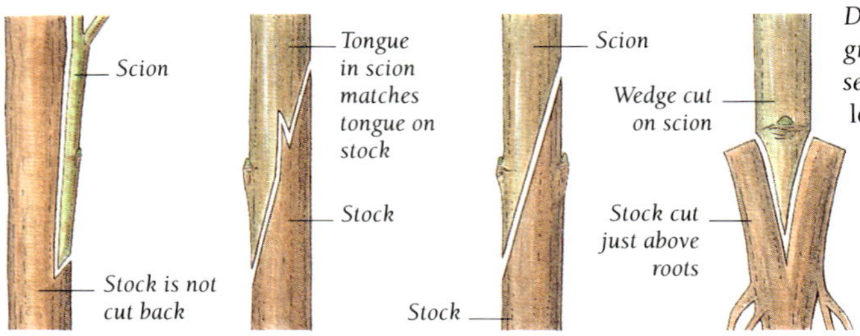

SPLICED SIDE-VENEER (*see p.109*)
WHIP-AND-TONGUE (*see p.59*)
WHIP (*see p.109*)
APICAL-WEDGE (*see p.108*)

Daphnes may be grafted using one of several techniques (see left). The rootstocks most widely used are two-year-old Daphne alpina, acutiloba, giraldii, laureola, *or* mezereum. *Keep newly grafted plants just moist for at least ten days.*

Elaeagnus *Autumn olive, Oleaster*

Semi-ripe cuttings from late summer to autumn
Hardwood cuttings from late autumn to late winter
Division in spring
Seeds in autumn

Cuttings from the deciduous and evergreen shrubs in this genus normally root well, but in some years they are prone to leaf drop and will not root. Plants that produce suckers may be divided. New plants should be ready to plant out in 2–3 years.

Cuttings

Elaeagnus x *ebbingei* and its cultivars root more reliably than *E. pungens*. With the latter, select material with large, bright, shiny leaves. Take nodal semi-ripe stem cuttings (*see p.95*), 3–4in (7–10cm) long and with 2–3 nodes, retaining only the top two leaves. Wound the bottom ¾in (2cm). Bottom heat at 59–68°F (15–20°C) speeds rooting, which takes 8–12 weeks.

Take hardwood cuttings (*see p.98*) of the most vigorous growth and root in a frost-free, humid environment. The cuttings should root in 12–20 weeks.

Division

E. commutata spreads by suckers. Lift, divide, and transplant suckers of a mature plant (*see p.101*).

Seeds

Gather seeds from ripe fruits and sow fresh in autumn (*see p.103*); they benefit from winter cold. *E. pungens* seeds ripen in spring and may germinate at once; if not, treat as autumn sowings.

Semi-ripe cuttings *One shoot of the current season's growth (here of* Elaeagnus x ebbingei*) provides several cuttings* (see left). *Reduce large leaves by half to reduce moisture loss* (see above).

Enkianthus

Cuttings in late spring to early summer
Seeds in winter to early spring

Root softwood cuttings from the mainly deciduous shrubs in this genus as for deciduous rhododendrons (*see p.138*). In colder areas, rooted cuttings may fail to overwinter because the growing season may not be long enough for the new wood to ripen fully. Treat seeds gathered from dry capsules as for rhododendrons (*see p.138*). New plants take 4–5 years to flower.

Epipremnum

Cuttings at any time
Layering at any time

These evergreen, woody climbers produce aerial roots along their stems; cuttings taken from such shoots root very easily.

Take softwood stem-tip (*see p.101*) or semi-ripe leaf-bud cuttings (*see p.97*), pot them individually, and provide bottom heat of 68°F (20°C). Mature plants may be had from cuttings in 2–3 years and from simple (*see p.106*) or air layering (*see p.105*) in 1–2 years.

ESCALLONIA

GREENWOOD OR SEMI-RIPE CUTTINGS from midsummer to autumn
HARDWOOD CUTTINGS from late autumn to late winter

Most of these mainly evergreen shrubs can be increased from greenwood or semi-ripe cuttings. Rooting of 4in (10cm) greenwood stem cuttings (*see p.101*) takes 4–8 weeks. Semi-ripe cuttings (*see p.95*) will also root reliably in a cold frame over winter.

Less vigorous cultivars with more twiggy growth root more readily from hardwood cuttings. Hardwood cuttings (*see p.99*) are also less prone to basal stem rot. They can be taken in one of two lengths: 8–10in (20–25cm) or 4in (10cm) (*see below*). Root in a frost-free, humid environment or, in mild areas, outdoors. The young plants should be large enough by the following autumn to lift and replant in the garden. It takes 2–3 years to obtain a flowering plant.

HARDWOOD CUTTINGS
If material is limited, take shorter 4in (10cm) cuttings. Trim leaves off the lower half of each stem. In a peat and bark mix, cuttings root in 6–10 weeks.

EUONYMUS *BURNING BUSH, SPINDLE TREE*

SOFTWOOD OR SEMI-RIPE CUTTINGS from late spring to late summer
GREENWOOD CUTTINGS in late spring
HARDWOOD CUTTINGS from autumn to late winter
SEEDS in autumn
GRAFTING in late winter

This genus includes deciduous and evergreen shrubs and climbers that root readily from cuttings. Greenwood cuttings are best for *Euonymus alatus;* hardwood cuttings for *E. japonicus* and its cultivars. Deciduous species can be raised from seeds. New plants mature in three years. Wear gloves when handling *E. europaeus* and other species that irritate the skin.

CUTTINGS

Softwood or semi-ripe cuttings (*see pp.100 and 95*), 2–4in (5–10cm) long, root within four weeks. Leaf drop can occur if material has powdery mildew on the foliage, so select only healthy material. Since rooting can take up to ten weeks, take greenwood cuttings (*see p.101*) of *E. alatus* as early as possible and from a shrub that still produces vigorous new growth each year. Hormone rooting compound is beneficial. Root hardwood cuttings (*see pp.98–9*) of *E. japonicus* and its cultivars in a frost-free, humid place. Plant out rooted cuttings in autumn.

SEEDS

Seeds harvested from ripe fruits (*see below*) and sown fresh in autumn should germinate in the following spring after a period of chilling (*see pp.103–4*).

GRAFTING

Use seedlings rootstocks of *E. europaeus* to spliced side graft (*see p.58*) its cultivars. Whip-and-tongue graft (*see p.59*) *E. fortunei* cultivars for a standard.

EUONYMUS SEEDS
These shrubs have very colorful fruits that split open to reveal their seeds in autumn. To collect the blood-red seeds of this Euonymus hamiltonianus *subsp.* sieboldianus, *tie a paper bag over a stem before the capsules split. Remove the fleshy, orange outer seed coats (arils) before sowing.*

OTHER SHRUBS AND CLIMBING PLANTS

DECAISNEA Sow seeds in autumn (*see p.103*).
DENDROMECON Root softwood cuttings (*see p.100*) in free-draining medium.
DESFONTAINIA Take semi-ripe cuttings (*see p.95*) from midsummer to autumn; bottom heat is not essential.
DEUTZIA Propagate as for *Philadelphus* (*see p.136*).
DIERVILLA Take softwood to semi-ripe cuttings (*see pp.100–01 and 95*).
DIPELTA Root greenwood to semi-ripe cuttings (*see pp.101 and 95*). Sow seeds in spring (*see p.104*).
DISANTHUS Take softwood cuttings as for *Hamamelis* (*see p.130*); overwintering rooted cuttings can be difficult. Simple layer (*see p.106*).
DRIMYS Root softwood to semi-ripe cuttings (*see pp.100–01 and 95*). Older plants may self-layer (*see p.107*).
DRYANDRA Root softwood cuttings (*see p.100*) in summer. Sow seeds 2–3 to a pot in spring (*see p.104*) at 64°F (18°C); some need smoke treatment (*see p.103*).
ECCREMOCARPUS Sow seeds in spring (*see p.104*) at 50–59°F (10–15°C). Seeds of *E. scaber* need light to germinate.
EDGEWORTHIA Root greenwood and semi-ripe nodal stem-tip cuttings (*see pp.101 and 95*) in summer in free-draining medium. Split bottom ¾–1in (1–2cm) of stem.
ELEUTHEROCOCCUS Take greenwood cuttings (*see p.101*) in early summer, or root cuttings as for *Celastrus* (*see p.122*). Divide suckers in late winter (*see p.101*). Sow seeds in autumn or spring (*see pp.103–4*).
ELSHOLTZIA Root softwood cuttings (*see p.100*) in spring. Cover with plastic, but avoid getting too humid. Bottom heat is not needed.
EPIGAEA Root greenwood cuttings (*see p.101*) in summer without bottom heat. Separate rooted layers (*see p.107*) in spring or autumn.
ERICA *See pp.110–11.*
EUPATORIUM Softwood cuttings as for *Olearia* (*see p.135*). Seeds in spring (*see p.104*).
EUPHORBIA Root greenwood stem-tip cuttings (*see p.101*) in free-draining medium with gentle bottom heat in summer. Seeds in spring (*see p.104*).
EURYOPS Root softwood to semi-ripe cuttings from spring to autumn as for *Caryopteris* (*see p.121*). Sow seeds in spring (*see p.104*) at 50–55°F (10–13°C).
EXOCHORDA Softwood cuttings in spring as for *Syringa* (*see p.142*). Seeds (*p.103*) in autumn.
FALLOPIA See *Polygonum* (*p.138*).
x FATSHEDERA Take cuttings as for *Hedera* (*see p.130*).

DRYANDRA QUERCIFOLIA

FATSIA

CUTTINGS at any time
SEEDS in autumn or spring

The only commonly grown species is the evergreen shrub, *Fatsia japonica* (syn. *Aralia japonica*). Cultivars must be increased from cuttings, which are awkward because of their size, but the species is more easily raised from seeds.

Prepare semi-ripe cuttings as shown (*see right*); if necessary, reduce the foliage. Treat as standard cuttings (*see p.95*); bottom heat of 59–68°F (15–20°C) aids rooting.

Sow seeds, extracted in late autumn from ripe black fruits, in pots and cover with vermiculite (*see p.104*). Germination takes 10–20 days at 59–68°F (15–20°C). Plant out after two years for sizeable plants in three years.

SEMI-RIPE FATSIA CUTTING
Select a young, vigorous, semi-ripe shoot (here of Fatsia japonica*). Remove the top 3–4in (8–10cm), or 3–5 nodes, of the stem by cutting just below a node with clean, sharp pruners. Remove all but the top two leaves and the growing tip; trim off the lower leaves at the base (see* inset*). Insert the cutting so that only the bottom nodes are buried.*

FORSYTHIA

Forsythia 'Northern Gold'

SOFTWOOD OR GREENWOOD CUTTINGS from spring to midsummer
SEMI-RIPE CUTTINGS from midsummer to early autumn
HARDWOOD CUTTINGS from late autumn to early spring
SEEDS in early spring
LAYERING in spring or autumn

These deciduous shrubs are some of the easiest to root as cuttings. The sprawling *Forsythia suspensa* self layers in the wild, so layering works well for the species and cultivars. Seeds also germinate readily. New plants take 18–36 months to reach flowering size.

CUTTINGS

Softwood or greenwood nodal stem-tip and stem cuttings in rooting medium (*see pp.100–01*) root in 2–4 weeks. Reduce the foliage by up to a half on longer-leaved cultivars. Rooting directly in pots (*see p.96*) and in a sun tunnel (*see p.39*) are suitable options.

Take semi-ripe cuttings (*see p.95*), about 4in (10cm) long if they are to be kept over winter in a cold frame.

Leave hardwood cuttings (*see p.98*) undisturbed until the following autumn; in colder areas, they root more quickly in a cold frame or frost-free greenhouse with bottom heat of 54–68°F (12–20°C).

SEEDS

Seeds require about four weeks of chilling (*see p.103*); in cooler areas, they germinate readily in the same spring if sown in containers in a cold frame.

LAYERING

Use simple layering (*see p.106*) or self-layering (*see p.107*) to produce new plants; layers root in 6–12 months.

FREMONTODENDRON

FLANNEL BUSH

SEMI-RIPE CUTTINGS in late summer
HARDWOOD CUTTINGS from late autumn to late winter
SEEDS in spring

Taking cuttings of these evergreen or semi-evergreen shrubs (syn. *Fremontia*) and their cultivars is challenging, but success is possible. Both species germinate readily from seeds. New plants reach flowering size in 12 months.

CUTTINGS

Take 3–4in (8–10cm), nodal stem-tip semi-ripe cuttings (*see pp.101 and 95*); retain the growing tip and only one other leaf. Use hormone rooting compound and a free-draining medium; rockwool plugs are an excellent alternative. Place in a heated closed case or under opaque plastic with bottom heat of 54–68°F (12–20°C). Regular fungicidal sprays, and medium kept on the dry side, will protect against botrytis. Internodal stem cuttings (*see p.94*) will root, but less successfully.

Hardwood cuttings (*see p.98*) will root in a frost-free place, but, for almost guaranteed success, take nodal stem-tip cuttings as above, but from fully ripened wood, and insert in rockwool plugs. A vigorous root system should develop in 4–6 weeks. Transplant into 3½in (9cm) pots immediately after roots are visible.

SEEDS

Sow seeds gathered from dry capsules directly into 3½in (9cm) pots (*see p.96*) to avoid root disturbance. Viable seeds germinate in 30 days with bottom heat of 59–68°F (15–20°C). Water seedlings sparingly at first to control damping off.

FUCHSIA

Fuchsia 'Garden News'

SOFTWOOD CUTTINGS at any time
SEMI-RIPE CUTTINGS from midsummer to early autumn
HARDWOOD CUTTINGS from late autumn to late winter
SEEDS in late winter

It is almost impossible for cuttings of the deciduous and evergreen shrubs and climbers in this genus to fail. Fuchsias can suffer from a range of pests and diseases when grown under cover, so take cuttings from clean, healthy plants only. Raising plants from seeds is an alternative for species fuchsias. New plants flower very quickly, usually the following year.

CUTTINGS

With softwood cuttings (*see right and p.100*), rooting is almost guaranteed. Nodal stem-tip, single-node, and internodal stem cuttings all root within 10–20 days. You can also root them in florist's foam (*see right*) or rockwool. With semi-ripe cuttings (*see p.95*), the secret to producing a good specimen is to pinch out new growth to a pair of leaves just above the last break of buds.

Hardwood cuttings (*see p.98*) of the vigorous *F. magellanica* and its cultivars root quickly. They can usually be lifted in spring. In cold areas, place the cuttings in a frost-free place.

SEEDS

Seeds gathered from fleshy fruits and sown in spring and covered with vermiculite (*see pp.103–4*) should germinate at 68°F (20°C) in three weeks. Growth at first is slow, but if started early and grown on in warmth the shrub will flower in its first year.

GARDENIA

Gardenia augusta 'Veitchii'

GREENWOOD AND SEMI-RIPE CUTTINGS at any time
SEEDS at any time

The shrubby species in this evergreen genus are easily raised from green- and semi-ripe wood (*see pp.101 and 95*), taken as nodal stem-tip cuttings. Cuttings resent root disturbance so are best rooted singly in cell trays or pots. They root in 6–8 weeks if kept humid with bottom heat of 68–77°F (20–25°C) and flower in 12–18 months.

Seeds germinate readily if sown fresh (*see pp.103–4*) and provided with bottom heat of 59–68°F (15–20°C). New plants take up to seven years to flower.

GENISTA *BROOM*

SOFTWOOD OR GREENWOOD CUTTINGS in early to midsummer
SEMI-RIPE CUTTINGS in midsummer
HARDWOOD CUTTINGS from autumn to midwinter
SEEDS in spring

These deciduous to evergreen shrubs (syn. *Chamaespartium*, *Echinospartium*) flower in their first or second year, depending on the cultivar. *Genista hispanica* is particularly successful from seeds.

CUTTINGS

Softwood and greenwood nodal stem-tip cuttings (*see pp.100–01*) of *G. tinctoria* and its cultivars root in 2–4 weeks.

Semi-ripe cuttings (*see p.95*) taken from *G. hispanica* root reasonably well when material is selected from young plants producing vigorous growth each season. Take 2–2¾in (5–7cm) cuttings at the point at which the growth begins to firm and the new foliage narrows. Apply hormone rooting compound and insert in free-draining medium. Keep humid with bottom heat of 59°F (15°C).

Hardwood cuttings (*see p.98*), 2¾–4in (7–10cm) long of *G. lydia*, if taken from well-ripened wood to avoid rot, root well in rockwool plugs. Heel cuttings (*see p.96*) can be slightly less mature. Treat them as for semi-ripe cuttings; rooting takes 8–12 weeks.

SEEDS

Gather seeds from pealike pods. Scarify the hard seed coats by sandpapering them and soaking in hot water (*see p.102*) before sowing in spring. Seeds should then germinate in 2–3 weeks.

SOFTWOOD CUTTINGS

To take internodal stem cuttings, divide a shoot into sections, each with about ½in (1cm) of stem above and below one set of leaves. These can also be split vertically to create more cuttings. Pinch out 1in (2.5cm) long growing tips for nodal stem-tip cuttings.

FUCHSIA CUTTINGS IN FLORIST'S FOAM

1 *Cut a block of florist's foam into 1in (2.5cm) cubes. Soak the cubes in a bowl of water for 10–15 minutes, then place them in a saucer or tray. Use a knitting needle to make a ½in (1cm) deep hole in the center of each cube. Prepare some stem-tip cuttings of fuchsia (see above).*

2 *Insert a cutting into each cube, taking care not to crush the stems. Each cutting should sit with the leaves just above the surface and the base in contact with the bottom of the hole. If the hole is too shallow, deepen it with the knitting needle – do not push in the cutting.*

3 *Add water to the saucer to a depth of ½in (1cm). Label and place the cuttings under a plastic bag, or cover, in bright indirect light at about 59°F (15°C) until rooted (see inset).*

4 *When their roots show through the florist's foam, pot the cuttings singly into 3in (8cm) pots of soilless potting mix. Cover the foam with ¼in (5mm) of mix to stop the roots from drying out. (If exposed, the foam acts as a wick, drawing moisture away from the roots.)*

OTHER SHRUBS AND CLIMBING PLANTS

FICUS Take greenwood to semi-ripe cuttings at any time as for *Hoya* (*see p.131*). Air layer anytime (*see p.105*).
FORTUNELLA Root semi-ripe cuttings in summer (*see p.95*) with bottom heat. Sow seeds in spring (*see p.104*).
FOTHERGILLA Take softwood cuttings in early summer as for *Hamamelis* (*see p.130*). Simple layer (*see p.106*).
GARRYA Take semi-ripe cuttings (*see p.95*) in summer and again in late autumn. Root in free-draining medium or in rockwool as for *Fremontodendron* (*see p.128*).
GAULTHERIA (syn. x *Gaulnettya, Pernettya*) Take semi-ripe cuttings in autumn as for *Ceanothus* (*see p.121*). Divide suckers (*see p.101*) in spring and autumn. Sow seeds as for *Rhododendron* (*see p.138*).
GEVUINA Semi-ripe cuttings as for *Olearia* (*see p.135*). Seeds in autumn (*p.104*).
GRAPTOPHYLLUM Semi-ripe cuttings (*see p.95*) in spring or summer. Sow seeds in spring (*see p.104*) at 66–75°F (19–24°C). Simple layer (*see p.106*) in summer.
GREVILLEA Heel cuttings (*see p.96*) from late summer to late winter. Seeds (*see p.103*) fresh, or soaked at 59°F (15°C) in spring. Whip graft (*see p.109*) to avoid rot, for early flower or weeping plant.
GRISELINIA Take semi-ripe and hardwood cuttings as for *Prunus laurocerasus* (*see p.138*). Seeds (*see p.104*) in autumn.
GYNURA Take softwood cuttings in spring or semi-ripe in autumn (*see pp.100 and 95*). Use free-draining medium and bottom heat of 68–77°F (20–25°C).
HALIMIUM As for *Cistus* (*see p.122*).
HALIMODENDRON Take root cuttings in winter as for *Celastrus* (*see p.122*). Sow seeds in spring (*see p.104*) in a frost-free place. Whip-and-tongue graft (*see p.108*) onto *Caragana arborescens* rootstock in late winter.

HAMAMELIS *Witch hazel*

CUTTINGS in spring
SEEDS in autumn
LAYERING in spring
GRAFTING in late summer

Softwood cuttings of these deciduous shrubs usually overwinter badly: take early nodal stem-tip cuttings (*see pp.100–01*) as soon as new growth is 2¾–4in (7–10cm) long. Bottom heat of 54–68°F (12–20°C) and hormone rooting compound speed rooting, in 6–8 weeks. Keep cuttings just moist and frost-free over winter.

Place ripe seed capsules in a covered tray: they explode to release seeds. The seeds are doubly dormant. Provide three months' warm, then three months' cold, stratification (*see p.103*); or, in cold climates, sow fresh seeds and overwinter them in a cold frame (*see p.103*). Simple layer (*see p.106*) suitable shoots.

Spliced-side graft (*see p.58*) cultivars onto two-year-old, pot-grown seedling rootstocks of *Hamamelis virginiana*, as low as possible to avoid suckers. Pot two-year-old *H. virginiana* seedlings in early spring as stocks for chip-budding (*see below and p.60*) and keep watered and in active growth. Transplant in the following autumn to flower in 4–5 years.

CHIP BUDDING

1 *Take buds of similar ripeness as on the rootstock; in cold regions, these will be at the base of the budstick (here of* Hamamelis × intermedia 'Moonlight'*). Prepare buds with a ⅛in (2.5mm) stalk and 1¼in (3cm) of bark.*

2 *Prepare a rootstock (here of* H. virginiana*) and position the bud. If needed, align the bud to the side of the cut on the stock (see inset) so the cambiums meet. Bind the bud in place. Keep in humid shade with 68°F (20°C) bottom heat. The bud should take in 4–6 weeks.*

HEBE

SOFTWOOD CUTTINGS from late spring to autumn
SEMI-RIPE CUTTINGS from midsummer to late autumn

These evergreen shrubs include some small alpine forms. All root well from cuttings, but semi-ripe material is better for many of the smaller-leaved species and cultivars.

Softwood cuttings (*see below and pp.100–01*) root in 3–4 weeks. Use of mist systems or hormone rooting compound can cause cuttings to rot. Hebes can suffer from downy mildew and a leafspot disease; to avoid this, pot cuttings as soon as rooted, overwinter in a well-ventilated, frost-free environment, and water sparingly. Plant out in spring.

Take semi-ripe cuttings (*see p.95*) from species such as *H. pimeleoides* and *H. rakaiensis*. *H. pinguifolia* cuttings may rot at the base then root at the medium surface. New plants flower in two years.

SOFTWOOD HEBE CUTTINGS

Hebes vary widely in size from dwarf to large shrubs. Take nodal stem-tip cuttings that are 2–3in (5–8cm) long with 1–2 pairs of leaves.

HEDERA *Ivy*

SOFTWOOD CUTTINGS at any time
SEMI-RIPE OR HARDWOOD CUTTINGS from late summer to late winter
LAYERING at any time
GRAFTING at any time

Stems of these evergreen climbers and trailing shrubs root readily in the wild and so are simple to grow from cuttings or by layering. Smaller-leaved species and cultivars may be grafted onto tree ivy (× *Fatshedera lizei*) to create a standard plant.

CUTTINGS

Take single-noded softwood cuttings, leaf-bud, or hardwood cuttings (*see pp.97–100*) from young stems for trailing plants or adult growth for bushy plants. Longer softwood cuttings of small-leaved *Hedera helix* cultivars ensure strong growth. Root 2–3 cuttings direct in a 3½in (9cm) pot (*see p.96*) and keep cool to avoid premature shooting. Rooting takes 4–8 weeks. Cuttings scorch easily.

LAYERING

Dig up self-layers of *H. helix* and *H. hibernica*, and serpentine layer *H. colchica* and its cultivars (*see p.107*).

GRAFTING

Apical wedge-graft (*see p.108*) or T-bud (*see below*) three scions onto the rootstock. T-budding is best done when the scion plant is in full growth. For a full head, pinch back new growth.

TOP-WORKING TO CREATE A STANDARD IVY

1 *Prepare a* × Fatshedera lizei *rootstock: make three staggered T-cuts around the stem, 3ft (90cm) from the base. Loosen the flaps of bark with the back of a knife blade.*

2 *As you make each T-cut, slice a bud (see inset) from a budstick taken from ripe wood of the Hedera. Slide the bud into the cut so it fits snugly; trim off the "tail."*

3 *Bind the grafted area with grafting tape. Keep in humid shade until the wounds callus (4–6 weeks). Four weeks after they take, cut back the stem to just above the grafts.*

HIBISCUS

Hibiscus syriacus 'Diana'

SOFTWOOD OR SEMI-RIPE CUTTINGS from early to late summer
HARDWOOD CUTTINGS from late autumn to midwinter
SEEDS in spring
LAYERING in spring and summer
GRAFTING in winter

Most of the deciduous and evergreen shrubs in this genus, such as *Hibiscus rosa-sinensis* and *H. syriacus* and their cultivars, root readily from cuttings. Hardwood cuttings are easy to take when pruning evergreen *Hibiscus*. Less easily rooted cultivars may be layered. Seedlings of *H. syriacus* vary, so they are used mostly as rootstocks. Grafts take readily and in favorable conditions grow quickly enough to be planted out the following autumn or spring. Plants may take three years to flower.

CUTTINGS

Take standard softwood stem-tip or semi-ripe cuttings (*see pp.100–01 and 95*). Bottom heat of 54–68°F (12–20°C) and hormone rooting compound improves success. Pot early cuttings into 3½in (9cm) pots; leave those rooted from midsummer undisturbed over winter. Hardwood cuttings (*see p.98*) of *H. syriacus* retain the leading bud and root well if frost-free and in deep pots.

SEEDS

Gather seeds from large, dry capsules. Spring-sown seeds (*see p.104*) germinate readily. Sow *H. syriacus* in a seedbed for rootstocks the following autumn.

LAYERING

Air layers (*see p.105*) of *H. rosa-sinensis* cultivars should root in 6–8 weeks.

GRAFTING

Use scion material up to two years old, and apical-wedge graft (*see p.108*) onto the stock at the union between root and stem. Pot successful grafts into 5½–7in (14–19cm) pots and grow on in a frost-free place.

HOYA *WAX FLOWER*

CUTTINGS at any time
LAYERING at any time

Plants in this large genus of evergreen shrubby climbers can be increased by nodal, semi-ripe cuttings (*see p.95*), 3in (8cm) long, which will root in 6–8 weeks at 68°F (20°C).The long lengths of stem are suitable for simple layering (*see p.106*), from pot to pot if necessary. Hoyas may flower quickly, or not for several years.

HYDRANGEA

SOFTWOOD CUTTINGS from late spring to midsummer
SEMI-RIPE CUTTINGS in midsummer
HARDWOOD CUTTINGS in winter
SEEDS in spring
LAYERING in spring

Most of the deciduous and evergreen shrubs and climbers root readily from almost any cutting. Exceptions are climbing *Hydrangea anomala* subsp. *petiolaris*, which layers easily, and *H. quercifolia*, which will freely germinate from seeds. Some hydrangeas will reach flowering size in their second year.

CUTTINGS

For most hydrangeas, length determines the type of softwood cutting (*see pp.100–01*) since the space between nodes varies, but any cutting roots in 2–4 weeks. Pinch out new growth to avoid leggy plants. *H. quercifolia* and *anomala* subsp. *petiolaris* need care: take 2–4in (5–10cm) nodal stem-tip cuttings; retain only the immature tip. Reduce foliage on *H. quercifolia* by up to a half.

SPLIT-STEM CUTTING
Use a clean, sharp knife or a scalpel to split the stems of softwood and semi-ripe cuttings lengthwise to double the amount of cuttings taken.

Do not trim leaves

Apply hormone rooting compound. Rooting can take up to 12 weeks. Root semi-ripe (*see p.95*) and hardwood cuttings (*see p.98*), which are good for *H. Villosa* (*syn. H. aspera* Villosa Group) and its cultivars (because the hairy leaves and stems are susceptible to rot), in a frost-free place.

SEEDS

Sow seeds, extracted from dry capsules, in containers (*see p.104*); cover lightly; keep cool and humid at 50°F (10°C).

LAYERING

Use serpentine layering (*see below and p.107*). Rooted layers should be ready to transplant within a year.

SERPENTINE LAYERING A CLIMBING HYDRANGEA

1 *Select a healthy shoot that is developing aerial roots (here of* Hydrangea anomala *subsp.* petiolaris*) from last year's growth. Mix equal parts peat and grit into the soil.*

2 *Peg down as much of the stem as possible, aerial roots downward. Lightly bury about 6in (15cm) of the stem. Keep the layer moist until new shoots appear, up to a year later.*

OTHER SHRUBS AND CLIMBING PLANTS

HARDENBERGIA Root soft- and greenwood cuttings (*see pp.100–01*) in summer without bottom heat. Take semi-ripe cuttings in summer or autumn (*see p.95*). Sow seeds as for *Clianthus* (*see p.124*).
HELIANTHEMUM Root greenwood cuttings in summer and autumn (*see p.101*). Sow seeds in spring (*see p.104*) in a frost-free place. New plants need plenty of light.
HELICHRYSUM Root softwood to semi-ripe cuttings (*see pp.100–01 and 95*) at any time; avoid getting them too wet. Sow seeds in spring (*see p.104*).
HELIOTROPIUM Greenwood cuttings in summer (*p.101*). Semi-ripe cuttings in summer (*p.95*). Seeds in spring (*p.104*).
HIBBERTIA Root greenwood and semi-ripe cuttings as for *Olearia* (*see p.135*).
HIPPOPHAE Greenwood cuttings (*see p.101*) in free-draining medium. Root cuttings as for *Celastrus* (*see p.122*). Sow fresh seeds outdoors in autumn (*see p.103*).
HOHERIA Root greenwood and semi-ripe cuttings (*see pp.101 and 95*) in summer and autumn in free-draining medium. Sow seeds in autumn (*see p.104*).
HOLODISCUS Greenwood cuttings (*see p.101*) in summer. Seeds in autumn (*see p.103*). Simple layer spring to summer (*see p.106*).
HOVEA Root greenwood to semi-ripe cuttings as for *Olearia* (*see p.135*). Sow seeds as for *Clianthus* (*see p.124*).
HUMULUS Leaf-bud cuttings (*p.97*) in spring to early summer. Golden forms may scorch; late-rooted cuttings overwinter badly. Serpentine layer in spring (*p.107*).

HYPERICUM *St. John's Wort*

Hypericum lancasteri

Softwood or semi-ripe cuttings from late spring to early autumn
Hardwood cuttings from late autumn to midwinter
Division in spring
Seeds in autumn or spring

The deciduous and evergreen shrubs in this genus are easily raised from cuttings or seeds to flower in 2–3 years; hardwood cuttings are best for taller shrubs. *H. calycinum* spreads by runners and can be divided.

Cuttings

Softwood and semi-ripe stem cuttings (*see pp.100 and 95*), about 2in (5cm) long, with 1–2 pairs of leaves, normally root in 3–6 weeks. For best results, select nonflowering shoots. With softwood cuttings, be careful not to damage the stem when removing the lower leaves. Direct rooting in pots (*see p.96*) is an option. For smaller species, such as *Hypericum olympicum*, cuttings may only be ¾–1¼in (2–3cm) in length.

If only a few plants are needed, root hardwood cuttings (*see p.98*) in deep pots; otherwise, root in a sheltered place such as a cold frame or under a sun tunnel (*see p.39*).

Division

Lift clumps of *H. calycinum* (*see p.101*) and replant or pot rooted pieces. This is best done before the new season's growth begins.

Seeds

Gather seeds from ripe capsules and sow in autumn in cool climates or in early spring (*see p.104*); lightly cover with vermiculite. Keep frost-free.

JASMINUM *Jasmine*

Jasminum angulare

Softwood or semi-ripe cuttings in spring and summer
Hardwood cuttings in winter
Layering in spring

These deciduous and evergreen shrubs and climbers are relatively easily increased by cuttings; cuttings of *Jasminum officinale* and *J. nudiflorum* are best from hardwood. Layering is an option, especially for species that produce aerial roots along the stems. It usually takes three years to obtain a good-sized flowering plant.

Cuttings

Softwood and semi-ripe cuttings (*see pp.100 and 95*) can be internodal to reduce the length of the cuttings. Remove part of the compound leaf to reduce the risk of botrytis. Hormone rooting compound aids rooting, which usually takes about four weeks. Cuttings rooted early with sturdy topgrowth are likely to overwinter better in cooler climates. Always take a few extra cuttings to avoid disappointment.

Take standard hardwood cuttings (*see pp.98–9*). In cold areas, root in a sheltered place such as in a cold frame or in deep pots left over winter in a frost-free greenhouse.

Layering

Select shoots with roots forming along their length and simple layer them (*see p.106*). A good root system should form within 12 months. Then sever from the parent plant and pot up or plant out.

KALMIA *Mountain laurel*

Greenwood cuttings in summer
Hardwood cuttings in midwinter
Seeds in winter to early spring
Layering in spring

Cuttings of these evergreen shrubs can be challenging and, although seeds germinate readily, seedlings need care. Layering is the most reliable option. New plants take up to five years to flower well.

Cuttings

Wound greenwood cuttings (*see p.101*) on both sides of the stem, then treat as rhododendrons (*see p.138*). Rooting is slow. Try hardwood cuttings (*see p.98*).

Seeds

Surface-sow seeds as for rhododendrons (*see p.138*). Seedlings require shade and a low-nutrient soil mix because they become scorched easily.

Layering

Simple layering (*see p.106*) produces rooted plants in 12 months and plants for the garden in another two years.

KOLKWITZIA *Beauty bush*

Softwood and greenwood cuttings in late spring or early summer

Kolkwitzia amabilis, a deciduous shrub, roots easily from cuttings to flower in three years. Treat the cuttings as for *Philadelphus* (*see p.136*). Avoid water shoots, and make the cuttings at least three nodes in length to increase the number of new shoots and improve success in overwintering.

LAPAGERIA
Chilean bellflower

Seeds in spring
Layering in spring and autumn

The best way to propagate this single species of evergreen climber, *Lapageria rosea* and its cultivars, is by layering. Shoots can be either simple or serpentine layered (*see pp.106–7*). Semi-ripe or basal cuttings are sometimes recommended, but where marginally hardy they are very reluctant to root and, if they do, rarely grow successfully, even in warm climates.

Soak the seeds for 48 hours prior to sowing individually into 3in (8cm) pots (*see pp.103–4*). Cover with ½in (1cm) of vermiculite and germinate at 59–68°F (15–20°C). New plants take 2–3 years to reach flowering size.

LAVANDULA *Lavender*

Softwood or semi-ripe cuttings from early summer to autumn
Hardwood cuttings from late autumn to late winter
Seeds in spring
Layering in spring

Often, these evergreen shrubs and subshrubs are so full of flower after the first one or two years that there is insufficient suitable new growth for cuttings, which often readily succumb to botrytis. Seed-raised species and cultivars are of variable habit and flower color. Layering is an option for older, leggy plants that are slow to produce new growth.

Cuttings

Take 2½–3in (6–8cm) softwood or semi-ripe cuttings (*see pp.100 and 95*) from young plants in early to midsummer, trim below a node, and strip off the bottom 1¼in (3cm) of foliage. Apply hormone rooting compound and insert in free-draining medium. Early-summer

LAVATERA *MALLOW*

SOFTWOOD OR GREENWOOD CUTTINGS from spring to autumn

Although it is possible to root cuttings of the deciduous and evergreen shrubs and subshrubs in this genus throughout the year, those taken before flower buds form from soft- and greenwood root most quickly and surely.

The length between nodes can be quite great, and mallows will root from internodal cuttings, so take cuttings (*see pp.100–1*) at a set length of 2½–3in (6–8cm), regardless of whether it means trimming above or below a node. This will ensure that the new plants are not leggy. Rooting takes 2–4 weeks. Mallow are also prime candidates for rooting directly in pots (*see p.96*). New plants flower in 1–2 years.

cuttings root reasonably under mist or unheated opaque plastic. Air cuttings regularly and spray with fungicide. Rooting takes 4–8 weeks. Take semi-ripe cuttings with a heel (*see p.96*) and root in a frost-free place.

Hardwood cuttings are taken as for semi-ripe cuttings, but after flowering and preferably from new flushes of growth (*see below*). In winter, they may take three months to root. Keep frost-free to prevent premature shooting. If this occurs, pinch new growth back to just above the original cutting to prevent rot or aphid attack.

SEEDS

Sow the seeds, gathered from dry seedheads, after four weeks of cold stratification (*see pp.103–4*).

LAYERING

Use mounding (*see p.290*) to obtain good-sized plants by the next spring. Plant them quite deeply to avoid legginess.

CUTTING BACK FLOWERING SHOOTS OF LAVENDER
Hardwood cuttings of lavender are best taken from new flushes of growth after blooming. Encourage formation of new shoots by trimming off all the flowering stems as their color fades. Take care not to cut back the shrub too hard, because lavenders do not break readily from old wood.

LIGUSTRUM *PRIVET*

SOFTWOOD OR SEMI-RIPE CUTTINGS from early to midsummer
HARDWOOD CUTTINGS from late autumn to midwinter
SEEDS in late autumn or early spring
LAYERING in spring or autumn

This genus includes deciduous and evergreen shrubs. Privet is often grown as a hedge, and the clippings make good cuttings. It takes three years to grow a good-sized plant.

Take nodal softwood and semi-ripe cuttings (*see pp.100 and 95*), 2¾–4in (7–10cm) long; retain the top two pairs of leaves. Rooting takes 3–6 weeks. They can be rooted directly in pots (*see p.96*).

Root hardwood cuttings (*see pp.98–9*) either in open ground or in a frost-free place. Do not worry if foliage drops; new leaves will appear in spring. *Ligustrum* produces 3ft (1m) or more of growth when young and vigorous, so it is possible to take very large cuttings (*see below*) to produce mature plants ready to go in the garden the following autumn, 1–2 years sooner than usual.

All privets may be simple layered (*see p.106*). Gather seeds from ripe berries and sow fresh (*see p.104*) in late autumn. Dry seeds germinate more uniformly if given 6–8 weeks of cold stratification (*see p.103*) in spring.

TAKING LARGE HARDWOOD CUTTINGS OF PRIVET

1 *Remove 2ft (60cm) long ripe shoots (here of* Ligustrum ovalifolium*), cutting at the base of the new growth, just below a node.*

2 *Trim off the soft tips and the foliage from the bottom half of the stems; cut all the shoots to a uniform length (see inset). Remove a sliver of bark, 1½in (3.5cm) long, from the base of each cutting with a clean knife or pruner blade. Space the cuttings in a slit trench 4in (10cm) apart so that the foliage is just clear of the soil. Firm in, water, and label.*

OTHER SHRUBS AND CLIMBING PLANTS

HYPOCALYMMA Take semi-ripe cuttings in summer (*see p.95*). Surface-sow seeds in spring (*see p.104*).

HYSSOPUS Take softwood to semi-ripe cuttings from spring to autumn (*see pp.100–1 and 95*).

ITEA Root evergreen species from nodal greenwood and semi-ripe cuttings as for *Ilex* (*see p.81*); deciduous species from softwood and greenwood cuttings (*see pp.100–1*). Surface-sow seeds in spring (*see p.104*).

IXORA Root semi-ripe cuttings (*see p.95*) in summer with bottom heat.

KENNEDIA Seeds in spring as for *Clianthus* (*see p.124*).

KERRIA Divide suckers (*see p.101*). Soft- to hardwood cuttings as for *Forsythia* (*see p.128*).

LANTANA Take greenwood and semi-ripe internodal cuttings (*see pp.101 and 95*) in summer and autumn. Cuttings root well in rockwool plugs.

LEPTOSPERMUM Root semi-ripe cuttings as for *Pittosporum* (*see p.137*). Sow seeds in autumn or spring (*see p.104*).

LESPEDEZA Take softwood and greenwood cuttings as for *Caryopteris* (*see p.121*). Sow seeds in autumn (*see p.103*); or store and sow in spring as for *Clianthus* (*see p.124*).

LEUCOTHOE Root greenwood and semi-ripe cuttings from midsummer to midwinter as for evergreen azaleas (*see Rhododendron, p.138*). Sow seeds as for *Rhododendron*.

LEYCESTERIA Place hardwood cuttings in a prepared bed in a cool, frost-free place in autumn to winter (*see p.98*). Seeds in autumn (*see p.103*).

LITHODORA Take greenwood nodal stem-tip cuttings from summer to early autumn (*see p.101*). Air foliage regularly.

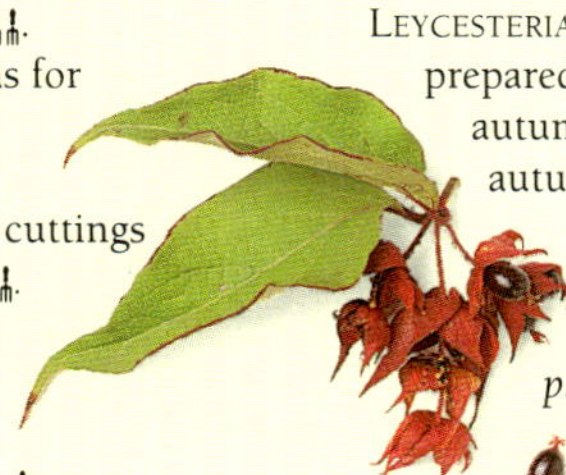

LEYCESTERIA FORMOSA

LONICERA *Honeysuckle*

Lonicera × heckrottii

SOFTWOOD, SEMI-RIPE OR LEAF-BUD CUTTINGS from late spring to late summer
HARDWOOD CUTTINGS from late autumn to midwinter
LAYERING in spring
SEEDS in autumn or spring

Honeysuckles may be evergreen or deciduous. Both shrubs and climbers may be grown from cuttings, and the climbers also respond well to layering. Flowering plants may be raised in three years.

CUTTINGS

Softwood and semi-ripe internodal stem-tip or stem cuttings (*see pp.100 and 95*) root in four weeks. Take cuttings 1¼–2in (3–5cm) long of climbers, such as *Lonicera japonica*, but 2½–3in (6–8cm) long of closer-noded shrubs (such as *L. pileata*). Take care to use material free from aphids and powdery mildew. Do not crowd the cuttings, which encourages botrytis. Semi-ripe cuttings of *L. pileata* and *L. nitida* root well if kept frost-free. You can also take leaf-bud cuttings (*see p.97*). Take standard hardwood cuttings (*see p.98*); 8–12in (20–30cm) cuttings of evergreens produce good-sized plants by the next autumn.

SEEDS

Seeds need cold to germinate; sow seeds extracted from berries fresh in autumn or refrigerate in moist peat for three months before sowing (*see pp.103–4*).

LAYERING

Serpentine layer (*see p.107*) suitable shoots; they take 6–12 months to root.

MAGNOLIA

Magnolia 'Ricki'

SEMI-RIPE CUTTINGS from late summer to autumn
SOFTWOOD OR GREENWOOD CUTTINGS in late spring to early summer
SEEDS in autumn and spring
SIMPLE LAYERING in spring
AIR LAYERING in autumn
GRAFTING in late summer, autumn, or spring

Many deciduous shrubs in this genus may be increased from nodal stem-tip cuttings of soft- or greenwood, in the same way as for tree magnolias (*see p.83*). At the base of each cutting make a light wound, no more than ¾in (2cm) long. Take 4–6in (10–15cm) semi-ripe cuttings of evergreen shrubs and treat as softwood cuttings; they root slowly in autumn and into winter. Sow the doubly dormant seeds as for tree magnolias.

Simple layer magnolias in spring (*see p.106*), and sever the rooted layers in the following spring. Air layering (*see p.105*) in autumn works well on the slower-growing species such as *M. stellata*.

For the gardener, grafting is often the best way to propagate magnolias. For smaller shrubs, use seed-raised *M. kobus* or *M. × soulangeana* grown from cuttings as rootstocks. Spliced side-veneer graft (*see p.109*) in autumn and early to mid-spring. Chip budding (*see p.60*) in late summer makes economical use of material. Plants mature in 4–5 years.

MONSTERA
Swiss cheese plant

LEAF-BUD OR STEM CUTTINGS at any time
LAYERING at any time

All of these evergreen, often epiphytic climbers produce aerial roots, making them suitable for layering, but cuttings also produce good results. It takes two years to obtain mature plants.

Take leaf-bud (*see right*) or stem (*see below*) cuttings, normally two nodes in length, and place in free-draining medium in a humid environment with 68–77°F (20–25°C) bottom heat. The leaf may be rolled up to stop the cutting from toppling. If you have more than one stem cutting, space them 1in (2.5cm) apart in the tray. Stem cuttings may also be inserted vertically in pots. Rooting takes 4–8 weeks. Protect new foliage from hot sun to prevent scorch.

To simple layer (*see p.106*), pin down a long shoot of the new growth into soil or an adjacent container filled with free-draining medium. Layers root fairly quickly (3–6 months), but sever new plants only once they are well established.

STEM CUTTING OF SWISS CHEESE PLANT
Choose a young stem that is just forming aerial roots. Cut a 2in (5cm) section as for leaf-bud cuttings (see right). *Fill a tray with soilless rooting medium. Press in the cutting so that it is half buried, with the bud uppermost.*

MAHONIA *Oregon grapeholly*

LEAF-BUD OR SEMI-RIPE CUTTINGS from midsummer to autumn
HARDWOOD CUTTINGS in winter
DIVISION in spring and autumn
SEEDS in autumn

Semi-ripe or hardwood cuttings from these evergreen shrubs are treated in similar ways. Wood taken once the first flush of growth has matured will root, but later cuttings root better. Plants flower after three years.

Prepare cuttings as leaf-bud cuttings (*see right and p.97*). Mahonias have quite short internodal growth, so a cutting can have two or more nodes. Make a small wound, about ½in (1cm) long, on one side of the stem; reduce the compound leaf to 2–3 pairs of leaflets. Root in free-draining medium; bottom heat of 59–68°F (15–20°C) improves rooting.

Mahonias can grow 12in (30cm) or more in a year, so several hardwood cuttings (*see p.98*) can be made from one stem. Divide clumping species such as *M. aquifolium* when not in active growth (*see p.148*).

Seeds often cross-pollinate, as do some taller *M. aquifolium* hybrids with *M. pinnata*, but seedlings are still worthwhile from home-gathered seeds. Gather ripe fruits in early summer, and clean and wash the seeds thoroughly before sowing (*see p.104*).

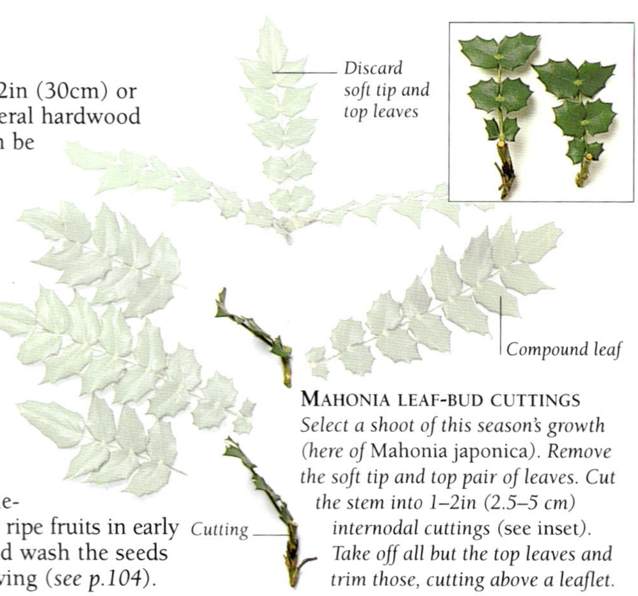

MAHONIA LEAF-BUD CUTTINGS
Select a shoot of this season's growth (here of Mahonia japonica*). Remove the soft tip and top pair of leaves. Cut the stem into 1–2in (2.5–5 cm) internodal cuttings (see inset). Take off all but the top leaves and trim those, cutting above a leaflet.*

MONSTERA LEAF-BUD CUTTING

1 Select a healthy, not quite mature leaf (here of Monstera deliciosa *'Variegata') with a good bud in the leaf axil. Cut straight across the stem just above the bud and about 1in (2.5cm) below the node, using a clean, sharp knife.*

2 Choose a pot that is no more than 1in (2.5cm) bigger in diameter than the stem. Fill with soilless rooting medium. Insert the stem vertically. Support the cutting with split stakes or roll up the leaf, stake it, and secure with a twist tie. Water and label.

NERIUM *OLEANDER, ROSE BAY*

GREENWOOD OR SEMI-RIPE CUTTINGS from late spring to early autumn
SEEDS in spring
LAYERING at any time

Nerium oleander is an evergreen shrub. To produce a flowering plant in two years, root 3in (8cm) greenwood or semi-ripe cuttings (*see pp.101 and 95*) direct in pots (*see p.96*) in a humid environment. Bottom heat of 54–68°F (12–20°C) speeds rooting, in 3–6 weeks. Cuttings also root in water (*see p.156*). Remove tips for bushy plants.

Gather seeds from beanlike pods in autumn. Sow in spring (*see p.104*) at 61°F (16°C) to germinate in two weeks. Oleanders hybridize readily (*see p.21*). Air or simple layering (*see pp.105–6*) produces a large plant but requires more time and effort than do cuttings.

OLEARIA *DAISY BUSH*

SOFTWOOD OR SEMI-RIPE CUTTINGS from summer to autumn
HARDWOOD CUTTINGS in winter

Among the evergreen shrubs in this genus, *Olearia stellulata* and similar weaker-growing species root reasonably well from softwood cuttings (*see p.100*) in free-draining medium in humid conditions, such as under plastic. Pot cuttings rooted early in the year, when hardened off, into 3½in (9cm) pots to avoid straggly plants. With hybrids such as *O. x haastii* and *O. x scilloniensis*, finding nonflowering shoots may be difficult; 2½–3in (6–8cm) semi-ripe cuttings (*see p.95*) root best. Leave the growing tips if possible, to prevent botrytis from setting in. Olearias also root well in rockwool (*see p.35*).

Hardwood cuttings (*see p.98*) of *O. macrodonta* root well. Make sure that the wood is fully mature at the base and root in a humid, frost-free place. If placed in a greenhouse, cover with plastic but do not provide bottom heat, which encourages rot. Large cuttings, 8–12in (20–30cm) long, will produce large plants ready to be planted in the garden the following autumn. New plants flower in 3–4 years.

OTHER SHRUBS AND CLIMBING PLANTS

LUPINUS Take softwood and greenwood basal cuttings (*see pp.100–1*) in spring. Too much humidity will rot the cuttings. Sow seeds in spring as for *Clianthus* (*see p.124*).
LYONIA Root greenwood and semi-ripe cuttings as for evergreen azaleas (*see Rhododendron, p.138*). Sow seeds as for *Rhododendron*.
MANDEVILLA Root softwood and greenwood cuttings (*see pp.100–1*) in early summer with bottom heat of 68–77°F (20–25°C). Sow seeds in early spring (*see p.104*) with bottom heat of 68–77°F (20–25°C).
MANETTIA Take softwood stem-tip cuttings (*see p.100–1*) in late spring or summer or semi-ripe cuttings (*see p.95*). Sow seeds in spring (*see p.104*) at 55–64°F (13–18°C).
MEDINILLA. Root greenwood cuttings (*see p.101*) in spring and summer, with humidity and 68–77°F (20–25°C) bottom heat. Sow seeds in spring (*see p.104*) at 66–75°F (19–24°C). Air layer any time (*see p.105*).
MELIANTHUS Take basal softwood cuttings (*see p.100*) in spring when new growth is no more than 6in (15cm) long. Divide clumps in early spring (*see p.101*). Sow seeds in spring as for *Abutilon* (*see p.118*).
MENZIESIA Root greenwood cuttings in summer as for evergreen azaleas (*see Rhododendron, p.138*). Sow seeds as for *Rhododendron* (*see p.138*).
METROSIDEROS Take semi-ripe cuttings as for evergreen *Ceanothus* (*see p.121*). Surface-sow seeds at 57°F (14°C) in spring (*p.104*).
MIMOSA Root nodal softwood cuttings (*see p.100*) in late spring. Sow seeds as for *Clianthus* (*see p.124*).
MIMULUS Take softwood to semi-ripe cuttings (*see pp.100–1 and 95*). Once rooted, harden off quickly, since they are prone to rot. Surface-sow seeds in early spring (*see p.104*).
MITCHELLA Take semi-ripe cuttings (*see p.95*) from late summer to autumn. Sow seeds in autumn (*see p.103*).
MYRICA Root nodal greenwood cuttings (*see p.101*) in early to midsummer with bottom heat. Take root cuttings as for *Celastrus* (*see p.122*). Sow seeds in autumn (*see p.103*). Simple layer (*see p.105*).
MYRTUS Root semi-ripe to hardwood cuttings as for *Pittosporum* (*see p.137*). For small-leaved species, which are more difficult to root, place ½–¾in (1–2cm) of fine grit on top of the medium. Sow seeds in autumn or spring (*see pp.103–4*).
NANDINA Take nodal greenwood cuttings (*see p.101*) in summer. Select wood just at the point at which the stem is darkening. Divide suckers (*see p.101*). Sow seeds in autumn (*see p.103*).
NEILLIA Root softwood to semi-ripe stem cuttings in summer as for *Philadelphus* (*see p.136*). Sow seeds in autumn (*see p.103*).
OEMLERIA (syn. *Osmaronia*) Take nodal softwood and greenwood cuttings in late spring as for *Amelanchier* (*see p.118*). Divide suckers as for *Amelanchier* (*see p.118*). Sow seeds in autumn (*see p.103*).
OSMANTHUS Root semi-ripe nodal stem-tip cuttings (*see p.95 and 101*) from late summer to winter. Where possible, take with a heel. Insert in free-draining medium or rockwool plugs with bottom heat. Sow seeds in containers in autumn (*see p.103*) and leave in a frost-free place.
OSTEOSPERMUM Take softwood to semi-ripe cuttings (*see pp.100–1 and 95*) at any time. Sow seeds in spring (*see p.104*).
OZOTHAMNUS Semi-ripe cuttings from late summer to winter as *Phlomis* (*see p.137*). Cuttings are prone to rotting off. Sow seeds in autumn (*see p.103*) in containers in a frost-free place.
PACHYSTACHYS Root softwood and greenwood nodal stem-tip cuttings (*see pp.100–1*) in summer.

MIMULUS AURANTIACUS

PAEONIA *PEONY*

Paeonia suffruticosa 'Reine Elisabeth'

SEEDS in summer
GRAFTING in late summer

This discussion refers to the shrubby deciduous tree peonies. Species come true from seeds but take several years to flower. Grafting is the best option. Plants flower in 2–3 years.

SEEDS

Sow seeds fresh (*see p.103*) in pots and provide two periods of chilling, such as two cold winters, with warmth between. Seeds are doubly dormant (roots emerge in the first year and seed leaves in the second). Guard against mice: they love the seeds. (*See also* Perennials, *p.204*.)

GRAFTING

A scion and rootstock of the same species avoids suckering; however, *Paeonia lactiflora* and *P. officinalis* stocks are often used. Take a piece of root about 4in (10cm) long and ½–⅝in (1–1.5cm) thick for a stock. Many stocks can be taken from one plant, and then discard the plant. Prepare a scion from a 1½in (4cm) single leaf-bud cutting with a bud in the axil. Make the cut in the stock to a depth of 1¼–1½in (3–4cm). Proceed as for a standard apical-wedge graft (*see p.108*).

In autumn, the grafts should be ready for potting. Grow on for a year in a frost-free place before planting out; make sure the union is underground to encourage the scion to root.

PARTHENOCISSUS *VIRGINIA CREEPER, BOSTON IVY*

SOFTWOOD OR SEMI-RIPE CUTTINGS from spring to midsummer
HARDWOOD CUTTINGS in winter
SEEDS in autumn and spring
LAYERING in spring

Cuttings of these vigorous, deciduous climbers can be a little awkward. Plants mature in three years.

CUTTINGS

Softwood cuttings (*see p.100*) may rot; semi-ripe ones (*see p.95*) root better but may fail to overwinter. Rooting takes 3–5 weeks. Cuttings of *Parthenocissus tricuspidata* should have several nodes to give them more overwintering buds from which to shoot away. Internodal cuttings 2½–3in (6–8cm) long of *P. quinquefolia* have only one node, but once rooted they grow away more readily. Cuttings from up to three-year-old hardwood (*see p.98*) root well in a frost-free place. Bottom heat can be used if the topgrowths remain cool; they are prone to premature bud burst.

SEEDS

Chill seeds extracted from black, fleshy fruit for two months, by sowing fresh in autumn or cold stratifying (*see pp.103–4*).

LAYERING

Many plants form aerial roots along the shoots; serpentine layer (*see p.107*) one such shoot to obtain several plants.

PARTHENOCISSUS TRICUSPIDATA 'LOWII'
Softwood or semi-ripe cuttings of this and other cultivars of Boston ivy should have at least 3–4 nodes; larger cuttings overwinter more easily.

PASSIFLORA *PASSIONFLOWER, GRANADILLA*

Passiflora 'Amethyst'

SOFTWOOD OR SEMI-RIPE CUTTINGS from spring to late summer
SEEDS at any time
LAYERING in spring

The mainly evergreen climbing plants in this genus are very easily increased from any type of softwood or semi-ripe cutting, including nodal stem-tip (*see p.101*), leaf-bud (*see p.97*), and semi-ripe stem (*see p.95*) cuttings. Rooting takes 3–4 weeks in a humid environment, but do not transplant until spring.

Cuttings may be rooted directly in pots (*see p.96*).

Ferment the seeds to kill fusarium disease: store ripe fruits for 14 days, mash, and leave pulp in warm place for 3 days. Clean seeds in a sieve under running water, then dry. Prior to sowing (*see pp.103–4*) at 68–77°F (20–25°C), soak the seeds for 24 hours in hot water to soften their hard coats. They should then germinate readily.

Very long shoots suitable for serpentine layering (*see p.107*) are produced every year. New plants fruit and flower freely after 2–3 years.

PHILADELPHUS
MOCK ORANGE

SOFTWOOD OR SEMI-RIPE CUTTINGS from late spring to midsummer
HARDWOOD CUTTINGS in winter
SEEDS in late winter or spring

Take softwood or semi-ripe, nodal stem-tip and stem cuttings (*see pp.100 and 95*) of these deciduous shrubs. The cuttings should be two internodes or about 3in (8cm) long; avoid thick, pithy water shoots and look out for tips distorted by aphids. Root semi-ripe cuttings in a tray or directly in pots (*see pp.95–6*). Rooting takes 4–6 weeks. Root hardwood cuttings (*see p.98*) in a frost-free place or on a heated bench.

Seeds germinate more freely if given 6–8 weeks chilling (*see p.103*) before sowing. Do not let seeds dry out.

SEMI-RIPE CUTTINGS
In spring, pot on cuttings (here of Philadelphus coronarius *'Aureus') rooted directly in pots, or plant out in a nursery bed.*

PHILODENDRON

SOFTWOOD OR SEMI-RIPE CUTTINGS at any time
SEEDS when ripe
LAYERING at any time

The evergreen, often epiphytic climbing shrubs in this genus naturally root from their stems, so they are easy to grow from cuttings or layers if kept warm and humid.

Leaf-bud, stem-tip, and stem cuttings (see *pp.95–101*) of soft- or semi-ripe wood, up to 4in (10cm) long, are all suitable (*see below*). The type of cutting is determined by the spacing between the nodes, which varies greatly. Rooting takes 4–6 weeks at 70–77°F (21–25°C). Cuttings require indirect light and misting during very warm weather.

TYPES OF CUTTING

PHLOMIS

SEMI-RIPE OR HARDWOOD CUTTINGS from midsummer to midwinter
SEEDS in spring

As with many gray-foliaged plants, cuttings of the evergreen shrubs and subshrubs in this genus are prone to rot if kept too wet; seeds of species germinate readily. Plants should mature in two years.

CUTTINGS

Take nodal stem-tip semi-ripe or hardwood cuttings (*see pp.95 and 98*), 4in (10cm) long, from nonflowering, current season's growth. Insert in free-draining medium and place under plastic. It is easy to kill cuttings if the medium and environment are too damp. Avoid bottom heat, which creates condensation that drips onto leaves, encouraging botrytis. Air the cuttings at least three times a week for 5–10 minutes. *Phlomis* root excellently under cover in the garden. Rooting takes 4–12 weeks.

SEEDS

Sow seeds in spring (*see p.104*) and cover with vermiculite. Germinate in 2–3 weeks at 59–68°F (15–20°C).

Extract seeds of species from ripe berries and sow immediately (*see pp.103–4*) with bottom heat of 68–77°F (20–25°C).

Air layering (*see below and p.105*), and simple layering (*see p.106*) provide large new plants in 12–18 months. Seeds or cuttings provide a good-sized plant in another year or so.

AIR LAYERING
Wound the stem when air layering a philodendron by bark-ringing the chosen shoot. Score two parallel cuts, about ½in (1cm) apart, around the stem. Take care not to cut too deeply into the pith. Then peel off the ring of bark to reveal the wood (see inset).

PIERIS

Pieris japonica

GREENWOOD OR SEMI-RIPE CUTTINGS from late spring to autumn
SEEDS in late winter or spring
LAYERING in spring

It can be hard to find good cutting material on these evergreen shrubs but is worth the effort, because only species are best raised from seeds. Plants flower in three years.

CUTTINGS

Once the new foliage loses its red or pink tinge, take thin nodal greenwood cuttings (*see p.101*), up to 3in (8cm) long, from a vigorous plant. Remove the tips and retain 4–5 leaves. Reduce larger leaves by half. With hormone rooting compound, free-draining, low-nutrient medium, and 54–59°F (12–15°C) bottom heat, rooting takes 6–8 weeks. Make ½–¾in (1–2cm) wounds on semi-ripe cuttings (*see p.95*).

SEEDS

Surface-sow seeds (*see p.104*); keep moist at 59°F (15°C). Seedlings grow slowly and are prone to scorch.

LAYERING

Simple layer (*see p.106*) in spring, but air layer (*see p.105*) at any time.

PITTOSPORUM

Pittosporum 'Garnettii'

SEMI-RIPE CUTTINGS in autumn
SEEDS in late winter
LAYERING in early spring
GRAFTING in late winter

The evergreen shrubs in this genus have more than one flush of growth, so it is easy to confuse an earlier flush with old wood. Take 2½–3in (6–8cm) semi-ripe cuttings (*see p.95*) from current season's growth. Cuttings can rot off at the base, but if inserted through a ¾in (2cm) layer of sharp sand on free-draining medium, they often root higher up the stem. Large-leaved and green species and cultivars root more easily. Rooting takes 8–12 weeks at 54–68°F (12–20°C). If leaf drop occurs, discard the cuttings and take a second batch.

Gather the sticky seeds when the capsules split, wash in soapy water, and sow (*see p.104*) at 59°F (15°C). Seedlings may be planted out after one season. Increase suitable shoots by air and simple layering (*see pp.105–6*).

Whip graft (*see p.109*) or spliced side graft (*see p.58*) onto a one-year-old *P. tenuifolium* seedling rootstock. Under plastic, the union calluses in six weeks; at this point, harden off and cut back the stock. Expect 12in (30cm) of growth in a year in sheltered conditions.

OTHER SHRUBS AND CLIMBING PLANTS

PARAHEBE Root greenwood cuttings in late spring and early summer in free-draining medium as for *Hebe* (*see p.130*). Sow seeds in spring (*see p.104*) in a frost-free place.

PARROTIOPSIS Root greenwood cuttings as for *Magnolia* (*see p.134*) in early summer. Sow seeds as for *Hamamelis* (*see p.130*).

PENSTEMON Take nodal softwood to semi-ripe cuttings (*see pp.100 and 95*) from spring to autumn. Sow seeds in autumn or spring (*see pp.103–4*).

PENTAS Take softwood cuttings (*see p.100*) at any time. Sow seeds in spring (*see p.104*) at 61–64°F (16–18°C).

PEROVSKIA Root nodal stem cuttings in spring before flowers form, as for *Caryopteris* (*see p.121*). Keep hardwood cuttings in winter frost-free (*see p.98*).

PETREA Semi-ripe cuttings (*see p.95*) in summer with bottom heat of 64°F (18°C). Simple or air layer (*pp.105–6*) in late winter.

x PHILAGERIA Layer as *Lapageria* (*see p.132*).

PHOTINIA Root nodal greenwood and semi-ripe cuttings (*see pp.101 and 95*) in free-draining medium from summer to winter. They root well in rockwool plugs and with high levels of rooting hormone. Sow seeds in spring (*see p.104*).

PHYGELIUS Take softwood basal cuttings in spring and nodal greenwood cuttings up to autumn (*see pp.100–1*). Sow seeds in spring (*see p.104*) at 50–59°F (10–15°C).

PHYLLODOCE As for heaths (*see pp.110–11*)

PHYSOCARPUS Softwood to semi-ripe cuttings from late spring to late summer as for *Caryopteris* (*see p.121*). Seeds in spring (*see p.104*) in a frost-free place.

PILEOSTEGIA Semi-ripe cuttings in summer and autumn as for *Escallonia* (*see p.127*). Simple or serpentine layer (*see pp.106–7*).

PIPER Greenwood cuttings (*see p.101*) in summer at 68–77°F (20–25°C). Seeds in spring (*see p.104*) at 68–77°F (20–25°C).

PIPTANTHUS Seeds as *Clianthus* (*see p.124*)

PISONIA Take greenwood to semi-ripe cuttings (*see pp.101 and 95*) in summer. Sow seeds in spring (*see p.104*). Air layer (*see p.105*) in spring.

PLUMBAGO Take softwood to semi-ripe stem cuttings (*see pp.100–101 and 95*) from spring to autumn. Seeds in spring (*see p.104*).

POLYGALA Root nodal softwood to semi-ripe cuttings (*see pp.100–1 and 95*) in spring and summer. Sow seeds of hardier species in autumn; sow seeds of tender species in spring (*see p.104*).

POLYGONUM *RUSSIAN VINE, MILE-A-MINUTE PLANT*

Polygonum baldschuanicum

SOFTWOOD OR SEMI-RIPE CUTTINGS from late spring to late summer
HARDWOOD CUTTINGS in winter
ROOT CUTTINGS in winter

These vigorous, deciduous climbers (syn. *Fallopia*) are very vigorous growers, yet softwood and semi-ripe cuttings (*see pp.100 and 95*) are surprisingly difficult to root. Some rot, while others fail to overwinter in colder climates. Take internodal cuttings no more than 2½in (6cm) long. Rooting takes 2–4 weeks and growth is slow. New plants take three years to reach flowering size.

With hardwood cuttings (*see p.98*), untangling the twisted mass of mature stems is usually the hardest part. They root well in deep pots or trays in a frost-free place such as a greenhouse. If shoots appear before roots are well developed, cover them with fleece to protect them from being scorched by the sun. Cuttings potted singly in 5½–7in (14–19cm) pots will be ready to plant in autumn. Root cuttings may be taken as for *Celastrus* (*see p.122*).

POTENTILLA *CINQUEFOIL*

GREENWOOD TO SEMI-RIPE CUTTINGS from late spring to late summer
HARDWOOD CUTTINGS in winter
SEEDS in autumn or spring

The deciduous shrubs in this genus (syn. *Comarum*) are easy to root from greenwood and semi-ripe stem cuttings (*see pp.101 and 95*), but they must not be allowed to dry out because the young foliage scorches easily.

Take cuttings 2–2¾in (5–7cm) long, and pinch out the growing tips if they are still soft. Rooting takes about three weeks. Nodal and internodal cuttings do equally well. Rooting directly in pots (*see p.96*) and under the protection of a sun tunnel (*see p.39*) are other options. Watch out for powdery mildew in spring and spider mite at the end of summer if raising plants under glass.

Similarly sized cuttings may be taken from hardwood (*see p.98*). These may be slightly larger than standard length for the more vigorous cultivars of *Potentilla fruticosa*, such as 'Gold Drop' and 'Klondike'. The cuttings root well in a cold frame or in a deep container on a heated bed in a frost-free greenhouse.

Shrubby potentillas may be grown from seeds (*see p.104*) but may take longer to flower, usually in two years, and produce variable offspring.

PRUNUS *ORNAMENTAL CHERRY*

SOFTWOOD CUTTINGS in late spring and early summer
SEMI-RIPE CUTTINGS from late summer to autumn
HARDWOOD CUTTINGS from late autumn to late winter
SEEDS in autumn or spring

There is a wide range of deciduous and evergreen shrubs in this genus. Flowering shrubs such as *Prunus tenella* and *P. glandulosa* root in 4–6 weeks from softwood basal cuttings (*see p.100*) taken from new 2½in (6cm) shoots as the flowers fade. Semi-ripe and hardwood cuttings (*see pp.95 and 98*) of the evergreen laurels, *P. laurocerasus* and *P. lusitanica*, root prodigiously if kept frost-free and humid. Reduce large leaves by half. Rooted cuttings may be potted in 5½–7in (14–19cm) pots in late winter and planted out the following autumn.

Gather seeds from ripe fruits. They need 2–3 months' cold to germinate: sow fresh in autumn or stratify in moist peat before spring sowing (*see pp.103–4*).

PYRACANTHA *FIRETHORN*

GREENWOOD OR SEMI-RIPE CUTTINGS from midsummer to early autumn
HARDWOOD CUTTINGS from late autumn to midwinter
SEEDS in autumn or spring

Several cuttings may be taken from one new shoot of the evergreen shrubs in this genus. In two or three years they will flower and fruit.

CUTTINGS

Greenwood or semi-ripe nodal stem cuttings (*see pp.101 and 95*), 2½–3in (6–8cm) long, root easily. Remove any soft tips and apply hormone rooting compound. Rooting takes 4–6 weeks.

Treat hardwood cuttings (*see p.98*) as above, but wound the bottom ¾in (2cm). Keep frost-free. Bottom heat of 54–68°F (12–20°C) speeds rooting. Larger cuttings, 8–12in (20–30cm) long, rooted in 5½–7in (14–19cm) pots, produce shrubs to plant out the next autumn. Cuttings taken in early winter may suffer from scab, preventing rooting.

SEEDS

Extract seeds from berries in autumn and winter (*see below*). The seeds need three months' cold stratification (*see pp.103–4*) before they will germinate.

GATHERING FIRETHORN SEEDS
Gather sprays of ripe fruits in autumn and winter. Squash them to remove most of the flesh, then wash by rubbing them in warm water. Sow fresh or store in moist sand in the refrigerator.

RHODODENDRON

Rhododendron 'Sappho'

SOFTWOOD OR GREENWOOD CUTTINGS from late spring to midsummer to
SEMI-RIPE CUTTINGS from midsummer to autumn
SEEDS in winter to early spring
LAYERING in spring and autumn
GRAFTING in winter

This genus includes a wide range of deciduous and evergreen shrubby azaleas and rhododendrons that can be propagated in a variety of ways. Times vary for first flowering, from 2–5 years or more.

CUTTINGS

To root deciduous azaleas, take softwood nodal stem-tip cuttings (*see p.100*) when the new growth is only an inch or two long, often when the shrubs are still flowering. Apply hormone rooting compound. Cuttings are susceptible to scorch, so shade heavily on bright, hot days. Placing cuttings under mist works well. Rooting takes 8–10 weeks. The greater the root growth before autumn the better, since overwintering small-rooted cuttings of deciduous azaleas is notoriously difficult. Placing rooted cuttings under fluorescent lights to extend the daylength in colder climates is beneficial.

For evergreen azaleas and dwarf rhododendrons, nodal greenwood cuttings (*see p.101*) root more easily.

Many of the evergreen, large-flowered hybrids root best from semi-ripe nodal cuttings (*see p.95*). Remove the tips, reduce larger leaves by up to a half, wound, and apply hormone rooting compound. Provide bottom heat of 54–68°F (12–20°C) for best results. Rooting takes 10–15 weeks.

SEEDS

Seeds from hand-pollinated plants often come true to type. Surface-sow the fine seeds (*see p.104*), gathered from dry pods, onto sieved acidic (ericaceous) soil mix. Ensure that the seeds do not

RHUS *SUMAC*

ROOT CUTTINGS in winter
DIVISION in late winter
SEEDS in winter and spring

For deciduous and evergreen shrubs and climbers in this genus (syn. *Toxicodendron*), root cuttings (*see Celastrus, p.122*) work very well, yielding saplings ready to plant out in a year. Sumacs sucker prolifically and so are easy to divide (*see p.101*). Soak the seeds in hot water for 48 hours and chill for three months (*p.103*) before sowing.

dry out by placing the pots or trays under mist, glass, or plastic wrap. Seeds need light to germinate. Bottom heat at no more than 61°F (16°C) reduces germination time. Leave small seedlings in the container until the following year, or transplant them into cells. Grow on under protection and shade as required in summer. Transplant spring-sown seedlings the following year.

LAYERING

Air (*see p.105*) and simple (*see p.106*) layering both work well, if suitable shoots are selected (*see below*).

GRAFTING

Spliced side-veneer (*see p.109*) in winter onto pencil-thick seedling rootstocks, either pot-grown or bare-root. Suckering from the stock can be a problem, so the union should be as low as possible. A rooted cutting of *R.* 'Cunningham's White' suckers less often. Plunge bare-root stocks in moist peat to encourage a fibrous root system and a good root ball to develop quickly. Callusing takes 6–8 weeks in a plastic tent at 59–68°F (15–20°C).

SELECTING SHOOTS FOR SIMPLE LAYERING *A healthy, strong stem with green, flexible shoots* (see left) *will bend more easily and root more readily when layered than older, woodier stems* (see right).

RIBES *FLOWERING CURRANT*

SOFTWOOD OR SEMI-RIPE CUTTINGS from late spring to midsummer
HARDWOOD CUTTINGS from late autumn to midwinter
BUDDING in mid- to late summer
GRAFTING in late winter

Cuttings of these deciduous and evergreen shrubs are taken from soft- or semi-ripe wood for ornamentals and from hardwood for fruiting currants and gooseberries (*Ribes uva-crispa* var. *reclinatum*). Standard gooseberries may be grafted. New plants mature or fruit in 2–4 years.

CUTTINGS

Softwood and semi-ripe stem and stem-tip cuttings (*see pp.100–1 and 95*) root reasonably well. Avoid using material affected with powdery mildew. For best results, take nodal stem-tip cuttings from 3–4in (8–10cm) of new growth, retaining the top two leaves. Apply hormone rooting compound, and protect young foliage from scorching.

Take hardwood cuttings of currants and gooseberries (*see right and p.98*). Insert cuttings of gooseberries and red- and whitecurrants (*R. rubrum*) to half their length. If desired, retain the top two leaves. Insert blackcurrant cuttings (*R. nigrum*) so that only two buds are above soil. Keep ornamental hardwood cuttings frost-free to ensure rooting.

GRAFTING

Chip bud or whip-and-tongue graft (*see pp.59–60*) gooseberry scions onto a rootstock such as *R. divaricatum* or *R. odoratum* at 3–4ft (1–1.2m). If chip-budding, insert two facing buds.

HARDWOOD CUTTINGS

PREPARING CUTTINGS *Cut ripe shoots of gooseberries and currants to length (see left). Retain all the buds on cuttings of blackcurrant (to produce plenty of shoots at or below ground level) and of gooseberry (to assist rooting). Remove all but the top 3–4 buds of red- and whitecurrant cuttings to prevent suckering.*

GOOSEBERRY CUTTINGS *Lift the rooted hardwood cuttings after one year. Rub out any shoots on the lower 4in (10cm) of the stem or any buds from the base of each cutting before planting them out. This will avoid formation of troublesome suckers when the bush establishes.*

OTHER SHRUBS AND CLIMBING PLANTS

PONCIRUS Root softwood to semi-ripe nodal cuttings (*see pp.100–1 and 95*) in summer. Sow seeds in autumn (*see p.103*).
PROSTANTHERA Take semi-ripe nodal stem-tip cuttings in late summer and autumn as for *Phlomis* (*see p.137*). Cuttings may rot. Sow seeds in spring (*see p.104*).
PROTEA Take semi-ripe stem-tip cuttings as for *Olearia* (*see p.135*). Sow seeds in spring (*see p.104*) at 50–59°F (10–15°C). Seedlings may damp off. Some species respond to smoke treatment (*see p.103*).
PTELEA Take greenwood nodal cuttings in early summer (*see p.101*). Sow seeds in autumn (*see p.103*).
PTEROSTYRAX Root softwood nodal cuttings in early summer as for *Caryopteris* (*see p.121*). Sow seeds in autumn (*see p.103*).
RHAMNUS Root semi-ripe to hardwood nodal cuttings (*see pp.95 and 98*) in autumn and winter in an open medium or rockwool plugs with 50–59°F (15–20°C) bottom heat. Sow seeds in autumn (*see p.103*).
RHAPHIOLEPIS Root greenwood nodal cuttings as for *Pyracantha* (*see p.138*). Sow seeds in autumn (*see p.103*).
RHODOTHAMNUS Root semi-ripe nodal cuttings (*see p.95*) in summer with 59–68°F (15–20°C) bottom heat. Sow seeds as for *Rhododendron* (*see p.138*).
RHODOTYPOS Root softwood to hardwood cuttings as for *Forsythia* (*see p.128*). Sow seeds in autumn (*see p.103*).
ROMNEYA For named cultivars, take root cuttings as for *Celastrus* (*see p.122*), but insert the root horizontally. Soak seeds in alcohol for 15 minutes (*see p.103*); sow in autumn. To avoid disturbing roots, transplant into cell packs.
ROSMARINUS Take semi-ripe and hardwood cuttings as for *Lavandula* (*see p.132*). Sow seeds in spring (*see p.104*).

RUBUS *BRAMBLES*

SOFTWOOD OR SEMI-RIPE CUTTINGS from spring to midsummer
HARDWOOD CUTTINGS in winter
ROOT CUTTINGS in autumn and winter
LEAF-BUD CUTTINGS in mid- to late summer
DIVISION from autumn to early spring
LAYERING from late summer to early spring

These deciduous and evergreen shrubs and climbers include raspberries (*Rubus idaeus*), blackberries (*R. fruticosus*), wineberries (*Rubus phoenicolasius*), and many hybrid berries. Although they are long-lived plants, they can carry viruses, so regular propagation maintains vigor. Blackberries can be invasive in some areas, such as Australia. Brambles root easily from all types of cuttings, but division is best for raspberries. For blackberries and hybrid berries, leaf-bud cuttings provide large numbers of new plants, and tip-layering is best where only a few plants are required. Fruit and flowers are usually produced after 2–3 years; divided raspberries fruit after one year.

CUTTINGS

Take softwood and semi-ripe cuttings (*see pp.100 and 95*) of ornamentals. They can be rooted directly in pots (*see p.96*). Cuttings inserted upside down root as well, if not better. Hardwood (*see p.98*) and root cuttings of deciduous species (*see Celastrus, p.122*) respond well.

Take leaf-bud cuttings (*see p.97*) where material is limited. Select a healthy section of cane about 12–18in (30–45cm) long, avoiding immature buds and choosing healthy buds with healthy leaves. Take a 1in (2.5cm) cutting, including a bud and about ½in (1cm) above and below it. Insert in a mix of equal parts peat and sand, in trays or pots, in a humid, frost-free place (or under mist). Rooting takes 6–8 weeks. In spring, pot or plant out in a nursery bed 12in (30cm) apart in rows 3ft (90cm) apart. They will be ready to plant out in the following autumn or spring.

DIVISION

This is best for raspberries. Lift mature plants in the dormant season and divide (*see p.101*), keeping at least one cane and a good root system with each piece. Plant in a new row, 15–18in (38–45cm) apart. Shorten the cane to 9in (23cm), just above a bud. For suckering species, divide rooted suckers (*see p.101*).

LAYERING

Tip layering (*see right*) is the best way to propagate blackberries. It utilizes the plant's habit of rooting from the tip when the canes touch the ground. For ornamental species, use serpentine layering (*see p.107*).

TIP LAYERING BRAMBLES

1 *In late summer, choose a vigorous, healthy cane, preferably at the edge of the plant. Bury the tip in a 4–6in (10–15cm) deep hole and firm. If needed, peg the cane down.*

2 *Keep the soil moist. The tip should root in a few weeks. Lift it at this stage and pot to grow on or leave it until spring and transplant. When severing the tip from the parent plant, retain about 9in (23cm) of the old stem.*

SALIX *WILLOW*

SOFTWOOD OR SEMI-RIPE CUTTINGS from spring to summer
HARDWOOD CUTTINGS from autumn to late winter
SEEDS in spring

The shrubby willows root very easily from cuttings. Take softwood or semi-ripe cuttings (*see pp.100 and 95*), and root in containers in humid conditions. They can also be rooted outdoors under cover (*see p.96*). More vigorous species may put on 3ft (90cm) of growth (or more) before autumn. For dwarf willows, take 1in (2.5cm) softwood cuttings in late spring to early summer.

Hardwood cuttings (*see p.98*) may be taken up to 8in–6ft (20cm–2m) in length, producing a mature plant a year or two earlier than standard cuttings. One way of obtaining young, straight shoots for large cuttings is to cut back a stock shrub almost to the ground each spring, a process known as stooling (*see p.56*).

If seeds are produced, they are viable for only a few days. Sow at once or store in damp peat in a refrigerator for no more than a month. Sow as for *Clematis* (*see p.123*) and keep moist at all times. The seeds should germinate in 1–2 days.

A LIVING FENCE
This fence, just coming into bud in spring, has been woven from 6ft (2m) hardwood cuttings of Salix viminalis. *The cuttings root readily to form a green fence. A few nurseries provide large hardwood cuttings, called sets, that can be inserted whole to form an almost instant windbreak on exposed hillsides.*

SAMBUCUS *ELDER*

SOFTWOOD OR SEMI-RIPE CUTTINGS from spring to midsummer
HARDWOOD CUTTINGS in winter
SEEDS in spring
GRAFTING in winter

The deciduous shrubs in this genus root easily from softwood or semi-ripe nodal cuttings (*see pp.100 and 95*) if suitable material is used. Avoid vigorous, pithy shoots, since these are likely to rot. Consider rooting directly in pots (*see p.96*). If possible, take hardwood cuttings (*see p.98*) with a heel, because large stems tend to be pithy and prone to rot. Root outdoors, or in containers in a frost-free place.

Gather the hard-coated seeds from the fleshy fruits (*see p.103*) as soon as they ripen in summer. If stored dry in a refrigerator, they remain viable for several years, but are best sown fresh in autumn (*see p.104*) where they will undergo a period of cold. Germination may occur in the first or second spring.

Spliced side graft colored cut-leaved cultivars, such as *Sambucus racemosa* 'Plumosa Aurea', onto one-year-old *S. nigra* seedlings (*see p.58*) for a good-sized plant by the following autumn.

SOLANUM

Solanum crispum 'Glasnevin'

SOFTWOOD OR SEMI-RIPE CUTTINGS from late spring to late summer
SEEDS in late winter to early spring

This genus (syn. *Lycianthes*) includes semi-climbing wall shrubs, both evergreen and deciduous, as well as the eggplant and potato (*see p.307*). Shrubby species are not usually difficult to root from cuttings. Winter cherries (*Solanum pseudocapsicum*) may be raised from seeds.

CUTTINGS

Solanum cuttings can suffer badly from botrytis and stem rots. It is best to take softwood and semi-ripe nodal stem cuttings (*see pp.100 and 95*), 2–4in (5–10cm) long, of the less vigorous new growth; select shoots with close-spaced nodes. Plants mature in 2–3 years.

SEEDS

Extract seeds from ripe fruits (*see p.103*) and sow fresh (*see p.104*), covering with ½in (1cm) of vermiculite. Provide 68°F (20°C) bottom heat to germinate within four weeks, and fruit in eight months.

SOPHORA

SEMI-RIPE CUTTINGS in late summer
SEEDS in autumn or spring

The deciduous and evergreen shrubs in this genus belong to the pea family, so the hard seeds must be treated before sowing. Success with cuttings depends on obtaining suitable material. Plants flower in 3–4 years.

CUTTINGS

Semi-ripe cuttings (*see p.95*) are best selected from plants that are still producing good new growth annually prior to flowering. Once the plant has reached maturity, when only enough growth is produced to bear the new flower buds, rooting becomes much more difficult. Insert cuttings 2–3in (5–8cm) long, where possible with a heel (*see p.96*), in free-draining medium. Apply hormone rooting compound and provide bottom heat of 59°F (15°C). Rooting takes 6–8 weeks. Harden off the seedlings, keep frost-free over winter, and pot in spring.

SEEDS

Gather seed and soak for 48 hours (*see p.103*) to remove the sticky coating. Sow fresh (*see p.104*) in warm climates or store dry in a refrigerator. Before spring sowing, soak in hot water for 24 hours.

SPIRAEA *SPIREA*

SOFTWOOD OR SEMI-RIPE CUTTINGS in spring to late summer
HARDWOOD CUTTINGS in winter
DIVISION when dormant

These deciduous shrubs all root readily from cuttings. Clump-forming species, such as *S. thunbergii*, may be divided. Plants flower in 2–3 years.

CUTTINGS

Take softwood and semi-ripe stem cuttings (*see pp.100 and 95*), 2–3in (5–8cm) long. Rooting takes 2–4 weeks. They may also be rooted directly in pots (*see p.96*) or in a sun tunnel (*see p.39*). With more vigorous species, such as *S.veitchii*, hardwood cuttings (*see p.98*) root well in a frost-free place or in a deep container placed on a heated bed in a frost-free greenhouse.

DIVISION

It is often a good idea to prune back the plant to within 12in (30cm) of the ground to make it easier to handle the clump before dividing it (*see p.101*).

STEPHANOTIS

Stephanotis floribunda

SEMI-RIPE CUTTINGS at any time
SEEDS in spring

These evergreen twining climbers and shrubs are easily increased from cuttings or seeds. New plants reach flowering size in 2–3 years.

CUTTINGS

Root semi-ripe nodal cuttings (*see p.95*), with 2–3 nodes, at a temperature of 70–77°F (21–25°C). Stem-tip cuttings also do well (*see p.101*). Several cuttings can be made from one shoot. Rooting takes 4–6 weeks. Cuttings require shading and misting during very warm weather to prevent scorch. Alternatively, place the cuttings under plastic.

SEEDS

Gather ripe seeds from the pods and sow fresh (*see pp.103–4*). Germination occurs at 68–77°F (20–25°C).

OTHER SHRUBS AND CLIMBING PLANTS

RUSCUS Take single-bud rhizome cuttings (*see p.149*) in early winter and grow on in a frost-free place. Divide clumps (*see p.101*) in early spring. Sow seeds in autumn (*see p.103*).

RUTA Root greenwood to semi-ripe nodal cuttings (*see pp.101 and 95*) in summer and autumn without bottom heat. Sow seeds in spring (*see p.104*).

SALVIA Take softwood to semi-ripe nodal cuttings (*see pp.100–1 and 95*). Surface-sow seeds in spring as for *Rhododendron* (*see p.138*).

SANTOLINA Take greenwood to hardwood nodal stem-tip cuttings (*see pp.101 and 98*). Seeds in autumn or spring (*see p.104*).

SARCOCOCCA Root greenwood to hardwood nodal cuttings as for *Buxus* (*see p.120*). Divide suckers (*see p.101*). Sow seeds in autumn (*see p.103*).

SCHIZOPHRAGMA Root greenwood nodal cuttings in summer as for *Pyracantha* (*see p.138*). Results can be variable. Seeds require three months of cold stratification (*see p.103*) before germinating.

SENECIO Root greenwood to hardwood cuttings of hardy species at any time as for *Lavatera* (*see p.133*). Take greenwood and semi-ripe cuttings (*see pp.101 and 95*) of tender species in summer and autumn. Sow seeds of hardier species in pots in spring (*see p.103*) in a frost-free place. Sow tender species in spring (*see p.104*) at 59–68°F (20–25°C).

SKIMMIA Take greenwood to hardwood nodal stem cuttings as for *Escallonia* (*see p.127*). Sow seeds in autumn (*see p.103*).

SOLANDRA Root greenwood to semi-ripe cuttings (*see pp.101 and 95*) in summer at 59–68°F (15–20°C). Sow seeds in spring (*see p.104*).

SORBARIA Take softwood to hardwood cuttings as for *Abutilon* (*see p.118*). Dig up rooted suckers (*see p.101*). Sow seeds in autumn (*see p.103*).

SORBUS Sow seeds in autumn (*see p.103*).

SPARTIUM Seeds as for *Clianthus* (*see p.124*).

STACHYURUS Root greenwood nodal or heel cuttings (*see pp.101 and 96*) in summer. Avoid vigorous shoots. Cuttings may root but fail to grow away in spring despite initial flowering. Seeds in autumn (*see p.103*).

STAPHYLEA Root greenwood nodal cuttings (*see p.101*) in summer. Sow seeds collected in autumn immediately to avoid drying out and loss of viability; they require periods of warm, then cold, stratification (*see p.103*).

STEPHANANDRA Nodal or internodal stem cuttings as for *Lavatera* (*see p.133*). Seeds as for *Staphylea* (*see above*).

STREPTOSOLEN Softwood stem-tip cuttings in early summer as for *Abutilon* (*see p.118*). Root semi-ripe cuttings in summer (*see p.95*). Simple layer in late summer (*see p.105*).

SWAINSONA As for *Clianthus* (*p.124*).

SKIMMIA JAPONICA 'RUBELLA'

SYMPHORICARPOS
SNOWBERRY

SOFTWOOD OR SEMI-RIPE CUTTINGS from late spring to early autumn
HARDWOOD CUTTINGS in winter
DIVISION from autumn to early spring
SEEDS in spring

These deciduous shrubs will root from 2–3in (5–8cm) long softwood or semi-ripe stem cuttings (*see pp.100 and 95*) in 2–4 weeks, maturing in 2–3 years. They may be rooted directly in pots (*see p.96*) or a sun tunnel (*see p.39*). Take hardwood cuttings as shown (*see right*).

Prune back, lift, and divide overgrown clumps (*see p.101*). Spring-sown seeds need warm, then cold, stratification (*see p.103*) to germinate the following spring.

HARDWOOD CUTTINGS OF SNOWBERRY

1 Hold 10–15 ripe shoots of current season's growth (here of Symphoricarpos albus*) together and cut into sections, each the length of the pruners. Tie the cuttings into bundles. Trim so that they are all the same length.*

2 Fill a pot with a free-draining medium (here equal parts potting mix and grit). Insert the bundles so that the lower half to two thirds are buried. Label. In early spring, plant out the rooted cuttings singly to grow on.

SYRINGA *LILAC*

Syringa vulgaris 'Président Grévy'

SOFTWOOD CUTTINGS in late spring
ROOT CUTTINGS in autumn
SEEDS in autumn or spring
LAYERING in spring
GRAFTING in late winter and mid- to late summer

Only cuttings from nonripened wood of the deciduous shrubs in this genus root, and seeds may be unreliable. Layering was the standard method until mist units arrived and is still easiest for the gardener. Lilacs are easy to graft, but suckers may be a problem. New plants take three years or more to flower.

CUTTINGS

Take stem cuttings (*see p.100*) from 2in (5cm) softwood shoots. With hormone rooting compound, free-draining medium, and bottom heat of 59°F (15°C), rooting takes 6–8 weeks. Root cuttings grow as easily as suckers: take as for *Celastrus* (*see p.122*), but insert singly in pots.

SEEDS

To ensure even germination, sow fresh seeds (*see p.104*) to chill over winter (*see p.103*). In early spring, apply 68°F (20°C) bottom heat. If spring-sown seeds (*see p.104*) germinate poorly, chill over winter to germinate next spring.

LAYERING

Simple layer (*see p.106*) with a 2in (5cm) tongue; lift in the following spring.

GRAFTING

Grow *Syringa vulgaris* rootstocks from root cuttings and cut back to 2in (5cm) to avoid suckering. Apical-wedge graft (*see p.108*) with a 2–4in (5–10cm) scion. In winter, whip graft (*see p.109*) onto bare-root two-year-old seedlings.

TAMARIX *TAMARISK*

SOFTWOOD CUTTINGS from late spring to midsummer
HARDWOOD CUTTINGS in winter
SEEDS in spring

The deciduous and evergreen shrubs in this genus have weak roots, which can be a problem with cuttings. Plants mature in three years.

CUTTINGS

Softwood cuttings (*see p.100*), 2–4in (5–10cm) long, root easily in free-draining medium, but foliage rots if kept humid for too long. Root singly in cells or pots to avoid weak roots dropping off when potting rooted cuttings.

Try rooting hardwood cuttings (*see p.98*) in deep trays in a frost-free place, then grow on for a year to allow a much bigger root system to develop. Then pot plants directly into 5½–7in (14–19cm) pots, or plant out in the garden.

SEEDS

Store seeds extracted from dry capsules in a refrigerator (*see p.102*) to preserve their viability. Spring-sown seeds (*see pp.103–4*) should germinate readily.

TIBOUCHINA

GREENWOOD CUTTINGS in summer
HARDWOOD CUTTINGS in winter
SEEDS in spring

The evergreen shrubs in this genus root easily from hardwood cuttings outdoors (*see p.98*) in free-draining soils in warm areas; otherwise, they need 59–68°F (15–20°C) bottom heat. Sideshoots of greenwood root well: insert nodal stem-tip cuttings (*see p.101*) in free-draining medium with bottom heat of 59–68°F (15–20°C). Rooting takes 6–10 weeks. Germinate seeds (*see p.104*) at 68–77°F (20–25°C).

VACCINIUM

SOFTWOOD OR SEMI-RIPE CUTTINGS from late spring to late summer
HARDWOOD CUTTINGS in winter
RHIZOME CUTTINGS in spring
DIVISION in autumn and spring
SEEDS in late winter
LAYERING in early spring

This genus includes evergreen and deciduous shrubs, many with edible fruit. They include bilberries (*Vaccinium myrtillus, V. caespitosum*) and whortleberries (*V. arctostaphylos, V. parvifolium, V. myrtillus*). The most popular of the genus, blueberries, are not easy but may be grown in several ways; cranberries are prostrate and suited to layering.

CUTTINGS

Highbush blueberries (*V. corymbosum*) root best from ½–¾in (1–2cm) softwood shoots (*see p.100*) or 4–6in (10–15cm) midsummer cuttings (*see p.95*). Retain the top 3–4 leaves; root in free-draining medium at 64–68°F (18–20°C). Pot in spring and grow on for a year.

Evergreens root best from semi-ripe material (*see p.95*). In areas with long, hot summers, hardwood cuttings (*see p.98*) of deciduous species can be taken from fully ripened wood. Root in a frost-free place or in deep pots.

Cut rhizomes of lowbush blueberries (*V. angustifolium* var. *laevifolium*) into 4in (10cm) pieces and root in perlite with 68°F (20°C) bottom heat, as for *Bergenia* (*p.190*).

OTHER METHODS

Divide mature clumps of the cowberry (*V. vitis-idaea*) and replant (*see p.101*). Surface-sow seeds on acidic (ericaceous) soil mix; cover with finely ground sphagnum moss, and keep moist until germination. Simple or self layer (*see pp.106–7*) cranberries (*V. macrocarpon*) and species that are difficult to root.

VIBURNUM

GREENWOOD CUTTINGS from late spring to early summer
SEMI-RIPE CUTTINGS from midsummer to autumn
HARDWOOD CUTTINGS in winter
SEEDS in autumn or in spring
LAYERING in spring
GRAFTING in late summer

The evergreen and deciduous shrubs in this genus fall into groups for propagation. Plants flower at various ages, from 2–3 years onward.

CUTTINGS

Greenwood cuttings (*see p.101*) are best for *Viburnum carlesii* cultivars and deciduous winter- and summer-flowering viburnums. For the former, take early cuttings; overwintering can be difficult. Insert nodal stem-tip cuttings, with a pair of leaves and three nodes, in free-draining medium. Halve large leaves. Hormone rooting compound improves rooting to 4–6 weeks. Root vigorous material directly in pots (*see p.96*). Pinch out terminal flower buds on new plants.

Evergreens root well from semi-ripe nodal or internodal cuttings (*see p.95*). Hormone rooting compound and gentle bottom heat speeds rooting to 6–8 weeks. Deciduous winter-flowering species also root from hardwood cuttings (*see p.98*) if kept frost-free and rooted in deep pots at 54–68°F (12–20°C). Internodal hardwood cuttings of evergreens, no more than 2½in (6cm) long, root well in 6–8 weeks in rockwool. Bottom heat of 54–68°F (12–20°C) and humidity speed rooting. Keep the rockwool moist at all times.

SEEDS

Sow seeds of species fresh (*see below*); they germinate more quickly with a period of warm, then cold, stratification (*see p.103*); seeds sown in spring (*see p.104*) germinate in the following year.

LAYERING

Many, especially the *V. carlesii* group, may be simple layered (*see p.106*).

GRAFTING

Whip graft (*see p.109*) scions of *V. carlesii* and *V.* x *burkwoodii* onto pot-grown *V. lantana* or *V. opulus* seedling rootstocks. Suckering can be a problem.

SOWING VIBURNUM SEEDS

1 *In late autumn, squash freshly collected ripe fruits (here of* Viburnum betulifolium*). Prepare a pot with soil-based potting mix. Scatter the pulp and seeds evenly on the surface.*

2 *Cover with ¼in (5mm) gravel and label. Leave in a cold place to encourage the seeds to germinate. This takes 6–18 months. Transplant singly into pots and grow on for two years.*

VISCUM *MISTLETOE*

SEEDS in early spring

These parasitic, evergreen shrubs may be found growing in apple orchards. Choose a mature, strong tree that will not be weakened by the parasite, of apple, ash, cedar, hawthorn, larch, linden, oak, or poplar. Squash some fresh berries and insert the very sticky pulp directly into a wound on the branch on which the mistletoe is to grow (*see below*). Seed germination and growth for the first couple of years are slow.

PLANTING MISTLETOE SEEDS

1 *Select a branch (here of an apple tree) 4in (10cm) or more in girth and 5ft (1.5m) from the ground. Make two short cross cuts in the bark; lift the flaps; push in some seeds (inset).*

2 *Cover the wound with a small piece of burlap or moss and secure with twine or raffia. This will protect the seeds from birds and from drying out until they germinate.*

OTHER SHRUBS AND CLIMBING PLANTS

SYMPLOCOS Root greenwood nodal cuttings as for *Pyracantha* (*see p.138*). Sow seeds as for *Staphylea* (*see p.141*).
SYNGONIUM Take softwood stem-tip (*see p.101*) or leaf-bud cuttings (*see p.97*) in summer.
TECOMANTHE Sow seeds at 64–70°F (18–21°C) in spring (*see p.104*). Root semi-ripe cuttings (*see p.95*) with bottom heat in summer. Serpentine layer (*see p.107*) in spring.
TELOPEA Root semi-ripe nodal stem-tip cuttings (*see pp.95 and 101*) in late summer and autumn in free-draining medium. Seeds have low viability; sow fresh, 2–3 seeds in a 3½in (9cm) pot at 77°F (25°C) (*see p.104*). Thin to one seedling; plant out after first flower in 2–3 years.
TERNSTROEMIA Root greenwood to semi-ripe nodal cuttings (*see pp.101 and 95*) in summer and autumn in free-draining medium. Seeds in autumn (*see p.103*).
TEUCRIUM Softwood to semi-ripe nodal cuttings (*see pp.100–1 and 95*) from summer to autumn. Sow seeds in spring (*see p.104*) at 68°F (20°C).
THUNBERGIA Greenwood nodal cuttings (*see p.101*) throughout summer. Seeds in spring (*see p.104*) at 68–77°F (20–25°C).
THYMUS *See* Culinary Herbs, *p.291*.
TRACHELOSPERMUM Root greenwood to semi-ripe nodal or internodal cuttings (*see pp.101 and 95*) in summer and autumn with 15–20°C (59–68°F) bottom heat. Simple or serpentine layer (*see pp.106–7*) spring.
UGNI Take semi-ripe cuttings as for *Callistemon* (*see p.121*).
ULEX Greenwood and hardwood cuttings as for *Genista* (*see p.129*). Soak seeds in hot water and sow in autumn or spring (*see pp.103–4*) with no bottom heat.
VINCA Take greenwood and semi-ripe internodal cuttings (*see pp.101 and 95*) at any time. For bushier plants, insert at least one and a half nodes below medium surface; new shoots then develop above and below surface. Avoid material with diseased black stem lesions. Divide clumps (*see p.101*) in early spring.
VITEX Root greenwood to semi-ripe cuttings (*see pp.101 and 95*) in summer with no bottom heat. Sow seeds in spring or autumn (*see pp.103–4*) in a frost-free place.

VITIS *GRAPE*

SOFTWOOD OR SEMI-RIPE CUTTINGS from late spring to midsummer
HARDWOOD CUTTINGS in late autumn or winter
SEED in spring
LAYERING in spring
GRAFTING in mid- to late winter

Genus of deciduous twining climbers. Many wine and dessert grapes are cultivars of *Vitis vinifera*. There are also hybrids between *V. vinifera* and *V. labrusca*. Most species root well from cuttings. *V. coignetiae* is difficult to root but responds well to layering. Grafting vines can be used to increase vigor or resistance to pests.

Take softwood or semi-ripe nodal cuttings (*see pp.100 and 95*), 3in (8cm) long with three nodes, from close-noded, thinner growth, which roots more quickly. Reduce foliage on large-leaved species by up to a half. Apply hormone rooting compound. Rooting takes about four weeks. Harden new growth before winter.

For all hardwood cuttings (*see above right and p.98*), check that the wood is still green in the center, since dieback can be a problem. In late autumn, before winter cold sets in, prepare vine eyes by making a cut above a bud and another 2in (5cm) below the bud. Insert in deep trays vertically with the bud on the medium surface, and root in a frost-free place or with bottom heat of 64°F (18°C). In early winter, take 2–3ft (60–90cm) cuttings from prunings, and tie them in bundles. Heel in, in a sheltered place, to two-thirds of their depth. In mid- to late winter, prepare standard-length cuttings (*see above*) from the prunings and root in pots (*see below*).

Sow seeds after a short period of chilling (*see pp.103–4*). Serpentine layer (*see p.107*) *V. coignetiae*.

Whip-and-tongue graft (*see p.59*) one or two scions onto suitable stocks in areas affected by the vine phylloxera (a serious pest affecting roots and leaves). Use the same graft for weak-growing cultivars.

ROOTED CUTTINGS *Hardwood cuttings may be taken in two lengths: with 3–4 buds or with one bud (vine eyes). The latter root less readily but yield a greater number of cuttings.*

STANDARD HARDWOOD CUTTINGS OF VITIS

1 *Root the cuttings (here of* Vitis vinifera*) in soil-based potting mix in a frost-free place with bottom heat of 70°F (21°C). A propagating blanket is ideal for large numbers.*

2 *When the cuttings break into bud in spring* (above left), *pot them singly* (above center). *Grow them on until the following spring* (above right) *before planting them out.*

WEIGELA

SOFTWOOD OR SEMI-RIPE CUTTINGS from late spring to midsummer
HARDWOOD CUTTINGS in winter
SEEDS in spring

These deciduous shrubs root very easily from cuttings. Take softwood and semi-ripe nodal stem cuttings (*see pp.100 and 95*), 2½–3in (6–8cm) long. Rooting takes about four weeks. Consider rooting directly in pots (*see p.96*) or in a sun tunnel (*see p.39*). In colder areas, semi-ripe cuttings root well in cold frames. Hardwood cuttings (*see p.98*) may be rooted in a sheltered place or in deep containers.

Extract seeds from the dry capsules and sow in spring as for *Phlomis* (*see p.137*) or in sheltered seedbed. They should germinate in a few weeks and produce flowering plants in 2–3 years.

WISTERIA

Wisteria × formosa

SOFTWOOD CUTTINGS from late spring to midsummer
HARDWOOD CUTTINGS in winter
ROOT CUTTINGS in late winter
SEEDS in early spring
LAYERING in spring
GRAFTING in late winter

These vigorous, deciduous, twining climbers are best increased by layering and cuttings.

CUTTINGS

Take softwood cuttings (*see p.100*), 2½–3in (6–8cm) long from less vigorous sideshoots with closely spaced nodes. Rooting takes 6–8 weeks. Harden the cuttings and encourage good root growth before winter. New shoots are unlikely to appear until the spring. Hardwood cuttings (*see p.98*) root best in a sheltered place or in deep pots in a frost-free greenhouse. Given bottom heat of 54–68°F (12–20°C), root cuttings (*see p.158*) ¾–1½in (2–4cm) long produce new shoots in 4–5 weeks.

SEEDS

Seed-raised plants are of varied quality and take years to flower and so are only useful as rootstocks. Soak dry seeds for 24 hours before sowing (*see pp.103–4*).

LAYERING

The long shoots produced annually are ideal for serpentine layering (*see p.107*).

GRAFTING

Apical-wedge graft (*see p.108*) onto two-year-old *Wisteria sinensis* seedlings, or onto lengths of root (*see below*). Plunge the graft into moist peat, keep humid, and provide 59–68°F (15–20°C) bottom heat. The union should callus in 3–6 weeks. Harden, then pot when the buds begin to swell.

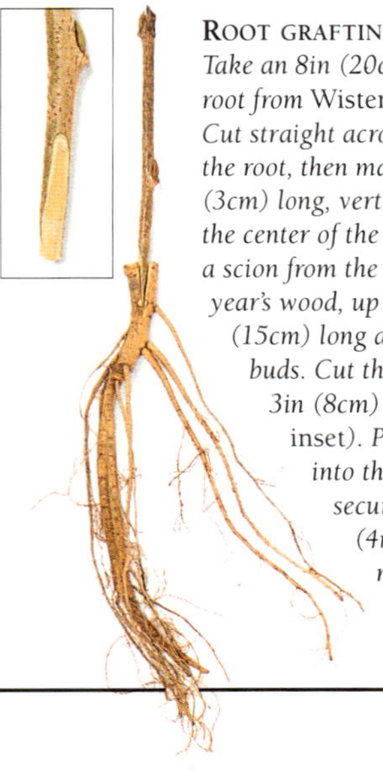

ROOT GRAFTING *Take an 8in (20cm) length of root from* Wisteria sinensis. *Cut straight across the top of the root, then make a 1¼in (3cm) long, vertical cut into the center of the root. Prepare a scion from the previous year's wood, up to 6in (15cm) long and with 2–3 buds. Cut the base into a 3in (8cm) wedge* (see inset). *Push the scion into the stock; secure with a ¼in (4mm) wide rubber band.*

YUCCA

SOFTWOOD CUTTINGS from late spring to summer
BUD CUTTINGS in early spring
DIVISION in late winter and early spring
SEEDS in spring

The evergreen shrubs in this genus make striking specimens. With the hardier, stemless species, it is possible to propagate from the swollen buds or "toes" produced on the roots, or from suckers. With the tender, stemmed species, you can use stem cuttings. New plants will be a good size in 2–3 years.

CUTTINGS

Young tender species often produce small shoots from the main stem that can be used as softwood cuttings (*see p.100*). Rooting takes 8–12 weeks.

For the tender *Yucca elephantipes*, you can take stem cuttings from mature shoots (*see below*). Cuttings may be placed horizontally in trays to induce young shoots, if none are available, for use as softwood cuttings. If the cuttings are to be grown on, they are best inserted vertically.

For root cuttings of hardier, stemless species, uncover the roots of a mature plant, or lift the entire plant, in early spring and cut off the swollen buds (*see below left*). If the buds are not yet breaking, dust with fungicide. Insert these individually into 3½in (9cm) pots, and cover well with soil mix. By autumn, you will have a well-established plant ready for planting out or growing on for another year in a 7in (19cm) pot.

DIVISION

For many of the smaller hardier, stemless species, division of suckers (*see below right*) works well. Shade new plants to prevent them from being scorched by the sun until established.

SEEDS

Soaking yucca seeds for 24 hours before sowing (*see pp.103–4*) can speed germination, but is not necessary. Provide bottom heat of 59°F (15°C).

TAKING YUCCA BUD CUTTINGS

1 Uncover the roots of a mature plant (here Yucca flaccida*). Remove swollen buds (toes) from the parent rhizome, cutting straight across the base of the toe.*

2 Pot each toe singly in a free-draining medium, at twice its depth. Water; label. With bottom heat of 59–68°F (15–20°C), the toe will root in 2–3 weeks (see inset).

DIVISION OF YUCCA SUCKERS

1 In spring, carefully uncover the base of a sucker (here of Yucca filamentosa*). Cut it off at the base, where it joins the parent rhizome. Dust the wounds with fungicide.*

2 Pot the sucker singly in a free-draining medium, such as equal parts soilless potting mix and fine grit. Label. Keep at 70°F (21°C) until rooted (12 weeks).

TAKING STEM CUTTINGS FROM A YUCCA

1 Remove a 1–3ft (30–90cm) section from a mature stem (here of Yucca elephantipes*), cutting between the leaf nodes.*

2 Strip all foliage from the stem. Cut the stem into cuttings, about 4in (10cm) long (see inset); trim alternately below a node and above a node with clean, sharp pruners.

3 Press the cuttings horizontally into a tray of moist soilless rooting medium so they are half buried, or insert single cuttings vertically into 3½in (9cm) pots. Keep humid at 70–75°F (21–24°C) until new shoots appear.

OTHER SHRUBS AND CLIMBING PLANTS

WESTRINGIA Root greenwood and semi-ripe cuttings (*see pp.101 and 95*) in summer and autumn in a very open medium with bottom heat of 59–68°F (15–20°C); do not allow the foliage to get too wet.
WIGANDIA Take greenwood cuttings (*see p.101*) in early summer. Sow seeds in spring or under cover in winter (*see p.104*) at 55–64°F (13–18°C).
XANTHOCERAS Take root cuttings as for *Celastrus* (*see p.122*). Sow seeds in autumn (*see p.103*).
XANTHORHIZA Take greenwood nodal cuttings (*see p.101*) in early summer. Divide clumps (*see p.101*) in spring and autumn. Sow seeds in autumn (*see p.103*).
ZANTHOXYLUM Take root cuttings as for *Celastrus* (*see p.122*). Divide rooted suckers (*see p.101*) in early spring. Sow seeds in autumn (*see p.103*).
ZENOBIA Root semi-ripe nodal cuttings (*see p.95*) in late summer in free-draining medium at 59–68°F (15–20°C). Sow seeds as for *Rhododendron* (*see p.138*).

Perennials

Propagating this hugely varied group of plants enables the gardener to keep existing plants healthy and vigorous, replace short-lived perennials as they fail, and build up stocks for an attractive border display

The term "perennial" strictly describes any plant that makes growth for three years or more, but in horticulture it is applied to non-woody perennial plants. Many make totally new herbaceous growth before flowering and seeding each year and die back in winter, especially in colder regions, but some are evergreen.

Perennials form a group of enormous value to the gardener, encompassing not only traditional border plants but alpines, water garden plants, ferns, and ornamental grasses including bamboos. Orchids and bromeliads are also perennials, grown mostly in warm-climate gardens or as house- or greenhouse plants in colder areas. These popular groups of plants are generally propagated using some specialized techniques.

The majority of perennials make new growth from the base, or crown; their roots or rhizomes spread (unless confined in containers) and the plants naturally form clumps, making division an obvious choice for propagation. Using division, the gardener can not only reinvigorate mature plants but acquire several small portions of the same plant, complete with their own roots and shoots, which can immediately be planted elsewhere in the garden as new plants. Commercial growers take very many small divisions from stock plants and grow them on in controlled environments; gardeners can often adopt these methods.

To give impact to plantings, perennials are often required in quantity – seeds or cuttings provide the means. Many perennials are easy to raise from seeds (spores can similarly be used for ferns), but new plants take longer to flower, and home-gathered seeds do not always come true to type. Cuttings raised in suitable conditions offer the best way of obtaining offspring that are clones of the parent, including cultivars with special characteristics such as particularly colored or large or double flowers; plants bred not to flower, such as the lawn chamomile 'Treneague'; foliage plants with finely cut, differently colored, or variegated leaves; single-sex plants; and sterile hybrids.

Dried thistle seeds
Like many sea hollies, Eryngium giganteum *does not readily tolerate root disturbance and is better raised from seeds. It is more poetically known as Miss Willmott's Ghost, because it would mysteriously appear in every garden this Victorian plantswoman visited: she scattered seeds of this, her favorite flower, wherever she went.*

Late-summer pollinators
Both the flower form and color range of Aster *attract bees and butterflies late in the season. These plants benefit from regular, even annual division, flowering more freely and being less prone to infection by powdery mildew.*

DIVISION

The easiest method of vegetative propagation for perennials is by division. It is the method most commonly used by gardeners for rejuvenating an old plant while providing extra plants and commercially for propagating many garden perennials in large numbers.

Most perennials should be divided every three to four years to keep them healthy and vigorous. Most of the late summer-flowering, fibrous-rooted plants, such as hardy chrysanthemum cultivars and Michaelmas daisies (*Aster*), flower best when divided annually or biennially. Perennials such as bearded irises produce new rhizomes each year. The clumps should be split and the divided rhizomes replanted every three years or so.

However, a few genera, such as peonies, *Podophyllum*, and to some extent hostas, prefer to be left alone and should be divided only for propagation.

Plants are divided in autumn or early spring, when they are not in active growth. Spring- and early summer-bloomers such as lily-of-the-valley (*Convallaria*), *Epimedium*, and *Uvularia* are left until after flowering. If necessary, most perennials can be divided at any time, except during hot, dry periods and freezing winter weather.

Early-summer division of some perennials works well, for example *Pulmonaria* and early-blooming bearded irises. At this time of year, new roots grow and any damage heals quickly, reducing the risk of rot. Potting the divisions may help them establish; keep them shaded. Some early-flowering plants, such as hellebores and peonies, form the following year's flower buds in mid- to late summer; divide these in late summer or early autumn to ensure flowers the next spring. All plants that are divided in summer should be watered thoroughly until they establish.

The secret of successful division at any time is always to have more root than shoot, to cut away excess foliage, and to keep the divisions moist and sheltered until established.

PREPARING THE SOIL

Division provides a good opportunity to improve the soil. Bulky organic matter, be it compost, leaf mold, or well-rotted manure, can be worked in where plants have been lifted. If replanting in the same site, add a little slow-release fertilizer such as bonemeal to give a good start to the new plants. Replanting divisions in a different site, however, helps maintain vigor and counteract any buildup of pests or of diseases in the soil.

SEPARATING PERENNIALS

Not all plants need to be lifted to separate them. A number of perennials naturally produce new plantlets around the parent, and these can simply be dug up and removed without lifting the parent plant. Some, such as strawberries, produce rooted runners (see p.150). Perennials such as bugle (*Ajuga*) form mats of individual rosettes; lift a mat and pull it apart gently into individual rosettes or lift just a few from the edge

DIVIDING PERENNIALS WITH MATURE CROWNS

1 Divide plants with a spreading rootstock, such as this Helianthus*, early in spring, just as the new growth is breaking. Lift the plant with a fork, inserting it well away from the crown to avoid damaging the roots.*

2 Shake the roots free of loose soil. Divide the plant into smaller pieces by chopping through the woody center with a spade. Try to avoid damaging the fresh, young growth around the perimeter of the plant.

3 Pull the divisions into smaller pieces with your hands. Make sure that each piece has a good root system and several new shoots. Discard the old, woody center and any other pieces without plenty of strong, new growth.

4 Replant the divided sections immediately, to the same depth as before, spacing them well apart to allow for new growth. Firm in lightly and water thoroughly, taking care not to wash away any soil and expose the roots.

SEPARATING CLUMPS WITH FIBROUS ROOTS

SMALL PLANTS *To divide a small perennial (here a gentian), lift the clump and gently pull it apart, using two hand forks held back to back. If the plant is very congested, cut it into pieces with a sharp knife.*

LARGE PLANTS *Some large perennials do not have woody crowns but become more and more congested at the center. Divide such plants (here a daylily) with two forks held back to back. Lever the forks backward and forward to loosen the roots.*

DIVIDING RHIZOMATOUS PERENNIALS

1 For perennials that have a thick rhizome (here an iris), lift the whole clump with a garden fork. Shake the roots free of soil and break the clump into manageable pieces with your hands.

2 With a clean, sharp knife, cut the new, young rhizomes from the clump. Make sure that each piece has a good root system and a fan of leaves. Discard the old, exhausted rhizomes in the clump.

3 Dust the cut surfaces of the rhizomes with a fungicide to prevent rot. Trim the roots by up to one-third. To prevent wind rock on irises, trim the leaves to about 6in (15cm) in a mitered shape.

4 Plant out the divisions. Settle them into the soil so that the top of the rhizome is just barely covered with soil. Firm in well and water regularly until established.

of the mat. While this is not division in the strict sense, the results are similar: the spread of the parent is restricted, and new plants obtained.

Dividing perennials

When lifting plants for division, shake or wash them free of soil, using a hose or a bucket of water. Cleaning the rootstock reveals any natural lines of division, so the plant can be split easily with minimum damage to roots, buds, or shoots.

Pulling the plants apart rather than cutting them does less damage. Small plants such as *Heuchera* and primroses and those with a loose clump of underground stems, such as *Dicentra formosa, Epimedium pinnatum,* and *Geranium sanguineum*, can be pulled apart into pieces. With some plants that have a large mass of roots, such as lily-of-the-valley, a hand fork is very useful for teasing out small pieces.

For larger fibrous-rooted perennials, the traditional method of splitting clumps using back-to-back garden forks (*see facing page, below*) is hard to beat. Perennials with a tight woody crown (*Astilbe*, hellebores, *Geranium pratense* cultivars, and *Trollius*), rhizomatous perennials, and those with fleshy roots, for example delphiniums, herbaceous peonies, and *Rheum*, need to be cut apart. A spade or an old, strong knife is ideal.

As much as possible, care should be taken to avoid damaging the roots during division. Treatment of root damage differs, depending on whether the perennial is a dicotyledon or a monocotyledon (*see page 17*). Most perennials are dicotyledons; if any damaged or oversized roots are trimmed neatly after division, root growth should continue unabated. Monocotyledonous perennials – in which single, large leaves, rather than leafy stems, arise from the crown, such as with hostas, rhizomatous irises, and *Lysichiton* – are unable to regenerate damaged roots. Cut such roots back to the crown to encourage formation of new roots.

The exposed roots of divided plants should never be allowed to dry out. If there is to be a delay between lifting and replanting, the divisions should be heeled in, either in a spare corner or a box of moist soil mix or peat. Plastic storage crates are ideal for this purpose.

Care of divisions

As a general rule, try to divide plants into good-sized portions, each with vigorous, new growth. If a plant is divided into many small pieces, the divisions will take longer to mature to flowering size than a few, larger pieces. Established clumps may have woody centers; these parts lack vigor and are best put on the compost pile. Also, discard any damaged portions.

Once the parent plant has been divided, trim off any dead or damaged material (*see facing page*). Use a clean, sharp knife to avoid introducing disease into cuts. Badly damaged roots or shoots can also be treated with a fungicide to protect against rot entering the wounds. Vigorous, healthy, and relatively undamaged divisions with three to five shoots and good roots can be replanted immediately (*see facing page*) or lined out for growing on in a nursery bed. Plant divisions in a nursery bed at about one-half to two-thirds of the usual spacing appropriate for a plant in the open garden.

Pot smaller pieces individually, each in a pot just larger than its roots, and place them in a sheltered place to grow on until they are established. Be aware though that many plants (particularly those with fleshy roots) that are fully hardy in the ground will die if their roots are exposed to severe cold while in pots. In colder climates, therefore, they will need to be plunged or taken under cover (*see pp.42–43*) over winter. When they are of a reasonable size, replant the divisions into prepared soil.

Very small divisions of hardy perennials should be encouraged to put on as much growth as possible before the end of the growing season. Pot them in a fertile, free-draining soil mix, such as one part fine grit to two parts soil-based potting mix, which will provide nutrients for growth, and place under cover where the temperature is higher than outdoors. This will extend their growing season. Provide shade in summer to protect the young plants from scorch, and keep well watered.

Benefits of division *Left to their own devices, perennials such as the* Heuchera *shown here can deteriorate in vigor and appearance as old, woody stems develop at the base of the plant. Flowering performance can also be impaired. To maintain the plant at its best, divide it every four years or so.*

Single bud divisions

In commercial propagation, some genera are reduced to single buds to maximize yields of new plants identical to the parent. It is most often practiced on monocots such as *Agapanthus*, daylilies (*Hemerocallis*), and hostas but also on many other perennial cultivars. Best results are obtained from division in spring just as the plants start into growth.

Single bud division (*see right*) can be undertaken by the gardener. Make sure that a good portion of root is taken with each division, and avoid inflicting any more damage than is necessary. Grow them on in a sheltered nursery bed, or pot them into deep 3½in (9cm) or, for larger plants, 5in (13cm) pots, making sure that each bud is covered to the same depth as it was before. Greater protection from extreme temperatures (*see pp.38–45*) is needed for these divisions in the early stages.

If more plants are wanted quickly, single fleshy buds of plants such as hostas may be divided in half vertically through the bud crown, but this does encourage rot; absolutely scrupulous hygiene is essential. Pot halved buds in deep 5in (13cm) pots and give bottom heat (*see p.41*) to increase growth and help the buds establish quickly.

Dividing container-grown plants

Division of container-grown plants is usually very successful. Plants with rooting stems, or runners, such as the mother of thousands saxifrage (*see right*), need not be removed from their pots at all but can be encouraged to develop new plantlets by pegging the runners into small pots of soil mix. Fleshy-rooted plants such as spider plants (*see below, right*) actually divide and reestablish better if container-grown, because it avoids the damage to the roots caused by lifting from the border. They can be divided at any time, but ideally after flowering or when dormant.

To divide a container-grown perennial, knock it out of the pot, then wash the soil mix from the roots, if preferred, to reveal the natural lines of division. Pull the plant into good-sized pieces (usually three or four). With potbound plants, it may be necessary to cut through the crown with a large knife and tease the roots apart from the top. Be careful not to cut into and damage the roots.

Trim any damaged roots on the divisions, according to whether the plant is a dicotyledon or monocotyledon (*see p.149*), and pot singly. Use a soil-based potting mix, which provides stability to the root ball and consistent levels of nutrients and is easily rewetted if the soil mix dries out.

SINGLE BUD DIVISIONS

Fleshy-rooted plants *Pull apart the crown, making sure each piece (here of a hosta) has a single, plump bud and a good root system. Line out the divisions in a nursery bed at the same depth as before and 6in (15cm) apart, or pot.*

Perennials with creeping rootstocks *Cut the rootstock (here of* Veronica austriaca*) into sections, each with a strong bud and a good root system. If necessary, trim the longer roots.*

PROPAGATION OF ROOTING RUNNERS

1 *Prepare a 3in (8cm) pot of moist rooting medium. Peg a runner (here of* Saxifraga stolonifera*) down so that the base of the plantlet is in contact with the soil mix surface.*

2 *Once rooted, usually after a few weeks, sever the runner close to the new plant. Grow on the plantlet until the roots fill the pot, then pot into soil mix.*

DIVIDING A CONTAINER-GROWN PLANT

1 *Water the plant well (here* Chlorophytum comosum*) and let it drain. Slide the plant from the pot and shake off the soil mix. Loosen the root ball from below; gently pry apart.*

2 *Trim any diseased or damaged thick roots from each division, leaving fibrous feeding roots intact. Pot singly into pots about ¾in (2cm) wider than the root ball* (see inset)*, using a similar soil mix.*

Sowing seeds

Seeds provide a simple and economical way of raising large numbers of perennials, although it has limitations. Many cultivars do not come true from seeds, and even commonly grown species display some natural, albeit acceptable, variation in the seedlings. However, there is always a chance of producing a seedling that is superior to its parents.

Some cultivars do, however, come reasonably true to type, including some delphiniums, lupines, and Oriental poppies (*Papaver orientale*). Seedlings with colored, marbled, or variegated leaves, such as *Heuchera* cultivars, vary in color, so poor forms need to be rogued out at an early stage.

Seeds also offer the only way of raising monocarpic species, such as *Meconopsis*, that die after the first flowering. Perennials that are very slow to increase vegetatively, such as *Hepatica* and *Pulsatilla*, may be raised in large numbers commercially from seeds.

Sorting seeds *Seeds can be cleaned using specialized stacking sieves. Lightly crush dry seedheads through a sieve with a mesh just larger than the seeds. The seeds fall through this top sieve and are caught in the sieve with a finer mesh below. Fine chaff sifts through and collects in the dish below.*

Gathering perennial seeds

Saving seeds from one's own plants is easily done by the average gardener. Many perennials produce seeds readily, often in papery capsules or pods. Gather from plants with the best characteristics of the form to ensure good-quality seedlings. Seedheads can ripen quickly, so watch them closely and gather the seeds before they are dispersed. Choose a dry day to ensure that the seeds are not damp and at risk of rot.

In some cases, for example with irises and peonies, seedheads are obvious and easily seen, whereas other seedheads, as with *Hepatica* and primrose (*Primula vulgaris*), are hidden among the foliage. Remove each seedhead and crush it between two pieces of wood or with your fingers to release the seeds over a clean sheet of paper. *Euphorbia* and some other perennials have seedpods that "explode" to eject the seeds or disperse them very rapidly; remove these seedheads on their stems as they turn brown and place in a paper bag. Always label bags of seeds when you gather them to avoid confusion later.

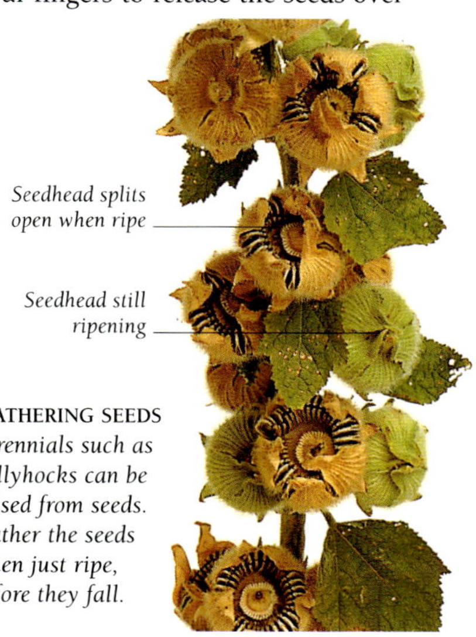

Gathering seeds *Perennials such as hollyhocks can be raised from seeds. Gather the seeds when just ripe, before they fall.*

Sorting and cleaning seeds

A simple way to clean gathered seeds is to place them in a shallow container and blow lightly over them to clean off dust and chaff, leaving the seeds behind. Use kitchen, homemade, or specialized (*see above*) sieves with metal gauze to clean seeds thoroughly for storing. An assortment of mesh sizes will be needed for differently sized seeds. Use one sieve to hold coarse chaff, a finer sieve to catch the seeds, and a tray to receive dust. Take care not to confuse seed sieves with kitchen sieves: some seeds are toxic.

Gather berries as soon as they are ripe of plants such as lily-of-the-valley (*Convallaria*) and *Polygonatum*, then macerate them. Place the berries in a sieve under running water and rub off the pulp. Alternatively, add the mashed berries to a bowl of water and stir well. The pulp and dead seeds usually float; viable seeds should sink. Pour off the pulp and dry the seeds on paper towels.

When to sow perennial seeds

Some seeds are best sown immediately after gathering. Seeds of perennials that flower in early to midsummer germinate more quickly and uniformly if sown fresh, for example lupines, primroses, or poppies (*Papaver*). Some perennials, such as *Meconopsis* or *Primula*, have very short-lived seeds. *Euphorbia*, gentians, and several others are best stored in a cool place until autumn and sown then. Seeds of later-flowering perennials, if sown in autumn, will not germinate until early spring. In most cases, such as for most chrysanthemums and asters, these seeds may be stored over winter and sown in spring.

Storing seeds

Seeds must be stored in a cool, dry place; humidity and warmth cause seeds to deteriorate and die. A good place to store seeds is in the refrigerator at 41°F (5°C). Place dry seeds in labeled paper packets in an airtight, plastic container.

A little desiccant, such as silica gel, placed in the container will remove excess moisture. Place a packet in with the seeds or, better still, sprinkle gel in the bottom of the container and sit the seed packets on a piece of metal gauze above the gel. Another option is powdered milk from a newly opened box, although this can be used only once. Both of these products absorb moisture from the air and reduce humidity. Avoid opening the container unnecessarily.

Seed viability

The usual reason for germination failure is that dead seeds are sown. Seeds fail for a number of reasons: the seeds may not be fertilized or (*continued on p.152*)

Testing seeds for viability *Add medium-sized or large seeds to a jar of water. Viable seeds sink to the bottom, while dead, hollow seeds float. After drying them off, sow the viable seeds immediately.*

SEEDS FROM DRIED BERRIES

Some perennial berries (here of Actaea spicata*) may be dried for storage. Before sowing, crush the dried berries with a wooden presser or weight, then sieve to sort the chaff from the seeds.*

SCARIFICATION BY SOAKING

Some seeds (here of lupines) have hard coats that are broken down naturally by moisture. Prepare them for sowing by soaking them for 24 hours in a saucer of cold water. Sow immediately.

(*continued from p.151*) may fail to fully develop, hybrid seeds may have defective genes, or seeds may be damaged by fungal or insect attack. After sowing, seeds may be killed by rot, rodents, or severe cold.

Treating dormant seeds

Some perennial seeds have built-in dormancy to delay germination in the wild until conditions occur that are beneficial for seedling development (*see pp.19–20*). There are several ways to break this dormancy before sowing to obtain a good rate of germination. Hard protective seed coats in perennials are most common in the pea family (Fabaceae). The seed coats must be scarified so that moisture can enter. Gardeners are often advised to file seed coats, but anyone who has tried this with dozens of lupine seeds knows it is painful and time-consuming.

A better way of scarifying larger seeds is to rub a batch with fine-grade sandpaper (*see* Shrubs and Climbing Plants, *p.102*).

With seeds gathered in cool, moist summers, it is often sufficient to soak the seeds (*see above*). If the seeds are large or from plants grown in hot, dry conditions, pour boiling water over them and allow to stand in the cooled water for 24 hours. Sow soaked seeds immediately; otherwise, they will die.

Many perennials, particularly those from mountainous or harsh climates, have seeds that do not germinate until after a cold period. The seeds must be chilled (stratified) before sowing in spring by placing them in a refrigerator, or sown in autumn in regions with cold winters (*see opposite*).

A few perennials, such as peonies, are doubly dormant and require a period of cold, then warmth, followed by a second spell of cold. If the seeds are not sown fresh, they take two years to germinate naturally. This can be overcome by subjecting the seeds to artificial temperature changes.

To override chemical inhibitors (*see p.19*) in the seeds of some perennials, the seeds are sown as soon as they are fully formed before the inhibitor is activated, sown after storing when it has broken down, or soaked in water for 48 hours to leach out the chemical, as with rhizomatous irises.

Preparing containers for sowing

Perennial seeds are often sown in pots or half pots of 3½in (9cm) to 5in (13cm). Seeds that germinate quickly

RAISING PERENNIALS FROM SEEDS

1 Fill a container, here a 5in (13cm) pot, with moist seed soil mix. Firm it gently to no more than ½in (1cm) below the rim.

2 Sow the seeds (here of Leucanthemum x superbum*) thinly and evenly from a folded piece of paper or from the packet.*

3 Cover with a shallow layer of sieved soil mix. Label and stand the pot in water until the surface darkens; allow it to drain.

4 Cover the pot with a sheet of glass or plastic wrap to prevent moisture loss. Place in a sheltered place at a suitable temperature.

5 When the seedlings have two seed leaves, transplant singly. Use degradable pots (see inset) for plants that dislike root disturbance.

6 As soon as the seedlings have a good root system, plant them out into their final positions or pot them on, as appropriate.

SOWING FINE SEEDS

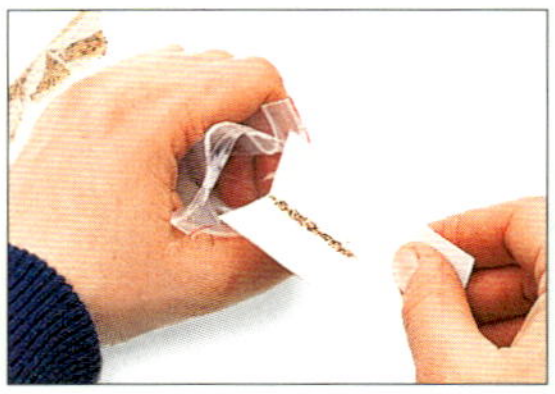

1 Very fine, dustlike seeds (here of Campanula*) can be mixed with fine sand to make it easier to sow evenly. Place the seeds and a little sand in a plastic bag and shake well.*

2 Fold a piece of clean paper in half to make a funnel and place some of the sand and seeds mixture on the crease. Gently tap the paper to sift the seeds over the soil mix.

VERMICULITE TOP-DRESSING

Seeds in containers may be covered with a ¼in (5mm) layer of fine-grade vermiculite instead of soil mix. This allows air and light to reach the seeds, reducing the risk of damping off (see p.46).

and easily, such as of delphiniums or lupines, or those of plants that dislike root disturbance, are best sown singly in cells or plug trays (*see p.31*); use one with cells large enough for seedlings to reach a good size before potting.

Soil-based seed soil mixes (*see pp.33–4*) are best for most perennials unless the seedlings will be transplanted soon after germination. A good home-made seed soil mix can be made of two parts sterilized soil, two parts peat or leaf mold, and one part sharp sand. For autumn sowings, equal parts coarse sand and peat, bark fiber, or soil works equally well.

To prepare a container for sowing, fill it generously with soil mix, tap to settle it, scrape off the excess, and firm with a presser or base of an empty pot.

Sowing seeds in containers

Take care not to sow (*see facing page*) too thickly, which could lead to spindly seedlings and damping off (*see p.46*). Cover with screened soil mix or, for seeds that need light to germinate or germinate quickly, top-dress with vermiculite (*see above*). Large seeds may be space-sown, pushed into the soil mix with a presser, and covered with ¼in (5mm) of soil mix. Seeds that must not dry out fare better when sown on moss (*see pp.165 and 208*).

After sowing, water containers using a fine rose or by standing the container for 30 minutes in a tray of water; this avoids disturbing the soil mix surface and seeds. Cover the container or place in a closed case to prevent moisture loss, and shade it from sun if necessary. Remove the cover after germination.

For most seed germination, an ideal temperature is 60°F (15.5°C). Keep seeds of very hardy plants at 50°F (10°C); they will germinate at lower temperatures, but it takes longer. Tender species need a minimum of 68°F (20°C). If containers are sown in autumn for stratification by winter cold, cover the

STRATIFYING SEEDS

In cooler climates, plunge pots of seeds up to their rims in an open bed of sand, bark fiber, or soil over winter so that cold will encourage the seeds to break their dormancy and germinate.

seeds with a shallow layer of fine gravel or coarse sand to discourage weeds and protect seeds from rain. Pack the containers into an open cold frame or sink in a plunge bed (*see above*). The bed keeps the soil mix moist and protects clay pots and plant roots from cold damage. Cover the containers with fine mesh to protect the seeds from birds and rodents.

Seeds of perennials can be fickle. Seeds that normally germinate quickly may not do so, and supposedly dormant seeds may germinate rapidly. It is wise to keep pots or trays of seeds for a year after the expected germination date.

Handling the seedlings

Seedlings need bright light and regular watering. If using rockwool plugs or another inert medium, feed the seedlings once they have two true leaves with a liquid fertilizer according to the manufacturer's instructions.

Transplant seedlings 30 or 40 to a tray or individually into plugs, cells, or pots (*see facing page*) as soon as they are large enough to handle. If the seedlings germinated under cover at a frost-free temperature, it is better to pot them when they are slightly larger. Always handle seedlings by the leaves. Use soil-based potting mixes (*see pp.33–4*) or a mix of three parts sterilized soil, two parts peat or leaf mold, and one part sharp sand.

Grow on the seedlings in a sheltered place until well established. Plant out fast growers into their final positions in the same year, but delay planting out slow developers until the next spring. These are better potted or grown on in a nursery bed for a year.

Sowing seeds outdoors

Easy perennials may be raised in a seedbed: the seeds are best spring-sown in drills as for annuals or biennials (*see pp.218–19*). If needed, thin the seedlings as they grow; when they are about 3in (8cm) tall, lift and plant them out.

Seeds that germinate slowly may rot if the soil mix decomposes, so these are better sown directly into a seedbed in a cold frame. Sow them in rows, label, and top-dress with fine gravel. Keep the bed moist and weed-free; be aware that organisms working through the bed may displace the seeds.

Seedlings may need potting or transplanting after only a few weeks; if left too long, they become crowded and drawn as they compete for light and air.

Hybridizing perennials

Many perennials, such as daylilies, irises, chrysanthemums, or hostas, can be hybridized (*see p.21*), sometimes with exciting results. It helps to focus on one group, research its characteristics, and have a specific aim, such as to produce larger-flowered, hardier *Agapanthus*.

Alternatively, simply plant suitable parents together, let the bees do the work, gather the seeds, and select from the resulting seedlings. Be ruthless and keep only the best examples.

TRANSPLANTING SELF-SOWN SEEDLINGS

Many perennials, such as these Oriental poppies (Papaver orientale), *naturally seed themselves about the garden.*

Use a trowel to lift each seedling with enough soil to avoid disturbing its root ball. Replant the seedlings immediately into prepared soil in a suitable site, firm gently, label, and water. Keep watered and shaded, if necessary, until they are established.

TAKING CUTTINGS

A wide range of perennials can be propagated from cuttings, using a variety of plant parts: stems, leaves, and roots. In most cases, some form of controlled environment – a heated closed case, greenhouse, or cold frame, for example – is necessary to encourage the cutting to regenerate missing parts, such as roots. If these conditions can be provided, cuttings are ideal for obtaining a number of new perennials that will be ready to plant out, and may even flower, in their second year.

Mature plants recover well from having a modest amount of cutting material removed, or stock plants can be cultivated especially for the purpose of providing cuttings. Good hygiene – clean, sharp tools, sterile growing media, and the prompt removal of dead or damaged material or of any cutting in a batch that shows disease – helps ensure success. With some perennials, you can take cuttings at almost any time of the year they are not in flower, whereas with others material is suitable only during a few weeks or even days. If taken after flowering, many cuttings will root and grow well. Cuttings from perennials that die down over winter should be taken early in the growing season so that the cuttings have plenty of time to form good root systems capable of coming through the next dormant period.

ROOTING MEDIA

Materials into which cuttings are inserted must give them support and be sterile, water-retentive, and well aerated: mixtures of peat and fine grit, perlite, vermiculite, or sand are among the most popular (*see p.33*). Several inert media can also be used: rockwool (*see p.35*) and vermiculite are popular for stem cuttings; for some tricky alpines, ground pumice is used (*see p.167*). Some easy-to-root plants will develop roots from stems that are simply suspended in water (*see p.156*).

PROTECTING CUTTINGS

Cuttings taken from the topgrowth of perennials are usually soft or semi-ripe, and it is essential that their tissues remain turgid (well supplied with water). In dry air or in wind, water will be lost from stem and leaf surfaces and the cutting will rapidly wilt, so a sheltered, humid growing environment is essential. In tropical and subtropical climates, stem cuttings may root well in open ground, but in other zones they must have protection in a greenhouse or plastic-film tunnel or, on a small scale, in a closed case or a cold frame or covered on a shaded windowsill.

Stem cuttings are in general more likely to root if provided with bottom heat, making the exposed growth cooler than the buried part. Care will be needed in the weaning of protected cuttings from warmth and high humidity to open-air conditions, and a period of hardening is essential: be careful, too, not to overwater cuttings until they are well established.

TAKING CUTTINGS FROM STEMS

Stem, stem-tip, and basal stem cuttings can all be used to propagate perennials; they may be soft-, green-, or semi-ripe wood, depending on the stage of growth. It does no harm to most garden plants to take shoots formed in the first flush of growth as cuttings, leaving the second for flowering. If you do this, delay any spring feeding until cuttings have been taken, because rooting will be improved if the stems are not too sappy. Take material where possible from the younger, more vigorous shoots at the edge of a clump.

Nonflowering shoots are always preferable, but with some plants, such as geraniums or impatiens, this is not always possible; remove flowers and buds from such cuttings.

TAKING STEM-TIP CUTTINGS FROM PERENNIALS

1 Select close-noded, healthy shoots from the current season's growth, here from a coleus (Solenostemon). *Remove each one by cutting just below a node, and 3–5in (8–13cm) below the shoot tip, with a clean, sharp knife.*

2 Place the cuttings in a plastic bag or bucket of water until they can be prepared. Trim off the lower leaves with a clean, sharp knife or pinch them off with your fingers. Take care not to leave any snags, which might rot.

3 To insert cuttings into the rooting medium (here rockwool), make small holes. For cells, as here, make one hole per cell. Insert each cutting so its leaves sit just above the surface. Firm in gently, water, and label.

Label left to right, front to back

4 Place the cuttings in a closed case or tent them under plastic (to keep humid) in bright light at a minimum temperature of 64–70°F (18–21°C). After about two weeks, the cuttings should have developed roots (see inset).

Four-week-old cuttings

5 Pot rooted cuttings singly into 4in (10cm) pots of soilless potting mix. Do not tease out the roots from rockwool modules. Label, water, and grow on in a warm, bright place.

PROMOTING ROOTING OF CUTTINGS

HORMONE ROOTING COMPOUND *To encourage root formation, prepared cuttings (here of* Salvia iodantha*) can be dipped into a hormone rooting powder or (as here) gel.*

HUMIDITY *For cuttings inserted in a pot, cover with a plastic bag held clear of the cuttings on split stakes. Secure the bag with a rubber band to keep it airtight. This maintains the humidity around the cuttings and prevents any moisture loss.*

Stock plants kept to supply cutting material should be young and vigorous. Do not use high-nitrogen fertilizers on stock plants, or cuttings from them will prove difficult to root.

The softer the growth, the faster it will root but the more vulnerable the cutting will be to pests and diseases and adverse conditions. Periodic checks for pests such as aphids on cuttings taken in late summer and early autumn, such as of violas and penstemons, is vital: pests weaken soft cuttings very quickly. Preventative sprays or drenches with a fungicide are also advisable.

With nearly all plants, the lower cut is made just below a leaf joint, where natural growth hormones (auxins) are more active in the initiation of roots. A hormone rooting powder or gel (*see above*) helps; most plants root well but more slowly without it.

STEM-TIP CUTTINGS

Soft- and greenwood cuttings are taken from new growth in spring to early summer, or from greenhouse plants soon after they start into growth. In mid- or even late summer, spring and early summer bloomers such as *Aubrieta* and violas that have been cut back after flowering will also produce suitable soft shoots. As might be expected from the name, the stems should be soft, almost succulent; if bent they will snap, or squash if pressed. Given the right conditions, softwood cuttings root quickly, usually in less than two weeks.

Semi-ripe cuttings are taken from shoots that are in active growth but where basal parts are beginning to ripen, usually from midsummer to mid-autumn. Such cuttings will bend without snapping and will not crush readily. These cuttings need protection from cold to root well, but they are more resistant to adverse conditions. Rooting takes longer, from four to eight weeks. Once the cuttings have rooted, they should be potted into a suitable soil mix (*see p.32*). A cold frame, greenhouse, or plastic-film tunnel can all be used for growing them on, or, in warm climates, a sand bed in a sheltered spot. In all cases, shade them from strong sun.

STEM CUTTINGS

On long main-stemmed perennials, such as *Lobelia cardinalis* hybrids and *Veronica*, one can get several cuttings from one stem by cutting it into sections 2–3in (5–8cm) long. The top of each cutting is trimmed just above a leaf and the base just below a leaf. Take off the bottom leaf from each cutting and perhaps one or two more on leafy stems, so that there is a sufficient length of bare stem to insert into the rooting medium. Treat stem cuttings thereafter exactly as for stem-tip cuttings.

METHODS FOR EASILY ROOTED PLANTS

A space-saving method when taking large numbers of stem cuttings from easily rooted plants, such as *Penstemon, Aster, Dianthus, Euphorbia, Phlox,* and *Lysimachia,* is the moss roll (*see below*), developed by professionals but very easy to use for home propagation.

Sphagnum moss may be replaced with coarse peat, finely shredded bark, or rockwool. The plastic may be folded over at the base before being rolled up to retain loose peat or bark, but the roll will need careful watering to avoid waterlogging and rot. Stand the roll in a closed case or tent it in a plastic bag. Water the roll regularly and thoroughly from above and allow it to drain.

Stem-tip cuttings of very easy-to-root perennials, for example *Penstemon, Gazania,* and *Tradescantia,* may be rooted in water (*continued on p.156*).

STEM-TIP CUTTINGS IN A ROLL

1 Cut a black plastic strip about 6in (15cm) wide and 2ft (60cm) long. Cover with a 1in (2.5cm) layer of damp sphagnum moss. Place the cuttings so their leaves sit just clear of the moss.

2 Space the cuttings on the "inside" end of the strip about 3in (8cm) apart, and gradually reduce the spacing to 2in (5cm) at the "outside" end. Roll up the strip, starting at the inside end.

3 When the roll is complete, secure with rubber bands, then label. Place the roll out of direct sun at a minimum of 70°F (21°C). Cover to keep the cuttings humid and water from the top as necessary to keep the moss moist.

4 When the cuttings show signs of growth, after 4–6 weeks, unroll the strip. Tease the cuttings out of the moss. Pot them singly in 3in (8cm) pots of soilless potting mix.

(*Continued from p.155.*) Place the cuttings in a jar of water (*see right*) on a greenhouse bench or windowsill. Shield from strong sun to reduce the growth of algae. Aftercare is as for stem-tip cuttings.

Basal stem cuttings

These consist of entire young shoots severed from the crown of the parent plant so that each retains a piece of parent tissue at the base. They are strong shoots in active growth and quick to form roots, unlike more mature shoots dedicated to producing flowers.

If taken very early in the season from summer-flowering plants such as asters, phlox, and salvias, basal stem cuttings should make reasonably sized flowering plants by summer or autumn of the same year. Commercially, this is popular because it cuts out a year's production. It also allows cuttings to put on the maximum amount of growth before the next dormant period, benefiting plants such as salvias that might otherwise not come through a harsh winter.

Basal stem cuttings of many perennials may be taken from the first flush of new growth in spring. Even earlier cuttings can be obtained by light forcing of plants that have been lifted and potted in the previous autumn (as with the delphinium below) and started into growth in a greenhouse, plastic-film tunnel, or cold frame. Some plants, including delphiniums, *Diascia*, and violas, can also be induced to form material suitable for basal stem cuttings later in the season: cut back flowered stems to the crown and top-dress with organic fertilizer to encourage the plant to produce sturdy, new shoots quickly.

Some perennials, notably lupines and delphiniums, have hollow stems that tend to rot in soil mix. It may be difficult to obtain good material from them for softwood cuttings, but taking basal stem cuttings seals the stems against rot. For hollow-stemmed cuttings, a light, open medium such as vermiculite or perlite (*see below*) is effective in preventing rot; regularly spray or drench the cuttings with fungicide.

Basal stem cuttings may also be taken from rootstocks, such as of chrysanthemums, that have been overwintered under cover; the rootstocks are usually then discarded

SOFTWOOD CUTTINGS IN WATER

1 Take softwood stem-tip cuttings about 4–6in (10–15cm) long from healthy, close-noded shoots (here of a coleus). Trim each cutting just below a node; remove its lower leaves. Place a piece of wire netting over a jar of water; insert the cuttings so their stems are in the water.

2 Keep filling up the water so that the lower stems of the cuttings are always submerged. After 2–4 weeks, the cuttings should have well-developed roots. Pot singly in 3in (8cm) pots of sandy potting mix. Water and label.

DELPHINIUM BASAL STEM CUTTINGS IN PERLITE

1 In spring, select new shoots that are about 3–4in (8–10cm) long. Cut off at the base, each with a piece of the parent's woody crown. Trim off all except the top two or three leaves.

2 With a clean, sharp knife, remove any damaged tissue or stubs from the bottom third of the stem of each cutting.

3 Fill a 6in (15cm) pan with moist perlite to within 1in (2.5cm) of the rim. Stand the pot in a saucer of water. Gently push in about eight cuttings so that they are half-buried.

4 Label the pot and stand in its saucer of water in a warm place out of direct sunlight. Keep the perlite constantly moist. The cuttings should root in 4–8 weeks and are ready for potting when the new roots are about ½in (1cm) long. Ease them out gently and give a light tap to knock any loose perlite off the roots.

5 Pot the rooted cuttings singly into 3in (8cm) pots of soilless potting mix at the same depth as before. Firm gently, label, and water. Grow on the cuttings for 6–8 weeks until they are established before planting them out.

BASAL STEM CUTTINGS

1 In spring, when the new shoots emerging at the base of the plant (here a Chrysanthemum*) are just* 3–4in (8–10cm) *tall, cut them cleanly through at the junction with the woody crown tissue.*

2 Remove the lower leaves and trim the bases, cutting straight across below a node if visible, or so the cuttings are 2in (5cm) *long. Treat the base of each cutting with hormone rooting powder or gel.*

3 Insert the cuttings into pots of rooting medium. Water well and label. Put the cuttings in a closed case or tent them in a clear plastic bag. Bottom heat speeds rooting.

4 When well rooted, usually after about four weeks, separate the cuttings. Aim to keep disturbance to the roots to a minimum. Pot the cuttings singly in potting mix (see inset).

because the new plants will have more vigor than the parent (*see above*).

Since these cuttings are usually taken early in the season, bottom heat (*see p.41*) improves rooting. A suitable propagating medium may be mixed from equal parts sand and peat. Hormone rooting compound often helps, as does dusting with a fungicide.

A cold frame, greenhouse, plastic-film tunnel or, in warm climates, a sand bed in a sheltered spot, shaded from hot sun, can be used for growing on the cuttings.

PART-LEAF CUTTINGS

1 Select a healthy, full-grown leaf and cut it into sections so that the veins in the leaf are wounded. Here a Streptocarpus *leaf is cut in half and the midrib discarded. Prepare a seed tray of free-draining rooting medium.*

2 Make shallow trenches in the medium, then insert the leaf cuttings in them, cut side down. Firm gently around the base of the cuttings. Put the tray in a closed case or seal in a plastic bag to prevent moisture loss.

LEAF CUTTINGS

Some plants can regenerate both roots and shoots from partial or whole leaves. Generally, variegated leaves cannot be used for leaf cuttings; new plants will be plain green. There are two types of leaf cutting. With the first, new plants form on the surface of a sectioned leaf, as in many *Streptocarpus* (*see left*) and *Sansevieria*.

The second utilizes a whole leaf and its stalk and, usually, a dormant bud at the base of the stalk where it joined the stem. On some, such as African violets, the bud is not crucial because a new one will form. In many, including *Ramonda* and petiolares-type alpine primroses, the bud must be preserved: without it, the cutting will root but a new rosette will not form. The buds are not visible; removing a leaf by holding it and drawing it downward (never tug) usually keeps the bud intact.

De-pot or dig up a plant and remove most of the soil mix or soil to get at outer leaves from rosettes: they may look messy but usually work well.

Leaf cuttings need a free-draining rooting medium, such as equal parts coarse sand or perlite and peat, and they may be inserted singly or several around the edge of a pot. They are usually taken early in the growing season, but cuttings of many tropicals and house plants such as *Peperomia* may be taken at most times of the year if given a period of warmth to initiate regeneration. Tropical cuttings must be kept in high humidity at around 68°F (20°C). New plantlets should start to form in a few weeks.

Nontropical species, such as those raised from whole-leaf cuttings, are taken in mid- to late spring. They are usually covered to maintain humidity but do not need extra heat at this time of year. By midsummer, new young plants should develop and can be potted in a suitable soil mix (*see p.32*).

WHOLE-LEAF CUTTINGS

1 Cut healthy, mature leaves (here of African violet, Saintpaulia*) from the parent plant, close to the base of the leaf stalk. Insert in pots of equal parts peat and coarse sand so that the base of each leaf just touches the surface.*

2 Water the cuttings, allow to drain, then label them. Cover to prevent moisture loss: here, clear plastic bottles are cut down to make improvised cloches. Shade the cuttings from direct sunlight.

3 Several plantlets should form around each leaf base. Remove the covers and allow the new plants to grow on until they are large enough to be teased out and potted individually in soil-less potting mix.

Root cuttings

While it is easier for a root cutting to develop shoots than a stem cutting to form roots, not all root cuttings develop new roots as readily as a stem cutting. Root cuttings are best taken from a plant when it is most dormant, in mid- to late autumn or early winter. Root cuttings cannot be used to increase variegated plants: although new plants will grow, their leaves will be plain green.

Plants with thick roots such as *Papaver orientale*, *Symphytum*, and *Verbascum* can be propagated by this method. It is often advised that root cuttings should be of pencil thickness, but in fact many perennials do not have many roots this thick, and thinner root cuttings are often just as, if not more, successful. The thinner they are, the longer they should be. With very thin-rooted plants such as phlox, choose the thickest roots and lay the cuttings horizontally on, rather than inserted upright in, the rooting medium.

Root cuttings from many suitable popular perennials should grow well in a cold frame. Extra protection may well be needed in cold weather to prevent the soil mix from freezing. Root cuttings from marginally hardy and tender plants should be kept at a minimum temperature of 45–50°F (7–10°C).

When new growth can be seen on cuttings in spring, check to see if they are well rooted before potting them: root cuttings produce shoots some time before any new root growth occurs, and cuttings must not be potted until a new root system has formed.

Minimizing root disturbance

Some plants, such as *Pulsatilla*, grow well from root cuttings, but the parent plant will suffer a check in growth from the root disturbance. The plants can be container-grown and encouraged to send down roots for cuttings into a sand or gravel bed (*see* Eryngium, *p.196*). If the plant is in the ground, cut around it some 4in (10cm) from the crown, lift it carefully, and replant elsewhere. Severed roots should be visible around the walls of the hole. Do not fill in the hole, but place a sheet of glass or clear, rigid plastic over it for protection, and mark it with stakes. Leave until new shoots are visible around the hole walls, then lift and pot the plantlets to grow on.

Layering perennials

A few perennials with a prostrate habit, such as scrambling phlox, or sprawling stems, such as pinks (*see* Dianthus, *p.193*), may be layered as for woody plants (*see p.106*). The best time is late winter, before growth begins, or autumn, after new growth is complete. Separate new plants in the next growing season.

ROOT CUTTINGS

1 Lift the plant (here an Acanthus) in late autumn when it is dormant and wash the roots free of soil. Choose strong roots, of medium thickness for the plant, and sever them from the parent, cutting as close to the crown as possible. Remove no more than one-third of the available root material from the parent plant.

2 Cut each root into sections that are 2–4in (5–10cm) long; making the thinner cuttings the longest. To make sure that you insert the cuttings the right way up, cut the base of each cutting at an angle and cut the top of each cutting straight across (see inset).

3 Prepare pots of rooting medium, water them, and allow them to drain. Treat the cuttings with a fungicide to prevent rot. Make holes as deep as the cuttings in the medium and insert them vertically, angled end down. The top of each cutting should be level with the surface.

4 Top-dress the cuttings with a ½in (1cm) layer of coarse sand or grit, label, and put them in a cold frame, closed case or, in warm climates, a sheltered place. Slow-rooting species may benefit from bottom heat. Water the medium only to prevent drying out until the cuttings show signs of rooting.

5 When new topgrowth appears, usually by the following spring, gently tease out the cuttings and check for root growth. When ready, pot the cuttings individually in 3in (8cm) pots filled with soil mix. Water them well, then label (see inset). Grow on the rooted cuttings until they are of sufficient size to plant out.

ALTERNATIVE METHOD FOR THIN ROOT CUTTINGS

Cut roots into sections 3–5in (8–13cm) long, depending on the plant. Cut straight across at both ends of each cutting. Lay the cuttings horizontally, about 1in (2.5cm) apart, on moist rooting medium in trays. Cover the cuttings with ¼in (5mm) of medium, firm, then allow to root (see steps 4–5).

FERNS

Ferns are primitive plants that, lacking flowers, reproduce by spores rather than by seeds. Increase from spores is the usual method of propagation where many plants are wanted. However, it is tricky and not always possible: spores may not form when cultural conditions are less than ideal; some ferns are sterile; and many crested or plumose cultivars do not come true from spores. Many ferns also reproduce by vegetative means, such as by rhizomes, bulbils, or plantlets. These can all be exploited by gardeners to increase stocks.

SPORES

The fern life cycle (*right*) has two phases; a sporophyte (spore-bearing) asexual stage, familiar as the fronded plants we grow, and a sexual gametophyte stage called the prothallus, produced when spores are dispersed from the fern and germinate. It is at this stage that fertilization takes place, enabled by water, since the male sperm must swim to the female egg; this is why ferns grow in moist places. An embryo develops, then a recognizable fern; when mature, the fern will produce spores, continuing the cycle.

GATHERING SPORES

Spores of most temperate fern species ripen in mid- to late summer; those of many tropical ferns ripen less seasonally through the year (*continued on p.160*).

LIFE CYCLE OF A FERN

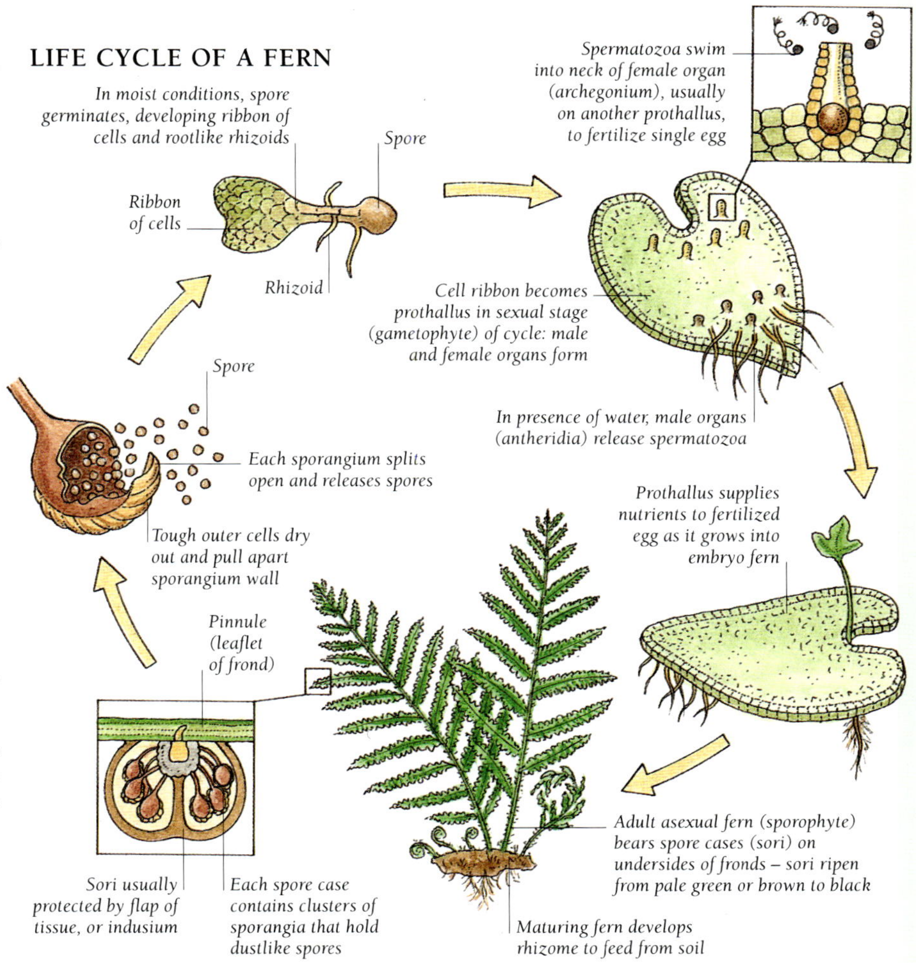

A–Z OF FERNS

ADIANTUM MAIDENHAIR FERN Sow fresh spores at 59°F (15°C) for hardier species, 70°F (21°C) for tender ones. Divide rhizomes (*p.162*) into large pieces (closely spaced nodes) in early spring. Root plantlets at frond tips of tropical species such as *A. caudatum*.
ANGIOPTERIS GIANT OR KING FERN Detach auricles (*p.163*).
ASPLENIUM (syn. *Ceterach, Phyllitis*) SPLEENWORT Sow spores as for *Adiantum*. Root bulbils or plantlets (*p.161*), on frond midrib on *A. bulbiferum*, at base of frond on hart's tongue fern (*A. scolopendrium*), especially sterile cultivars such as 'Crispum'. Divide (*p.162*) hardier species in spring. Root plantlets at frond tips of *A. rhizophyllum*.
ATHYRIUM LADY FERN Sow spores as for *Adiantum*. Root tiny bulbils (*p.161*) from base of frond stalks. Divide side-crowns (*p.162*) without lifting parent (especially *A. filix-femina* cultivars that do not come true).
BLECHNUM HARD OR WATER FERN Spores in late summer at 59°F (15°C). Divide (*p.162*) in spring: only *B. penna-marina* and *B. spicant* establish easily in colder areas. Take plantlets from stolons (*p.162*).
CIBOTIUM Sow green spores as soon as ripe at 70°F (21°C).
CYATHEA (syn. *Alsophila*) TREE FERN Sow fresh spores at 59–64°F (15–18°C). Take offsets from trunks or roots (*p.163*).
CYRTOMIUM Sow spores at 61°F (16°C).
CYSTOPTERIS BLADDER FERN Sow spores at 61°F (16°C). Root bulbils (*p.161*), under frond midribs of *C. bulbifera*. Divide rhizomes (*p.162*) in spring.
DAVALLIA Sow spores as for *Adiantum*. Divide creeping rhizomes or root aerial rhizomes (*p.162*).
DICKSONIA Sow spores as for *Cibotium*. Take offsets from trunks (*p.163*).
DIPLAZIUM Sow fresh spores at 70°F (21°C). Root bulbils (*p.161*) of *D. bulbiferum*. Detach plantlets from creeping roots (*p.162*) of *D. bipinnatifidum* and *D. esculentum*.
DRYOPTERIS BUCKLER FERN Sow fresh spores at 59°F (15°C). Divide in spring or autumn (*p.162*), especially cultivars and forms.
LYGODIUM CLIMBING FERN Sow spores as for *Cibotium*. Divide (*p.162*) before growth begins. Layer climbing stems (*p.163*).
MARATTIA As for *Angiopteris*.
MATTEUCCIA Sow fresh spores at 59°F (15°C). Divide or detach side-crowns early spring.
NEPHROLEPIS SWORD FERN Sow spores as for *Cibotium*. Take plantlets from runners, esp. of cultivars and root aerial stolons (*p.162*).
ONOCLEA SENSITIVE FERN As for *Matteuccia*.
OSMUNDA Sow green spores as soon as ripe at 59°F (15°C). Divide in spring or autumn.
PELLAEA Spores at 55–64°F (13–18°C).
PLATYCERIUM Sow spores as for *Cibotium*. Detach plantlets once distinct "nest" forms.
POLYPODIUM As for *Matteuccia*.
POLYSTICHUM HOLLY, SHIELD FERN Sow spores as for *Matteuccia*. Take bulbils (*p.161*) from base of midribs. Divide (*p.162*) in spring, esp. sterile forms like 'Pulcherrimum Bevis'.
PTERIS BRAKE Sow fresh spores at 70°F (21°C). Divide rhizome (*p.162*) in spring.
THELYPTERIS Sow fresh spores at 59°F (15°C). Divide (*p.162*) in spring or summer.
WOODSIA Sow fresh spores at 59°F (15°C). Divide (*p.162*) when dormant.
WOODWARDIA CHAIN FERN Sow spores at 59°F (15°C) in late summer or early autumn. Divide (*p.162*) in spring. Take bulbils (*p.161*) from upper frond surface.

PROPAGATING FERNS FROM SPORES

1 *Select a frond (here the brown-spored* Adiantum raddianum *'Fritz Luthi') with ripe sporangia (see right). Cut off the frond with a clean, sharp knife. Place it in a clean folded sheet of paper or envelope in a warm, dry place for 2–3 days to collect the spores.*

UNRIPE

RIPE

TOO RIPE

2 *Gently tap the spores onto the surface of a sterilized mixture of equal parts peat and sharp sand, or two parts sphagnum moss to one of coarse sand, in a 3in (8cm) pot. Cover with clear plastic wrap.*

3 *Keep the pot in a closed case at the appropriate temperature in indirect light. After 6–9 months, lift small "patches" of the green prothalli that have developed on the surface.*

4 *Set the patches up to ¾in (2cm) apart in slight depressions in a pot of fresh soil mix. Spray with sterilized water, cover, and place the pot in the same propagating environment as before.*

5 *When the young fronds are large enough to handle, pot them into cells or trays of moist, soilless potting mix. Keep in a humid environment, then pot on when small fronds develop.*

(*Continued from p.159.*) The sori, or spore-bearing bodies, are visible on the underside of the fronds (*see p.159 and above*). A few ferns, as in *Onoclea*, produce special spore-bearing fronds. Unripe sori are usually pale green or pale brown, with a granular surface. As sori ripen, their color darkens and the sporangia within swell and split to shed the spores. When just a few of the sori are open and are shaggy in appearance, the frond is ready for propagation.

To gather spores, place a fertile frond, or section of frond, in a clean envelope and keep in a warm, dry atmosphere. Do not use plastic bags; they encourage dampness and molds. When the spores are released, they have the appearance of dust. Before sowing, they should be separated from any debris such as scale remnants or leaf hairs, which can contaminate the spore culture.

Examination with a hand lens will reveal minute particles of uniform size: these are the spores, and the rest is debris. Either use a fine sieve, or tip the mass onto a clean sheet of paper. Hold the paper at an angle of 45°. Debris will travel rapidly down the surface while the spores move slowly; with a little practice, the spores can be kept on the paper while the debris falls off.

Contamination with algae, mosses, and fungi is a major cause of poor viability and death of prothalli. If you are having problems, try sterilizing the spores in a ten percent solution of sodium hypochlorite (standard household bleach) in distilled water for 5–10 minutes. Drain, rinse in sterile, boiled and cooled water, and dry the spores on filter paper for 24–48 hours.

Green spores, as in *Lygodium* and *Osmunda*, have very short viability and must be sown within 48 hours of gathering. Only spores that are brown when ripe can be stored; they may remain viable for 3–5 years if properly prepared. To store spores, transfer to a labeled plastic film canister containing a packet of desiccant, then keep in a refrigerator at 39–41°F (4–5°C).

SOWING SPORES

The easiest and most successful sowing medium is a mix of two parts sphagnum moss with one part coarse sand. Sterilize a pot with boiling water or ten percent sodium hypochlorite solution (*as above*) and fill with the mixture, then sterilize it by pouring boiling water over the surface. Cover at once with plastic wrap, allow to cool completely, then surface-sow the spores (*see above*) thinly. Re-cover immediately with fresh plastic wrap, or seal the pot in a new plastic bag. Place in a closed case in indirect light. Germinate hardy and cool-temperate ferns at 59–68°F (15–20°C) and tropical ferns at 70–81°C (21–27°F) (*see* A–Z of Ferns, *p.159*).

Within 2–26 weeks, a velvety green haze of young prothalli should appear on the surface of the medium. If it is slimy, there may be algal contamination. Some growers recommend discarding such cultures, although often a few ferns survive. If moss grows, weed it out with tweezers, and water from below with a ten percent solution of potassium permanganate to control the infestation.

In the spring after sowing, clumps of young prothalli can be "patched off" into sterile, soilless seed mix. Put in a new plastic bag, seal, and grow on in indirect light and closed conditions, until tiny, recognizable fronds appear.

Alternatively, leave the prothalli in place and apply a very dilute balanced liquid fertilizer, a quarter of "normal" strength, each month. Patching off can then be delayed until tiny fronds of the adult ferns are clearly visible. They are sturdier, easier to handle, and better able to withstand disturbance at this stage.

When the young fronds are growing well, transplant into a tray in soilless mix. Water them in carefully and grow on under a bell jar or closed case. Once established, harden off by gradually admitting more light and air. When 2–3in (5–8cm) tall, pot them singly into 2–3in (5–8cm) pots. Grow on in bright indirect light, shaded from bright sun and sheltered from wind. Provide minimum temperatures to suit each species. Most new ferns are large enough to plant out in 2–3 years.

VEGETATIVE PROPAGATION

The methods of vegetative increase described here will produce offspring identical to the parent fern, providing a means of building up stocks of cultivars that never produce spores or do not come true from spores.

Bulbils and plantlets
Many ferns produce bulbils, which look like fat, round seeds, some of which develop into plantlets with roots while still on the parent frond. Bulbils and plantlets may develop at frond tips, on or under the midrib, over the entire upper surface of the frond, or at the base of the midrib. In their native habitats, they weigh down the frond to ground level to root and extend the colony.

Propagating from mature bulbils
Most bulbils mature toward the end of the growing season, between late summer and autumn. A bulbiferous frond may be detached and pinned onto a tray containing a moist mixture of soilless seed mix, or equal parts peat and sharp sand (*see right*), where the bulbils will root. If plantlets have already developed, it is not necessary to retain the leaflets of the parent frond (*see right, below*).

Alternatively, the frond can be pinned down *in situ* while still attached to the parent plant, so that the bulbils root into the surrounding soil while receiving sustenance from the parent. Once they have 3–4 fronds, detach and pot them to grow on (*see steps 4 and 5, right*). The young ferns should be large enough to harden off and plant in 3–4 months, or in late spring or early summer outdoors in colder climates.

Propagating from dormant bulbils
The bases of the old fronds of some ferns, notably *Asplenium scolopendrium* and its cultivars, remain fleshy and green. When detached near the rhizome and planted, they produce a cluster of white bulbils near the base that can be grown on to make new plants.

In spring, lift the parent fern and clean the soil from the base to expose the old, apparently dead, frond bases. Snap the frond cleanly away at its point of attachment to the rhizome. Trim away dead material with a scalpel or sharp knife to leave a section about 2in (5cm) long, with green, living material at the base. Insert this upside down, with the green tissue pointing upward just above the surface, into a tray of soil-based seed mix that has been sterilized with boiling water and allowed to cool. Place the tray in a new plastic bag, inflate, and seal. Keep in bright indirect light at 59–68°F (15–20°C).

Within 1–3 months, each leaf base will form green swellings that develop into small, white bulbils. When they develop roots, remove the frond from the plastic bag, detach the bulbils, pot singly (*step 5, right*), and grow on in a closed case or plastic bag as for plantlets grown from mature bulbils (*see above*).

GROWING FERNS FROM BULBILS

1 In the autumn, select a frond (here of Asplenium bulbiferum*) that is weighed down by bulbils and cut it off near the base. Tiny new fronds may already be emerging from the bulbils* (see inset).

2 Prepare a tray with moist, soilless seed mix. Peg down the frond on the surface of the mix with wire staples (see inset). *Make sure that the ribs of the frond are in close contact with the surface.*

3 Water the tray, allow to drain, label, and put in an inflated, sealed, clear plastic bag. Keep in a warm, light place out of direct sun or in a closed case in shade: hardy species at 59–68°F (15– 20°C), tropical ones at 75–81°F (24–27°C).

4 When the bulbils have rooted, take the tray from the bag or closed case and remove the wire staples. Lift each plantlet, holding it by the frond. Cut the new plantlet free from the frond with a knife, if necessary.

5 Fill 3in (8cm) pots with moist, soilless potting mix. Carefully pot individual plantlets. Keep in a warm, light place; water regularly and give a half-strength liquid feed monthly. Pot them on as they develop.

FRONDS WITH ROOTING PLANTLETS

FROND WITH PLANTLETS *In some cases, bulbils develop fronds and root systems while still attached to the parent plant (here of* Diplazium proliferum*). The frond can be removed and used for propagation.*

PREPARING THE FROND *Remove mature leaflets and any dead matter on the frond by pinching them off. Pin the frond onto a tray of soil mix* (see step 2 above) *and pot plantlets individually when they show new growth.*

DIVIDING AERIAL RHIZOMES OF FERNS

1 Select a strong, new rhizome (here on a Davallia solida *cultivar) with plenty of healthy young fronds. Remove a section 6–12in (15–30cm) long, cutting straight across the rhizome with pruners.*

2 Cut the rhizome into sections about 2–3in (5–8cm) long. Trim off the fronds, which may otherwise rot. Each section should have at least one growth bud (see inset). Longer sections tend to be more successful.

3 Fill a seed tray with a moist mix of equal parts soil, bark, fine grit or coarse sand, and peat. Firm lightly, then gently press or peg the rhizome sections about 1in (2.5cm) apart into the surface. Label.

4 Keep humid in a closed case, heated if necessary to 70°F (21°C). When the sections are well rooted and are producing fronds, usually within 4–6 months, pot them individually into moist, soilless potting mix. Label and grow on in humid shade.

Simple division of ferns

Dividing established ferns is simple and ideal when only a few plants are wanted. It may be the only practical means of propagation for sterile forms such as *Polystichum setiferum* 'Pulcherrimum Bevis'. Division sets back the parent and is best done in early to midspring, to give it a full growing season to recover.

Ferns that have upright rhizomes, each with a crown or "shuttlecock" of fronds at its apex, can be divided to separate side-crowns that form around the main crown. It is essential that the divisions consist of completely intact single crowns with roots. In some ferns, as with *Matteuccia struthopteris* or *Athyrium filix-femina*, side-crowns arise 6–12in (15–30cm) or more from the main crown and can often be detached without lifting the parent. With other ferns, lift the plant as growth begins and divide as for herbaceous perennials (*see p.148*), separating individual crowns. Trim away dead fronds and any damaged rhizomes, and rub cut surfaces with garden lime to seal the wounds.

Replant the parent and large divisions of vigorous hardy ferns at once in their permanent sites, and keep well watered until reestablished. Pot small divisions, and those of delicate or tender ferns, in 3in (8cm) pots in free-draining, soilless potting mix containing a slow-release fertilizer. Place in a shaded, sheltered site until new growth appears; outdoors or in a cold frame for hardy species, and under glass at an appropriate temperature for tender ferns. Keep evenly moist but do not overwater. Most can be planted out after three months.

Division of fern rhizomes

Ferns possessing rhizomes that creep sideways, either below, at, or above the soil surface, can be divided simply by cutting up the rhizome with a clean, sharp knife or pruners in early to midspring. Each section can be only 2–3in (5–8cm) long but must have one or more growing points and a root system. Pot them individually into soilless potting mix, and grow on in sheltered shade. Keep them well watered until they start into growth, which is usually within 2–3 months.

Terrestrial ferns, such as *Phegopteris connectilis* or *Gymnocarpium dryopteris,* usually have their rhizomes beneath the soil, with fronds appearing from the nodes. Growth buds are seldom visible on underground rhizomes. In this case, ensure that each section has 2–3 healthy fronds, and a small root ball, at least 2in (5cm) across, with an intact clump of soil. On short-creeping rhizomes, the nodes are often congested, making short sections difficult to take. Slightly larger divisions taken from well-established colonies are most likely to be successful.

When dividing ferns with surface rhizomes, as in *Polypodium*, it is vital that each section has good roots. When replanting or potting, ensure that the rhizome is set at the same level as it was before lifting; it will rot if buried.

Many epiphytic and lithophytic (rock-dwelling) ferns, such as *Davallia*, produce aerial rhizomes that will produce roots and new fronds if severed and pegged down on soil mix (*see above*) in early spring. Alternatively, pin them down on open ground while still attached to the parent fern and sever each plantlet when rooted.

Propagation from stolons

Some ferns, for example *Blechnum*, spread to form colonies by subterranean stolons, runners that produce new plantlets at their apex and sometimes at the nodes. Detach young plantlets from the parent colony in spring, ensuring that each has a well-developed root system. Pot into soilless potting mix with a little added slow-release fertilizer, keep evenly moist, and grow on in a sheltered, shady site. When they are growing well, usually after 2–3 months, plant out. Young plants may be slow to grow; in colder climates, if they have not made good growth by summer, overwinter in a frost-free place and plant out in the following spring.

Some *Nephrolepis* have aerial stolons, trailing stems that root where they touch the soil. Promote this habit by pinning down stolons during the growing season into 2–3in (5–8cm) pots in equal parts peat or fine bark and sharp sand. Keep evenly moist at 55°F (13°C). In late winter or early spring, when plantlets begin to show growth, detach them from the parent, pot, and grow on.

Some species, notably *N. cordifolia*, produce small, scaly tubers at intervals along the stolons. Remove these with a short length of stolon when repotting in late winter or early spring, then treat as above, potting each tuber with a length of stolon at the same depth as before.

Propagation from auricles

Ferns in the tropical family Marattiaceae, which includes *Angiopteris*, *Christensenia*, and *Marattia*, form enormous, upright rhizomes topped by massive fronds up to 15ft (5m) tall. At the swollen base of each frond stalk, they bear a pair of fleshy, earlike growths known as auricles that produce new plants from dormant buds. They can be induced to root, if detached, to form a new plant. Auricles may be detached at any time, especially in the tropics; elsewhere, they make most rapid growth if taken in late winter or early spring. Root them in a mixture of peat and sand (*see below*), or insert the base in moist sand and top with a layer of sphagnum moss to half the auricle's depth. Keep humid in a closed case or under mist at 75–81°F (24–27°C) and in bright, indirect light.

It takes 2–6 months (less in tropical regions) before new growth appears. The auricles form visible buds, then roots and finally shoots. In temperate areas, it may take 12 or more months to form plants large enough to transplant. Once fronds are recognizable, pot into a lime-free mix of one part soil, two parts sharp sand, three parts leaf mold, three parts medium-grade bark, and one part charcoal. Keep the plants moist at all times and in high humidity.

Layering

Layering can be used for *Lygodium*, the climbing ferns. Their fronds arise from a climbing rachis (frond midrib) with nodal joints. When the frond is growing actively, between early spring and early summer, pin a node onto the surface of a pot of moist, sharp sand. Keep it evenly moist, at a minimum of 59–68°F (15–20°C) in bright, filtered light, with high humidity. When strong new growth emerges at the tip of the frond, sever the layer and pot into equal parts leaf mold or peat, soil-based potting mix, osmunda fiber, and charcoal.

Separating offsets

Some tree ferns produce offsets from their trunks (*Dicksonia* and *Cyathea*) or from the roots (*Cyathea*). These usually develop very slowly unless the parent's main growing point is damaged. They can be grown on if severed cleanly from the parent trunk in spring.

Center the offset in a pot in a moist mix of one part each of soil, medium-grade bark, and charcoal, with two parts sharp sand and three parts leaf mold. Set it just deep enough so that it sits upright. Place in a closed case with high humidity at 59–68°F (15– 20°C), in bright, filtered light. Harden off once the offset begins to show new growth.

PROPAGATION FROM AURICLES

1 *In late winter or early spring, select a young, vigorous plant* (such as the *Angiopteris* in the foreground), *preferably with loosely packed auricles at the base. Auricles from mature plants* (in the background) *root less readily.*

2 *Remove a healthy, undamaged auricle by cutting between it and the parent rhizome with a clean, sharp knife. Fill a 2–3in (5–8cm) clay pot with a moist mix of equal parts coarse sand and peat.*

3 *Trim any roots or snags on the auricle* (see inset) *and dust the cut surface with fungicide. Insert the auricle, base downward, so that the bottom half is buried below the surface. Water in and label.*

4 *Keep in a warm, bright, humid place. Adventitious buds should form within 2–6 months. Pot, or plant out, when a strong root system and small fronds have developed* (see above), *usually in 12–18 months.*

Alpine plants

There is much similarity between the methods used to propagate alpines and those used for larger perennials and shrubs. The most obvious difference, and the one that raises most problems, is one of scale. Cuttings are especially small and fussy: some may be no more than ¼in (5mm) long.

The other key difference relates to the conditions alpines prefer. Whether from high mountains or low altitudes, the most important environmental element most alpines have in common is very good drainage. In cultivation, including when being propagated, they prefer a growing medium that is water-retentive yet very free-draining. Standard soil mixes are generally unsuitable. Extra grit or sand must be added; pure sand or even ground pumice is used for cuttings of certain plants.

Growing from seeds

For many alpines, seeds are best sown the moment they are ripe, not only for those species whose seeds have short viability, such as primroses. Seeds sown fresh in early to midsummer (especially those of *Adonis*, *Androsace*, *Anemone*, *Codonopsis*, *Corydalis*, *Dionysia*, *Hepatica*, *Incarvillea*, *Meconopsis*, *Primula*, *Pulsatilla*, and *Ranunculus*) may germinate in only 2–3 weeks and develop into strong, healthy new plants by autumn. If seeds cannot be gathered or purchased fresh, they are best sown either in winter or early spring.

As with other plant groups, the seeds of many species will come true to type, but that of many cultivars will not; usually their seedlings will be inferior, but, just occasionally, an exceptionally fine plant may arise. Whenever several plants in the same genus grow in close proximity, hybrids are likely to occur, especially with *Aquilegia*, *Celmisia*, *Geranium*, *Lewisia*, *Meconopsis*, *Penstemon*, *Primula*, *Saxifraga*, and *Viola*.

Gathering and storing seeds

Alpine seeds should be gathered as soon as they are ripe (especially genera such as *Geranium* and *Euphorbia* that scatter seeds far and wide), cleaned, and sown fresh or stored in a cool, dry place, or in an airtight box in a refrigerator.

Gathering seeds of cushion alpines often requires patience and diligence (which is why the seeds are scarce and valuable): by the time the fruits are ripe, they may be buried among the new leaf rosettes. You may need a hand lens to locate them, and tweezers to pry leaf rosettes apart gently and to remove the tiny fruits or individual seeds.

Preparing seeds for sowing

Some alpine seeds will not germinate until they have received a period of cold stratification (*see* p.152–3), simulating natural alpine conditions. In colder climates, winter in the open garden usually provides all the cold that is necessary: pots of seeds can be left in a ventilated cold frame. Winter-sown seeds can germinate quickly, and the seedlings may need protection (*see p.45*). Alternatively, cheat the seasons by putting seeds in the refrigerator for a time (*see facing page*), then taking them outside to a cold frame to germinate.

Hard-coated alpine seeds are usually far too small to chip or scarify (*see also p.152*), but some seeds can be soaked before sowing to aid germination, especially older, fleshy seeds that have become wrinkled and shrunken in storage; *Cyclamen* and *Tropaeolum* seeds are good examples. Soak the seeds for 12–24 hours in tepid water (adding a drop of liquid soap helps water uptake), then drain and sow immediately.

Sowing seeds of alpines

Hygiene is especially vital with alpines: seeds and seedlings are tiny and easily swamped by weeds, liverworts, and mosses. Soil mixes and pots must be clean, if not sterile. A good all-purpose seed soil mix for alpines consists of equal parts of soil-based seed mix or sterilized soil and either fine sharp grit or coarse sand. Use horticultural sand: coastal sand contains salt, which will kill seedlings. If using a peat-based mix, or for alpines that demand very sharp drainage such as *Acantholimon* and *Dionysia*, double the amount of grit or sand.

Seeds from cushion plants

Fruits – capsules – on cushion or mat-forming alpines (here Androsace hirtella*) can be tiny and hidden among the new growth. Gather the fruits, capsules, or single seeds using tweezers.*

Pot sown with fine seeds of alpines

Put a layer of broken pots or rock chips in the bottom, then fill to within ¾in (2cm) of the rim with soil mix. A good mix is one part peat-based seed mix to two parts fine grit or coarse sand. Water well, then allow to drain. Sow the seeds finely over the surface in a ⅛in (2–3mm) layer of fine horticultural sand.

Sowing alpine seeds

Sow seeds evenly over the surface, covering all but fine seeds (see left) with a little soil mix. Add ¼–½in (5–10mm) of fine grit to protect the seeds. Water and label. Transplant seedlings when they produce two true leaves, top-dressing with a ½in (1cm) layer of fine grit (see inset).

SEED STRATIFICATION

Sow seeds as normal (see facing page, below). *Seal the pot in a plastic bag to keep the soil mix moist. Place in the bottom of a refrigerator for 4–5 weeks. Remove the bag and place outdoors.*

Thin-sowing is essential, tapping seeds carefully from the hand or packet (larger seeds can be placed individually). Most seeds sown in soil mix need covering with a very fine dusting of mix, but care must be taken not to bury the seeds. Very fine seeds can be mixed with dry fine sand to help distribute the seeds thinly and evenly. For such seeds, no soil mix covering is needed. A thin layer of fine, sharp grit helps retain moisture and suppresses mosses and liverworts, and it also prevents the seeds from being washed out by watering or, if pots are in the open, heavy rain. Place the labeled pots in a cool, partly shaded position outdoors: a cold frame is ideal.

Germination of seeds

This varies enormously from species to species: it may take place within days of sowing, or anything up to four years later. Erratic germination can pose a problem, especially if seeds continue to germinate in the same pot over a period of a year or more. Ideally, carefully tease out and transplant early seedlings, then fill in gaps in the seed pot with more soil mix and return it to its previous position to await further germination.

Care of seedling alpines

Once they are large enough to handle, the majority of seedling alpines should be transplanted carefully. If the seeds germinate in early winter, however, it is best to leave them undisturbed until spring. Some alpines are best left in their seed pots for a year or more.

Many alpines develop an extensive root system when they are very young, and transplanting must be done with great care to avoid damage. Although in some cases seedlings are only ¼–½in (5–10mm) tall, as with other seedlings, handle only the leaves to avoid damaging the fragile young stems. Transplant into trays, individual pots, or cells; the latter are best for the majority of tufted and cushion-forming alpines. Use the same free-draining soil mixes as for sowing seeds. Firm the mix only gently, water it thoroughly, and allow to drain. Make a hole large enough to contain the roots, insert each seedling, filter in more soil mix, and firm gently. Cover the mix right up to the neck of the plant with a ¼–½in (6–12mm) layer of fine grit. This keeps the surface of the soil mix cool and weed-free but, more importantly, ensures perfect drainage around the neck, which is otherwise prone to fungal attacks.

Hardy gesneriads from seeds

This group, which includes *Haberlea*, *Jankaea*, and *Ramonda* (and, culturally speaking, dwarf rhododendrons), needs special treatment. The seeds are almost dustlike and must be surface-sown; the seedlings are very prone to desiccation and vulnerable to infections. Seeds are best sown as for fern spores (*see also p.160*) on live, finely chopped sphagnum moss (*see below*) or on sterilized peat-based seed soil mix, then germinated in an enclosed environment.

If using soil mix, fill a pot with it and firm, then water with boiling water to sterilize the mix. Allow it to drain and cool, then sow thinly on the surface, as for moss (*see below*).

Cover the container immediately after sowing, either in a closed case or tented and sealed in a plastic bag, or in a clear plastic container with a lid. Seal a loose lid with tape. Leave in a cool, shaded place. The seeds do not usually need watering for a long time, but, should it become necessary, water from below or lightly mist over the top. Do this quickly: the more often the lids are removed and the longer they are left open, the greater the chance of infection with spores of various mosses and fungi.

The seedlings develop very slowly and should be left undisturbed still in their sealed container until the second or even third year. Transplant them into peat-based mix and gradually wean them from their protected environment.

SOWING SEEDS ON MOSS

1 With scissors on a clean surface, chop up a few handfuls of sphagnum moss into 1in (2.5cm) pieces and place in a clean, glass bowl. Use as much green, fresh moss as possible.

2 Fill the bowl with boiling water to sterilize the moss; then allow it to cool. Squeeze out the excess moisture. Place a 1–2in (2.5–5cm) layer of the moss in a small, sterilized container.

3 Scatter the seeds on top of the moss. Fine seeds can be sown more evenly using a folded piece of paper or cardboard. Seal the container with a lid, then label (see inset). *Place in a cool, shady place or in a shaded cold frame.*

4 The seeds should germinate after 4–6 weeks (see inset). *Ventilate the container by removing the lid at regular intervals to prevent damping off. Grow on for 2–3 years until the seedlings become large enough to handle.*

Taking cuttings

Cuttings are a good way of propagating many alpines, especially named hybrids and cultivars, which are unlikely to come true from seeds. As with larger plants, stems, leaves, and roots can all be used, but the cushion and rosette- and mat-forming alpines all require special techniques. Expensive equipment is unnecessary, since most alpines can be increased with simple methods and some very basic equipment, although tweezers and a scalpel are useful tools for dealing with tiny pieces of plant material. Stem cuttings may be ⅛–¼in (3–5mm) long, but smaller cuttings 1/16–⅛in (1–3mm) long often need to be taken, even smaller for choice *Dionysia*, *Saxifraga*, and *Gentiana*.

The prime rules for taking any cuttings apply equally to alpines: use very clean, sharp cutting tools; select healthy, nonflowering material; never allow cuttings to dry out, either when preparing them or when growing them on; and keep pests and diseases at bay.

Hormone rooting compounds can be helpful, especially for woody alpines such as many dwarf ericaceous plants, daphnes, and alpine willows (*see* Shrubs and Climbing Plants, *pp.118–145*), but many cuttings root satisfactorily without them.

A good medium for cuttings of many alpines is made with equal parts of a standard soil-based rooting medium and coarse sand. Even this may not be free-draining enough for certain alpines: pure horticultural sand or even ground pumice (*see opposite*) can be used for difficult-to-root plants such as *Dionysia* and some *Saxifraga*.

Most prepared cuttings may be inserted in pots, pans, or trays in suitable medium, sand, or pumice. They should be spaced in rows in trays or around the perimeter of a pot or pan. Label each container and water in the cuttings with a fungicide. Cuttings root satisfactorily in a sheltered place, usually at 50–59°F (10–15°C) out of direct sunlight. They should also be covered to keep them humid and avoid moisture loss. Suitable sites are a cool, well-lit windowsill, under a glass jar or clear plastic bag, in an unheated closed case or shaded cold frame, or even on a bench in a greenhouse or alpine house. Gentle bottom heat of 55–64°F (13–18°C) is not vital, but it speeds rooting.

While the cuttings are rooting and growing on, any that show signs of distress, dying back, or of fungal infection should be removed quickly, otherwise the whole batch of cuttings may be affected. Pot the cuttings once they have rooted: this will be indicated by renewed shoot growth or roots appearing through the base of the pot.

Stem-tip cuttings

These are essentially similar to those taken from larger herbaceous plants. Softwood cuttings are taken from young, green shoots in active growth in the spring or early summer before the new shoots begin to harden and ripen. Greenwood cuttings are slightly more mature: leafy shoots where growth has slowed but not hardened and is still quite soft and sappy. They are taken in early summer. As these shoots mature, they become firm, or semi-ripe. Shoots of the current year's growth that are fully ripened and woody furnish hardwood (or from evergreens, ripewood) cuttings of many alpine plants. These cuttings can be taken from midsummer until autumn, depending on the plant.

Trim the cuttings to just below a node (except for *Clematis*, which should be internodal) and trim off lower leaves close to the stem. Soft growing tips can be pinched out, especially if wilting.

Basal and rosette cuttings

These are the most important of all for alpine plants, since many are rosette-forming cushions and carpets. Take the

TAKING CUTTINGS OF ALPINES

1 Select strong, nonflowering shoots (here from Gypsophila repens*) and take cuttings from different areas on the plant. Place the cuttings in a plastic bag to prevent wilting.*

2 Trim the cuttings as indicated below, using a clean, sharp knife or scalpel. Fill a pot with gritty rooting medium, insert the cuttings to the required depth (see below)*, and firm in.*

TYPES OF CUTTINGS OF ALPINE PLANTS

Basal *Take new 2–3in (5–7cm) shoots (here of* Primula*) from the plant base, with new leaves and a short stem. Trim base below a node.*

Softwood *Take the soft tips of new, green shoots (here of* Gypsophila*) in active growth. Cuttings should be 1–3in (2.5–7cm) long.*

Greenwood *Take 1–3in (2.5–7cm) lengths from soft tips (here of* Erodium*) when growth slows down. Trim the lower ½in (1cm) of the cutting.*

Rosette *Take new rosettes at the plant edges (here of* Saxifraga*). Cut ¼–½in (5–10mm) below the leaves. Trim lower third of stem.*

Semi-ripe *From stems that are just hardening but not yet woody (here of* Phlox*), take 1¼in (3cm) lengths. Strip the bottom ½in (1cm) of stem.*

Ripewood *Take from fully ripe, new shoots (here of* Dryas*) about 1in (2.5cm) in length. Trim to leave about ½in (1cm) of stem clear at the base.*

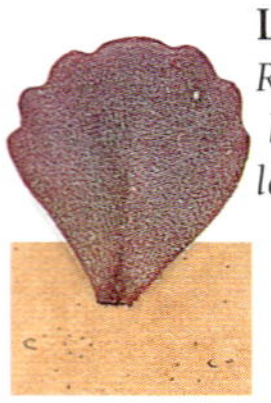

Leaf *Remove mature, healthy, undamaged leaves (here of* Sedum*). Cut each leaf as close to the base of the plant or stem as possible.*

Self-rooting *Brush away surface soil around the edge of the plant and lift rooted pieces (here of* Veronica*). Trim off sideshoots and straggly roots.*

TAKING ALPINE ROOT CUTTINGS

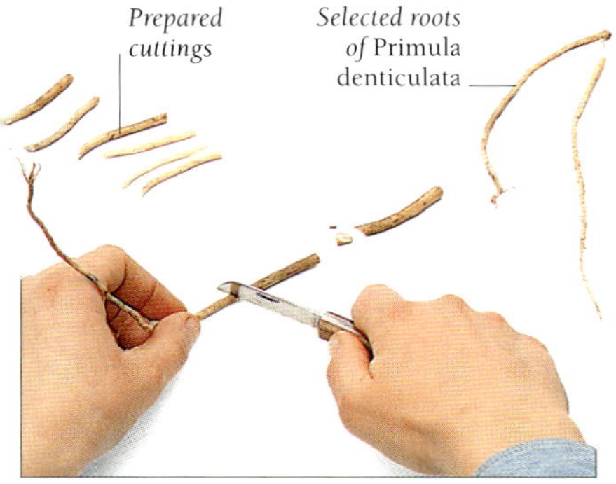

1 *In late autumn, lift a healthy plant. Cut off thick, healthy roots close to the crown. Cut each one into 1½–2in (4–5cm) pieces, making an angled cut at the lower end.*

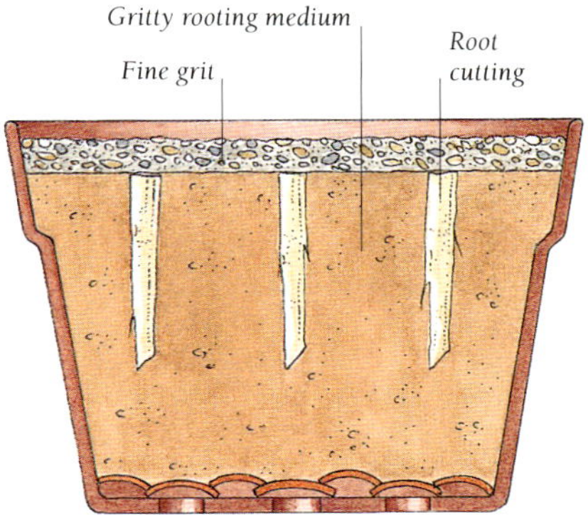

2 *Put drainage material in the base of a large half pot. Fill with rooting medium. Insert the cuttings so the straight ends are flush with the surface. Layer ½in (1cm) of fine grit on top.*

cuttings in late spring and in summer. Handle parent plants with care, for they are easily bruised, and any damage may invite in fungal infections. The cuttings often have very short stems, so they need to be taken and trimmed with care. Rosette cuttings are best placed in rows in trays or in pots. Rooting is slow and rather spasmodic.

Dionysia is often particularly difficult to root, being prone to rotting off. For these and several other plants (*see box, below*), some commercial growers advocate using crushed pumice instead of rooting medium (*see below*). Cuttings will require only occasional watering. This is best accomplished by placing pots in a deep tray of water for an hour.

Self-rooted cuttings

Many alpines form mats or tufts that root down at intervals or produce creeping, rooting stems (runners) or rhizomes. Removing rooted portions is simple and has the advantage of not disturbing the parent plant unduly. Take the cuttings in late spring and summer when the plants are in active growth by cutting off pieces with a sharp knife. Self-rooted cuttings do not need to be covered once potted.

Leaf cuttings

A few alpines can be propagated from single leaves, particularly those that have firm or fleshy foliage; summer is the best time. Selected leaves should be mature and healthy with no sign of dieback or yellowing. Insert the bottom quarter or third of the leaf upright in the medium, or preferably at 45° (with the upper leaf surface uppermost).

Water sparingly until the cuttings root to avoid the possibility of rot. Pot on each cutting once new leaves or shoots appear at the base of the leaf.

Root cuttings

A few alpine plants, including *Anchusa caespitosa*, *Morisia*, and *Primula denticulata*, can be grown from root cuttings (*see left and p.158*). Select only the thickest and healthiest roots. The best time for this is in late autumn and winter. Pure sharp sand is an alternative to rooting medium for some plants. Keep slightly moist, but not wet. Pot cuttings once new growth appears.

Division

Many alpine perennials, including some alpine *Dianthus*, can be propagated by simple division, in the same way as their larger relatives (*see p.148*). Being smaller, alpines need to be handled with greater care; some easily fall apart when lifted. Most suitable are those alpines that form clumps with a mass of fibrous roots, such as alpine *Achillea* and *Campanula*, *Arenaria*, *Celmisia*, and *Gentiana acaulis*. Unsuitable for division are the majority of cushion alpines (cushions are easily ruined by lifting), particularly alpines with a central crown or a simple taproot, such as *Androsace* and *Dionysia*.

Lift plants in early spring as growth starts, or after they have flowered. Remove some of the soil to expose the roots. Tease the plant apart into sizeable pieces, ensuring that each separated portion has plenty of sustaining roots. Replant immediately: if planting in the same area, first work over the soil lightly and add some compost and bonemeal. Smaller portions that inevitably separate, or larger pieces with few roots, can be potted as for cuttings and grown on under cover, for example in a cold frame, until well established.

ROSETTE CUTTINGS IN GROUND PUMICE

1 *Select a healthy rosette from the edge of the plant (here* Dionysia aretioides*). Steady the rosette with tweezers and cut the stem ¼–½in (5–10mm) below the shoot tip.*

2 *Carefully trim off the lower leaves from the lower third of each rosette (see inset). Dip the base of each cutting in hormone rooting compound.*

3 *Fill a 2in (5cm) clay pot with ground pumice to within ½in (1cm) of the rim. Water from below and allow to drain. Insert cuttings ½in (1cm) apart. Firm and label.*

GROUND PUMICE

Finely ground pumice, derived from Icelandic volcanic rock, is totally sterile and is sufficiently water-retentive for alpines. It is available from alpine suppliers in some areas.

Plants to root in pumice

ANDROSACE (syn. *Douglasia*) Small cushion species: *A.ciliata*, *A. cylindrica* and *A. vandellii*
CELMISIA *C. sessiliflora*
DIONYSIA especially *D. curviflora*, *D. tapetodes*, *D. microphylla*, *D. freitagii*
DRABA *D.rigida* var. *bryoides*, *D. mollissima*
GYPSOPHILA *G. aretioides*
MYOSOTIS *M. pulvinaris*
RAOULIA All species
SAXIFRAGA Small, rare, cushion types, especially softer types: *S. cebennensis*, *S. oppositifolia*, *S. poluniniana*, *S. pubescens*

Water garden plants

True aquatic plants are those that grow with their roots, and often part or all of their topgrowth, permanently submerged in either water or saturated soil. They include bog plants such as *Lysichiton*, which thrive in waterlogged soil; marginals (such as *Iris laevigata*), which grow in shallow water; water weeds such as *Myriophyllum*, submerged plants that help oxygenate the water; deep-water floating-leaved plants such as waterlilies (*Nymphaea*); and surface-floaters (for example, *Pistia stratiotes*), whose roots trail freely, absorbing nutrients from the water.

Methods of propagation

Most aquatic plants reproduce readily by vegetative means. Many multiply by producing new plantlets, either on floating stems or from questing roots. In tropical and subtropical areas especially, certain aquatic plants (such as the water hyacinth, *Eichhornia crassipes*) thrive so well that they are regarded as invasive weeds and even clog waterways.

In small ponds, plants must be thinned and divided regularly to avoid crowding, and this may result in more plants than the pond can accommodate. Replant only the younger and most vigorous portions and discard old, unproductive parts to rejuvenate the entire planting. In garden ponds, aquatics may be grown in meshed planting baskets, which makes it easier to lift and divide clump-forming plants, such as some *Cyperus*, and rhizomatous plants, such as cattail (*Typha*). Standard plastic pots with many drainage holes may also be used. Free-floating plants and loosely rooting submerged weeds can be thinned and separated by combing or netting them from the water.

Other propagation methods, such as seeds or cuttings, often require more aftercare, with new plants needing to be raised in controlled conditions that mimic their growing environment.

There are special, soil-based aquatic mixes available for water garden plants, but a heavy soil or soil-based potting mix is also suitable.

Division

Division is certainly the simplest means of increase for fibrous-rooted plants such as sedges and other marginals, plus certain tuberous and rhizomatous plants including waterlilies. Plantlets may be separated from many aquatics without lifting the parent. In general, divide plants in active growth, preferably in late spring, so that the wounds heal quickly. With some exceptions, it is best not to divide dormant plants, because low water temperatures increase the risk of rot.

Take care not to increase algal blanket weed in the process; tiny traces of it are easily overlooked, so thoroughly wash the stems, foliage, and roots of divisions to ensure they are free of fine algal filaments before you replant.

Dividing waterlilies

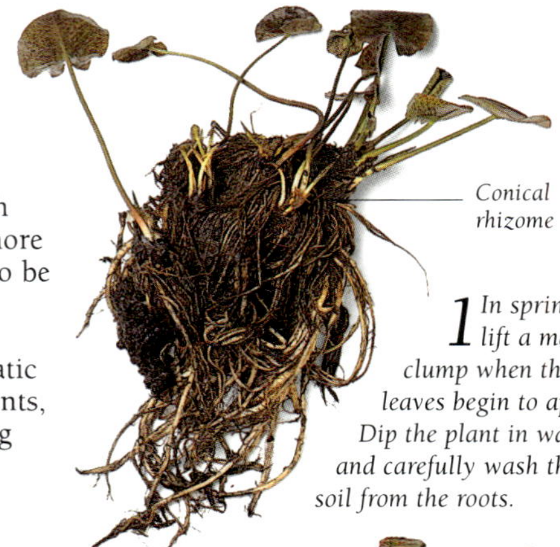

1 In spring, lift a mature clump when the leaves begin to appear. Dip the plant in water and carefully wash the soil from the roots.

2 Cut the rhizome into sections, each with 2–3 growth buds. Trim away any damaged or overlong roots. Pot each section and keep in shallow water until they show signs of growth.

A–Z of plants for the water garden

Acorus Divide rhizomes in spring.
Alisma Water plantain Divide rhizomes in spring. Sow seeds fresh or store dry for spring sowing at 59°F (15°C).
Aponogeton Divide rhizomes in spring; grow on at 59°F (15°C). Sow fresh seeds at 59°F (15°C).
Butomus Flowering rush, Water gladiolus Divide in early spring; grow on bulbils. Sow fresh seeds at 59°F (15°C).
Calla Bog arum Divide in spring. Sow fresh seeds at 50°F (10°C).
Caltha Marsh marigold Divide in late summer or early spring. Sow fresh seeds at 50°F (10°C).
Cyperus Divide in spring. Plantlets in summer. Sow seeds in spring; tender species at 70°F (21°C). Take cuttings when in growth.
Eichhornia Water hyacinth Detach offsets in summer; overwinter at 45°F (7°C).
Houttuynia Divide rhizomes or plantlets in spring. Sow seeds fresh at 50°F (10°C). Take cuttings in late spring.
Hydrocharis Frogbit Plantlets in spring or summer. Sow seeds fresh at 50°F (10°C).
Iris Divide rhizomes after flowering. Sow seeds fresh at 50°F (10°C).
Lagarosiphon (syn. *Elodea*) Take cuttings in spring or early summer. Can be invasive.
Lysichiton Divide in spring after flowering. Sow seeds fresh or in spring at 50°F (10°C).
Mentha aquatica Watermint Divide in spring or autumn. Sow seeds in spring at 50°F (10°C). Cuttings in spring or summer.
Menyanthes trifoliata Bogbean Divide in spring. Sow seeds fresh at 50°F (10°C). Cuttings in spring.
Nelumbo Lotus Divide in spring. Sow scarified seeds at 77°F (25°C) in spring.
Nuphar Yellow pond lily Divide in spring.
Nymphaea Waterlily Divide in spring. Plantlets in summer. Sow seeds fresh or in spring; hardy species at 50–55°F (10–13°C), tropical ones at 73–81°F (23–27°C). Root-bud cuttings in spring or early summer.
Orontium Golden club Divide in spring. Sow seeds fresh at 50°F (10°C).
Peltandra Arrow arum Divide in spring.
Pistia Water lettuce Plantlets in summer.
Pontederia Pickerel weed or rush Divide in late spring. Sow seeds fresh at 50°F (10°C).
Potamogeton As for *Lagarosiphon*.
Ranunculus aquatilis, *R. lingua* Divide in spring or late summer. Sow seeds fresh at 50°F (10°C). Cuttings after flowering.
Sagittaria Arrowhead Detach plantlets or tubers in spring. Sow seeds fresh at 50°F (10°C).
Stratiotes aloides Detach plantlets in summer or turions in autumn.
Typha Cattail Divide in spring.
Victoria Giant waterlily Sow seeds in winter or early spring at 84–90°F (29–32°C).

Eichhornia crassipes

Dividing clump-forming plants
Some clump-forming perennials, mainly marginal plants such as sedges (*Carex*), may be simply lifted and pulled apart by hand as for any fibrous-rooted perennial (*see p.148*). Lift the entire clump, then pull or cut off sections, about a handful in size, with good roots. Discard the older, central part of the clump, then replant the new divisions.

Small divisions may be potted to grow on until established; place the pots in a larger container filled with water up to the level of the soil mix. Keep frost-free over winter where necessary.

Dividing rhizomes and tubers
A number of water garden plants have rhizomatous or tuberous roots. Divide these in spring or early summer. Hardy waterlilies (except for *Nymphaea tetragona*, which is raised from seeds) are often increased in this way, but even if you do not need to increase stocks, it is a good idea to lift and divide waterlilies every few years to rejuvenate them. Some have a roughly conical rhizome around which new growth points develop; you can cut away as little as a single one of these with a sprout of leaves and some fibrous roots to pot and grow on (*see facing page*). Rhizomes of other waterlilies such as *N. odorata* and *N. tuberosa* extend horizontally, with sprouts of leaves and roots at intervals. Although they look different from conical rhizomes, the principle is the same. Cut the rhizome into sections, each with some leaf and root growth attached.

Replant the divisions in containers just below soil level, in fresh aquatic soil mix. Return large divisions to their permanent positions. Raise them on bricks to enable the young stems to reach the surface and gradually lower them as the stems grow. Keep small divisions frost-free over winter under shallow water, just deep enough to allow their stems to float freely. As the new growth appears, gradually increase the depth, always ensuring that the tips of the shoots and the unfurled leaves are at the surface.

All rhizomatous and tuberous aquatic plants are divided in much the same way. Some rhizomes are easy to pull apart by hand, but with others you will need a sharp knife. Irises, often divided in autumn, usually require cutting. Make sure that each division includes a section of rhizome with roots and a fan of leaves, as for garden irises (*see p.149*). Trim back the leaf fan to about 3–4in (8–10cm), then replant.

DETACHING OFFSETS

1 In spring, remove vigorous plantlets from the floating parent plant by snapping through the long, connecting stems.

2 Place the plantlet in the water; support it for a little until it floats upright. Air sacs at the base of the leaf keep it buoyant, and new shoots should soon develop.

SEPARATING WATERLILY PLANTLETS

1 After flowering, select a healthy plantlet with good roots. This one has formed on the flower stem, but other waterlilies produce plantlets at the bases of the leaves. Pull the plantlet up and away from the rest of the plant. The stem should break without much resistance, because it begins to rot and the plantlet starts taking up nutrients through its own roots.

2 These plantlets are from flowering shoots: they are at differing stages of development but can all be grown on to form new plants. Trim off the old flower stem and any damaged material. Fill a basket or large pot with aquatic soil mix or heavy soil.

3 Insert each plantlet up to its crown in the soil mix and secure them with wire hoops. Cover with a thin layer of gravel, leaving growing points exposed (see inset), then label. Grow on in shallow water.

Separating plantlets
Many aquatic plants produce young plantlets; these may be detached from the parent and grown on independently. Many types of free-floating plant reproduce in this way, developing offsets that detach naturally and float away or quickly root into muddy shallows. Some form clumps of rosettes, such as *Pistia*; break off the offsets (*see above left*) to hasten the process.

Other plants, such as *Stratiotes aloides* and some, mostly tropical, waterlilies, form plantlets on long flowering stems that must be severed (*see left*). Some tropical waterlilies may produce a plantlet on almost every leaf, at the top of the leaf stalk, that may even bloom while still attached to the parent. You can detach the plantlet easily once the leaf starts to disintegrate, or root it by pinning the leaf down onto a pot of aquatic soil mix as for other perennials (*see p.150*). Either detach the leaf from the parent and keep the pot in shallow water or position a pot under the leaf and allow it to root before cutting it free.

The dwarf paper reed, *Cyperus papyrus* 'Nanus', forms plantlets in its flowerheads. Encourage these to root by bending the stalk and burying the flowerhead in a partly immersed container of soil. Once the plantlets root, they may be divided and potted separately to grow on.

GATHERING AND SOWING SEEDS OF WATER GARDEN PLANTS

1 *Gather seeds from ripe seedheads in summer or autumn. Cut off dry capsules (here of* Iris laevigata*), and break them open. Seeds should be sown immediately upon gathering; if this is not possible, store them in vials of water.*

2 *Fill a 5in (13cm) pot with gently firmed aquatic soil mix or soil-based potting mix, then sow the seeds evenly over the surface. Cover with a ¼in (5mm) layer of fine grit: this will help retain moisture. Label.*

3 *Stand the pot in a large bowl that is a little deeper than the pot. Add water to the bowl until it just covers the pot. Place in bright light at the appropriate temperature for the plant until the seeds germinate* (see inset).

SEEDS

Raising aquatic plants from seeds can be quite a slow process, with some taking 3–4 years or more to reach flowering size, but it is useful if you require a large number of plants or where it is not possible to take divisions or cuttings. It is suitable for many plants that are valued for their flowers, such as waterlilies, lotuses (*Nelumbo*), *Aponogeton distachyos,* and *Orontium aquaticum*. As with other plants, seeds of cultivars may not come true to type.

GATHERING SEEDS

Gather seeds of water garden plants as soon as they are ripe in summer or in autumn. It is best to sow the seeds immediately, but if necessary they may be stored in vials of clean water in a cool, dark place for sowing in spring. Storing seeds in moist peat is not recommended. Seeds of only a very few water plants, such as *Alisma* and *Mentha*, can be dried for later sowing.

Some plants set seeds freely, such as the water plantain (*Alisma plantago-aquatica*), while others, such as cattails (*Typha*), may yield fertile seeds only occasionally or, as with tender water-lilies, only in warm climates. Some water plants bear fruits or berries, which must first be macerated to extract the seeds (*see pp.151–2*).

With the exception of *Nymphaea tetragona*, hardy waterlilies set seeds infrequently, while tropical kinds generally seed freely. To save seeds, enclose a pod in a muslin bag (*see above right*). Never let the seeds dry out; sow them by smearing them in their aqueous jelly over the surface of the growing medium. Wash off the jelly if you wish to store the seeds over winter.

GATHERING WATERLILY SEEDS

To harvest the seedpods, wrap some muslin loosely around the bud as soon as the flower fades. Secure it with twine around the stem to keep the seed mass intact as it sinks to the bottom. The seeds are held in an aqueous jelly that disperses as the seedpod ripens and disintegrates (see right). *Retrieve the seeds after 2–3 weeks.*

SOWING SEEDS

First prepare pots or deep trays with aquatic soil mix, soil-based potting mix, or sieved garden soil (*see p.152*). Do not add fertilizer, because it encourages algal growth, which could smother the seedlings. Sow the seeds evenly on the surface and cover with their own depth of fine grit. Seedlings need wet soil, so stand the pot or tray in a larger container of water so that it is partially submerged or just covered, as in its natural habitat (*see top of page*). Seeds of hardier plants may germinate without artificial heat if covered with a sheet of glass raised enough to allow air circulation, in a bright, sheltered place. Less hardy species germinate best at about 59°F (15°C); tender species at 70°F (21°C) and above. Some germinate more readily with gentle bottom heat.

When the first pair of true leaves appears, transplant the seedlings into individual pots (*see p.152*), then immerse them in water as before under glass, protected from cold if necessary, for another year. Transfer the young plants to their permanent positions once the water has warmed up in spring.

Hybridizing water garden plants

Species of waterlilies and water irises may produce some pleasing seedlings if hybridized (*see also p.21*). To keep seeds pure, transfer pollen from a two or three-day-old bloom to the liquid in the center of a waterlily bloom that is on the point of opening. Protect the pollinated flower from insects by enclosing it in muslin.

Cuttings

Most submerged aquatics do not develop woody stems, so all cuttings are of soft growth, best taken in spring or summer. Fast-growing submerged plants, for example *Lagarosiphon* and *Potamogeton crispus*, should be regularly replaced by young stock raised from cuttings.

Cuttings are usually softwood stem-tip cuttings, prepared in a similar way to other perennials (*see pp.154–5*). Take cuttings material by pinching or cutting off healthy, young shoots. Remove the lower leaves from cuttings of marginal plants. Trim rosettes as for *Cyperus* (*see below*). Cuttings of submerged plants can be tied into bunches of six and either potted or thrown into muddy wildlife ponds to root. Root cuttings of other plants singly, for example of water mint (*Mentha aquatica*) and water forget-me-nots (*Myosotis scorpioides*). Insert the cuttings into pots or trays in soil, then submerge them in shallow water in a warm, shaded place. Cuttings of marginals will root in jars of water (*see p.156*). You may be able to plant out rooted cuttings after 2–3 weeks.

Root-bud cuttings

When you lift rhizomatous or tuberous plants from the water, or buy them bare-root, you may see small, rounded swellings with emerging shoots on the roots; these root buds, also called "eyes," may be used for propagation. With tuberous waterlilies and plants such as *Acorus*, pare out just the root bud with a sharp knife (*see below*). With rhizomes, such as *Nuphar*, take a 3–4in (8–10cm) section as well as the growing point.

Pot the buds in pots or seed trays. Keep submerged under glass as for seeds (*see facing page*), potting on as necessary and raising the water level as the shoots grow (keeping the tips at the surface). Keep cool but frost-free over winter; transplant as growth begins in spring.

New plants from winter buds

Some aquatics, such as *Hydrocharis* and *Hottonia*, produce nodulelike root buds, called winter buds or turions. As the parent becomes dormant in early winter, these naturally float free and sink to the bottom where they stay until spring. Then, the winter buds rise to the surface and develop into new plants. To facilitate this process, detach the winter buds and pot them (*see below left*). In spring, when the emerging buds float to the surface, gather them and pot into containers in soil or aquatic soil mix.

Bulbils

Certain rhizomatous plants, such as *Butomus umbellatus*, form bulbils on the rhizomes, which are similar in function to root buds. Bulbils may be detached and potted (*see below*) to grow on.

PREPARING ROSETTE CUTTINGS

Select a new, fully mature leaf (here of Cyperus involucratus*) and cut the stem 2in (5cm) below the rosette. Hold the rosette in one hand and trim the tops of the bracts (*see inset*) with sharp scissors. Pot the cutting.*

TAKING ROOT-BUD CUTTINGS

1 *Cut out the swollen root bud with its growing point from the rootstock. It may be necessary to cut through the neighboring leaf stalks to preserve the bud. Use a sharp knife; fungal infections are less likely to enter clean cuts.*

2 *Fill a 4in (10cm) basket with aquatic soil mix or sifted topsoil. Press in the bud (*see inset*) so that the growing tip is just visible. Top-dress with coarse grit to hold it in place. Immerse so the grit is just below the water.*

WINTER BUDS (TURIONS)

At the end of the growing season, detach the winter buds from the parent plant (here frogbit, Hydrocharis morsus-ranae*). Cover with their own depth of soil mix in a pot, and keep the pot covered with 6in (15cm) of water. Keep cool, but frost-free, over winter.*

PROPAGATING FROM BULBILS

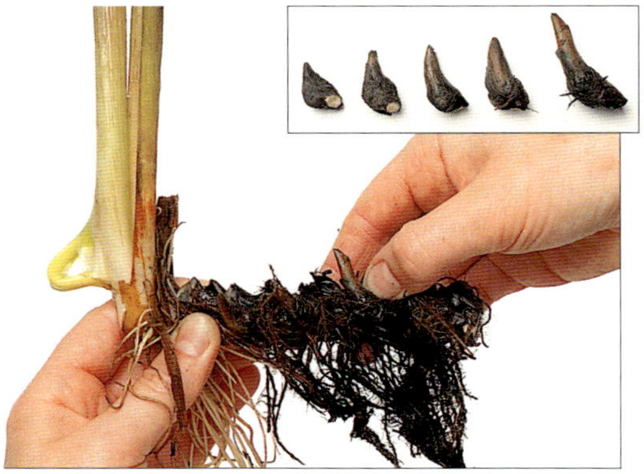

1 *In spring, when dividing marginals (here a flowering rush,* Butomus umbellatus*), carefully pry off bulbils (*see inset*) from the rhizomes. Use your thumbnail and take care not to snap off the bulbil tips, which are soft.*

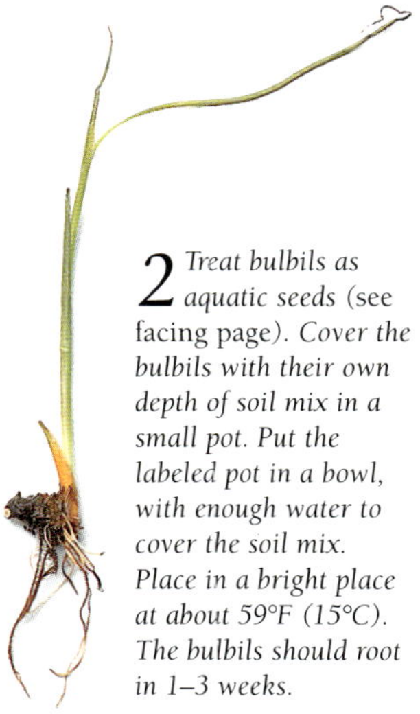

2 *Treat bulbils as aquatic seeds (*see facing page*). Cover the bulbils with their own depth of soil mix in a small pot. Put the labeled pot in a bowl, with enough water to cover the soil mix. Place in a bright place at about 59°F (15°C). The bulbils should root in 1–3 weeks.*

BROMELIADS

These evergreen perennials may be terrestrial, saxicolous (cling to rocks), or epiphytic (cling to trees) and originate mainly from tropical regions of the Americas. Habitats range from desert to rainforest. Many are rosette- or urn-shaped, with central "vases" that trap rainwater. Some epiphytic *Tillandsia* (known as airplants) lack vases and obtain water from the air via minute, spongelike, silvery scales covering the foliage. A few (xerophytic) species are cactuslike, thriving in arid, dry deserts.

The more popular bromeliads, such as *Billbergia, Neoregelia,* and *Tillandsia,* are neat, decorative plants that in cold climates make attractive greenhouse, conservatory, or indoor plants. In warm regions, they may be grown outdoors and are used for landscaping in tropical countries. No bromeliads are frost-hardy although a few, for example *Dyckia, Hechtia,* and *Puya,* are nearly so.

Propagation is usually by division of offsets – the fastest and easiest method and for most people the only practical one, since seeds are of short viability and rarely available unless set by your own plants. Bromeliads need lime-free soil and water. If tap water is alkaline, use clean rainwater or cooled, boiled water for both mist-spraying and watering. If alkaline water is used for spraying, the calcium deposits will mark the leaves.

DIVISION

The natural cycle of a bromeliad is to reach maturity, flower once, and then die. Offsets form around the base of mature plants, and after flowering the parent persists for a year or so, while the offsets draw nourishment from it. In this way, a large clump builds up from several generations of offsets.

In cultivation, growers often detach offsets far too early, in order to neaten a plant. These small, immature offsets are very slow to root and require intensive care. Removal is often difficult when they appear between leaves, as with some *Tillandsia* and *Cryptanthus.* Treat immature offsets like unrooted cuttings (*see below*), growing them on in high humidity at a constant 70°F (21°C).

It is far better to leave offsets attached to the slowly deteriorating parent until they reach two-thirds of their full size, by which time they will have established an independent root system. This is especially true for *Vriesea splendens* and its close relatives, which produce just one offset in the center of the vase; the only way to detach it for propagation is to peel off the leaves that form the vase, destroying the parent.

The best time to divide offsets is soon after growth starts in spring. Knock the clump out of its pot and divide it (*see below*), discarding the remains of the parent and potting the offsets singly. A flowering-sized plant can often be had within a year. Use much the same technique with airplants and other epiphytes mounted on cork bark or

DIVISION OF TERRESTRIAL BROMELIADS

1 Lift a plant with mature rooted offsets (here Cryptanthus praetextus*), or knock it out of its pot. Wear gloves, if necessary. Gently pry apart the offsets; discard the old woody center.*

2 Plant out or pot rooted offsets singly. Immature offsets with only root initials (see inset) may form in leaf axils: treat the bases of these offsets with hormone rooting compound and insert in bromeliad seed mix to root.

3 For rooted offsets, prepare a pot with a suitable soil mix, such as equal parts of soil-based mix, coarse bark, and pumice granules. Insert the offset, firm gently, water in, and label.

DIVISION OF EPIPHYTIC BROMELIADS

1 Most epiphytic bromeliads produce offsets at the base of the plant (here Neoregelia carolinae*). Select mature offsets that have begun to form roots for propagation.*

2 Remove an offset, cutting straight across the base of its stem. Dust the cuts with fungicide. Wire the offset onto a suitable mount to root or pot as for a terrestrial (see above).

OFFSETS IN LEAF AXILS

The offsets of some bromeliads (here Tillandsia cyanea*) form in the leaf axils. Strip off the outer leaves to expose the base of a mature offset, then gently pull it away.*

GATHERING SEEDS FROM BROMELIADS

BERRIES *Leave the berries (here of an* Aechmea *hybrid) on the plant until they start to fall naturally, so the seeds are fully ripe. Pulp the berries, remove the seeds, and wash them in warm water with a little detergent added to clean off the sticky coating.*

FLUFFY SEEDHEAD *The papery capsule opens to reveal a fluffy seedhead (here of* Tillandsia tectorum*). Seeds are fully ripened when the plumes lift effortlessly from the stalk, ready to float on the air. Sow the seeds with the plumes attached* (see below).

driftwood, where offsets are much more accessible. Leave them in place until they are two-thirds of the parent's size. They are ready for division when they will come away easily without pulling.

GROWING ON ROOTED OFFSETS

Rooted offsets from terrestrial species should be potted, as may a number of epiphytes such as *Aechmea, Billbergia,* and *Neoregelia* if it suits the grower. A very free-draining soil mix is vital to avoid rot. Try equal parts of peat and coarse sand with a little added horticultural charcoal, or equal parts of peat, perlite, and coarse sand.

Humidity is also essential: keep the vases of offsets filled with water, especially during summer, but take care not to overwater the soil mix. Epiphytic offsets can also be wired onto driftwood, cork bark, or tree-fern stem. Wedge airplant offsets in crevices on branches.

SEEDS

Raising bromeliads from seeds is rewarding for the gardener and is used for mass production and hybridization at nurseries. However, many bromeliads are self-sterile; unless two or more plants of the same species flower simultaneously, it is rare for viable seeds to be set in a small collection. Many *Tillandsia,* such as *T. butzii*, are self-fertile so are most likely to set seeds.

Bromeliad flowers appear at various times from the vases of mature plants. With some plants, such as *Guzmania sanguinea*, *Neoregelia carolinae* 'Tricolor', and *Tillandsia ionantha*, the top leaves of the rosette turn red when the plant is about to flower. In the wild, flowers are pollinated by hummingbirds, bats, and insects so are best hand-pollinated in cultivation to encourage seeds to set.

Seeds may be contained in papery capsules that split to disperse plumed or winged seeds on the wind. Others are carried in berries and have a jellylike covering (this makes the seeds stick to tree bark when birds wipe their beaks while eating the fruits). *Tillandsia* seed capsules take from six months to a year to mature; the plumed seeds are ready for gathering within a few days of the capsules opening (*see above right*). Berries should be left on the plant until fully mature (*see above left*), then the seeds carefully separated from the flesh and any jelly coating washed off before sowing, since it may inhibit germination.

SOWING SEEDS

Bromeliad seeds should be sown fresh because they are viable for only a month or two – or a few weeks for plumed seeds. Professional growers sow onto orchid seedling mix, which has a very small particle size. Many free-draining, fine, sterilized seed soil mixes are also suitable, as are the mixtures recommended for offsets (*see above*).

Scatter seeds thinly over the surface of a prepared tray of mix; leave seeds from berries on the surface, but anchor plumed or winged seeds with a very fine layer of coarse grit. Cover with a sheet of glass to retain humidity and sheets of styrofoam to retain warmth and give shade. Minimum temperatures for germination are 66–81°F (19–27°C).

Gardeners may also sow epiphytic seeds onto bundles of conifer twigs, which are slightly acidic (*see below*), or push them into crevices in fir cones.

Bromeliad seedlings grow and form roots very slowly; in many epiphytes the original roots disappear some time later. Allow at least five months between sowing and moving on the seedlings. Transplant to about 1in (2.5cm) apart and grow on close together in trays (except for airplants). This creates a more favorable growing environment than potting small plantlets individually. Seedlings may be transplanted several times before potting.

When they are large enough to handle, pot seedlings singly. Epiphytic seedlings may also (*continued on p.174*)

SOWING SEEDS OF EPIPHYTIC BROMELIADS

1 *Take some twigs from a conifer, such as a cypress or juniper, and make into a bundle with a little moist sphagnum moss. Tie the bundle with twine, raffia, or wire.*

2 *Pull apart freshly collected, fluffy seedheads (here of a* Tillandsia*) and scatter the plumes evenly over the bundle. They should adhere to the moss or can be tied in with more raffia.*

3 *Use a mist-sprayer to lightly water the bundle. Label the bundle and suspend it lightly in a shaded, warm place with 100 percent humidity, such as a closed case or mist-propagation bench. Keep the bundle moist by mist-spraying it regularly, or daily submerging it in clean rain water.*

SOWING IN A CONTAINER

Prepare a seed tray or pot with free-draining mix, such as equal parts peat, perlite, and coarse sand. Spread the plumed seeds over the surface. Cover with a thin layer of grit to keep the seeds in contact with the mix.

(*continued from p.173*) be transferred to pieces of tree-fern stem or cork bark.

Use a very free-draining, lime-free potting mix for all seedlings. A fine grade of orchid mix, equal parts of peat and coarse sand, or equal parts of peat, perlite, and coarse sand is best for the first potting. Coarser orchid mixes combined with a little coarse sand can be used for potting on larger plants. Use a standard or even taller pot to provide excellent drainage. At all stages, it is vital plants are not potted too deeply; the lower leaves should be totally clear of the mix. It usually takes three years or more for new plants to flower.

Other methods

The long, rootless strands of Spanish moss (*Tillandsia usneoides*) can be propagated by perhaps the easiest of all cuttings: simply snip about 12in (30cm) from the end of an established clump, hang it up in the warm, humid conditions in which the plant thrives naturally, and allow to grow on.

Ananas, including edible pineapple and miniature decorative cultivars such as *A. comosus* 'Variegatus', produce fruits after the flowers on the stem that emerges from the center of the mature vase. At the top of each mature fruit is a tuft of foliage that may be sliced off and rooted (*see right*). (Fruits retailed in stores may have had the growing tip removed to prevent them from being propagated.)

Pineapples can also be increased from shoots that develop in leaf axils, called suckers when they appear low down on the main stem and slips when they arise on the fruit stem (*see top right*). They do not develop if left on the parent but can be detached and rooted for new plants.

PROPAGATING PINEAPPLES FROM CUTTINGS

Select healthy slips or suckers, either below the fruit (see left) or at the base of the stem. Detach any of these with a sharp knife and dip the cut surfaces in a fungicide. Allow to dry for a few days. Trim off the lower leaves and insert the cuttings in pots of sandy compost (see below) to root at 70°F (21°C). Pot them on into 6in (15cm) pots when they have rooted.

PROPAGATING PINEAPPLES FROM CROWN SHOOTS

1 *Use a sharp knife to scoop out the crown shoot of a ripe pineapple with about ½in (1cm) of the fruit attached. Dip the wound in fungicide and allow to dry for several days.*

2 *Insert the cutting into a pot of rooting medium and keep at a minimum temperature of 70°F (21°C). The cutting should root and be ready to pot on within a few weeks.*

A–Z OF BROMELIADS

ABROMEITIELLA Terrestrial; divide offsets in spring or summer. Sow winged seeds in spring at 81°F (27°C).
AECHMEA Epiphyte; divide offsets in early summer. Sow seeds from berries as soon as ripe at 70°F (21°C).
ANANAS PINEAPPLE Terrestrial; root slips or suckers or crown shoots (*see above*) at any time.
BILLBERGIA Epiphyte; divide offsets in summer. Sow seeds from berries as soon as ripe at 81°F (27°C).
BROMELIA Terrestrial; divide in late spring or early summer. Sow seeds as for *Billbergia*.
CANISTRUM As for *Billbergia*.
CATOPSIS Epiphyte; divide offsets in late spring; bottom heat aids rooting. Sow plumed seeds as soon as ripe at 81°F (27°C).
CRYPTANTHUS EARTH STAR, STARFISH PLANT Terrestrial; detach offsets from leaf axils in early summer. Sow seeds as for *Billbergia*.
x CRYPTBERGIA Terrestrial; divide offsets in spring.
DYCKIA Terrestrial, xerophyte; divide in late spring or early summer. Sow winged seeds in early spring at 81°F (27°C).
FASCICULARIA Terrestrial, epiphyte, xerophyte; divide offsets in spring or summer. Sow seeds from berries in winter or spring at 81°F (27°C).
GUZMANIA Epiphyte; divide offsets in midspring. Sow plumed seeds at 81°F (27°C) in midspring.
HECHTIA Terrestrial, xerophyte; divide offsets in spring. Sow winged seeds as soon as ripe at 70–75°F (21–24°C).
NEOREGELIA (syn. *Aregelia*) Terrestrial, epiphyte; divide offsets in spring or summer. Sow seeds from berries as soon as ripe at 81°F (27°C).
NIDULARIUM BIRD'S NEST BROMELIAD Epiphyte; as for *Neoregelia*.
ORTHOPHYTUM Saxicolous; divide offsets in spring. Sow seeds as for *Billbergia*.
PITCAIRNIA Terrestrial; divide offsets in late spring or early summer. Sow winged seeds in spring at 66–75°F (19–24°C).
PUYA Terrestrial; sow winged seeds as soon as ripe at 66–75°F (19–24°C).
QUESNELIA Terrestrial, epiphyte; as for *Neoregelia*.
TILLANDSIA AIR PLANT Epiphyte; divide offsets in spring. Seeds as for *Billbergia*. Take cuttings of *T. usneoides* at any time.
VRIESIA Epiphyte; divide offsets in spring. Sow seeds as for *Pitcairnia*.
WITTROCKIA Terrestrial, epiphyte; offsets in spring or summer. Sow seeds as for *Pitcairnia*.

Ornamental grasses

Grass, in the form of a closely mown lawn, has long been valued for its durability but has often been regarded as merely a foil for more interesting planting. Yet the grass family includes an extraordinary diversity of ornamental plants. Some species are valued for their architectural form, such as *Miscanthus sinensis*; others for their foliage color, including glaucous blue fescue (*Festuca glauca*); for variegation, such as green-and-white striped gardener's garters (*Phalaris arundinacea* 'Picta'); for attractive stems, for example the Chilean bamboo (*Chusquea culeou*); or for their flowerheads (inflorescences), such as the feathery heads of *Cortaderia selloana*.

True grasses belong to the Poaceae family and almost always have hollow, rounded stems, with solid nodes at regular intervals. This is most obvious in woody-stemmed bamboos (subfamily Bambusoideae). Rushes and sedges look similar but are not true grasses; they belong to other botanical families.

Flowers are borne in spikes, panicles, or racemes. Many grasses flower when two years old or so, but bamboos remain vegetative for decades. They will eventually begin to flower: at first, only a few canes will have inflorescences, but these will increase in number quite considerably in subsequent years. Once flowering begins, a bamboo will decline in vigor and then often die.

Propagating perennial grasses

Perennial grasses are common plants and, in some cases, can be invasive weeds, so it is often assumed that they are easy to propagate. They can be, provided that a few basic principles are followed. There are two main methods of increase: by division or from seeds.

Division must be used to increase all bamboos, which rarely flower; variegated grasses, which lose their variegation if raised from seeds; and grasses such as *Miscanthus* that fail to set seeds in colder climates. Division is also a useful means of rejuvenating mature grasses that are congested and bare at the center.

DIVIDING SMALL CLUMPS

If necessary, cut down the foliage by a half to three-quarters to about 6–8in (15–20cm) so the grass is easier to handle. Lift the clump with a fork and divide it into 2–4 pieces, either by hand or using two hand forks. Replant the divisions either in the garden or in a nursery bed or pot singly in sandy soil mix. Label the divisions and water well.

Division

Division of grasses can be a simple process and should succeed, provided that it is carried out at the correct time of the year. Grasses produce new growth buds, some of which are quite large, in summer; these lie dormant until the following spring. In general, it is best to divide grasses just as the buds start into growth, usually in midspring. This is especially important for bamboos; if divided at other times of the year, the success rate is generally poor because of the risk of rot or drought. Other grasses, if grown on light soils or in warm climates, may be divided in autumn.

Division of small grasses

For small, clump-forming grasses, cut back the foliage for easier handling, then lift the clump. Shake off loose soil from the roots, or wash the roots clean, to make it easier to separate them. Divide the clump into good-sized sections, as shown above. Trim any overlong or damaged roots from each division.

If the clump is tightly packed or tough, as with *Miscanthus*, use a sharp knife or a spade to cut through the roots. This will inflict less damage to the roots than pulling the rootstock apart.

Division of bamboos

Bamboo roots are sensitive to drought, so choose a cool, overcast day for division to prevent drying out. It is also wise to wear heavy gloves; bamboo leaves contain silica and are very sharp.

Some bamboos have long, thin rhizomes with shoots all along their length; these spread out to form a loose clump that can be invasive. Divide this type as shown below, taking strong, new rhizomes from the edge of the clump.

Other bamboos have short, thick rhizomes, with shoots at the tips, that form a tight clump. (*Continued on p.176.*)

DIVISION OF RHIZOMATOUS BAMBOOS

1 In spring, loosen the soil around a clump of bamboo to expose the rhizomes, with their new buds, at the edge of the clump. Sever these from the parent plant, using pruners.

2 Cut the rhizomes into pieces, each with at least one bud. Pour some fungicidal powder into a small dish and dip the cut surfaces into it (see inset).

3 Pot each piece individually into a free-draining soil mix, with the rhizome just below the surface of the mix and the shoots exposed. Firm in, label, and water well.

DIVIDING LARGE GRASS CLUMPS

1 *Look for an offset clump (here of* Arundo donax*) of strong shoots and plump buds. Dig a trench, at least a spade blade's deep, around it to expose the roots.*

2 *Scrap away the soil to reveal the rhizomes running between the offset to the main clump. Use loppers, an ax, or a mattock to sever them, then lift the offset.*

3 *Divide the offset into pieces, each with at least 3–4 buds. Trim the rhizomes to form neat root balls. Replant at the same depth as before, water in, and label.*

PROPAGATION FROM SINGLE BUDS

Small pieces of rhizome that are broken off during division may be grown on, provided that each has a healthy growth bud (see right*). Discard any with weak buds* (left)*. Grow on in pots in a frost-free place or in a nursery bed for a year before planting.*

(*Continued from p.175.*) If possible, lift the entire clump. Using pruners or a large knife, divide the rhizomes into pieces, each with several growth buds. Take care not to damage any fibrous roots. Cut the stems down to 12in (30cm) to reduce water loss. With a large, tough clump of bamboo, it may be more practical to take off an offset clump at the edge of the plant (*see below*).

Dividing large grass clumps

Large clumps of tall grass can be divided using two back-to-back forks, as for other fibrous-rooted perennials (*see p.148*) or, if the rootstock is tough, with loppers, a mattock, or an ax. Established clumps of bamboos and other grasses that are too large to lift usually have offset clumps that can be separated, as shown above.

Choose an offset clump and cut the stems down to 2ft (60cm) for easier handling. When digging out the offset clump and dividing it, be careful not to damage any of the growth buds at the base of the stems; they are sometimes brittle and easily snapped off. Discard any woody sections, and trim damaged roots or rhizomes.

Any single-budded pieces (*see above right*) that become detached from the clump may be grown on but need more care and time to establish than usual.

Growing on divisions

Grass divisions may be replanted in the garden, lined out in a nursery bed, or potted, depending on their size and local conditions. If planting out, choose a sunny site with free-draining, moisture-retentive soil; very fertile soil encourages foliage at the expense of flowering.

Small or tender divisions are easier to manage if potted; use a free-draining soil mix (*see p.34*). Keep the potted divisions cool and moist and out of sun and drying winds until established. A closed cold frame is ideal; when signs of new growth appear, open the frame. Most bamboos and grasses will be ready for planting out after a year.

Sowing seeds

If grasses are allowed to seed in the garden, the resulting seedlings tend to crowd out established plants, and it is almost impossible to identify seedling grasses or distinguish desirable kinds from weeds. Gather well-developed, healthy inflorescences just before their seedheads are fully ripened to extract seeds for sowing (*see below*).

Grasses may be sown directly into outdoor beds, but the seedlings must be rigorously thinned to give each room to develop. It is better to plant container-grown seedlings (*see p.152*). Some grass seeds are large so can be space-sown. Keep them at the required temperature (*see* A–Z of Ornamental Grasses, *facing page*). Most grass seeds germinate in a week if sown fresh. Transplant seedlings, one to a pot or cell, as soon as they are large enough to handle. Transfer pots of established seedlings to a frost-free place to grow on. Plant out in midspring.

Sowing lawns

Lawns are popular in cool-temperate regions, but less so in areas of low summer rainfall, because they require regular irrigation. Lawn seed mixtures vary, depending on region and climate and what quality of lawn is required.

Modern breeding has produced improved selections of tough, perennial ryegrass that tolerate close mowing and produce a hard-wearing, fine turf, ideal for family gardens. Fine fescues, bents, and bluegrasses are more suitable for quality lawns where appearance is paramount. If extending a lawn under trees, choose a mixture that includes shade-tolerant species and cultivars.

In areas with dry summers, clover is sometimes added to the seed mixture because it remains green, while in hot regions, drought-tolerant grasses such as

GATHERING GRASS SEEDS

Gathering *Cut stems (here of* Miscanthus*) once the inflorescences have fluffed up fully* (above right)*. If cut too soon* (above left)*, the inflorescence will contain no seeds.*

Extracting *Keep the grass stems in a cool, dry place for a few days to allow the seeds to finish ripening. Strip off the seeds from each spike; they should come away easily. Sow at once or store until spring. Sow 3–5 seeds to a 3in (8cm) pot, or individually in cell packs, in free-draining, soilless seed mix.*

Cynodon dactylon, *C. transvaalensis*, and *Digitaria didactyla* are used, although they may turn brown in winter.

A lawn may be in use for decades, so if creating a new one prepare the site thoroughly. Start well in advance of early autumn or spring sowing. First remove any roots, large stones, and weeds, then rototill or dig over and level the area, incorporating well-rotted organic matter to a depth of 10in (25cm). Spot-treat any perennial weeds that appear in the next few months. In heavy, clay soils, it may be necessary to improve drainage with gravel or drainage pipes. In dry areas, install irrigation.

Just before sowing, firm the soil with a roller or by treading. Rake to remove small stones and lumps and to create a fine tilth. Sow in early autumn or spring, after rainfall or irrigation.

For large areas, it is convenient to use a spreader, but small lawns may be sown by hand. For even sowing, mark out the area into equally sized sections (*see right*). Weigh out a volume of seeds for one section, and place in a measuring container. You can then measure, rather than weigh out, subsequent amounts of seeds. Mixing the seeds with an equal amount of sand and scattering them from a plastic pot is quick, easy, and ensures even coverage.

If the area is small, cover to protect it from birds and keep moist. Remove the cover as soon as germination occurs. In warm, moist conditions, seedling grass should be growing well by late autumn or early summer.

SOWING A LAWN

1 Mark out the site into sections of equal size. Measure out enough seeds for one section. Scatter half the seeds across and half down the area, sowing by hand or from a pot (see inset).

2 Lightly rake over the surface of the sown area to cover the seeds. If needed, protect the area from birds with plastic sheeting or netting. In dry weather, water the site regularly.

3 Germination should occur in 7–14 days. Once the grass is about 2in (5cm) tall, use a lightweight mower with very sharp blades to cut it to a height of 1in (2.5cm).

SOWING WITH A SPREADER

For large areas, a spreader is useful. Sow half the seeds one way and half at right angles to this. For a defined edge, lay plastic sheeting and push the spreader just over it.

A–Z OF PERENNIAL ORNAMENTAL GRASSES

Sow seeds of following genera (nonvariegated forms only) at a minimum temperature of 50°F (10°C). Divide in spring.

AGROSTIS

ALOPECURUS Foxtail grass

CALAMAGROSTIS Reed grass

DACTYLIS

DESCHAMPSIA Hair grass

ELYMUS Wild rye

FESTUCA Fescue

GLYCERIA.

HOLCUS

LEYMUS (syn. *Elymus*)

MELICA Melick

MILIUM *M. effusum* 'Aureum' comes true from seeds.

MOLINIA

PENNISETUM Fountain grass

PHALARIS

PHRAGMITES Giant reed

PHYLLOSTACHYS (bamboo) Pot divisions with at least two growth buds; keep in a closed frame until new shoots appear. Pot on when pots fill with roots; plant out after two years.

POA Meadow grass, spear grass Peg down ripe flowerheads of *P. alpina* var. *vivipara* to obtain rooted plantlets (*see p.150*).

SASA (bamboo)

SESLERIA

Sow seeds of following genera (nonvariegated forms only) at a minimum temperature of 59°F (15°C). Divide in spring.

ARUNDINARIA (bamboo)

ARUNDO Divide. Take single-noded cuttings from new stems in spring; place horizontally on rooting medium in trays, as for root cuttings (*see p.158*); keep moist at 59°F (15°C) to root.

BAMBUSA Bamboo

BOUTELOUA

CHIMONOBAMBUSA (bamboo) Take rhizome sections (*see p.175*).

CHIONOCHLOA Distinct male and female plants; fertilized seeds from females are viable.

CHUSQUEA (bamboo) Take rhizome sections (*see p.175*).

CORTADERIA Pampas grass, Tussock grass Sow fertile seeds from female plants; less common self-fertile types often self-sow. Divide as for large grasses; cut into smaller pieces; grow on in pots at 60°F (15.5°C).

CYMBOPOGON

DANTHONIA

DENDROCALAMUS (bamboo) Sow seeds at 64°F (18°C). Take sections of stem (culm); place them horizontally in sphagnum moss at 70°F (21°C) to root.

ERAGROSTIS Love grass

FARGESIA (bamboo) Take rhizome sections (*see p.175*).

HAKONECHLOA MACRA

HELICTOTRICHON

HIMALAYACALAMUS (bamboo) Sow seeds at 64°F (18°C).

IMPERATA

MISCANTHUS

OPLISMENUS Take stem cuttings from semiripe, nonflowering shoots in late summer (*see p.154*).

PLEIOBLASTUS (bamboo)

PSEUDOSASA (bamboo)

SACCHARUM (syn. *Erianthus*) Sow at 70°F (21°C). Take single-node stem cuttings in spring as for *Arundo*; root at 64°F (18°C).

SEMIARUNDINARIA (bamboo) Take rhizome sections (*see p.175*).

SHIBATAEA (bamboo) Take rhizome sections (*see p.175*).

SORGHASTRUM

STENOTAPHRUM Remove rooted plantlets (*see p.150*) produced on shoots from underground stems in autumn.

STIPA (syn. *Achnatherum*) Spear, feather, or needle grass

YUSHANIA (syn. *Sinarundinaria*) (bamboo)

For annual grasses, see Annuals and Biennials *(pp.220–29)*.

ORCHIDS

All orchids belong to the huge family Orchidaceae, with some 835 genera, 25,000 species, and many thousands of hybrids. Many, with flowers of fabulous shape and spectacular color, are among the finest of cultivated ornamental plants. During their evolution, orchids adopted different modes of growth and adapted to their habitats by becoming epiphytic or terrestrial. These physical adaptations are significant both in terms of their cultural needs and in the methods used for propagation.

EPIPHYTIC ORCHIDS *Many cultivated orchids are tropical epiphytes, such as this* Cattleya aurantiaca. *In the wild, it grows on a tree and absorbs moisture from the air. Decaying leaf litter in the tree crotches and along the branches provides nutrients, and the warm, humid climate allows the orchid's anchoring roots to be exposed without harm.*

EPIPHYTIC ORCHIDS

Most cultivated orchids are epiphytes and a few are lithophytes, that is, occurring on or among rocks. Epiphytic orchids grow on trees, but they are not parasitic. They use aerial roots to absorb moisture from the air and take nutrients from decayed leaf litter that collects in branch crotches and on the trunk. The aerial roots also act as anchorage, often adhering to the bark for part of their length before hanging freely in midair. Epiphytes display one of two growth habits: sympodial or monopodial.

In sympodial orchids, the terminal growth ends in a flower spike, or inflorescence. Increase in the plant's size arises from lateral buds, known as "eyes," on pseudobulbs, which are found at the base of previous growths. Orchids with a monopodial growth pattern have extended stems or rhizomes, and all new growth arises from the growing tip. Flower spikes occur on the stem at the base of mature leaves.

The conditions in their native habitats enable epiphytes to survive with their roots exposed to the elements. Epiphytic orchids occur in warm, humid rainforests at low altitudes or at sea level, as well as in cooler, high-altitude rainforests. This indicates the range of temperatures needed for cultivation and propagation. Cool-growing orchids need minimum temperatures of 50–55°F (10–13°C); the intermediate-growing orchids, 57–66°F (14–19°C); and warm-growing orchids, 68–75°F (20–24°C).

For most epiphytes, a mix made up of three parts fine granulated bark to one part perlite and one part charcoal serves for both potting and vegetative propagation (*see also pp.33–4*).

COMMERCIAL METHODS OF RAISING ORCHIDS

Meristem culture permits the commercial production from one orchid of thousands of identical offspring by culturing growth cells, taken from a dormant bud, in a laboratory (*see below and p.15*).

Raising orchids from seeds also involves skilled laboratory work. In the wild, the tiny seeds rely on sugars that are produced by symbiotic microfungi to provide them with energy to germinate. In cultivation, the seeds can be germinated on agar-based media that contain all the necessary nutrients. Seeds must also be gathered and germinated under totally sterile conditions to avoid their being killed by airborne bacteria. In flower, seedlings naturally vary, and the best are selected for meristem culture. It is possible for the gardener to grow orchids from seeds, but it requires special equipment and some degree of skill.

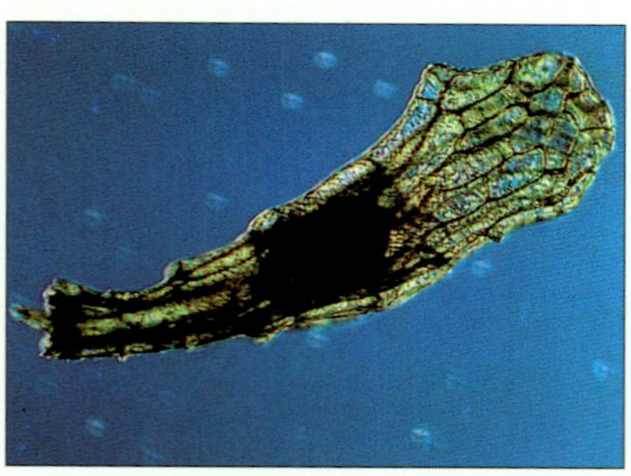

ORCHID SEED *One orchid can produce a million tiny seeds. They are very vulnerable to airborne bacteria and so must be gathered and sown in completely sterile conditions.*

MERISTEM CULTURE *Cells from the growth bud of an orchid pseudobulb are cultivated in sterile conditions on a special nutrient gel to produce large numbers of tiny plantlets.*

TERRESTRIAL ORCHIDS

Terrestrial, or ground-dwelling, orchids predominate in cooler climates where epiphytic orchids are not able to exist. There are also many tropical terrestrials, for example *Habenaria*. Terrestrial orchids are mostly deciduous and have one of two principal growth habits. They are either rhizomatous or produce underground tubers, each supporting a leaf rosette and a central flowering stem: The plant is dormant in winter and remains so until spring.

Adopting the dormancy habit, along with possessing underground storage organs, confers greater cold tolerance than is seen in the epiphytes. Most so-called hardy orchids are terrestrials, and, although some are hardy in many areas, few can tolerate very damp winter conditions and so are more safely grown in a cold greenhouse or alpine house.

Most terrestrials require a free-draining mix, which may contain soil, grit, peat, leaf mold, osmunda fiber, or fine bark.

SYMPODIAL ORCHIDS

Sympodial orchids include those, such as *Cattleya*, that have pseudobulbs (swollen, food- and water-storage organs), which bear leaves and flowers. A dormant, leafless pseudobulb is known as a backbulb. Backbulbs can be used for propagation, since removal from the rhizome usually activates dormant eyes. Not all sympodials have pseudobulbs; a few produce leafy growths instead, such as *Paphiopedilum*.

Propagation of sympodial orchids with pseudobulbs is most usually by removal of single backbulbs or by division. Backbulbs take a few years to flower, while divisions of a large plant may bloom in the following season, provided that each division has at least four pseudobulbs. The basic techniques are similar for all sympodial epiphytes with pseudobulbs, but variations are made to accommodate differences in

DIVIDING PSEUDOBULBS OF SYMPODIALS

1 In spring, an orchid (here a Cymbidium*) with eight or more pseudobulbs may be divided into two. Knock the plant out of its container. Shake the excess mix from the roots.*

2 Push the pseudobulbs apart slightly in the center and, with a sharp pruning knife, cut down through the woody rhizome that joins them. Pry the plant apart into two sections.

3 Remove any leafless backbulbs from the divided sections. Discard any that are old and shriveled. Plump backbulbs may be potted separately (see below) *to grow on.*

4 Trim off any dead roots, using clean, sharp pruners. Trim back longer healthy roots, but be sure to retain at least 6in (15cm) of living root to anchor each plant in its new pot.

5 Repot each divided section in a container that is just a little larger than its root ball. Hold the base of the pseudobulbs level with the rim of the pot, then fill in with orchid bark.

structure and habit. With some orchids, such as in *Odontoglossum*, increasing by backbulbs is rarely successful because they seldom produce enough dormant eyes. In this case, it is possible to propagate from a leading pseudobulb (*see p.180*). Other sympodials, as in *Dendrobium*, form adventitious growths – small plantlets that may be separated and potted (*see p.181*).

Dividing pseudobulbs of sympodials

A well-grown plant produces one or more new pseudobulbs annually, each of which will live for several years. Each new pseudobulb grows from the base of the previous one, on a tough connecting rhizome. To flower in its first year, new growth depends on the young pseudobulb obtaining nutrients from the more mature pseudobulbs, even after forming its own roots and leaves. So, if plants are to flower in the season after division, each piece must have four or more plump, green pseudobulbs. Any shriveled, brown pseudobulbs are dead and should be discarded.

Division of most sympodial orchids follows a similar pattern to that shown above. Division is carried out in spring, when the parent plant is being repotted. Knock the plant out of its container and remove the oldest, leafless pseudobulbs to leave at least four on each division. Separate the pseudobulbs by placing a clean, sharp pruning knife between them and pushing down vertically to cut through the rhizome.

In most genera, the rhizome connecting the pseudobulbs is so short that it becomes visible only during this procedure, but it is essential not to slice through soft tissue at the base of the pseudobulb, which will render it useless. To avoid this, push the pseudobulbs apart firmly with fingers and thumb before inserting the knife. Cut off the dead roots, but leave some living roots to anchor each division in its pot. Pot each division with the pseudobulbs sitting on the surface of the mix so that new growth, which should appear within six weeks, does not rot away.

Propagation from single backbulbs

As a pseudobulb ages after flowering, it eventually drops its leaves but is still alive and has sufficient reserves to sustain further growth. Some orchids lose all their leaves at once; (*continued on p.180*)

PROPAGATING SINGLE BACKBULBS

1 Pot up plump, healthy backbulbs (see inset) *singly in 3in (8cm) pots of orchid mix. Sit the backbulb on the surface of the mix to avoid rotting the dormant growth buds.*

2 Place the backbulb in a cool, shaded position and keep moist. Within six weeks, the buds should start into growth, and after 2–3 months the backbulb should have a new shoot.

DIVIDING A LEADING PSEUDOBULB

1 *In spring or autumn, when it is not in full growth or completely dormant, knock the plant (here a* Burrageara*) out of its container. Carefully tease out the mix from the roots to reveal the leading pseudobulb.*

2 *Place the root ball on its side. Use a clean, sharp scalpel or knife to cut down through the rhizome between the leading pseudobulb and the backbulbs. Carefully pull free the leading pseudobulb; if necessary, cut through the roots.*

3 *Trim off any damaged roots and old or dead backbulbs from both sections. Repot the main plant into a pot ½in (1cm) larger than the root ball. Pot the leading pseudobulb in as small a pot as possible.*

(*continued from p.179*) others shed one leaf at a time over two or three years. While still attached to the main plant, its role is to support new growth and flowers. But if leafless backbulbs are separated from the parent plant while still green and plump, they may be used for propagation, provided that four pseudobulbs are left on the parent plant.

Sever single backbulbs from the parent plant with a clean, sharp pruning knife, taking care not to damage the softer tissue at its base. Where the backbulb is covered with basal leaf bracts, peel these away until a dormant bud, or "eye," is visible at the base (*see right*). Depending upon the type of orchid, there may be one or several. *Cymbidium* orchids will have several eyes, with the strongest ones at the base of the backbulb and weaker ones higher up.

Remove any dead roots from beneath the backbulb, but leave about 2in (5cm) of good roots to anchor it in its pot. Pot it (*see p.179*) in orchid mix and grow on in a closed case. Keep the case at a temperature to suit the individual orchid, according to whether it is cool-, intermediate-, or warm-growing (*see p.178 and* A–Z of Epiphytic Orchids, *pp.181 and 183*).

A new green shoot should appear within six weeks, and, after a further four weeks or so, new roots should emerge. At this stage, remove the plant from the case and place it in the greenhouse or indoor growing area in good light. After a further six months the plant can be "dropped on," that is, potted into a larger container, without disturbing the mass of mix or the new, growing roots. Pot again after one year and, from then on, as necessary until the plant is mature.

At some stage during this time, the original pseudobulb will become exhausted. It will shrivel and die and can then be removed from the young growing plant and discarded. The new plant should reach flowering size after approximately four years.

Sometimes, two dormant buds will grow on at the same time from the same pseudobulb. Such plants are "double-leadered." In a few years, each leader will form an independent plant, so that there are two within one pot. When it becomes possible to leave four or more pseudobulbs on each piece, they can be divided. Plants reduced to less than four pseudobulbs are unlikely to bloom again until sufficient strength has been built up, which may take several years.

Dividing a leading pseudobulb

With some groups of orchids, notably the *Odontoglossum* group, propagation by backbulbs is seldom successful. An alternative, although risky, method of propagation is by removal of the leading pseudobulb. It must be attempted only with strong, healthy plants with leaves on all, or most, of its pseudobulbs.

The *Odontoglossum* group includes all species of the genus *Odontoglossum* as well as closely related genera, hybrids (including intergeneric hybrids), and any cultivars derived from them, for example x *Odontocidium*, which is an intergeneric hybrid between *Odontoglossum* and *Oncidium*. All plants with *Odontoglossum* species in their parentage may be increased in the same way.

Propagate from leading pseudobulbs in spring or autumn, when the plant is neither in full growth nor dormant, and the leading pseudobulb has new shoots about 6in (15cm) tall. Knock the plant out of its pot and separate the leading pseudobulb from the rest of the plant by cutting through the connecting rhizome. Tease apart the roots gently. If necessary, cut through them, but take care not to damage the pseudobulbs.

Pot the leading pseudobulb with its own roots into as small a pot as will comfortably hold it. Replant the rest of the plant into a pot a little larger than the root ball. New growth should appear from the base of the second pseudobulb and go on to flower when mature.

Propagation of the Cattleya group

The *Cattleya* group are epiphytic, sympodial orchids. The term applies to all species of *Cattleya* as well as other closely related genera and intergeneric hybrids between them, such as x *Laeliocattleya*. All orchids with *Cattleya* species in their parentage are propagated in the same way. The group produces short rhizomes and erect, stout to slender pseudobulbs, each with one or two semi-rigid leaves.

They can be increased by separation of backbulbs in the usual way and can also be divided into equal parts of four or more pseudobulbs, where each has a

DORMANT EYES

When dividing pseudobulbs and backbulbs, look for dormant "eyes" at the base (here of a Cattleya*). These should be fat and green; if shriveled or brown, they are dead. There should be at least one healthy eye on each pseudobulb or backbulb to be propagated.*

TAKING CUTTINGS OF DENDROBIUM

1 *Remove a 10in (25cm) long section of a healthy cane. Cut with a sharp knife just above a leaf node or at the base of the cane.*

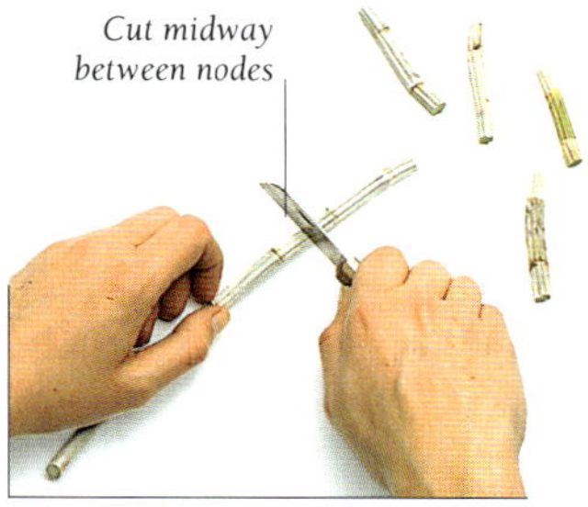

2 *Cut between the leaf nodes of the cane, dividing it into pieces about 3in (8cm) long. Each cutting should have at least one node.*

3 *Fill a seed tray with moist sphagnum moss. Lay the cuttings on the moss, cover, and keep in a humid, warm place.*

4 *The cuttings should root in a few weeks, producing plantlets. Once they are large enough to handle, pot them individually.*

new growth (*see p.179*). Sometimes, however, the older pseudobulbs or backbulbs lack new growth. If so, they can be started into growth by cutting through the rhizome between the pseudobulbs, without lifting them, in early autumn. Leave the divisions in place until the following spring. Separate and repot them when new growth appears on each division, but before new roots grow out from the bases of the new growth, to flower 2–3 years later.

ORCHIDS WITH CANELIKE PSEUDOBULBS

At first glance, some sympodials, notably *Dendrobium*, seem to be monopodial, because their leaves grow at the ends of long, seldom-branching stems. In fact, the "stems" are canelike pseudobulbs; they may have leaves growing from nodes on the cane or from the cane's tip. Flowers develop from nodes along the canes, usually in spring. *Dendrobium* and *Thunia* with canes will produce new growth from dormant buds at the nodes so can be increased from "stem" cuttings (*see above*), which flower in 2–3 years.

Sometimes, *Dendrobium* produce adventitious growths, or small plantlets, from nodes on the cane. These, too, can be used for propagation (*see right*). Most plantlets flower in 2–3 years.

DIVIDING ORCHIDS WITHOUT PSEUDOBULBS

Some sympodials, such as *Paphiopedilum* and *Phragmipedium*, do not develop pseudobulbs. Both are challenging to propagate; they have no backbulbs and do not respond well to division. Some species are also notoriously reluctant to flower before they produce multiple shoots, usually in 4–5 years.

These orchids can be divided, when they have at least four growths, by cutting through the thick rhizomes before growth begins in late winter or early spring, in much the same way as dividing pseudobulbs (*see p.179*). However, it is advisable to attempt this only with mature, well-developed plants, so that the multiple growths needed for flowering remain on the parent plant.

PROPAGATING FROM ADVENTITIOUS GROWTHS

1 *Choose a plantlet with strong, healthy roots (here a* Dendrobium*) and sever it from the parent stem with a clean, sharp knife.*

2 *Pot the plantlet in a 3in (8cm) pot of fine orchid mix. Make sure that the roots (see inset) sit just below the surface.*

A–Z OF EPIPHYTIC ORCHIDS

Ada Cool-growing sympodial; divide plant or remove backbulbs (*see p.179*).
Aerides Cool- to intermediate-growing monopodial; as for *Vanda* (*see p.183*).
Angraecum Propagation not recommended.
Anguloa Cradle or Tulip orchid Cool-growing sympodial; divide plant or remove backbulbs (*see p.179*) in spring.
x *Angulocaste* Cool- to intermediate-growing sympodial; as for *Anguloa*.
Arachnis Scorpion orchid Warm- or intermediate-growing monopodial; take stem sections as for *Vanda* (*see p.183*).
Ascocentrum Intermediate-growing monopodial; as for *Vanda* (*see p.183*).
Barkeria Cool-growing sympodial; divide as for *Paphiopedilum* (*see left*) in spring.
Brassavola Intermediate-growing sympodial; divide stemlike pseudobulbs of large plants in spring.
Brassia Cool-growing sympodial; divide plant or remove backbulbs (*see p.179*).
x *Brassocattleya* Intermediate-growing sympodial; remove single backbulbs (*see p.179*) in spring.
x *Brassolaeliocattleya* Intermediate-growing sympodial; remove single backbulbs (*see p.179*) in spring.
Bulbophyllum Cool-, intermediate- or warm-growing sympodial; divide backbulbs (*see p.179*) in spring.
Cattleya Intermediate-growing sympodial; divide or remove single backbulb (*p.179*).
Coelogyne Cool- or intermediate-growing sympodial; divide plant or remove backbulbs (*see p.179*) in spring.
Cymbidium Cool-growing sympodial; divide plant or remove single backbulbs (*p.179*).
Dendrobium Cool- to intermediate-growing sympodial; take stem cuttings in spring or remove plantlets (*see above*).
Dendrochilum Golden chain orchid Cool-growing sympodial; divide plant or remove single backbulbs (*see p.179*) in spring.
Dracula Propagation not recommended.
Encyclia Cool-growing sympodial; divide plant or remove single backbulbs (*see p.179*) in spring.
Epidendrum Cool- or intermediate-growing sympodial; divide as for *Paphiopedilum* (*see left*) in spring. A few are terrestrial.
Laelia Cool- or intermediate-growing sympodial; occasionally divide backbulbs (*see p.179*) in spring.
x *Laeliocattleya* Cool-growing sympodial; divide plant or remove backbulbs (*see p.179*) in spring.
Lemboglossum Cool-growing sympodial; divide backbulbs (*see p.179*) in spring.
(*Continued on p. 183.*)

Monopodial orchids

Instead of pseudobulbs, these orchids have an upward-growing stem or rhizome with new leaves produced at intervals from the growing tip. Some, for instance *Phalaenopsis*, have a short rhizome and, as new leaves develop at the top, older leaves below are shed, so that at any one time the plant bears 3–6 leaves. Orchids with this habit are self-regulating in size and never become unduly tall. Other monopodials, such as vandas, produce a much longer rhizome with many leaves appearing in pairs in succession from the apex, while the rhizome grows continually taller. With either growth habit, normal division is impossible.

While many monopodials do not increase as readily as sympodials, they do have a natural ability to reproduce if the growing tip, where the new leaves form, becomes rotten or damaged. If this occurs, a plant may produce new growth from a point lower down on the stem. This ability may be exploited for propagation. Only *Phalaenopsis* orchids produce new plantlets on flowered stems (*see below*), while others produce plantlets at various points along the rhizome or near the base.

Taking stem sections

Monopodial orchids, such as in *Vanda*, that produce a long, upward-growing rhizome may be propagated when the parent plant reaches a certain size and stage in its development. As the plant grows, new leaves are made at the tip and old ones are shed from the base. Eventually, the lower portion of the stem becomes bare and leafless, with aerial roots emerging from the axils of old leaf bases. At this stage, the top part of the plant may be removed, together with its aerial roots, to encourage the lower, leafless portion to produce new growth (*see facing page*). This is also a good way of managing plants that have become too tall and top-heavy, but it does carry some risk to the parent plant so should be done only when absolutely necessary.

In spring, at the start of the growing season, cut through the rhizome with a sharp knife and repot the top portion of the plant. Place in humid shade with a nighttime minimum of 61–66°F (16–19°C); mist-spray regularly with nonalkaline water for a few weeks to avoid the sections drying out.

Wrap the lower stem in damp moss to encourage one or more new roots and shoots to form. Cover the moss with clear plastic and tie in place. Keep the moss damp. New growth should appear in a few weeks, at which point the plastic and moss should be removed.

Alternatively, leave the leafless lower portion of the plant in its container and place in a closed case at the appropriate temperature (*see p.178 and* A–Z of Epiphytic Orchids, *pp.181 and 183*). Within a few weeks, a new plant should begin to grow from a node near the stem base. After 6–12 months, when the new plant has at least two pairs of leaves and its own roots, it can be removed from the old stem and potted.

Propagating from plantlets

Some monopodial orchids reproduce freely and naturally by producing new plantlets at various points along the rhizome or near the stem base. These can be left on the plant until they are established and have their own leaves and roots. At this stage, the plantlets can be removed and potted separately without any risk to the parent (*see left*); most will flower in 1–2 years.

Phalaenopsis species have short, upward-growing rhizomes, each with 3–6 oval, fleshy leaves. They rarely produce new growths from their base naturally but may do so if the center of the plant becomes damaged or rotten. The flower spikes, which appear from the base of the leaf, are unusual in that their stems have nodes on the lower portions, each with a tiny potential growth eye beneath a covering bract.

When the first flowering from the stem tip has finished and has been cut off, the lower nodes may be stimulated to produce a second flowering stem.

Propagating Phalaenopsis from keikis

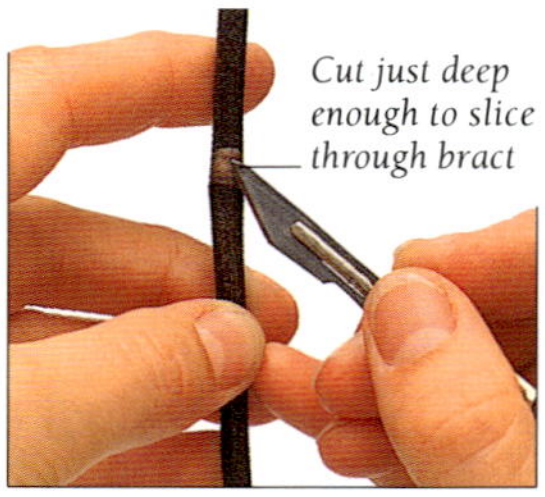

1 Wash your hands and use a sterilized scalpel. Select a leaf node, then make a vertical cut down the center of the bract that covers the node. Do not cut into the bud beneath.

2 Using sterilized tweezers, peel back and pull away the two halves of the bract to expose the eye. Do not leave any snags. Remove the bracts from 3–4 nodes on the stem.

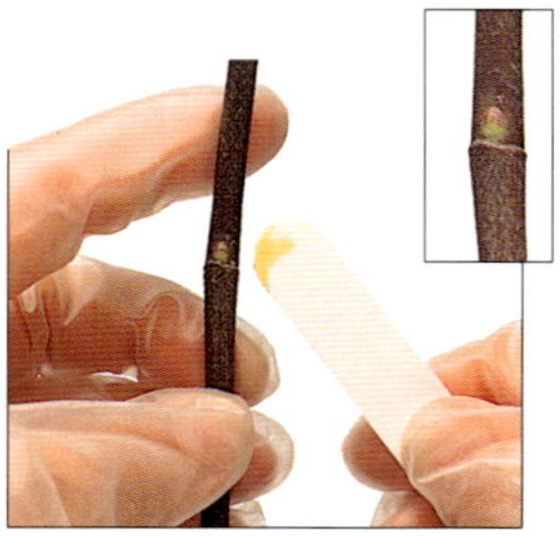

3 Use a sterilized plant label or a spatula to smear a little keiki paste (growth hormone) over each prepared eye (see inset) and the exposed tissue around it.

4 After 6–8 weeks, the treated nodes should produce tiny plantlets. Lay the stem across some small pots of orchid mix. Peg each plantlet singly into a pot and keep moist to encourage it to root into the mix.

5 After 12–18 months, when the plantlets are at least 3in (8cm) tall, they may be detached from the parent plant. Cut the parent stem next to the plantlet and cut back to its base. The new plant should flower in two years.

Rooted Phalaenopsis plantlets

Some Phalaenopsis, *particularly* P. lueddemanniana, *occasionally produce plantlets from the old flowered stems. Separate the plantlet from the parent by severing the stem 1in (2.5cm) below the plantlet. Prepare a 3in (8cm) pot of orchid mix, then sit the plantlet on the surface. Anchor the aerial roots to the surface with wire staples.*

TAKING A STEM SECTION OF VANDA GROUP ORCHIDS

1 *Vanda* and allied orchids have a single stem. When this becomes top-heavy, the plant (here *V. tricolor* var. *suavis*) may be cut into sections to encourage new growth from the lower stem.

2 *Remove one or two portions of the stem, cutting straight across the stem between leaf nodes with pruners. Make sure that the section has some healthy aerial roots.*

3 *Wrap the leafless lower stem in a ½in (1cm) layer of moist sphagnum moss to encourage new shoots. Secure the moss in place with twine, then wrap in clear plastic. Keep the moss moist.*

4 *Pot the top stem section in orchid mix. Sit the base of the stem just in the mix and support it with a sturdy stake until it roots. Do not bury the aerial roots, because they will be prone to rot.*

5 *Keep the stem section in the shade at a minimum of about 64°F (18°C). Spray it frequently to avoid dehydration until the new roots establish.*

This can be useful in lengthening the flowering period by several weeks or even months. It sometimes occurs naturally to such an extent that stems need to be removed altogether if the plant is not to flower itself to death.

Nodes on the lower flowering stem can be encouraged to produce plantlets, or keikis, instead of flowers, by treating the nodes with keiki paste (available from some orchid specialists). This compound contains rooting hormones and growth-promoting vitamins. However, it can be quite difficult to maintain the sterile conditions that are essential for success.

As soon as the first blooms fade, remove the top, flowered portion of the stem. Select a node and remove the bract carefully as shown (*see left*). Coat the bud and the tissue immediately around it sparingly with keiki paste. Treat 3–4 nodes per stem and only two stems per plant. New plantlets should develop within 6–8 weeks. Leave them on the stem until new leaves and roots have grown. Peg down each plantlet onto a small pot of mix and allow the plantlet to root directly into the new pot before detaching it from the parent stem.

A–Z OF EPIPHYTIC ORCHIDS

(*Continued from p.181.*)

LYCASTE Cool-growing, sympodial epiphytic or terrestrials. Divide plant or remove single backbulbs (*see p.179*) in spring.

MASDEVALLIA Propagation not recommended.

MAXILLARIA Cool-growing sympodial; divide plant or remove single backbulbs (*see p.179*) in spring.

MILTONIA Cool- or intermediate-growing sympodial; remove single backbulbs (*see p.179*) in spring.

MILTONIOPSIS PANSY ORCHID Cool-growing sympodial; divide when large enough (*see p.179*) in spring.

x *ODONTIODA* Cool-growing sympodial; as for *Odontoglossum*.

x *ODONTOCIDIUM* Cool-growing sympodial; as for *Odontoglossum*.

ODONTOGLOSSUM Cool-growing sympodial; divide leading pseudobulb (*see p.180*).

x *ODONTONIA* Cool-growing sympodial; as for *Odontoglossum*.

ONCIDIUM Cool- or intermediate-growing sympodial; divide those with pseudobulbs or remove single backbulbs (*see p.179*) in spring. Divide others when large enough.

PAPHIOPEDILUM SLIPPER ORCHID Cool- or intermediate-growing sympodial epiphytes or terrestrials; divide by cutting through rhizomes (*see p.181*).

PHALAENOPSIS MOTH ORCHID Warm-growing monopodial; remove rooted plantlets or propagate keikis any time (*see p.182*).

PHRAGMIPEDIUM Cool- or intermediate-growing sympodial; divide by cutting through rhizomes (*see p.181*) in spring.

ROSSIOGLOSSUM Propagation not recommended.

x *SOPHROLAELIOCATTLEYA* Intermediate-growing sympodial; divide plant or remove single backbulbs (*see p.179*) in spring.

SOPHRONITIS Propagation not recommended.

STANHOPEA Cool-growing sympodial; divide plant or remove single backbulbs (*see p.179*) in spring.

VANDA Intermediate- to warm-growing monopodial; stem sections (*see above*).

x *VUYLSTEKEARA* Cool-growing sympodial; as for *Odontoglossum*.

x *WILSONARA* Cool-growing sympodial; as for *Odontoglossum*.

Terrestrial orchids

Commercial techniques for propagating hardy terrestrial orchids from seeds have produced an increasing range of available species and, once acquired, many are easy to propagate vegetatively. Terrestrials are either rhizomatous (with rhizomes and, often, pseudobulbs that are similar to those of epiphytic sympodial orchids) or tuberous (producing a leaf rosette from a bud at the top of an underground tuber). The propagation method depends on the growth habit.

A suitable mix may be made of equal parts soil, coarse sand, mixed peat and leaf mold, and fine bark, with a little bonemeal added.

Dividing rhizomatous terrestrials

Most rhizomatous terrestrials are propagated in spring, just before growth begins. All divisions need food reserves if they are to establish as a new plant, so terrestrials are divided into pieces with a leading shoot and 2–3 pseudobulbs, on much the same principle as sympodial epiphytes (*see p.179*). Terrestrial orchids often grow with their pseudobulbs partially buried in the soil: when replanting, set the pseudobulbs at the same depth as before. The divisions may be planted out in similar conditions to the parent plant or potted in pans and grown on in the greenhouse.

Rhizomatous orchids that have no pseudobulbs may be divided into sections, each with 2–3 years' of growth behind the leading shoot. These annual growths can be counted by the joints on the rhizome. *Cypripedium* do well if divided toward the end of the growing season, when their food reserves are distributed evenly through the rhizome. There is less risk of damaging any new growth, and the plants reestablish well before the onset of dormancy.

Most rhizomatous species regularly produce side growths from the main rhizome and provide plentiful material for propagation. A few branch rarely, producing a single, continuously elongating growth, which makes normal division difficult. When these rhizomes show four or more annual growth joints, they can be induced to shoot from the dormant buds by cutting only halfway through the rhizome early in the growing season. Do not cut through the rhizome completely: the aim is simply to reduce the dominance of the growing tip and induce formation of sideshoots. Leave each division of at least two growths in place until the beginning of the next growing season. If successful, active buds should begin to shoot in the spring. Lift the plant, separate the sections, and pot individually. Grow on in the same conditions as the parent.

Propagating pleiones

Members of the genus *Pleione* may be epiphytic, lithophytic, or terrestrial. They form tight clumps of single, small pseudobulbs that are in fact separate plants, rather than a succession of differently aged pseudobulbs on a connecting rhizome. The pseudobulbs flower in spring, then die back over the summer while a new pseudobulb forms, ready to flower in the following spring. Only occasionally do pseudobulbs persist for a second winter to produce new shoots in spring.

Clumps of *Pleione* may be lifted and divided in autumn (*see below*). The pseudobulbs usually fall apart naturally;

Dividing clumps of terrestrial pseudobulbs

1 *Some terrestrial orchids, such as these* Pleione formosana, *form tightly packed clumps when mature. These can be lifted and divided in the autumn, while the pseudobulbs are dormant, to provide new plants.*

2 *Lift the dormant pseudobulbs carefully, using a tool to ease them out from the clump. Take care to avoid damaging the roots. Any old, shriveled pseudobulbs should be discarded, because they will not produce healthy new growth.*

3 *Clean off any dead matter, and remove any loose papery tunics from the viable pseudobulbs. Remove dead roots using a clean, sharp knife, but take care not to damage the new and healthy roots* (see inset).

4 *Prepare 5–6in (13–15cm) pans of a free-draining, soilless potting mix. Space five pseudobulbs on the mix. Cover the roots with mix so that the growing "eyes" at the base are just above the surface. Water and label.*

Pleione bulbils

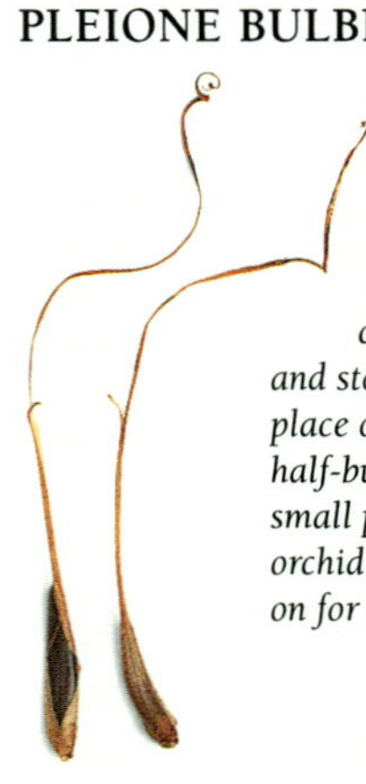

Bulbils form where the leaf grew at the top of the old pseudobulb. In late autumn, collect the bulbils and store in a cool, dry place over winter. In spring, half-bury the bulbils in a small pan of free-draining orchid mix and grow on for a year.

DIVIDING TERRESTRIAL ORCHIDS WITH TUBERS

1 Lift the plant (here a Dactylorhiza*) at any time from early autumn to early spring. Gently wash off the soil to reveal the tubers. Cut the underground stem between the old and the new tuber with a sharp knife.*

2 Replant the parent and water well. Plant out the new tubers at the same depth as they were before, spacing them about 6in (15cm) apart. Water and label.

if they do not, gently push them apart until they separate. A plant may also produce bulbils (*see box, facing page*) at the point from which the old leaf was shed. The bulbils may be detached and used to increase stock.

Propagating tuberous orchids

The growth of tuberous orchids is similar to that of other tuberous plants, and, like them, they vary in their ability to produce new tubers. Some, like *Ophrys*, rarely do so, while *Dactylorhiza* may form substantial colonies of offsets. Where new tubers are formed naturally, clumps may be lifted and divided at any time during dormancy (*see above*). Many growers prefer to do this in early autumn to avoid damaging young roots, which begin growth early in the year. After division, plant out the parent plant and the offsets where they are to flower.

Orchids such as *Ophrys* and *Orchis* that are reluctant to produce new tubers, usually forming only one tuber a year to replace the old, can be coaxed to do so by one of two forms of division. "Summer" propagation is used just as the flowers begin to fade, from early spring onward, depending on the species. Lift a plant from the soil and detach the new tuber from the rosette, cutting the underground stem, or stolon, that connects them just above the new tuber's bud. The new tuber will be plump and firm, as distinct from the old, brown, and shriveled one.

Repot the rosette and old tuber, with most of its root system intact. Pot the new tuber separately; treat it as if it is dormant and keep cool and dry. The old shoot (with its flower spike removed to prevent energy being expended on seed production) is kept in growth to allow more new tubers to be produced before dormancy.

"Winter" propagation utilizes the unflowered rosette as it reaches full leaf development. By this stage, a new tuber should have begun to form below the rosette. Remove the rosette and new tuber together by cutting through the bottom of the stem that arises from the old tuber. Take care to leave a small portion of stem with one or two roots still attached to the original tuber. The rosette should flower normally and sustain the growth of the new tuber. The old tuber will then develop one or more growths from dormant axillary buds on its stem, which will in turn produce their own tubers. This operation can be performed without removing the plant from the soil or its container, since the two new plants formed are left to complete their growth naturally.

Stem cuttings of terrestrials

A few terrestrials, such as *Ludisia discolor*, have fleshy, segmented stems that root from the nodes as they touch the ground. This ability makes them easy to increase by stem cuttings (*see below*). *Ludisia* is subtropical in origin, so, after the cuttings callus, pot in terrestrial orchid mix and grow on in a shaded closed case with high humidity and bottom heat of 68°F (20°C).

LUDISIA STEM CUTTING

*The stems of the terrestrial jewel orchid (*Ludisia discolor*) readily produce adventitious roots. Take 3–5in (8–13cm) stem-tip cuttings, cutting below a node, and leave in a cool, dry place for 48 hours to callus before potting.*

A–Z of terrestrial orchids

Bletilla Mostly cool-growing (*B. striata* is hardy in Zones 5–8) and rhizomatous; divide in spring as for *Pleione* (*see facing page*). Flowers in first year.
Calanthe Mostly warm- or cool-growing terrestrials (*C. discolor* is hardy in Zones 7–9) and rhizomatous; divide just before growth begins in spring, as for sympodial epiphytes (*see p.179*); divisions must have a leading shoot and at least two pseudobulbs. Flowers in first year.
Cypripedium Lady's slipper orchid Rhizomatous; divide rhizomes into sections in spring or autumn (*see facing page*). Flowers in 1–2 years. Generally hardy in Zones 3–7.
Dactylorhiza Marsh orchid, Spotted orchid Tuberous; divide when dormant (*see above*). Flowers in 1–3 years. Some hardy in Zones 5–8.
Epipactis Helleborine Rhizomatous; divide rhizomes (*see facing page*) when dormant in early spring. Some hardy in Zones 4–8. Flowers in first year.
Goodyera Jewel orchid Mostly cool-growing, rhizomatous; divide in spring as for *Ludisia*; keep shaded, cool, and humid until established. Stem cuttings as for *Ludisia*. Flowers in 1–3 years.
Habenaria Warm-growing, tuberous; divide in autumn or spring as for *Dactylorhiza*. Flowers in 3–4 years.
Ludisia Jewel orchid Warm-growing, fibrous-rooted; take stem cuttings (*see above*). Flowers in 1–3 years.
Ophrys Tuberous; slow to increase, use "summer" and "winter" propagation. Some hardy in Zones 7–9. Flowers in 3–4 years.
Orchis Tuberous; slow to increase, use "summer" and "winter" propagation. Flowers in 3–4 years. Some hardy in Zones 5–7.
Pleione Rhizomatous, epiphytic or terrestrial; divide pseudobulbs (*see facing page*) to flower the next year. Propagate from bulbils to flower in 3–5 years. Hardy in Zones 9–10.
Serapias Tuberous; spreads by stolons that produce new tubers at their tips – detach and replant new tubers in spring. Flowers in first year. Hardy in Zones 8–9.

A–Z OF PERENNIALS

ACANTHUS
BEAR'S BREECHES

DIVISION in spring or in autumn
SEEDS in spring
CUTTINGS from mid- to late autumn

All *Acanthus* may be divided, especially variegated forms. They increase naturally from roots left in the soil, so all except variegated plants are easy to propagate from root cuttings. Species can be raised from seeds. Use deep pots for seedlings and cuttings; *Acanthus* dislike root disturbance.

DIVISION

Cut clumps into 2–4 pieces (*see p.148*). Autumn division in areas with cold, wet winters is not advisable. Plants divided in autumn may flower the next year; spring-divided plants in two years.

SEEDS

Sow the seeds (*see p.151*) at 59°F (15°C). Pot seedlings or line out in a nursery bed to flower in three years. Protect new plants from severe cold in the first winter.

CUTTINGS

Take 2–3in (5–8cm) root cuttings from mature, healthy plants (*see p.158*). Cuttings flower in two years.

RIPENING SEEDHEADS
The tall flower spike (here of Acanthus spinosus*) ripens from the base, each flower producing large, shiny black seeds.*

ACHILLEA *YARROW*

Achillea 'Taygetea'

DIVISION in spring
SEEDS in autumn or in spring
CUTTINGS in spring or in early autumn

Both border and alpine forms of this genus are propagated in similar ways. They may be divided in the usual way (*see p.148*) to flower in their first season or into single bud divisions (*see p.150*) for more plants. It may be possible to take self-rooted cuttings (*see p.166*) from alpines without lifting the parent. Sow seeds (*see p.152*) at 59°F (15°C); seedlings often flower in the first year. Take semi-ripe cuttings (*see p.154*) in early autumn or basal stem cuttings (*see p.156*) in spring from alpines and border perennials for flowers in a year.

ACHIMENES *HOT-WATER PLANT, CUPID'S BOWER*

DIVISION in autumn or in early spring
SEEDS in early spring

This tender genus has been extensively hybridized: many cultivars are grown. The plants are dormant in winter, surviving as scaly rhizomes. The rhizomes (small, nodular swellings commonly called tubercles) increase in number naturally and can be gathered while the plant is dormant in autumn or winter (or when dividing the plant in spring) and used for propagation (*see below*).

To increase the yield of new plants, cut the tubercles in half before potting. Plants flower in the same year.

All species can be grown from seeds to flower in two years. Sowing seeds of cultivars or of plants that have been deliberately hybridized (*see p.21*) can result in interesting color variations. Sow on moss as for alpines (*see p.165*) at 64°F (18°C) in spring as the daylight hours are lengthening; short days induce dormancy.

PROPAGATING ACHIMENES PLANTS FROM TUBERCLES

1 In the autumn after the foliage has died down, remove the dormant plant from its pot or lift it from the border. Tease apart the roots and detach the tubercles from the dead roots.

2 Discard the parent plant. Half-fill a seed tray with moist peat. Scatter the tubercles evenly over the surface. Cover with ½in (1cm) of peat. Label and store in a cool, dry place.

3 In spring, prepare a 5in (13cm) pot with soilless potting mix. Lay about five tubercles on the surface. Cover with ¼–½in (5mm–1cm) of vermiculite, label, and water well with tepid water. Keep at about 59°F (15°C).

Pot plantlets singly or grow on as one plant

4 Water sparingly until shoots appear, usually about three weeks later. After 8–10 weeks, the plantlets (here of A. erecta) should have several pairs of leaves (see inset) and, after 12 weeks (above), may be potted singly, if desired.

AETHIONEMA *STONE CRESS*

SEEDS in autumn or in early spring
CUTTINGS from late spring to early summer

The woody-based perennials in this genus (syn. *Eunomia*) tend to be rather short-lived, but most stone cresses come readily from seeds. Special forms and cultivars must be increased from cuttings.

SEEDS

Some stone cresses, such as *Aethionema grandiflorum* and *A. saxatile* and their cultivars, will self-sow in the garden, especially when grown on raised beds. Sow seeds (*see p.164*) in autumn in a cold frame (of hardy types only in cold climates) or in spring at 50°F (10°C). Plants will flower within two years.

CUTTINGS

Take softwood stem-tip cuttings, 1¼–2in (3–5cm) long (*see p.166*). Put in bright but indirect light; if too shaded, new shoots will become drawn. Pot singly once rooted; plant into final positions in the late summer or following spring.

AGAPANTHUS

AFRICAN BLUE LILY

Agapanthus 'Blue Giant'

DIVISION in spring
SEEDS in autumn or spring

Species and cultivars in this genus may all be divided, especially those with variegated foliage. They are set back by frequent root disturbance, and older plants reestablish slowly from division; three- or four-year-old plants are an ideal age. Gathered seeds may not come true to type but can yield some interesting variations.

DIVISION

Lift clumps and divide into 2–4 pieces using back-to-back forks (*see p.148*). Trim off any damaged roots. Substantial divisions should flower in the same year. Plants may be divided into single crowns to grow on in nursery beds or pots. Protect from severe cold in the first winter, if needed, and plant out in spring. In warm climates, plants may flower in 12 months, but most take 2–3 years.

SEEDS

Seeds sown at 61°F (16°C) (*see p.151*) should germinate within three weeks. Grow on established seedlings in a cold frame and, if necessary, protect from cold; in spring, transfer to a nursery bed. The new plants should flower in the third year.

GATHERING AGAPANTHUS SEEDS
Cut flowerheads "in the green" when the seedpods are swollen but before they split open. Keep in a box in a warm, dry place until the seeds have been released.

DIVIDING AGAPANTHUS
After dividing into sections, carefully trim off any old stems and damaged root tissue, using a clean, sharp knife to cut straight across each root. Dust the wounds with fungicide, such as sulfur dust, to guard against rot (see inset).

ALCHEMILLA *LADY'S MANTLE*

Alchemilla mollis

DIVISION in spring
SEEDS in autumn or spring

These perennials prefer full sun, and most readily self-sow. Most are hardy in much of North America; a few from southern Africa are less hardy. The fibrous-rooted clumps of any species or cultivar are easily divided (*see p.148*). Pull them apart and replant, or divide into single crowns with strong roots and pot them or line them out in nursery beds; the new plants should flower in the same year.

If raising the hardier species from seeds, the best results are obtained from an autumn sowing (*see p.152*), followed by exposure to winter cold. Spring-sown seeds of less hardy plants kept at 60°F (15.5°C) will germinate within three weeks and may flower the same season.

SEEDLINGS OF ALPINE LADY'S MANTLE
Lady's mantle (here A. alpina*) often self-sows in the garden. Lift the seedlings carefully, as soon as they are large enough to handle, and transplant.*

OTHER PERENNIALS

ABELMOSCHUS Sow seeds (*see p.151*) in spring at 60°F (15.5°C).
ACAENA Divide in early spring or autumn (*see p.167*). Sow seeds (*p.164*) in gritty soil mix in autumn, in a cold frame. Take stem-tip cuttings (*p.166*) or self-rooted cuttings or runners (*p.148*) in late spring.
ACANTHOLIMON Seeds (*see p.164*) when ripe or in early spring; put in cloche or cold frame; seeds have low viability. Take semi-ripe cuttings (*p.166*) in late summer; remove lower, spiny leaves with scalpel; cuttings rot easily. Use very gritty soil mix; shelter in a cold frame; do not overwater.
ACIPHYLLA Division (*see p.148*) in spring may be possible. Sow seeds fresh (*p.151*) in autumn; put in cloche or cold frame. Do not overwater.
ACONITUM Divide (*see p.148*) in early spring. Sow seeds (*p.151*) in autumn; put in cold frame or cloche; germination may be slow.
ACTAEA Divide rhizomes (*see p.149*) in spring. Sow seeds (*p.151*) outdoors in autumn; germination may be slow.
ADONIS Divide after flowering; dust large cuts with fungicide (*see p.148*). Seeds (*p.151*) when ripe in gritty soil mix; put in cloche or cold frame; old seeds germinate erratically.
AESCHYNANTHUS Sow ripe seeds (*see p.151*) at 70°F (21°C); short viability. Softwood cuttings (*p.154*) any time.
AGASTACHE (syn. *BRITTONASTRUM*) Sow seeds (*see p.151*) in spring at 60°F (15.5°C). Take semi-ripe cuttings (*p.154*) in summer or autumn.
AGLAONEMA Divide in spring (*see p.148*). Sow ripe seeds (*p.151*) at 70°F (21°C).
AJUGA Divide (*see p.148*) or detach rooted plantlets in spring or in early autumn. Sow seeds (*p.151*) in spring at 50°F (10°C).
ALCEA Sow seeds (*see p.151*) in spring or summer at 60°F (15.5°C).
ALOCASIA Divide in spring (*see p.149*). Sow seeds (*p.151*) in spring at 77°F (25°C).
ALONSOA As for *Diascia* (*see p.194*).
ALPINIA As for *Alocasia* (*see above*), but sow seeds when ripe.
ALTERNANTHERA Divide in early autumn or spring (*p.148*). Semi-ripe stem-tip cuttings (*p.154*) in early autumn; softwood cuttings of overwintered plants in early spring.
ALYSSUM Sow seeds (*see p.151*) in autumn or early spring. Semi-ripe cuttings (*p.166*) in late summer; use rooting compound and gritty soil mix.
ANACYCLUS Sow seeds (*see p.151*) in spring at 60°F (15.5°C). Take basal stem cuttings (*p.156*) in spring.
ANAGALLIS Detach self-rooted layers (*see p.24*) at any time; best in summer. Sow seeds (*see p.151*) in spring at 50°F (10°C).
ANAPHALIS Divide in spring (*see p.148*). Sow seeds (*see p.151*) in spring at 50°F (10°C). Take basal stem cuttings (*p.156*) in spring.
ANCHUSA Divide into single crowns in spring (*see p.148*). Seeds in spring (*p.151*) at 50°F (10°C). Take root cuttings of cultivars (*p.158*) in autumn. Root cuttings (*p.167*) in late winter, or rosette cuttings (*p.166*) each with a piece of stem in late summer, of *A. cespitosa*.

***ACONITUM NAPELLUS* SEEDHEADS**

ANDROSACE *Rock jasmine*

Androsace pyrenaica

Division in early summer
Seeds in autumn or when ripe
Cuttings from early to midsummer

Perennial alpines in this genus (syn. *Douglasia*) rot if too wet, especially if cold. Dense cushion types are best raised from seeds; larger, mat-forming types flower more quickly if divided or grown from cuttings. Tweezers are useful; seeds are tricky to find and cuttings are tiny.

Division

Divide plants such as *A. lanuginosa*, *A. sarmentosa*, and *A. sempervivoides* after flowering (*see p.167*) into single or several rosettes, to flower the next year.

Seeds

Sow seeds (*see p.164*) as soon as ripe, if possible; old seeds tend to have poor or erratic germination. Use gritty soil mix, which must be sterile to avoid weeds or disease overwhelming the tiny seedlings. Sow in pots and keep in a sheltered place outdoors. Seedlings are initially slow to develop; delay transplanting them until the following spring or even the next one. Plants flower in 2–3 years.

Cuttings

Take stem-tip or rosette cuttings (*see p.166*) of larger, leafier types; root in a gritty soil mix. Cushion-forming types are tricky. Take single rosette cuttings or small clumps that have roots and insert in pure gritty sand or ground pumice (*see p.167*). Plants flower in two years.

ANEMONE *Windflower, Anemone*

Anemone hupehensis

Division in spring or in late summer
Seeds when ripe or in spring
Cuttings in autumn or in winter

Rhizomatous anemones tend to flower in the spring; fibrous-rooted, herbaceous species usually flower in late summer or autumn. (For tuberous species, *see p.261*.) Woodland anemones divide well, but Japanese anemones may suffer a check in growth and are better grown from root cuttings. They may also produce plantlets around the parent where roots are damaged: these can be lifted and transplanted with care.

Division

Divide late-flowering types, such as *Anemone multifida*, in spring. Cut clumps into 2–4 sections and replant where they are to flower. Spring or early summer bloomers, such as *A. canadense*, are better divided immediately after flowering. The first group should flower the same year, the latter in the next year.

Divide rhizomatous species (*see p.149*) when dormant or, to locate them without causing undue damage, as their leaves die down. Cut the rhizomes into sections, each with at least one bud, and replant immediately before they dry out. They should flower in the following season.

Seeds

Anemone seeds germinate most successfully if sown thinly as soon as they are ripe. Fresh, spring-sown seeds (*see p.151*) kept at 60°F (15.5°C) should germinate in three weeks. Seed-raised plants flower in their second or third season. Sow in moist, gritty soil mix (adding leaf mold for woodland species such as *A. apennina* and *A. nemorosa*).

Transplant fibrous-rooted seedlings when large enough to handle. Seedlings of rhizomatous anemones are best left to grow on in their pots for 12 months before transplanting; liquid feeds during this period, when they are in active growth, help seedlings grow strongly.

Woodland species, for example *A. apennina*, some forms of *A. nemorosa*, and *A. multifida*, often self-sow.

Cuttings

To avoid disturbing Japanese anemones, uncover the edge of the clump and take root cuttings (*see p.158*). They usually flower in 2–3 years. For *A. sylvestris*, pot a plant in spring; in autumn, lift it and slice the root ball across, about 2in (5cm) below the crown. Repot both parts, lightly covering the cut roots on the lower root ball with ½in (1cm) (of grit or soil mix; after a month or so, shoots will appear. Both parts may be divided and planted out in spring.

Gathering anemone seeds
Some anemones have woolly seedheads (here of A. multifida*). Some seeds will fall out naturally; the remainder can be sown within the "wool."*

ANTHURIUM

Anthurium andraeanum

Division in early spring
Seeds in autumn or spring

These evergreen, tender perennials, many of which are epiphytic, may be divided (*see p.148*) to flower in 1–2 years. Take care not to damage the fragile roots. Sow seeds (*see p.151*), as soon as they are ripe or in spring, at 77°F (25°C); they may take several months to germinate. Seed-raised plants take several years to reach flowering size.

ARMERIA *Thrift, Sea pink*

Division in autumn or in early spring
Seeds in autumn or in early spring
Cuttings in late summer

Perennial thrifts are cushion- or mat-forming plants; most are quite hardy. The woody crowns may be divided (*see p.149*); plants are also easily raised from seeds (*see p.151*) in a cold frame. When taking cuttings (*see p.166*), use semi-ripe, leafy basal stems, 1¼–2in (3–5cm) long, from the edge of the plant. Bottom heat is not necessary, but aids rooting, as will hormone rooting compound.

ARTEMISIA *Mugwort, Wormwood, Sagebrush*

Division in spring
Seeds in autumn or in spring
Cuttings in late summer or in spring

The herbaceous or woody-based perennials in this genus are easily divided, and some forms root rather easily from cuttings. Seed-raised plants take longer to mature.

Division

Lift and divide clumping plants, such as *A. lactiflora* and *A. ludoviciana* (syn. *A palmeri*), into moderate-sized pieces for replanting at once (*see p.148*); they make effective plants the same season.

Seeds

Sown seeds (*see p.151*) may be placed in a cold frame – or at 61°F (16°C) to germinate within two weeks. Plant out seedlings in the following spring.

Cuttings

Take stem tips or heeled sideshoots as greenwood cuttings (*see p.154*) in late summer, except from *A. absinthium* 'Lambrook Silver', which roots best from softwood cuttings taken in spring. Plant out in the next spring to mature in 1–2 years. *A.* 'Powis Castle' will not survive severe winters; take cuttings in summer.

ASPIDISTRA *CAST-IRON PLANT*

DIVISION in spring

All species are essentially tender. Divide the woody rootstock using a knife (*see p.148*) to cut clumps into small pieces of rhizome with roots. Pot the divisions singly; keep at 59°F (15°C) until new roots are growing strongly.

ASTER

DIVISION in spring
SEEDS in spring
CUTTINGS in spring

Perennials in this genus (syn. *Crinitaria, Microglossa*) benefit from annual or biennial division, which makes them less prone to mildew. Divide the tight, woody crowns with a spade or back-to-back forks (*see p.148*). Crowns pulled apart into single rooted shoots, replanted 2–3in (5–8cm) apart, normally flower in the same year. Seeds sown (*see p.151*) at 59°F (15°C) should germinate in two weeks and flower in their second year. Pink-flowered cultivars usually produce mauve offspring. Basal shoots work best as cuttings (*see p.156*), but stems can be used if material is scarce. Root the cuttings in pots or a moss roll (*see p.155*) in a closed case or on a mist bench; pot and grow on in a cold frame.

AUBRIETA *AUBRETIA*

Aubrieta 'Joy'

DIVISION after flowering or in early autumn
SEEDS when ripe or in early spring
CUTTINGS in late summer and in early autumn

There are 12 species of mat- or mound-forming plants in this genus, but only cultivars of *Aubrieta cultorum* are commonly grown. Taking cuttings is the most reliable method of propagation for cultivars.

DIVISION

Clumps may be carefully lifted and divided (*see p.148*). Cut back the foliage on divisions to reduce moisture loss.

SEEDS

Aubretias are easily raised from seeds (*see p.151*), but the seedlings will vary.

CUTTINGS

Take ripewood cuttings when the shoots are well matured by the summer sun. Ripe shoots are brittle: use a scalpel or craft knife when preparing cuttings (*see right*). Do not pull off the lower leaves, or the stem may break; instead, use a sharp blade, cutting upward. Alternatively, cut back foliage after flowering and take semi-ripe cuttings from the new growth. Insert cuttings up to their leaves in gritty soil mix in pots or trays and place in a covered nursery bed. Pot as soon as well-rooted (in 3–5 weeks) to grow on, then plant out later in the autumn or the following spring.

TAKING RIPEWOOD CUTTINGS OF AUBRETIA
Select strong, nonflowering shoots, no longer than 2in (5cm), preferably half this length. Trim the lower half of each cutting of leaves, cutting upward close to the stem. Make an angled cut at the base below a node. Remove any yellow leaves, which may rot, from the rosette.

OTHER PERENNIALS

ANEMONOPSIS MACROPHYLLA Divide with care in spring (*see p.148*). Sow seeds (*p.151*) as soon as ripe; winter cold needed to break dormancy; germination can be erratic.
ANGELICA Sow seeds (*see p.151*) in spring at 50°F (10°C).
ANIGOZANTHOS Divide in warm areas in autumn, or in spring (*see p.148*). Sow seeds (*p.151*) when ripe or in spring at 59°F (15°C); germination can be slow, hot water (*p.152*) or smoke treatment (*p.20*) helps.
ANTENNARIA Divide (*see p.148*) after flowering or detach rooted plantlets; pot small pieces (*p.149*). Sow seeds (*p.151*) when ripe or in spring, in gritty soil mix; keep in a cold frame. Do not overwater.
ANTHEMIS Sow seeds (*see p.151*) in spring at 59°F (15°C). Take semi-ripe cuttings of herbaceous types (*p.154*) in early autumn. Take basal stem cuttings of alpines (*p.166*) in late spring or early summer.
ANTHERICUM Divide (*see p.148*) after flowering. Seeds (*p.151*) in spring at 50°F (10°C).
ANTHRISCUS As for *Angelica*. *See also* Chervil, *p.290*.
ANTIRRHINUM Sow seeds (*see p.151*) in autumn or spring at 59°F (15°C). Softwood cuttings in late spring; semi-ripe cuttings in early autumn (*p.154*).
AQUILEGIA Sow seeds fresh in late spring or early summer (*p.151*) at 50°F (10°C); sow old seeds in autumn and expose to winter cold; gather seeds from isolated plants; hybridizes and self-sows very freely. Take basal stem cuttings (*p.166*) in early summer of choice alpines.
ARABIS Divide in autumn or early spring (*see p.167*) or detach rooted pieces of mat-forming species. Sow seeds (*p.164*) in autumn, or in spring at 50°F (10°C). Root stem-tip cuttings (*p.166*) in summer.
ARCTOTIS (syn. *Venidioarctotis, Venidium*) As *Gazania* (*p.197*).
ARENARIA As for *Arabis*.
ARISARUM Divide rhizomes (*see p.149*) as plants die down in summer. Sow seeds as soon as ripe (*p.151*) at 59°F (15°C).
ARISTEA Detach rooted leaf fans (*p.149*) in early spring. Seeds (*p.151*) in spring at 61°F (16°C).
ARNICA As *Anthericum*.
ARTHROPODIUM Divide in spring (*see p.148*). Sow seeds (*p.151*) in spring at 50°F (10°C).
ARUNCUS Divide (*see p.148*) in spring. Seeds (*p.151*) in autumn at 50°F (10°C).
ASARINA PROCUMBENS (syn. *Antirrhinum asarina*) Sow seeds in spring (*see p.151*) at 16°C (61°F). Take stem-tip cuttings (*p.154*) in spring or summer.
ASCLEPIAS Sow seeds (*see p.151*) in spring at 59°F (15°C).
ASPARAGUS Divide (*see p.148*) when dormant. Extract seeds from berries and sow (*pp.151–2*) in spring at 59°F (15°C). (*See also* Vegetables, *p.294*.)
ASPHODELINE Divide carefully after flowering (*see p.148*); divisions taken at other times are prone to rot. Sow seeds in spring (*p.151*) at 59°F (15°C).
ASPHODELUS As for *Asphodeline*.
ASTILBE Divide carefully in early spring (*see p.148*). Seeds have short viability; sow (*p.151*) in autumn; expose to winter cold.
ASTRANTIA Divide in spring (*see p.148*). Seeds (*p.151*) when ripe or in spring at 50°F (10°C).
AURINIA Sow seeds (*see p.151*) in autumn or early spring at 50°F (10°C). Take 1¼–2in (3–5cm) greenwood stem-tip cuttings (*p.166*) in late summer.
AZORELLA Sow seeds (*see p.164*) in gritty soil mix when ripe or in autumn, or in early spring at 50°F (10°C). Take rosette cuttings (*p.166*) in spring or summer.

AQUILEGIA 'CRIMSON STAR'

BEGONIA

Begonia 'Organdy'

DIVISION in early spring
SEEDS when ripe or in spring
STEM CUTTINGS in autumn or in spring
LEAF CUTTINGS from late spring to early summer

Most perennials in this genus are tender. Rhizomatous begonias, such as *Begonia bowerae*, *B. manicata*, and *B. rex* may be divided. The popular Semperflorens begonias used as bedding are usually grown from seeds, although basal stem cuttings can be taken. Leaf cuttings root readily from *B. rex*, *B. masoniana*, and many others, possibly all species and forms. For tuberous begonias, *see p.262*.

DIVISION

Divide rhizomes (*see p.149*) into sections with at least one growing tip and pot individually. Older, leafless portions of rhizome may be cut into 2in (5cm) pieces and lined out in trays of rooting medium. Keep moist at 70°F (21°C). When shoots and roots have formed, usually after six weeks, they can be potted singly and the temperature reduced to 59°F (15°C). Plants should reach a good size in six months.

SEEDS

In cool climates, sow the fine seeds (*see p.151*) at 70°F (21°C) in spring; in warm regions, sow also when seeds ripen. Do not cover the seeds – light is required for germination. The seedlings appear after 2–3 weeks and are transplanted as soon as they are large enough to handle. *B. semperflorens* should flower in 3–6 months; other species may take a year.

CUTTINGS

Stem-tip cuttings (*see p.154*) can be taken from all stem-forming begonias. They should root within a month at 70°F (21°C). Cuttings from most of the winter-flowering begonias are best taken in spring.

Leaf cuttings (*see p.157*) are prepared with a portion of stalk, 1in (2.5cm) long, inserted into the soil mix so that the leaf rests on the surface. At 70°F (21°C), plantlets form in about six weeks. To produce more plants from the leaf, cut through the main veins or cut the leaves into small squares (*see below*).

TAKING LEAF CUTTINGS FROM BEGONIAS

1 Select a fully grown, healthy leaf (here of a Rex begonia). Using a sharp knife, cut off the leaf stalk and then straight across each of the main veins on the underside of the leaf.

2 Pin the leaf, cut side down, onto the surface of a tray of rooting medium or vermiculite; label. Keep humid at 70°F (21°C) until plantlets develop, usually in two months.

3 When the plantlets are large enough to handle, lift the leaf and carefully separate the plantlets. Take care to preserve some medium around the roots of each one. Pot individually into 3in (8cm) pots of soilless potting mix to grow on. Water and label.

SQUARE LEAF CUTTINGS

Cut squares, about 1in (2.5cm) across, from a large, healthy leaf. Each square must have a main vein running through it. Pin them, veins downward, into a tray of rooting medium and treat as in steps 2 and 3 (left).

BERGENIA *ELEPHANT'S EARS*

DIVISION in autumn or spring
SEEDS in spring
CUTTINGS in autumn or spring

Older plants of these perennials form a mass of woody, creeping rhizomes, often on the soil surface, with leaves only at their tips. If just a few plants are required, these may be detached. For large numbers of new plants, take rhizome cuttings.

DIVISION

After flowering or in autumn, lift and sever new plantlets from the ends of the long rhizomes (*see p.149 and below*) and replant, leaving the parent in place. Plantlets flower the next year.

SEEDS

Sow seeds (*see p.151*) in trays. They will germinate, without extra heat, in 3–6 weeks. New plants flower after two years.

DIVIDING BERGENIAS
Divide plants in early spring, ensuring that each piece has a good rosette of leaves and about 6in (15cm) of rhizome with roots. Trim off larger leaves to reduce water loss. Replant deeper than before if the parent rhizomes were on the surface.

CALCEOLARIA
SLIPPER FLOWER

SEEDS in spring and summer
CUTTINGS in early autumn or spring

Perennials in this genus are sometimes grown (for annuals, *see p.221*). Many species, and modern cultivars of *Calceolaria integrifolia* (syn. *C. rugosa*), may be raised from seeds, surface-sown at 61°F (16°C) to germinate in two weeks (*see p.151, or for alpines p.165*). Seedlings need cool, airy conditions.

Take semi-ripe heel cuttings (*see p.154, or for alpines p.166*) in autumn and overwinter with cold protection, or overwinter stock plants to supply cuttings in spring. They root easily in two weeks. Plant out in late spring.

Detach individual rosette cuttings (*see p.166*) from alpine species in summer and root in a gritty soil mix.

BERGENIA RHIZOME CUTTINGS

1 Cut older pieces of leafless rhizome into 1½–2in (4–5cm) sections, each with several dormant buds. Trim any long roots. Half-bury the sections, buds uppermost, about 2in (5cm) apart in trays in moist perlite or soil mix. Label.

2 Keep the cuttings at a humid 70°F (21°C) in a heated closed case. After 10–12 weeks, plantlets (here of B. cordifolia*) should have rooted. Pot singly or line out in a nursery bed.*

CUTTINGS

When dividing *Bergenia,* cut the remaining, older parts of the rhizomes, which are devoid of leaves, into sections. Place in trays of soil mix or perlite with their upper surfaces exposed (*see above*). After watering, place them in a heated closed case or cover with a sheet of plastic or glass to prevent dehydration. Keep shaded at 70°F (21°) to root. The new plants can be planted out in spring. Expect flowering within 12–24 months.

CAMPANULA *BELLFLOWER*

Campanula raineri

DIVISION in early autumn or in spring
SEEDS in autumn or spring
CUTTINGS in late spring or in early summer

The perennials in this genus include alpines as well as sturdy herbaceous plants. Some smaller types, such as *Campanula rotundifolia*, self-sow invasively and are a ready source of divisions and cuttings.

DIVISION

Divide the fibrous or woody crowns (*see p.148*) to increase cultivars and good forms. Self-rooted shoots or plantlets on runners may be detached from the fringes of many *Campanula,* especially the alpine species (*see p.167*), without lifting the parent plant. Keep potted sections in a sheltered place to establish.

SEEDS

Sow the fine seeds thinly (*see p.152*) and cover lightly. Spring-sown seeds should be kept at 60°F (15.5°C); if sown in autumn, pots or trays of seeds may be placed in a cold frame. Plant out seedlings of more robust perennials in the summer or autumn of the first year. Overwinter seedlings of smaller alpines (*see p.164*) in their containers and pot them in the spring. Sow *C. pyramidalis* and *C. medium* as biennials (*see p.221*).

CUTTINGS

Nearly all alpine species may be grown from basal stem cuttings (*see p.166*), inserted in gritty soil mix, preferably in late spring. Roots should form, without bottom heat, in 2–3 weeks. Take stem-tip cuttings of herbaceous species (*see p.154*) from new growth after flowering. Take root cuttings (*see p.158*) from *C. glomerata* in winter.

ALPINE BELLFLOWER CUTTING
Rosette cuttings about ½in (1cm) long may be taken from many alpine bellflowers (here of Campanula cochleariifolia*).*

CANNA

DIVISION in spring
SEEDS in spring

These tender plants must be lifted to overwinter dry under cover in cold climates. Divide the rhizomes (*see p.149*) and start them into growth at 61°C (16°C) for flowers in the same season. File or hot-water treat the seeds to break their seed-coat dormancy before sowing them. Sow the seeds (*see p.151*) at 70°F (21°C). Seed-raised plants usually flower in their second year.

CARDAMINE *BITTERCRESS*

DIVISION after flowering or in early autumn
SEEDS when ripe or in early spring
CUTTINGS in early spring

Many of the perennials (syn. *Dentaria*) in this genus have fragile rhizomes: divide with care; any fragments can be potted. Sow seeds (*see p.151*) at 50°F (10°C); keep rhizomatous seedlings in their pots for a year. Weighting a leaf of *C. pratensis* or its cultivars onto soil may induce a plantlet to form; this species also forms bulbils (*see p.26*) below or at soil level.

OTHER PERENNIALS

BELAMCANDA Divide (*see p.148*) in spring. Sow seeds (*p.151*) in spring at 59°F (15°C).
BELLIS Divide cultivars after flowering (*see p.148*). Sow seeds (*p.151*) for spring bedding in midsummer.
BERTOLONIA Seeds (*see p.151*) in spring at 70°F (21°C). Stem-tip cuttings (*p.154*) in spring.
BIDENS Sow seeds (*see p.151*) in spring at 59°F (15°C). Take stem-tip cuttings (*p.154*) in spring or in early autumn.
BLANDFORDIA Separate clumps in spring or after flowering (*see p.149*). Sow fresh seeds (*p.151*) in spring at 59°F (15°C).
BOLAX Detach rooted offsets (*see p.166*). Sow ripe seeds (*p.164*); keep in a cold frame.
BOLTONIA Divide (*see p.148*) in early spring. Sow seeds (*p.151*) in spring at 59°F (15°C).
BORAGO Divide *B.pygmaea* (*see p.148*). (Annuals, *see p.291*.)
BOYKINIA Divide (*see p.167*) in late winter or early spring. Sow seeds (*p.164*) in spring; keep in a cold frame.
BRACHYSCOME (syn. *Brachycome*) Sow seeds (*see p.164*) in spring at 64°F (18°C); few viable seeds are produced. Take basal stem cuttings (*p.166*) in spring.
BRUNNERA Divide after flowering (*see p.149*). Seeds (*p.151*) in spring at 50°F (10°C). Take root cuttings (*p.158*) in winter.
BULBINE As for *Belamcanda*.
BULBINELLA Divide (*see p.148*) in autumn. Sow ripe seeds (*p.151*); keep in a cold frame.
BUPHTHALMUM Divide in spring (*see p.148*). Sow seeds in spring (*p.151*) at 50°F (10°C).
BUPLEURUM As for *Buphthalmum*.
CALAMINTHA Divide in spring (*p.148*) or lift rooted stems. Seeds (*p.151*) in spring at 50°F (10°C). Take semi-ripe cuttings (*p.154*) in early autumn.
CALANDRINIA Sow seeds in spring at 59°F (15°C), as for *Lewisia* (*see p.202*). Sow seeds of alpines in autumn (*p.164*); overwinter in sheltered place to break dormancy for best results. Root rosette cuttings of alpines (*p.166*) in sand in summer; suitable shoots may be few.
CALATHEA Divide (*see p.149*) in late spring. Sow seeds (*p.151*) in spring at 70°F (21°C).
CALLISIA (syn. *Phyodina*) Divide (*see p.148*) in spring. Seeds in spring (*p.151*) at 63°F (17°C).
CAREX Divide in spring (*see p.148*); pot or grow on single rooted shoots in nursery bed (*p.149*). Sow short-lived seeds (*p.151*) in autumn if possible, or in spring at 59°F (15°C).
CARLINA Sow seeds (*see p.151*) in spring at 59°F (15°C).
CATANANCHE Divide in mid-spring (*see p.148*). Sow seeds (*p.151*) in spring at 59°F (15°C). Take root cuttings (*p.158*) in winter.

CELMISIA
NEW ZEALAND DAISY

SEEDS when ripe or in autumn
CUTTINGS in late spring

Perennials in this genus are self-sterile; they usually set seeds only if several plants grow together. Sow seeds (*see p.164*) at 50°C (10°C). Keep moist and semi-shaded until established. Take rosette cuttings (*see p.166*); some species root well in pumice (*see p.167*). It may be possible to detach rooted rosettes from larger plants: treat as cuttings until established. Divisions or cuttings must never dry out: mist them daily but do not overwater, which leads to rot.

CHLOROPHYTUM
SPIDER PLANT

PLANTLETS at any time
DIVISION in spring

Variegated forms of *Chlorophytum comosum* are the most commonly grown of these tender plants. Their attraction lies in the plantlets that often develop at the ends of old flowering stems. Plantlets develop immature roots while still on the plant and may be detached and potted. If unrooted, remove with a portion of stem, insert into pots of soil mix and keep at 59°F (15°C); they should root within ten days.

Division (*see p.150*) produces mature plants more quickly. Grow on the new divisions at 59°F (15°C).

CHRYSANTHEMUM

Chrysanthemum 'Yvonne Arnaud'

DIVISION in spring
SEEDS in spring
CUTTINGS in spring

Of the large-flowered perennials, or florist's chrysanthemums, in this genus (syn. *Dendranthema*), the Korean types are fairly hardy; most others are much less hardy. (For annuals, *see p.222*.) It may be possible to pull apart the rootstock (stool) of hardier types (*see p.148*). If replanted in fertile soil, divisions should flower in the same season with renewed vigor.

Sow seeds (*see p.152*) of cushion and cascade chrysanthemums at 59°F (15°C). Seeds germinate in two weeks, and plants flower in the same year.

Take 2–3in (5–8cm) basal stem cuttings from garden plants (*see pp.156–7*) or, for larger numbers, from stock plants overwintered in pots under cover. Root in trays of rooting medium at 50°F (10°C). Pot rooted cuttings and grow on at 50°F (10°C). Plant out or pot on in late spring to flower the same year.

CONVALLARIA *LILY-OF-THE-VALLEY*

Convallaria majalis

DIVISION in spring or in autumn
SEEDS in autumn

The thin, creeping rhizomes of *Convallaria majalis* can be invasive. They are best divided (*see p.149*) after flowering, although they tolerate division at any time when not in active growth. Pull apart the rhizomes into rooted portions, each with a bud, and replant them at once. For a large number of plants, treat rhizomes as cuttings (*see below*). Plants rapidly establish to flower the following spring.

Plants are rarely seed-raised because it is so slow. First extract the seeds by macerating the berries (*see p.151*). Germination outdoors takes at least two winters; plants flower after three years.

RHIZOME CUTTINGS

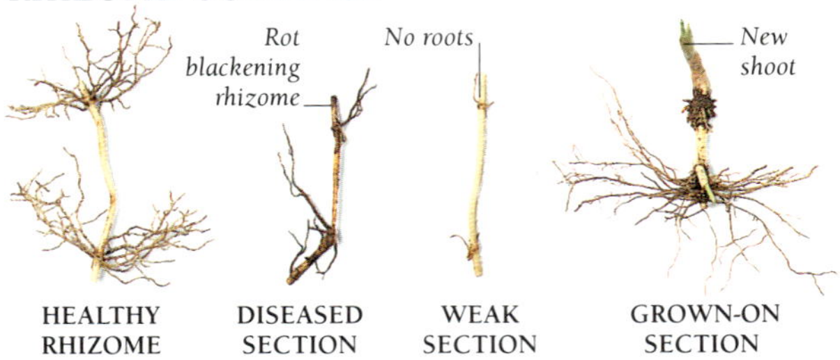

Cut rhizomes into 2–3in (5–8cm) sections, each with roots and some dormant buds. Discard any diseased or weak sections. Treat them as for thin root cuttings (see p.158). *The cuttings should develop shoots in spring and may be planted out in autumn.*

CORYDALIS

DIVISION in spring or in early autumn
SEEDS in early summer or in autumn

Many of the perennials in this genus (syn. *Pseudofumaria*) are quite hardy, but some of the fibrous-rooted types, such as *Corydalis tomentella*, are more suited to alpine house conditions. Rhizomatous types such as *C. cheilanthifolia* can be divided; others are best grown from seeds. (*For tuberous species, see p.264.*)

DIVISION

Lift and divide dormant rhizomes (*see p.149*) carefully. The stems are sappy and fragile and easily damaged by handling. Replant large divisions immediately. Pot small pieces to plant out the next year.

SEEDS

Sow seeds (*see p.151*) as soon as they are ripe or in autumn; older seeds have poor viability. Allow them to germinate in a sheltered place outdoors. Transplant seedlings into small pots when large enough to handle. Many self-sow readily; transplant seedlings carefully.

CORYDALIS SEEDLINGS
Fresh seeds should germinate in a few weeks at about 59°F (15°C), but old seeds tend to germinate slowly or erratically. Keep the pot for two years to allow all the seedlings to come up.

DELPHINIUM

Delphinium 'Fanfare'

DIVISION in spring
SEEDS in spring
CUTTINGS in late spring

The easiest way to propagate perennial delphiniums is by division. Several of the cultivars do come fairly true from seeds; others yield variable offspring that may still be of value. Most delphiniums are quite hardy.

Divide mature clumps into 2–4 pieces, discarding the woody center (*see p.148*). Divisions flower the same year.

Sow seeds in pots (*see p.151*) at 55°F (13°C). Seedlings appear in 14 days, although old seeds germinate erratically. New plants may flower in 18 months.

Take basal stem cuttings from 3in (8cm) long shoots (*see p.156*); these new shoots should not yet be hollow, one of the factors that make cuttings prone to rot. Insert in rooting medium (some growers put a layer of fine sand in the bottom of the hole) or in perlite (*see p.156*). Keep at 59°F (15°C) and pot when rooted, after about ten days. Plant out in nursery beds in early summer.

DIANTHUS *CARNATION, PINK*

DIVISION in spring or in autumn
SEEDS in spring, early summer or in autumn
CUTTINGS from mid- to late summer
LAYERING from mid- to late summer

The perennial species are mostly quite hardy and are increased in various ways according to the type. They can be subjects for hybridizing (*see p.21*). (*See also* Annuals and Biennials, *p.223*.)

DIVISION

Some spreading and mat-forming species and cultivars root naturally as they grow. These can be divided after flowering into large portions (*see p.148*), each with up to 20 shoots and some roots. The new plants will flower the next year.

SEEDS

Sow seeds (*see p.151*) of pinks grown for summer bedding, such as Chinese or Indian pinks (*D. chinensis*) in spring at 59°F (15°C) to germinate within ten days. Sow sweet Williams (*D. barbatus*) as biennials (*see p.219*) in early summer; transplant in midautumn. Sow alpines in pots in cold frames in autumn or spring. A few species self-sow.

CUTTINGS

Semi-ripe cuttings may be taken from all *Dianthus* (*see below, left*), especially small and alpine species. A hormone rooting compound is helpful. Insert in pots of rooting medium in a frame or closed case; keep moist but not wet. Rooting takes 2–3 weeks at 59°F (15°C); plants will flower the next year.

LAYERING

Carnation stems may be layered (*below*) into the soil or a plunged pot of rooting medium and should root in eight weeks.

CUTTINGS FROM PINKS

Hold a nonflowering shoot near the base and pull out the tip. It should break easily at a node, giving a cutting 3–4in (8–10cm) long with 3–4 pairs of leaves. Remove the lowest pair (see inset).

LAYERING BORDER CARNATIONS

1 *Choose a strong, nonflowering shoot. Strip the leaves from all except the top 3in (8cm) of the stem. Make a 1in (2.5cm) sloping cut just below the leaves to form a tongue* (see inset).

2 *Prepare the soil below the cut with equal parts of coarse sand and moist peat. Gently bend the stem so that the tongue opens out, push it into the soil, and pin securely in place.*

OTHER PERENNIALS

CATHARANTHUS Sow seeds (*see p.151*) in spring at 70°F (21°C). Semi-ripe cuttings (*p.154*) in summer and early autumn.
CENTAUREA Divide in spring (*see p.148*). Sow seeds (*p.151*) in spring at 50°F (10°C). Take root cuttings (*p.158*) in winter.
CENTRANTHUS Divide in spring (*see p.148*). Sow seeds (*p.151*) in spring at 50°F (10°C).
CERASTIUM Divide in spring (*see p.148*). Seeds in autumn or spring (*p.151*) at 59°F (15°C). Take soft stem-tip cuttings (*p.154*) in early summer.
CHAMAEMELUM Divide in early autumn or spring (*see p.148*). Sow seeds (*p.151*) in spring at 50°F (10°C).
CHELONE Divide in spring (*see p.148*). Sow seeds (*p.151*) in spring at 59°F (15°C). Take softwood stem-tip cuttings (*p.154*) in late spring.
CHIASTOPHYLLUM OPPOSITIFOLIUM (syn. *Cotyledon simplicifolia*) Divide after flowering or in early spring (*see p.148*). Sow seeds (*p.151*) in autumn in pots; keep in a cold frame. Softwood cuttings (*p.154*) early summer.
CHRYSOGONUM VIRGINIANUM As for *Centranthus*.
CIMICIFUGA Divide in spring (*see p.148*), especially colored-leaf forms. Sow seeds (*p.151*) in autumn; germinates poorly.
CIRSIUM As for *Centranthus*.
CLAYTONIA Sow seeds (*see p.151*) as soon as ripe, in a shaded cold frame. Some self-sow.
CLITORIA Sow seeds in spring after hot-water treatment (*see pp.151–2*) at 70°F (21°C). Take semi-ripe cuttings (*p.154*) in late summer.
CLIVIA Divide if not in flower (*see p.148*). Sow seeds (*p.151*) in spring at 70°F (21°C).
CODONOPSIS Sow fine seeds thinly (*see p.151*) when ripe or in autumn, in a cold frame; leave seedlings in pots for a year. Most flower in the third year.
COLEUS See *Solenostemon* (*p.209*).
CONVOLVULUS Divide alpines (*see p.167*) in spring. Sow seeds (*p.151*) in spring at 59°F (15°C). Take semi-ripe cuttings (*p.155*) in early autumn. Take heel cuttings in summer from alpines (*p.166*) such as *C. boissieri*.
COREOPSIS Divide in spring (*see p.148*). Sow seeds (*p.151*) in spring at 50°F (10°C). Basal stem cuttings (*p.156*) in spring.
COSTUS Divide in spring (*see p.149*). Sow seeds (*p.151*) in spring at 70°F (21°C). In late winter before growth starts, cut rhizomes into 2in (5cm) pieces as *Bergenia* (*p.191*).
CRAMBE Seeds (*see p.151*) in spring at 50°F (10°C) or outdoors. Take root cuttings in late autumn (*see p.158 and p.299*).
CRASPEDIA Divide in spring (*see p.148*). Seeds of alpines in early spring (*p.151*) at 50°F (10°C); seeds often have low viability.
CTENANTHE As for *Maranta* (*see p.202*).
CURCUMA As *Maranta* (*p.202*).
CYNOGLOSSUM Divide in spring (*see p.148*). Sow seeds (*p.151*) in spring at 59°F (15°C).
DARMERA (syn. *Peltiphyllum*) Divide rhizomes after flowering (*see p.149*). Sow seeds (*p.151*) in spring at 50°F (10°C).
DIANELLA Divide rhizomes (*see p.149*) in midspring. Sow cleaned seeds in spring (*pp. 151–2*) at 59°F (15°C).

CATHARANTHUS ROSEUS 'PACIFICA PUNCH'

DIASCIA *TWINSPUR*

SEEDS when ripe or in spring
CUTTINGS in spring or in late summer

Diascia cordata

Named hybrids of perennial *Diascia* are most commonly grown. Plants are self-sterile and do not produce seeds unless more than one clone or species is grown. Sow seeds (*see p.151*) at 59°F (15°C) to germinate within ten days. Plants flower in the same year. Deliberate hybridization (*see p.21*) can have interesting results.

Take softwood stem-tip cuttings (*see right and p.154*) in spring, or from the regrowth on plants trimmed after flowering. In cold climates, semi-ripe cuttings taken late in the season need protection over winter until late spring in the following year.

DIASCIA SOFTWOOD CUTTINGS

Diascia cuttings are best taken in spring or from regrowth on pruned stock plants; otherwise, the stems tend to be hollow and rot when inserted in a rooting medium. Hollow stems may survive to root if you trim each cutting just below a node.

DIEFFENBACHIA *DUMB CANE*

CUTTINGS in spring
LAYERING in spring

These tender perennials are usually increased from cuttings and are probably the only herbaceous perennials that may be air layered. Wash your hands after handling dumb canes or wear gloves: the sap can cause an allergic reaction.

CUTTINGS

Plants often become straggly with age, but basal sideshoots and the leafy stem tips can be taken as cuttings (*see p.154*). Insert in pots of rooting medium in a closed case at 70°F (21°C). These cuttings should root within three weeks. If covered with a plastic bag and left on a windowsill in a warm room, cuttings will root, but in about six weeks. You can take stem cuttings, too, cutting the main stem into sections, each with a single node (*see right*). New shoots should appear within six weeks. The severed main stem of the parent plant should also produce fresh growth, as long as the lowest bud is retained.

LAYERING

Air layering (*see* Shrubs and Climbing Plants, *p.105*) can be used to root shoots while still on the plant. Remove any leaves with their stalks 4–6in (10–15cm) below the stem tip. Make two parallel cuts ¼in (5mm) apart around the stem; peel off the ring of skin. Slip a clear plastic bag, with the bottom cut open, over the stem, then tie or tape one end below the wound. Pack the bag with moist sphagnum moss, then secure above the moss. After three months or so, roots should be visible. Sever the rooted section, then pot to grow on.

DIEFFENBACHIA CUTTINGS

1 *You can use all the topgrowth from a single plant (here* Dieffenbachia seguine*), removing sideshoots and cutting through the main stem just above the lowest node.*

2 *Trim all but the top 2–3 leaves from any sideshoots and from the main stem. Cut the main stem into 2in (5cm) sections, cutting each just below a node.*

3 *Prepare some pots with moist, firmed rooting medium. Insert the stem-tip cuttings so that the leaves rest just above the surface. Press the stem cuttings horizontally into the medium, buds uppermost, one-third buried. Keep the rootstock in its pot.*

DIONYSIA

SEEDS in summer or in winter
CUTTINGS from late spring to midsummer

Apart from *Dionysa involucrata* and *D. teucrioides*, all species need two types of plant (as for primroses), pin- and thrum-eyed (*see p.206*), to be grown to produce seeds. Seeds of tight "cushion" forms lie deep within the leaf-rosettes: gather them in summer using tweezers.

Sow seeds in a very gritty soil mix (*see p.164*) the moment they are ripe or in winter, then keep in an airy, slightly shaded cold frame to germinate. Transplant seedlings into a mix of one part peat, one part soil, and three parts fine grit. To avoid wetting the plants, immerse the pots up to their rims in water, then allow to drain. Plants flower after their second season.

Take single rosette cuttings, ¼–⅝in (5–15mm) long (*see pp.166–7*); insert in crushed pumice or horticultural or fine sand. Keep in a partly shaded cloche or cold frame. Avoid watering until rooted.

ECHINOPS *GLOBE THISTLE*

DIVISION in spring
SEEDS in spring
CUTTINGS in late autumn

The perennials in this genus are easy to raise from seeds; alternatively, propagate named cultivars by division or from root cuttings.

Divide the woody clumps using a sharp knife or a spade (*see p.148*). Plants will flower the same summer.

Sow seeds (*see p.151*) of species in pots and keep at 59°F (15°C). Expect germination in two weeks. Transplant seedlings singly into pots; line out in a nursery bed in late spring. Seed-raised plants should flower in the second year.

Root cuttings (*see p.158*) may be taken from all species and cultivars. Choose pencil-thick roots and cut into 2–3in (5–8cm) sections.

GATHERING GLOBE THISTLE SEEDS
When the seedheads are dry and brown, cut off the flowering stems and pick off the seeds for drying and storing.

EPIMEDIUM *BARRENWORT*

Epimedium grandiflorum 'Lilafee'

DIVISION in spring
SEEDS in spring
CUTTINGS in winter

Large clumps of these mostly woodland plants are often divided; rhizome cuttings are easier to take from young plants. Seeds gathered from garden plants are likely to be hybrids.

DIVISION

After flowering, pull or cut large clumps into moderate-sized pieces (*see p.148*). Divisions flower in the following spring.

SEEDS

Only forms of *Epimedium davidii*, some forms of *E. grandiflorum*, and some new cultivars are self-fertile. Seeds may be set and gathered if more than one species is grown. Ripening pods split and drop their seeds while still green, so watch carefully. Sow seeds (*see p.151*) in pots in a cold frame as soon as ripe to germinate in four weeks, for flowers after three years.

CUTTINGS

Take rhizome sections and treat as root cuttings. Lift a clump and wash off the soil with a strong jet of water. Cut off old leaves. Carefully separate individual rhizomes; cut these into 2–3in (5–8cm) pieces and trim any overlong fibrous roots. Lay cuttings on the surface of a prepared tray; cover with soil mix. Keep in a sheltered place until they have roots and shoots. Plants flower in 2–3 years.

EPISCIA *FLAME VIOLET*

DIVISION in spring and in summer
SEEDS in spring
CUTTINGS in early or midsummer

All of these evergreen perennials (syn. *Alsobia*) are tender. The creeping mats of foliage spread by means of rooting, above-ground stems, or stolons. Plantlets are produced at the tips of these stolons and can be detached, potted singly, and grown on. Rooted plantlets will flower in the same season.

Surface-sow seeds on moss, as for *Sarracenia* (*see p.208*) at 70°F (21°C). Plants may flower in the second season.

Take softwood stem-tip cuttings from nonflowering shoots (*see p.154*) for flowers in the following year. Rooting is aided by bottom heat of 70°F (21°C).

EREMURUS *DESERT CANDLE, FOXTAIL LILY*

Eremurus robustus

DIVISION in summer or in early autumn
SEEDS in spring

Although quite hardy, the young growth of these plants is often damaged by spring frosts. They have fleshy, thick, but shallow roots that are very fragile and difficult to lift without damage. Only mature clumps of many crowns should be divided.

DIVISION

Lift the wide-spreading roots carefully once the leaves have died down. Use a sharp knife to divide the plant into individual, rooted crowns, and trim off the dying stems. If any large roots are damaged, trim them and dust the wounds with fungicide. Replant the crowns immediately (*see right*), or line out young crowns in nursery beds. Place the starfishlike crowns on coarse sand to help prevent rot, especially on heavy soils. Use deep trays instead of pots to grow on small crowns; keep them in a sheltered place, protected from severe cold. They may flower in two years.

SEEDS

Sow seeds (*see p.151*) to germinate at 59°F (15°C), or sow in early summer and place pots in a sheltered place, such as a cold frame. Fresh seeds germinate in two weeks, but older seeds are erratic and slower. Plants bloom in 3–5 years.

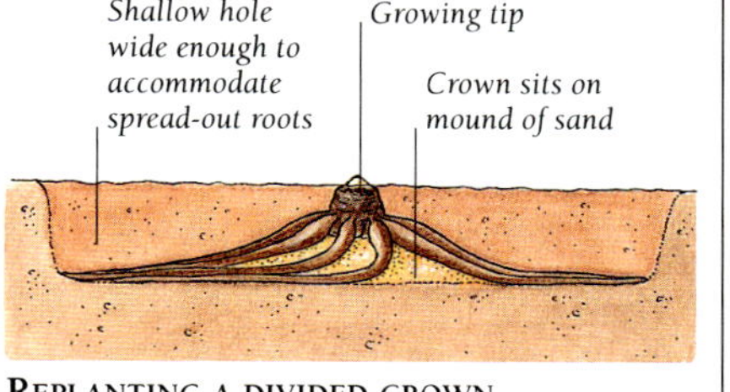

REPLANTING A DIVIDED CROWN
Dig a planting hole, wider than the roots and 6in (15cm) deep. Make a 2–3in (5–8cm) mound of coarse sand in the bottom. Sit the crown on top so that its growth bud is at soil level. Fill in.

OTHER PERENNIALS

DICENTRA Divide rhizomes in early spring or early autumn (*see p.149*), or alpines such as *D. eximia* when dormant in summer (*p.167*). Seeds when ripe or in spring (*p.151*) at 50°F (10°C).
DICTAMNUS ALBUS (syn. *D. fraxinella*) Divide in spring (*see p.148*). Seeds (*p.151*) fresh or in spring at 59°F (15°C).
DIETES Divide after flowering (*see p.149*); may be difficult to reestablish. Seeds in autumn or spring (*p.151*) at 59°F (15°C).
DIGITALIS Surface-sow seeds (*see p.151*) in spring at 50°F (10°C).
DIONAEA Divide (*see p.148*) in spring. Sow seeds (*p.151*) in spring at 54°F (12°C) as for *Sarracenia* (*p.208*); plants may take over five years to flower. Take leaf cuttings (*p.157*) in late spring or early summer: lay leaf flat on live, moist sphagnum moss; cover with thin layer of chopped moss; keep humid at 70°F (21°C).
DIPLARRHENA Divide after flowering (*see p.148*) into leaf fans with roots. Sow seeds at 59°F (15°C) in spring (*p.151*).
DODECATHEON Divide in early spring (*see p.167*). Sow seeds when ripe or in late summer (*p.164*). If bulblets form at base (*see p.26*), detach in autumn, pot and grow on. Treat single roots with dormant buds similarly.
DORONICUM Divide (*see p.149*) after flowering. Sow seeds at 50°F (10°C) in spring (*p.151*).
DRABA Divide in early spring (*see p.148*). Sets seeds readily; sow (*see p.164*) when ripe or in early spring; keep in a cold frame. Take rosette cuttings (*p.166*) in late summer; they need good drainage and may be rooted in pure sand. Water from below.
DROSERA Sow seeds (*see p.151*) on two parts peat to one part sharp sand as soon as ripe, at 50–55°F (10–13°C). Take leaf cuttings as for *Dionaea*.
DRYAS Sow seeds (*see p.151*) the moment they are ripe. Take 1–2in (2.5–5cm) ripewood cuttings as for *Aubrieta* (*see p.189*) in late summer; in pots or trays of free-draining gritty soil mix. Layer strong stems in early summer; cover with peat and coarse sand.
ECHINACEA Divide in spring (*see p.148*). Seeds (*p.151*) in spring at 59°F (15°C). Take root cuttings (*p.158*) in winter.
ENSETE Sow seeds as for *Musa* (*see p.204*).
EOMECON CHIONANTHA Divide (*see p.148*) after flowering. Sow seeds (*p.151*) in spring at 50°F (10°C).
EPILOBIUM (syn. *Chamaenerion*) Divide in spring (*see p.148*). Divide mat-forming alpines (*p.167*) in early spring as growth begins. Seeds (*p.151*) in spring at 50°F (10°C). Take soft stem-tip cuttings (*p.154*) in spring.
ERIGERON As *Aster* (*see p.189*).
ERINUS Sow seeds (*see p.164*) when ripe or in spring at 50°F (10°C). Take rosette cuttings (*p.166*) in spring.
ERODIUM Divide (*see p.148*) in spring. Sow seeds (*p.151*) as soon as ripe; keep in a cold frame. Basal stem cuttings in spring (*p.156*). Semi-ripe stem-tip cuttings (*p.154*) in summer.

ERYNGIUM *Sea holly*

Eryngium giganteum

Division in spring
Seeds in autumn or spring
Cuttings in late autumn

The fleshy roots of most of the perennials in this genus make very successful cuttings, although the plants are severely set back by root disturbance. The short-lived *E. giganteum* is monocarpic and can be increased only from seeds.

Division

Divide the tight, woody crowns just before growth starts (*see p.148*), using a knife to separate each crown with as many roots as possible. Line out in a nursery bed or replant in the border. They may be slow to establish, but some species may flower in the same season.

Seeds

Sow seeds (*see pp.151–2*) of species in spring at 50°F (10°C). Seedlings should emerge in two weeks; new plants flower in their second year – or third year for some species. Freshly gathered seeds germinate more evenly than old seeds: sow as soon as they are ripe, in autumn, to germinate in the following spring.

Cuttings

Take cuttings from thick roots (*see p.158*), cut into 2–3in (5–8cm) pieces. Lay horizontally on trays of soil mix and cover with more mix. Keep above freezing over winter. When shoots and fibrous roots appear in the following spring, pot the new plants singly to flower in their second season. Bundles of cuttings can also be stored upright in pots of sand, barely covered, over winter. In spring, when they sprout, line them out in a nursery bed to grow on. Small plants may also be scooped, as for *Primula* (*see p.206*).

To obtain cutting material without disturbing the parent's roots, place a container-grown plant (the pot must have big drainage holes) on a sand bed. When strong roots have grown into the sand through the holes, remove the pot by cutting under it with a sharp knife (*see below*). Lift the roots from the sand to use as cuttings or allow them to grow on until spring, then transplant them.

Obtaining material for root cuttings
In spring, place a container-grown plant (here Eryngium agavifolium*) on a sand bed that is at least 6in (15cm) deep to encourage the plant to root into the sand. In late autumn, slice under the pot to cut through the roots and free the pot. Lift the roots from the sand to use as cuttings.*

ERYSIMUM *Wallflower*

Erysimum 'Bredon'

Seeds in midsummer
Cuttings in summer

Some of the evergreen perennials in this genus were formerly known as *Cheiranthus*. Species and short-lived cultivars of wallflowers (*Erysimum cheiri*) and Siberian wallflowers (*E.* x *allionii*) are usually raised from seeds. Take cuttings from double-flowered wallflower cultivars such as 'Bloody Warrior', cultivars that do not set seeds such as 'Bowles' Mauve', and other improved forms of species.

Seeds

Short-lived perennials grown as bedding are sown as biennials (*see also p.219*). Sow seeds thinly in rows in seedbeds in midsummer, then transplant seedlings in early to midautumn.

Cuttings

Take semi-ripe stem-tip cuttings (*see p.154*) from nonflowering shoots. Insert in pots of rooting medium and root under cover with minimal or no heat. Pot the rooted cuttings singly, after a few weeks. Protect them over winter from severe cold in a cold frame, where necessary.

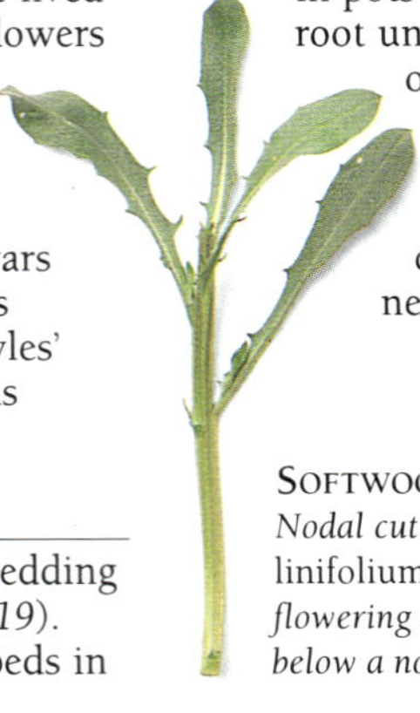

Softwood wallflower cutting
Nodal cuttings (here of Erysimum linifolium*) root easily. Remove a non-flowering shoot with 3–4 nodes, cutting below a node. Trim off the lower leaves.*

EUPHORBIA *Spurge*

Euphorbia schillingii

Division in early spring or from spring to summer
Seeds in autumn or spring
Cuttings in summer or in autumn

Perennials in this huge and very varied genus are tender to very hardy. Wear gloves when handling *Euphorbia*, since the milky sap can irritate the skin. Most herbaceous *Euphorbia* may be divided; species increase readily from seeds. Cuttings may also be taken from most species, but especially selected forms. (*For succulents, see p.246.*)

Division

Those flowering in spring and early summer, such as *Euphorbia polychroma*, are divided (*see p.148*) after flowering. Divide late bloomers, for example *E. sikkimensis*, in early spring. Single bud division (*see p.150*) is possible with fibrous-rooted species.

Seeds

Sow seeds (*see p.151*) at 59°F (15°C). Germination can be erratic; seedlings may appear over several months. To overcome this, sow in autumn and expose to winter cold; seeds should then germinate more evenly in spring.

Cuttings

Take stem-tip cuttings (*see p.154*) from mature growth after flowering. Take 2–4in (5–10cm) long shoots and allow to stand for an hour for the milky sap to dry before inserting in trays of rooting medium – or in a moss roll (*see p.155*). Place in a sheltered place such as a cold frame; excess humidity can cause rot. Cuttings take up to one month to root. Pot singly and plant out in spring.

FITTONIA *Nerve plant*

Division in spring
Seeds in spring
Cuttings in spring or in late summer

These tender, evergreen perennials have freely rooting, creeping stems. Divide established plants (*see p.148*), pulling the clumps into small, rooted pieces. Pot these individually and keep at 64°F (18°C) until established, when the temperature can be lowered to 59°F (15°C). Seeds should germinate in three weeks if sown (*see p.151*) in containers at 64°F (18°C).

Take softwood stem-tip cuttings (*see p.154*) from new shoots in spring or from mature shoots in late summer, and insert into trays or pots. At 64°F (18°C), rooting should take 14 days.

FRAGARIA *STRAWBERRY*

Fragaria x *ananassa* cultivar

DIVISION in late summer
SEEDS in early spring or in late summer
LAYERING in summer

These perennials include the fruiting strawberry and the alpine strawberry. Most strawberries produce plantlets on creeping, rooting stems ("runners," or stolons), a natural method of increase which can be encouraged by layering to provide a convenient method of propagation. Some strawberries do not produce runners, however, and must be increased by division or from seeds. Strawberries are susceptible to virus infection, and it is important to propagate only from healthy plants.

DIVISION

Some perpetual-fruiting cultivars do not produce many runners, so clumps may be propagated by standard division (*see p.148*). New plants should fruit in the following summer.

SEEDS

Alpine strawberries such as 'Baron Solemacher' do not produce runners and must be raised from seeds (*see p.152*)

GATHERING ALPINE STRAWBERRY SEEDS
Allow ripe fruits of alpine strawberries (here of Fragaria vesca *'Semperflorens') to dry. Rub gently over a clean dish to gather the seeds.*

ROOTING RUNNERS OF STRAWBERRIES
Keep the soil moist and remove all the flowers from a plant to encourage runners. As they form, peg the runners down to aid rooting. In late summer, carefully lift the rooted plantlets, sever them from the parent, and pot or plant out.

sown at 64°F (18°C) in early spring. Fresh seeds may be sown outdoors, or under the protection of a cold frame if needed, in late summer. New plants flower and fruit in the following year.

LAYERING

Many strawberries have runners that root into the soil; runner production coincides with the end of fruiting on cropping plants. Plantlets form on these stems as they grow. When the plantlets are well rooted, they may be easily severed from the parent plant. This self-layering habit can be encouraged. Stems may be layered onto the soil (*see above*) or into pots sunk into the bed.

For best results, keep some plants specifically for layering. Plant these 3ft (90cm) apart and remove the flowers. Keep the soil moist to encourage runners to develop and root. Peg runners with wire staples into the soil or into 3in (8cm) pots filled with soil-based mix and plunged level with the soil surface. Plant rooted plantlets into their final positions in late summer and autumn for a good crop in the following season.

GAILLARDIA *BLANKET FLOWER*

Gaillardia 'Kobold'

DIVISION in early spring
SEEDS in spring
CUTTINGS in late autumn

Perennials in this genus tend to be short-lived, especially on heavy soils. Most new plants flower in one year; cultivars can be divided or grown from cuttings. (*For annuals and biennials, see p.224.*)

DIVISION

Divide the tight crowns into individual, rooted shoots (*see p.150*).

SEEDS

To save seeds, gather ripe flowerheads and dry for several days; the seeds in the centers should then drop out very easily. Sow the seeds (*see p.151*) at a minimum temperature of 59°F (15°C); they should germinate within ten days.

CUTTINGS

Perennial cultivars can be propagated from root cuttings (*see p.158*). Remove the thickest roots from the perimeter of a clump to avoid disturbing the parent. Cut into 2–3in (5cm–8cm) lengths and root with bottom heat of 50°F (10°C).

GAURA

DIVISION in spring
SEEDS in early spring
CUTTINGS in spring or in summer

Perennials in this genus thrive in a hot, sunny position with free-draining soil. They are generally short-lived, except for *Gaura lindheimeri*. Divide plants (*see p.148*) to flower in the same season.

Sow the seeds in containers at 50°F (10°C) (*see p.152*). Take basal stem cuttings in spring or semi-ripe heel cuttings in summer (*see pp.154–7*). Plants raised from seeds or cuttings flower in their first or second season.

GAZANIA

Gazania rigens var. *uniflora*

SEEDS in spring
CUTTINGS from late summer to early autumn

Many perennials in this genus can be raised from seeds sown at 64°F (18°C) in free-draining soil mix (*see p.152*) to grow as annuals. Seedlings appear in 14 days and flower in the same season. *Gazania rigens* (syn. *G. splendens*) does not set seeds. Many cultivars will not come true.

Take basal stem or semi-ripe stem-tip cuttings (*see pp.154–6*), if possible from nonflowering shoots or remove the flower buds. Cuttings root readily, even in water; use a free-draining rooting medium to avoid rot. Keep humid, but well-ventilated, until rooted (usually in 2–3 weeks), then pot them. Keep frost-free before planting out in late spring.

OTHER PERENNIALS

EUPATORIUM Divide in spring (*see p.148*). Seeds (*p.151*) in spring at 59°F (15°C). Basal stem cuttings (*p.156*) in spring.
EVOLVULUS Seeds at 64°F (18°C) in spring (*see p.151*). Take semi-ripe cuttings in early autumn (*p.154*).
FELICIA (syn. *Agathaea*) Sow seeds (*p.151*) in spring at 59°F (15°C). Take semi-ripe cuttings (*p.154*) in early autumn.
FILIPENDULA Divide in spring (*see p.149*). Seeds (*p.151*) in spring at 50°F (10°C). Take root cuttings (*p.158*) in winter.
GALAX URCEOLATA (syn. *G. aphylla*) Divide in spring (*see p.148*); slow to reestablish. Seeds (*p.151*) in spring at 50°F (10°C).
GALEGA Divide (*see p.148*) in autumn or spring. Soak seeds in cold water; sow at 59°F (15°C) in spring (*pp.151–2*).
GALIUM Divide after flowering (*see p.148*). Sow seeds (*p.151*) when ripe or in spring; keep in a cold frame.

GENTIANA *GENTIAN*

Gentiana sino-ornata

DIVISION in early spring or after flowering
SEEDS from summer to early autumn or in early spring
CUTTINGS in spring or in summer

Most perennial gentians are rather long-lived and produce copious amounts of seeds, which are the prime means of propagation. Some, such as *Gentiana saxosa* and *G. septemfida*, may self-sow. Larger species such as *G. asclepiadea* tolerate division (*see p.148*). Others, especially mat-forming alpines such as *G. acaulis*, and autumn-flowering ones such as *G. veitchiorum* and *G. sino-ornata*, increase in the wild by rooted offshoots. Fleshy-rooted types with dense crowns, such as *G. purpurea* and *G. lutea*, resent disturbance once established, so are best raised from seeds or cuttings. For the autumn gentians, use organic-rich, acidic or neutral, free-draining but moist soil mix; spring gentians prefer a less organic, neutral to alkaline mix.

DIVISION

Divide rooted offshoots carefully (*see below*) in early spring to avoid divisions rotting over winter. Lift each plant and tease it apart into small pieces with several shoots and fleshy (thong) roots. Sometimes, offshoots can be detached without disturbing the parent. Replant or pot them immediately. Divide larger plants in the usual way (*see p.148*). All new divisions will die if they dry out; spray with water twice daily during dry periods. Plants should flower within a year if damage is kept to a minimum.

SEEDS

Seeds decline in viability fairly quickly so are best sown (*see p.152*) as soon as ripe. Autumn-flowering gentians need an acidic seed soil mix. Sow the fine seeds thinly to avoid damping off (*see p.46*). They germinate in 4–5 weeks, but the tiny seedlings often develop slowly. Transplant seedlings singly into pots once large enough to handle. New plants flower in 2–5 years.

CUTTINGS

Take softwood stem-tip or basal stem cuttings, especially of autumn-flowering gentians. Insert in pots in a mix of equal parts coarse sand and peat and keep at 59°F (15°C). Once rooted, pot the cuttings individually and grow on in a cold frame or alpine house (*see p.154*).

DIVIDING ALPINE GENTIANS

1 *Divide mat-forming species (here* Gentiana acaulis*) as growth begins in spring. Lift the plant and gently pull it apart into "thongs," each with roots and a crown of leaves (see inset).*

2 *Grow on the thongs in a nursery bed in gritty soil, spaced 6in (15cm) apart, or in pots of free-draining potting mix, for one year. Plant them out in the following spring.*

GERANIUM *CRANESBILL*

DIVISION in late summer, autumn or early spring
SEEDS when ripe or in early spring
STEM CUTTINGS in late spring or in late summer
ROOT CUTTINGS in autumn

Division every 3–4 years helps the perennials in this genus maintain vigor. Species hybridize readily, and some self-sow. All species and some cultivars may be raised from seeds. Only a few species, including *G. sanguineum* and *G. macrorrhizum*, form stems suitable to use as cuttings; take root cuttings from *G. pratense*, *G. phaeum*, and *G. sanguineum*.

DIVISION

Divide (*see p.148*) to flower in the first year. Loose, fibrous clumps are easily pulled apart. Tight, woody rootstocks must be cut or pried apart. Single bud divisions (*see p.150*) are possible.

SEEDS

Seed sown at 59°F (15°C) should germinate within 14 days (*see p.151*). Plants should flower the following year.

CUTTINGS

Take basal stem cuttings (*see p.156*) in spring or when growth has ceased. Cut at, or just below, ground level. Stems of trailing plants such as 'Ann Folkard' can be cut into sections in spring, each with one node. Root in trays in shade at 59°F (15°C). Rooted cuttings flower in a year.

Take root cuttings from alpines (*see p.167*), 1in (2.5cm) long; scatter like large seeds over soil mix in a tray and just cover. Root in a cold frame outdoors and transplant in spring. Some species, especially alpines, can be increased from self-rooted cuttings (*see p.167*).

RIPENING GERANIUM SEEDHEADS
Ripe seedheads eject the seeds suddenly, so check daily and gather the pods when they turn brown but before the "beak" unfurls. Keep them in a paper bag until they release the seeds.

GUNNERA

Gunnera manicata

DIVISION in spring or summer
SEEDS in summer, autumn

Divide large types (*see p.148*) before growth starts into single crowns in midspring, or sow seeds as soon as ripe from round fruits in autumn (*see p.151*) at 59°F (15°C). Divide mat-forming alpines (*p.167*) in early spring or late summer. Seeds of alpines are rarely fertile; sow fresh (*see p.164*) in pots in a cold frame.

OTHER PERENNIALS

GERBERA Divide old plants (*see p.148*) into single rosettes in spring. Sow seeds (*p.151*) in spring at 59°F (15°C).
GEUM Divide (*see p.149*) in spring. Sow seeds (*p.151*) in autumn outdoors or in spring at 50°F (10°C).
GILLENIA As for *Geum*.
GLAUCIUM Sow seeds (*see p.151*) direct in autumn or in spring at 59°F (15°C).
GLECHOMA Divide in spring (*see p.149*). Detach rooted plantlets at any time (*see p.24*). Sow seeds (*p.151*) in spring at 50°F (10°C). Take softwood stem-tip cuttings

GYPSOPHILA *BABY'S BREATH*

SEEDS when ripe or in spring
CUTTINGS in spring or in summer
GRAFTING in late winter

Most perennials in this genus are quite hardy, but a few are less so. Species are normally grown from seeds; grow cultivars, which do not come true from seeds, from cuttings. However, double-flowered cultivars of *Gypsophila paniculata* do not root readily from cuttings and are most successful if grafted. Larger herbaceous *Gypsophila* are deep-rooted and resent disturbance.

SEEDS

Sow seeds (*see p.151*) of perennial species in pots as soon as they ripen or in spring, and keep at 59°F (15°C). Slugs (*see p.47*) and snails may attack seedlings. (*For annuals, see p.224.*)

CUTTINGS

Take strong basal shoots (*see p.156*), if possible, or softwood stem tips (*see p.154*) as cuttings. Root at 64°F (18°C) in a mix of coarse sand and soil. Plants will flower in the following season.

GRAFTING

For grafting (*see below*), a two-year-old seedling of *G. paniculata*, with vigorous roots, is used to provide the rootstock. Lift a plant of the chosen cultivar in autumn, pot, and keep in a frost-free greenhouse to force growth slightly. By late winter, there should be strong, new growth on the cultivar, which can be used to provide scions for grafting. Keep grafted plants under cover until late spring, when they can be planted out. They will flower well in the next season.

GRAFTING *GYPSOPHILA PANICULATA*

1 Lift a two-year-old, seed-raised plant. Clean the soil from the roots. Remove a 3–4in (8–10cm) length from a ½in (1cm) thick root, cutting straight across the top end and at an angle at the base.

2 Trim any fibrous roots from the root section and cut back lateral roots to ½in (1cm). Make a ½–¾in (1–2cm) vertical cut into the top of the stock with a clean, sharp knife.

3 Take a 2–3in (5–8cm) long basal shoot from the cultivar to use as a scion. Remove the bottom pair of leaves and cut the base into a ½–¾in (1–2cm) long wedge shape.

4 Pot the stock in rooting medium and firm in. Gently push the base of the scion into the cut on the stock so they fit snugly together. Check that the edges of the stock and scion align on at least one side.

5 Secure the graft with plastic grafting tape or raffia to hold it firmly in place. Bind the entire graft to prevent drying out. Label the pot, then water thoroughly and allow to drain.

6 Cover the pot with a clean plastic bag kept clear of the graft by four split stakes to avoid rot. Keep in a light place at about 59°F (15°C) for 4–6 weeks until new growth appears.

of variegated *G. hederacea* cultivars (*p.154*) in spring. Can be invasive.
GLOBBA Divide (*see p.149*) in spring. Sow seeds (*p.151*) in spring at 70°F (21°C).
GLOBULARIA Divide in spring; tease away small rooted shoots from the edges of low, hummock-forming kinds that dislike disturbance (*see p.167*). Sow seeds (*p.164*) in autumn; keep in a cold frame. Take rosette cuttings (*p.166*) in late summer; bottom heat of 59–64°F (15–18°C) helps.
GLYCYRRHIZA Divide in late winter, as for *Paeonia* (*see p.204*). Sow seeds in spring at 59°F (15°C); soak first in cold water for 24 hours (*pp.151–2*).
HAASTIA Sow seeds (*see p.164*) when fresh in summer; keep in a cold frame; germinates in a few weeks; leave seedlings for one year before transplanting. Take rosette cuttings (*p.166*) in early summer. New plants are very susceptible both to drying out and to rotting.
HABERLEA As for *Ramonda* (*p.207*).
HACQUETIA EPIPACTIS (syn. *Dondia epipactis*) Divide after flowering (*see p.149*). Sow seeds (*p.164*) when ripe; keep in a cold frame; often self-sows.
HEDYCHIUM (syn. *Brachychilum*) Divide rhizomes while still dormant in early spring (*see p.149*). Sow seeds (*p.151*) in spring at 70°F (21°C).
HEDYSARUM Sow seeds (*see p.164*) in spring at 59°F (15°C) after soaking in hot water to break dormancy (*p.151*).

GERBERA JAMESONII CULTIVARS

HELENIUM *SNEEZEWEED*

Helenium 'Sonnenwunder'

DIVISION in spring
SEEDS in spring
CUTTINGS in spring

Most perennial *Helenium* quickly form large clumps. These are easily increased by division every 3–4 years, which also maintains the vigor of each plant. Cut the rootstock (*see p.148*) into good-sized portions.

Most garden *Helenium* are cultivars and will not come true from home-gathered seeds. Sow seeds (*see p.151*) in spring at a temperature of 59°F (15°C). Seedlings should emerge in about a week and be transplanted in early to midsummer. They often flower in the next year.

To increase stock of cultivars more quickly, take basal stem cuttings (*see p.156*) from new growth when the new shoots are about 3in (8cm) tall. Rooted cuttings may flower in the same season.

HEPATICA

DIVISION in late winter or in spring
SEEDS in early summer or in late winter

These woodland plants are slow to increase by vegetative means; sowing seeds is recommended, except for named cultivars. Divide mature plants in late winter or after flowering (*see p.148*). Each crown must have good roots if it is to establish well. Sow seeds (*see p.151*) the moment they are ripe, or in late winter, in pots in a cold frame. Plants flower after about three years.

HELIANTHUS *SUNFLOWER*

Helianthus 'Capenoch Star'

DIVISION in spring
SEEDS in spring
CUTTINGS in late spring

The several perennials in this genus are easily divided (*see p.148*); the rootstocks may be woody or spread by underground stems (stolons), which can be invasive. Plants will flower the same season. Sow seeds (*see p.151*) of species at 59°F (15°C) to germinate in 7–10 days; plants should flower in 2–3 years. Take basal stem cuttings (*see p.156*) from 3in (8cm) shoots; at 59°F (15°C), they should root within 14 days. Plants may flower in the same year. For annual sunflowers, *see p.224*; Jerusalem artichokes, *see p.302*.

HELICHRYSUM

DIVISION in spring
SEEDS in spring or in summer
CUTTINGS from summer to early autumn

Perennials in this genus are susceptible to rot if kept too moist, so take care to provide drainage and ventilate well. Fibrous-rooted clumps of perennials, for example *H. thianschanicum* (syn. *lanatum*), may be divided (*see p.148*) into 2–4 sections. Expect flowers later in the same year.

Gather ripe seedheads the moment they become fluffy, before the seeds blow away. Sow (*see p.151*) at 55–61°F (13–16°C). Seedlings should appear after two weeks, and plants will flower within two years. Sow seeds of alpines as soon as they are ripe in summer.

Take semi-ripe stem-tip cuttings (*see p.154*) of new, nonflowering growth and root at 59°F (15°C) in trays. Transplant the cuttings when rooted, usually in about 14 days, or delay potting until late spring. Provide cold protection where necessary over winter. New plants will flower in the following year. Rosette cuttings (*see p.167*) may be taken from the alpine *H. milfordiae*.

HELLEBORUS *HELLEBORE*

DIVISION after flowering
SEEDS in summer

The Lenten rose (*Helleborus orientalis*, *H.* x *hybridus*) hybridizes freely, but the seedlings are usually attractive; for true offspring of cultivars, plants must be divided. Other species come true.

DIVISION

Divide hybrids such as *H.* x *nigercors* when new growth is mature (*see p.148*). Young clumps of *H. orientalis* and other species can be pulled apart, but older plants and other species need cutting or back-to-back forks. Well-rooted pieces should flower in the following spring.

SEEDS

Most species set seeds, and many self-sow (*see below*). Sow at once (*see p.151*) in a seedbed or in trays; they germinate best if exposed to winter cold to break dormancy. They may start to germinate in autumn or the spring and flower in 2–3 years. Dry, old seeds germinate erratically, if at all. If seeds cannot be sown fresh, store in moist sand or moss. Good subjects for hybridizing (*see p.21*).

GATHERING HELLEBORE SEED CAPSULES
Test a seed capsule (here of Helleborus orientalis*) by gently squeezing; if it splits to reveal dark seeds, it is ready to harvest. Wear gloves to guard against the irritant sap. Keep the capsules dry and warm until they split* (inset).

SELF-SOWN HELLEBORE SEEDLINGS
Seedlings of many species (here Helleborus argutifolius*) may be found at the base of the plant in spring. When each seedling has at least one true leaf, carefully lift it and transplant in moist, fertile soil in dappled shade.*

HEMEROCALLIS *DAYLILY*

DIVISION in early spring
SEEDS in autumn or in spring

The majority of daylilies are very hardy, but most of the evergreen types are less so. Divide congested clumps with forks (*see p.148*), trim off damaged roots completely, and replant. Single bud divisions (*see p.150*) are possible; these can be "topped," as for hostas (*see facing page*). Sow seed of species (*see p.151*) at 59°F (15°C) to germinate in 14 days, especially if seeds are fresh. Plants flower from the second year. Seedlings from cultivars vary but may be pleasing.

HEUCHERA *CORALBELLS*

DIVISION in spring
SEEDS in spring

If not divided regularly, these perennials decline in vigor. Division also preserves the color and leaf variegation of cultivars, but a small number of variegated seedlings also come true, and others may be attractive. After dividing a crown (*see below and p.148*), discard the old, woody center. Sow seeds (*see p.151*) at 50°F (10°C). Some of the cultivars, such as 'Palace Purple' come true. Plants flower the next year.

DIVIDING A HEUCHERA
Lift the plant once in new spring growth. Take small, vigorous sections from around the edge, each with good roots and 2–3 shoots (see inset).

OTHER PERENNIALS
HELICONIA Divide in spring (*see p.149*). After hot-water treatment, sow seeds in spring at 70°F (21°C) (*pp.151–2*).
HELIOPSIS As *Helianthus* (*see facing page*).
x HEUCHERELLA Divide in autumn or spring (*see p.148*).
HOUTTUYNIA CORDATA Divide in spring (*see p.148*). Sow seeds (*p.151*) in spring at 50°F (10°C). Take softwood cuttings (*p.154*) in spring.
HYPOESTES Sow seeds (*see p.151*) in spring at 64°F (18°C). Soft stem-tip cuttings in spring or semi-ripe in summer (*p.154*).
IBERIS Sow seeds (*see p.151*) in autumn. Take semi-ripe cuttings (*pp.154 and 166*) in midsummer.
IMPATIENS Sow seeds (*see p.151*) of bedding species and cultivars at 61°F (16°C) in spring (*for annuals, see p.225*). Take soft stem-tip cuttings (*p.154*) in spring or summer.
INCARVILLEA (syn. *Amphicome*) Sow seeds (*p.151*) fresh, or in spring; keep in a cold frame.
INULA Divide in autumn or spring (*see p.148*). Sow seeds (*p.151*) in spring at 50°F (10°C). Take basal stem cuttings (*p.156*) in spring.
IPOMOEA (syn. *Mina, Pharbitis*) Sow seeds (*see p.151*) in spring at 70°F (21°C) in bright light (*for annuals, see p.225*). Take softwood cuttings (*p.154*) in spring.
IRESINE Stem cuttings in autumn; stem-tip cuttings in spring (*see pp.154–5*).

HOSTA *PLANTAIN LILY*

Hosta 'Halcyon'

DIVISION in spring
SEEDS in spring

Most form fibrous-rooted clumps, though some are rhizomatous or have creeping, rooting stems (stolons). They can take time to recover from root disturbance, so divide only when new plants are needed or when plants have outgrown their space.

DIVISION

Break dense clumps apart with a spade (*see right*); tease loose, fleshy-rooted clumps apart carefully by hand (*see p.22*) to minimize root damage. Single buds (*see p.150*) may be potted or lined out in a nursery bed. Plants will be multicrowned the following year, especially if "topped" (*see below*) at the same time. Cuts are made through the buds of young divisions lined out in a nursery bed; a multibudded crown will form around the damaged bud. This may flower in the following season and provides material for further division.

DIVIDING A LARGE HOSTA CLUMP
If the clump to be divided has a tough, dense rootstock, chop it into pieces with a spade. Make sure that each piece has 1–3 good buds and trim any damaged roots with a knife.

SEEDS

Hostas set seeds freely; gather the flower spikes as the lowest pods begin to shed seeds. Seedlings show much, sometimes interesting, variation, although most species come true from seed. Seedlings from variegated plants retain only one color. Sow seeds (*see p.151*) at 59°F (15°C); keep seedlings in a cold frame. Plants flower in 2–3 years.

PROPAGATING HOSTAS BY "TOPPING"

1 When the buds begin to shoot in spring, scrape away the soil from around the base of each bud to expose the crown. Use a clean, damp cloth to wipe clean the base of each crown, taking care not to disturb its roots.

2 Carefully make a small, vertical cut through the crown of each bud by pushing through the clean, sharp blade of a scalpel or knife. If the crown is thick enough, make a second cut at right angles to the first.

3 Treat each cut with hormone rooting compound, then insert a toothpick to keep each wound open. Cover the crowns with soil to the same depth as before, firm, and water well. Keep moist throughout the growing season.

4 By autumn, dormant buds should form around the healed cuts and, in the following spring, the new buds will produce new shoots (see above). *Divide the crowns in the autumn or in spring into pieces, each with its own bud.*

IRIS

Iris bulleyana

DIVISION in spring, midsummer, or autumn
SEEDS in spring

The fibrous-rooted and rhizomatous perennials benefit from being divided every 3–4 years. The species and new hybrids are raised from seeds. (*For bulbous irises, see p.271.*)

DIVISION

Divide moisture-loving irises such as Siberians in spring or autumn (*see p.148*). Lift rhizomatous kinds, such as bearded iris, in midsummer and cut rhizomes into sections, each with roots and a fan of leaves (*see p.149*); replant, with tops barely covered, 6in (15cm) apart. Flowers will be sparse the next year, but good thereafter. Cut rhizomes without growing points into pieces about 3in (8cm) long and put into trays, leaving the tops exposed. Shoots will soon appear. They will take two years to flower.

SEEDS

Iris seeds have germination inhibitors; soak in cold water for 48 hours before sowing (*see p.151*) in autumn in pots at 61°F (16°C) to germinate in spring. Seedlings begin to flower within two years. Never let seedlings of moisture-loving species dry out.

LEWISIA *BITTEROOT*

SEEDS from mid- to late summer or in early spring
ROSETTE CUTTINGS in summer
LEAF CUTTINGS in summer

The principal means of increasing these alpines is from seeds. *Lewisia cotyledon* cultivars, evergreen species, and several others form offsets that can be used as cuttings. Excess moisture is fatal, so water seedlings and cuttings carefully.

SEEDS

Sow seeds (*see p.164*) when ripe or in spring in a free-draining soil mix of one part sterilized soil to two parts each of leaf mold and sharp sand. Place in a cold frame. *L. tweedyi* germinates slowly and erratically. Some species hybridize readily; seeds may not come true to type, but seedlings can be very beautiful.

CUTTINGS

Remove offsets with as much stem as possible (*see p.166*). Root in pots in gritty soil mix or lime-free sand, in a shaded closed case or cold frame. Leaf cuttings (*see p.166*) may be rooted in the same conditions but are slow to establish and rot readily if overwatered.

LOBELIA

DIVISION in spring
SEEDS in autumn or in spring
CUTTINGS in spring or in summer

Some short-lived perennials (mostly *Lobelia erinus* cultivars) are grown as bedding, but the border perennials, some quite hardy and others less so, may be divided or grown from cuttings.

DIVISION

Separate the crowns of plants such as *L. siphilitica*, *L. cardinalis*, and *L. laxiflora* by hand, or with a hand fork and knife (*see p.148*), for flowers in the same year.

SEEDS

Sow seeds (*see p.151*) of hardier types as soon as ripe, in a sheltered place. Sow less hardy perennials thinly; at 59°F (15°C), seedlings emerge in a few weeks. Most seedlings flower in the first year.

CUTTINGS

Take stem-tip or stem cuttings (*see pp.154–5*) from border perennials in summer. Flowering stems of *L. siphilitica* and *L. cardinalis* can be cut into 2in (5cm) lengths; remove the lower leaves. They root in three weeks at 64°F (18°C). Protect over winter. Plants flower the next season. For more plants, split cuttings vertically, retaining leaves on each. Take basal stem cuttings (*see p.156*) of double forms of *L. erinus* in spring.

PATCHING SEEDLINGS OF BEDDING LOBELIA
Large numbers of seedlings for summer bedding are tedious to transplant. To save time and ensure a dense drift of plants, sow seeds less thinly and transplant seedlings in small clusters, or patches.

LUPINUS *LUPINE*

Lupinus 'The Chatelaine'

SEEDS from early spring to midspring
CUTTINGS mid- to late spring

Of the perennials, only cultivars of *Lupinus polyphyllus* are widely grown. Unusually, many modern hybrid selections, such as the Gallery Series, and some cultivars will breed true from seeds. Cuttings are the best means of vegetative increase. Many lupines dislike hot weather, moist soils, and root disturbance.

SEEDS

For even germination, soak seeds for 24 hours in cold water before sowing (*see p.152*) at 59°F (15°C). The seeds are large and may be space-sown in a seedbed (*see p.153*) or in individual pots to avoid root disturbance when potting on. Germination should occur within ten days. Plant out in late spring.

CUTTINGS

Take new shoots as basal stem cuttings (*see p.156*) when about 3in (8cm) tall. At a temperature of 59°F (15°C), rooting takes 10–14 days. To avoid the risk of rot, try rooting the cuttings in perlite instead of medium, as for delphiniums (*see p.156*). Pot rooted cuttings and grow on in a sheltered place such as a cold frame. Plant out in early summer to flower in the following year.

LYCHNIS *CAMPION, CATCHFLY*

DIVISION in summer or in autumn
SEEDS in early spring
CUTTINGS in spring

Divide perennials, except *Lychnis* × *haageana*, in this genus (syn. *Viscaria*) after flowering (*see p.148*). Divisions flower in the same or next season. Sow seeds (*see pp.151–2*) at 50°F (10°C); seeds of alpines are best sown as soon they ripen. Plants grown from seeds flower in 1–2 years. Some species, such as *L. coronaria*, self-sow freely. A large number of seedlings from color forms should come true. Take basal stem cuttings (*see p.156*).

MARANTA *PRAYER PLANT*

DIVISION in spring
SEEDS in spring
CUTTINGS in spring

Divide established plants of these rhizomatous, tender perennials, pulling the clumps apart (*see p.148*). Grow on divisions at 64°F (18°C) in humidity and bright, indirect light until they are established. Sow seeds (*see p.151*) to germinate at 64°F (18°C) in two weeks.

Take basal stem cuttings (*see p.156*) when new shoots are 3–4in (8–10cm) tall. Remove the lowest leaves and insert the cuttings in pots or trays in rooting medium. With humidity and bottom heat of 64°F (18°C), cuttings should root within two weeks.

MECONOPSIS

BLUE, HIMALAYAN, AND WELSH POPPIES

Meconopsis betonicifolia

DIVISION in late summer or in early autumn
SEEDS in summer, early autumn or in spring or

Of the often short-lived perennials in this genus, the Welsh poppy, *Meconopsis cambrica,* is easy to raise from seeds since it self-sows freely. The prized blue-flowered species, such as *M. betonicifolia*, are more difficult; some are monocarpic. Selected forms and sterile hybrids are divided.

DIVISION

Once growth has ceased, divide plants (*see p.148*) into single rosettes. Handle the crowns carefully: they bruise easily, which can lead to rot.

SEEDS

Sow seeds of *M. cambrica* in autumn and expose to winter cold to germinate in spring. Gathered seeds (*right*) of other species usually come true, although they tend to hybridize. Seeds have short viability: gather and sow them as soon as they ripen (seedlings from summer sowings need winter protection), or store seeds dry in the refrigerator and sow in early spring. For best results, do both. Sow the seeds in cells in soilless seed mix and cover them only lightly with vermiculite. Keep them moist but not wet. Sowing on moss (*see p.208*) prevents the seeds from drying out. At 59°F (15°C), germination takes three weeks. Pot or plant out seedlings in acidic soil mix or lime-free soil.

GATHERING MECONOPSIS SEEDS
As soon as the seed capsules turn brown, cut them off and leave to dry in a warm place until the tops open (see inset)*. Shake out the seeds onto a clean piece of paper, then sow at once.*

MIMULUS

MONKEY FLOWER

DIVISION in spring
SEEDS in autumn or in spring
CUTTINGS in spring or in autumn

Most perennials in this genus (syn. *Diplacus*) are short-lived and so should be propagated regularly. Established plants may be divided. All are easy to raise from seeds but hybridize freely, so seedlings may vary.

DIVISION

Perennial herbaceous species can be divided (*see p.148*); some have creeping rootstocks.

SEEDS

Surface-sow the tiny seeds (*see p.151*) in spring at 43–54°F (6–12°C). Germination usually occurs within two weeks. Hardy species may also be sown in autumn in pots for early flowers; protect during winter in a cold frame. *Mimulus* self-sow freely.

CUTTINGS

Take softwood stem-tip cuttings (*see p.154*). Cuttings root within three weeks and may flower later in the same season.

OTHER PERENNIALS

JANCAEA (syn. *Jankaea*) As for *Ramonda* (*see p.207*).
JEFFERSONIA (syn. *Plagiorhegma*) Divide (*see p.148*) in spring; slow to establish. Sow seeds (*p.151*) as soon as ripe, at 50°F (10°C). Slow-growing.
JUNCUS Divide in spring just as growth begins (*see p.148*). Sow seeds (*p.151*) as soon as ripe or in spring at 50°F (10°C).
KIRENGESHOMA Divide in spring (*see p.149*). Sow seeds (*p.151*) in spring at 50°F (10°C). Old seeds germinate erratically and slowly. Take basal stem cuttings (*p.156*) in spring.
KNAUTIA Divide in spring (*see p.148*). Sow seeds (*p.151*) in spring at 59°F (15°C). Basal stem cuttings (*p.156*) in spring.
KNIPHOFIA Divide in mid- to late spring; replant large portions, but pot and grow on small rooted shoots (*see pp.148–9*) Sow seeds (*p.151*) in spring at 59°F (15°C).
LABLAB PURPUREUS (syn. *Dolichos lablab*) *See* Vegetables, *p.302*.
LAMIUM (syn. *Galeobdolon, Lamiastrum*) Divide in spring (*see p.148*). Sow in spring in a seedbed or at 50°F (10°C) in pots (*pp.151–3*). Take stem-tip cuttings (*p.154*) in summer.
LATHYRUS Divide in spring (*see p.148*). Sow seeds in spring at 59°F (15°C); soak first for 24 hours in cold water (*pp.151–2*). For *L. odoratus, see p.226*.
LEONTOPODIUM Divide in spring (*see p.148*). Sow seeds (*p.151*) as soon as ripe or in autumn.
LEUCANTHEMUM As for *Knautia*.
LEUCOGENES Sow fresh seeds (*see p.151*) at once in organic-rich, free-draining, acidic to neutral soil mix; germination is usually poor. Take semi-ripe stem-tip cuttings (*p.154*) in late summer.
LIATRIS As for *Knautia*.
LIBERTIA As for *Liriope*, but seeds are in capsules.
LIGULARIA As for *Knautia*.
LIMONIUM As for *Knautia*.
LINARIA As for *Knautia*.
LINUM Sow seeds at 59°F (15°C) in spring (*see p.151*). Softwood cuttings in mid-spring or semi-ripe cuttings (*p.154*) of woody-based species in summer.
LIRIOPE Divide in spring (*see p.149*). Sow seeds extracted from berries (*pp.151–2*) in spring at 50°F (10°C).
LOTUS (syn. *Dorycnium*) Seeds in spring (*see p.152*) at 59°F (15°C); soak first for 24 hours in hot water. Semi-ripe cuttings (*p.154*) in late summer.
LUNARIA Divide *L. rediviva* in spring (*see p.148*). Sow seeds direct in spring (*p.152*). (*For annuals, see p.227.*)
LUZULA As for *Juncus*.
LYSIMACHIA Divide in spring (*see p.148*). Sow seeds (*p.151*) in spring at 50°F (10°C). Stem-tip cuttings (*p.154*) from late spring. Root semi-ripe cuttings of *L. nummularia* in early autumn in medium or moss roll (*pp.154–5*).
LYTHRUM As for *Knautia*.
MACLEAYA (syn. *Bocconia*) Divide in spring (*see p.149*). Sow seeds (*p.151*) in spring at 59°F (15°C); self-sows freely. Take rhizome sections in winter and treat as root cuttings (*p.158*).
MALVA Sow seeds (*see p.151*) in spring at 50°F (10°C). Take basal stem or stem-tip cuttings (*pp.154–6*) in spring.
MARRUBIUM Sow seeds (*see p.151*) in autumn or spring in pots at 50°F (10°C); germination is erratic. Basal stem cuttings (*p.156*) in late summer.
MAZUS Divide in spring. Sow seeds (*p.164*) when ripe or in early spring in pots at 50°F (10°C). Detach self-rooted cuttings (*see p.167*) in spring.
MELISSA Divide in spring (*see p.148*). Seeds (*p.151*) in spring at 50°F (10°C). Take semi-ripe cuttings (*p.154*) in late summer.
MENTHA *See* Mints, *p.291*.
MONARDA Divide (*see p.149*) in midspring; single bud divisions are possible (*p.150*). Seeds in spring (*p.151*) at 50°F (10°C). Take stem-tip or basal stem cuttings in late spring (*pp.154–6*). May flower in first year.
MORISIA MONANTHOS (syn. *M. hypogaea*) Sow seeds (*see p.151*) in winter or early spring in pots; keep in a cold frame. Take root cuttings (*p.158*) in winter months.

KNIPHOFIA 'ALCAZAR'

MUSA Banana, Plantain

Division in spring
Seeds when ripe

Despite their treelike appearance, these are tender herbs, although *Musa basjoo* is a bit hardier than most. They produce offsets, or suckers, which may be removed for propagation (*see below*). Pot offsets singly and keep at 70°F (21°C) until established. Shelter new plants from wind if needed.

Before sowing the large seeds (*see p.151*), file each carefully on one side, then soak in hot water and allow to cool for 24 hours. Sow one per pot and keep at 75°F (24°C). Expect germination within a month. Grow on seedlings at the same temperature. New plants can grow 10ft (3m) in a year.

Banana fruits and male flower
Cultivars (here Musa *'Lady's Finger') grown chiefly as ornamentals rarely set seeds, but if they do, gather and sow as soon as they ripen.*

PROPAGATING FROM BANANA SUCKERS

1 Clear the soil away to expose the sucker's point of origin (here of Musa basjoo*). Use a large, sharp knife to cut downward and detach the sucker with as many of its roots as possible.*

*2 Dust the cut surfaces with a fungicide (*see inset*). Fill in the soil around the parent plant. Remove any large or damaged leaves from the sucker to reduce water loss. Pot in a container just a little larger than the rootstock, at the same depth as before. Label, water, and grow on in a warm, shaded place.*

PAPAVER Poppy

Division in summer
Seeds in summer or in spring
Cuttings in late autumn

Perennial poppies are mostly quite hardy. Monocarpic species, such as *P. triniifolium*, and smaller ones, such as *P. atlanticum*, are difficult to divide but seed freely, so are best raised from seeds, which come reasonably true. Double or Oriental types are mostly cultivars of *P. orientale* or *P. bracteatum* and give mixed results from seeds so are divided or increased from cuttings. (*For annuals, see p.228.*)

Division

Separate a clump into single crowns, each with some strong roots (*see p.148*), for flowers next year.

Seeds

Gather the seedpods just as they turn brown, before the cap lifts. The small seeds need light to germinate: surface-sow (*see p.151*) as soon as they are ripe or in spring at 50°F (10°C) to germinate in ten days. Transplant seedlings as soon as they are large enough to handle: they dislike root disturbance. Seed-raised plants flower in the following season.

Cuttings

Oriental poppies reproduce naturally from broken roots left in the soil, so root cuttings usually succeed. They should be 3in (8cm) long, inserted vertically into free-draining soil mix (*see p.158*). Keep in a sheltered place over winter. When the new shoots have good roots in spring, line out in a nursery bed or pot singly. Alternatively, root them in sand, as for *Eryngium* (*p.196*). Rooted cuttings flower in the following year.

PAEONIA Peony

Division in early autumn
Seeds in autumn

Divide perennials (*for shrubs, see p.136*) in autumn by separating the tough roots into pieces (*see p.149 and right*), each with one to several plump, terminal buds. Move them only when necessary; it can take more than two years for divisions to bloom. Cover the buds with no more than an inch of soil, then mulch lightly.

The seeds (*see p.151*) are doubly dormant. Sow them in pots and leave outdoors to expose them to winter cold, or chill the seeds (*see p.152*) for several weeks in the refrigerator before sowing. During the first summer roots develop, but the seeds then require a second period of cold before shoots will appear. Plants may take five years to reach their full flowering size.

Dividing peonies
*When red, swelling buds appear, lift the crown and wash off the soil. Take care not to bruise the fleshy roots. Cut the crown into sections, each with 1–5 buds (*see inset*). Dust the cuts with fungicide to prevent rot. Replant at least 8in (20cm) apart with the buds just below the surface.*

Peony seedheads
Some peonies (here Paeonia cambessedesii*) produce black and red seeds in the same pods. Only the black seeds are fertile, so discard the others when gathering seeds for sowing.*

PELARGONIUM

Pelargonium 'A Happy Thought'

SEEDS in late winter or in mid-spring
SOFTWOOD CUTTINGS from spring to autumn
SEMI-RIPE CUTTINGS in late summer or in autumn

Commonly known as geraniums, perennial cultivars of the zonal, regal, ivy-, and scented-leaved geraniums are more popular than the less showy succulent species (*see p.249*). They are tender and generally perpetuated from year to year by taking cuttings in cold climates, discarding the parent. The single-flowered F1 hybrids of zonal geraniums, commonly used for bedding, are raised from seeds.

SEEDS

F1 hybrids flower quickly from seeds sown (*see p.151*) in late winter at 70°F (21°C). Seedlings appear in 7–10 days; grow them on at 59°F (15°C). Sow other types in midspring at 59°F (15°C).

CUTTINGS

Take softwood stem or stem-tip cuttings after flowering to root in 7–10 days. Rooted cuttings need a minimum of 45°F (8°C) over winter; plant out after frost. For early cutting material, in autumn lift, trim, and pot a few plants. Keep fairly dry and frost-free. In late winter, water and keep at 64°F (18°C) to force into growth. Soft cuttings taken then root in seven days. In cool to warm climates, traditional semi-ripe cuttings (*see p.154*) are less likely to rot, but slow; they root at 59°F (15°C).

PENSTEMON

SEEDS in early spring
CUTTINGS in summer or early autumn

Sow seeds (*see p.151*) of border perennials in this genus at 59°F (15°C), and those of alpines (*see p.164*) in a cold frame. It is well worth gathering seeds from good forms; they come fairly true. Penstemons are good subjects for hybridization (*see p.21*).

PENSTEMON HARTWEGII
Seedlings of border penstemons, such as this, should come fairly true, so they are well worth gathering.

Take semi-ripe stem-tip cuttings (*see p.154*) of all short-lived perennials in late summer to early autumn. Those of smaller alpines should be 1–2in (2.5–5cm) long; border types at least twice as long. In trays, pots or even in water, they should root in two weeks at 59°F (15°C). They may also be rooted in a moss roll (*see p.155*) to save space. Pot in free-draining, gritty soil mix to avoid rot, and protect rooted cuttings from cold.

Softwood cuttings of alpines taken in early summer can root well and may flower in the same year.

PEPEROMIA

DIVISION in spring
SEEDS in spring
CUTTINGS at any time

A wide range of selections in this tender genus are in cultivation. Variegated cultivars must be divided to retain the variegation. Seeds are rarely available. Plants with stems, such as *P. obtusifolia* (Magnoliifolia Group), may be increased from stem-tip cuttings; those without, such as *P. caperata*, from leaf cuttings.

DIVISION

Divide (*see pp.148–50*) into 2–4 pieces. Pot singly; keep humid until established. Bottom heat of 64°F (18°C) helps.

SEEDS

Sow seeds (*see p.151*) at a temperature of 70°F (21°C). Transplant the seedlings singly into pots when large enough to handle (usually in 3–4 weeks) and grow on at 64°F (18°C).

CUTTINGS

Take softwood stem-tip cuttings (*see p.154*) and insert around the edge of a pot. Place in a propagator or in a plastic bag and keep at 21°F (18°C). Cuttings should root within three weeks.

To take leaf cuttings (*see p.157*), select mature leaves and remove them with about 2in (5cm) of stalk (petiole). Insert around the edges of small pots filled with equal parts of coarse sand and peat, to a depth of about ½in (1cm). Cover to keep humid. It takes about four weeks at 70°F (21°C) for roots to grow, and as long again for plantlets to develop, from the bases of the petioles.

OTHER PERENNIALS

MYOSOTIDIUM HORTENSIA (syn. *M. nobile*) Divide carefully after flowering (*see p.148*). Sow seeds (*p.151*) as soon as ripe or in spring at 59°F (15°C).
MYOSOTIS Sow seeds (*see p.151*) in early summer at 50°F (10°C). Soft stem-tip cuttings (*p.154*) in summer of species such as *M. colensoi* and *M. pulvinaris*. (*For annuals, see p.227.*)
NAUTILOCALYX Sow seeds in spring on moss (*see p.208*) at 63°F (17°C). Take stem-tip cuttings (*p.154*) in summer.
NEMESIA Sow seeds (*see p.151*) in spring at 59°F (15°C). Take soft or semi-ripe stem-tip cuttings (*p.154*) in summer. (*For annuals, see p.228.*)
NEPENTHES Sow seeds in spring (*see p.151*) at 81°F (27°C). Take semi-ripe cuttings (*p.154*) in spring. Air layer in summer, as for *Dieffenbachia* (*p.194*).
NEPETA Divide (*see p.148*) in spring or autumn. Sow seeds in spring (*p.151*) at 50°F (10°C). Take soft stem-tip cuttings in early summer; semi-ripe cuttings in early autumn (*pp.154–5*).
NIEREMBERGIA Divide in spring (*see p.148*). Sow seeds (*p.151*) in spring at 59°F (15°C). Take soft stem-tip cuttings in early autumn; keep frost-free in first winter (*p.154*).
OENOTHERA Divide fibrous-rooted species in spring (*see p.148*). Sow seeds (*p.151*) in spring at 50°F (10°C). Take softwood cuttings (*p.154*), especially of taprooted species in late spring.
OMPHALODES Divide after flowering (*see p.148*). Sow seeds (*p.151*) in spring at 50°F (10°C) or in autumn; sow seeds of *O. lucilliae* and keep in a cold frame.
OPHIOPOGON As for *Liriope* (*see p.203*).
ORIGANUM *See* Culinary Herbs, *p.291*.
OSTEOSPERMUM Sow seeds (*see p.151*) in spring at 64°F (18°C). Take softwood cuttings in spring; semi-ripe cuttings in late summer (*pp.154–5*).
OURISIA Divide in spring (*see p.149*). Sow seeds (*p.151*) in equal parts grit, soil, and leaf mold as soon as ripe or in spring; keep in a cold frame.
OXALIS Divide rhizomatous and fibrous-rooted plants in early spring or just after flowering (*see pp.148–9*). Sow seeds (*p.151*) in spring at 55–64°F (13–18°C). (*For bulbous and tuberous species, see p.275.*)
PACHYSANDRA Divide in spring (*see p.148*). Take semi-ripe cuttings (*p.154*) during summer and autumn.
PARAQUILEGIA Sow seeds (*see p.151*) as soon as ripe in pots in gritty soil mix; keep in a cold frame. Take basal stem cuttings (*p.156*) in early summer; they do not always root.
PARNASSIA Divide in autumn or spring (*see p.148*). Sow seeds (*p.151*) in autumn in pots; keep in a cold frame.
PERICALLIS Sow seeds (*see p.151*) at 59°F (15°C) in spring or summer.

PETUNIA

Petunia 'Red Carpet'

SEEDS in spring
CUTTINGS in summer

The cultivars in this genus are popular bedding plants. Although perennial, they are usually raised from seeds as annuals. Sow seeds (*see p.151*) at 59°F (15°C) in light to germinate in ten days for flowers in the same season.

Perennials, especially the recent selections such as Surfinias for which seeds are not available, may be increased from softwood stem-tip cuttings (*see p.154*). Overwinter new plants under cover if necessary.

PHLOX

Phlox paniculata 'Graf Zeppelin'

DIVISION in spring or in early autumn
SEEDS in early spring
CUTTINGS in early spring, in late spring or in autumn

Division and basal stem cuttings from perennials in this genus produce flowering plants in the same year. Aerial parts of phlox are prone to nematode infestation, which is often not easily detectable, so herbaceous border kinds in particular should be increased from root cuttings. Seeds do not usually transmit nematode infestations, either. (*For annuals, see p.228.*)

DIVISION

Divide only healthy herbaceous phlox in spring (*see p.148*); alpines in early autumn. Mat-forming alpines do not respond well to division. Single bud divisions (*see p.150*) are also possible.

SEEDS

Sow seeds of species (*see p.151*) at 59°F (15°C) to germinate in 7–10 days. Shade seedlings of woodland species. Plants flower in the second year.

CUTTINGS

Alpines that have suitable shoots, and woodland species, may be increased from basal stem cuttings in early spring (*see p.156*). They will root at 59°F (15°C).

Alternatively, take softwood stem-tip cuttings in late spring; this is a good way of increasing mat-forming alpines. Cuttings of smaller alpine species (*see p.166*) may be only 1in (2.5cm) long; root them in a mixture of equal parts sharp sand and sterilized soil.

In autumn, lift border phlox and take 1in (2.5cm) cuttings (*see p.158*) from thicker roots; place horizontally in trays.

PRIMULA *PRIMROSE*

Primula veris

DIVISION in early spring or after flowering
SEEDS in midspring or in late summer to autumn
CUTTINGS in winter
SCOOPING in late winter

A huge and varied genus of sometimes short-lived perennials, which are increased in a variety of ways.

DIVISION

Regular division keeps cultivars of *P. vulgaris* and Polyanthus primroses healthy but can weaken other species. Pull apart fibrous-rooted clumps into single, rooted crowns or rosettes. Divide species with woody rootstocks such as *Primula allionii* with a knife (*see p.148*). Pot alpines, or replant larger divisions, to grow on. Cut back by half the large-leaved types, such as bog primroses and candelabras, to reduce moisture loss.

SEEDS

All species may be raised from seeds (*see p.164*). Seed-raised primroses have the advantage of being virus-free, but some garden species, especially *P. elatior*, *P. veris*, *P. vulgaris*, and candelabra types, hybridize readily unless isolated. In general, seeds are set only if both pin-eyed (long style, short stamens) and thrum-eyed (short style, long stamens) plants of the species are grown.

The seeds are short-lived so are best sown fresh, but seeds may be sown in spring at 59°F (15°C). For most primroses, a moist, organic-rich, yet free-draining soil mix is ideal.

SCOOPING ALPINE PRIMROSES

1 *Select vigorous plants (here of* Primula denticulata*) just as they start into growth. Use a sharp knife to cut or scoop out the crown of each plant and expose the top of the roots.*

2 *Use a fine brush to dust the cut roots with fungicide (see inset) to guard against rot. Cover each clump of scooped roots with a shallow layer of sharp sand.*

PULSATILLA *PASQUE FLOWER*

SEEDS as soon as ripe or in autumn
CUTTINGS from spring to autumn or in winter

These plants are slow to propagate by vegetative means but are easy to raise from seeds. Once established, they should not be disturbed; division and root cuttings are both challenging but worthwhile methods of increasing rare or unusually fine forms, especially of alpines. Seeds give excellent results if they are sown fresh.

SEEDS

Sow seeds (*see p.164*) from the feathery seedheads the moment they are ripe. The plumes tend to push the seeds out of the soil mix as they germinate: trim off the plumes before sowing or gently push the seeds back down. Seeds of *P. halleri* and *P. vulgaris* germinate in 10–14 days, and the seedlings flower in the following year. Other species may not germinate until the following spring, whenever seeds are sown. Do not allow seedlings to become potbound.

CUTTINGS

Lift and divide (*see p.167*) strong, multi-crowned plants into individual shoots, or rooted pieces, in spring after flowering, or in autumn. Each shoot should have a 2–3in (5–8cm) stem and a few roots, if possible. Pot in equal parts of sharp sand and peat, making sure that the bud is just above the surface of the soil mix. Place in a semi-shaded cold frame; keep moist, not wet. Provide more light when new growth is visible.

In winter, take root cuttings (*see p.167*) from a vigorous, multicrowned plant. Remove only the thickest, healthy roots and discard the parent, which will not recover. Cut the roots into 1¼–2in (3–5cm) lengths. Insert in a gritty soil mix so that the upper ends are just level with the surface. Keep moist but not wet. Pot after shoots appear.

Material for cuttings can be obtained without disturbing a container-grown parent plant by allowing it to root into a sand bed, as for *Eryngium* (*see p.196*).

Germination is most successful if the seeds are exposed to light (cover them only lightly with vermiculite, not soil mix) and kept moist and not too warm.

CUTTINGS

Root cuttings (*see p.167*) can be used to propagate color forms of *P. denticulata*; cut thicker roots of the parent plant into 1½–2in (4–5cm) pieces. Take rosette or single leaf cuttings of Petiolaris primroses as for *Ramonda* (*see below*).

SCOOPING

Scooping, either in open ground (*see below*) or in pots, is useful for alpines such as *P. denticulata* and leafy primroses, which produce a leafy tuft at soil level. Treat the removed topgrowths as rosette cuttings (*see p.166*).

3 *When the new shoots are 1–2in (2.5–5cm) tall, lift each plant. Take care not to damage its roots. Pull it apart gently into single rosettes, each with strong roots. Treat as rosette cuttings.*

RAMONDA

DIVISION in early summer
SEEDS in early or midsummer
CUTTINGS in summer or early autumn

These evergreen perennials rot if exposed to winter moisture. Divide congested plants carefully with a sharp knife into individual, rooted rosettes (*see p.167*); pot and grow on before planting.

Ramonda set abundant, dustlike seeds, which are easily lost once the small seed capsules ripen. Sow the seeds thinly (*see p.164*) as soon as ripe on organic, moist soil mix. Leave seedlings undisturbed for the first winter and transplant when large enough to handle in the spring.

Small rosette cuttings, or even single leaves, may be severed (*see p.166*) retaining as much stem as possible – at least ½in (1cm). Insert them in gritty soil mix or in equal parts of sharp sand and peat in a shaded propagating frame outdoors. They are slow to root. Plants may bloom in the following year but will flower more freely after 18 months.

RANUNCULUS *BUTTERCUP, CROWFOOT*

DIVISION in autumn or in spring
SEEDS in spring or from summer to autumn

Most perennials in this large genus are quite hardy; *Ranunculus asiaticus* is much less so. Buttercups increase naturally from seeds; division is often quicker. (*For aquatic species, see p.168.*)

DIVISION

Divide herbaceous plants after flowering, most alpine species in spring. Separate each plant into single, rooted crowns (*see p.148*). Pot alpine divisions; replant or line out in a nursery bed herbaceous border kinds, such as *R. aconitifolius*.

SEEDS

Sow seeds of *R. asiaticus* in early spring at a temperature of 59°F (15°C). The seedlings may flower in the first summer before they die down for the winter.

In most other species, seed dormancy must be broken. When the seeds are ripe in summer or autumn, they quickly fall away, often while still green. They are best gathered just before this point, immediately sown in pots, and then exposed to winter cold (*see pp.151–2*). Use a gritty, soil-based seed mix.

Place in a sheltered place such as a cold frame. Fresh seeds often germinate in the following spring but older (black or brown) seeds, and seeds of some Australasian species, take two or more years to germinate.

SAINTPAULIA *AFRICAN VIOLET*

Saintpaulia 'Bright Eyes'

DIVISION in spring
SEEDS in spring
CUTTINGS in spring or at any time when plants are in growth

The easiest way to raise African violets is by leaf cuttings. Division may be used for any of these tender perennials; some specialized flower-color patterns (chimeras) are propagated from flower-stalk plantlets.

DIVISION

Carefully tease apart rosettes, making sure each has roots (*see p.167*). Pot and tent in plastic bags for three weeks in a shaded, warm place until established.

SEEDS

Sow seeds on a layer of moss spread over seed soil mix (*see p.165*). At 70°F (21°C) germination occurs in 2–3 weeks. Seedlings develop slowly; when large enough to handle, pot singly. Once established, grow them at 59°F (15°C).

CUTTINGS

Take fully developed, new leaves with their stalks (petioles) as cuttings. Insert in pots, either singly or several around the edge (*see p.157*). Roots will be produced after a month and plantlets a month later. Detach the plantlets from each petiole and pot individually when they are large enough to handle.

OTHER PERENNIALS

PHLOMIS Divide in spring (*see p.148*). Seeds (*p.151*) in spring at 59°F (15°C).
PHORMIUM Divide in spring (*see p.148*); pot and grow on leaf fans with roots. Sow seeds (*p.151*) in spring at 64°F (18°C).
PHYSALIS Divide in spring (*see p.148*). Sow cleaned seeds (*p.151*) in spring at 59°F (15°C).
PLECTRANTHUS Sow seeds (*see p.151*) in spring at 70°F (21°C). Semi-ripe cuttings in late summer as for *Solenostemon* (*p.209*).
PODOPHYLLUM Divide (*see p.149*) in spring. Sow seeds (*pp.151–2*) in autumn.
POLEMONIUM Divide in early spring (*see p.148*). Sow seeds (*p.151*) in spring at 50°F (10°C).
POLYGONATUM Divide in spring (*see p.149*). Sow seeds (*p.151*) in autumn; keep in a cold frame; germination may be slow and erratic.
POTENTILLA (syn. *Comarum*) Divide herbaceous plants (*see p.148*) in spring. Sow seeds (*p.151*) when ripe in spring; keep in a cold frame.
PRUNELLA As for *Polemonium*.
PULMONARIA Divide after flowering or in spring (*p.149*). Seeds (*p.151*) in spring at 50°F (10°C). Take root cuttings in winter.
RAOULIA Divide mat in spring or early summer (*see p.167*). Sow seeds (*p.164*) thinly in rich, gritty soil mix in spring. Softwood cuttings (*p.166*) in summer of new ½–¾in (1–2cm) shoots; rooting erratic.
RHEUM Divide in late winter as *Paeonia* (*see p.204*). Sow seeds (*p.151*) at 50°F (10°C) in autumn. (*For vegetable, see p.306.*)
RODGERSIA Divide in spring (*see p.149*). Sow seeds in spring on moss as for *Sarracenia* (*p.208*) at 50°F (10°C).
RUDBECKIA Divide in spring (*see p.149*). Sow seeds (*p.151*) in spring at 50°F (10°C). Basal stem cuttings (*p.156*) in spring. (*For annuals, see p.228.*)

RUDBECKIA FULGIDA VAR. *SPECIOSA* 'VIETTE'S LITTLE SUZY'

SALVIA Sage

Salvia splendens Cleopatra Series

DIVISION in spring
SEEDS in spring
BASAL STEM CUTTINGS in late spring
STEM-TIP CUTTINGS in late summer or in early autumn

Perennial species from this large genus of quite hardy to very tender plants may be raised from seeds. Divide border perennials such as *Salvia nemorosa* and *S.* x *superba*. Take basal stem cuttings from border plants, for example *S. guaranitica* (syn. *S. concolor*). For annuals, *see p.228*; for the culinary sage, *S. officinalis*, *see p.291*.

DIVISION

To divide established plants (*see p.148*), cut the woody rootstock into 2–4 pieces with a knife and replant.

SEEDS

Seed pods ripen successively from the base of the flower spike and shed their seeds within two days; gather ripe pods frequently. Sow seeds (*see p.151*) at 61–64°F (16–18°C). Protect seedlings from cold, if necessary.

CUTTINGS

Take basal stem cuttings (*see p.156*) from new shoots that are about 3in (8cm) tall. Root at 59°F (15°C) to flower in the same season. Take soft and semi-ripe stem-tip cuttings (*see p.154*) from new, nonflowering growth. Pot rooted cuttings and keep frost-free over winter. Plant out in late spring.

SANSEVIERIA *Snake plant*

DIVISION in early spring
CUTTINGS at any time

Of these tender plants, only *Sansevieria trifasciata* and its forms are commonly grown in temperate areas. Variegated cultivars can be propagated only by division to perpetuate the leaf-patterning (cutting-raised plants have unvariegated leaves).

DIVISION

Divide large clumps with a spade or sharp knife when plants are dormant or about to start into growth (*see p.148*). This may be almost any time, but early spring is preferable. Pot into small pots, keep as warm as possible, and water sparingly until plants establish.

CUTTINGS

Prepare leaf cuttings (*see right and p.157*) from newly mature, healthy leaves. Cut each leaf horizontally into pieces, then insert these in pots or trays of sandy rooting medium. It does not matter if cuttings in any row touch. Place in bright, indirect light at about 70°C (21°C); leave uncovered and keep the medium just moist. If the cuttings are basal end down in the compost, new roots and shoots should develop from the bases in 6–8 weeks.

LEAF CUTTINGS OF *SANSEVIERIA*
Prepare a tray with a mix of equal parts peat and sand. Cut newly mature leaves (here of Sansevieria trifasciata*) into 2in (5cm) sections* (see left). *Insert the cuttings, lower edge downward, in the medium in rows. Space the rows 2in (5cm) apart.*

SARRACENIA *Pitcher plant*

DIVISION in spring
SEEDS in spring

Sarracenia purpurea is quite hardy; other species are much less so. Do not let divisions or seedlings dry out.

DIVISION

Divide large clumps just before new growth begins (*see p.148*). Cut off rooted crowns with a sharp knife, pot in live sphagnum moss (if possible) and keep moist at a temperature of 59°F (15°C).

SEEDS

Seeds germinate well if fresh, moist, and exposed to light – old seeds germinate erratically, if at all. Cold stratification (*see p.152*) improves results from old seeds. For a reliably moist environment that mimics the natural habitat of these bog plants, surface-sow seeds on moss (*see below*). Keep the seeds moist by sinking the pot in a larger one of moss, kept permanently damp, or cover with a sheet of glass or plastic, water from below, and ventilate regularly. Rainwater is best since it is lime-free. Germination takes 2–3 weeks at 61°F (16°C). When large enough to handle, pot seedlings singly in sphagnum moss or soil mix.

SOWING PITCHER PLANT SEEDS ON MOSS

1 Fill a 3½in (9cm) pot with soilless seed mix to within ¾in (2cm) of the rim and firm. Rub some moist sphagnum moss through a fine-mesh sieve to give it a fine texture.

2 Kill weeds seeds in the moss by soaking it in boiling water. When it is cool, squeeze out the excess water. Add a ¼in (5mm) layer of this moss to the pot of soil mix.

3 Plunge the prepared pot into a larger one filled with moist sphagnum moss. Sow the seeds thinly over the surface of the inner pot. Place in humid, bright shade at 61°F (16°C).

SAXIFRAGA *SAXIFRAGE*

Saxifraga sancta

DIVISION in spring or autumn
SEEDS in autumn or spring
CUTTINGS in late spring or
BULBILS in early summer

Division is the easiest way to increase these plants, except for the cushion plants. Mat- or cushion-forming types may be grown from cuttings; species from seeds.

DIVISION

Carefully tease apart (*see p.148*) fibrous-rooted clumps such as *Saxifraga fortunei* (syn. *S. cortusifolia* var. *fortunei*) in mid-spring before growth begins, for flowers in the same year. Pull off rooted rosettes or offsets of species such as *S.* x *urbium* and *S. paniculata* (syn. *S. aizoon*) after flowering; grow on in pots or nursery beds. Stems of *S. stolonifera* can be encouraged to form plantlets (*see p.150*).

SEEDS

Sow fresh seeds in pots, covered lightly with grit. Those sown in autumn and exposed to winter chill in a cold frame (*see p.152 and p.164*) germinate more evenly. Spring-sown seeds germinate in 2–3 weeks. Plants flower in 2–3 years.

CUTTINGS

Treat rosettes without roots as cuttings (*see p.166*); remove with ½–1in (1–2cm) of stem; root at 59°F (15°C) in gritty soil mix for flowers the next year. Cuttings from alpines may be tiny; root them in pure sand or pumice (*see p.167*).

BULBILS

S. granulata produces bulbils in leaf axils (*see p.26*) as it dies down in summer. Store in moist sand and "sow" in early spring in trays in seed soil mix at 50°F (10°C). Plant out in the following year.

SHORTIA

DIVISION in late spring
SEEDS when ripe or in early spring
BASAL STEM CUTTINGS in early summer
STEM-TIP CUTTINGS in late summer

These alpines (syn. *Schizocodon*) are set back by disturbance, develop slowly, and are very vulnerable to drying out. Divide after flowering (*see p.148*). If available, sow seeds (*see p.164*) at 50°F (10°C) in rich, acidic to neutral soil mix; do not disturb seedlings in the first year.

Take basal stem cuttings or stem-tip cuttings (*see p.166*) from strong, 1½–2½in (4–6cm) shoots; insert in pots in equal parts of sharp sand and organic soil mix. Rooting of cuttings is slow and not always successful.

SISYRINCHIUM

DIVISION in spring or in early autumn
SEEDS from summer to autumn or in spring

Divide perennials in this genus, especially variegated forms, ensuring each leaf-fan has roots (*see p.149*). Many self-sow prolifically. Sow seeds (*see p.151 and p.164*) as soon as they are ripe or in spring at 59°F (15°C).

SMITHIANTHA *TEMPLE BELLS*

DIVISION in late winter
SEEDS in spring

The rhizomes of these tender plants increase readily; divisions (*see p.149*) flower within a year. If stock is scarce, cut the rhizomes in half.

Sow the seeds on a layer of fine sphagnum moss over seed soil mix as for *Sarracenia* (*see facing page*) at 70°F (21°C). Germination takes 10–14 days but the seedlings grow slowly. Lower the temperature to 64°F (18°C) when the seedlings are established.

SOLENOSTEMON *COLEUS, FLAME NETTLE, PAINTED NETTLE*

SEEDS from early spring to early summer
CUTTINGS from early spring to late summer

Of these tender plants, cultivars and hybrids of *S. scutellarioides* (syn. *Coleus blumei*) are the most popular and widely grown.

SEEDS

Seeds (*see p.151*) provide an easy way to raise hybrids. Most come fairly true; some have pleasing variations; discard poor seedlings. Surface-sow seeds and keep moist, at 64°F (18°C), in good light to germinate in 10–14 days. Grow on established seedlings at a minimum temperature of 59°F (15°C).

CUTTINGS

Take softwood stem-tip cuttings (*see p.154*) from named cultivars. They root readily in a free-draining medium such as rockwool, or even in water on a bright, warm windowsill (*see p.156*). They root in 10–14 days at 64°F (18°C).

OTHER PERENNIALS

SANGUISORBA Divide in spring (*see p.149*). Sow seeds (*p.151*) in autumn; keep cool in cold frame; germination may be erratic.
SAPONARIA Divide in spring (*see p.148*). Seeds (*p.151*) in spring at 50°F (10°C). Soft stem-tip cuttings (*p.154*) in spring.
SCABIOSA Divide in midspring (*see p.148*). Seeds (*p.151*) in spring at 59°F (15°C). Basal stem cuttings (*p.156*) in late spring.
SCHIZOSTYLIS Divide in spring (*see p.148*). Seeds (*p.151*) in spring at 59°F (15°C).
SCROPHULARIA Divide in spring, especially variegated plants (*see p.148*). Sow seeds (*p.151*) in spring at 50°F (10°C). Take basal stem cuttings (*p.156*) in spring.
SCUTELLARIA Divide in spring (*see p.148*). Sow seeds (*p.151*) in spring at 50°F (10°C) or as soon as ripe. Take softwood cuttings in late spring or basal stem cuttings in spring (*pp.154–6*).
SELAGINELLA Divide carefully in spring (*see p.149*). Sow spores as for ferns (*p.159*). Take stem-tip cuttings in spring (*p.154*); they root quickly in organic, moist soil mix at 70°F (21°C).
SEMIAQUILEGIA As for *Aquilegia* (*see p.189*).
SENECIO As for *Schizostylis*.
SIDALCEA Divide in spring (*see p.148*). Sow seeds (*p.151*) in spring at 50°F (10°C). Take basal stem cuttings (*p.156*) in spring.
SILENE Divide (*see p.148*) after flowering. Sow seeds (*p.151*) as soon as ripe or at 50°F (10°C) in spring. Take basal stem cuttings in spring (*p.156*); ½in (1cm) long of alpines.
SMILACINA Divide after flowering (*see p.148*). Sow seeds (*p.151*) in autumn and expose to cold; germinates slowly.
SOLDANELLA Divide (*see p.148*) regularly after flowering to keep vigorous. Sow seeds (*p.151*) as soon as ripe in moist, organic soil mix; keep in a cold frame.
SOLEIROLIA (syn. *Helxine*) Divide in late spring (*see p.148*).
SOLIDAGO As for *Scabiosa*.
x SOLIDASTER LUTEUS (syn. x *S. hybridus*) Divide in late winter (*p.148*).
SPATHYPHYLLUM Divide in spring (*see p.149*). Sow seeds (*p.151*) as soon as available at 75°F (24°C).
SPHAERALCEA (syn. *Iliamna*) Sow seeds (*see p.151*) in spring at 59°F (15°C). Take basal stem cuttings (*p.156*) in spring.
STACHYS (syn. *Betonica*) Divide in spring (*see p.148*). Single bud divisions are possible (*p.150*). Sow seeds (*p.151*) in spring at 59°F (15°C).
STOKESIA LAEVIS Divide in midspring (*see p.148*). Sow seeds (*p.151*) in autumn or spring at 59°F (15°C). Take root cuttings (*p.158*) in late winter.
STRELITZIA Detach rooted suckers carefully after flowering, as for *Musa* (*see p.204*). Sow seeds (*p.151*) in spring at 70°F (21°C).

STRELITZIA REGINAE

STREPTOCARPUS *CAPE PRIMROSE*

Streptocarpus caulescens

DIVISION in spring ⅄
SEEDS in spring ⅄⅄
CUTTINGS from spring to autumn ⅄

Some of the tender perennials in this genus are monocarpic. The multiple-leaved species and cultivars may be divided or grown from leaf cuttings. Seeds are useful for raising new hybrids and especially species that produce only a single leaf, such as *Streptocarpus grandis*. A few species, for example *S. saxorum,* have stems, the tips of which can be taken as cuttings.

DIVISION

Cut or pull established clumps apart (*see p.148*). Pot each rooted crown singly. Kept at 15°C (59°F), they root well in three weeks and flower in the same year.

SEEDS

Sow seeds on a layer of fine moss as for *Sarracenia* (*see p.208*) at a temperature of 70°F (21°C). Seedlings will appear in 10–14 days but develop slowly at first. Flowers will appear in the second year and often in the first.

CUTTINGS

Take stem-tip cuttings from healthy plants (*see p.154*) at any time when they are in growth. Kept at 59°F (15°C), the cuttings should root in 2–3 weeks. New plants will flower in the same season.

To take leaf cuttings, cut a mature leaf in half along the midrib (*see p.157*) or for a greater number of plants, into smaller sections (*see below*). Insert each section vertically, cut or basal edge down, into a deep tray of rooting medium at 64°F (18°C). Plantlets appear along the cut veins in about four weeks; when they are well developed, detach them and pot singly to grow on.

LEAF CUTTINGS OF CAPE PRIMROSE
Cut a leaf into chevrons or transverse sections at least 1in (2.5cm) deep. Stand the cuttings, basal end downward, in rows in a tray of rooting medium. Lightly firm, label, and water.

TRADESCANTIA

Tradescantia zebrina

DIVISION in spring ⅄
SEEDS in spring ⅄⅄
CUTTINGS at any time ⅄

The hardier species respond well to being divided. Tender types are more often propagated from cuttings. All species may be raised from seeds, although variegated forms do not come true.

DIVISION

In cold climates, divide (*see p.148*) hardy border kinds only. Pull apart the compact, fleshy crowns carefully. Roots may be fibrous or tuberous.

SEEDS

Sow seeds (*see p.151*) and keep at 59°F (15°C), or 64°F (18°C) for tender species. Seedlings should appear in as little as seven days. Plants flower in their first or second season.

CUTTINGS

Stem cuttings (*see pp.154–6*) of creeping forms, for example the variegated *Tradescantia fluminensis*, root easily, even in jars of water on a windowsill, if they are taken from plants in active growth. Alternatively, insert four cuttings around the edge of a pot in rooting medium. In two weeks, they may be potted on as one plant.

THALICTRUM *MEADOW RUE*

Thalictrum aquilegiifolium

DIVISION in midspring ⅄
SEEDS as soon as ripe or in early spring ⅄⅄

The majority of the rhizomatous perennials in this genus are quite hardy, although a few are less so. The popular cultivar 'Hewitt's Double' is sterile and can be increased only by division. Divide the rhizomes carefully as growth begins (*see p.149*), Divisions can be slow to re-establish and may not flower until the second year. Sometimes rhizomes with some roots and buds at the edges of a clump may be detached without necessarily lifting the parent. Pot and grow on in part shade until established.

Gather seeds just before they ripen and turn brown; once ripe, they are rapidly dispersed. They are best sown fresh: older seeds germinate erratically because of embryo dormancy (*see p.152*). Sow the seeds (*see p.151*) in a sheltered place such as a cold frame. Seed-raised plants take 2–3 years to reach flowering size.

TOLMIEA *PIGGYBACK PLANT*

DIVISION in spring ⅄
PLANTLETS at any time ⅄

Tolmiea menziesii is the only species. Mature plants can easily be divided in spring (*see p.148*). An alternative is to exploit the natural process by which new plantlets form on the leaves, at the point where the blade (lamina) and stalk (petiole) meet – hence the common name. Detach a leaf with plantlet when the plant is in active growth and pot (*see below*) or, in open ground, weigh the leaves onto the soil with stones. After a few months, sever the leaf stalks to detach rooted plantlets as for rooted runners (*see p.150*).

PROPAGATING PIGGYBACK PLANTLETS

1 *Snip off a healthy leaf (here of* Tolmiea menziesii *'Taff's Gold') with a plantlet at the top of the leaf stalk (petiole). Retain ½–1in (1–2.5cm) of the petiole. Fill a 3in (8cm) pot with a mix of equal parts peat and sand.*

2 *Fold down the leaf around the base of the plantlet to meet the petiole. Bury the leaf and petiole so that the plantlet sits just on the surface (see inset) and firm. Water and leave in a light, warm place to root (usually 2–4 weeks).*

TRICYRTIS *Toad lily*

DIVISION in early spring
SEEDS in autumn
CUTTINGS from mid- to late summer

These plants have rhizomes or creeping, rooting stems (stolons). The tough clumps of rhizomes can be lifted and cut apart when dormant (*see p.149*), or rooted stolons may be lifted and detached. Plants may flower in the same year. All species can be raised from seeds. These ripen late in the growing season so are not always available in cold climates. Seeds should be sown immediately and exposed to winter cold (*see p.152*); germination may be delayed. Expect flowers in three years.

One plant may furnish several stems for leaf-bud cuttings (*see p.154 and below*), inserted into a gritty rooting medium. In humid conditions, a bulbil the size of a wheat grain will form in the leaf axil of each cutting before winter, and the leaf will die. In spring, new plants emerge. Pot or plant out to flower in two years.

TAKING STEM CUTTINGS OF TOAD LILIES

1 Toad lilies occasionally produce tiny bulbils in the leaf axils, often forming plantlets (see inset). *To exploit this, take stem cuttings in early summer just as flower buds are beginning to form and the stems (here of* T. hirta*) stiffen. Remove a long, healthy, nonflowering stem.*

2 Discard the soft tip of the stem and divide the remainder into sections, cutting straight across the stem above each leaf node. Each cutting retains one leaf that will provide food for the developing bulbil. Prepare a cell or seed tray with gritty rooting medium.

3 Insert the cuttings so that the leaves sit on the surface and do not touch. Place in a humid, shaded place with gentle bottom heat.

4 The leaves will die away as the cuttings root and bulbils form. New shoots may form before the cuttings become dormant over winter (see inset). *Keep them just moist until spring.*

TRILLIUM

DIVISION after flowering
SEEDS when ripe or in winter
SCORING after flowering

Divide rhizomes into pieces (*see p.149*), each with at least one bud and some roots. They may reestablish slowly. Slice rhizomes of robust species into 1¼–2in (3–5cm) lengths or score them *in situ* (*see below*); side-buds form which may be removed after a year and potted. Sow seeds in pots (*see p.151*) and expose to winter cold. Germination is slow; plants take five years to flower.

SCORING TRILLIUM RHIZOMES
Score around the exposed rhizome, just below the growing point. Dust the cut with fungicide, cover, and leave for a year. Lift the rhizome and detach and pot the offsets (see inset) *singly.*

OTHER PERENNIALS

STROBILANTHES Divide in spring (*see p.148*). Seeds (*p.151*) in spring at 59°F (15°C). Take basal stem or soft stem-tip cuttings (*pp.154 and 156*) in spring.
STROMANTHE Divide in spring (*see p.149*). Seeds (*p.151*) in spring at 70°F (21°C).
STYLOPHORUM Divide after flowering (*see p.148*). Sow seeds (*p.151*) in spring at 59°F (15°C).
SYMPHYANDRA Sow seeds (*see p.151*) in winter and early spring at 59°F (15°C).
SYMPHYTUM Divide (*see p.148*) in spring; only way to increase variegated forms. Seeds (*p.151*) in spring at 50°F (10°C). Take root cuttings (*p.158*) in winter.
TACCA Divide rhizomes in spring (*see p.149*) or when plants start into growth. Surface-sow seeds (*p.151*) in spring at 77°F (25°C).
TANACETUM (syn. *Balsamita, Pyrethrum*) Divide in spring (*see p.148*). Sow seeds (*p.151*) in spring at 50°F (10°C). Take basal stem cuttings in spring.
TELLIMA GRANDIFLORA Divide in spring (*see p.148*). Sow seeds (*p.151*) as soon as ripe.
TETRANEMA Divide in spring (*see p.148*). Sow seeds (*p.151*) as soon as ripe or in spring at 64–70°F (18–21°C).
THERMOPSIS Divide (*see p.149*) in spring or autumn. Soak seeds for 24 hours in cold water, then sow (*see p.151*) in spring at 59°F (15°C); germination often poor.
THLASPI Sow seeds (*p.151*) when ripe or in early spring in pots; keep in a cold frame. Soft stem-tip cuttings (*p.154*) in spring.
THUNBERGIA Sow seeds (*see p.151*) in spring at 70°F (21°C). Take semi-ripe cuttings (*p.154*) in early autumn.
TIARELLA Divide in spring (*see p.149*). Sow seeds (*p.151*) in autumn; keep in a cold frame.
TOWNSENDIA Sow seeds (*see p.164*) as soon as ripe in pots in gritty soil mix; keep in a cold frame. Take rosette cuttings (*p.166*) in spring with as much stem as possible. Often short-lived; propagate regularly.
TRACHELIUM (syn. *Diosphaera*) Sow seeds (*see p.164*) of *T. caeruleum* and alpines in spring at 50°F (10°C). Take softwood cuttings (*p.154*) in spring.
TRIFOLIUM Divide (*see p.148*) or detach rooted stems in spring. Sow seeds in spring at 50°F (10°C) after soaking in cold water for 24 hours (*pp.151–2*).
TROLLIUS Divide after flowering (*see p.148*). Sow seeds (*p.151*) as soon as ripe or in spring; may take two years to germinate.

TROPAEOLUM

Tropaeolum speciosum

DIVISION in spring
SEEDS in autumn to
LAYERING in late winter or in early spring

The most widely grown herbaceous perennial in this genus is the flame nasturtium (*Tropaeolum speciosum*). For annuals *see p.229*; for tuberous-rooted species *see p.278.*

DIVISION

Divide rhizomes before new growth begins (*see p.149*); pull them apart and curl long sections into pots. Small pieces may be treated as root cuttings (*see p.158*). Most *Tropaeolum* resent root disturbance, and success is variable.

SEEDS

Seeds of perennials have short viability, and germination is often erratic. Sow (*see p.151*) as soon as ripe, one seed to a pot to avoid root disturbance. If needed, store seeds in moist peat. Soaking older seeds in cold water for 12–24 hours may improve germination. Keep in a cold frame. Seed-raised plants may take 3–5 years to bloom.

LAYERING

Simple layer (*see p.106*) long shoots, covering them with 1in (2.5cm) of soil.

UNCINIA *HOOK SEDGE*

DIVISION in spring
SEEDS in autumn or in spring

These perennials form clumps, sometimes rhizomatous, that can be carefully divided (*see pp.148–9*). Seeds have short viability; sow them (*see p.152*) still in their husks as soon as they are ripe at a minimum of 59°F (15°C). Plant out the seedlings in the following spring; in cold climates, make sure this is after any risk of late frosts has passed.

VERATRUM

Veratrum album

DIVISION in early spring or in autumn
SEEDS in autumn

Divide rhizomes (*see p.149*) of these plants with care: all parts are toxic, and the sap may irritate skin. Sow the seeds (*see p.151*) as soon as they are ripe, then expose to winter cold. The seedlings may take several years to emerge will develop slowly and take years to flower.

VERBASCUM *MULLEIN*

DIVISION in spring
SEEDS in spring
CUTTINGS in late autumn

Perennials in this genus (syn. *Celsia*) that form substantial clumps, such as *Verbascum nigrum*, can be divided. Cultivars will not come true to type from seeds, but the resulting seedlings may include attractive plants. Short-lived perennials such as *V.* 'Helen Johnson' do not form large clumps; root cuttings offer an alternative to division. (*For annuals and biennials, see p.229.*)

DIVISION

Divide clumps (*see p.148*) before they start into growth, to flower that year.

SEEDS

Sow seeds at 59°F (15°C) to germinate in 10–14 days. Seedlings usually flower in the second year. Some *Verbascum* self-sow freely in the open garden.

CUTTINGS

Lift a plant and take 2in (5cm) root cuttings from healthy, thicker roots (*see p.158*). Place horizontally in a tray of soil mix and pot when rooted in spring. Discard the parent. Container-grown plants may be rooted into a sandbed as for *Eryngium* (*see p.196*). Rooted cuttings flower in the following year.

VERBASCUM 'GAINSBOROUGH'
Rosette-forming perennials, such as this cultivar, occasionally produce offset rosettes. These may be carefully detached and replanted without the need to disturb the parent plant.

VERBENA *VERVAIN*

Verbena 'Sissinghurst'

DIVISION in spring
SEEDS in spring
CUTTINGS in late summer

Most of the species and cultivars in this genus are grown as bedding from seeds, such as *Verbena* x *hybrida* cultivars. Bedding *Verbena* and many other species can be increased by cuttings. Divide fibrous-rooted plants, for example *V. corymbosa* and *V.* 'Homestead Purple'.

DIVISION

Divide mature clumps (*see p.148*) for flowers in the same year. Prostrate stems may root where they touch the soil; the plantlets may be detached, potted, and grown on (*see p.150*).

SEEDS

Sow seeds (*see p.151*) at 70°F (21°C). Germination takes 14 days, and seedlings flower in the same year. *V. bonariensis* (syn. *V. patagonica*) often self-seeds.

CUTTINGS

Take semi-ripe stem-tip cuttings (*see p.154*), from nonflowering growth if possible. At 59°F (15°C), cuttings root within 14 days. Keep the cuttings in bright light and overwinter with cold protection, where necessary.

VERONICA *SPEEDWELL*

DIVISION in early spring or in autumn
SEEDS in spring
CUTTINGS in late spring

Most of the herbaceous perennials in this genus are quite hardy. Protect those with woolly leaves, such as *Veronica bombycina*, from winter moisture. Many have a spreading habit, often rooting from stems, so they respond well to division. All species may be raised from seeds. Take basal stem cuttings from species that flower in summer, such as *V. longifolia*.

DIVISION

Divide small, mat-forming species such as *V. spicata* (*see p.166*) in spring, or detach rooted portions for flowers in the same year. Divide (*see p.148*) early-flowering species (*V. gentianoides*) after flowering to bloom next year. Clumps may be divided into single buds (*see p.150*).

SEEDS

Sow seeds (*see p.151*) at a temperature of 59°F (15°C) and cover very lightly to allow some light to reach the seeds. Cultivars will not breed true to type.

CUTTINGS

Take basal stem cuttings (*see p.156*) when new shoots are 3in (8cm) tall; at 59°F (15°C), they root in two weeks. Take stem cuttings from tall-stemmed plants (*see p.156*). Rooted cuttings may flower in the same season.

VIOLA *PANSY, VIOLET, VIOLA*

Viola tricolor

DIVISION in early spring, or in autumn or late winter
SEEDS in spring or in midsummer
CUTTINGS from late spring to late summer or in autumn
MOUNDING in summer

Perennials in this genus are sometimes short-lived, but most of them are fairly easy to propagate.

DIVISION

Divide (*see p.148*) clumps of *V. odorata* after flowering in early spring. Pull apart *Viola* cultivars into 2–4 pieces. Mat-forming species such as *V. riviniana* are easily divided; they flower the same year if split in autumn or late winter.

SEEDS

Sow seeds (*see p.151*) of most species in early to midspring and keep at 59°F (15°C). Sow winter-flowering pansies in midsummer. Seedlings should appear in 10–14 days; transplant when large enough to handle. Stemless alpines such as *V. jooi* are best left in the seed pans until the following spring, then carefully transplanted. Some species self-sow and hybridize freely. Many violets set viable seeds from insignificant (cleistogamic), greenish flowers, which never open.

CUTTINGS

Named cultivars may be sterile but root well from 1–2in (2.5–5cm) stem-tip cuttings. During flowering, stems of pansy and viola cultivars elongate and become hollow and stem cuttings will not root, so take cuttings in spring from new shoots. Insert them in equal parts of sharp sand and soil at 59°F (15°C); they will root within 14 days. Pot once they show renewed leaf growth.

Alternatively, three weeks before taking cuttings in autumn, cut back plants and take stem-tip cuttings from the regrowth. Keep rooted cuttings frost-free with good light over winter.

MOUNDING

Species may also be top-dressed with gritty soil mix, or mounded (*see below*), to encourage the stems to root. These rooted stems may then be detached, potted and grown on as for cuttings.

MOUNDING A CLUMP OF VIOLA
Work in a mix of equal parts fine grit and peat to cover the bottom half of the shoots in a mature clump (here of Viola cornuta*). Keep moist for 5–6 weeks until the shoots root into the soil mix. Detach the shoots and pot to grow on.*

WAHLENBERGIA

DIVISION in spring
SEEDS in early spring or in late summer
CUTTINGS in spring or in early summer

Often short-lived, perennials in this genus must be regularly propagated. Mat-forming plants may be divided (*see p.167*), and rooted suckers may be detached from *W. gloriosa*. Sow the tiny seeds when ripe or in early spring (*see p.164*) at 59°F (15°C). Take basal stem cuttings from strong new shoots (*see p.166*); root in a free-draining soil mix in a sheltered place such as a cold frame. Take soft stem-tip cuttings (*see p.166*) in summer and root at 59–64°F (15–18°C). Most new plants flower in the first year.

ZANTEDESCHIA *CALLA LILY*

DIVISION in spring
SEEDS in spring

Zantedeschia aethiopica and its cultivars are slightly cold-tolerant, but most species are tender. They form large clumps of tuberous rhizomes, which are easily divided. Of the cultivars, *Z. aethiopica* 'Green Goddess' is the only one that comes true from seeds.

DIVISION

In cold climates, dormant rhizomes of all species can be boxed up in trays of moist sand in a temperature of 59°F (15°C) until the buds begin to swell. When these are visible, cut the rhizomes into pieces, each with at least one bud. Dust the cut surfaces with fungicide. Replace the rhizomes in the sand at the same temperature to root, when they can be potted or planted.

Large clumps of *Z. aethiopica* and of other species and cultivars overwintered *in situ* in warm climates may also be lifted and split just as growth begins (*see p.148*). Divisons flower in the same year.

SEEDS

Sow one seed to a 3in (8cm) pot (*see p.152*) and keep moist at 70°F (21°C) to germinate in a few weeks. Keep the seedlings in active growth as long as possible. Expect flowers in 2–3 years.

ZANTEDESCHIA AETHIOPICA 'CROWBOROUGH'
When planted in moist soil or at pond margins, this calla lily forms large clumps. These may be lifted and divided as for rhizomatous irises (see p.149) *in spring just as they start into growth.*

ZAUSCHNERIA
CALIFORNIA FUCHSIA

DIVISION in spring
SEEDS in spring
CUTTINGS in late spring

Divide (*see p.148*) these plants with great care. Sow seeds (*see p.151*) at a temperature of 59°F (15°C); bottom heat improves germination. Take softwood stem-tip or basal stem cuttings (*see pp.154 and 156*). New plants flower in the first season.

OTHER PERENNIALS

UVULARIA Divide after flowering (*see p.149*). Sow fresh seeds (*p.151*) in autumn; keep in a cold frame; old seeds germinate slowly and erratically.
VALERIANA Divide in spring (*see p.148*). Seeds (*p.151*) in spring at 50°F (10°C). Basal stem cuttings (*p.156*) in spring.
VANCOUVERIA Divide in spring (*see p.149*). Sow ripe seeds (*p.151*); keep in a cold frame.
VERONICASTRUM Divide in spring (*see p.148*). Seeds and cuttings as for *Veronica* (*see facing page*).
WALDSTEINIA Divide after flowering (*see p.149*). Sow seeds (*p.151*) in autumn.
WULFENIA Divide in autumn or early spring into single rosettes, each with roots (*see p.167*). Sow seeds (*p.164*) in early spring in pots at 59°F (15°C).
XEROPHYLLUM Sow fresh seeds in autumn (*see p.151*) and expose to winter cold; germination is slow and erratic.

ANNUALS AND BIENNIALS

Although short-lived, annuals and biennials make rewarding subjects for propagation – with a little effort and in a short space of time, seed-raised plants ranging from creeping mats to climbers can color the summer garden

Annuals naturally germinate, flower, set seeds, and die within one growing season. Biennials produce only foliage in the first year; in the second year they flower, set seeds, and die. Because of the nature of their life cycles, the only way to increase these plants is from seeds.

Fortunately, most annuals and biennials are easy to raise from seeds. The seeds rarely become dormant, as do those of longer-lived plants, so they need no special treatment before sowing. They germinate easily and rapidly, providing a display of color very soon after sowing – some annuals flower within a few weeks.

The method of sowing – in containers or *in situ* – is dictated largely by the hardiness of the plants, the local climate, and how the plants are to be displayed. Annuals and biennials may be grown in their own border, as part of a bedding design, in containers, or as pot plants for greenhouses and conservatories. Biennials need longer-term care than annuals: the seedlings must be grown on for a season and are often raised in nursery beds before planting out.

FERTILIZED FLOWER
*Once pollinated and fertilized, the ovary at the center of a flower of Love-in-a-mist (*Nigella damascena*) swells and changes color. It develops into an attractive inflated seed capsule that can be dried for flower arrangements.*

Annuals and biennials are dedicated to only one means of reproduction, and, if they are suited to the climate, many produce prodigious quantities of seeds and self-sow with ease. Many popular garden species produce seedlings that, if not completely true to type, are nonetheless pleasing. This offers plenty of opportunity for gathering seeds, utilizing self-sown seedlings, trying your hand at hybridizing, or simply allowing the plants to naturalize in the garden.

ELEGANT SEEDHEADS
*Bells of Ireland (*Moluccella laevis*) is named for the large, green calyces that surround the white flowers. As the seeds ripen, the calyces become white and papery.*

SOWING SEEDS

Annual and biennial seeds may be sown under cover or outdoors, depending on their hardiness and local conditions. When buying seeds, you may choose F1 hybrid seeds for their uniformity, but naturally or open-pollinated seeds are usually quite acceptable and less costly. With home-collected seeds, bear in mind that only seeds of species come true to type. Hybrid seeds will differ in varying degrees from the parents.

BUYING SEEDS

If possible, check the date on the packet to make sure that the seeds are from the current season's crop. Seeds are often supplied in foil packets to keep them fresh. Once a packet is opened, the seeds begin to deteriorate, so they are best sown at once. However, if the packet is sealed with tape and kept in cool, dry conditions, most annual and biennial seeds remain viable for a year or more. Seeds of members of the pea family (Fabaceae) last longer. If exposed to moisture, light, or warmth, the seeds' viability will decline rapidly.

Seeds may be bought that are treated (*see right*) to make them easy to handle and to reduce the need for thinning. Some seeds, especially very fine seeds of F1 hybrids, are individually coated to form pellets that are large enough to space evenly when sowing. Water them well after sowing to dissolve the coatings and enable moisture to reach the seeds so they can germinate.

Water-soluble seed tapes work on the same principle. Lay a tape along the bottom of a drill, cover it with soil, and water in. Untreated seeds may be mixed into a gel, supplied in a kit or made from wallpaper paste, for fluid sowing. The gel is squeezed through a bag to distribute seeds evenly along the bottom of a drill (*see also* Vegetables, *p.284*).

Some hybrid seeds that are difficult to germinate may be primed before sale. The germination process has been started but arrested at a critical stage and the seeds dried partially.

SAVING YOUR OWN SEEDS

It is best to take seeds from vigorous, healthy plants with good flowers: these are likely to produce the best seedlings. Deadhead others to prevent them from forming seeds. Gather ripe seeds as soon as the seedpods turn from green to brown or black but before they open and shed their contents. On a dry day, pick the seedheads, either singly or on stalks, and lay them out to dry in a warm place. If they do not open when dry, gently crush pods and capsules to release the seeds (*see below*). Once separated from the chaff, seeds may be stored in packets or envelopes in a cool, dark place, such as a refrigerator (*see below right*), until sowing time. Allow at least 6 weeks to pass before sowing.

WHEN TO SOW ANNUALS AND BIENNIALS

In regions that experience frost, annuals may be started indoors in late winter, spring, or early summer in containers under cover, in temperatures of 55–70°F (13–21°C), according to the genus (*see pp.220–29*), and planted out when all danger of frost is past. They may also be sown direct in the open ground (*see p.218*) in spring where they are to flower, when the soil has warmed up to at least 45°F (7°C). They may also be sown in containers in areas where the open garden soil is heavy and wet, which may cause the seeds to rot.

Biennials are sown under glass or (more commonly) outdoors in a nursery bed from late spring to midsummer, depending on how fast they grow. The seedlings are transplanted in nursery rows to grow on, then planted in their

PURCHASED SEEDS

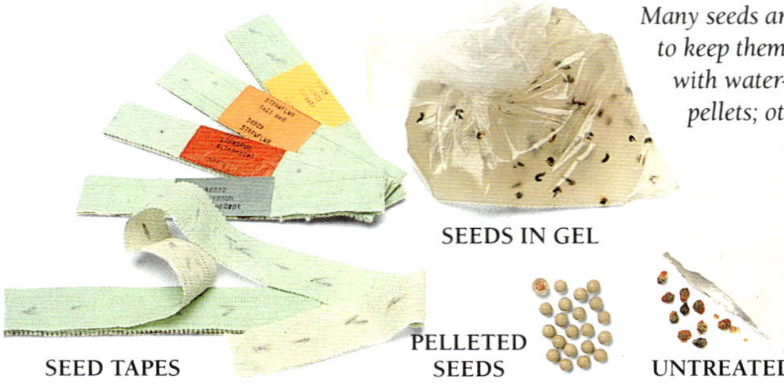

Many seeds are sold in airtight foil packets to keep them fresh. Some seeds are coated with water-soluble clay paste to create pellets; others are embedded in water-soluble tapes. Kits can be used to suspend seeds in gel. Pellets, tapes, and gels enable seeds to be spaced evenly so little thinning is needed.

GATHERING AND STORING SEEDS

SEED CAPSULES *Choose a dry day to gather ripe capsules to ensure the seeds are not damp. If the capsules are open or split, tip or shake the seeds onto a piece of paper for sowing or storing.*

DRYING SEEDHEADS *When seed capsules or pods turn brown, cut them off and place in paper-lined boxes or trays. Leave in a warm, sunny spot until completely dry, then extract the seeds.*

EXTRACTING SEEDS *Place dried seedheads into a sieve and hold over a piece of paper. Gently break up the seedheads; the seeds will fall through the fine mesh, leaving the chaff behind.*

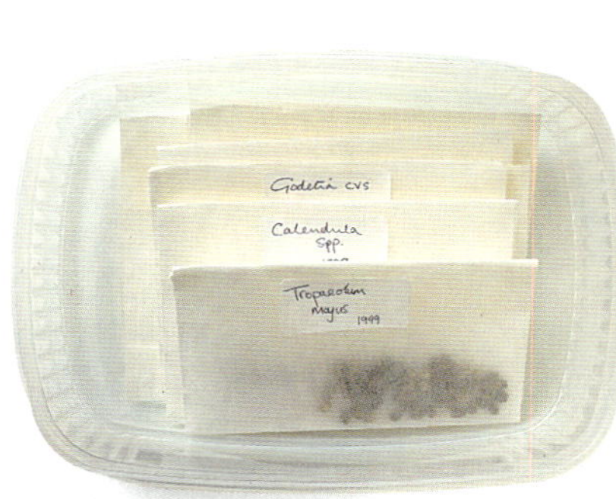

STORING SEEDS *Place cleaned seeds in sealed and labeled paper packets. Store in a plastic box, with a lid, in the bottom of the refrigerator at a temperature of 34–41°F (1–5°C).*

SOWING ANNUAL SEEDS IN A TRAY

1 Prepare a tray with seed soil mix. Stand it in water until the mix surface is moist. Allow to drain thoroughly. Sow the seeds thinly on the surface, tapping them from a fold of paper.

2 Cover all but very fine seeds with a layer of soil mix equal to approximately twice their thickness. Use a sieve to obtain a fine texture. Alternatively, use vermiculite (see below right).

3 Place a piece of glass, plastic, or plastic wrap over the tray to maintain moisture. Cover with netting or newspaper to shade it from direct sun. When germination starts, remove both covers.

Always handle seedlings by leaves

4 When the seedlings (here marigolds) are large enough to handle, gently knock them out of the container. Lift each seedling, keeping as much soil mix around its roots as possible.

5 Transplant each seedling into a prepared container (here a 24-pack), making a hole large enough for the roots. Gently firm the soil mix around the seedling. Water and label.

USING VERMICULITE

Vermiculite allows air and light to reach the seeds, so it is useful for covering seeds that require light to germinate. It also reduces the risk of damping off. Sow as usual in a pot or tray (see step 1) *and cover with ¼in (5mm) of fine-grade vermiculite.*

flowering positions in summer or autumn (*see p.219*).

In warm, frost-free climates, large seeds of annuals and biennials may be sown direct in the open ground as soon as the soil is warm enough, where they are to flower or in nursery beds. Fine or expensive seeds are better sown in containers, where growing conditions are more easily controlled, as are seeds of less vigorous plants. Make successive sowings for outdoor plantings to achieve a longer flowering season.

Sowing in containers

Pots, pans, seed trays, and cell packs are suitable, depending on the amount or type of seeds to be sown. Too large a container wastes space and soil mix; one too small can lead to thick sowing, causing damping off (*see p.46*) and weak seedlings. Large seeds may be sown in rockwool cells to create plug plants. Degradable pots are useful for plants that dislike root disturbance.

To prepare the container, fill it to its brim with seed soil mix (*see p.34*). Tap the container to get rid of any air pockets. Firm a soil-based mix reasonably well with your fingertips, particularly in the corners, before leveling the surface to about ¼in (5mm) below the rim, using a flat wooden board or presser. Firm soilless mix only very lightly before leveling. Thoroughly moisten the soil mix by standing the container in water or watering it overhead using a watering can fitted with a fine rose. Add a suitable fungicide to the water to avoid damping off. Allow the container to drain.

Sow seeds straight from the packet, a fold of paper, or your palm. Tap gently to release the seeds slowly, and sow thinly and evenly over the soil mix. Space-sow large or pelleted seeds one by one. Mix tiny seeds with equal parts of fine, dry sand to ensure even sowing.

No covering is necessary for fine seeds sown with sand – just press the seeds into the soil mix surface with a presser or empty container of the same size. Cover other seeds with a layer of soil mix or fine-grade vermiculite (*see above*) to keep the seeds in contact with the moist mix. If the covering layer is dry, moisten it with a mist-sprayer. Stop the mix from drying out by covering the container with plastic wrap or a sheet of glass or plastic or by placing it in a closed case. If necessary, shade the container from direct sun.

Germinating the seeds

The temperature and light needed for germination varies according to the genus (*see pp.220–29*). In cool climates, a heated closed case on the greenhouse bench is ideal, but a windowsill in a warm room suffices for a wide range of annuals. Check the container regularly and remove the lid or coverings as soon as germination occurs. Place the container in full light, but shade the seedlings from strong sun. Keep the soil mix moist at all times to maintain steady growth until the seedlings are ready to transplant.

Transplanting the seedlings

Container-raised seedlings should be transplanted into larger containers before they become overcrowded so they have room to develop before being planted in their flowering positions. The seedlings will suffer less of a check in growth if transplanted as soon as they can be handled, even if they are quite small (*continued on p.218*).

Sowing in a degradable pot

Sow three seeds in a 2in (5cm) degradable pot. Water and label. When seedlings appear, thin to one per pot. Plant out the entire pot when the seedlings are established.

PREPARING THE GROUND FOR SOWING

1 Remove all debris and weeds from dug soil. Firm the whole area by shuffling forward with both feet together, until it is flat and free of air pockets. Pay particular attention to edges.

2 Rake over the area in all directions to create a fine tilth, ready for sowing. This especially helps broadcast seeds settle between the fine furrows. If the soil is dry, water it thoroughly.

SOWING SEEDS IN ROWS IN A BORDER

1 First use stakes or twine to mark out a grid on the seedbed. Then sprinkle grit or sand on the soil to mark out the sowing areas; using a bottle (see inset) *will control the flow of sand. Alternatively, score the soil with a stick.*

2 Using a line of string or a stake as a guide, draw out drills about 1in (2.5cm) deep with a hoe in each sowing area. Scatter the seeds thinly and evenly along the drill (see inset). *Space-sow pelleted or large seeds individually.*

3 Carefully rake the soil back over the drills without dislodging the seeds. Firm with the back of the rake. Label each sowing area and water with a watering can fitted with a fine rose.

4 Initially, the seedlings may look sparse and appear to be growing in regimented patterns, but they will soon blend together to form a dense and informal planting.

(*Continued from p.217*) Seedlings grown on in cell packs are easy to handle and suffer little check to growth when planted out. Other suitable containers are biodegradable and plastic pots up to 3½in (9cm) in size, and deep seed trays. Seedlings that are destined to be grown in pots should be transplanted first into 3½in (9cm) pots, then potted on into 5–7in (13–18cm) pots.

To transplant seedlings, first water the container and allow it to drain. Tap the container on a hard surface, which should loosen the soil mix so it can be removed intact. Lift out each seedling by inserting a thin stake or similar tool under the root system, taking care not to cause it any damage. Always hold a seedling by the leaves to avoid bruising stems or growing tips.

Make a hole in the soil mix of the prepared container that is large enough to accommodate the roots and stem so that the seed leaves sit just above the soil mix. Firm in each seedling gently. Space the seedlings 1½–2in (4–5cm) apart or one to each cell. Keep any smaller seedlings at one end of the tray so that they do not need to compete with stronger ones and have a better chance of developing evenly.

Water the seedlings with a fine-rosed can to settle the roots. Place in slightly warmer conditions to help them to establish quickly. Keep them watered and, in sunny weather, shade with newspaper or netting to avoid scorch.

HARDENING OFF SEEDLINGS

New plants raised under cover in cool climates will have relatively soft growth, so they need to be gradually acclimatized to outdoor conditions, or hardened off (*see p.45*), for a couple of weeks before planting out. Hardened frost-tender annuals may be planted out once all danger of frost has passed. If conditions prevent planting out, pot on the plants or feed regularly so they continue to develop healthily.

SOWING SEEDS OUTDOORS

Annuals may be sown outdoors in prepared borders, in gaps in established borders, or in nursery beds for cutting or transplanting. Biennials are usually sown in nursery beds. Avoid very fertile soil; it promotes leaf growth at the expense of flower production. Most annuals and biennials prefer a sunny site.

Prepare the soil well before sowing, when the surface is sufficiently dry so that footwear remains clean and there is no danger of overcompaction. If the soil is lacking in nutrients, apply a balanced fertilizer at 2oz/sq. yd (70g/sq. m) or use a liquid fertilizer during growth. Immediately before sowing, when the soil is moist but not waterlogged, prepare the soil surface (*see above left*).

MARKING OUT A BORDER

In a border, annuals are best grown in bold, informal groups. Make a plan before sowing, giving consideration to height, habit, and flower color. Bear in mind that larger annuals need more sowing space than smaller ones.

Divide the sowing area into a grid to help transfer the plan accurately to the ground, then mark out drills at the appropriate spacings in each section (*see left*). Alternatively, make drills spaced 6–9in (15–23cm) apart throughout the whole area before marking out the plan, or broadcast-sow each section.

SOWING SEEDS IN DRILLS

Although rows of seedlings may initially seem too formal, they are easier to weed, being readily distinguished from weed seedlings, and to thin (*see facing page*).

Using the corner of a hoe, draw out the drills, usually 3–6in (8–15cm) apart, depending on the eventual size of the plant. Alternatively, press a long stake or the back of a rake firmly into the soil.

In practice, sowing depth is not too critical, but drills should be no more than 1in (2.5cm) deep. They should also be of a uniform depth for even germination. Make the drills less deep on heavy clay soil. If the soil is very dry, soak each drill before sowing.

Sow the seeds by hand or fluid-sow them along the drills, then cover (*see facing page*). Sow old seeds more thickly, because the germination rate is likely to be low. If there is no prospect of rain, water in the seeds well with spray from a fine-rosed watering can. Keep the soil moist and weed-free to obtain the best rate of germination.

Broadcast-sowing seeds

This method (*see below*) is best used when sowing among other plants, for example in gaps in borders. Weeding can be more difficult in the early stages, since a hoe cannot be used. Sow the seeds thinly on the prepared surface and rake them in lightly to keep them in contact with the soil. Label and water in well.

Thinning seedlings

Even with the most careful sowing, seedlings will need thinning (*see below left*) to avoid overcrowding. Many annuals shed copious amounts of seeds, so self-sown seedlings may also need thinning. The best time to thin is when the soil is moist and the weather mild. If the final spacing is 8in (20cm) or more, thin in several stages so the growing seedlings protect each other.

Use the strongest thinnings to fill sparse areas caused by uneven sowing or poor germination, or transplant elsewhere in the garden. Annuals with taproots such as *Clarkia*, *Gypsophila*, and poppies do not transplant well. After thinning, water in gently but well.

Nursery beds

Biennials are often raised in outdoor nursery beds and transplanted to their flowering positions when large enough (*see below*). It is usual to sow the seeds from late spring to midsummer; transplant them in summer to another nursery bed to grow on. In autumn, the young plants are transferred to their flowering positions. Annuals may also be raised in nursery beds for cutting.

Protecting outdoor sowings

Before and after germination, it may be necessary to protect annuals and biennials against rodents, birds, or cats. Lay twiggy sticks over the soil surface. Alternatively, construct a cage using wire netting (*see p.45*). Bend the edges down so that the netting is held above the emerging seedlings. You can protect autumn-sown annuals and biennials against cold or excess moisture by using cloches (*see p.39*).

BROADCAST-SOWING SEEDS

*1 Use a rake to give the soil a fine tilth (*see facing page*). Scatter the seeds thinly and evenly over the prepared seedbed by hand, with a seed sower, or straight from the packet.*

2 Rake over the area at right angles to cover the seeds: use light strokes so that they are disturbed as little as possible. Label the area. Water the soil using a fine-rosed watering can.

THINNING ANNUAL AND BIENNIAL SEEDLINGS

Individual seedlings *To thin seedlings in drills (here of larkspur), press down on the soil around the strongest seedlings, while pulling out the unwanted, weaker ones. Refirm and water.*

Seedling groups *Lift clumps of seedlings (here of sweet William). Separate them, retaining plenty of soil around the roots of each seedling. Replant singly into the bed at even spacings.*

RAISING BIENNIAL SEEDLINGS

1 Sow biennials (here wallflowers) in drills in a prepared seedbed; keep them well-watered. In a month or so, when the seedlings are 2–3in (5–8cm) tall, lift them using a hand fork.

2 Plant out the seedlings in a nursery bed 6–8in (15–20cm) apart, in rows 8–12in (20–30cm) apart. Allow space in each planting hole for the roots. Firm in, label, and water.

3 In autumn, when the new plants are growing well, water the nursery bed if it is dry, then carefully lift the plants. Transplant them to their flowering positions, in well-prepared soil.

A–Z OF ANNUALS AND BIENNIALS

Seeds germinate in either light or darkness unless specified. For perennials grown as annuals, see A–Z of Perennials (pp.186–213).

AGERATUM *FLOSS FLOWER*

SEEDS from late winter to early spring

The annuals in this genus may become naturalized in gardens and in the wild in subtropical and tropical climates. The seeds are produced in a papery seed capsule and are easily extracted (*see p.216*) when ripe.

A germination temperature in the region of 70°F (21°C) is required, and the seeds should take five days to germinate in light. Transplant the seedlings if necessary within seven to ten days. Floss flowers usually take 12 weeks or more to reach flowering size.

AMBERBOA *SWEET SULTAN*

SEEDS from early to midspring or in autumn

The seeds of these annuals and biennials are carried in papery seedheads and are fairly large and easily handled. They germinate at 70°F (21°C) within ten days of sowing in darkness. Seedlings are transplanted, if necessary, within a similar period.

Transplant all seedlings sown in containers into pots or cells (*see p.217*) to avoid root disturbance when planting out. In cold climates, autumn sowings need protection under cover. Amberboas flower in 12–14 weeks.

BRACHYSCOME

SWAN RIVER DAISY

SEEDS from midwinter to early spring

Collect seeds from the papery, disklike seedheads of the annuals in this genus (syn. *Brachycome*) as for *Helianthus* (*see p.224*), and dry them before storing (*see p.216*).

Surface-sow the seeds (*see p.217*), because light is necessary for a good rate of germination. This usually takes 15 days at a temperature of 70°F (21°C). Swan river daisies should flower 12–14 weeks after sowing.

AMARANTHUS

SEEDS from mid- to late spring

The annuals and short-lived perennials in this genus are wind-pollinated and often hybridize and seed about very freely. In some climates, *Amaranthus* can be invasive, but self-sown seedlings are easily removed or transplanted as for *Digitalis* (*see p.223*).

The tassel-like flowers are followed by brightly colored seedheads. Small seeds are carried deep within the tassel and cannot normally be seen. The best way to collect the seeds is to "milk" the tassels (*see below*). Alternatively, remove the flowerheads, place them in a paper-lined box, and leave in a warm, dry place for a week or so until the seeds fall out.

Clean the glossy black or pink seeds by tossing them in a bowl and gently blowing off the chaff as it rises to the top; the seeds will fall to the bottom.

Most *Amaranthus* germinate at 70°F (21°C) in ten days, but Chinese spinach (*A. tricolor*) requires a minimum of 77°F (25°C). If needed, transplant the seedlings within seven days (*see below*). If they are transplanted at a later stage, the plants will not be vigorous and will probably flower prematurely instead of after the usual 12 or more weeks.

Love-lies-bleeding (*A. caudatus*) may be sown outdoors where they are to flower in midspring; thin the seedlings to 2ft (60cm) apart.

▲ AMARANTHUS SEEDLINGS
Prick out Amaranthus *seedlings as soon as they have two or four leaves. If the seedlings are disturbed at a later stage, the new plants will not thrive.*

◀ GATHERING SEEDS
When the flowers (here of Amaranthus caudatus*) begin to change color (here from deep red to yellow), the seeds are ripe. Hold a tray beneath the flowerhead and gently "milk" the tassels so that the seeds* (see inset) *fall into the tray.*

OTHER ANNUALS AND BIENNIALS

ADLUMIA FUNGOSA Sow as soon as ripe in sheltered place or outdoors (*see p.229*).
ADONIS Sow as for *Centaurea* (*see p.222*).
AGROSTEMMA Sow as for *Nigella* (*see p.228*); flowers best in poor soil.
AGROSTIS Sow as for *Briza* (*see p.221*).
AIRA Sow as for *Briza* (*see p.221*).
ALCEA Sow as for biennial *Dianthus* (*see p.223*).
AMMI Sow as for *Centaurea* (*see p.222*).
ANCHUSA Sow seeds of annuals and biennials as for *Ageratum* (*see above*). *A. capensis* is best sown direct.
ANGELICA Sow seeds of biennials as soon as they are ripe; light and a temperature of 50–60°F (10–15.5°C) are needed for germination. Transplant seedlings as soon as they are large enough to handle; older seedlings resent root disturbance. Self-sown *A. archangelica* seedlings come fairly true. (*See also* Culinary Herbs, *p.290.*)
ANODA Sow as for *Gaillardia* (*see p.224*).
ANTHRISCUS Sow annuals and biennials as for *Centaurea* (*see p.222*). Sow direct in well-drained soil.
ARGEMONE Sow as for *Tagetes* (*see p.229*).
ASPERULA Sow as for *Centaurea* (*see p.222*).
ATRIPLEX Sow as for *Centaurea* (*see p.222*), but successively from spring to early summer.
BAILEYA Sow as for *Centaurea* (*see p.222*).
BARBAREA Sow seeds (*see p.219*) of biennials as soon as they are ripe.
BASSIA Sow as for *Callistephus* (*see p.221*).
BORAGO Sow as for *Centaurea* (*see p.222*).
BROMUS Sow seeds direct outdoors in spring at 50°F (10°C).
CALOMERIA (syn. *Humea*) Sow as for *Cleome* (*see p.222*), but as soon as the seeds are ripe.

BRACTEANTHA
STRAWFLOWER

Bracteantha bracteata cultivar

SEEDS in early to late spring

The annuals take 16–20 weeks to flower. Seeds are produced in a large, papery seedhead and are easily removed (*see p.216*) when dry. Although the seeds are fairly large, do not cover them with more than their own depth of soil mix or vermiculite because they need light to germinate. This takes five days at 70°F (21°C). Transplant the seedlings, if necessary, within seven to ten days.

BRASSICA

SEEDS from early to midspring

The commonly grown ornamental cabbages or kales (*B. oleracea* cultivars) belong to this genus. They are quite cold-hardy and are grown as biennials or annuals. Seeds are easily removed from the dried heads (*see p.216*) and will germinate rapidly at 70°F (21°C), in five days. If necessary, transplant the seedlings (*see p.217*) within seven days. Ornamental cabbages mature in approximately 16 weeks. (*See also* Vegetables, *p.296*.)

BRIZA QUAKING GRASS

SEEDS in early autumn or midspring

Collect the seeds of annual grasses in this genus as soon as the decorative seedheads become fully ripened (*see below*). Germination requires a temperature of 60°F (15.5°C) and takes 12 days. If necessary, transplant the seedlings (*see p.217*) within 10–14 days. Seedling grasses generally flower within 14 weeks.

GATHERING QUAKING GRASS SEEDS
Gently pull the seedhead (here of Briza minor*) through one hand so that the seeds fall into a bag beneath. (Clean plastic bags are fine for gathering, but not for storing, seeds.)*

BROWALLIA AMETHYST VIOLET, BUSH VIOLET

SEEDS from early to late spring or in late summer

The seeds of the annuals in this genus take 15 days to germinate. Surface-sow the seeds, because light is necessary for good germination. Kept at a temperature of 70°F (21°C), the seeds should germinate in 10–14 days. Plants flower in 16 weeks.

CALCEOLARIA POUCH FLOWER, SLIPPER FLOWER

SEEDS in spring or midsummer

There are perennials, biennials, and annuals in this genus. To extract the fine seeds, crush the rounded seed capsules (*see p.216*). Sow annuals in spring and biennial seeds in midsummer to obtain flowers in the following spring and early summer. The seeds require light and a temperature of 70°F (21°C) to germinate in 15 days. If needed, transplant seedlings in seven to ten days.

Flowering takes up to 36 weeks, but the Anytime Series flowers in 16 weeks at any time of year in suitable climates. (*See also* Perennials, *p.190*.)

CALENDULA ENGLISH MARIGOLD, POT MARIGOLD

Calendula officinalis 'Art Shades'

SEEDS in early to midspring or in autumn

Annuals in this genus are quite hardy and self-sow freely: seedlings of cultivars do not come true, but the variations may be acceptable. Transplant self-sown seedlings as for *Digitalis* (*see p.223*). Take care to preserve all viable parts of the large seeds when collecting them (*see below*).

Seeds are best direct-sown outdoors (*see p.218*) at a temperature of 70°F (21°C); they germinate in ten days in darkness. If needed, transplant seedlings in seven days. Protect autumn sowings from severe cold in colder climates. Calendulas flower in 10–12 weeks.

STRUCTURE OF CALENDULA SEEDS
Calendula *seeds frequently break into three parts when they are gathered or while they are stored. Each part can be sown as a viable seed, so take care not to discard them with the chaff.*

CALLISTEPHUS
CHINA ASTER

Callistephus chinensis Pompon Series

SEEDS in early to late spring or in early summer

The single species of *Callistephus* and its cultivars are annuals. Sow seeds outdoors in midspring at 50–60°F (10–15.5°C) after the last frosts, or raise plants under cover in containers (*see p.217*). Sow in the early summer to obtain autumn-flowering plants. Most China asters bloom for a fairly short time, so make successive sowings for a longer period of flowering.

The seeds are fairly large but should not be covered with more than their own depth of soil or soil mix. Germination takes eight days at 70°F (21°C); transplant seedlings, if necessary, within another seven to ten days. Flowers appear about 20 weeks after sowing.

CAMPANULA
BELLFLOWER

SEEDS in late spring to early summer or in autumn

Canterbury bells (*Campanula medium*) is a showy biennial. The seeds are carried in a rounded seed capsule, concealed in the calyx at the base of the flower. It is easier to crush the entire capsule and sow the results than sort out the tiny seeds from the chaff.

Surface-sow the seeds (*see p.217*), because they need light to germinate. This takes 20 days at 70°F (21°C). Transplant seedlings within four weeks as soon as they are large enough to handle, for flowers in 12 months. In regions with very mild winters, sow direct in autumn for spring flowers. (*See also* Perennials, *p.191*.)

BIENNIAL CAMPANULA SEEDLINGS
Grow on seedlings (here Campanula medium*) in nursery beds for the first season while they put on vegetative growth (*see above*). Plant out into their flowering positions in autumn.*

CAPSICUM *Pepper*

SEEDS in mid- to late spring

The annuals are mainly cultivated crops, but some with brightly colored fruits are also used ornamentally. The flat seeds are produced in fleshy fruits. To collect them in summer, slowly dry some ripe peppers to allow the seeds to mature, then extract the seeds. Wear gloves to avoid irritating the skin. (*See also* Vegetables, *p.298.*)

Sow the seeds the following spring at a temperature of 70°F (21°C). Germination takes ten days; if needed, transplant seedlings within a week. The plants start fruiting in 16–20 weeks.

CLARKIA

Clarkia 'Brilliant'

SEEDS in early spring or autumn

Seeds of these taprooted annuals (syn. *Godetia*) are carried in capsules that soon scatter the seeds once they are ripe. Sow direct (*see p.218*) to avoid disturbing the roots. At 70°F (21°C), seeds germinate in five days. Protect autumn-sown seedlings over winter where marginally hardy (*see p.39*). *Clarkia amoena* seeds come fairly true. Flowers in 12 weeks.

CLEOME *Spider flower*

SEEDS in midspring

Only annuals in this genus are usually cultivated. The very tender *Cleome hassleriana* (syn. *C. pungens*, *C. spinosa*) and its cultivars are most popular.

Sow seeds (*see p.217*) at about 70°F (21°C). They should germinate in ten days, but germination sometimes can be erratic. If this is the case, wait until the first seedlings have two true leaves before transplanting. Seedlings that are raised under cover are best grown on individually in 3½in (9cm) pots to prevent root disturbance when planting them out. Plants flower in 16–18 weeks.

CELOSIA *Cockscomb*

SEEDS from midspring to early summer

Cultivars of *Celosia argentea* are grown as annuals. Dry the feathery plumes of the seedheads and shake out the seeds over clean paper.

Germination takes ten days at a temperature of 70°F (21°C). Transplant seedlings within seven days, if needed. If sowing seeds in containers (*see p.217*), do not allow the seedlings to become too established before transplanting, because they do not like root disturbance. Pot the seedlings individually into small 3½in (9cm) pots. The plants take 12–14 weeks to flower.

CENTAUREA *Knapweed*

Centaurea cyanus

SEEDS in early spring

Of the annuals and biennials, the annual cornflower (*Centaurea cyanus*) and its cultivars are most popular. Self-sown seedlings come fairly true; treat as for *Digitalis* (*see facing page*). The largish seeds are easily extracted and are best sown direct (*see p.218*) to flower in 12 weeks. They germinate in ten days at 64°F (18°C) in darkness. If necessary, transplant seedlings (*see p.217*) in 10–14 days.

CHRYSANTHEMUM

SEEDS from early to late spring or in autumn

Some annuals in this genus are quite hardy. Sow the large seeds in early spring in containers (*see p.217*) or direct in late spring for flowers in 12–14 weeks. In frost-free areas, sow direct (*see p.218*) in autumn for early flowering. Seeds germinate in 11 days at 70°F (21°C). Transplant, if needed, in seven to ten days. (*See also* Perennials, *p.192.*)

CONVOLVULUS *Bindweed*

SEEDS from early to late spring

The most commonly grown annual in this large genus is *Convolulus tricolor* (syn. *C. minor*) and its cultivars. The seeds form in a rounded seed capsule. Convolvulus flowers 12–14 weeks after sowing outdoors.

If starting the seeds under cover (*see p.217*), the large seeds may be sown singly in plug trays of rockwool (*see below*) instead of soil mix for minimum root disturbance when transplanting. Seeds germinate at 70°F (21°C) in about five days.

If needed, transplant the seedlings (*see p.217*) within seven days. For seedlings raised in rockwool, simply drop the plug into the center of a preformed rockwool block so the roots can grow into the block without check.

SOWING CONVOLVULUS SEEDS IN ROCKWOOL

1 *Large seeds such as those of* Convolvulus tricolor *may be sown in a tray of rockwool plugs. Stand the tray in a drip tray and soak the rockwool with water. Allow to stand for 30 minutes, then drain off the excess.*

2 *To sow the seeds, make a hole about ¼in (5mm) deep in the center of each rockwool plug, using a small tool. Drop one seed into each prepared plug.*

3 *Push a little wad of loose rockwool fiber into each hole to fill it, making sure that there is no air space left above the seed. The dry fiber will absorb moisture from the rockwool plug. Label and place in a warm bright place.*

4 *The seedlings should reach the seed-leaf stage in 10–14 days* (see above)*. Grow them on until the roots show through the rockwool. Then plant out as rockwool plugs or pot into a rockwool block* (see inset).

CONSOLIDA *Larkspur*

SEEDS in early and late spring or in autumn

The seeds of these self-sowing annuals are poisonous and are produced in a long seedpod. They are best sown direct outdoors (*see p.217*). Successive sowings are recommended to provide a long season of flowering, especially when cut flowers are required. Autumn sowings will give flowers in late spring, but in colder areas protect seedlings over winter.

Seeds sown at 55°F (13°C) take 20 days to germinate. If necessary, transplant the seedlings (*see p.217*) within seven to ten days. Flowers appear in 12–16 weeks.

COREOPSIS *Tickseed*

SEEDS from early spring to early summer

The annuals in this genus self-sow. Seeds form in papery, disklike heads and are easily removed when dry, as for *Helianthus* (*see p.224*). When sown, they take five days to germinate at a temperature of 70°F (21°C) in light.

Transplant the seedlings (*see p.217*), if necessary, as soon as they are large enough to handle. The plants should come into flower within 12–16 weeks. *Coreopsis tinctoria* (syn. *Calliopsis tinctoria*) prefers sandy soil.

DIANTHUS *Pink, Carnation*

SEEDS in late spring and early summer

The annuals and biennials in this genus naturally hybridize very readily, so there is often a good deal of variation, often quite pleasing, in seedlings from home-collected seeds (*see p.216*). Many *Dianthus* are also good subjects for deliberate hybridizing (*see p.21*). Seeds are formed in a capsule.

Sow seeds outdoors (*see p.218*) at a temperature of 70°F (21°C); germination takes five days. Biennials flower 12 months after sowing, but some can be sown as annuals; annuals flower in 16 weeks. (*See also* Perennials, *p.193*.)

DIGITALIS *Foxglove*

SEEDS in late spring

The deep, tubular flowers of foxgloves attract nectar-seeking bees, which pollinate the plant. Seeds are produced in great quantity in papery capsules to enable the foxgloves to self-sow with ease. Self-sown seedlings can be lifted and transplanted (*see below*).

Cultivars come reasonably true to type although there is some, usually pleasing, variation. Collect the ripe, brown seed capsules just before they split and release the seeds. These, like all parts of the plant, are poisonous, so take care when sorting and cleaning them (*see p.216*).

Biennial foxgloves require a temperature of 70°F (21°C) in light to germinate; this should take 20 days. If needed, transplant seedlings within seven days.

Seedlings with dark stems are more likely to have purple flowers. Some cultivars flower 20 weeks after sowing, but usually they flower the following year in late spring and early summer.

SELF-SOWN SEEDLINGS

1 Foxgloves (here Digitalis purpurea*) readily self-sow around the garden. Seed capsules form along each flower spike in early or midsummer and, when ripe, they split open to shed copious amounts of small seeds.*

2 Look for seedlings at the foot of the parent plants in late summer or early autumn. Choose a cool, damp day to avoid drying out the seedlings' roots, and transplant those with at least four leaves into better flowering positions.

3 Lift the seedlings with a hand trowel so that each retains a good ball of soil around its roots. This protects the roots from damage and ensures that the seedlings establish rapidly.

4 Transplant the seedlings at least 12in (30cm) apart. Replant each seedling at the same depth as before, with its roots well spread out. Firm it in gently, water, and label.

OTHER ANNUALS AND BIENNIALS

CARTHAMUS Sow annuals as for *Centaurea* (*see p.222*); biennials as for *Callistephus* (*see p.221*).
CENTAURIUM (syn. *Erythraea*) Sow annuals and biennials at 50°F (10°C) when seeds ripen or in midautumn.
CEPHALIPTERUM Sow as for *Bracteantha* (*see p.221*).
CHIRITA Sow seeds of annuals (*see p.217*) in succession from late winter to spring, at 66–75°F (19–24°C).
CLADANTHUS Sow as for *Callistephus* (*see p.221*).
COIX Sow as for *Zinnia* (*see p.229*).
COLLINSIA Sow as for *Clarkia* (*see p.222*). Thin autumn sowings in spring. Self-sown *C. bicolor* seedlings come fairly true; seeds are best sown direct.
COLLOMIA Sow as for *Clarkia* (*see facing page*).
COTULA Surface-sow (*see p.217*) seeds of annuals at 55–64°F (13–18°C) in spring.
CREPIS Sow seeds of annuals (*see p.218*) as soon as the seeds ripen at 50–59°F (10–15°C).
CYNOGLOSSUM Sow seeds of annuals and biennials outdoors in midspring. Needs light to germinate. *C. amabile* is best sown direct.
DIMORPHOTHECA Sow as for *Brachyscome* (*see p.220*), but cover the seeds with soil mix.

DOROTHEANTHUS

ICE PLANT, LIVINGSTONE DAISY

SEEDS from early to midspring

Seeds of these annuals are produced in a fleshy capsule that should be dried thoroughly before removing the fine seeds. Sow them at a temperature of 70°F (21°C) for germination in ten days and flowers in 16 weeks. Transplant the seedlings, if needed, in seven to ten days. In colder regions, if sowing in containers under cover (*see p.217*), harden the seedlings well (*see pp.218 and 45*) before planting them out.

ERYSIMUM *WALLFLOWER*

SEEDS in late spring or early summer

The few annual and biennial species produce seeds freely in long pods. They are easily removed once the pods have been dried (*see p.216*) and have split open. Sow the seeds at 70°F (21°C) to germinate in five days. When transplanting the seedlings (*see p.219*), trim the taproots to promote formation of fibrous roots to help plants establish more easily after planting. (*See also* Perennials, *p.196*.)

GAILLARDIA

BLANKET FLOWER

SEEDS in early spring

The annuals in this genus bloom heavily. The seeds, produced in papery cases, are fairly large and easily handled. Sow in containers in colder climates (*see p.217*). Germination takes 20 days at a temperature of 70°F (21°C). Seedlings are transplanted, if necessary, within seven to ten days. Plants flower in 16 weeks. (*See also* Perennials, *p.197*.)

GYPSOPHILA *BABY'S BREATH*

Gypsophila elegans

SEEDS in early to mid-spring

The annuals in this genus are easy to propagate from seeds; germination can take up to ten days. They are best sown direct (*see p.218*) because they do not transplant well. Sow at 70°F (21°C). If necessary, transplant the seedlings as soon as they are large enough to handle. The annuals flower in 12–15 weeks. (*See also* Perennials, *p.199*.)

HELIANTHUS *SUNFLOWER*

SEEDS from late winter to early spring

The flowerheads of the annuals in this genus are often large and can be 12in (30cm) or more across. The large seeds form in a disklike seedhead in the center of the flower and are easily extracted (*see below*). Bear in mind, however, that the cultivars hybridize very freely and therefore may not come true from collected seeds. Sunflowers are worth experimenting with to create new hybrids (*see p.21*).

Sunflowers resent root disturbance, so sow direct (*see p.218*) or singly in pots (*see p.217*) or rockwool plugs (*see* Convolvulus, *p.222*). Germination is reliable and takes five days at an optimum temperature of 70°F (21°C). If transplanting is necessary, carry out within seven days and replant a little deeper than before to support the seedling stems. Sunflowers bloom in 16–20 weeks. (*See also* Perennials, *p.200*.)

EXTRACTING RIPE SEEDS

1 *In late summer or early autumn, choose a sunflower head (here of* Helianthus annuus*) that is about to go over and cut it off. Carefully rub off the chaff from among the ripe seeds in the center of the flowerhead.*

2 *Grip the flowerhead firmly in both hands and bend it so that the seed mass opens up slightly. Hold the flowerhead over a clean sheet of paper and stroke it firmly with one hand. The seeds should pop out and fall onto the paper.*

ESCHSCHOLZIA *CALIFORNIA POPPY*

SEEDS from early to late spring and in early autumn

The annuals are quite hardy and produce seeds very freely, so self-sown seedlings that are fairly true to type readily arise. They do not transplant well, however, so it is best to gather the seeds before they are scattered (*see below*). Sow the seeds direct outdoors (*see p.218*).

Germination usually takes ten days at a temperature of 60°F (15.5°C). Carefully transplant seedlings singly, if necessary, within seven days. Sow successive batches of seed for a prolonged flower display. In colder climates, protect autumn-sown seedlings in winter. California poppies generally flower in 12–16 weeks.

GATHERING CALIFORNIA POPPY SEEDHEADS

UNRIPE SEEDHEADS *To gather the seeds, remove the long, thin pods as soon as they turn color from green to brown in early to midsummer, before they burst open and scatter the seeds.*

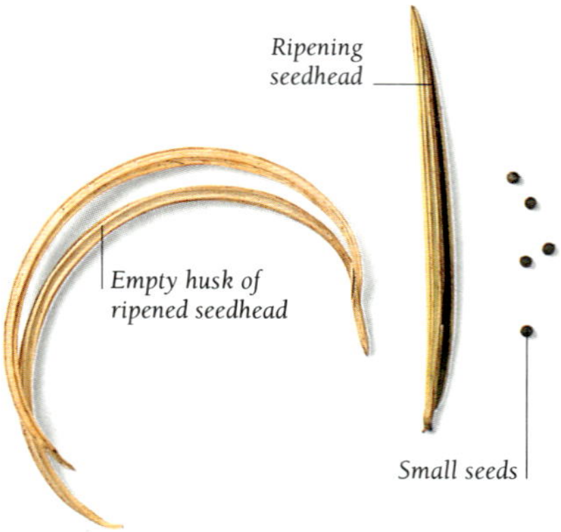

RIPE SEEDHEADS *As each capsule dries in the sun, tension builds up within its walls. Eventually, the capsule explodes, ejecting the seeds with great force to disperse them as far from the parent plant as possible.*

IBERIS *Candytuft*

Iberis amara

SEEDS from early spring to early summer or in autumn

The annuals in this genus produce great quantities of seeds in pods after flowering in spring or summer. Sow the seeds outdoors (*see p.218*) in successive batches for a long and continuous display, and in autumn for early flowering in the following year. The seeds germinate readily in eight days at a temperature of 70°F (21°C). Candytuft plants take 12–16 weeks to flower.

IPOMOEA *Morning glory*

SEEDS from midspring to early summer

The climbing annuals, which are most often grown from this genus, are quite tender. The seeds, produced in rounded capsules, are large and easily handled but are toxic if ingested. Soak them in tepid water for 24 hours before sowing and keep them at a temperature of 64°F (18°C) to ensure good germination. This usually takes five days.

Sow the seeds singly in containers (*see p.218*) in cool climates, outdoors in warm climates. If needed, transplant the seedlings in seven days. Morning glories (syn. *Mina, Pharbitis*) like a fertile soil mix. They flower in 16 weeks.

IPOMOEA TRICOLOR 'HEAVENLY BLUE'
Morning glories, once germinated, require a minimum temperature of 45°F (7°C) and fertile soil; they flower abundantly during summer.

IMPATIENS *Balsam, Busy Lizzie*

SEEDS from early to late spring

The annuals range from very tender species such as *Impatiens balsamina* to hardier ones such as *I. glandulifera*. The latter can be quite invasive.

The ripened seed capsules burst open and violently eject their seeds. The best way to collect the seeds is to tie a tiny bag over each capsule as soon as it changes color. Remove the bag once the capsule has released its seeds.

Germination requires a temperature of 70°F (21°C) in light and takes 15 days. Transplant the seedlings, if necessary, within a similar period of time. *Impatiens* seedlings are prone to damping off (*see p.46*), and they scorch in hot sun. They take 12–16 weeks to flower.

RIPENING IMPATIENS SEEDHEADS
When ripe, the walls of each seedhead split apart and coil backward so suddenly that the seeds are ejected several feet from the plant.

LAGURUS *Hare's tail*

SEEDS in spring or autumn

The only species of Hare's tail, *Lagurus ovatus*, is grown for its fluffy flowerheads, or inflorescences, which, when dried, remain intact for a considerable time. Hare's tail grass is a good choice for poor, sandy soils in full sun. In some regions, it has naturalized and become a weed. Collect the seeds in the same way as for *Briza* (*see p.221*) as soon as the flowerheads ripen and become fluffy in the summer.

Sow the seeds direct (*see p.218*) in spring for flowers in 12 weeks.In colder climates, autumn sowings should be made in containers (*see p.217*) and placed in a sheltered place over winter.

Seeds need a minimum temperature of 64°F (18°C) for germination, which normally takes ten days. If necessary, transplant seedlings within 10–14 days.

OTHER ANNUALS AND BIENNIALS

DOWNINGIA Sow seeds of annuals as for *Phlox* (*see p.228*).
DRACOCEPHALUM Sow as for *Centaurea* (*see p.222*).
ECHIUM Sow seeds (*see p.217–9*) at 55–61°F (13–16°C); annuals in spring, biennials in early summer.
EMILIA (syn. *Cacalia*) Sow seeds of annuals as for *Callistephus* (*see p.221*).
ERAGROSTIS Sow as for *Briza* (*see p.221*), but in midspring.
EUPHORBIA Sow annuals in spring as for *Nigella* (*see p.228*), biennials as for *Erysimum* (*see facing page*). (*See also* Cacti and Other Succulents, *p.246*.)
EUSTOMA (syn. *Lisianthus*) Sow seeds (*see p.217*) of annuals and biennials at 55–61°F (13–16°C) in autumn or late winter.
EXACUM Sow annuals and biennials as for *Browallia* (*see p.221*), but lightly cover seeds with soil mix.
FELICIA (syn. *Agathaea*) Sow seeds of annuals as for *Impatiens* (*see above*).
GILIA Sow as for *Calendula* (*see p.221*).
GLAUCIUM Sow as for *Calendula* (*see p.221*). Resents root disturbance.
GOMPHRENA Sow seeds of annuals as for *Impatiens* (*see above*).
HELIOPHILA Sow as for *Centaurea* (*see p.222*). For winter-flowering container plants, sow in early spring or autumn at 61–66°F (16–19°C).
HESPERIS Sow seeds of biennials in spring in final position (*see p.218*); germination requires a temperature of 50–59°F (10–15°C). Self-sown *H. matronalis* seedlings come fairly true.
HIBISCUS Sow seeds of annuals (*see pp.217–8*) at 64°F (18°C) in spring; soak seeds in hot water for an hour before sowing. (*See also* Shrubs and Climbing Plants, *p.131*.)
HORDEUM Sow as for *Briza* (*see p.221*).
HYOSCYAMUS Sow seeds (*see pp.217–9*) of annuals and biennials in spring. Taprooted seedlings resent root disturbance, so sow in flowering positions. Henbane often self-sows freely.
IONOPSIDIUM Sow seeds of annuals in spring, summer, or autumn (*see p.217*). Plant often self-sows.
IPOMOPSIS Sow seeds of annuals and biennials (*see pp.217–8*) at 55–61°F (13–16°C) in early spring or in early summer.
ISATIS Sow seeds of annuals and biennials (*see pp.217–8*) in autumn or spring at 13–18°C (55–64°F). Self-sows freely.
LAGENARIA Sow seeds of annuals as for *Capsicum* (*see p.222*), but soak seeds in tepid water before sowing.

LATHYRUS *Sweet pea*

Lathyrus 'Mars'

SEEDS from midautumn to midwinter or from early to midspring

The most commonly grown annual in this genus is the sweet pea, *Lathyrus odoratus*, most often a climber. The seeds, produced in long pods, are large and easily handled. Pick seedpods when they turn pale brown and rattle. Dry them (*see p.216*) until they split and release the seeds.

In Hardiness Zones 8–9, sweet peas are best sown in midautumn or late winter, but early spring sowing can still give good results.

For the best flowers, the ground should be enriched some time before sowing. Dig over the soil in a trench or block, depending on if the stake supports are to be erected as a trellis or tepee. If the soil is heavy, prepare it in autumn for spring sowing so it can be broken down by frost action, or raise the bed.

Sow direct in the open ground (*see below right*) in early to midspring or in autumn in warm areas. In cold regions, sow in containers (*see bottom left*) in autumn and winter and germinate in a sheltered place, such as a cold frame lined with 2in (5cm) of gravel. The optimum germination temperature is 55°F (13°C) in darkness.

To aid germination, soak the seeds overnight in tepid water. Sow the seeds immediately; if left too long, they are prone to rot. Some black seeds of cultivars are impervious to water and must be chipped (*see below left*) to allow moisture to reach the seed embryos. However, some growers consider both soaking and chipping unnecessary. Germination takes 15 days.

Seedlings that have not been raised in individual containers are transplanted into open ground or are first potted individually into deep 3in (8cm) pots when they are about 2in (5cm) tall. At all times they must be grown as cool as possible, being given protection only if the weather is very cold. In warm conditions, the seedlings grow too quickly and become leggy, or they die.

Whereas it is not necessary to pinch out the tips of autumn-sown seedlings, it is useful for those raised in winter or spring to encourage sideshoots (*see bottom center*). For exhibition-quality plants, allow one shoot to develop, support it with a stake, then remove all tendrils and sideshoots to concentrate growth into flower production.

Sweet peas should start flowering within 12–14 weeks, depending on time of sowing, but autumn sowings will not flower until spring or early summer.

Sweet peas are good plants to hybridize, and many amateur gardeners have produced some excellent cultivars. Pollinate the chosen seed parent (*see right*) and protect it from insect pollination by tying a muslin bag over it for a few days. Collect the seeds in late summer. (*See also* Hybridizing, *p.21*.)

CHIPPING SEEDS

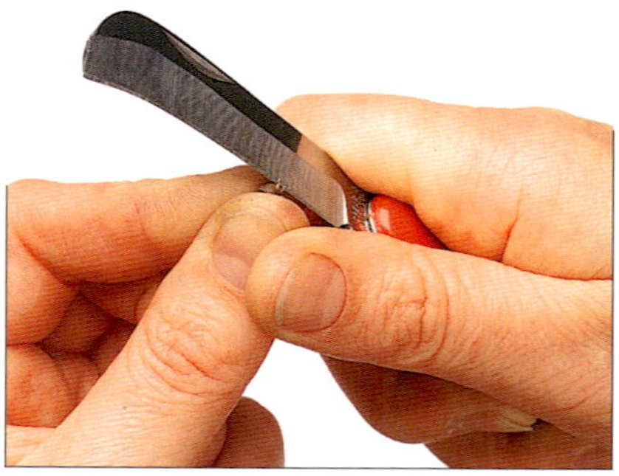

Chip the hard coats of black seeds by using a clean, sharp knife to cut away a small piece of each seed coat, or use a soldering gun to burn a tiny hole. Take care to make the cut well away from each seed's scar (hilum).

SOWING SWEET PEA SEEDS OUTDOORS

PREPARING THE SOIL *Dig over the soil, in a trench or block, according to how the seeds are to be sown. Add 3–4in (8–10cm) of well-rotted manure or compost to the bottom of the trench. Allow to settle for at least four weeks.*

DIRECT-SOWING UNDER A TEPEE *First construct a tepee of six 8ft (2.5m) stakes. Make a hole about 1in (2.5cm) deep on both sides of each stake. Sow a few seeds in each hole, cover over, and firm. Water in if the soil is dry.*

SOWING SWEET PEA SEEDS IN CONTAINERS

1 *Sow sweet pea seeds in deep containers that allow room for the seedlings' roots. Fill 5in (13cm) pots with seed soil mix, and space-sow 5–7 seeds per pot. Cover the seeds with ½in (1cm) of fine-grade vermiculite, label, and water.*

2 *Leave the seeds in a cool, sheltered place; in colder climates, a cold frame is ideal. To promote bushy growth, pinch out growing tips when the seedlings have two or more pairs of leaves. Plant out as soon as the roots are visible.*

USING TUBE POTS

To avoid disturbing the seedlings' roots, sow the seeds in tube pots instead of standard pots. Almost fill the tube pots with seed soil mix. Sow the seeds singly and cover with ½in (1cm) of mix. Label and water.

HYBRIDIZING SWEET PEAS

1 *Choose a stem on the seed parent (here* Lathyrus *'Mars') that has one or two unopened flowers. Pinch off open flowers; they are already pollinated (sweet peas are self-pollinating). Also remove any immature flowers.*

2 *Hold back the wings of the seed-parent flower to expose the keel. Using a needle or a safety pin, pry open the keel to reveal the ten stamens with their pollen-bearing anthers.*

3 *Use fine tweezers to pinch off all the stamens from around the central stigma. Take care not to damage the stigma or to leave any snags that could encourage rot.*

4 *Take a fully open flower of the pollen parent (here* Lathyrus *'Margaret Joyce'). Holding it by its wings, place its keel over the seed parent's stigma. Shake the pollen flower to transfer its ripe pollen to the seed parent's stigma.*

LAVATERA *MALLOW*

SEEDS from early to late spring or early summer

These annuals and biennials have disklike seedheads. Sow annuals in spring and biennials in early summer in a sheltered place. The seeds take 14 days to germinate at 70°F (21°C). Transplant seedlings, if necessary, within seven days. Annual mallows flower in 12–16 weeks. (*See also* Shrubs and Climbing Plants, *p.133*.)

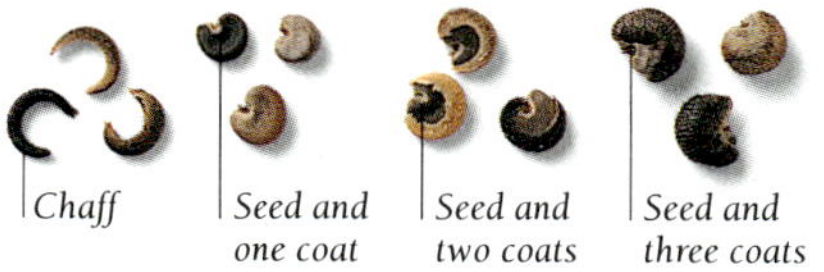

SORTING SEEDS FROM THE CHAFF
Mallow seeds have three coats or layers of chaff; some layers may fall away. When storing or sowing seeds, be sure to discard all loose chaff.

LINARIA *TOADFLAX*

SEEDS from early to midspring or in summer

The annuals in this genus are the most often grown, although there are some biennials, which are sown in early summer. Seeds are produced in dry capsules. Sow outdoors (*see p.219*); the seeds are relatively small, so take care not to sow them too thickly.

The optimum temperature for germination is 55°F (13°C). Seedlings appear in ten days; if necessary, transplant them as soon as they are large enough to handle. Most plants take 12 weeks to flower. Annual toadflax self-sows very freely; transplant the seedlings as for *Digitalis* (*see p.223*).

LUNARIA *HONESTY, MONEY PLANT*

SEEDS in early summer

Lunaria annua (syn. *L. biennis*) may be annual or biennial, but it is usually grown as a biennial. Being very free-seeding, it naturalizes very readily, and self-sown seedlings are easily transplanted, as for *Digitalis* (*see p.223*). The prominent flat, translucent seedheads are valuable for dried flower arrangements.

Dry the seedheads thoroughly before extracting the seeds (*see below*). The seeds take 14 days to germinate at 64°F (18°C). Transplant the seedlings, if necessary, within two weeks. If grown as a biennial, flowering is in late spring or early summer of the following year.

GATHERING HONESTY SEEDS
In summer, when most of the flat seedheads take on the appearance and texture of silvery tissue paper, the seeds are ripe. Cut off a flower stem and peel away the outer skin from each side of a seedhead. Pick the large flat seeds from the central, inner membrane.

OTHER ANNUALS AND BIENNIALS

LAYIA Sow seeds of annuals as for *Calendula* (*see p.221*).
LEGOUSIA Sow as for *Calendula* (*see p.221*).
LEUCANTHEMUM Sow as for *Centaurea* (*see p.222*).
LIMNANTHES Sow as for *Calendula* (*see p.221*), but protect autumn sowings over winter in colder regions. Self-sown *L. douglasii* seedlings come fairly true.
LINANTHUS Sow as for *Centaurea* (*see p.222*).
LINDHEIMERA Sow as for *Centaurea* (*see p.222*).
LINUM Sow as for *Centaurea* (*see p.222*). Flowering flax (*L. grandiflorum*) dislikes root disturbance, so sow seeds direct (*see p.218*).
LOBELIA Sow seeds of annuals (*see p.217*) at 59–77°F (15–25°C) in late winter and early spring. Readily self-sows in suitable climates. (*See also* Perennials, *p.202*.)
LOBULARIA Sow seeds of annuals (*see p.218*) in early to late spring at 50–59°F (10–15°C). Self-sown *L. maritima* seedlings come fairly true.
LONAS Sow as for *Centaurea* (*see p.222*).
LUPINUS Sow as for *Centaurea* (*see p.222*) after nicking the seeds or soaking them for 24 hours. (*See also* Perennials, *p.202*.)
LYCHNIS (syn. *Viscaria*) Sow as for *Erysimum* (*see p.224*).
MALCOLMIA Sow seeds of annuals (*see p.218*) from late spring at 4–6 weekly intervals for succession of flowers; germinates at 50–59°F (10–15°C). Self-sown *M. maritima* seedlings come fairly true to type.
MALOPE Sow as for *Centaurea* (*see p.222*). Self-sown *M. trifida* seedlings generally come fairly true.
MALVA Sow seeds of annuals and biennials as for *Centaurea* (*see p.222*) or *Erysimum* (*see p.224*).

MATTHIOLA *GILLYFLOWER, STOCK*

Matthiola 'Giant Excelsior'

SEEDS from midwinter to midspring or in midsummer

Annuals in this genus are best raised in containers (*see p.217*) under cover in colder climates, but there are different cultivars for different seasons. Seeds are produced in abundance in long, narrow pods and germinate in ten days at 70°F (21°C).

Transplant seedlings within a week or so. Double-flowered cultivars can be selected at the seedling stage. Move all the seedlings to a place below 50°F (10°C): those seedlings whose seed leaves become yellowish green will then develop double flowers.

In cold regions, protection (*see p.39*) over winter will be necessary for biennial stocks grown for autumn transplanting. Annual stocks flower in 12–16 weeks; biennials the following spring.

MYOSOTIS *FORGET-ME-NOT*

SEEDS in late spring or early summer

The biennial cultivars of *Myosotis sylvatica* are most often grown. They self-sow freely and come reasonably true to type. Lift spent plants and lay them under shrubs or in woodland so they can shed their seeds and become naturalized. To save seeds, lay the entire plant in a paper-lined seed tray to dry (*see p.216*); the seeds should fall into the bottom of the tray.

Sow the seeds outdoors (*see p.219*) or in containers (*see p.217*). Sow seeds of *M. arvensis* in spring. Germination occurs at 55°F (13°C) in darkness in about five days. Transplant the seedlings to a nursery bed, then in their flowering positions in autumn. Biennials flower in spring of the following year.

NICOTIANA *FLOWERING TOBACCO*

SEEDS in early to late spring

Annuals in this genus produce seeds in oval capsules in summer and autumn. The seeds are very fine and need light for germination; mix them with fine sand and surface-sow them (*see p.217*). They require a temperature of 70°F (21°C) in order to germinate in 20 days. Seedlings are transplanted, if necessary, within seven days. Flowering tobaccos take 12 weeks to reach flowering size.

NIGELLA *LOVE-IN-A-MIST, DEVIL-IN-A-BUSH*

SEEDS from early to midspring or early to midautumn

These quite hardy annuals have inflated seed capsules; gather them as they ripen (*see below*). They also self-sow freely, producing copious amounts of seeds that scatter on the ground around the plant. *Nigella damascena* seedlings come fairly true; lift and transplant them as for *Digitalis* (*see p.223*).

Sow seeds outdoors (*see p.219*) when the soil temperature reaches 64°F (18°C). Seeds germinate readily within ten days. If necessary, seedlings should be transplanted in seven to 14 days. Autumn-sown seedlings need protection (*see pp.39–40*) over winter in colder climates. Plants flower in 12–16 weeks, or in the following spring if they are autumn-sown.

GATHERING NIGELLA SEEDS

1 In summer, when the seed capsules begin to turn brown, cut them off and place them in a saucer or tray lined with clean blotting paper or newspaper. Leave them in a warm, sunny place until the seedheads are completely dry.

2 Shake out the small seeds from the dried capsules onto some clean paper. If necessary, sieve through a fine-meshed sieve to winnow out any chaff. Store the seeds in labeled paper packets in a cool, dry place.

PAPAVER *POPPY*

Papaver rhoeas Shirley Series

SEEDS from early to midspring or from late spring to early summer

There are annual and biennial poppies. The distinctive "pepper pot" seed capsules produce large quantities of seeds and readily self-sow. *Papaver rhoeas* seedlings come fairly true. Gather capsules as they change color, and lay in trays to ripen. Simply shake out the seeds (*see p.216*).

Sow annuals in spring and biennials later. They germinate readily, in 20 days at 55°F (13°C) in light. The tap-rooted seedlings resent root disturbance so are best sown direct or transplanted once they have two true leaves, or within seven days. Annuals flower in 12 weeks, biennials the following spring or summer. (*See also* Perennials, *p.204*.)

PHLOX

SEEDS from early to late spring

There are a few annuals in this genus. The seeds, produced in oval capsules, germinate within ten days at a temperature of 64°F (18°C) in darkness, and the seedlings are transplanted, if necessary, within a week. Annual phlox flower in 12–16 weeks. (*See also* Perennials, *p.206*.)

RESEDA *MIGNONETTE*

SEEDS early to midspring or early to midautumn

Most often grown is the fragrant annual *Reseda odorata*. To collect seeds, remove and dry flower spikes before the small seed capsules split (*see p.216*). Seeds germinate at 70°F (21°C) in five days. If needed, transplant seedlings in seven to ten days. Protect autumn sowings over winter in colder regions (*see pp.39–40*). Annuals flower in 12–16 weeks, autumn sowings in spring.

RUDBECKIA *CONEFLOWER*

SEEDS from early to midspring

The seeds of these annuals are easily removed from papery seedheads. If raising in containers, do not sow too deeply. Seeds germinate in 20 days at 70°F (21°C). If needed, transplant seedlings within seven days. Coneflowers take 20 weeks to flower.

SALVIA *SAGE*

SEEDS in early to late spring

The annual *Salvia coccinea* and *S. splendens* (scarlet sage) are the most widely grown. Save seeds as for *Reseda* (*see above*). They germinate at 70°F (21°C) in light in 15 days. Transplant seedlings in seven to ten days for flowers in 16 weeks. (*See also* Perennials, *p.208*.)

SCHIZANTHUS *BUTTERFLY FLOWER, POOR MAN'S ORCHID*

Schizanthus pinnatus

SEEDS in early spring to early summer or in late summer

These showy annuals and biennials flower in 12–16 weeks. Sow annuals in spring for summer flowers or in late summer for winter-flowering container plants. Cover seeds only very thinly. Germination at 70°F (21°C) in light is in seven days. Transplant seedlings, if needed, within a week.

TROPAEOLUM *NASTURTIUM*

SEEDS from midspring to early summer

Most of the annuals self-sow readily and come fairly true; transplant as for *Digitalis* (*see p.223*). To save the large seeds, pick them individually when ripe and dry before storing (*see p.216*). Germination takes eight days at 64°F (18°C) in darkness. Transplant the seedlings, if needed, within a week. Nasturtiums flower best on poor soils in 12–16 weeks. Some *Tropaeolum majus* cultivars, such as 'Hermine Grashoff', are increased not from seeds but from basal stem or stem-tip cuttings (*see pp.154–7*).

VERBASCUM *MULLEIN*

SEEDS from early to late spring or early summer

Most species are biennials, but a few are annuals. To save seeds, remove and dry flower spikes before the seed capsules split (*see p.216*). Mix seeds with fine sand, then surface-sow at 55°F (13°C). Germination takes 14 days. Transplant the taprooted seedlings, if necessary, as soon as possible afterward – into individual pots if raising them in containers. Some plants may flower in 20 weeks from an early sowing, later sowings the following year. (*See also* Perennials, *p.212.*)

TAGETES *MARIGOLD*

SEEDS early to late spring

Marigolds produce copious amounts of large seeds in feathery seedheads. Cultivars freely hybridize and do not come true from collected seeds, but the seedlings are often pleasing; it is worth experimenting with creating your own hybrids (*see p.21*).

To save seeds, pick and dry entire seedheads (*see p.216*) once they mature. Sow seeds without removing the "tails." Seeds germinate easily, at 70°F (21°C) in only five days. If needed, transplant the vigorous seedlings within seven days. Flowers appear in 8–12 weeks.

HARDENING OFF MARIGOLD SEEDLINGS
In colder climates, seedlings that have been raised indoors need to be hardened off under a cover or in a cold frame for a few weeks before planting out. Ventilate the seedlings more each day.

ZINNIA

SEEDS from early to midspring

All species in this genus, including the annuals, are quite tender. The seeds, produced in disklike seedheads, are large and easily handled. To save seeds, cut the entire flowerhead after the petals have faded and dry before removing the seeds as for *Helianthus* (*see p.224*).

Sow at a temperature of 70°F (21°C). Germination is rapid, within five days. Transplant the seedlings (*see p.217*), if necessary, within seven days; they dislike root disturbance, so pot them singly into cells or degradable pots. Zinnias flower in 16–20 weeks.

OTHER ANNUALS AND BIENNIALS

MENTZELIA Sow annuals as for *Centaurea* (*see p.222*).
MOLUCCELLA Chill seeds of annuals at 34–41°F (1–5°C) for two weeks, then sow (*see p.218*) at 55–64°F (13–18°C) in spring.
NEMESIA Sow seeds (*see p.217*) of annuals at 60–70°F (15.5–21°C) from early to late spring. Germination may be erratic above 68°F (20°C). Leave woolly covering on seeds; they germinate best in total darkness.
NEMOPHILA Sow seeds of annuals (*see p.218*) from early to late spring at 50–59°F (10–15°C). Seedlings dislike root disturbance. Self-sows freely.
NICANDRA PHYSALODES Sow as for *Centaurea* (*see p.222*). Self-sows freely.
NOLANA Sow as for *Callistephus* (*see p.221*).
OENOTHERA Sow annuals as for *Centaurea* (*see p.222*), biennials as for *Erysimum* (*see p.224*), or in early autumn. Self-sown *O. biennis* seedlings come true.
OMPHALODES Sow annuals as for *Centaurea* (*see p.222*). Self-sown *O. linifolia* seedlings come fairly true.
ONOPORDUM (syn. *Onopordon*) Sow seeds of biennials (*see p.219*) at 50–61°F (10–16°C) in late spring or early summer where they are to flower. Self-sown *O. acanthium* and *O. nervosum* seedlings come true.
PANICUM Sow annuals as for *Chrysanthemum* (*see p.222*).
PERILLA Sow seeds as for *Chrysanthemum* (*see p.222*).
PHACELIA Sow annuals as for *Nigella* (*see facing page*); sow biennials direct in autumn.
PLATYSTEMON CALIFORNICUS Sow as for *Centaurea* (*see p.222*). Seedlings come fairly true.
POLYPOGON Sow as for *Briza* (*see p.221*).
PORTULACA Sow as for *Dorotheanthus* (*see p.224*).
PROBOSCIDEA (syn. *Martynia*) Sow as for *Tagetes* (*see above*).
PSYLLIOSTACHYS Sow biennials as for *Tagetes* (*see above*) and annuals as for *Rudbeckia* (*see facing page*).
RHODANTHE (syn. *Acroclinium*) Sow as for *Rudbeckia* (*see p.228*).
SALPIGLOSSIS Sow as for *Tagetes* (*see above*).
SANVITALIA Sow as for *Calendula* (*see p.221*).
SCABIOSA Sow seeds of annuals and biennials as for *Calendula* (*see p.221*), but in spring.
SEDUM Sow as for *Centaurea* (*see p.222*).
SILENE Sow seeds (*see p.217–9*) of annuals at 50–59°F (10–15°C) in autumn or spring. Self-sown *S. armeria* seedlings come fairly true.
SILYBUM Sow seeds of annuals or biennials direct (*see p.218–9*) in late spring or early summer. Thin to 2ft (60cm).
SMYRNIUM Sow seeds (see *p.218*) of biennials in flowering position at 50–59°F (10–15°C) in autumn or late spring. Germination is erratic.
THYMOPHYLLA Sow seeds of annuals and biennials as for *Matthiola* (see *facing page*).
TITHONIA Sow as for *Zinnia* (*see above*).
TRACHYMENE (syn. *Didiscus*) Sow at 70°F (21°C) in midspring; germination may be slow.
TRAPA Collect ripe seeds of annuals in autumn. Store frost-free in wet moss or water over winter. Sow in spring at 55–64°F (13–18°C) in wet soil mix. (*See also* Water Garden Plants, *p.170.*)

SCABIOSA ATROPURPUREA COCKADE SERIES

CACTI AND OTHER SUCCULENTS

The sculptural, often bizarre forms of this extraordinary group of plants belie the comparative ease with which many in cultivation may be propagated.

Succulents evolved to survive in habitats with extreme conditions, particularly periods of drought. They store water in specialized tissue in swollen roots, stems, or leaves. Many desert species have tiny leaves, or no leaves at all, to retain moisture; others are rainforest epiphytes, living in trees and absorbing water through strap-like stems. Cacti make up one family of stem succulents, distinguished by a unique feature: the areole, a padlike bud from which flowers, shoots, and spines grow. All cacti are succulents, therefore, but not all succulents are cacti.

Other succulents span many plant families and so are very diverse in form, from stark, cactuslike barrels to treelike leafy species, and also in the ways they may be propagated. Some techniques, such as stem and leaf cuttings, are broadly similar to those used on herbaceous perennials but with the advantage that succulent cuttings do not wilt as quickly. However, the fleshy cuttings are very susceptible to rot, so good hygiene is essential for success. In the wild, many succulents increase by forming spreading clumps of rosettes, globular offsets, or tubers – these may be divided in various ways, according to their habit. Special grafting techniques exploit the singular anatomy of cacti, making it possible to enhance flowering and improve growth rates of slow or difficult cultivars. Grafting also provides a means of perpetuating the exotic deformities of the monstrose, cristate, or neon-colored forms.

Raising species from seeds is slower than vegetative propagation but is an easy and economical way to build up a collection. It also helps conserve stocks of the increasing numbers of succulent species that are now endangered in the wild.

SAGUARO CACTUS IN FLOWER
This cactus, Carnegiea gigantea, *takes 150 years to grow 40ft (12m). After 40 years, the first flowers appear, setting 10 million seeds a year; only one seedling survives in five years. Seeds germinate readily in cultivation.*

MEXICAN HAT PLANT
This succulent, Kalanchoe daigremontiana, *produces tiny plantlets at its leaf margins. In the wild, they would drop off and root nearby. To propagate these, carefully pick off the plantlets and plant them in a gritty cactus soil mix.*

SOWING SEEDS

The majority of cacti and succulents are relatively straightforward to raise from seeds. Most germinate quite quickly if kept warm and moist and, although they are relatively slow-growing, it is interesting to watch the new plants develop. Most species are best sown in late winter so that the seedlings are as large as possible before they become dormant in the following winter. In colder climates, sow seeds under cover and use a closed case if possible. The seeds should germinate in spring when the warmer temperatures encourage plants to make active growth.

GATHERING SEEDS

Commercial seeds are available, but gathering and sowing fresh seeds usually yields better results. Most cacti seeds are small and round but some, such as those of prickly pears (*Opuntia*), are large and have very thick coats; they may take up to two years to germinate. A few, such as those of *Pediocactus*, need a period of 2–4 weeks chilling in the refrigerator, at about 37°F (3°C), to trigger germination, but these are the exceptions rather than the rule.

If gathering seeds, take care to let the seedpods ripen on the plant; if harvested too early, many of the seeds may not have developed sufficently to germinate when sown. If seeds need to be stored, keep them cool and dry in a paper envelope. Sieve dry seeds to remove any chaff, which could cause rot later. Remove as much pulp as possible from seeds of fleshy fruits, then squash the wet seeds onto a paper towel and allow them to dry.

Seedpods of succulents vary widely. Plants in the crassula family mostly have small pods, which become papery and dry when ripe; these contain tiny, dustlike seeds. Shake them out over a sheet of paper.

Mesembryanthemums have buttonlike capsules that also turn brown when ripe; moisten the capsules to help them open and release the seeds. Euphorbias have pods with three chambers, each of which contains one round seed. When ripe, the pod suddenly bursts to eject the seeds far from the plant; to gather them, tie a small paper bag over a ripening pod.

TYPES OF SEEDHEAD
Some dry seedpods split open to release seeds, while woody pods open when moistened by rain. Others have fluffy "parachutes"; each plume is carried in the wind to distribute its seed. Seeds in fleshy fruits are eaten by animals and dispersed in the droppings – ready-made seedbeds.

SOWING SEEDS AND TRANSPLANTING SEEDLINGS

1 *Fill the container, here a 5in (13cm) pan, to within ½in (1cm) of the brim with free-draining cactus seed soil mix. Firm lightly.*

2 *Sprinkle seeds evenly over the soil mix surface by gently tapping the packet. If the seeds are tiny, mix them with fine sand first.*

3 *Use a fine mist-sprayer to lightly moisten the surface of the soil mix, making sure not to overwater or disturb the seeds.*

LARGE SEEDS

Press each seed into the soil mix and sow at twice the seed's own depth. Space seeds about ½in (1cm) apart so they have enough room to develop.

4 *Top-dress with a thin layer of fine grit. Label and place a clear plastic bag over the pot. Keep at a minimum temperature of 70°F (21°C) and in partial shade.*

5 *Transfer the seedlings to a bright place at 59°F (15°C). When the seedlings are beginning to crowd each other, carefully lift a clump of them from the pot.*

6 *Divide the clump into single seedlings, keeping as much soil mix around the roots as possible (see inset). Set each plant into a 2½in (6cm) pot of cactus soil mix.*

7 *Top-dress each pot with a ¼in (5mm) layer of fine grit. Label. Keep the pots at a minimum temperature of 59°F (15°C) and water sparingly after a few days.*

TRANSPLANTING SUCCULENTS

When transplanting succulent seedlings (here of Gasteria croucheri*), lift them out individually from the seed tray. Take care not to damage their fragile roots or leaves.*

Sowing seeds

The majority of cacti and succulents are quite slow to grow once they have germinated, so it makes sense to sow seeds in small containers to save space. A 2in (5cm) pot is ideal for 25–30 seeds or a 5in (13cm) pan for 50–100 seeds, while a seed tray is large enough for 1,000 seeds.

Sow the seeds as shown (*see facing page*). Use an open, free-draining soil mix to avoid rot. A specialized cactus soil mix is fine; alternatively, make a mix of one part very fine (⅛in or 3mm), sharp grit or coarse sand to two parts of potting mix, peat, or sterilized soil. The grit may be sold as bird grit in pet stores. Shell grit is too limy. Unless sterilized first (*see p.33*), vegetable matter, such as leaf mold, can contain fungal and bacterial spores, which introduce disease to seedlings.

Cover the surface of the soil mix and seeds with a shallow layer of grit to help keep the seeds in close contact with the soil mix and discourage rot as the seedlings develop. Sharp sand is used sometimes instead, but it is less suitable because it has a tendency to solidify and retain water and may also encourage algae and moss to develop.

Water the seeds after sowing, either by spraying carefully (*see facing page*) or from below. Do this by immersing the container in a dish of water to about half its depth for about an hour, then remove it and allow it to drain. To provide the seedlings with protection against damping off (*see p.46*), add a general-purpose fungicide to the water.

Put the container in a warm place, such as a closed case, but shielded from direct sun. Seeds in single pots may be sealed in clear plastic bags instead of a closed case. Keep at 70–86°F (21–30°C), depending on the species (*see* A–Z of Cacti and other Succulents, *pp.242–51*). Many types of seeds will germinate in 2–3 weeks; lower temperatures tend to extend this period. In hot conditions, above 90°F (32°C), germination is very poor, and the seeds will lie dormant until the temperature drops.

Keep the soil mix fairly moist until the first seeds have germinated, then move them to a cooler environment, at a minimum of about 59°F (15°C). Once the seedlings appear, remove them from the closed case or plastic bags.

Seedling care

Keep the containers of seedlings in a warm, lightly shaded area. They should be watered regularly and not be allowed to dry out. Take care not to saturate the soil mix, however, because keeping the seedlings continuously wet will soon make them start to rot.

After germination, the seedlings will appear to do very little for 1–3 months while they develop their root systems. Many cactus seedlings will look like very small peas at about six months old. After this stage, they should double in size every three to six months, being about 1–2in (2.5–5cm) in diameter in 2–4 years after sowing. The tall species of columnar cactus usually grow more quickly than this.

Small seedlings have a very delicate root systems that are easily damaged during transplanting. It is therefore best to leave the seedlings undisturbed for as long as possible until they become quite crowded, provided there are no other reasons for transplanting them, such as signs of an infection or any algae or moss growth on the soil mix.

Transplanting seedlings

After several months to two years, when the seedlings are large enough to handle comfortably, lift them from the container and gently tease them apart. Cactus seedlings have very soft spines and can generally be handled without protective gloves, but avoid touching and bruising their delicate roots.

Seedlings that are 1in (2.5cm) or more in diameter should be potted into 2–2½in (5–6cm) pots. Smaller seedlings will grow better if planted in rows in seed trays or pans, spaced about twice their own diameter apart. They can then be grown on again until crowded before they need to be potted individually. In all cases, use a gritty cactus soil mix.

After transplanting, allow seedlings to settle and heal any damaged roots for a few days before watering. Place in a bright position, but keep out of full sun until the seedlings have established and show visible signs of new growth, then treat as adult plants. Small plants will benefit from protection from strong sun.

POLLINATING FLOWERS BY HAND

Many cacti and succulents are not self-fertile and must be fertilized by pollen from another plant; usually two flowering plants of the same species are needed to produce seeds that should come true to type. Many species will cross-pollinate with another species from the same genus, but the resulting seedlings will differ from both parents, often being intermediate between the two. Seedlings of hybrid parents typically show even greater variation. Plants grown under cover or those being used for hybridization (*see p.21*), must be pollinated by hand (*see right*).

1 Cross-pollinate plants grown under cover when the male anthers are ripe and laden with pollen. Use a small, clean paintbrush to gather the pollen from the anthers of a flower on one plant – the pollen parent.

2 Transfer the pollen to the ripe, sticky female stigma on a flower of another plant (here an Epiphyllum*) of the same species or cultivar (or of a different species but same genus if producing a new hybrid).*

Division

Dividing cacti and other succulents is a relatively straightforward and fast way of obtaining new plants of a decent size. The technique is particularly useful for propagating hybrids, selected forms, and variegated plants, which are unlikely to come true from seeds.

There are various methods of division, depending on the type of rootstock. Some plants form clumps of offsets, which develop their own root systems; others spread by means of underground stems, or stolons, which produce plantlets a little way from the parent; carpeting or trailing species often root at intervals along the stems; and other succulents increase from tubers.

The easiest way to decide how to divide a plant is to lift it or knock it out of its pot, shake off as much of the soil or soil mix as possible, and inspect the roots. The basic principle for all division is to separate a vigorous plant into a few sections, each of which has its own roots and growing point or shoots.

Many succulents have fleshy roots, which may easily rot if damaged during division and then allowed to stay wet. It is therefore wise to let divisions of plants settle in their new containers or positions for a few days before watering them, in order to allow any root damage a chance to heal.

Dividing succulent rootstocks

Some clump-forming succulents with a crown of shoots, such as *Sedum spectabile* (syn. *Hylotelephium spectabile*), may be treated as herbaceous perennials (*see p.148*). Divide a clump at the start of the growing season, as shown below, making sure that each section has at least one healthy growing point and some healthy, vigorous roots.

Dividing clump-forming succulents

1 Scrape away soil mix around the parent (here Haworthia cymbiformis*) to reveal the base of each offset. Detach an offset by cutting straight across the joint with the parent. Allow the wound to callus* (see inset).

2 Fill a 6cm (2½in) pot with cactus soil mix and insert each cutting. Top-dress with fine grit, label, and keep in a warm spot in partial shade. When new growth appears (see inset)*, pot on.*

Division of succulent offsets

Many types of succulent form clumps by producing offsets around the parent plant. These usually develop much more quickly while attached to the parent, but periodically dividing the clump creates "instant" new plants. The best time to divide most clump-forming plants is at the start of the growing season in spring or early summer (*see also* A–Z of Cacti and other Succulents, *pp.242–51*).

When dividing the plant, first lift it or remove it from its container and shake off as much soil mix as will come away easily from the roots. It is then easy to select and detach offsets that have already rooted, before replanting the parent and the offsets. Alternatively, take offsets from the perimeter of a plant without lifting it, as shown above.

Succulents such as *Agave*, *Gasteria*, and *Haworthia* are very easy to divide because their offsets usually have developed independent root systems and so make good growth once potted.

Some large-growing succulents, such as certain types of *Agave* and *Aloe,* may produce large, densely rooted offsets that become difficult to separate from the parent. With these plants, you may need to use a sharp knife, pruners, or even back-to-back forks (*see p.148*) to pry apart a clump. Check the divisions for any loose or thin, discolored roots – these are often dead and should be removed. Untangle the remaining roots so that you can spread them out evenly in the new planting holes, or in the new containers if repotting.

Dividing succulent rootstocks

1 Divide the plant (here Sedum spectabile*) as it comes into growth in the spring. Lift the whole plant with a fork, taking care not to damage the roots and fleshy leaves. Shake off as much soil as possible from the roots.*

2 Pull apart the plant into pieces, each with a root system about the size of a large hand. Discard any woody, old growth from the center of the plant. Replant each piece, spacing them about 2ft (60cm) apart, and water in if dry.

Division of mat-forming succulents

Some mat-forming or trailing members of the crassula family, for example *Adromischus*, *Crassula*, *Sedum*, and some *Echeveria*, root along their stems wherever they come into contact with the soil to form a rooted mat.

Established plants may be simply cut into smaller clumps with a sharp knife; the divisions may then be potted or replanted. By contrast, many of the carpeting mesembryanthemums rarely produce roots from their stems unless they are severed, so their offsets must be treated as stem cuttings (*see p.236*).

Dividing stoloniferous succulents

Some succulents, for example some species of *Agave*, spread by thick, underground stems, or stolons, which run out from the base of the parent plant and end in a new rosette. Once the rosettes have developed a set of leaves, they will normally have produced their own roots from the stem at the base of the rosette. It is best to leave very small shoots attached to the parent because they will develop much more quickly.

Remove the older, rosette-bearing underground stems from the base of the parent plant with a sharp knife, then shorten them by cutting just beneath the new roots of the rosette. Allow the cut surfaces to dry in a warm, airy place for a couple of days before potting the rosettes individually.

Other succulents that spread by stolons include members of *Kleinia* and *Senecio*; divide these as for rosettes.

Propagating cacti from offsets

Most clump-forming cacti have just a single root system and produce offsets without independent roots, with the exception of very mature plants. Unrooted offsets may, however, be cut off from the parent plant and treated as standard stem cuttings (*see p.237*). Some *Echinopsis*, *Gymnocalycium*, and *Rebutia* are exceptions, producing offsets with roots even when they are quite small. Few clumping *Mammillaria* have rooted offsets, except for the very small-headed species (*see also* A–Z of Cacti and other Succulents, *pp.242–51*). Epiphytic cacti cannot be divided.

Offset-forming cacti are easy to divide by simply breaking up the clump into suitably sized pieces and treating them as succulent offsets (*see facing page*). Once potted, keep them at a minimum of about 64°F (18°C), and water them sparingly until new growth is visible.

Dividing tuberous succulents

Some succulents increase from tubers, which are underground storage organs. Tubers are sometimes produced on the fibrous roots of the parent, as with some species of *Pelargonium*. Other succulents, such as *Ceropegia*, develop tubers just below soil level wherever the stems of the parent plant root into the soil.

Most tuberous succulents have a dormant period, usually in winter, during which they often die back to the tuber. This is the best time to divide them, in most cases. However, many *Pelargonium* are dormant in summer; divide this group in late summer before the plants come back into growth. Species that make active growth in summer (usually those from regions with summer rainfall) are best divided in spring. Divide deciduous *Ceropegia* in spring; evergreen types at any time the weather is warm, ideally in late spring. Tuberous *Senecio* and *Kleinia* should be divided in spring or summer.

Divide stem tubers, such as those of *Ceropegia*, as shown below. Make sure that each tuber has at least one shoot or growing point. To divide root tubers, simply lift the plant and pull away some healthy tubers. If the rootstock is very dense, cut through the roots to avoid tearing the tubers. Pot immediately, as for stem tubers (*see below*), but cover the tubers with a thin layer of soil mix.

Some of these tuberous plants may be difficult, so care is needed to reestablish them successfully. It is particularly important not to overwater the soil mix, because this can lead to rot.

Division of plantlets

Some *Pelargonium*, such as certain scented-leaf forms including the rose-scented geranium (*Pelargonium graveolens*), produce plantlets along their rootlike stems. In open beds, the plantlets can become invasive, so they are easy to propagate. Sever the stems between the plantlet and the parent, lift, and pot singly as for tubers.

DIVISION OF TUBERS

1 *In late spring to summer, dig out some mature tubers, each with a growing point, from the parent plant (here* Ceropegia linearis *subsp.* woodii*). Allow to dry for a few days in a bright, warm, and airy place.*

2 *Fill a 3in (8cm) pot with gritty, free-draining cactus soil mix to within ½in (1cm) of the rim. Insert each tuber so that its roots are buried in the mix and the tuber sits on the surface. If planting more than one tuber in a pot, make sure that they are not touching.*

3 *Top-dress with a layer of fine gravel around the tuber. Label the pot, and water lightly. Place in a bright, airy position, out of direct sunlight, and at a minimum temperature of 61°C (16°C). Water sparingly, keeping the soil mix only slightly moist until the tuber sends out new shoots (this is usually in 2–3 weeks).*

TAKING CUTTINGS

Some cacti and other succulents do not flower readily in cultivation, and commercial seeds are often not readily available, so taking cuttings offers a reliable way of increasing many of these plants. Succulent cuttings have the advantage that, because of their fleshy tissue, they can retain nutrients and water while they become established.

Unusual forms, such as variegated, monstrose, or cristate (crested) plants, and hybrids, can usually be propagated only from cuttings to preserve their distinctive characteristics.

There are various types of cuttings, the most suitable depending on the plant's form and growth habit. Succulents are generally propagated by stem, leaf, or rosette cuttings, while cacti are raised from globular, columnar, or flat stem cuttings. Many clump-forming species produce unrooted offsets, which may also be treated as cuttings.

TAKING SUCCULENT STEM CUTTINGS

1 In early to midspring, choose a healthy sideshoot (here of a Kalanchoe). Using a clean, sharp knife, make a straight cut as close to the base of the stem as possible.

2 Trim the shoot to about 2in (5cm) long, removing the leaves from the bottom ½in (1cm) of stem if necessary. Leave the cutting in a warm, dry place for about 48 hours to allow it to callus.

3 Prepare a 3in (8cm) pot with gritty soil mix (see below). Insert the cutting into the grit top-dressing so that the leaves are just clear of the surface.

SELECTING SUITABLE MATERIAL

When selecting cuttings, you will increase the chances of success if you take care to choose suitable material from the parent plant. Take cuttings from tissue that is semi-ripe or ripe rather than very young; cuttings that are very small, or taken from immature tissue, are more prone to rot. On the other hand, cuttings that are too large (with the exception of some of the columnar cacti), or from material that is old and woody, take a long time to root.

In most cases, remove material for the cuttings using a sharp knife. It is important that knives and surfaces are clean (*see p.30*) to avoid introducing disease through the cuts. With some leaf cuttings, however, it is better to pull off the leaf. Once you have taken a cutting, allow the cut surface to form a callus by leaving it in a warm, dry, airy place. This may take up to several days, depending on the thickness of the cutting and on the time of year.

SUITABLE ROOTING MEDIA

A suitable rooting medium for cacti and succulents would consist of two parts cactus soil mix to one of fine grit. With succulents, it is important that the cuttings have just enough moisture to encourage rooting without being wet, which will quickly rot them. Using soil mix with a layer of fine grit or fine gravel on top allows any excess moisture in the mix to evaporate through the gravel, providing enough water for rooting while leaving the base of the cutting comparatively dry. Similarly, when potting a cutting, insert it into the soil mix just deep enough for it to stay upright; if too deep in the mix, the base of the cutting may rot before it has rooted.

SUCCULENT STEM CUTTINGS

Most small, slender-stemmed succulents with a bushy habit, especially those in the crassula family, root easily from cuttings. They are prepared in a similar way to herbaceous cuttings (*see above and p.154*). Larger cuttings are treated as for cactus stem cuttings (*see p.238*).

Take the cuttings from stems that have ripened and lost their bright, juvenile color, as shown (*see above*). Trim the cuttings so that they are 2–3in (5–8cm) in length. Longer cuttings tend to collapse and bend during rooting and do not make good plants. Allow the cuttings to callus so that they form hard skins over the wounds.

Take a pan or seed tray and prepare it as shown (*see left*). Gently push the cuttings through the fine grit into the soil mix. Keep slightly damp; many will root in one to three weeks if kept warm. Succulent cuttings are much more prone to damping off (*see p.46*) in high humidity, so do not place them in a closed case. If the conditions are not warm enough, apply gentle bottom heat of 70°F (21°C).

SUCCULENT LEAF CUTTINGS

Some types of succulent, for example many species of *Crassula*, *Kalanchoe*, and *Echeveria* (all members of the crassula family), may be propagated

POT PREPARED FOR CUTTINGS
Cacti and succulent cuttings root most successfully in a free-draining soil mix. Use a pot three-quarters filled with a gritty cactus soil mix and topped with fine grit. The top-dressing will protect the stem of the cutting from rot, while the base of the cutting roots into the soil mix.

TAKING SUCCULENT LEAF CUTTINGS

1 Remove a mature, healthy leaf (here of Pachyphytum oviferum) *by pulling it gently sideways from the stem. Allow the wound to callus (see inset) by leaving the leaf for a few days in a warm, dry place.*

2 Prepare a 5in (13cm) pan (or a seed tray) with gritty soil mix and fine grit (see facing page). Push the base of each leaf deep enough into the grit for the leaf to stand up. Space the cuttings about ½in (1cm) apart.

3 Label and place in a bright, warm, airy position. Keep slightly moist. After 1–6 months, the leaves should have rooted and produced new plantlets (see inset).

from leaf cuttings. Many of these plants have their axillary buds (those in the axil of the leaves) more firmly attached to the leaves than the stems. The buds are not generally visible, but by gently easing a mature, healthy leaf slowly sideways from the stem, it should come away with the axillary bud attached.

Take the cuttings, selecting firm, fleshy leaves, and pot them as shown above. Place them in a bright position but shielded from direct sun, and keep them slightly damp. The minimum temperature requirement varies according to the species (*see* A–Z of Cacti and other Succulents, *pp.242–51*).

The leaves should start to produce roots after two to four weeks. After a month or more, tiny new plantlets will develop around the base, usually in clusters. When these are large enough to handle, split them and treat as succulent stem cuttings (*see facing page*).

Leaf cuttings will also often root on damp newspaper. Simply fold a sheet of newspaper and place it in the bottom of a seed tray. Spray with water and drain off the surplus. Lay the leaves on top, then keep in a bright, airy place; spray with water occasionally. When the leaves form roots, pot them as shown above.

SUCCULENT ROSETTE CUTTINGS

Some rosette-forming succulents, such as *Echeveria*, *Haworthia*, and *Sempervivum*, consist of clumps of rosettes. These rosettes may be severed at the base where they join the parent plant, and rooted as shown (*see right*).

WHEN TO TAKE CACTI STEM CUTTINGS

The best time of year to take cuttings of most cacti, especially in colder climates, is in late spring when the warmer, drier weather arrives and the plants have started to grow strongly. It then gives them a chance to establish for as long as possible before the following winter.

SUCCULENT ROSETTE CUTTINGS

1 Using a clean, sharp knife, cut 2–3in (5–8cm) from the top of a young rosette of leaves (here of Echeveria *'Frosty'). Trim off the bottom leaves (see inset) and allow to callus for a few days.*

2 Prepare a standard 3in (8cm) pot (see facing page) or a deep seed tray. Gently push the stem of the cutting through the fine grit top-dressing into the soil mix below, so that the leaves sit just above the surface. Label the pot.

3 Place the cuttings in a bright, airy position, with bottom heat of 70°F (21°C) if possible. Do not enclose them in a closed case, because high humidity can cause rot. Most cuttings root within 1–3 weeks.

TAKING FLAT STEM CUTTINGS

1 Cut a flattened, leaflike stem (here of an Epiphyllum*) into 9in (23cm) sections with a clean, sharp knife. Allow them to callus for a few days in a warm, dry place. Fill a pot (the smallest one that a cutting will stand up in) one-third full of cactus soil mix.*

2 Cover the soil mix with a shallow layer of fine grit, then push the cutting into the mix below. Fill the pot to just below the rim with more fine grit, to support the cutting. Make sure that each cutting is planted with the end that was nearest the parent plant in the pot.

3 Label and keep in a bright spot, but out of direct sun, at a temperature of 64–75°F (18–24°C). Occasionally mist-spray with water but do not overwater, because this may make the cuttings rot. The sections should root in 3–12 weeks, depending on the plant and season.

GLOBULAR STEM CUTTINGS

Many globular cacti such as *Echinopsis* and some *Mammillaria* produce offsets that may be detached and treated as cuttings to make extra plants, although they usually look more attractive when grown on as large clumps.

Take a cutting by easing a sharp knife between the offset and the parent plant. Cut through the base of the offset at its narrowest point. Allow the cuttings to callus for two days or more.

Prepare a pot or seed tray in the usual way (*see p.236*). Gently push each cutting down into the grit until it touches the soil mix. Place in an airy spot at about 70°F (21°C), and water sparingly. The cuttings should root in three weeks to three months.

COLUMNAR CACTI STEM CUTTINGS

Most types of columnar cacti, and some *Euphorbia* and *Stapelia*, may be grown from stem cuttings; it may be necessary to use the main stem because many of these plants do not branch until mature. Cut a section from the top of a stem as shown (*see right*). Leave in a dry, airy spot to callus. In summer, this may take only a few days, but at other times of the year it may take considerably longer.

Pot the cutting as shown, filling in around it with fine gravel to hold it steady. Water sparingly to keep the soil mix from drying out completely. This helps to reduce the risk of rot, because the base of the cutting is not in contact with wet soil mix. The moisture evaporating from the mix is trapped in the gravel, encouraging rooting.

Leave the pot in a bright and airy place at a minimum of 64–75°F (18–24°C), depending on the species. The cuttings should root in 3–12 weeks.

TAKING COLUMNAR STEM CUTTINGS

1 Cut a section of stem from the top of the plant (here Echinopsis pachanoi*), from 3in (8cm) to 6ft (2m) long, depending on the size of the plant. Trim the base and allow to callus (see inset) for 1–4 weeks.*

2 Use the smallest pot that the cutting will stand up in. Fill the bottom 1in (2.5cm) with cactus soil mix, then a ½in (1cm) layer of fine gravel. Stand the cutting on the gravel. Fill with gravel, label, and water lightly.

When the cuttings are showing signs of active growth, tip the pot sideways to remove the gravel, and replace it with soil mix. Once the plant has developed a good root system, it may be potted into a larger container that better suits its proportions.

FLAT STEM CUTTINGS

Some epiphytic (forest) cacti, such as *Epiphyllum* and Christmas cacti (*Schlumbergera*), usually root easily from sections of their flat, leaflike stems. These cacti generally prefer a more humid environment than desert types, and they prefer partial shade.

In late spring or early summer, after flowering, remove a whole, mature stem from the parent plant at the base, and cut it across its width into sections (*see top of page*). Allow the cuttings to callus for a few days. Prepare a pot as shown, then carefully push each cutting about 1–2in (2.5–5cm) through the grit into the soil mix. Up to about ten cuttings, spaced evenly apart, may be rooted in a 5in (13cm) pot. Keep slightly moist in a warm, shady position until rooted.

Grafting

This process involves propagating a plant by taking a cutting (the scion) and uniting it with the base (the rootstock or stock) of a more vigorous species. While it is relatively easy to graft many cacti, most other succulents are more difficult to treat in this way. The fundamental principles are the same, but specific techniques vary according to the plants used. The best time of year to carry out grafting is at the start of the growing season, from late spring to midsummer.

Reasons for grafting

When grafted, many slow-growing and difficult species become easier to cultivate and flower more readily; in some cases, growth rates increase by as much as ten times. Plants that do not grow well on their own roots outside their natural habitat, or that grow so slowly from seeds that they are almost impossible to increase in this way, are best grafted.

Grafting is used to propagate unusual cacti such as the cristate (crested) or the monstrose forms, as well as cultivars that have been bred without chlorophyll, such as the neon cacti. A plant lacking chlorophyll cannot manufacture any food for itself, so it is grafted onto a green stock, which supplies nutrients for both the stock and scion.

How grafting works

The stems of many cacti and other succulents possess two principal types of tissue, the xylem and the phloem, separated by a concentric ring between them (*see box, p.240*). This ring is the cambium, which in old stems may be woody. Inside the ring is the xylem, which conducts nutrients and water through the plant from the roots. On the outside is the phloem, which stores sugars and water and deals with waste products. Xylem, cambium, and phloem together form the vascular bundle. For a graft to unite successfully, the xylems, cambiums, and phloems of both stock and scion must be in contact.

Suitable rootstocks

Most grafts must use a rootstock and scion from within the same plant family. To increase the chances of success, both stock and scion should be healthy and growing well. With a little practice, you may expect a success rate of over 90 percent. However, many growers resort to this method only to try to propagate a plant that is already ailing, in which case a success rate of 30 percent or less is more likely. Generally, a fast- and easy-growing plant is used for the stock.

For cacti, a three-sided *Hylocereus* species is often used commercially as a stock. In warm areas, it is ideal for rapid growth, but it needs a winter minimum of 59°F (15°C), higher than many people keep their collections in colder climates. The taller *Echinopsis* species (formerly *Trichocereus*), such as *Echinopsis pachanoi*, *E. scopulicolus*, and *E. spachiana*, are robust and easy to grow, and so make much better stocks for cold climates.

Flat grafting

This is by far the most common type of graft, because it is easy and quick to use and generally gives excellent results. For grafting, you need a sharp knife with a blade that is rigid enough not to bend but thin to make the cut as cleanly as possible and avoid crushing the cells on either side of the cut. There are many cheap, disposable (*continued on p.240*)

FLAT GRAFTING

1 In late spring to midsummer, cut straight across the top of a vigorous stock plant (here Echinopsis scopulicolus*) using a clean, thin-bladed knife. Leave a 1–2in (2.5–5cm) tall rootstock in the pot.*

2 Using the knife, chamfer the edges of the stock. This is done by trimming off each of the corners, making a diagonal cut upward about ¼in (5mm) below the cut surface. Do not touch the wound with your hands.

3 Take a stem cutting from the scion plant (here Rebutia caniguerali*i f.* rauschii*) that is ½–1in (1–2.5cm) in diameter and no taller than it is broad. If the skin is very tough, chamfer the edges a little.*

4 Place the scion on the stock and gently "screw" the two surfaces together. This ensures that any air bubbles are eliminated and the exposed tissues are in close contact. Secure in place with two rubber bands. Label.

5 Leave the pot in a bright, airy place out of direct sunlight. Keep the soil mix slightly moist. Remove the rubber bands when there are signs of active new growth, usually after about two weeks.

GRAFTING CUTS

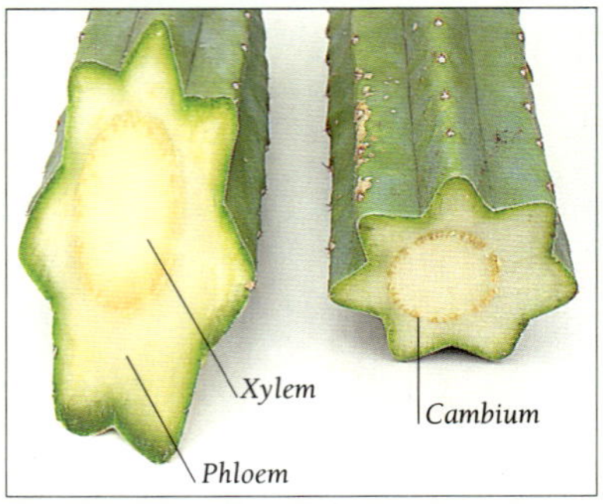

A straight cut made across the stem will expose sufficient amounts of the different types of tissue in a thick-stemmed cactus for flat grafting (see above, right). Using an angled cut (above, left) exposes a larger area of tissues, which increases the chances of a successful union when side grafting species with slender stems.

(*continued from p.239*) craft knives or scalpels available that are all excellent for use in grafting. Make sure that you have everything on hand before you start, and work quickly to complete the operation with as little contamination as possible. Sterilize the knife blade by standing it in alcohol or denatured alcohol (*see also p.30*).

Cut down the cactus that you have selected for the rootstock (*see p.239 and box, below*), and prepare it as shown (*see page 239*). Bear in mind that short stocks usually look much better than tall ones. When you have made the cut, make sure that the vascular bundle, xylem, and phloem are all exposed. Some cacti have sunken growing points, and cutting the stock too near the tip of the stem may leave the growing point intact – with disastrous results. The tip of the stock will continue to grow through the scion and will overwhelm it. If the stock has a hard skin, chamfer the edges a little so that when the tissue shrinks it will not become concave and pull away from the scion.

Now quickly prepare the scion (the plant you want to propagate). Cut the base cleanly and, if it has a very tough skin, chamfer the edges as for the stock. Position the scion on top of the stock; make sure that at least part of the xylem and phloem of the scion matches up with those of the stock. Once you have joined the scion and stock, lightly rotate ("screw") the scion to expel any excess sap or air bubbles, then secure in place.

There are various ways of holding the two cut surfaces together with a little pressure until they have united. Broad rubber bands are ideal for small grafted plants in pots, but check that they are not so tight that they cut into the scion.

Larger cactus grafts or those growing in open ground may be held together using an old piece of nylon stocking, stretched into a rope. Hook one end over the spines on one side of the stock, take it over the scion, then pull it tight and hook the other end to spines on the other side of the stock. Alternatively, apply the required pressure by using two lengths of string, weighted at the ends, draped over the scion at right angles.

Place the newly grafted plant in a bright, airy position at 66°F (19°C), shielded from full sun. The graft should unite in two to three weeks. Water the plant according to the stock plant's requirements, but try to keep water away from the cut surfaces. Signs of active new growth will soon be apparent if the graft is successful, after which you can remove the ties. Grow the plant for about a month in light shade, then treat as normal.

SIDE GRAFTING

This technique is used for grafting slender-stemmed species, such as *Echinopsis chamaecereus*, or those with a narrow central core, which makes it difficult or impossible to carry out a conventional flat graft. Cutting a slender-stemmed scion at a shallow angle so that the cut surface is a long oval (*see box, far left*) provides a larger

SIDE GRAFTING

Make an oblique cut on the stock and scion and press the cut surfaces together. Secure with a cactus spine or clean needle and bind with raffia or rubber bands. Support the grafted plant with a thin stake and twine. Treat as for a flat-grafted plant.

POPULAR ROOTSTOCKS FOR GRAFTING CACTI

In theory, any cactus may be grafted onto any other type of cactus, but the following are the more popular rootstocks.

CEREUS (any species) Short-lived as stock, tending to last only 3–5 years.

CLEISTOCACTUS WINTERI Quite good for small-growing plants, but may offset freely.

ECHINOPSIS (most species) Ideal as stock in colder climates. Tall-growing species (syn. *Trichocereus*) are easier to use than globular ones. *E. pachanoi* and *E. scopulicolus* both give sturdy and robust growth. Stock is slow to offset and tolerates temperatures as low as 45°F (7°C). *E. spachianus* is also popular, but offsets freely.

EPIPHYLLUM HYBRIDS New growth (cylindrical or four-angled) is useful for small seedling scions. Stock has limited useful life.

HARRISIA (any species) Slender stock, useful for small scions.

HYLOCEREUS (any species) Popular with commercial growers grafting in high temperatures, but not good for cold climates.

MYRTILLOCACTUS GEOMETRIZANS Popular with some commercial growers. Stock needs at least 50°F (10°C) in winter. Its vigor wanes after 3–4 years.

PERESKIOPSIS (any species) Very slender, cylindrical stems make excellent stocks for grafting young seedlings, but after one year or even less scion will need to be regrafted onto stock with larger diameter.

SELENICEREUS (any species) Very slender, cylindrical stems make particularly good stocks for grafting epiphytic or forest cacti. Long lengths may be used to make tall standards. Minimum temperature of 43°F (6°C) required.

ECHINOPSIS CHAMAECEREUS F. LUTEA

APICAL-WEDGE GRAFTING

1 Cut a shoot 2–3in (5–8cm) long from the scion plant (here a Christmas cactus) by cutting it straight through at a joint.

2 Cut the top 1–3in (2.5–8cm) from a stem on the stock plant (here a Selenicereus). Make a fine, vertical cut ¾in (2cm) deep into the vascular bundle.

3 Use a thin-bladed knife to pare slivers of skin from both sides of the base of the scion to form a tapered end. Make sure that the central core is exposed.

4 Insert the scion into the slit at the top of the stock so that the exposed tissues of both are in close contact. Push a long cactus spine through the grafted area.

5 Put a weakened clothes pin across the join to hold the graft firmly in place. Label and leave in partial shade. Remove the pin and spine once the graft has united.

BINDING A GRAFT WITH RAFFIA

You may prefer to use raffia to bind the graft instead of the cactus spine and clothes pin shown in step 5. Do not tie the raffia too tightly, or it may crush the tissue of stock and scion.

area of xylem and phloem to unite with those on the stock. The scion may then be secured in place as on a flat graft, with gentle pressure applied by using rubber bands; the resulting grafted plant is very one-sided, however, and so is not particularly pleasing.

The better option is to use a more slender stock, such as of *Pereskiopsis* or *Selenicereus*, and cut both the stock and scion diagonally. As when flat grafting, check that parts of the xylem and phloem correspond, and "screw" the scion gently onto the stock to expel any air bubbles. It may not be practical to secure the graft with rubber bands, so hold the scion in place on the stock with a cactus spine (*as shown, left*) or a clean needle, then bind them together with raffia or a rubber band or clamp them using an old clothes pin that has a weakened spring.

Side grafting is an ideal method for producing a tall standard plant with a treelike stem, such as for the rat's tail cactus (*Rhipsalis*), allowing room for the long stems to trail (*see p.250*). Root a plant of *Selenicereus* up to 4ft (1.2m) in length; once it is growing actively, it is ready to use as a stock. Secure the stock to a sturdy stake to keep it straight and help support the weight of the graft, then side graft a *Rhipsalis* scion onto it.

Apical-wedge grafting

This technique, which is also sometimes known as split grafting, may be used instead of a flat graft, but it is difficult to cut the stock and scion at exactly the same angles so that they match up well. It is therefore usually reserved for those cases where a flat graft would be unsatisfactory and is especially suitable for cacti with flat, leaflike stems and other epiphytes, as well as some slender-stemmed succulents. Like side grafting, this method is also often used to create a standard, using scions such as the Christmas cactus (*Schlumbergera*).

For the rootstock, use a slender plant such as *Pereskiopsis* or *Selenicereus* grown to the required length. Tie in to a sturdy stake for support. Take a cutting one or two stem segments long from the scion plant. Two scions may be grafted back to back onto the same stock; this produces a plant with a well-balanced head more quickly than a single scion.

Prepare the stock and scion(s) as shown above. When inserting the scion into the top of the stock, take care to match the cut surfaces as closely as possible. Secure the scion in place and apply light pressure by clamping the graft with a weakened clothes pin or by binding it with raffia. Place the grafted plant in an airy position, out of full sun, at 66°F (19°C). Water as normal for the stock plant. The two plants should unite within a few days.

Grafting other succulents

Although exactly the same methods are used, grafting succulents is generally far more complex than grafting cacti. Both scion and stock should be from the same plant family, but because of the huge diversity of most of these families, some stocks may be compatible with the scion, while others are not. As with cacti, use a stock from a plant that is easy-growing and vigorous. The following scions and stocks generally may be grafted successfully.

Adenia The more difficult and rarer species are grafted onto *Adenia glauca*.

Adenium New color hybrids are grafted onto *Adenium obesum*, and rarer species onto oleanders (*Nerium*).

Ceraria These may be grafted onto *Portulacaria afra*.

Ceropegia, Stapelia Scions of these are grafted onto *Ceropegia linearis* subsp. *woodii* and *Stapelia grandiflora*.

Euphorbia, Monadenium These are usually grafted onto one of the cactus-like species such as *Euphorbia ingens* and *E. canariensis*.

Pachypodium Madagascan species may be grafted onto *Pachypodium lamerei*.

A–Z OF CACTI AND OTHER SUCCULENTS

AEONIUM

SEEDS in early spring or in autumn
CUTTINGS in spring or in autumn

Many of the plants in this genus (syn. *Megalonium*) tolerate dry cold to a minimum of 50°F (10°C) but rot in damp conditions. Mature rosettes, and in some cases the entire plant, may die after flowering. Species that are predominantly solitary, such as *Aeonium tabuliforme* (syn. *A. bertoletianum*, *Sempervivum complanatum*) and *A. spectabile*, can usually be raised only from seeds. Cuttings may be taken from any plant once it is large enough.

SEEDS

Aeonium seeds are minute and dustlike: even a small pinch will produce hundreds of seedlings if the seeds are fresh and viable. Viability of stored seeds rapidly declines to only one or two percent. The tiny seedpods are papery when ripe in summer. To sow the seeds, mix with a little fine sand and sow (*see p.232*) to germinate at 66–75°F (19–24°C).

CUTTINGS

Take cuttings while the plant is in active growth. Some of the taller species with sturdy stems, such as *A. arboreum* (syn. *Sempervivum arboreum*), lend themselves to propagation from large stem cuttings (*see right and p.236*). Cut each stem 3–12in (8–30cm) below the leading rosette; the more rigid the stem, the longer the cutting may be.

Once the cuttings have callused, set them individually, 2–3in (5–8cm) deep, in fairly small pots of gritty cactus soil mix. Keep just moist. Cuttings taken in spring or early autumn root rapidly in 1–2 weeks and make good-sized plants in 1–2 months.

Treat cuttings that have slender stems, such as *A. sedifolium* (syn. *Aichryson sedifolium*, *Sempervivum masferreri*) and *A. haworthii* (syn. *Sempervivum haworthii*), as rosette cuttings (*see p.237*). Although it is a member of the crassula family, this succulent does not root from single leaves.

AEONIUM STEM CUTTINGS
Take a cutting (here of Aeonium arboreum*), severing the stem at least 3in (8cm) below the leading rosette. Allow to callus for 1–3 days. Pot in cactus potting mix. Cut off any sideshoots at the main stem, and treat in the same way.*

AGAVE

SEEDS from spring to summer
DIVISION from spring to summer (clumps)
(single rosettes)

The hardier members in this genus tend to have bluish leaves; more tropical, light green-leaved or variegated cultivars are slightly less hardy. They tolerate a minimum of 41–50°F (5–10°C), depending on the species. Some are monocarpic, dying once they have flowered; with other species, each rosette dies after flowering. Agaves are easy to raise from seeds, if available. Most species offset readily, lending themselves to division.

SEEDS

In cultivation, they set seeds rather erratically; hand-pollination may help (*see p.233*). If fertilized, they produce seed capsules that swell as they ripen. When sowing the large, flat seeds (*see p.232*) at 70°F (21°C), cover them with a ¼in (5mm) layer of fine grit to keep them in contact with the soil. It takes 2–3 years to raise a small plant.

DIVISION

Agave increase by underground stems, or stolons, from which new rosettes, or offsets, are produced. Wait until each offset has a complete rosette of leaves; by then, it should have its own root system. These plants have vicious spines and daggerlike teeth, so it is advisable to wear protective gloves and sleeves when handling them. Divide young plants as shown below for good plants in 2–5 years. Keep each division just moist until well established, usually in 1–3 months.

Mature plants of species that freely offset, for example *A. americana* (syn. *A. altissima*) and its cultivars, soon make large, tightly packed clumps. These may be divided with a knife into smaller sections or individual offsets (*see p.234*).

DIVIDING AGAVE OFFSETS

1 *Lift or knock out the parent plant (here* Agave americana *'Variegata') and lay on its side so you can reach below the spiny leaves. Remove the loose soil and old or dead roots.*

2 *Select a healthy offset and separate it from the parent, cutting through the connecting stolon with a clean, sharp knife just below the offset's roots. Replant the parent. Place the offset in a warm, bright, airy spot for a few days until the wound calluses over.*

3 *Pot the offset in gritty cactus soil mix. Top-dress with a shallow layer of small gravel. Do not water for the first week.*

ASTROPHYTUM

Astrophytum myriostigma

SEEDS in spring or summer
GRAFTING in late spring to late summer

The entire genus may be relatively difficult to propagate because they are slow-growing and have poor root systems. Adding calcium (for example in the form of lime) to the soil or soil mix aids growth of new roots. These cacti tolerate a minimum of 50°F (10°C).

Seeds germinate easily, often in 4–5 days, if fresh and sown at 70°F (21°C). They are helmet-shaped and produced in red or green fruits. Unusually, viable seeds do not sink when placed in water because they contain air pockets. Before sowing (*see p.232*), liberally sprinkle the surface of the soil mix with ground lime; this greatly increases the survival and growth rate of seedlings.

The sand dollar cactus, *Astrophytum asterias* (syn. *Echinocactus asterias*), is prone to rot if too wet and to shrivel if too dry; it grows better if grafted as a seedling. The slender, young stems of *Pereskiopsis* make ideal rootstocks.

When grafting, as shown below, it is essential to work quickly and unite each scion and stock before the sap dries up. This happens after 15–30 seconds. The stocks may produce suckers later on; remove these as soon as they appear. Plants reach a good size in 2–4 years.

GRAFTING ASTROPHYTUM SEEDLINGS

1 For a seedling graft, a suitable rootstock, such as a 4–6in (10–15cm) tall Pereskiopsis spathulata, *and* Astrophytum *seedlings (here of* A. asterias*) are required. Prepare the rootstock by cutting it back to about 1–2in (2.5–5cm) and trimming off the sideshoots.*

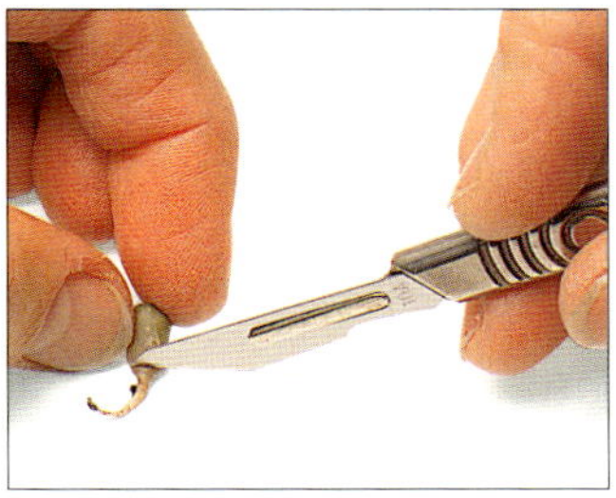

2 Immediately after the rootstock is prepared, lift a seedling to use as a scion. Use a sterilized scalpel or a sharp, thin-bladed knife to cut off the roots at the base. Work as quickly as possible.

3 Gently press the prepared scion onto the top of the stock, to one side so that as much of the water-storing tissue and central transport tissue are aligned as possible. Rotate the scion gently to remove any trapped air bubbles; the sap should hold it in place.

4 Place the grafted plant in a humid chamber, here a bottle cloche over a saucer with a little water. Keep at a minimum of 70°F (21°C) in bright, indirect light. The graft should show signs of active growth in 2–3 weeks (see inset).

CEPHALOCEREUS

SEEDS in spring
CUTTINGS from spring to summer

These cacti, hardy to 50°F (10°C), are fairly rare in cultivation apart from the old man cactus (*Cephalocereus senilis*). Plants may take ten years or more to reach 12in (30cm) in height and 50 years to reach 5ft (1.5m). Because of their slow growth and usually solitary stems, they are normally raised from seeds. Taking a cutting is worth doing only to save a plant that has rotted at the base. Most benefit from additional lime in the soil or soil mix.

SEEDS

Use a very free-draining soil mix of two parts cactus mix and one of fine grit, because these cacti are very susceptible to overwatering. Sow the seeds (*see p.232*) at 66–75°F (19–24°C).

CUTTINGS

If taking a columnar stem cutting, cut the stem above the site of the rot and inspect the cut surface. If there is any discoloration, trim the cutting until the tissue is clean. Allow the wound to callus for 2–3 weeks until it is firm and dry. Pot into fine gravel and water sparingly only in warm weather until active growth is visible; this may take up to two years.

OLD MAN CACTUS *The spines on this species,* C. senilis, *become longer and thicker as it matures (see left). It will not flower or fruit until it is twenty years old or more, so it is generally grown from purchased seeds.*

OTHER CACTI AND SUCCULENTS

ADENIA Sow seeds (*see p.232*) in spring at 66–75°F (19–24°C). Take stem cuttings (*p.236*) in summer. Apical-wedge graft (*p.241*) rare or difficult cultivars onto *A. glauca* stocks.
ADENIUM OBESUM (syn. *A. arabicum, A. micranthum, A. speciosum*) Seeds (*see p.232*) at 61°F (16°C) in spring. Flat or side graft (*pp.239–41*) rare or colored cultivars on species.
ADROMISCHUS As for *Crassula* (*p.245*).
AICHRYSON Sow seeds (*see p.232*) in spring at 66–75°F (19–24°C). Take rosette cuttings (*p.237*) in spring or early summer.
ALOE Sow seeds (*see p.232*) at 70°F (21°C) in spring to autumn. Divide offsets (*p.234*) just before season of growth in spring or autumn. Take cuttings as for *Gasteria* (*p.247*).
APOROCACTUS Sow seeds (*see p.232*) at 70°F (21°C) from spring to summer. Cuttings as for *Epiphyllum* (*p.246*).
ARGYRODERMA As for *Haworthia* (*see p.247*).
ARIOCARPUS Sow seeds (*see p.232*) from spring to summer at 75°F (24°C). Graft seedlings as for *Astrophytum* (*above*).
BROWNINGIA (syn. *Azureocereus*) As for *Cereus* (*see p.244*).
CALYMMANTHIUM As for *Cereus* (*see p.244*).
CARNEGIEA GIGANTEA Seeds at 70°F (21°C) in spring (*p.232*).
CEPHALOPHYLLUM As for *Conophytum* (*see p.245*).
CERARIA Seed and stem cuttings as for *Cotyledon* (*p.245*).

CEREUS

SEEDS in spring or in summer
CUTTINGS in spring or in summer

These mostly tall, columnar cacti are easy to raise from seeds. They grow up to 4ft (1.2m) a year and branch freely, so a single cutting will give a decent plant almost instantly. *Cereus* tolerate short periods of 25°F (-4°C).

SEEDS

The flowers open at night and are pollinated by moths. Hand-pollinate plants grown under cover (*see p.233*). Allow the plumlike fruits to ripen and soften before extracting the dark seeds. Sow (*see p.232*) at 66–75°F (19–24°C) for good-sized plants in ten years.

CUTTINGS

Because the columnar stems are rigid, it is possible to take cuttings up to 6ft (2m) long. The monstrose form of *Cereus hildmannianus* (often mistakenly called *C. peruvianus*) is best increased by cuttings (*see right and p.238*), although it reproduces fairly readily from seeds. The larger the wound on the cutting, the longer it takes to callus. After potting, keep the soil mix slightly moist in warm weather. Cuttings root in 1–12 months.

TAKING A CEREUS STEM CUTTING

1 Wear thick gloves and wrap a folded cloth around the chosen stem (here a monstrose form of Cereus hildmannianus*) to steady it. Use a large knife to remove a 3in–3ft (8cm–1m) length, cutting straight across the stem.*

2 Place the cutting on a wire tray or on styrofoam blocks to prevent the spines from being damaged. Leave it in a warm, dry place to allow the cut surface to callus. This will take at least 2–3 weeks in summer and a little longer at other times of the year.

3 Choose a pot that is slightly larger than the base of the cutting. Fill the bottom third with cactus soil mix, then add a 1in (2.5cm) layer of fine gravel. Stand the cutting on the gravel and fill around it with more gravel to the top. If necessary, support it with one or more sturdy stakes. Label and keep the soil mix slightly moist.

CEROPEGIA

SEEDS in spring
DIVISION from spring to summer (stem tubers) (root tubers)
CUTTINGS from spring to summer (sticklike species) (climbing or trailing species)

The many succulents in this genus grow best with a minimum of 39–64°F (4–18°C). When sowing seeds (*see p.232*), cover them with fine grit to ensure moist conditions for germination. Most germinate rapidly at 75–81°F (24–27°C). Fresh seeds often germinate in less than a week.

Most tuberous species produce offset tubers at the roots of the parent tuber. Lift the plant, remove the offset tubers, and pot, for new plants in 2–3 months. Detach tubers that form along the stems without lifting the parent (*see p.235*).

To propagate sticklike species such as *Ceropegia dichotoma*, take 4–6in (10–15cm) cuttings with at least three nodes, severed just below a leaf node scar. Pot as stem cuttings (*see p.236*) to root in 1–2 months, but do not let the bases touch the soil mix.

Take stem cuttings also from slender-stemmed, climbing, and trailing species, or coil longer cuttings, as shown above, and root at 61°F (16°C). Coil cuttings of the heart or rosary vine (*C. linearis* subsp. *woodii*), each with 1–2 tubers.

Larger tubers make good rootstocks for flat grafting the milkweed family.

STEM CUTTINGS OF TRAILING CEROPEGIA

1 Three-quarters fill a 5in (13cm) pan with cactus cuttings soil mix. Loosely coil a 10–12in (25–30cm) length of stem; peg it on the surface.

2 Cover with ¼in (1cm) of soil mix. Firm and water. Place in a bright, warm, dry spot; keep just moist until new shoots appear in 1–2 months.

3 Once the new shoots are 4–6in (10–15cm) tall, cut the stem into sections, each with its own shoot and roots. Trim off the old stem. Pot each rooted cutting into a small pot of cactus soil mix.

OTHER CACTI AND SUCCULENTS

CHEIRIDOPSIS As *Haworthia* (*see p.247*).
COPIAPOA Sow seeds (*see p.232*) at 66–75°F (19–24°C) from spring to summer; slow. Take stem cuttings as for *Mammillaria* (*p.248*).
CORRYOCACTUS (syn. *Erdisia*) Seeds and cuttings as for *Cereus* (*see above*).
CYPHOSTEMMA Sow seeds (*see p.232*) at 64–70°F (18–21°C) from spring to early summer.
DELOSPERMA As for *Conophytum* (*see facing page*).
DIOSCOREA (syn. *Testudinaria*) Sow seeds (*see p.232*) in autumn at 66–75°F (19–24°C). Cuttings are very difficult.
DISCOCACTUS Sow seeds as for *Gymnocalycium* (*see p.247*). Divide offsets as for *Mammillaria* (*p.248*).
DISOCACTUS As for *Epiphyllum* (*see p.246*).
DROSANTHEMUM As for *Conophytum* (*see facing page*).
DUDLEYA As *Aeonium* (*p.242*).

CLEISTOCACTUS

SEEDS from spring to summer
CUTTINGS from late spring to summer
GRAFTING from spring to summer

Seeds are produced in green, yellow, or red berries. Sow them (*see p.232*) to germinate at 70°F (21°C).

The rigid stems of upright species such as the silver torch (*Cleistocactus strausii*) furnish columnar stem cuttings up to 6ft (2m) long (*see p.238*). Cuttings from clumping species such as *C. winteri* with slender, arching stems are easier to manage if only up to 2ft (60cm) long. Support cuttings with stakes to prevent them from bending while they root, usually 1–4 months. It takes 2–3 years to produce a good-sized plant.

Crested, or cristate, *Cleistocactus* forms may be flat grafted to preserve their characteristics (*see right and p.239*). Cleistocactus tolerate a minimum of 50°F (10°C).

FLAT GRAFTING A CRISTATE FORM

1 When flat grafting a cristate Cleistocactus, *take a fan-shaped section of the crest (here of* C. winteri) *to prepare as a scion. Cut off the sides of the crest and then the base to create a roughly rectangular scion about ¾–1½in (2–4cm) wide. If the sides are not taken off, they will grow into the soil and rot.*

2 Prepare a suitable rootstock (here a 1½in (4cm) Echinopsis scopulicolus*). Unite the scion and stock, taking care to align the cambium layers. Secure with rubber bands until signs of new growth appear. Grow on in a bright place at 61°F (16°C).*

3 After one year or so, the grafted plant should have developed the convoluted form of its parent. Eventually the crest will grow down to the base of the scion and the corrugations will spill over and conceal the rootstock beneath.

CONOPHYTUM

Conophytum bilobum

SEEDS in autumn
CUTTINGS in spring or in late summer to early autumn

These succulents prefer temperatures above 50°F (10°C). Gather the minute seeds in autumn and surface-sow (*see p.232*) at 70°F (21°C) in humid shade at once to allow seedlings the maximum time for growth before summer dormancy.

The best time to take stem cuttings (*see p.236*) is in late summer or early autumn when the plants first show signs of coming out of dormancy. Separate the heads and cut each at the base. Keep moist at 66°F (19°C) to root in 2–4 weeks. If a plant has not come out of dormancy by late autumn, the stems are probably dead; treat the heads as cuttings and keep dry in cool weather. They root rapidly when warm and moist in spring and flower in 3–5 years.

CORYPHANTHA

SEEDS in spring or in early summer
DIVISION from late spring to early summer

Most of these cacti are solitary or offset slowly so are best raised from seeds (*see p.232*). Gather large, brown seeds from the green seedpods and sow at 66–75°F (19–24°C). A good-sized plant will develop in about five years.

A few species, such as *Coryphantha elephantidens*, produce multiheaded clumps with numerous offsets. Rooted offsets may be divided (*see p.235*) and replanted or potted singly or in clumps.

COTYLEDON

SEEDS in early spring
CUTTINGS from spring to summer

Most species in this genus may be raised from the dustlike seeds (*see p.232*), sown at 66–75°F (19–24°C).

Take stem cuttings (*see p.234*) from bushy forms such as the panda plant (*Cotyledon tomentosa*). Semi-ripe, 2–3in (5–8cm) long stems give best results; longer cuttings bend while they root and make untidy plants. If kept moist, the cuttings should root in 3–4 weeks and be ready for planting out in 2–3 months. Many species may be increased from leaf cuttings (*see p.235*). Leaves that have dropped off may not retain their axillary buds, so always take fresh leaves from the plant. Plantlets form in 1–3 months.

CRASSULA

SEEDS from spring to summer
DIVISION from spring to summer
STEM CUTTINGS from spring to summer
LEAF CUTTINGS from spring to summer

This diverse genus contains a wide range of succulents that grow best at a minimum of 41–50°F (5–10°C). Raising most of them from seeds is very unpredictable. Taking stem cuttings is probably the easiest means of increase; leaf cuttings are fairly easy, but slow. Some low, clumping species such as *Crassula schmidtii* may be divided.

SEEDS

Crush the minute, dry seedpods to gather the dustlike seeds. They tend to be short-lived; germination rates vary from 1–2 to 100 percent (*see p.232*).

DIVISION

Mat-forming species that readily root from the creeping stems may be lifted and divided. Gently pull or cut the plant into suitable pieces and repot or replant them (*see p.234*). Within a few weeks, the divisions should fill out and make neat, new clumps.

CUTTINGS

Take 2–4in (5–10cm), semi-ripe stem cuttings (*see p.236*). Large bushy plants with thick stems, such as the silver jade plant (*C. arborescens*) or dollar plant (*C. ovata*, syn. *C. argentea*), are rooted from 5–10in (13–25cm) cuttings. Trim off some leaves to avoid stems bending under the weight while rooting. If taking leaf cuttings (*see p.237*), use fresh leaves just above the point of active growth. They take a year or so to form a plant.

ROOTING LEAVES
In the wild, Crassula leaves that fall on the ground often take root and develop into new plants. Single leaves may be taken as cuttings.

CRASSULA NEALEANA

ECHEVERIA

SEEDS from spring to summer
DIVISION from spring to summer
ROSETTE CUTTINGS from spring to late summer
STEM OR LEAF CUTTINGS from spring to summer

Sow seeds of species in this genus (*see p.232*) at 61–66°F (16–19°C). Mat-forming plants that root along the stems may be divided (*see p.234*). Take rosette cuttings (*see p.237*) from plants that produce offsets. Those with few or no offsets may be increased by leaf cuttings (*see p.237*) taken from the main stem near the base of the rosette. Leaves of many showy hybrids and a few species will not come away cleanly from the main stem; instead, use lower leaves from flower stems, before the flowers open. Older plants may be ungainly; cut the stems 3in (8cm) below the rosettes and treat as stem cuttings (*see p.236*).

ECHINOCEREUS *HEDGEHOG CACTUS*

Echinocereus stramineus

SEEDS in spring or summer
CUTTINGS from late spring to summer

Cacti in this genus with dense, comblike spines, such as *Echinocereus reichenbachii*, are fairly slow-growing and best raised from seeds (*see p.232*) sown at 70°F (21°C). Those with open spination, such as *E. cinerascens* and *E. pentalophus* (syn. *E. procumbens*), tend to be faster growing and make fine clumps: these cacti can also be increased from columnar stem cuttings.

Sever a stem near its base and trim to 2–4in (5–10cm). Leave for 1–2 weeks to callus, then treat as standard cuttings (*see p.238*). They may take 1–3 months to root and produce a good plant in 1–2 years. It is possible to take cuttings from the slower-growing species, but they may take up to two years to root and are very prone to rot. Most species tolerate temperatures to 45°F (7°C) if dry, but prolonged cold marks plants badly.

ECHINOPSIS

SEEDS from spring to summer
GLOBULAR STEM CUTTINGS in spring or summer
COLUMNAR STEM CUTTINGS from spring to early summer

This genus, hardy to 50°F (10°C), includes cacti formerly classified as *Lobivia* and *Trichocereus*. Species may be raised from seeds. The type of cutting depends on the plant habit. Tall-growing species make good rootstocks.

SEEDS

To set seeds, flowers must be hand-pollinated (*see p.233*). Fruits take 2–4 months to ripen, then split to reveal the seeds; sow (*see p.232*) at 70°F (21°C). Most globular species are suitable for hybridizing (*see p.21*). Try crossing *E. oxygona* with highly colored species such as *E. aurea* or *E. arachnacantha*.

CUTTINGS

Globular echinopsis and species such as the peanut cactus (*E. chamaecereus*) produce numerous offsets that fall away at the touch of a finger. Take globular stem cuttings (*see p.238*). If taking stem cuttings from columnar cacti (*see p.238*), sever each stem 12–18in (30–45cm) from the base to allow for new growth. Trim cuttings to less than 4ft (1.2m) and allow to callus for 3–6 weeks.

ECHINOPSIS CALOCHLORA *Although many* Echinopsis *are globular in shape, others, such as this* E. calochlora, *are columnar in habit when young. As they mature, they form large sprawling clumps of creeping stems. These* Echinopsis *may be increased by columnar stem cuttings.*

EPIPHYLLUM *ORCHID CACTUS*

Epiphyllum crenatum

SEEDS in spring or summer
CUTTINGS from spring to late summer

For best results, sow seeds (*see p.232*) of species fresh at 70°F (21°C). Hybrids may be cross-pollinated (*see p.233*) easily, but the seedlings vary greatly in hue and form. Seed-raised plants flower after 4–7 years.

By far the easiest way to increase orchid cacti is by flat stem cuttings (*see p.238*). Cut stems into 6–9in (15–23cm) lengths. Very short cuttings usually take an extra 1–2 years to flower. The cuttings should root in 3–6 weeks; those rooted early in the year often flower in the following spring. All *Epiphyllum* need a minimum of 50–59°F (10–15°C).

EUPHORBIA

SEEDS from spring to summer
CUTTINGS from midspring to midsummer

Succulents in this genus are tender, many needing a minimum 45–59°F (7–15°C). Their milky sap is very irritant and can cause blindness if rubbed in the eye; it is hardened by water but can be washed off with warm soapy water. Dip cuttings in, and spray the parent with, water to coagulate sap at the wounds. The seeds are normally rare and costly. (*See also* Perennials, *p.196*.)

SEEDS

The seedpods explode when ripe, so tie paper bags over them to gather seeds (*see p.232*). Viable seeds germinate well at 59–68°F (15–20°C). Keep seedlings and plants at a minimum 61°F (16°C).

CUTTINGS

Globular species such as *E. globosa* and *E. obesa* sometimes form offsets. Sever these in midspring to midsummer and treat as cactus stem cuttings (*see p.238*).

Some thick-stemmed, cactuslike *Euphorbia*, such as *E. canariensis*, are fairly easy from cuttings; other small, slow-growing ones are more challenging. Take stems up to 6ft (2m) long from late spring to early summer; avoid unripened growth. Allow to callus for 1–2 weeks or more, then treat as cactus stem cuttings. They should root in 1–6 months.

In late spring, take up to 6in (15cm) long stem cuttings (*see p.236*) from bushy, slender-stemmed species such as the crown of thorns (*E. milii*). They should root in 3–6 weeks. Do not disturb the cuttings until active growth is visible, because the new roots are very brittle. Cuttings produce attractive new plants in about a year.

GASTERIA

SEEDS in spring or in autumn
DIVISION in spring to autumn
CUTTINGS from spring to summer

This recently revised genus of rosette-shaped succulents now contains just 16 species. It is best to avoid propagating the plants while they are flowering. They need a minimum of 45°F (7°C).

Gasterias take about three years to make decent, small plants from seeds. Sow (*see p.232*) at 66–75°F (19–24°C).

Most *Gasteria* offset fairly freely to form closely packed mounds. They need to be divided (*see p.234*) with a knife, so the parent plant must first be lifted or knocked out of its pot (*see right*). Allow the cuts on the offsets to callus for two days in a warm, airy place, then pot to grow on. Older offsets often have their own roots; make sure the neck of each sits in the grit top-dressing and the roots are in contact with the soil mix. Pot young offsets with no roots in equal parts of fine grit and cactus soil mix and keep slightly moist. Offsets taken in early spring make good plants in a year.

Gasterias will root from leaf cuttings (*see p.237*), but they are not always successful and are rather slow. Take fresh leaves from about halfway up the plant. Set the cuttings in small pots of almost pure gravel. Water frequently to prevent drying out. Plantlets should appear in 3–6 months at the bases of the leaves and take 1–2 years to form plants.

DIVIDING OFFSETS
Lift the plant (here Gasteria carinata *var.* verrucosa*) and select a young, healthy offset. Shake off as much soil mix as possible from its roots. Use a sharp knife to sever the offset* (see inset) *at the point where it is attached to the parent plant.*

GYMNOCALYCIUM

SEEDS from spring to autumn
DIVISION from spring to autumn
GRAFTING from late spring to summer

These cacti prefer a minimum of 50°F (10°C). Most species are easy to grow from seeds. One or two species, such as *Gymnocalcium andreae* and *G. bruchii*, offset quite freely and may be divided. Grafting is necessary to increase the brightly colored neon cacti cultivars.

SEEDS

The plum-shaped fruits ripen to green, blue, or red, and seeds vary from very small to large. Sow the seeds (*see p.232*) at 66–75°F (19–24°C). Many smaller species flower in 2–4 years.

DIVISION

Lift and divide them as for *Gasteria* (*see above and p.235*). They should make flowering plants in 2–3 years.

GRAFTING

Neon cacti lack chlorophyll and so cannot sustain themselves. Each must be flat-grafted onto a green rootstock that is taller than normal so that it can sustain itself and the scion (*see below and p.239*).

GRAFTED NEON CACTUS
To create this plant, flat graft a scion from the neon cactus (here Gymnocalycium mihanovichii *'Red Cap') onto a 4–6in (10–15cm) tall* Echinopsis *rootstock. Keep the plant out of full sun to protect the tender, colored scion from scorching and fading.*

HAWORTHIA

SEEDS in spring or in autumn
DIVISION in spring or in autumn
CUTTINGS from spring to autumn

Viability of seeds rapidly declines after six months, but fresh seeds (*see p.232*) germinate well, for plants in 2–3 years. Many species offset freely and may be divided (*see p.234*): separate rooted rosettes; break clumps (*H. attenuata*, *H. cymbiformis*) into sections; divide stolons of species such as *H. tessellata* and *H. limifolia*. Sever offsets of taller species (*H. glauca*, *H. reinwardtii*) at the base; treat as stem cuttings (*see p.236*). Some root from leaf cuttings (*see p.237*); it is slow (1–2 years for a plant) but useful for plants that do not offset.

HOYA WAX FLOWER

Hoya carnosa

SEEDS in spring or summer
CUTTINGS from spring to summer

Most of these succulent and semisucculent plants need a minimum of 50°F (10°C). Tufted seeds are carried in long pods. If sown fresh (*see p.232*) and kept moist at 70–81°F (21–27°C), they can germinate in a few days. Most, however, are increased by cuttings. Cut a length of stem just below a leaf node and 3–4 nodes long. Dip the base in hormone rooting powder, which also helps to stop the milky sap from leaking. Treat as stem cuttings (*see p.236*) to root in 2–6 weeks. New plants flower in 1–2 years.

OTHER CACTI AND SUCCULENTS

ECHINOCACTUS Sow seeds (*see p.232*) from spring to early autumn at 70°F (21°C).
ESCOBARIA Sow seeds as for *Gymnocalycium* (*see above*). Treat offsets as for *Mammillaria* (*p.248*).
ESPOSTOA As for *Cereus* (*see p.244*).
FAUCARIA As for *Haworthia* (*see above*).
FEROCACTUS Sow seeds (see p.232) in spring at 50–68°F (10–20°C).
GIBBAEUM As for *Haworthia* (*see above*).
GLOTTIPHYLLUM As *Haworthia* (*see above*).
GRAPTOPETALUM As for *Echeveria* (*see facing page*).
HAAGEOCEREUS Sow seeds and take stem cuttings as for *Cereus* (*see p.244*).
HARRISIA Sow seeds and take cuttings as for *Cleistocactus* (*p.245*).
HATIORA Take stem cuttings (*see p.238*), 2–3 pads long, from spring to autumn; take 3–5 pad cuttings from club-shaped stems.
HELIOCEREUS As for *Epiphyllum* (*see facing page*).
HYLOCEREUS As for *Epiphyllum* (*see facing page*).
JATROPHA As for *Euphorbia* (*facing page*).
JOVIBARBA Sow seeds (*see p.232*) in early spring at 50°F (10°C). Take rosette cuttings (*p.232*) in spring and summer.

KALANCHOE

Kalanchoe blossfeldiana

SEEDS in spring to autumn
STEM CUTTINGS from spring to autumn
LEAF CUTTINGS from spring to summer
PLANTLETS from spring to autumn

Seeds of *Kalanchoe* (including *Bryophyllum*) may be extremely viable or very weak; sow them (*see p.232*) at 70°F (21°C).

The easiest way to propagate bushy plants such as *K. blossfeldiana* is from stem cuttings (*see p.236*). Allow the cuttings to callus for 24 hours. They should root in 1–2 weeks. Take cuttings after flowering to obtain new, flowering plants in the following spring.

A number of small, leafy species, such as *K. pumila*, are grown from leaf cuttings (*see p.237*) and root in 2–6 weeks. Some large, fleshy-leaved species, such as *K. beharensis*, root very readily from mature leaves (*see top right*) to form new plants in 1–2 years.

Some species formerly classified as *Bryophyllum* have slightly notched leaf edges from which adventitious buds are produced. These buds fall to the ground in the wild and form new plantlets; they seem to root anywhere. *K. tubiflora* and *K. daigremontiana* are easy to propagate in this way (*see right*). Grow plantlets in clumps or pot singly for new plants in 3–6 months. *Kalanchoe* requires a minimum of 50°F (10°C).

TAKING KALANCHOE LEAF CUTTINGS

1 *Remove healthy leaves with stalks intact (here of* Kalanchoe beharensis*) from the parent plant. Thread onto a length of wire and hang in a warm, airy place, out of direct sun. Make sure that the leaves do not touch each other.*

2 *Plantlets should form at the base of the leaf stalks after 3–6 months. Once these are large enough to handle, detach them and pot them individually in 2in (5cm) pots of cactus potting mix to grow on. Label and water.*

KALANCHOES FROM ADVENTITIOUS BUDS

1 *Any time between spring and autumn, gently pull away some plantlets, or adventitious buds, from the notched leaf margins (here of* Kalanchoe tubiflora, *syn.* K. delagoensis*). The plantlets root very readily, even in carpet.*

2 *Three-quarters fill a 2in (5cm) pot with cactus soil mix. Add a ½in (1cm) layer of fine grit. Set about six plantlets on top. Keep slightly moist in a bright, airy place out of direct sun. They should root within a few days.*

LITHOPS *LIVING STONES*

Lithops karasmontana

SEEDS in autumn or spring
CUTTINGS in early summer

These succulents are slow-growing and very prone to rot. Because of this, they need some care in propagation. *Lithops* are hardy to 54°F (12°C).

Because of their slow growth, most *Lithops* are raised from seeds (*see p.232*), which germinate easily in most cases. The seedpods ripen in the summer; crush them to gather the small seeds and sow at 66–75°F (19–24°C) for new plants in 2–3 years. The difficulty lies in protecting seedlings from rot.

Offsets of one or more heads may be removed from larger clumps and treated as globular stem cuttings (*see p.238*). Many of the cuttings may rot, so be sure it is worth splitting the parent clump. Allow the heads to callus for a few days, then pot in small gravel. Keep slightly moist, but not wet; roots should appear in 1–2 weeks. It takes 1–2 years to form a new plant.

MAMMILLARIA
PINCUSHION CACTUS

SEEDS from spring to autumn
DIVISION from spring to summer
CUTTINGS from spring to summer

Self-fertile species often set seeds, taking up to a year to form mostly red, candle-like pods. Gather seeds when the pods are soft, and sow (*see p.232*) at 66–75°F (19–24°C). Seeds remain viable for 5–10 years. Seedlings flower in 2–5 years.

Mammillarias form clumps with age, but the offsets usually do not root while still attached to the parent. Very small-headed clumps such as *M. vetula* (syn. *M. magneticola*) may be rooted, however, and lifted and divided into sections (*see p.235*). Allow any cuts to callus for a few days before repotting or replanting.

Most offsets are treated as globular stem cuttings (*see p.238*) for new plants in 2–5 years. The heads of some freely offsetting species, such as *M. gracilis* and the strawberry cactus (*M. prolifera*), fall away at the slightest pressure. Other clumps should be lifted and suitable offsets severed with a knife. These cacti need a minimum of 45–50°F (7–10°C).

OTHER CACTI AND SUCCULENTS

KLEINIA Seeds (*see p.232*) at 68°F (20°C) in spring or summer. Divide stolons or tubers (*p.235*) in spring or summer.
LAMPRANTHUS As *Conophytum* (*see p.245*).
MALEPHORA As *Conophytum* (*see p.245*).
MATUCANA Sow seeds as for *Gymnocalycium* (*see p.247*).
MELOCACTUS Seeds as for *Gymnocalycium* (*see p.247*). In colder areas, graft seedlings as *Astrophytum* (*p.243*). Flat graft (*p.239*) small plants late spring to midsummer.
MONADENIUM Sow seeds (*see p.232*) at 66–75°F (19–24°C) in spring. Stem cuttings (*p.236*) in spring or summer.
NEOPORTERIA Sow seeds as for *Gymnocalycium* (*see p.247*).
NOLINA Sow seeds (*see p.232*) at 66–75°F (19–24°C) in spring. Cuttings difficult.
OREOCEREUS (includes *Borzicactus*) Sow seeds (*see p.232*) at 70°F (21°C) in spring or summer.
OROYA Sow seeds as for *Gymnocalycium* (*see p.247*).
PACHYCEREUS (includes *Lophocereus*) Seeds or cuttings as for *Cereus* (*see p.244*).
PACHYPHYTUM As for *Echeveria* (*see p.246*).

OPUNTIA *Prickly pear*

SEEDS from spring to summer
CUTTINGS from spring to summer

Some of these reproduce so readily in favorable conditions (some are hardy to -10°F/-23°C) that they have become weeds in some regions. Avoid contact with the painful barbed spines and smaller spines, called glochids.

The large, hard-coated seeds are produced in often edible fruits. They can take up to two years to germinate and then may yield a poor percentage of seedlings. Sow (*see p.232*) at 70°F (21°C) for a decent plant in 3–5 years.

Many *Opuntia* have flat, oval, pad-like stems, which root very readily as stem cuttings. Take them as shown (*see right*) and keep them slightly moist at 66°F (19°C). The cuttings should root in 2–6 weeks and should form a good-sized plant in 2–3 years.

OPUNTIA STEM CUTTINGS

1 Wear thick gloves and use a paper collar to guard against the barbed spines. Use a sharp knife to sever a pad, cutting straight across a joint. Leave the cutting in a warm, dry place for 2–3 days to allow the wound to callus (see inset).

2 Two-thirds fill a small pot with soil mix, topped with a layer of fine grit. Stand the cutting on it. Add more grit.

PARODIA

Parodia magnifica

SEEDS from spring to autumn
CUTTINGS from spring to summer
GRAFTING spring to summer

Most of these tend to be solitary until quite old, so the best method of increase is from seeds. A few, such as *Parodia ottonis*, freely produce offsets, which may be used as cuttings. Special forms are best grafted. Cacti in this genus (syn. *Eriocactus, Notocactus, Wigginsia*) are hardy to 41–50°F (5–10°C).

SEEDS

Seeds are produced in spiny berries or red pods. Those in the Notocactus group are easy to raise from seeds. Sow them (*see p.232*) at 19–24°C (66–75°F) to germinate in 2–3 weeks. Seedlings of the Parodia group are slow-growing for the first two years but then grow rapidly and soon catch up with other species. New plants flower in 3–5 years.

CUTTINGS

Sever offsets at the bases and treat as globular stem cuttings (*see p.238*) for new plants in 2–3 years. Offsets of *P. ottonis* form at the ends of short stolons. Lift the parent plant, and they should come away very readily.

GRAFTING

Cuttings of misshapen forms will root, but as grafted plants they are less prone to rot. Flat-graft (*see p.239*) monstrose stems; graft sections of crested (cristate) forms as for *Cleistocactus* (*see p.245*) for an attractive plant in 2–3 years.

PELARGONIUM *Geranium*

SEEDS in autumn or in late winter
DIVISION in spring to summer
CUTTINGS from spring to summer

Of succulents in this genus, the species are easy to raise from seeds. Most fleshy-stemmed and shrubby forms are grown from cuttings. Tuberous species or plantlets may be divided. These plants prefer a minimum of 50°F (10°C). New plants flower in 1–3 years. (*See also* Perennials, *p.205*.)

SEEDS

Remove the "parachutes" from the small seeds to sow (*see p.232*) at 66–75°F (19–24°C); germination occurs in 5–25 days. In hot weather, seeds of many succulents lie dormant so are best sown after summer. Seedlings may damp off (*see p.46*) if chilled or in poor light.

DIVISION

Separate root tubers of mature plants as shown below for new plants in 1–2 years. Treat as adult plants, but water sparingly until new growth is visible. Some species, such as *P. graveolens*, form plantlets on underground stems: these are easy to lift and divide (*see p.235*).

CUTTINGS

For shrubby succulents, take 2–4in (5–10cm) semi-ripe cuttings (*see p.236*); cut below a leaf scar. Dip in weak hormone rooting compound; dry for 24 hours. Set in soil mix, water in, then do not water for two weeks. If they do not root, keep just moist and roots should appear. For those with thick, fleshy stems, allow cuttings to callus for about a week, then treat as above.

DIVISION OF PELARGONIUM ROOT TUBERS

1 In its growing season, lift the parent plant (here Pelargonium lobatum*) or remove it from its pot. Cut or break off one or more tubers from the roots. Half-fill a small pot with cactus potting mix and add a shallow layer of fine grit.*

2 Lay the tuber on top and cover with more grit. Place in a bright, airy spot at 66°F (19°C); keep the soil mix slightly moist. A new shoot should be produced from each tuber after 2–3 weeks.

REBUTIA

Rebutia wessneriana

SEEDS in spring and in autumn
DIVISION from spring to early summer
CUTTINGS from spring to early summer
GRAFTING from late spring to late summer

Most of these (including *Sulcorebutia* and *Weingartia*) tolerate dry cold to 15–25°F (-17 to -4°C) and are easy to increase by seeds, division, or cuttings.

SEEDS

Sow seeds (*see p.232*) at 70°F (21°C) for flower in two years or so. Avoid sowing in midsummer; temperatures over 84°F (29°C) seem to inhibit germination.

DIVISION

Several species, such as *Rebutia albiflora*, make mats of small heads, which root down on their own. Simply break a clump into sections (*see p.235*) for new plants in 1–2 years. Allow to callus for two days, then replant or pot.

CUTTINGS

Most species offset freely into clumps. Sever offsets at their bases and treat as globular stem cuttings (*see p.238*).

GRAFTING

Flat-grafting (*see p.239*) onto columnar *Echinopsis* is best for forms that rot easily, such as *R. canigueralii* f. *rauschii*, or do not root readily, such as *R. heliosa*.

SCHLUMBERGERA
CHRISTMAS CACTUS

SEEDS in spring
CUTTINGS in spring and summer
GRAFTING in midsummer

These cacti must be cross-pollinated to set seeds. The grapelike fruits soften when ripe. Sow seeds (*see p.232*) at 66–70°F (19–21°C) for plants in 3–4 years. For flowering plants in one year, take flat stem cuttings (*see p.238*), 2–3 whole segments long, as the plant starts into growth. They root very readily. Root three cuttings back-to-back in a pot for a bigger, more balanced plant. Christmas cacti may be apical-wedge grafted (*see p.238*) onto an upright rootstock, such as *Selenicereus*, to create a standard in 2–3 years. Plants are hardy to 41°F (5°C).

RHIPSALIS
MISTLETOE CACTUS

SEEDS from spring to autumn
CUTTINGS from spring to autumn
GRAFTING from late spring to midsummer

This genus includes cacti formerly known as *Lepismium*; all grow best with a minimum of 45°F (7°C). Most may be raised from seeds. Taking cuttings is usually quick and easy. *Rhipsalis* may also be grafted to create a standard with a head of pendent stems.

SEEDS

Most *Rhipsalis* flower fairly easily and produce tiny, bright berries, which take about six months to ripen and become sticky. Wash the seeds in warm, very slightly soapy water, dry, and sow at once (*see p.232*) at 66–70°F (19–21°C) for flowering plants in 3–5 years.

CUTTINGS

To take a stem cutting, detach a slender stem at a joint and cut it into 4–6in (10–15cm) long sections. Treat as for flat stem cuttings (*see p.238*). The cuttings should root in 3–6 weeks and will make nice plants in 1–2 years.

GRAFTING

For the rootstock, use a piece of stem from a *Selenicereus* (*see facing page*), and stake firmly. Prepare the stock and scion as shown above (*see also p.240*). Once active new growth is visible, usually 2–3 weeks later, remove the raffia. Growth is usually fairly rapid thereafter, producing an attractive plant in 1–2 years.

SIDE GRAFTING RHIPSALIS

1 Prepare a 2–4in (5–10cm) scion from a species such as Rhipsalis pilocarpa *(see left) for side grafting onto a slender columnar cactus rootstock (here* Selenicereus*).*

2 Place the scion and stock together so that the cambium layers meet; if necessary, place the scion to one side of the stock. Press slightly to remove any air bubbles. Pin in place with a cactus spine (see inset) and bind the graft with raffia. Stake if necessary and grow on.

OTHER CACTI AND SUCCULENTS

PERESKIA Sow seeds (*see p.232*) in spring at 66–75°F (19–24°C). Take stem cuttings (*p.236*) from late spring to summer.
PILOSOCEREUS Sow seeds and take cuttings as for *Cereus* (*see p.244*).
PLEIOSPILOS As for *Haworthia* (*see p.247*).
PTEROCACTUS Sow seeds as for *Gymnocalycium* (*see p.247*). Take cuttings as for *Mammillaria* (*p.248*).
RHODIOLA As for *Sedum* (*see facing page*).
RUSCHIA As for *Conophytum* (*see p.245*).
STAPELIA As for *Haworthia* (*see p.247*).
STENOCACTUS (syn. *Echinofossulocactus*) Sow seeds as for *Gymnocalycium* (*see p.247*). Take cuttings as for *Mammillaria* (*p.248*).
STENOCEREUS Sow seeds and take cuttings as for *Cereus* (*see p.244*).
STOMATIUM As for *Haworthia* (*see p.247*).
STROMBOCACTUS Sow seeds (*see p.232*) at 70°F (21°C) in spring; seedlings may be difficult to establish.
SYNADENIUM As for *Euphorbia* (*see p.246*).
THELOCACTUS Sow seeds as for *Gymnocalycium* (*see p.247*).
TREMATOSPERMA Sow seeds (*see p.232*) in spring at 70°F (21°C). Cuttings are difficult.
TRICHODIADEMA As for *Conophytum* (*see p.245*).
UEBELMANNIA Sow seeds (*see p.232*) at 75°F (24°C) in spring. Graft seedlings from late spring to midsummer onto *Pereskiopsis* rootstocks as for *Astrophytum* (*see p.242*).
VILLADIA As for *Cotyledon* (*see p.245*).
WEBEROCEREUS As for *Epiphyllum* (*see p.246*).

SEDUM *Stonecrop*

SEEDS from spring to autumn
DIVISION in spring or in late summer
CUTTINGS from spring to summer

The succulent species in this genus (syn. *Hylotelephium*) are easy to propagate. The method depends on the habit of the plant. Many are quite hardy, but tender species need a minimum of 41°F (5°C).

SEEDS

Sow seeds (*see p.232*) of hardier species, such as *S. acre*, at 55–61°F (13–16°C), tender species at 59–64°F (15–18°C). Seed-raised plants flower in 1–3 years.

DIVISION

Divide deciduous, clumping species such as *S. spectabile* in spring (*see p.234*). Lift mature mat-forming species, for example *S. lydium*, to find how far along the stems the mat has rooted, then divide it with a sharp knife into sections, each with some rooted stems. Divisions should flower in one year.

CUTTINGS

Most species root very readily from cuttings, usually in 1–6 weeks. Tender plants, such as *S. rubrum*, *S. hintonii*, and *S. morganianum*, are easily rooted from leaf cuttings (*see below and p.237*) for a small plant in one year. They can also be increased from stem cuttings (*see p.236*) to obtain plants more quickly, in 2–3 months. Cut 2–3in (5–8cm) from the tips of the stems and allow the cuttings to callus for a day. Take ¾–1¼in (2–3cm) long cuttings of hardier, creeping forms, such as *S. spurium*.

Rosette cuttings (*see p.237*) of hardier, rosette-forming sedums such as *S. spathulifolium* flower in 1–2 years.

PROPAGATING SEDUM FROM LEAF CUTTINGS

ADVENTITIOUS ROOTS *Many species, such as this* Sedum rubrotinctum, *readily produce adventitious roots from the stems and leaves. Single leaves from these plants may be rooted in trays lined with damp newspaper before potting.*

TAKING LEAF CUTTINGS *Flick off plump leaves from the stem. Place on damp newspaper in bright shade at 61°F (16°C). In 3–4 weeks, the leaves should form roots and plantlets* (see inset) *at their bases. Pot in pans to grow on.*

SELENICEREUS

Selenicereus grandiflorus

SEEDS from spring to autumn
CUTTINGS from spring to summer

The larger-flowered *Selenicereus* are known as Queen of the Night. The species that have cylindrical stems, such as *S. grandiflorus*, make good rootstocks for side grafting (*see p.240*) other epiphytic cacti. Minimum 59°F (15°C).

Seeds are not always available since they take so long (5–10 years) to become a flowering plant, but they should be sown (*see p.232*) at 61–66°F (16–19°C) as soon as ripe or in spring.

Most *Selenicereus* are fairly easy to increase from cuttings, for mature plants in 2–5 years. Take 2½–4in (6–10cm) stem sections; treat as flat stem cuttings (*see p.238*) to root in 3–6 weeks.

SEMPERVIVUM *Houseleek*

SEEDS from spring to autumn
DIVISION in summer to autumn
CUTTINGS in summer to autumn

Some of these succulents are hardy to -30°F (-34°C). The rosettes die after flowering, but the plants offset freely to form a spreading carpet.

Flowers must be hand-pollinated (*see p.233*) to set seeds, but only a limited number of seeds may still be produced. Crush the tiny, dry fruits to gather the seeds. Once they are sown, leave the seeds in a sheltered spot, such as a cold frame, to germinate.

Most *Sempervivum* form a number of offsets each spring on long, slender stolons. These often have their own roots and may be detached and potted or replanted (*see p.234*). Offsets establish more quickly in 4–6 weeks if kept moist and out of direct sun. Treat unrooted offsets as rosette cuttings (*see p.237*).

SENECIO

SEEDS from spring to summer
DIVISION from spring to late summer
CUTTINGS from spring to summer

Succulents in this genus, which now includes tender species of *Kleinia*, *Notonia*, and *Othonna*, are hardy to a minimum of 42–50°F (6–10°C). New plants reach a good size in 1–3 years.

Break the parachutes of hairs off the seeds before sowing (*see p.232*). Cover them with a layer of fine grit. They should germinate in 2–4 weeks.

A number of sticklike species, such as *Senecio articulatus, syn. Kleinia articulata* (candle plant), spread by stolons. Single stems or clumps may be separated from the plant (*see below*). Choose stems with adult characteristics. If the shoots have no roots, add a thin grit layer to the soil mix; sit the shoot on this. Tuberous species, such as *Senecio oxyriifolius*, may also be divided (*p.235*).

Take 4–6in (10–15cm) stem cuttings (*see p.236*) from species with thick stems and 5–10cm (2–4in) stem-tip cuttings from thinner-stemmed species.

DIVIDING A SENECIO

1 Lift the parent plant or remove it from its pot. Select a well-developed shoot at the edge of the clump. Cut or break it off with a length of underground stem (stolon). This may already have roots. Replant the parent plant.

2 Allow the shoot to callus for 24 hours. Pot so that its roots are just covered with cactus soil mix halfway in a 3½in (9cm) pot. Fill in around the shoot with fine gravel to the rim. Label and grow on as for stem cuttings (see p.236).

Bulbous Plants

Most bulbous plants are best planted in bold groups or naturalized in sweeping drifts to make the most of their flowering display; propagating them enables the gardener to build up large stocks quickly and inexpensively

The propagation of bulbous plants is almost an act of faith, since so much of what happens is out of sight. Most techniques, however, are simple and can be achieved in a small space with only basic tools and soil mixes, and large stocks of plants can be built up quickly in many cases. Young bulbous plants that you have raised yourself settle well in the garden, which is not always the case with large, purchased ones.

The term bulbous plant is a broad one, used here to embrace true bulbs, corms, and tubers, fleshy structures that store food and water to tide the plants through dormant periods when they retreat underground. An understanding of the plant's annual cycle of growth and dormancy is often a good guide as to when to propagate it.

Many of these plants reproduce naturally by means of offsets, and therefore division of offset clumps is a widely used method of propagation in cultivation. Seeds are recommended for increasing species and some tubers that do not lend themselves to vegetative propagation, although patience is required because seedlings can take several years to reach flowering size.

There are several propagation techniques that are unique to bulbous plants, such as scaling, twin-scaling and chipping, scooping and scoring, and sectioning, all of which exploit the ability of the dormant storage organ to produce new bulblets, cormels (cormlets), or tubers. Some bulbs form bulbils or bulblets naturally; these offer a way of increase that is similar but much quicker than seeds. A few bulbs can be increased from cuttings.

Rhizomatous plants are sometimes grouped together with bulbous plants, but in this book they are found in the Perennials chapter (*see pp.146–213*).

Exotic bulb
There are only two species of Veltheimia, *both of which are bulbs found in South Africa. This is* V. bracteata. *It is easily propagated from seeds or offsets and, unusual for bulbous plants, from leaf cuttings.*

Ornamental onion
Allium cristophii *is a particularly decorative member of the onion family. Its large seedhead is actually a spherical umbel of many small seedpods, which split open when ripe to release their black seeds. The seedheads dry very well for ornamental use.*

DIVISION

Bulbs and corms increase naturally by forming clumps of small bulbs or cormels (cormlets) that draw nutrients from the parent plant. Most are attached to the storage organ itself (offsets), but some form on other parts of the plant (bulblets and bulbils). It is simple to propagate these plants by splitting them. Many tubers do not increase in this way but instead grow steadily larger; these must be raised from seeds (*see p.256*) or, in a few cases, from cuttings (*see individual genera, pp.260–79*). A few tubers (notably dahlias) form clumps that can be divided like perennials.

Many garden bulbs produce so many offsets that they eventually become overcrowded; as they compete for space, light, and moisture, new bulbs fail to thrive or flower, becoming "blind." Division keeps them healthy and strong.

Some bulbs, such as *Cardiocrinum giganteum*, take several years to flower and then die, leaving a few offsets for increase. A few (*Lilium candidum*, *Crocus tommasinianus*, *Nerine*, and some *Sternbergia*) flower best if congested; divide them only to increase stocks.

Most bulbous plants have a dormant season and are best divided just at its onset, after the foliage has died down, but many can be divided just as they start into growth. Evergreen bulbs and corms, such as *Dierama*, *Cyrtanthus*, and *Lloydia*, should be divided immediately after flowering. The period of dormancy varies, depending on the species' native climate. For example, a *Crinum* is dormant in spring, a snowdrop in summer, and a tulip until late summer.

DIVIDING OFFSETS

Most offsets usually form within the parent bulb's tunic, or skin, if there is one; they are attached to the basal plate, from which the roots grow.

Some bulbs, such as daffodils and lilies, produce their offsets to the sides of the parent. In the case of tulips, the offsets are often directly beneath. Most corms, such as in gladioli, form around the basal plate, while others (*Crocosmia*) develop "chains" of corms.

The size of offsets varies. *Crinum*, for example, produce quite large offsets. Deep digging around the parent plant is necessary to free the perennial roots before careful removal of the offsets (*see below*). Some *Allium* produce quantities of tiny offsets that are easily separated from the parent by the very act of digging up the bulbs.

Take care when lifting parent bulb or corms or knocking them out from pots: many are fragile and easily damaged. Clean off the soil and detach the offsets (*see below*). In nearly all cases, they can be removed by hand, but tightly packed clumps, such as with *Anemone nemorosa*, *Corydalis*, and *Eranthis*, may need to be cut free with a knife. If you wound the parent bulb, dust the exposed area lightly with a fungicide before replanting to protect it from rot.

Offsets that are close in size to the parent bulb, and can thus be expected to flower the following year, can be replanted directly into their flowering positions. Prepare the site first by forking it over and clearing away any debris and perennial weeds. Work in some well-rotted organic material to condition the soil, as well as a good commercial bulb fertilizer.

DIVIDING LARGE BULBOUS OFFSETS

1 In spring, before active growth begins, lift a clump of bulbs (here of Crinum) with a garden fork. Shake off any excess soil from the roots.

Pull the clump apart and select large bulbs with healthy, well-developed offsets. Discard any that are withered, misshapen, or show signs of disease.

2 Pull or cut the offsets carefully from each bulb, taking care to preserve any roots. Dust damaged basal plates with fungicide.

3 Prepare 6in (15cm) pots with a moist, sandy soil mix. Pot each offset individually, up to its neck. Label and water the pot.

DIVIDING SMALLER BULBOUS OFFSETS

1 Lift a clump of mature bulbs. Select the healthy bulbs, and reject those that are dead or that show signs of pests or diseases.

2 Separate any pairs or clumps of bulbs with large offsets into single bulbs by gently pulling them apart, without damaging the roots.

3 Clean the bulbs by rubbing them with finger and thumb to remove any loose, outer tunics. Dust the bulbs with fungicide.

4 Pot the divided bulbs. Plant the bulbs at twice their own depth, and space them at least their own width apart.

DIVISION OF STOCK-PLANT CORMS

1 To encourage the production of cormels (here of gladioli), shallowly plant mature corms in spring. Plant in rows in a nursery bed 1in (2.5cm) deep and 4in (10cm) apart.

2 During summer, remove the flowerheads to prevent their wasting energy on producing unwanted seeds.

In autumn, or when foliage begins to die down, carefully lift the corms with a hand fork. The corms should have produced large numbers of cormels around their bases.

Cormels should come away easily

3 Pull off the cormels. The cormels will probably vary in size, but most of them will be viable. Discard any shriveled cormels; store the rest frost-free in dry peat over winter.

4 In spring, draw out drills, 4in (10cm) apart and 1in (2.5cm) deep, in a free-draining nursery bed. Put cormels 2–3in (5–8cm) apart, cover, water, and label. Grow on for 2–3 years.

CORMELS IN SEED TRAYS

Cormels can be planted in seed trays in moist, gritty soil mix instead of being lined out in a bed. Space the cormels 1in (2.5cm) apart, then cover with ½in (1cm) of soil mix.

Small offsets are best grown on in a more controlled environment. Some can be lined out in nursery beds, but small quantities are more easily managed if they are potted. Many should reach flowering size after two years and can be planted out in spring or autumn.

Sort container-grown offsets, once divided, according to their size, and repot in a similar soil mix.

POTTING OFFSETS

Bulbous plants need a free-draining soil mix; otherwise, they are prone to rot. Most are best in a mixture of equal parts soil-based mix and fine grit. For lime-hating species such as *Lilium speciosum*, make up a mixture of one part pulverized bark, five parts acidic soil mix, and five parts lime-free small gravel.

Use pots that allow for two years' growth. Either plastic or clay pots are suitable, but clay pots dry out faster and so will need more watering. Most bulbs or corms should be covered to twice their own depth; some, like crocuses, pull the bulbs down to the correct level as the roots grow. Pot small offsets in groups of five or more, large ones singly.

AFTERCARE OF OFFSETS

Young bulbs and corms need protection from extreme heat and cold. In colder climates, most are best in pots in a cold frame (*see p.40*) that shelters them from winter cold and keeps out pests and weeds. Cold frames can overheat, so keep them ventilated during hot, dry spells and shade them if necessary. Tender offsets, especially corms, may need to be kept in a warm greenhouse for part of the year.

Nursery beds are suitable in warmer regions, where they may need shading, or for hardy bulbs and corms in cold climates, where protection must be given during periods of severe cold. Control pests such as bulb fly and mice that eat bulbs, as well as weeds.

While the young plants are in active growth, feed and water them regularly. It is a good idea to sink pots in a plunge bed (*see p.257*) or a nursery bed to keep a more even temperature around the pots and prevent them from drying out quickly, so that less watering is needed.

During their dormant period, most bulbs and corms should be kept barely moist. Water them only to stop the soil mix from drying out completely. Shade summer-dormant bulbs and corms in hot weather to avoid overheating. Some, however, such as some fritillaries, must never be allowed to dry out.

SHALLOW PLANTING OF STOCK PLANTS

Gladioli are propagated commercially by shallowly planting stock corms to stimulate production of cormels. This technique (*see above*) can be used for other bulbs and corms such as crocuses, irises, or *Watsonia*: it takes a little longer than simple division but is ideal if large numbers of offsets are needed.

BULBLETS AND BULBILS

A few bulbs, such as *Iris reticulata*, *Ixia*, some *Ipheion*, and *Oxalis*, form bulblets (tiny bulbs) around the parent. Stem-rooting lilies and many *Allium* species form bulblets on the stem below ground. Lift the parent and separate and pot the bulblets as for offsets (*see facing page*).

Other genera produce tiny bulbs, or bulbils, in the leaf axils (*Calochortus* and lilies) or flowerheads (*Gagea* and some *Allium*). They are shed naturally, often in late summer. Gather them from the ground or snap off the plant. Pot them and grow on as for cormels (*see above*).

Sowing seeds

Seed-sowing may seem a slow way to increase bulbous plants, but it can be rewarding. It makes it easy to build up large stocks, and after two or three years, successive sowings will give a new batch of flowers each year. Rare species are usually only available as seeds. The best way to propagate woodland species, which do not tolerate drying out or root disturbance, is from fresh seeds.

Bulbous plants increased vegetatively lose vigor over time and fall prey to disease, especially lilies and related genera such as *Nomocharis*. They can be renewed by seed-raised bulbs, which are always virus-free even if the parent is not. Cultivars may set fertile seeds but do not come true and may yield only a small number of garden-worthy plants.

Gathering and storing seeds

Seeds of most bulbous plants are large and easy to handle. The seed capsules are usually on the old flowered stems. A few bulbous plants have inconspicuous capsules at ground level (for instance, crocuses) or produce berries (such as *Arisaema* and *Arum*) that in the wild are eaten by small mammals or birds.

Ripe capsules (*see below*) quickly shed their seeds; watch them closely. Gather the capsules (*see below*) and shake the seeds into a paper bag. Like capsules, berries are ripe when they turn color – squash them to extract the seeds. Wash off any pulp in warm water, then spread the seeds on paper towels to dry.

Freshly sown seeds germinate quite evenly, usually by the following spring, although nearly all remain viable for a season if kept cool. Store the seeds in paper bags at 41°F (5°C) – the crisper compartment of a refrigerator is ideal. In colder climates, it is often impractical to sow seeds of tender subjects when fresh, because of severe winters.

Sowing seeds

Cut a small sample of seeds in half to gauge how many are viable: fertile seeds will be fleshy and pale or translucent. Seedlings form storage organs quickly, so most seed trays are too shallow. A 3½in (9cm) pot or 5in (13cm) pan is best. Mix equal parts of soil-based seed soil mix (*see p.34*) and fine grit or coarse sand for clay pots. For lime-hating bulbs, mix equal parts peat (or coir) and fine lime-free grit (such as aquarium gravel); add a soluble feed suitable for lime-hating seedlings. With plastic pots, use six parts of grit to four of soil mix to avoid waterlogging.

Fill the pot to three-quarters of its depth with soil mix (*see below*). Water it by spraying the surface or by standing it in a tray of water until the surface becomes moist by capillary action, then allow it to drain. Sprinkle the seeds evenly over the soil mix. Seeds that are large enough to handle, as with some fritillaries and lilies, may be set on end, about ¼in (5mm) apart.

Cover the seeds with soil mix and top-dress with fine grit to deter slugs and snails, inhibit growth of liverworts, and deflect heavy rain so the soil mix surface does not pan. Label the pot.

RIPENING SEEDHEADS

Most bulbous seed capsules (here of Fritillaria imperialis) *are green when unripe* (see left) *and brown and dry when ripe* (see inset). *Harvest the seeds as soon as the capsules ripen.*

GATHERING SEEDS

Cut the ripe capsules from the parent plant (here Alstroemeria). *Keep in a paper bag in a dry, airy place for up to two weeks. The capsules will split open, releasing the seeds* (see inset).

SOWING SEEDS

1 *Prepare a pot with free-draining seed soil mix and firm* (see inset). *Tap the packet to sow the seeds evenly over the surface.*

2 *Use a sieve to scatter a thin layer of fine soil mix over the seeds. There should be just enough mix to cover the seeds.*

3 *Cover the soil mix with fine grit or aquarium gravel to the pot rim. Add it carefully to avoid disturbing the seeds.*

4 *Label the pot, then stand it in a shady area, or plunge it in a sand bed* (see facing page), *to keep the soil mix from drying out.*

USING PLUNGE BEDS

Sink pots of seeds up to the rims in a bed of coarse sand or grit, in a cold frame or under greenhouse staging. Group them according to the plants' dormant periods to make watering easier.

POTTING BULBOUS SEEDLINGS

1 *One-year-old seedlings (here of* Fritillaria meleagris) *are often not sufficiently well developed to pot. After the growing season, allow the foliage to die back and stop watering.*

2 *In the second year, when the young bulbs or corms are dormant, repot them in fresh, gritty bulb soil mix. Place them at twice their own depth and spaced their own width apart.*

DEVELOPMENT OF BULBOUS SEEDLINGS

After two years, seedlings (here of Calochortus tolmiei) *may vary noticeably in size. The largest will have germinated in the first year, whereas the smallest may not have germinated until the second year.*

Sort the smaller from the larger seedlings and pot them separately; all should develop satisfactorily.

Germinating seeds

Seeds are often spurred into germination as snow melts in the wild. A winter freeze for hardy seeds or above-freezing chill for tender seeds, even if in the refrigerator, then a period at around 50°F (10°C) aids germination. Tender seeds need a frost-free environment; some also have specific temperature and light needs for germination to take place (*see* A–Z of Bulbous Plants, *pp.260–79*). All seeds must be kept moist; if they dry out after germinating, they will die; on the other hand, they rot in prolonged moisture. Their growth is also checked by extreme heat or cold, so spring sowings may be less successful than autumn sowings.

A plunge bed (*see above*) keeps pots from drying out and moderates the soil mix temperature, so it does not overheat in summer or freeze in winter. Water the plunge medium so moisture can soak through clay pots by capillary action; water plastic pots directly but sparingly. Alternatively, keep the pots in a cool, shady area, such as the lee of a wall or in a cold frame. Control any worm (*see p.40*), insect, or mammal activity (*p.47*).

Bulbous seed leaves are often grass-like in appearance. Some seeds sprout within a few weeks, but the majority of autumn sowings will not show any signs of germination until the first mild spell in late winter. Some bulbous plants, such as *Paris*, stay dormant for a year; others, such as *Arisaema* and *Colchicum*, germinate erratically over a few years.

Care of seedlings

Group seedlings according to their dormant periods. Most need to be barely moist when dormant; a few, such as lilies and some crocuses, need watering all year. To bulk up seedlings rapidly, keep them in growth as long as possible by feeding and watering them regularly in the growing season. Bulb or tomato fertilizer is good, since it has a high potassium and low nitrogen content, which aids storage organ development without promoting leaf growth. When the leaves begin to wither, stop feeding.

All bulbous plants resent root disturbance, so leave the seedlings for two growing seasons before potting, unless they are overcrowded. Seeds that germinate erratically may be left longer.

Growing on seedlings

Pot seedlings when they are dormant and the soil mix is nearly dry. Carefully knock out the pot of seedlings: as you separate them, note the position of the growing points, because some bulbous plants, such as *Erythronium* and some *Corydalis*, look similar at both ends and it is easy to plant them upside down.

To exclude worms, cover the pot base with a piece of screening. Add ½in (1cm) of coarse grit for fast drainage, then three-quarters fill the pot with a soil-based potting mix combined with an equal part of fine grit. For lime-hating plants, use acidic soil mix. Top it with ½in (1cm) of fine sand to keep each basal plate or base in a free-draining area and make it easier to see the tiny storage organs when repotting. Space the storage organs (*see above*) to allow for two more years' growth before planting out. Cover them with soil mix, then with a ½in (1cm) layer of fine grit. Water well and place in a sheltered place outdoors or under cover, depending on the temperature needs of the species.

Plant out very large seedlings in a nursery bed to grow on or in their final positions, where they should flower more quickly. Prepare the soil first with grit and well-rotted organic matter.

Self-sown seedlings

Many bulbous plants seed themselves outdoors, but it may be difficult to identify seedlings naturalized in grass. Most are best left *in situ* and divided only if congested (*see p.254*). Lift rare or tender seedlings while in growth; keep the root ball intact and pot (*see above*).

Hybridizing

Some bulbous plants may be hybridized (*see p.21*) successfully, particularly those with prominent stamens and stigmas, such as daffodils, irises, lilies, and tulips.

Scaling and Chipping

Scaling, twin-scaling, and chipping are methods of propagation that are unique to bulbs. The storage organ itself is broken or cut into pieces, each of which yields a new bulb. It is a more exacting method than division (*see p.254*), since a controlled environment, with moisture, aeration, and warmth, is essential for success. It is the best way, however, of increasing stocks of bulbs that do not readily increase by offsets or set seeds in cultivation.

Scaling and chipping can be performed on good-quality purchased bulbs as well as bulbs dug up from the garden. The young bulbs settle well in the garden, which is not always the case with more mature, purchased bulbs. Lily scaling, unlike seed raising of bulbs, affords no protection against the transfer of disease, so only plants that are vigorous and free of disease should be used.

Bulbs that have loosely packed scales, such as all lilies and some fritillaries, may be scaled, with the scales being removed by hand. Bulbs with a tighter structure, such as daffodils, hyacinths, and *Nerine*, must be cut into pairs of scales. Small bulbs or nonscaly bulbs, for example *Hippeastrum*, may be cut into chips. A piece of the basal plate must be retained on each section for twin-scaling and chipping to succeed, but with scaling this is not necessary.

The optimum time for scaling and chipping bulbs is when their food reserves are at maximum, during the dormant stage before new root growth starts. This is usually in late summer or early autumn for spring to summer-flowering bulbs and in spring for those that flower in autumn or winter.

Scaling bulbs

After the topgrowth dies down, lift a few mature bulbs and clean off the soil. Select only healthy, vigorous ones for scaling. Pull off and discard withered or damaged outer scales, then snap off the scales in succession as shown below. Usually a few scales are removed and the parent bulb is replanted after treating with fungicide. For a large quantity of new plants, scale the entire bulb.

Treat the scales with fungicide, then place them in a suitable medium in a plastic bag. This may be a peat and perlite mixture or ten parts vermiculite moistened with one part water. The bag is sealed, retaining as much air as possible to allow the scales to "breathe," and left in a dark place at 68°F (20°C).

For bulbs from cold climates, such as *Lilium martagon* and North American lilies, the scales may well need, after six weeks' warmth, a further six weeks at 41°F (5°C) to simulate winter and stimulate bulblet production. The crisper section of the refrigerator is ideal.

A traditional alternative to the plastic bag is to insert the scales to half their depth in pans or trays filled with equal parts of vermiculite or peat and sharp sand. Keep the scales humid under a cover or in a closed case at 68°F (20°C) in the greenhouse. This makes it easier to check the scales for rot.

Check the scales after a few months for new bulblets (*see below*); leave the scales attached to the bulblets if new roots have grown on the bulblet's tiny

Scaling bulbs

1 Lift virus-free bulbs in late summer or early autumn, before root growth starts. Clean the bulb and snap off the required number of outer scales as close to the basal plate as possible. Replant the parent bulb immediately.

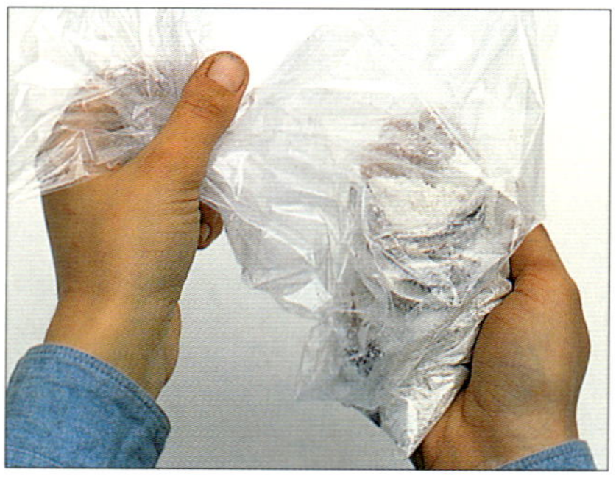

2 Put some fungicidal powder in a clear plastic bag. Add the scales (here of a lily) and shake the bag gently to coat the scales thoroughly with the powder. Alternatively, soak in fungicidal solution and drain.

3 Prepare a mixture of equal parts perlite and moist peat substitute or peat in a second, clear plastic bag. Add the coated scales. Inflate the bag, then seal and label it. Keep the bag in a dark place at a temperature of 68°F (20°C).

4 When bulblets have formed, usually by the spring, take the scales out of the bag. If the scales are soft, gently pull them off. If they are still firm, or if roots are emerging from the basal plate or scale callus, leave the scale attached.

5 Pot the bulblets in equal parts soil-based potting mix and fine grit, singly or several to a pan. Water, label, then top-dress with grit. Keep them in a cool, shady place over summer, then overwinter them in a cold frame.

6 Pot the bulbs into larger pots each spring or autumn. If grown several to a pan, gently separate the bulbs first (see above). *When the new plants reach flowering size, plant them out either in the garden or in large containers.*

TWIN-SCALING BULBS

1 *Select a clean, healthy, dormant bulb (here of a daffodil). Remove the brown, outer scales and cut off any old, fibrous roots or dead tissue, keeping the basal plate intact. Slice off the nose of the bulb with a clean, sharp knife.*

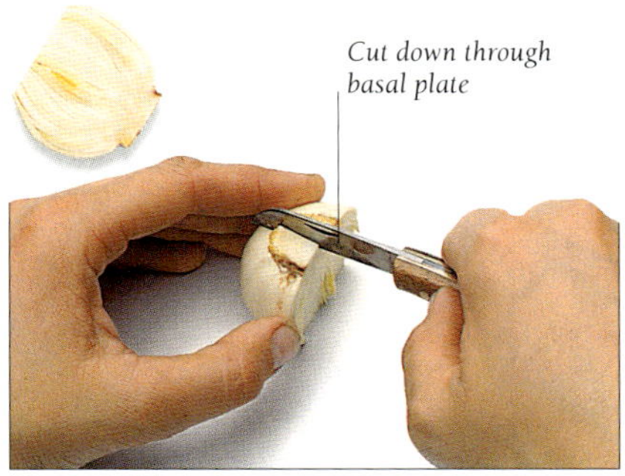

2 *Turn the bulb upside down and cut it vertically in half, and then into quarters. Depending on the size of the bulb, you can divide it into eight or more segments, provided that each retains a piece of the basal plate.*

3 *Peel back pairs of scales from each piece; cut them free at the base with a scalpel. Each pair of scales should have a piece of the basal plate attached (see inset). Dip the twin-scales in fungicidal solution and allow to drain.*

basal plate as well as on the callus at the end of the scale. Whether separated or attached, pot the bulblets individually or several to a pan, depending on their size. Insert them into a free-draining soil mix (*see facing page*), covering them with their own depth of mix. Use acidic soil mix for lime-hating species, or mix one part of ground bark to five of soil mix. Most new plants flower in three or four years.

TWIN-SCALING

When twin-scaling bulbs (*see above*), scrupulous hygiene is essential to prevent any disease from entering the new plants through cut surfaces. Wash your hands carefully (or wear surgical gloves) and use a sterilized cutting board and tools. Wipe the knife blade with denatured alcohol between each cut (*see also p.30*).

Select high-quality, dormant bulbs and clean as shown above. Remove any old, outer scales. Cut the bulb into segments and split each of these into pairs of scales, starting with the outer two scales. For this task, a sharp, thin-bladed knife or scalpel is essential to keep damage to the bulb tissue to a minimum. Larger bulbs may yield up to forty twin-scales. Treat the twin-scales thereafter as for scales (*see facing page*), but check them regularly and remove any twin-scales that show signs of rot. In about 12 weeks, bulblets should form on the top of the basal plate. Treat them as scales.

CHIPPING

In chipping, the bulb is cut downward to produce 8–16 "chips" rather like the segments of an orange (*see right*). Hygiene is as important for chipping as for twin-scaling. The treated chips may be placed in a bag or a tray, as for scales, to form bulblets. Pot the chips and grow on at the recommended temperature for the species (*see* A–Z of Bulbous Plants, *pp.260–79*) to flower in 2–3 years.

CHIPPING BULBS

1 *Dig up a healthy bulb (here a* Hippeastrum*) when dormant and clean it. Remove any papery outer skin and trim back the roots with a clean, sharp knife without cutting into the basal plate. Cut back the growing tip.*

2 *Holding the bulb with the basal plate uppermost, cut it into 8–16 similarly sized sections ("chips"), depending on the size of the bulb. Make sure that each chip retains a piece of the basal plate.*

3 *Soak the chips in a fungicidal solution, made up according to the manufacturer's instructions, for up to 15 minutes to kill any bacteria or fungal spores. Allow the chips to drain on a rack for about 12 hours.*

4 *Place the chips in a clear plastic bag containing ten parts of vermiculite to one part of water. Inflate the bag, then seal and label it. Keep the bag in a dark place at 68°F (20°C). Check the bag periodically and remove any chips that show signs of rot.*

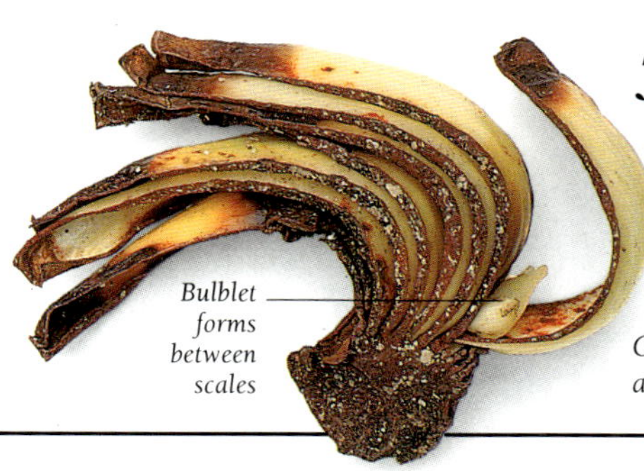

5 *After about 12 weeks, bulblets should form just above the basal plate. Pot the chips individually in 3in (8cm) pots in free-draining, soil-based potting mix. Insert each chip with its basal plate downward and the bulblets covered by about ½in (1cm) of soil mix. Leave the scales exposed; they will slowly rot away as the bulblets develop. Grow on in a sheltered position, in conditions appropriate to the individual species.*

A–Z OF BULBOUS PLANTS

ALLIUM *ORNAMENTAL ONION*

Allium hollandicum

DIVISION in late summer
BULBILS in late summer
SEEDS in late summer to autumn or spring
CHIPPING in early summer

Most of these perennials are bulbous plants, but a few are rhizomatous (*see* Perennials, *p.149*). They flower in spring, summer, or autumn. Propagate species such as *A. flavum* and *A. mairei* by division of offsets, and all others except sterile hybrids from seeds. Many self-seed readily in sunny, free-draining sites. A few have bulbils in the flowerheads (*see below*) or may be chipped. All types of propagation should yield a flowering plant in two to five years.

DIVISION

Many species, such as *Allium moly*, produce offsets very prolifically – some are tiny and form on the rooting portion of the stem so may easily be lost in careless lifting or repotting of the parent bulb. After the leaves die down, detach the offsets (*see pp.254–5*) to pot or replant, according to their size.

Take care to note the position of the growing points, which are not always conspicuous, before detaching them.

SEEDS

Gather seeds of large-flowered *Allium* by removing the entire flower stalk (*see below*). For smaller seedheads, shake the seeds directly into a paper bag. Sow the seeds fresh or store at 41°F (5°C) and sow in the spring (*see p.256*). Most germinate in 12 weeks, but some take up to a year. Take care when potting on seedlings to keep the growing points upright; they are not very obvious.

CHIPPING

Chip (*see p.259*) distinctly colored cultivars such as *A. hollandicum* 'Purple Sensation' to retain the true color.

ALLIUM BULBILS *Some ornamental species, such as* A. roseum, A. sphaerocephalon, *and* A. vineale *(shown here), sometimes produce aerial bulbils in the flowerhead. Pull off the bulbils gently. Grow them on in pots in moist, gritty soil mix, spaced 1in (2.5cm) apart and covered to a depth of ½in (1cm).*

GATHERING ALLIUM SEEDS

1 *Gather seeds when the flowerhead turns brown, before the seedpods open. Tug gently at the flower stalk; if it comes away readily at the base, it is ripe. Cover the wound with some soil to stop pests from entering the plant.*

2 *Line a cardboard box with paper. Hang the flower stalk upside down in a cool, airy place so that the flowerhead is suspended just above the lining of the box. The ripening seed capsules will open to shed seeds onto the paper.*

ALSTROEMERIA *PERUVIAN LILY*

DIVISION in late summer or autumn
SEEDS in late summer

These perennials produce white starchy tubers, which sometimes appear like creeping rhizomes. Species are best increased by seeds because the tubers are so delicate and are easily damaged; named cultivars can be increased only by division. Peruvian lilies are good subjects for experimenting with hybridization (*see p.21*) because many of the seedlings show pleasing variations. Flowering plants may be expected in 2–3 years.

DIVISION

Offset tubers are often connected very tenuously to the parent crown. When dividing a plant, lift the crown with great care, before the leaves have quite died down (*see p.254*). It is best not to split the crown into very small pieces if replanting immediately in open ground.

SEEDS

Alstromeria seeds should be sown fresh; it is hard to break the dormancy of seeds once they have been dried and stored. The seed capsules "explode" to scatter their seeds when ripe. For the best harvest of fresh seeds, cover the ripening seedhead for a few days with a small pillowcase or a cloth bag secured around the stalk; the seeds will be caught in the bag. Alternatively, cut the entire flower stalk and hang it up to dry and release its seeds (*see right*).

For the best rate of germination, sow the seeds immediately (*see p.256*). Keep them at a minimum temperature of 68°F (20°C) for four weeks, then remove the seeds and, using a knife, chip each outer case above the embryo, which shows as a dark spot. Resow the seeds and keep them at about 50°F (10°C).

The new tubers are easily damaged, so plant out the seedlings by the potful, as for *Erythronium* (*see p.267*).

GATHERING ALSTROEMERIA SEEDS
As soon as the seedhead has dried fully, cut the stem at its base and tie a paper bag around the seedhead. Hang it upside down in an airy place for two weeks to gather the seeds.

AMARYLLIS

Amaryllis belladonna 'Hathor'

DIVISION in spring
SEEDS in autumn

The only species, *Amaryllis belladonna*, is a bulbous perennial, hardy to 23°F (-5°C), but needs long, hot summers to flower well. It hybridizes easily with other members of the Amaryllidaceae family, such as *Crinum*, *Brunsvigia*, and *Nerine* (*see p.274*). Seeds from named cultivars do not come true, so the bulbs must be divided; some may be chipped. New plants flower after three years.

DIVISION

The parent bulbs may be 8in (20cm) deep in the ground, so care is needed when lifting them. Separate the large offsets (*see p.254*) and grow on in pots, keeping them just moist until they are established in autumn.

SEEDS

The fleshy seeds often germinate while still on the stem and must be gathered promptly, before they wither and die, and sown immediately. Sow them singly in 3in (8cm) pots, just covering them with soil mix or coarse sand (*see p.256*), and keep at 61°F (16°C). To hybridize *Amaryllis* with other genera, *see p.21*.

CHIPPING

Slow, large-flowered cultivars can be increased by chipping (*see p.259*) if there are not many offsets.

ANEMONE *WINDFLOWER*

DIVISION in mid- to late summer
SEEDS in summer

There is a wide range of tuberous species in this genus. Offsets are produced 2–3 years after a plant begins flowering. The species self-sow very readily, and seedlings from cultivars of *Anemone blanda*, which are grown for their variation of color, are often quite acceptable. (*See also* Perennials, *p.188*.)

Divide the offsets after the leaves die down (*see p.254*). Plant them where they are to flower, about 1in (2.5cm) deep, to flower the next year, or pot and plant out when in full growth in the spring.

The seedheads are often woolly or hairy and are best sown fresh. Remove as many of the hairs as possible prior to sowing by rubbing the seeds in your hands with a little dry sand. Sow in trays in seed soil mix (*see p.256*) and leave in a cool, sheltered place. Germination can be erratic; the first seedlings should appear in the following spring. Most should flower beginning in the third year.

ARISAEMA *JACK-IN-THE-PULPIT*

Arisaema candidissimum

DIVISION in autumn
SEEDS in autumn
SECTIONING in spring

These tuberous perennials produce hooded, sometimes bizarre-looking inflorescences composed of a spadix ("Jack") within a spathe (the "pulpit').

Tiny, scalelike offsets produced around the disk-shaped parent tuber can be removed (*see p.254*) and potted to flower in 2–4 years. The smallest offsets are best left attached to the parent until the following year.

Since there are no garden cultivars, all *Arisaema* can be raised from seeds. Remove the berries from the plant as soon as they have turned red and are ripe, and squash them to release the seeds. The flesh of the berries may inhibit germination; wash the seeds thoroughly and spread them to dry on paper towels for 24 hours in a warm, airy place. Sow the seeds immediately in trays (*see p.256*). In any case, germination is often slow and erratic and it is worth keeping all sown seeds for up to four years before finally discarding them. *Arisaema sikokianum*, however, germinates readily from fresh seeds. Seedlings may be slow to reach flowering size, usually in 3–5 years.

Some gardeners also section the tubers when they are dormant, as for *Caladium* (*see p.262*).

ARUM *LORDS AND LADIES*

DIVISION in early summer
SEEDS in late summer to autumn

These mainly spring-flowering tuberous perennials form tight clumps and may be lifted and separated when dormant (*see p.254*) after flowering. This can be done even though the parent tuber has sent up 5–6 berrying stalks: it could have 50 dormant offsets around it. *Arum creticum* in particular responds well to division.

The seeds germinate best if sown fresh (*see p.256*). Extract the seeds from the berries, as for *Arisaema* (*see above*), but wear gloves to protect against the caustic juice. Plants flower in 3–4 years.

ARUM BERRIES
The berries (here of Arum italicum*) appear in summer before the autumn leaves. Gather them for their seeds when they turn red or orange.*

BABIANA

DIVISION in autumn
SEEDS in autumn

This member of the Iridaceae family is among the hardiest of the Cape bulbs; the corms may be left outdoors at temperatures down to 23°F (-5°C).

Lift and divide established corms (*see p.255*) and pot in equal parts of soil-based mix and sharp sand, or plant outdoors at a depth of 8in (20cm). Keep them well watered over winter. Flowers may be produced in the following year. *Babiana ambigua* forms aerial corms in the leaf axils: in the wild, these drop to the ground as the foliage dies. Remove them when the foliage discolors and treat as cormels (*see p.255*).

Gather the seeds, which ripen to black, and sow them immediately in trays of seed soil mix combined with an equal part of sharp sand. They should germinate within four weeks at 55–59°F (13–15°C). Transplant the seedlings individually into deep pots of equally free-draining soil mix. The contractile roots will pull the developing corms down to the appropriate depth. Seed-raised plants flower in the second year.

OTHER BULBOUS PLANTS

ALBUCA Divide offsets (*see p.254*) when dormant. Sow seeds (*see p.256*) at 55–64°F (13–18°C).
x AMARYGIA PARKERI (syn. x *Brunsdonna parkeri*) Divide offsets as for *Amaryllis* (*see above*).
AMORPHOPHALLUS Divide offsets if produced, when dormant (*see p.254*). Sow ripe seeds (*see p.256*) at 66–75°F (19–24°C).
ANEMONELLA THALICTROIDES Divide well-established plants (*see p.254*) in autumn. Sow fresh seeds (*see p.256*) in summer.

BEGONIA

BULBILS in late summer or spring
SEEDS in late summer or spring
SECTIONING in spring
CUTTINGS in spring

The tuberous perennials in this genus include the Tuberhybrida, Multiflora, and Pendula begonias, of which there are many named cultivars. All are tender and dormant in winter. Some species, such as *Begonia sutherlandii*, produce bulbils; these provide an easy means of propagation. Seedlings are prone to damping off (*see p.46*), so controlled conditions are needed for success; sectioning and cuttings are less tricky. Most new begonias flower in the first summer after propagation. (*See also* Perennials, *p.190*.)

BULBILS

If bulbils develop in the leaf axils, gently detach them when they are fully developed. Surface-sow them immediately as for seeds (*see p.256*) on moist soilless mix, or store them dry in perlite or vermiculite at 41°F (5°C) for potting in the following spring.

BEGONIA SEED CAPSULE *One begonia plant can produce many thousands of fine, dustlike seeds. Mix the seeds with fine sand to sow them evenly.*

SECTIONING TUBEROUS BEGONIAS

1 After the leaves die back in autumn, lift the dormant tubers and clean them. Dust the crowns with fungicide and store in boxes of dry sand.

2 In spring, space the tubers 2in (5cm) apart and 1in (2.5cm) deep in a tray of moist, sandy soil mix. Keep them at 55–61°F (13–16°C).

3 When shoots appear, cut each tuber into pieces, each with at least one shoot and some roots. Dust the cuts with fungicide; allow to callus.

4 After a few hours, pot each section singly in a mixture of equal parts peat and perlite or fine grit, so the top of each tuber is level with the surface.

5 Lightly firm and water, and label each pot. Keep the tubers at a minimum of 64°F (18°C) in a humid, bright place until established (see left).

SEEDS

Sow fresh seeds (*see p.256*) only when the daylight hours are lengthening; if not, store at 41°F (5°C) and wait to sow in spring. Surface-sow seeds in pans of peat-based soil mix (or a peat-free alternative). Water, then cover the pan with a sheet or glass or clear plastic and keep it at 64–68°F (18–20°C). The seeds should germinate quickly, at which time the sheet of glass should be removed.

Three to four weeks after sowing, pot the seedlings singly in a mix of equal parts peat and sand, with a little slow-release fertilizer. Feed with a tomato fertilizer diluted to half-strength. Begonias make good subjects for hybridizing (*see p.21*).

SECTIONING

Large tubers with several growing points can be sectioned (*see above*) before planting in spring. Each section should

CALADIUM *ANGEL WINGS*

DIVISION in spring
SECTIONING in spring

Generally, only named cultivars of these tender tuberous perennials are grown; these must be propagated vegetatively to retain the colorful foliage variations. Most, including *Caladium bicolor* cultivars, produce offsets. The first leaves on each new plant often revert to the species and will look atypical, but in a few months the foliage will show its true colors. These are rainforest plants, so the tubers will not survive drying out.

DIVISION

Lift the tubers before growth begins and snap or cut off any offsets (*see far right and p.254*). Grow on as for sections.

SECTIONING

Lift the often spherical tubers before growth begins and cut them into sections (*see right*). Cut as cleanly as possible to minimize damage to the tuber tissue. Root the sections in free-draining soil mix, such as equal parts peat and sharp sand or perlite.

CUTTING UP CALADIUM TUBERS

1 Use a clean, sharp scalpel to cut each tuber into sections, each retaining a dormant growth bud. Press gently and smoothly on the scalpel to obtain a clean cut.

2 Dust the cut surfaces of each section with a fungicide, such as sulfur dust, or immerse them in a suitable fungicidal solution. Leave for several days on a wire tray to dry and callus.

3 Prepare some 5in (13cm) pots with a free-draining, soilless mix. Pot each section singly, growth bud uppermost, and cover with its own depth of soil mix. Lightly water and label.

4 Place the potted sections in a humid place at a minimum of 68°F (20°C), such as in a heated closed case. The tubers should produce shoots in 7–10 days.

BASAL STEM CUTTINGS
Overwinter a tuber as shown in steps 1–2 (see left). When the shoots are 2in (5cm) tall, cut them out of the tuber, so that each has a piece of tuber at the base (see inset). Pot them singly.

have at least one growing point and some good roots. It is best not to be too greedy: only existing roots will develop; rootless sections of tuber are not able to produce new ones. When strong new shoots appear, pot them into the same soil mix as for seedlings and gradually harden off (*see p.45*) in a sheltered place.

CUTTINGS

Before replanting, or as new growth emerges in early spring, cut individual shoots from the tuber, each with a piece of tuber at the base (*see above*). Pot these basal stem cuttings singly in equal parts peat and perlite and keep moist and humid at a temperature of 64°F (18°C). After a month, check for rooting, then treat as seedlings.

During summer, cut off 4in (10cm) nonflowering sideshoots to use as stem cuttings. Root as for basal stem cuttings.

CALADIUM OFFSETS

Instead of sectioning a tuber, slice off its nose to encourage it to form offsets from the dormant buds. Pot the tuber as for sections (see left). In the spring, knock out the tuber, divide it into single offsets, and pot singly.

5 When the shoots have one or two true leaves, usually a few weeks later, pot each plant into 3½in (9cm) pots to grow on. Place each tuber at the same depth as before. Water in and label.

CALOCHORTUS *FAIRY LANTERN, MARIPOSA*

Calochortus venustus

DIVISION in autumn
BULBILS in autumn
SEEDS in autumn

Most of these bulbous perennials will not tolerate dampness or cold when dormant. All may be propagated from seeds, since there are no garden hybrids. Some species, for instance *Calochortus barbatus* (syn. *Cyclobothra lutea*) and *C. uniflorus*, often produce bulbils in the leaf axils. Division may be necessary when offsets become so congested that flowering is inhibited. It can take four years to produce flowering-size bulbs.

DIVISION

The parent bulb produces offsets after flowering, usually preventing the parent from flowering the next year. Remove the offsets (*see p.254*) and pot in a very free-draining mix that is not too rich to avoid overly lush, soft growth. Equal parts of soil-based potting mix and coarse grit would be suitable, or even a bed of coarse sand or ground pumice. Keep dormant offsets dry, and delay watering until late autumn.

BULBILS

For bulbil-producing species, collect the dying, brown foliage and tease out the bulbils. Treat as lily bulbils (*see p.273*).

SEEDS

Sow seeds in pots (*see p.256*) as soon as they ripen. Keep them dry, but exposed to cold, over winter. The seeds should germinate easily in spring, often before the parent bulbs show signs of growth.

CAMASSIA *QUAMASH*

DIVISION in autumn
SEEDS in autumn

Some species from this small genus of bulbous perennials, for example *Camassia leichtlinii*, have a number of cultivars, which can be increased only by division. Lift the bulbs after flowering and detach the offsets (*see p.254*). They should flower after two years.

All species come easily from seeds, which are produced freely; indeed, the species will self-sow if the seeds are not gathered. Self-sown seedlings are to be found near the base of the parent plant but do not need to be transplanted. They take little room and grow well, particularly among shrubs. If sowing (*see p.256*) the seeds, do not allow the container to dry out. Seed-raised plants can reach flowering size in three years.

CHIONODOXA *GLORY OF THE SNOW*

Chiondoxa forbesii

DIVISION in autumn
SEEDS in autumn

These bulbous perennials offset very readily to produce a very good display in a relatively short time. Divide clumps when they become crowded, every 3–4 years, after the leaves have died down (*see p.254*). Offsets will flower after two years.

Chionodoxa also set seed profusely each year. If left to self-sow, a colony soon takes hold. Alternatively, gather the seeds and sow in trays (*see p.256*) for flowers in the third year.

CHLIDANTHUS

DIVISION in autumn
SEEDS in spring

Chlidanthus fragrans is the only species; it is a tender, bulbous perennial. Offsets can be divided while dormant (*see p.254*) to flower in two years. Apply a tomato fertilizer when the new plants are in active growth.

Gather ripe seeds in autumn and store for spring sowing (*see p.256*); in cold climates, winter light is too poor for seedlings. Sow at 55–64°F (13–18°C) in trays. Keep seedlings barely moist in the winter, then treat as offsets. Lift self-sown seedlings in autumn, pot, and grow them on in a frost-free situation.

OTHER BULBOUS PLANTS

BELLEVALIA As for *Muscari* (*see p.274*).
BONGARDIA CHRYSOGONUM Sow seeds when ripe in summer (*see p.256*). Tiny tubers form deep in pot.
BRIMEURA Divide bulbs (*see p.254*) and sow ripe seeds in summer (*see p.256*).
BRODIAEA Divide corms in late summer or autumn (*see p.254*). Sow seeds at 55–61°F (13–16°C) in summer (*see p.256*).
BULBOCODIUM As for *Colchicum* (*p.264*).
CARDIOCRINUM Sow seeds in deep trays when ripe in autumn (*see p.256*). Shoots appear some time after germination; seedlings can take seven or more years to flower. After flowering, bulb dies but offsets may be divided (*see p.254*).
CHASMANTHE Sow seeds when ripe at 55–61°F (13–16°C) in summer (*see p.256*). Divide corms in spring (*see p.255*).
x CHIONOSCILLA ALLENI Divide bulbs in summer (*see p.254*).

COLCHICUM *Autumn crocus, Meadow saffron*

DIVISION in late summer or autumn
SEEDS in autumn

These cormous perennials are famous for their showy flowers that appear without leaves. Large-flowered hybrids very rarely produce a better-flowered form when raised from seeds, so they are best divided. Division every 3–4 years also maintains flowering. Alpine species are best grown from seeds.

DIVISION

Clumps of colchicums may be divided as for bulb offsets while dormant in summer (*see p.254*) but will stand division while in flower, when they are easier to locate (*see below*). Remove the papery tunics, which can inhibit growth. A few species, such as *Colchicum psaridaris*, have underground stems (stolons) and should be lifted with care.

SEEDS

Gathered seeds germinate readily if sown fresh (*see p.256*) in pots of soil-based mix. Keep them in a cool, shady position with some exposure to cold. Stored seeds are not so successful and may not produce seedlings until up to four years after sowing.

DIVIDING COLCHICUMS IN FLOWER

1 Lift a mature clump carefully, digging to a spade-blade's depth to preserve the roots. Shake off excess soil from the bulbs and pull them apart. Clean off any dead matter and the strong outer tunics.

2 Enrich the soil with a little bonemeal, compost, or some well-rotted leaf mold. Replant the bulbs in scattered, small groups at the same depth as before. Space the bulbs about ½in (1cm) apart. Firm them in gently and water around, not on, the bulbs.

COLOCASIA *Taro*

DIVISION in spring
SECTIONING in spring
CUTTINGS in spring

Offsets of these tender, evergreen tuberous perennials may be divided (*see p.254*) and grown in rich soil or in pots at a minimum temperature of 70°F (21°C) and high humidity. Large tubers may be sliced into sections, each with a growing bud; treat as for *Caladium* (*see p.262*). Take basal stem cuttings from tubers starting into growth, as for begonias (*see p.262*), but grow on in humid heat. (*See also* Vegetables, *p.299*.)

OTHER BULBOUS PLANTS

COMMELINA Divide tubers in spring. Sow seeds in spring at 55–64°F (13–18°C) (*see p.256*).
CRINUM Divide in spring (*see p.254*). Sow in spring at 70°F (21°C) (*see p.256*).
CYPELLA Divide bulbs and bulbils when dormant (*see p.254*). Sow ripe seeds (*see p.256*) at 45–55°F (7–13°C).
CYRTANTHUS Divide evergreen bulbs (*see p.254*) in spring, usually after flowering. Sow seeds when ripe (*see p.256*).

CORYDALIS

DIVISION in autumn
SEEDS in summer

The most commonly grown of the tuberous perennials in this genus (syn. *Pseudofumaria*) are *Corydalis cava* (syn. *C. bulbosa*) and *C. solida* (syn. *C. halleri*). Their tubers "split" readily into two when mature; lift and divide them as for bulbous offsets (*see p.254*) to flower the next year. You may need to use a knife. Take care to note the growing points, which are not obvious.

Species with large tubers, such as the Leonticoidus group, rarely offset and are best raised from seeds (*see p.256*). Vigilance is needed to gather ripe seeds before they are shed (*see below*). Sow immediately or store for spring sowing, to flower in two years. Germination may be erratic. Take care to pot seedling bulbs with growing points uppermost.

SEEDPODS
Ripe pods often stay green and shed seeds quickly. Hang stems of closed pods in a paper bag to gather the black seeds as the pods split open.

CROCOSMIA

Crocosmia masoniorum

DIVISION in spring or late summer
SEEDS in autumn
SECTIONING in spring

There are numerous cultivars of these corms (syn. *Antholyza*, *Curtonus*). They form large clumps, which are more vigorous and free-flowering if divided every 3–4 years. Seed-raised plants are worthwhile only from species. New cultivars are constantly being introduced; sectioning provides a way of bulking up stocks from a few corms. New plants flower in the following year.

DIVISION

Crocosmia readily form congested mats of corms in "chains," with younger corms developing on top of older corms. Contractile roots pull the chains deeper into the soil. Normally the clumps are divided into chains after flowering (*see below*) or in spring, but if offsets are few

DIVIDING A MATURE CLUMP

1 When the foliage dies down after flowering, lift a mature clump (here of Crocosmia masoniorum*). Dig at least 12in (30cm) down to avoid damaging the corms or roots.*

3 Tease the chains of corms apart. Clean off any dead or diseased matter and old stems. Corms may be ½–2in (1–5cm) in diameter. Pot smaller corms in soilless potting mix at the same depth as before, to bulk up for a year.

or rare, the chains may be split into individual corms. Stock plants may be planted shallowly to obtain quantities of corms for division (*see p.255*).

Some *Crocosmia*, such as *C.* 'Lucifer' or 'Jackanapes', produce underground stems (stolons) from buds on the corms; new plants then form on the ends of the stolons. When dividing these from the parent plant, retain any portion of stolon with good fibrous roots with each offset.

SEEDS

Sow the large seeds as soon as they are ripe in soil-based potting mix (*see p.256*). Cultivars sometimes self-sow; grow the seedlings apart to preserve the true cultivar strain. Crocosmias make good subjects for hybridizing (*see p.21*).

SECTIONING

Before new growth appears, corms of cultivars may be cut into sections, as for begonias (*see p.262*). Pot them or line them out in a nursery bed to grow on.

OF CROCOSMIA

2 *Carefully pull the tightly matted clump apart to loosen the chains of corms. If the clump is very congested, pull it apart with back-to-back forks.*

4 *Prepare a planting site with plenty of well-rotted organic matter. Replant the larger chains of corms at the same depth as before, but at least 3in (8cm) deep and about 3in (8cm) apart. Water them in thoroughly and label.*

CROCUS

DIVISION in late summer
SEEDS in late summer

Both spring- and autumn-flowering forms of these cormous perennials can be divided in late summer. Species may also be raised from seeds. *Crocus tommasinianus* self-sows readily and flowers best in congested clumps; divide it only when necessary. Alpine species, such as *C. gargaricus*, must be kept watered while dormant. New plants take 2–3 years to flower.

DIVISION

Crocuses generally form small corms around the parent; in bad conditions, the corm produces many tiny cormels and no flowers. Some (*C. nudiflorus*, *C. scharojanii*) form cormels on the ends of underground stems, or stolons; take care the cormels do not fall out of the pot. Lift and divide corms (*see p.255*) and grow on in pots or plant directly in the garden. Plant stock bulbs shallowly to promote cormel formation (*see p.255*).

CROCUS SEED CAPSULES
As the seeds ripen, each seed capsule gradually emerges from below soil level at the base of the flowering stem. Remove it before it splits open, then dry in a paper bag to gather the seeds.

SEEDS

A good rate of germination is possible with fresh seeds. Sow the large seeds in trays (*see p.256*). Keep the seedlings well watered throughout the year; plant out after two years. Self-sown seedlings can be left to grow on *in situ*.

CYCLAMEN

Cyclamen cilicium

SEEDS from midsummer to late winter
SECTIONING in late summer

Some of these tuberous perennials, such as *Cyclamen coum*, are rather hardy, while others are tender, such as *C. persicum*. Seeds are the only reliable method of producing new plants and a lot cheaper than buying quantities of tubers. Seed-raised F1 *C. persicum* hybrids can flower in as little as eight months. Sectioning is generally less successful but may be the only method available to the gardener of increasing stock of rare or named cyclamens. Vigorous garden plants are best left undisturbed.

SEEDS

Cyclamen seeds are slow to ripen. Those of summer- and autumn-flowering species, such as *C. hederifolium* (syn. *C. neopolitanum*), ripen the following summer. In most cases, the stems that bear the seed capsules coil down, pulling the capsules to ground level. (*C. persicum* does not coil.) A sticky coating, which may be pale brown, darkening with age, attracts ants, which then quickly distribute the seeds.

Cyclamen seeds are best sown fresh (*see right*). Sow immediately after soaking: light at this stage sends seeds into a second dormancy that is difficult to break. Sow the large seeds in a mix of equal parts seed soil mix and sharp grit (*see p.256*). Water, allow to drain, then seal the pots in clear plastic bags. Keep at a minimum temperature of 61°F (16°C), in a lightly shaded place.

Remove the bags once germination occurs. Transplant the seedlings as soon as they are large enough to handle. Alternatively, if the seedlings are not crowded, leave them for a year and pot the tubers singly when dormant (this option is not for *C. persicum* hybrids).

SECTIONING

The tubers of a few species, notably *C. trochopteranthum* (syn. *C. alpinum*), have numerous growing points on the top of the tubers. Lift the tubers when dormant and cut them into sections, as for *Caladium* (*see p.262*).

CYCLAMEN SEEDS
Gather seed capsules as they begin to split (see inset). Shake out the seeds. Soak for 12 hours in warm water with a little dishwashing liquid to soften the seed coats and dissolve the mucus.

DAHLIA

Dahlia 'Conway'

DIVISION in spring
SEEDS in early spring
CUTTINGS in late winter or spring

There are thousands of garden hybrids of these tuberous perennials; few species are grown. Dahlias are very frost-sensitive; in cold climates, they are lifted after the first frost, stored at a minimum of 37°F (3°C), then planted or propagated in spring. Make sure that the stored tubers are cleaned of all soil and are just barely moist; otherwise, fungal infections may set in.

Clumps of tubers are easily divided but, for a greater quantity of plants, may be increased by cuttings. Some bedding dahlias may be raised from seeds. New plants normally flower in the same year.

DIVISION

Dig up a clump of tubers before spring growth commences, or bring them out of storage. Divide them into sections using a clean, sharp knife, and make sure that each division has at least one strong, healthy dormant bud ("eye") and one tuber. Dust all the cut surfaces with fungicide. Plant the divisions 4–6in (10–15cm) deep in their flowering positions immediately to grow on.

BASAL STEM CUTTINGS OF DAHLIAS

1 In late winter, start some dahlia tubers into early growth. Insert them into a box of soil mix, leaving the tops of the tubers exposed. Keep them moist in a lightly shaded position at a minimum temperature of 54°F (12°C).

2 When the new shoots are about 10cm (4in) tall, cut them out of the tuber, retaining a small piece of tuber on each. Trim the leaves from the base of each cutting (see inset). Root 5–6 cuttings in a 5in (13cm) pot.

SEEDS

Sow seeds (*see p.256*) and keep at a minimum 61°F (16°C) at all times for rapid germination. Transplant the seedlings singly into pots and plant outdoors when nighttime temperatures are 54°F (12°C) or above.

Dahlias are easy to hybridize (*see p.21*), but the seedlings will vary wildly; many will be discarded in the attempt to produce a worthwhile form.

CUTTINGS

Basal stem cuttings (*see above*) can be taken under cover in late winter from tubers forced into growth. Take new shoots with a piece of tuber at the base of the stem, then discard the tuber.

Insert the cuttings up to the leaves in a free-draining soil, such as equal parts coarse sand and peat (or peat substitute) and keep humid at about 66°F (19°C). When the cuttings show signs of growth, gradually reduce the humidity. Pot the cuttings singly in 3½in (9cm) pots in soilless mix. Harden them off (*see p.45*) before planting out.

Alternatively, a tuber may be used as a stock plant to take several series of cuttings throughout the spring (*see below*). After lifting the tuber in autumn, pot it and keep in a frost-free place during the winter. Move it into a position with a minimum temperature of 50°F (10°C) in early spring to stimulate the dormant buds to shoot.

TAKING CUTTINGS FROM DAHLIAS

1 Bring overwintered tubers into growth in late winter. Remove the first shoots when they are 3–4in (8–10cm) tall in early spring. Cut above the lowest node to leave a bud on the tuber.

2 Prepare the cuttings by trimming the base just below a node and removing all but the top two leaves. Take care to preserve the dormant buds, or eyes, in the leaf axils (see inset, right).

3 Insert the cuttings singly into containers of soilless rooting medium. Here, they are inserted into individual biodegradable pots. Firm them in gently, water, and label.

4 Keep the cuttings at a minimum of 61°F (16°C) at night. They should root in 2–3 weeks. When their roots are well developed (see inset), *pot the cuttings or, if weather permits, plant out in their final positions.*

5 Keep the tuber in a warm and moist place. The remaining buds should produce a new flush of shoots. Several batches of cuttings may be obtained from a stock tuber in this way. The tuber will benefit from a foliar feed if it is planted out.

DIERAMA *ANGEL'S FISHING ROD, WANDFLOWER*

DIVISION in early spring or late summer
SEEDS in autumn

These evergreen cormous perennials can be divided but resent the disturbance, so it is best to leave a plant until it is really congested. They must not be allowed to dry out when dormant in spring.

The corms form in chains, as with *Crocosmia* (*see p.264*), and should be divided in the same way, with care, after flowering. Replant the chains 4in (10cm) deep. They will be in the ground for some time, so make sure that it is well prepared and fertilized. Divisions take 1–2 years to flower freely again.

Sow seeds (*see p.256*) when ripe. Transplant the seedlings singly, grow on in a frost-free place, and plant out the following spring to flower in 2–3 years.

ERANTHIS *WINTER ACONITE*

Eranthis hyemalis

DIVISION in spring
SEEDS in late spring
SECTIONING in spring

These clump-forming perennials have knobby tubers. Many of the dry tubers sold in autumn fail to come into growth in spring. Damp-packed tubers will produce better plants. Dividing tubers in the green (that is, immediately after flowering in spring and before the leaves die down) seems harsh, but it is successful. Treat the offsets as for *Galanthus* (*see p.269*). You may need to cut the tubers apart with a knife. They will flower in the following year.

Seeds ripen very quickly in spring and are soon scattered to form a colony. If left to itself, the common winter aconite, *Eranthis hyemalis*, will seed prodigiously to form large colonies. If allowing plants to self-sow in grass, do not clear away the first few mowings, which may be full of seeds. To grow the plant elsewhere, gather the brown seeds as soon as the pods open. They need sowing immediately outdoors or in a pan (*see p.256*), to flower in 2–3 years.

Sterile hybrids, such as *E. hyemalis* Tubergenii Group 'Guinea Gold', may be sectioned if there are not many offsets. Treat tubers as for *Caladium* (*see p.262*).

OTHER BULBOUS PLANTS

DICHELOSTEMMA (syn. *Brevoortia*) Divide corms in late summer (*see p.254*). Sow seeds at 55–61°F (13–16°C) when ripe (*see p.256*).

ERYTHRONIUM *DOG'S-TOOTH VIOLET, TROUT LILY*

DIVISION in autumn
SEEDS in autumn

The bulbs of these clump-forming perennials look like long teeth. They do not tolerate being disturbed or drying out, so seeds are the best method of increase. *Erythronium dens-canis* self-sows in favorable conditions. Mature clumps may be divided if necessary.

Chipping has been recommended, especially for species that offset very slowly, but it is not very practical because the tubers are so thin and the basal plates so small.

DIVISION

Choose a cool, damp day to divide the bulbs (*see right*) to ensure they do not dry out. Take care to note the position of the growing points, which are not always conspicuous. Replant the bulbs immediately or insert in deep pots; contractile roots will draw the bulbs down into the soil mix. If they are out of the ground for any time, keep the bulbs in a plastic bag containing moist perlite or peat. Divided bulbs should flower in the following year.

Forms of *E. americanum* are best planted individually because they are very quick to spread by means of underground stems (stolons).

DIVIDING ERYTHRONIUM CLUMPS
The long, thin bulbs of Erythroniums *form congested clumps. Lift them carefully and tease out clusters of bulbs from the clump. Enrich the soil with well-rotted organic matter. Replant the bulbs at the same depth, but 2cm (¾in) apart.*

SEEDS

Gather the seeds from the pods when ripe and sow the seeds (*see p.256*) in pots of moist and rich seed soil mix (*see p.34*). The seedling bulbs grow quite slowly. They are best planted out as a potful (*see below*) when two years old in order to avoid disturbing their roots through repeated potting, and to avoid planting them upside down (their growing points are not obvious). They should flower two years later.

TRANSPLANTING ERYTHRONIUM SEEDLING BULBS

1 *Grow on seedling bulbs in the same pot for two or three years. Then, when they are dormant, carefully slide out the entire mass of soil mix and bulbs from the pot.*

2 *Plant the mass of bulbs into a prepared bed of moist, acidic soil, so that the top of the mass is at least 1in (2.5cm) below the surface and cannot dry out. Label and water.*

EUCHARIS

DIVISION in spring
SEEDS in autumn

In warm climates, these tender bulbous perennials are evergreen and can be grown outdoors. Otherwise, a humid, warm greenhouse or house, and a large pot of soil-based potting mix, enriched by a weekly liquid feed, must be its home. Most are increased by division in cold climates because seeds are only occasionally produced.

Detach the offsets (*see p.254*), pot them individually, and grow on at 59°F (15°C). Remove any flower stems that form until the bulbs reach full size, with a diameter of about 3in (8cm). After two years, the offsets should flower.

Gather ripe seeds and surface sow at once in pots (*see p.256*). Germinate them at 77°F (25°C) with high humidity. Transplant seedling bulbs in autumn. They should flower after 3–4 years.

EUCOMIS *PINEAPPLE FLOWER, PINEAPPLE LILY*

Eucomis bicolor

DIVISION in autumn or spring
SEEDS in autumn

The large bulbs of these unique-looking plants are best not divided until they are obviously congested. Divide any offsets (*see p.254*) and keep frost-free over winter before planting out in spring, or divide in spring. They flower after three to five years.

Sow the fleshy seeds (*see p.254*) as soon as they ripen in soilless seed mix at 61°F (16°C). The seedlings grow rapidly and need regular potting to avoid checking their growth. Protect from low temperatures for the first two years.

FREESIA

DIVISION in autumn
SEEDS in autumn

Numerous hybrids have been selected from the species of these cormous perennials. They resent being disturbed while in full growth. When the foliage dies down, lift or repot mature corms and divide as for bulb offsets (*see p.254*).

Gather seeds when ripe and soak them in warm water for 24 hours until the seeds are swollen to soften the hard seed coats before sowing in containers (*see p.256*). For optimum germination, keep them dark and provide bottom heat (*see p.41*) of 55–64°F (13–18°C). Once the seedlings emerge, which can take one or many months, pot them up individually and grow on at a minimum of 41°F (5°C) to flower within the year. Seedling corms do not thrive if allowed to dry out or if exposed to temperatures much above 50°F (10°C).

GAGEA

DIVISION in autumn
BULBILS in autumn
SEEDS in autumn

Many of these bulbous perennials produce small offsets in profusion that can easily be detached and grown on (*see p.254*). They produce flowering plants in two years.

Some species, such as *Gagea fistulosa*, sometimes produce bulbils, instead of flowers, which fall to the ground in summer. Others, such as *G. villosa*, form bulbils in the axils of the basal leaves. Pick off the bulbils as they turn brown or collect them from the ground. Treat them as lily bulbils (*see p.273*) for flowers in 2–3 years.

The seeds are quite small but are easily collected and sown (*see p.254*). Seedling bulbs take 3–4 years to flower. Some, such as *G. lutea* and *villosa*, self-sow in favorable conditions and make good subjects for naturalizing in the garden.

FRITILLARIA *FRITILLARY*

Fritillaria meleagris

DIVISION in autumn
SEEDS in autumn
SCALING AND CHIPPING in late summer
SCOOPING AND SCORING in late summer or early autumn

Many fritillaries are quite hardy, except for a few Californian species that will suffer damage below 41°F (-5°C). The bulbs vary greatly in size, from the diminutive *Fritillaria minima* to the very large *F. imperialis*. Propagation depends on the size and type of bulb. *F. camschatcensis* and Himalayan and Chinese species need to be watered during dormancy. New plants flower after three years.

DIVISION

Offsets vary greatly in size: some are true offsets, as with *F. pyrenaica*, and may be replanted direct after division (*see p.254*). Other species, for example *F. acmopetala*, *F. crassifolia*, *F. pudica*, and *F. recurva*, have tiny offsets, produced in abundance and best described as "rice." These are best grown on in containers as for cormels (*see p.255*).

SEEDS

Some species self-seed readily and come true to type. Gather the papery winged seeds when ripe, and sow in the usual way (*see p.254*). They need exposure to fluctuating temperatures to germinate: keep them at 28°F (-2°C) at night and 50°F (10°C) by day. Grow them on in containers for two years before planting.

SCALING AND CHIPPING

Scaly bulbs such as *F. camschatcensis* lend themselves to scaling (*see p.258*) to form new bulblets. The scales may also be chipped (*see right and p.259*) for a larger number of bulblets. Chipping is useful for rare bulbs where cross-pollination is impossible and no seeds are forthcoming. The number of scales or chips depends on the size of the bulb.

SCOOPING AND SCORING

Lift large bulbs when they are dormant, clean off any soil or dead material, and check that each is not damaged or diseased. Scoop them as for hyacinths (*see p.271*) or score as shown below to encourage formation of bulblets. Treat the bulblets thereafter in the same way as for offsets (*see above*).

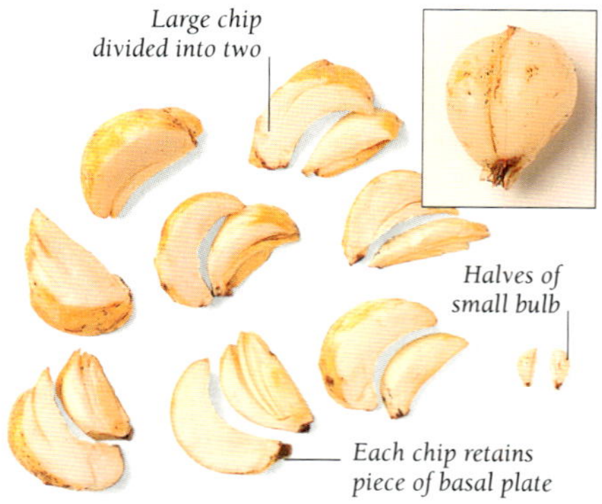

CHIPPING FRITILLARIES
Fritillaria bulbs can be cut into wedges, or chips. Cut larger, open-scaled bulbs (here Fritillaria imperialis*) into eight or so chips, and then divide each chip in two by cutting through the basal plate between the scales. Snap very small bulbs such as* F. acmopetala *(see inset) in two.*

SCORING LARGE FRITILLARY BULBS

1 Hold the bulb (here of Fritillaria imperialis*) upside down. With a scalpel, make two cuts across the basal plate and base. Make the cuts the same depth as the basal plate and at right angles to each other. Dust with fungicide.*

2 Prepare a pot saucer or seed tray with a ¾in (2cm) layer of moist, coarse sand. Rest the bulb on the sand. Label. Keep in a warm, dry place. Bulblets should form along the cuts in 8–10 weeks.

GALANTHUS *Snowdrop*

DIVISION in spring
SEEDS in summer
TWIN-SCALING in summer
CHIPPING in early summer

After a few years, these bulbs form congested clumps, so division is advisable to improve vigor. Seeds are produced only in mild weather that favors pollinating bees; some species self-sow freely in favorable conditions. Forms and cultivars are numerous and often in short supply; large numbers of new bulbs may be obtained by twin-scaling. Snowdrops also respond very well to chipping; this produces fewer new plants than twin-scaling but results in flowering plants more quickly. Water the bulbs even when dormant. New plants flower after three years.

DIVISION

Lift and divide clumps after flowering but while the leaves are still in growth or "in the green" (*see above*). These divisions establish more successfully.

DIVIDING SNOWDROPS "IN THE GREEN"
Lift clumps of snowdrops, taking care not to damage the roots, and pull the clumps apart. Replant single bulbs into prepared soil at the same depth as before. Firm, label, and water in.

The common snowdrop, *G. nivalis*, can be naturalized in woodland in this way.

SEEDS

To ensure germination, gather the seeds as the capsules split open. They should be sown immediately (*see p.256*) to avoid the seeds becoming dormant and less ready to germinate. Double-flowered snowdrops do not set seeds.

TWIN-SCALING SNOWDROPS
One bulb may yield up to 32 twin-scales. After bulblets form (about 12 weeks), they may be rooted (see inset) and overwintered in a deep tray in soilless potting mix before planting.

TWIN-SCALING AND CHIPPING

Divide the bulbs into pairs of scales (*see p.259 and above*).The bulbs can also be cut into about eight "chips" (*see p.259*). New bulblets are best grown on in a lightly shaded nursery bed of organic soil outdoors, at a minimum of 28°F (-2°C). Alternatively, grow on the bulblets in deep seed trays or pots in a frost-free place for a year and then plant out.

GLADIOLUS

DIVISION in autumn
SEEDS in late summer
SECTIONING in summer

Only a few species of these cormous perennials are grown, but there are thousands of garden hybrids. Gladioli very readily produce cormels for division. Species can also be increased by seeds and hybridize (*see p.21*) readily. Any hybrid may be sectioned to preserve the form. New plants should flower in the second year.

DIVISION

Detach cormels from garden plants once the flowering stems have died back. Alternatively, plant stock corms shallowly in a nursery bed to obtain greater numbers of cormels (*see below*). The cormlets may be stored indoors over winter, lined out in a nursery bed in spring, and grown on for a year before planting.

SEEDS

Gather the seeds and sow fresh (*see p.256*) in deep containers. Keep the seedlings in growth in the first winter by maintaining a minimum temperature of 59°F (15°C). Allow the young corms to die back in the following autumn, store them dry and frost-free overwinter, and plant them out in the following spring.

SECTIONING

Lift dormant corms and cut them into sections, as for *Caladium* (*see p.262*). Gladioli are susceptible to molds and rots, so always treat the cut surfaces with fungicide. Grow on the sections as for cormels (*see above*).

CORMELS FROM STOCK PLANTS

1 Plant corms shallowly in a nursery bed in spring (see p.255). In summer, remove the flower spikes before they fade and waste energy on seed production. Cut off each flower spike just above the leaves. This encourages the corms to produce more cormels.

2 In autumn, lift the stock corms. Gently detach all the cormels from each corm. Clean and store the cormels over winter, then line them out to grow on.

GLORIOSA

Gloriosa superba 'Rothschildiana'

DIVISION in spring
SEEDS in early spring

This single species, *Gloriosa superba*, has fingerlike tubers, which are produced in abundance. All forms are tender. Rooted tubers flower in two years, seed-raised plants in 3–4 years.

Take care when handling the tubers, because they can irritate the skin. The tubers multiply quickly. Divide them as for bulbous offsets just before growth starts (*see p.254*). Replant the tubers just below the surface of the soil or repot in soil-based mix with added grit. Grow on in frost-free conditions.

Sow in containers (*see p.256*) in seed soil mix combined with an equal part of sharp sand, and provide bottom heat (*see p.41*) of 66–75°F (19–24°C). Germination should occur in a few weeks.

OTHER BULBOUS PLANTS

FERRARIA Divide corms in autumn (*see p.255*). Sow seeds (*see p.256*) in autumn at 43–54°F (6–12°C) in bright light.
GALTONIA Divide offsets (*see p.254*) in autumn when dormant. Sow seeds when ripe (*see p.256*) in summer; keep frost-free for two years and water when dormant.
HABRANTHUS Divide the few offsets (*see p.254*) when dormant. Sow seeds as soon as ripe (*see p.256*) at 61°F (16°C).

HAEMANTHUS *Blood lily*

Haemanthus coccineus

DIVISION in early spring
SEEDS in spring

Offsets are produced slowly, so these tender bulbs can be divided only every few years. Seed-raised plants flower in 3–5 years, offsets in two years. Keep evergreen bulbs just moist and deciduous species dry when dormant.

DIVISION

Sideshoots sometimes appear before offsets are fully formed, but they can be divided in the second year. Just as they start into growth, uncover the offsets and tease away from the parent bulb. Pot singly in soilless mix with their necks just above the surface; use deep pots to allow the large roots room to grow. Keep in the pots until flowering; blood lilies flower best when potbound.

SEEDS

Extract the large seeds from the fleshy fruits and sow (*see p.256*) in sandy soil mix. Provide 61–64°F (16–18°C) bottom heat (*see p.41*). Water and feed the seedlings well to keep them in leaf for as long as possible and build up the bulb. When the leaves die, stop watering and keep dry and frost-free over winter.

HYACINTHOIDES *Bluebell*

DIVISION in autumn
SEEDS in autumn

In very favorable conditions, these bulbous perennials (syn. *Endymion*) seed themselves prodigiously. They are therefore easy to naturalize, but they can also become invasive. The storage organs are completely replaced annually; the husk of the old bulb is found beneath the new one. New plants should flower in the following year.

DIVISION

Large clumps are often located at a considerable depth in the soil, so take care not to sever the stems when lifting a clump for division (*see p.254*). Once lifted, the numerous bulbs are easily separated. Replant them immediately, spaced singly 2in (5cm) apart, to cover a large area.

SEEDS

Gather the seeds when ripe, then sow immediately. They are best sown in large quantities in drills in a seedbed as for cormels (*see p.255*) and transplanted into their flowering positions two years later while they are dormant. Self-sown seedlings can be left to grow on *in situ*. The contractile roots soon pull the bulbs well below the surface.

HIPPEASTRUM *Amaryllis*

Hippeastrum cultivar

DIVISION in late winter or in early spring
SEEDS in autumn
CHIPPING in summer

The 60 or so species of these mainly tender bulbs may be raised from seeds, but the many hybrids must be divided to obtain true-to-type plants. New plants flower in 2–3 years.

DIVISION

Lift the plants before they come into active growth and pull away large offsets (*see p.254*). Leave smaller ones attached to the parent bulb to bulk up until the following year. Pot the offsets individually in rich soilless mix, water thoroughly, and grow on at a minimum temperature of 55°F (13°C). They need good light to grow on, otherwise the stems become elongated. Water freely while in growth, but keep them dry and frost-free when dormant.

SEEDS

Sow the seeds when ripe (*see above right*) in containers (*see p.256*) and keep at a minimum temperature of 61°F (16°C) for rapid germination. Pot the seedling bulbs when their leaves are 5–6in (13–15cm) long and grow on as for offsets (*see p.255*). Encourage them to rest in winter by watering less.

HIPPEASTRUM SEEDHEAD
The seedhead forms relatively quickly after the flower fades. Collect and sow the seeds as soon as they are ripe, before they are dispersed.

CHIPPING

The large bulbs are an ideal shape for chipping (*see p.259*) and can be cut into as many as 16 chips.

HYACINTHUS *Hyacinth*

DIVISION in autumn
TWIN-SCALING AND CHIPPING in late summer
SCOOPING AND SCORING in late summer

Only cultivars of this bulbous perennial, *Hyacinthus orientalis*, are commonly grown. They must all be increased vegetatively because their color and vigor is the result of years of selection. The easiest way is by division of offsets. However, hyacinths reproduce slowly, so various methods of cutting the bulbs may be used if no offsets are available. The rate of success depends on keeping the bulbs free from rot. Hyacinths are much hardier in the ground than in containers. New plants flower in two to three years.

DIVISION

Lift and divide offsets when the foliage has died down. Dig down deeply around the clump, as for *Roscoea* (*see p.276*), because the offsets often lie deep in the soil. Throw the cleaned offsets onto the ground and replant where they land for a natural grouping. Allow the topgrowth to die away naturally. Water and feed the offsets regularly while they remain in active growth.

TWIN-SCALING AND CHIPPING

In late summer, slice large bulbs into 16 sections. They can be twin-scaled or chipped (*see p.259*). Unlike other chipped bulbs, hyacinth chips do not rot away very readily after the new bulblets form. When the bulblets have developed, therefore, pot the chips singly, placing them horizontally instead of vertically in the soil mix (*see below*), so that the old scales are completely buried. This will encourage them to rot away more quickly.

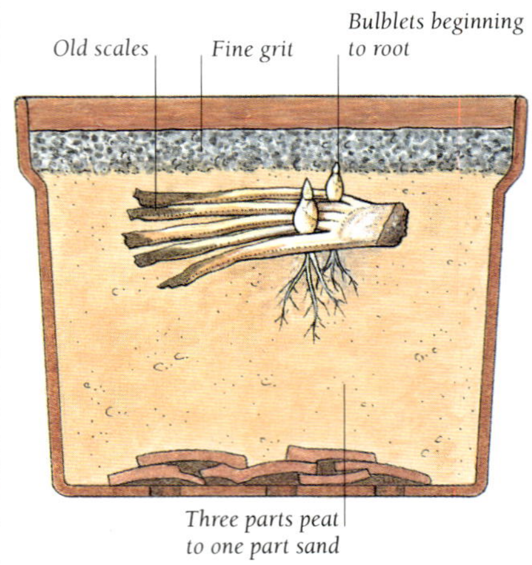

POTTING A HYACINTH CHIP
Once bulblets form, place the chip horizontally in a half pot or pan of free-draining soil mix. Cover with ½in (1cm) of mix and ½in (1cm) of fine grit to ensure the chip rots off. Grow on for a year before repotting or planting out.

SCOOPING AND SCORING

These methods involve wounding the basal plates. With the first, most of the basal plate is scooped out (*see below*). Alternatively, make deep cuts in the basal plate, as for fritillaries (*see p.268*). When bulblets form, detach to grow on, or pot the bulb upside down in gritty soil mix, with the bulblets just buried. After a year, detach and grow them on.

SCOOPING HYACINTHS

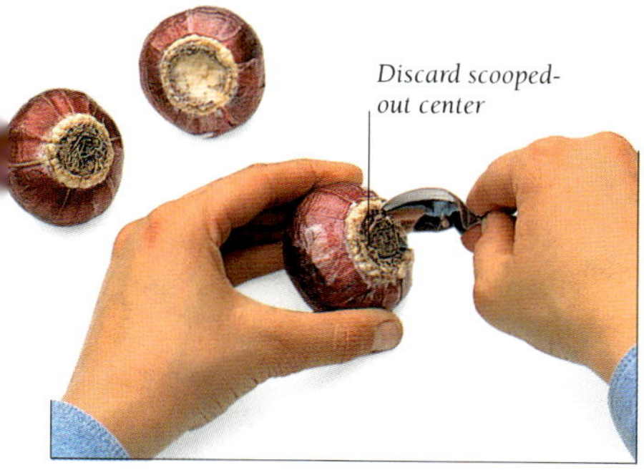

1 Scoop out the center of the basal plate of each dormant bulb, using a sterilized, sharpened teaspoon or scalpel. Leave the outer rim of each basal plate intact. Dip the cut surfaces in fungicide to reduce the risk of rot.

2 Fill a tray or saucer with moist, coarse sand. Set the prepared bulbs, basal plates uppermost, into the sand. Keep them in a warm, dark place, and water the sand occasionally to keep it damp.

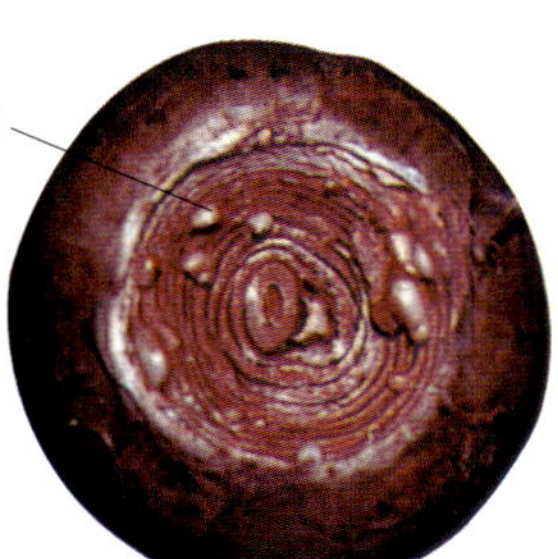

3 After three months, bulblets should form on the scooped basal plate. When they are large enough to handle, detach and set them in rows in a tray of soilless rooting medium. Cover with 1in (2.5cm) of medium and treat as seeds.

HYPOXIS STARFLOWER

Hypoxis angustifolia

DIVISION in autumn
SEEDS in autumn or spring

These cormous perennials produce new corms annually, so they lend themselves to division. Seeds are useful if you require larger quantities of plants for a woodland setting. New plants should flower after three years.

Lift offset corms (*see p.254*). Replant the corms singly in free-draining soil or pot them in equal parts coarse sand and soilless potting mix. If necessary, protect them from late spring frosts.

Gather seeds just as they begin to turn black in cup-shaped capsules; cut off the entire stalk as for *Alstroemeria* (*see p.260*). Sow seeds (*see p.256*) at a minimum of 50°F (10°C) to ensure germination. Seeds may be stored at 41°F (5°C) over winter if needed. If attempting to transplant self-sown seedlings, take care not to mistake them for grass.

IPHEION

Ipheion uniflorum 'Wisley Blue'

DIVISION in autumn
SEEDS in summer or spring

Ipheion uniflorum and its cultivars are the most commonly cultivated of these bulbous perennials. They are prolific, producing masses of offsets. Some are tiny. Lift after the foliage has died down to divide (*see p.254*). This is the only way to produce cultivars true to type. New plants should flower after 1–2 years.

Gather the seeds in summer. Sow the seeds (*see p.256*) immediately or in spring in a sandy seed soil mix. Container-grown *Ipheion* often self-sow in plunge beds under cover; the strap-like, slightly succulent seedlings are easily identified for transplanting.

OTHER BULBOUS PLANTS

HERBERTIA As for *Tigridia* (*see p.278*).
HERMODACTYLUS TUBEROSUS (syn. *Iris tuberosa*) Separate tubers in autumn, as for Juno irises (*see right*).
HYACINTHELLA As for *Muscari* (*see p.274*).
HYMENOCALLIS (syn. *Ismene*) Divide the few offsets (*see p.254*) when dormant. Seeds in spring (*see p.256*) at 66°F (19°C).
IXIA Detach tiny cormels (*see p.255*) in autumn. Sow seeds (*see p.256*) in autumn and keep frost-free.

IRIS

Iris magnifica

DIVISION in autumn
SEEDS in late summer to autumn
CHIPPING in late summer

The bulbous perennials in this genus fall into three groups: Juno, Reticulata, and Xiphium irises. They have many cultivars, which can be propagated only vegetatively: Juno irises are chipped, while Reticulata and Xiphium irises are best divided. All the species can set seeds, which come true. All bulbous irises die back after flowering and are summer-dormant. New plants take three years to flower. (*See also* Perennials, *p.202*.)

DIVISION

Reticulata irises form tiny bulblets around the parent bulb, inside netlike tunics. This group of irises is prone to disease, so check the offsets carefully (*see below*). In areas with dry summers, plant the offsets outdoors; in other areas, pot them (*see p.254*). If large numbers of offsets are required, plant stock bulbs shallowly as for corms (*see p.255*).

SEEDS

The large seeds are best gathered and sown (*see p.256*) as soon as they are ripe. They should germinate early in the spring as the parent bulbs flower. Some irises, such as *I. reticulata* or *I. winogradowii*, form seed capsules at soil level; treat these as for crocuses (*see p.265*). They can be hybridized easily (*see p.21*); when selecting seedlings, choose them for vigor and form as well as color.

CHIPPING

Juno irises can be increased by chipping (*see p.259*). Cut the basal plate with great care to avoid damaging the fleshy true roots, which are only tenuously attached. A new bulb may also be grown from a root, if it is cut out together with a dormant bud on a piece of basal plate. Dust cut surfaces with fungicide and pot the root carefully in equal parts coarse sand and soil-based potting mix.

DIVIDING IRISES
Reticulata irises, such as Iris histrio, *are particularly prone to disease, so it is important to discard any bulbs that show signs of disease when dividing a clump of offsets.*

IXIOLIRION

DIVISION in autumn
SEEDS in autumn

The small white bulbs of these perennials are readily increased from offsets (*see p.254*). Seeds, which are produced in abundance, yield larger quantities of plants but are slower to reach flowering size, usually in three years. Gather the seeds as soon as they ripen and sow immediately (*see p.256*). They usually germinate well in the following spring.

LACHENALIA *CAPE COWSLIP*

Lachenalia aloides

DIVISION in late summer or early autumn
BULBILS in late summer
SEEDS in spring or summer

These bulbous perennials are native to South Africa. They are winter growing and, in cold areas, need excellent light conditions to keep growth compact and foliage markings attractive. New plants will often flower in their second year.

Cape cowslips produce numerous offsets. Divide them after three years when the foliage dies down (*see p.254*). If potted or replanted in a mix of equal parts soil-based potting mix and fine grit, they will grow quickly.

Some Cape cowslips, for example *Lachenalia bulbifera* (syn. *L. pendula*) produce bulbils (*see below*).

Gather the fleshy seeds as soon as they ripen and sow immediately (*see p.256*) in free-draining soil mix. The pan, once watered, needs to be kept just moist and at a minimum of 59°F (15°C) in bright light to ensure a good rate of germination. Pot the seedlings singly when they are large enough to handle. Keep them in active growth over winter in a bright, frost-free place.

CAPE COWSLIP BULBILS
The hard, round bulbils (here of Lachenalia bulbifera*) form in clusters at the base of the old stems. Gather these once the leaves die down and treat as for lily bulbils* (see right).

LEUCOCORYNE

DIVISION in summer or autumn
SEEDS in summer

Offsets are not freely produced by these tender bulbous perennials, so seeds are a better method of producing new plants in quantity. New plants should flower after three years.

Lift and divide offsets (*see p.254*) at the onset of dormancy after spring flowering. Replant or repot but keep them dry and rested until the end of dormancy, then water them to start them into growth in the late autumn. Keep them in active growth over winter, in bright light at 50°F (10°C).

Gather the seeds when ripe and sow immediately, barely covering the seeds in soil mix because they need light to germinate. Keep seedling bulbs well fed and watered and in growth for as long as possible. When they become dormant, allow the soil mix to dry out.

LEUCOJUM *SNOWFLAKE*

DIVISION in late summer to early autumn
SEEDS in late spring or in late autumn

Some of these bulbous perennials prefer a moist, partly shaded site; smaller forms require sun and well-drained soil. The exact timing of propagation depends on whether the plant flowers in summer to autumn or in spring. Lift mature plants when the leaves die down, and divide the offsets (*see p.254*). Alpine or dwarf species may be raised from seeds. For best results, sow fresh seeds (*see p.256*) in sandy soil mix; alternatively, store the seeds at 41°F (5°C) to keep them viable.

SNOWFLAKE IN FLOWER
Whether propagated by division or raised from seeds, most snowflakes (here Leucojum vernum *var.* vagneri*) should flower in 2–3 years.*

OTHER BULBOUS PLANTS
LLOYDIA Treat as for *Fritillaria* (*see p.268*); keep *L. serotina* watered throughout dormancy.

LILIUM *LILY*

Lilium x *dalhansonii*

DIVISION in early spring or in autumn
BULBILS in late summer
SEEDS in autumn
SCALING in late summer
CUTTINGS in late spring or in midsummer

Except for hybrids of *Lilium longiflorum* and *L. formosanum*, and a few other species, the bulbous species and the thousands of hybrids are quite hardy. Not all groups of lilies can be propagated in the same way. The garden hybrids can be raised only vegetatively, the method depending on the form and group of the lily, but care must be taken to use only virus-free stock. All species lilies can be raised from seeds. It is slow and requires care but yields vigorous, virus-free plants. Some lilies, such as *Lilium speciosum*, do not tolerate lime and need to be raised in acidic soil mixes. All lilies need to be kept moist throughout dormancy.

DIVISION

Some species, notably *L. speciosum* in all its forms, produce offsets at the side of the large parent bulb that reach flowering size in 2–4 years. Detach these in autumn (*see p.254*) and grow on in acidic soil mix with equal parts of sharp sand in pots or nursery beds. *L. candidum* flowers best in congested clumps, so divide only when necessary.

Some lilies, such as *L. auratum*, *L. bulbiferum*, *L. canadense*, *L. lancifolium* (syn. *L. tigrinum*), *L. longiflorum*, *L. pardalinum*, and *L speciosum*, produce rooted bulblets, usually below ground at the base of the old flowering stem. Lift the bulb while it is dormant in early spring to remove the bulblets (*see below*). Pot the bulblets and place in

INCREASING LILIES FROM BULBLETS
Lift the dormant bulb and detach the bulblets (see inset) *from the old stem. Replant the parent bulb. Prepare pans of moist, soil-based potting mix and insert the bulblets at twice their own depth. Cover with a layer of grit, then label.*

COLLECTING AND ROOTING LILY BULBILS

1 *Ripe bulbils come away easily from the leaf axils. Select healthy, vigorous plants – bulbils can transfer disease. Throughout late summer, pick the bulbils from the stems as soon as they mature.*

2 *Fill a pan with moist, soil-based potting mix. Gently press the bulbils into the surface. Cover with a ½in (1cm) layer of coarse sand or fine grit. Label. Grow on in a frost-free place until the following autumn.*

ROOTING LILY BULBILS IN A TRENCH

Lift the bulb, taking care to preserve the roots. Make a trench that slopes away from the bulb; work in some compost and coarse sand. Lay the stem in the trench and cover so that only the tip is exposed.

a shaded, frost-free place and treat thereafter as for seeds in pots (*see p.256*). Plant out in the following autumn to flower in 3–4 years. Alternatively, in early autumn, before the stems die back completely, wrench the stems out of the ground to avoid disturbing the parent bulb. Pot the bulblets or plant out *in situ*.

BULBILS

The tiny bulbils that form in the leaf axils of some lilies root readily and produce a flowering plant in three years. Some species can be induced to form bulbils by disbudding just before flowering. Bulbil-forming lilies include *L. bulbiferum*, *L. chalcedonicum*, *L. lancifolium* (syn *L. tigrinum*), *L. leichtlinii*, *L. sargentiae*, *L.* x *testaceum*, and some hybrids.

Gather the bulbils as they ripen (*see above*), root them in pans, then plant out the entire pan of young bulbs the following autumn. Alternatively, the parent lily may be buried in a trench after flowering (*see above right*) so that the bulbils root along its length. Lift the young bulbs and replant in the spring.

SCALING

Most lilies, particularly the hybrids, are increased commercially by this method. It is quite easy for the gardener (*see p.258*) if done in late summer so that good growth can be achieved before winter. Some species, for example *L. pardalinum* and *L. washingtonianum*, have so many scales that they often shed scales naturally when lifted. *L. martagon* and other species from harsh climates benefit from a period of cold below 27°F (-3°C) to start the scales into growth.

SEEDS

Gather pale or brown seedpods, dry them, and sow the seeds fresh (*see p.256*). Lily seeds may be stored and sown in spring but will not germinate as well. Seeds of some lilies, such as *L auratum*, *L. candidum*, *L. henryi*, *L. japonicum*, and *L. martagon*, germinate quite quickly but appear dormant until leaves appear in the following growing season; this is hypogeal germination (*see p.20*). Keep the pots moist and lightly shaded for at least two years to check if seeds have germinated. The seeds will die if they dry out. Pot on seedling bulbs regularly to allow vigorous growth. They should reach flowering size in 4–5 years. Lilies also may be hybridized easily (*see p.21*).

CUTTINGS

It has been discovered that a few lilies can be grown from leaf cuttings; these include *L. longiflorum* and *L. lancifolium* and their cultivars. Pull off vigorous leaves after the lily has come into growth and treat as an herbaceous cutting (*see below*). Cuttings may also be taken in midsummer. Keep the cuttings humid, but ventilate regularly and check for rot.

LILIES FROM LEAF CUTTINGS

1 *Select healthy, newly mature leaves (here of* Lilium longiflorum*). Firmly grasp each one close to the stem and gently peel it off, so that it comes away with a "heel." Place the cuttings in a plastic bag to prevent moisture loss.*

2 *Prepare a dilute fungicidal solution. Wear latex gloves to avoid contaminating the cuttings and to protect your skin from the chemicals. Completely immerse each leaf cutting in the solution.*

3 *Insert three cuttings in an 3in (8cm) pot of moist vermiculite so that one-third of each cutting is buried. Label and keep humid and shaded at 59–64°F (15–18°C).*

4 *In 5–6 weeks, the cuttings should root and bulblets form at the bases. Tease the cuttings from the vermiculite. Pot singly into soilless potting mix at the same depth.*

5 *Label the cuttings and water well. Keep them moist in a frost-free place in bright light to keep them in growth for a year before planting them out.*

LYCORIS

Lycoris radiata

DIVISION in summer
SEEDS in autumn

The perennial roots of these bulbous perennials resent being disturbed, so they are best propagated from seeds, although it takes longer (3–7 years after sowing) to obtain a flowering plant. Gather the seeds when ripe and sow them immediately (*see p.256*). Keep frost-free, ideally at 45–54°F (7–12°C), to ensure good germination.

Division of offsets before flowering (*see p.254*) should be done with great care to avoid damaging the roots, and it will always set back the plants. It is better practice to top-dress and feed an established plant for many years rather than attempting to divide it.

MERENDERA

DIVISION in summer
SEEDS in spring or autumn

Offsets are freely produced by these cormous perennials. The plants flower very erratically, so be sure to divide by late summer before they begin to flower. Break open the blackish tunics that encase the corms, then detach the cormels (*see p.255*). Pot them in free-draining soil mix and keep well watered while they are in active growth (but dry when dormant) to ensure they flower well in the following year.

Since they form at ground level, the seed capsules are not obvious. Gather the seeds and sow as soon as they are ripe (*see p.256*).

MORAEA *PEACOCK FLOWER*

DIVISION in autumn
SEEDS in autumn or spring

In spring and summer, these cormous perennials produce numerous short-lived, irislike flowers in clusters. Some species can withstand temperatures to 20°F (-7°C). Tropical species require a minimum temperature of 12°C (54°F). In frost-free conditions, they can be evergreen. New plants flower in 2–3 years.

Cormels are freely produced. Lift the parent plants when dormant, or when growth is least active, in autumn. Grow on the cormlets in containers or in nursery beds (*see p.255*). Gather the seeds when ripe; timing depends on the flowering season of the species. Sow the seeds immediately (*see p.256*); they usually germinate very rapidly. Transplant when large enough to handle.

MUSCARI *GRAPE HYACINTH*

Muscari neglectum

DIVISION in autumn
SEEDS in autumn

These bulbous perennials (syn. *Muscarimia*) are easily grown. In fact, they can be too successful as colonizers, and for this reason they need careful placement.

DIVISION

Numerous offsets are produced each year; divide them (*see p.254*) to start new colonies that will flower in two years.

SEEDS

Seed-raised plants do not flower for 2–3 years, but seeds are useful for alpines, such as *Muscari comosum*, that have few offsets. Species with large bulbs, such as *M. muscarimi* (syn. *M. moschatum*), have semi-permanent roots that resent being disturbed; these are also best raised from seeds, but may be left to self-sow freely. Gather seeds in summer; sow (*see p.256*) in autumn direct or in nursery beds.

NERINE

DIVISION in spring
SEEDS in autumn
CHIPPING in late summer

Some of these bulbous perennials are evergreen. *Nerine bowdenii* and its cultivars are useful as cut flowers. They are best left undisturbed and divided only when congestion affects flowering. Some smaller nerines, such as *N. filifolia* and *N. pudica*, can be raised from seeds; larger bulbs are suitable for chipping.

DIVISION

Nerines form a solid mat of offsets after 4–5 years. Divide in spring (*see right and p.254*), not after the leaves die down, when the flower buds may be damaged. Lift a clump carefully, separate out single offsets, and replant with their necks just showing, to flower within a year or two.

SEEDS

Nerine seeds germinate very quickly, often while still on the stem. Keep a watch for the fleshy seed capsules forming on dying flower stems and

NARCISSUS *DAFFODIL*

Narcissus rupicola

DIVISION in autumn
SEEDS in from late spring to early autumn
TWIN-SCALING AND CHIPPING in late summer

There are 50 or so species and thousands of cultivars of these bulbous perennials. For the gardener, division is the easiest method of increase. In fact, the bulbs can become so congested they rise up in a mound and must be lifted to maintain the flowering display.

Twin-scaling or chipping may suit cultivars that are slow to increase, for example *Narcissus pseudonarcissus* subsp. *moschatus* (syn. *N. alpestris*). Seed-sowing is best for rare species that need to be conserved.

DIVISION

Most daffodils increase naturally by offsets; large ones may be separated and replanted (*see p.254*) in soil improved with well-rotted organic matter, to flower again in two years. Discard any old, misshapen bulbs. Pot small offsets and grow on for two years before replanting them.

SEEDS

Gather seed capsules as soon as they split, from late spring to early summer. Cut off the capsules rather than pulling them off, to prevent pests from entering the parent bulb. Sow the seeds (*see p.256*) immediately in deep pots. Germination usually occurs upon the first rains in autumn. Keep the seedlings moist and frost-free. Seedlings flower in 2–4 years. Species self-sow readily.

Seedlings from naturally pollinated seeds or cross-pollinated cultivars (*see p.21*) can be worthwhile. Daffodils are fairly easy to hybridize, because the stamens and stigmas are very accessible.

TWIN-SCALING AND CHIPPING

Daffodil bulbs consist of a series of broad scale leaves and are suitable for twin-scaling (*see below and p.259*) if many new plants are required. Treat the twin-scales as single scales (*see p.258*) when growing them on.

Chipping (*see p.259*) is easier in preparation since it demands fewer cuts, but it produces fewer bulbs. A large bulb may be cut into 16 or so chips to flower in three years.

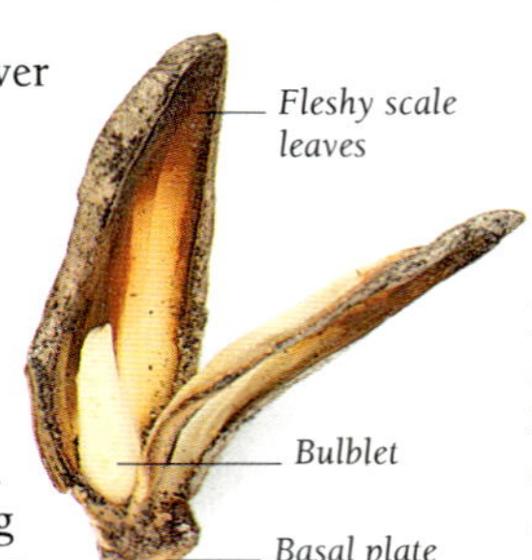

TWIN-SCALING
Cut a large daffodil bulb into 30 or more twin-scales. Once bulblets form on most of the twin-scales, discard any failures and pot the rest.

DIVIDING NERINE

1 *Lift a mature clump, digging deep to avoid damaging the bulbs and roots. Separate the clump using back-to-back forks, then carefully tease out single bulbs from each piece.*

2 *Discard any diseased bulbs, then clean the healthy offsets. Replant the offsets at the same depth as before in prepared soil. Space them about 2in (5cm) apart. Label and water.*

gather the seeds as soon as they ripen. Sow (*see p.256*) immediately, otherwise they will perish. Lightly cover the seeds with soil mix and germinate at a temperature of 50–55°F (10–13°C). Keep the seedling bulbs frost-free, and do not allow the soil mix to dry out. Pot them individually or plant them out after a year. Seed-raised *Nerine* should flower in 3–5 years.

CHIPPING

Lift large bulbs in late summer and cut them into 16 chips (*see p.259*). Once the chips have started into growth and have been potted, water the young plants only when they are in active growth. Do not allow the dormant bulbs to become desiccated, however. Keep them frost-free until they are large enough to plant out after two years.

NOMOCHARIS

SEEDS in autumn
SCALING in late summer

This beautiful relative of the lily has bulbs that are scaly and easily damaged when moved, but this does make them easy to propagate. The scales are very easily removed, after flowering but before the leaves die down, to produce new bulblets (*see p.258*).

If disease-prone stocks need renewing, new plants are best raised from seeds because seeds are unlikely to transmit the disease. Gather and sow the seeds as soon as they are ripe at 45–50°F (7–10°C) for the best results (*see p.256*). Keep the seedling bulbs well watered throughout the year; they should flower within four years.

ORNITHOGALUM *STAR-OF-BETHLEHEM*

DIVISION in autumn
SEEDS in autumn

Many of the European species of these bulbous perennials are quite vigorous; one in particular, *Ornithogalum umbellatum*, is extremely invasive in many areas. The South African species are much less hardy. The chincherinchee, *O. thyrsoides*, is most commonly grown. Offsets are freely produced and are white and almost greasy to the touch. Leave plants undisturbed for three years, then divide after the foliage dies down (*see p.254*).

Gather the seeds from the flowering spikes when the seed capsules change color from green to brown (*see below*). Sow them immediately (*see p.254*) to obtain flowering plants in 3–4 years. They can also be left to self-sow and build up a colony.

RIPENING SEED CAPSULES
As the seed capsules ripen, the stem (here of Ornithogalum nutans*) gradually dies and falls to the ground, ensuring that the seeds spill safely into the soil when released.*

OXALIS *SHAMROCK, SORREL*

DIVISION in autumn
SEEDS in autumn

The storage organs of these plants may be bulbs, rhizomes, or tubers. Like some of their herbaceous cousins, some have a highly effective means of seed dispersal and have become invasive weeds in some areas.

The bulbs or tubers vary greatly in habit, size, and appearance. Some are scaly rhizomes, such as *O. enneaphylla*; others have netlike tunics, such as *O. adenophylla*, while some (*O. obtusa*) are surface-growing. They all can be divided as for bulbous offsets (*see p.254*) to produce flowers the next year. (For how to divide nonscaly rhizomes, *see* Perennials, *p.149*.)

Some species, such as *O. valdiviensis*, have capsules that burst to scatter seeds; gather seeds as for *Alstroemeria* (*see p.260*). Choice species are more discreet; the seeds must be carefully gleaned from ground-level seed capsules. Sow (*see p.256*) at 55–64°F (13–18°C) for flowers in 2–3 years.

OXALIS OBTUSA
This species spreads slowly, forming a mat. It sends out underground stems, or runners, that produce bulbils. Lift these when dormant and grow on as for lily bulbils (see p.273).

OTHER BULBOUS PLANTS

MILLA Separate corms (*see p.255*) when dormant. Sow seeds (*see p.256*) in spring at 55–64°F (13–18°C).

NECTAROSCORDUM Sow seeds (*see p.256*) when ripe in autumn. May become invasive if left to self-sow.

NOTHOLIRION If bulbils are produced, treat as for lilies (*see p.273*). Sow seeds (*see p.256*) when ripe in late summer.

NOTHOSCORDUM Divide offsets (*see p.254*) when dormant in autumn.

PANCRATIUM Divide offsets (*see p.254*) when dormant; take care not to damage parent bulbs. Sow ripe seeds (*see p.256*) in autumn at 55–64°F (13–18°C).

PAMIANTHE

DIVISION in winter
SEEDS in autumn

The deciduous *Pamianthe peruviana* is the only commonly grown species of this sometimes evergreen, bulbous perennial. It requires a minimum of 50°F (10°C) and should never dry out, but it does require a rest period in winter with reduced watering. New plants should flower in 3–4 years.

The bulb is composed of large, fleshy scales; it spreads slowly by underground stems (stolons) that push the scales apart. Lift these scales and treat them as bulbous offsets (*see p.254*) when growth is at its slowest in winter.

The seeds takes a year to ripen in the capsules before they can be harvested and sown. Germination is rapid if they are kept humid at 61–70°F (16–21°C).

POLIANTHES *TUBEROSE*

DIVISION in autumn
SEEDS in autumn

The tuberose, *Polianthes tuberosa*, has been cultivated for several centuries but is now lost from the wild in Mexico. The tender tubers usually bloom only once but produce many offsets each year after flowering. Separate these when the tubers are dormant (*see p.254*) and replant in well prepared, very fertile soil; the soil must be warm. Store offsets in a warm, dry place if needed until spring.

Sow seeds as soon as they ripen at a temperature of 66–75°F (19–24°C). Provide the seedlings with a minimum nighttime temperature of 50°F (10°C).

ROMULEA

Romulea bulbocodium

DIVISION in autumn
SEEDS in autumn

A widespread cormous genus, this includes European species such as *Romulea bulbocodium* (syn. *R. grandiflora*) and South African corms such as *R. macowanii*. Nearly all are winter-growing and spring-flowering, so they may be potted and watered at the same time.

In some cases, the offsets are almost as large as the parent corm and are quick to reach flowering size the next year if divided as for bulbs (*see p.254*).

The long seedpods retain the large, brown seeds until well into autumn, even after ripening. Sow the seeds fresh (*see p.256*) at 45–54°F (6–12°C) or outdoors under cover to ensure even germination in spring and flowers in three years.

ROSCOEA

DIVISION in spring or autumn
SEEDS in spring

At first glance, this genus appears to be nonbulbous; however, the roots are tuberous, and the plants are monocotyledonous (*see p.17*). *Roscoea* withstand temperatures of -4°F (-20°C) if planted deeply. In wet areas, they are prone to rot, so protect them against heavy rain. Seeds produce flowering plants in 2–3 years, but some, such as *Roscoea* 'Beesiana', are sterile and must be divided.

DIVISION

Roscoea may be divided in spring, but it is easier to do it just as the foliage turns color and begins to die back, as for an herbaceous perennial (*see right*). Separate the thin tuberous roots and replant the divisions in soil prepared with plenty of well-rotted organic matter to flower in the following summer.

SEEDS

Gather ripe seeds in late summer or autumn (*see below*). Sow immediately in warm climates or store at 41°F (5°C) for spring sowing (*see p.254*) in cool climates. Germination is usually rapid, and the seedlings can be transplanted into pots or a nursery bed in summer.

ROSCOEA SEEDHEAD
The swelling seed capsules gradually weigh down the stems toward the ground. Gather the seeds as soon as they turn yellowish brown.

DIVIDING A ROSCOEA CLUMP

1 On a cool, damp day, dig a trench at least a spade blade's depth around the plant (here Roscoea *'Beesiana') to avoid damaging the fleshy roots. Lift the plant, using a fork.*

2 Divide a clump into sections, using back-to-back forks if needed. Each section should have good roots and 6–12 healthy growth buds. (The old shoots indicate where the buds are.)

3 Cut away damaged roots and dead matter. Dust the wounds with fungicide. Replant the sections into prepared soil, 6in (15cm) deep and 6–12in (15–30cm) apart. Water and label.

SCILLA *SQUILL*

DIVISION in early autumn
SEEDS in autumn
CHIPPING in late summer

The European and Asiatic species of these bulbous perennials are quite hardy, whereas South Africans are tender. The bulbs are slow to form offsets and division (*see p.254*) is an easy, if slow, form of increase. It is best done in autumn when divisions soon root; this applies to autumn-flowering species also.

Scilla set seed readily, especially *Scilla autumnale*, and self-sow in favorable conditions. Seeds may be gathered in late summer and sown (*see p.256*) in autumn to germinate in spring and flower within three years. Leave self-sown seedlings *in situ*.

Some species with large bulbs, such as *Scilla peruviana*, may be propagated by chipping. Slice the bulbs into 16 chips (*see p.259*). They flower in 2–3 years.

SINNINGIA

SEEDS in spring
SECTIONING in spring
BASAL STEM CUTTINGS in spring
LEAF CUTTINGS in late spring or early summer

Sinningia speciosa and its cultivars, commonly known as gloxinas, are tender tuberous perennials. They prefer a minimum of 64°F (18°C); in cold climates, store the tubers dry over winter. In growth, the tubers need warm, indirect sunlight and a rich soil mix. New plants flower within a year.

Surface-sow (*see p.256*) the tiny seeds on a peat-based seed soil mix. Keep in bright, indirect light at a minimum of 59°F (15°C). Pot the seedlings singly in a rich, soilless potting mix.

Seedlings are prone to fungal attack, so if only a few plants are needed, cut tubers into sections, before growth starts, as for begonias (*see p.262*).

To take basal stem cuttings, nestle some tubers, buds uppermost, into a tray in soilless potting mix, so they are half-buried and almost touching, in early spring. Leave in a light place at 64–68°F (18–20°C) for 2–4 weeks and keep the soil mix just moist. When shoots appear, take cuttings (*see above*) and pot singly in soilless mix with the tuberous "eye" just covered.

TAKING BASAL CUTTINGS OF GLOXINIAS
Start tubers into growth to obtain new shoots about 4cm (1½in) tall. Cut them out of the tuber with a clean, sharp knife, retaining a small piece of tuber at the base of each cutting (see inset).

Cuttings of whole or part leaves (*see below*) may be taken. New tubers form at the base of leaf stalks or cut veins; some may fail to root and grow.

GLOXINIA LEAF CUTTINGS

1 Select a mature, healthy, undamaged leaf that is as flat as possible. Cut it from the plant. Use a clean scalpel to divide the leaf into transverse sections, each about 1½in (4cm) wide. Half-fill a seed tray with a soil mix such as equal parts peat and sharp sand or perlite.

2 Lay the cuttings flat on the soil mix surface. Secure with wire hoops over the main veins to keep the cuttings in close contact with the soil mix. Label, water, and cover to keep humid.

3 Keep the cuttings out of direct sunlight at a temperature of about 64°F (18°C). In 3–4 weeks, tiny tubers should begin to form. Allow the old leaves to rot away naturally, then pot the tubers at twice their own depth to grow on.

WHOLE LEAF CUTTING

Remove a leaf with its stalk and a small piece, or heel, of the main stem at the base. Place it upright in a prepared pot so that the leaf sits on the surface. Label, water, and cover with a plastic bag held clear of the leaf with split stakes. Treat as in step 3.

OTHER BULBOUS PLANTS

PUSCHKINIA As for *Chionodoxa* (*see p.263*).
RHODOHYPOXIS Divide tubers in spring (*see p.254*). Sow seeds at 45°F (7°C) in spring.
SAUROMATUM Separate offset tubers when dormant in winter (*see p.254*).
SCADOXUS As for *Haemanthus* (*see p.270*).

SPARAXIS HARLEQUIN FLOWER

DIVISION in late summer
SEEDS in autumn or in spring

In the Northern Hemisphere, the corms of harlequin flowers may be kept dry in winter and planted in spring, to ensure they flower in summer and do not revert to their autumn-to-winter growth pattern. In mild areas, plant them in autumn for spring flowers.

Cormels are freely produced and can be separated when dormant (*see p.255*). In cold climates, delay sowing seeds (*see p.256*) until spring, because the plants need warmth to grow. New plants should flower within three years.

SPREKELIA *AZTEC LILY, JACOBEAN LILY*

DIVISION in late summer
SEEDS in spring

The cultivated stock of the only species, *Sprekelia formosissima*, has become infertile, but seeds have now been re-introduced from the wild. This tender bulb is dormant in winter.

A few offsets are usually encased in the bulb tunic. These can be separated (*see p.254*) in late summer and potted individually or lined out in a nursery bed. They resent root disturbance. Take care not to keep the dormant bulbs too dry or they will become desiccated. On the other hand, if they get too wet, they will rot. Offsets will flower in 2–3 years.

If available, sow seeds (*see p.256*) when the threat of frost has passed. In warm climates, seeds should germinate freely if sown fresh.

STERNBERGIA *AUTUMN DAFFODIL*

DIVISION in late summer or early autumn
SEEDS in autumn to spring
CHIPPING in summer

The bulbs of some species flower best in mature, congested clumps, so divide them only when necessary. The bulbs are dormant only for a short time; lift them to divide the offsets (*see p.254*) and pot them or grow them on in a nursery bed in a sunny site. New plants take 3–4 years to reach flowering size.

The best method of increase is from seeds, which are produced in capsules at soil level. Sow the seeds (*see p.256*) at 55–61°F (13–16°C) as soon as they are ripe to germinate in the first autumn.

One species in particular, *Sternbergia candida*, is rare in the wild and not quick to multiply. Chipping (*see p.259*) is a way of bulking up rare stocks more quickly. Cut each bulb into as many as eight chips.

TECOPHILAEA *CHILEAN BLUE CROCUS*

DIVISION in late summer
SEEDS in late summer

The two species of cormous perennials are thought to be extinct in the wild. They need frost-free conditions in winter when in growth; during summer dormancy, they must be kept barely moist. They take 2–3 years to flower.

Lift the corms and detach the cormels to grow on (*see p.255*). The more tender *Tecophilaea violiflora* must have complete frost protection (*see pp.38–45*). *Tecophilaea* rarely set seeds in cooler climates. Although they are not rare in cultivation, the corms are costly. It is therefore worth the effort of hand-pollinating the flowers in spring to ensure seed set.

Gently brush a soft paintbrush over the central stamens of every flower to transfer the pollen from one flower to another. Sow the seeds (*see p.256*) in frost-free conditions as soon as they ripen; they germinate quite quickly.

TIGRIDIA *PEACOCK FLOWER, TIGER FLOWER*

DIVISION in spring or in autumn
SEEDS in spring

Tigridia pavonia and its cultivars are the most commonly grown of these tender bulbous perennials. They are prone to viruses, so seeds provide a way of avoiding disease if necessary.

DIVISION

Divide the bulbs (*see p.254*) every 3–4 years in spring or, in cooler climates where they are overwintered under cover, in autumn. The offsets vary in size; replant larger ones with the parent bulbs to flower in the same year. Take care to discard any offsets that have been affected by viruses. Pot smaller offsets or line them out in a nursery bed, as for cormels (*see p.255*), to grow on.

SEEDS

Gather the seeds in summer and sow (*see p.254*) fresh in warm areas or in spring in cold climates at a minimum of 59°F (15°C). Keep seedlings moist, and in bright light shaded from hot sun, to flower within 2–3 years.

TIGRIDIA PAVONIA SEEDHEADS
This species produces long, upright seedpods in late summer. The wind shakes the brown ripened pods, which then scatter seeds like a salt shaker.

TRITELEIA

Triteleia laxa

DIVISION in early autumn
SEEDS in autumn

In dry, warm summers, the cormous perennials in this small genus will self-sow to some extent. New plants should flower within 3–5 years.

DIVISION

Separate offset corms when dormant as for bulbous offsets (*see p.254*). The offsets may have several layers of fibrous coats; discard older layers, but do not denude the corms completely.

SEEDS

Seeds are best sown as soon as ripe (*see p.256*) at 55–61°F (13–16°C). Transplant seedlings 18 months later into a raised bed with very free-draining soil.

TRITONIA

DIVISION in autumn
SEEDS in autumn or in spring

Tritonia have affinities to *Crocosmia* but are generally more tender. They are very easy to please. Cultivars must be divided to maintain the stock, but species come easily from seeds. New plants flower in two years.

DIVISION

The plants are in active growth in winter, so they should be lifted and divided in autumn. The corms are produced in chains as with *Crocosmia*; separate them in the same way (*see p.264*).

SEEDS

The small, black seeds can be sown as soon as they ripen in equal parts soil-based seed mix and coarse sand at a temperature of 59°F (15°C). If this is not possible, store the seeds in a cool, dark, dry place and delay sowing until spring.

TROPAEOLUM

Tropaeolum polyphyllum

DIVISION in early spring
SEEDS in spring
CUTTINGS in spring

Many of the tuberous perennials in this genus are tender, although a few are hardier. Seeds are easy but not always available in cold areas. (*See also* Annuals and Biennials, *p.229*.)

DIVISION

The tubers can be very large and deeply set in the ground, with spreading clumps and threadlike shoots that travel some distance below the surface before emerging. Lifting and dividing offsets can be quite a tricky task.

Before the delicate shoots start into growth underground, lift the dormant tubers and very carefully separate as for bulbous offsets (*see p.254*). Replant the offsets at the same depth as the parent tuber to flower the next year. If growing on tubers in containers, use deep pots.

SEEDS

Pick the large, fleshy seeds from the cuplike capsules. Store over winter and sow in spring (*see p.256*) in frost-free conditions. Germination is often erratic. Seed-raised plants flower in three years.

CUTTINGS

The tubers of *T. polyphyllum* lie very deep in the soil, so lifting them is quite a chore. Instead, take stem-tip cuttings as for herbaceous perennials (*see p.154*).

TULBAGHIA

DIVISION in spring
SEEDS in late summer or in spring

The bulbous or rhizomatous perennials are clump-forming and usually deciduous, although some are semi-evergreen. They are mostly summer-growing and are vigorous plants that benefit from regular division to maintain them at their best. Tulbaghias do not seed freely in cold climates.

DIVISION

Tease apart bulbous clumps in spring, even if they still have some foliage, and pot them to grow on (*see p.254*).

SEED

Gather the seedheads in late summer and dry to extract the seeds. These may be sown (*see p.256*) as soon as they are ripe. Stored seeds are best sown in the spring to avoid any danger of frost. The seeds germinate very readily in a few weeks, and seedlings often reach flowering size within two years.

TULIPA *Tulip*

DIVISION in autumn
SEEDS in autumn

The thousands of cultivars of this bulb are best divided, especially because many are lifted and stored dry during summer in cool or wet areas. The 100 or so species come true to type from seeds, but some patience is needed since seedling bulbs may take six years to flower.

DIVISION

The ideal time to separate the offsets (*see p.254*) is when the bulbs are lifted to be stored dry in a tray over summer. Commercially this is still practiced, although tissue culture (*see p.15*) is now used for new cultivars. In some species, offsets form on the ends of roots directly beneath the parent bulb and sink into the soil ("droppers"), so take care when lifting them. Replant offsets too deeply – 8in (20cm) – rather than too shallowly, or they may not flower. Plant shallowly as for corms to promote offsets on stock plants (*see p.255*), or cut small notches into the basal plate to encourage offsets.

WILD TULIPS
In the wild, tulips (here Tulipa tschimganica*) grow in soil that is baked in the heat. When dormant, some tulips must be kept completely dry.*

SEEDS

The papery, winged seeds are best sown in autumn and need a period of cold to germinate evenly. Tulips hybridize easily (*see p.21*). Most cultivars are sterile or produce few good seedlings.

VELTHEIMIA

DIVISION in autumn
SEEDS in autumn or spring
CUTTINGS in late autumn

The two large bulbous perennials of this genus are tender. They are summer-dormant, and young plants need long, bright days to grow well; this is not always easy to achieve in winter in cool climates. New plants can flower within three years.

Veltheimia resent being disturbed, so wait until flowering diminishes, then divide the offsets (*see p.254*). Replant them in sandy soil or equal parts soil-based potting mix and coarse sand. Make sure that the top of the "necks" of the offsets are exposed.

Sow seeds (*see p.256*) at 66–75°F (19–24°C) singly in pots. Use deep 1¼in (3cm) pots to allow the seedling roots space to grow away quickly.

Mature leaves may be treated as cuttings (*see below*). Once bulblets have formed, carefully tease them out of the soil mix and pot up singly. Grow on in shade at 41–45°F (5–7°C).

TAKING VELTHEIMIA LEAF CUTTINGS

1 *Take a newly mature leaf (here of* Veltheimia bracteata, *syn.* V. capensis*). Cut through its base with a scalpel or sharp knife, taking care not to cut into leaves beneath. If desired, cut the leaf into 1½–2½in (3–6cm) sections.*

2 *Fill pots or trays with moist sharp sand or equal parts potting mix and vermiculite or fine grit. Insert the cuttings vertically, just deep enough to stand up. Keep humid at 68°F (20°C) for 8–10 weeks until bulblets form.*

WATSONIA

DIVISION in spring
SEEDS in autumn

Watsonia corms are generally hardy to about 20°F (-7°C). They are scarce in commerce; seeds may be the only option. They flower in three years.

Watsonia form clumps with chains of corms, similar to *Crocosmia*, and are divided in the same way (*see p.264*). In cold climates, lift summer-flowering species before the first frosts, divide them, and store dry over winter, then replant in spring. If large numbers of corms are required, plant stock corms shallowly in a nursery bed (*see p.255*).

The seeds are produced in long pods. Gather them when ripe and store until autumn. Sow (*see p.256*) at 55–64°F (13–18°C); keep the seedlings frost-free.

ZEPHYRANTHES

Zephyranthes grandiflora

DIVISION in spring (evergreen species) or in autumn (deciduous species)
SEEDS in spring or autumn

Among these bulbous perennials, *Zephyranthes candida* is the hardiest, surviving temperatures to 20°F (-7°C). They are commonly known as rain or wind flowers. Evergreen clumps flower best if left undisturbed but must be divided eventually. Deciduous offsets are more easily divided. New plants flower in two years.

DIVISION

When an evergreen clump such as of *Z. candida* becomes congested, it is best lifted and divided (*see p.254*) before active growth begins, in much the same way as for herbaceous perennials (*see also* Roscoea, *p.276*) Divide deciduous spring-and summer-flowering species once they begin dying down in autumn.

SEEDS

The large, flat, black seeds persist for a long period in the capsule. Gather them when ripe; this varies from spring to autumn, depending on the species and level of rainfall. Sow the seeds (*see p.256*) in spring at 55–64°F (13–18°C).

OTHER BULBOUS PLANTS
ZIGADENUS Divide bulbs (*see p.254*) when dormant in late autumn or spring. Sow seeds (*see p.256*) when ripe or in spring at 55–64°F (13–18°C).

VEGETABLES

As well as the excitement of raising a new plant, propagating vegetables brings the added reward of an edible harvest, often within a few months. To flavor your vegetables and other dishes, stock the garden with culinary herbs.

Vegetables may be perennial, biennial, or annual plants, but most are grown as annual crops. The principal, and generally easy, method of propagation therefore is from seeds, which may be sown in various ways, depending on the crop and the climate. The traditional method of sowing vegetable seeds outdoors is in drills in a separate vegetable plot, but they may also be sown in deep beds to avoid the need for digging, in containers, or in informal patches in an ornamental kitchen garden. Some methods of seed sowing, such as fluid-sowing and intercropping, are peculiar to the propagation of vegetables.

Vegetables are usually sown direct or transplanted as seedlings into their permanent site. It is therefore particularly important to provide the optimum soil conditions for the best possible crop. This involves preparing the soil, rotating crops to avoid buildup of pests and diseases, and sowing appropriate cultivars for the required harvest time. Vegetables may be classed as cool-, temperate-, or warm-climate crops; sowing times will vary depending on the climate.

Some vegetables, such as asparagus and cardoon, are perennial; these may be propagated by other means, such as cuttings of various kinds, division, or grafting. Tuberous vegetables, such as potatoes or Jerusalem artichokes, are generally increased from seed tubers; in some cases, specially bred seed tubers are available that are certified free of viruses to ensure a healthy crop.

With some vegetables, such as leeks, it is worth allowing a few plants to go to seed to sow next year. Some vegetables cross-pollinate freely, but others will come fairly true to type from home-gathered seeds; many are specially raised hybrids that produce inferior results if grown from gathered seeds.

Culinary herbs (*see pp.287–91*) are cultivated in much the same way as other herbaceous or woody plants and so may be propagated in a number of ways, depending on the plant. Annuals and biennials must be raised from seeds; herbaceous perennials may be increased from cuttings or by division; woody herbs may also be layered.

RED-HOT CHILI PEPPERS
Chili peppers such as this Capsicum annuum *'Hot Mexican' cross-pollinate more readily than sweet peppers, so it is advisable to grow parent plants at least 70 ft (20 meters) apart from other cultivars. Gather seeds from fully ripened fruits.*

PUMPKINS AND SQUASHES
This diverse group of annual vegetables is easy to propagate. If the seeds are to be gathered, hand-pollinate the female flowers and remove male flowers to prevent cultivars from cross-pollinating. Squash and pumpkin seeds must be fully mature to ensure germination.

SOWING SEEDS

Most vegetables are grown as annual crops and therefore are raised from seeds, generally with good results. Many F1 hybrids are produced by crossing two selected parents. The hybrids are more vigorous, produce larger crops, and may be of superior quality to open- or naturally pollinated cultivars. Research in recent years has enabled resistance to pests and diseases to be bred into many cultivars, although quite a few people feel the flavor has been sacrificed. For this reason, many gardeners grow the so-called "heirloom" cultivars, all of which are open- or naturally pollinated, and use natural, "organic" methods for controlling pests and diseases.

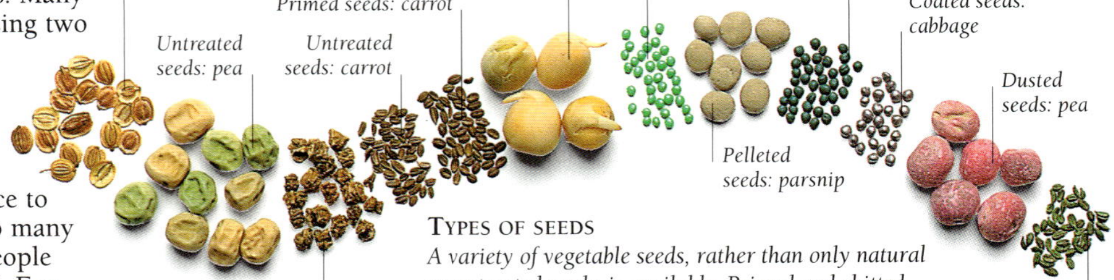

TYPES OF SEEDS
A variety of vegetable seeds, rather than only natural or untreated seeds, is available. Primed and chitted seeds guarantee even germination; pelleted seeds are easy to handle; coated seeds protect against disease.

BUYING VEGETABLE SEEDS

Always buy seeds that have been stored in cool conditions and are preserved in sealed packets. Commercial seeds are tested for viability, cleanliness, and purity before reaching the consumer. They are available in a variety of forms, although primed and chitted seeds may be difficult to find.

UNTREATED OR "NATURAL" SEEDS These have simply been harvested, dried, and cleaned. They generally vary in size and are sometimes graded into specific sizes for drilling, using seed sowers (*see p.28*).

PRIMED OR "SPRINTER" SEEDS These are specially treated to germinate 1–2 weeks earlier than natural seeds. Primed seeds are also larger and easier to space along a drill or sow individually in containers. They are ideal for sowing early carrots or parsnips when conditions are poor.

CHITTED (SPROUTED) SEEDS These are pregerminated and sold in small plastic containers to be sown at once in pots or trays. They are useful for seeds that are difficult to germinate. Any seeds may be pregerminated at home (*see p.284*) to give them an early start.

PELLETED SEEDS These are coated with clay to form small balls and are easier to handle than untreated seeds, particularly small seeds such as those of cabbages, carrots, and cauliflowers. They are often treated with a fungicide or insecticide. Pelleted seeds need moister conditions than untreated seeds to break down the coatings so the seeds can germinate.

COATED AND DUSTED SEEDS These are treated with fungicide. As with all such seeds, wear gloves or wash your hands after sowing.

DRYING SEEDPODS
In damp climates, pull up stems with seedpods (here beans) and hang them by their roots in an airy, dry, frost-free place. Once dried, remove the pods and extract the seeds.

GATHERING SEEDS

Instead of buying seeds, you can gather them from plants in your garden. F1 hybrids do not come true to type, but gardeners who are not concerned with uniformity can experiment with open-pollinated seeds. Some vegetables are more worthwhile from home-gathered seeds than others (*see* A–Z of Vegetables, *pp.292–309*).

Some vegetables are self-pollinating, while others need to be cross-pollinated. In the garden, there will be a certain amount of natural cross-pollination, so self-pollination is never 100 percent. To ensure purity of seeds, either grow only one variety of each vegetable, or isolate the different varieties of self-pollinators from one another. Brassicas and corn can be grown for seeds only in large quantities. Each variety must be grown in a large block – about 50 plants for brassicas and 100 plants for corn – to ensure the purity of the seeds.

Some vegetable seeds, such as carrots, parsley, and parsnip, can be sown immediately after they ripen, whereas others, such as beans, squash, tomatoes, and corn, must be stored. Allow the seeds to ripen fully before harvesting. Gather seeds in pods while still on the stalks and dry them thoroughly (*see below, left*). Seeds contained in fleshy fruits need to be cleaned before drying. Some seeds may need special treatment (*see* A–Z of Vegetables, *pp.292–309*).

STORING SEEDS

Seeds deteriorate with age, losing their viability and vigor, which results in poorer germination and reduced yields. If stored, they are best preserved in cool, dark, dry conditions at about 34–41°F (1–5°C): never in a kitchen drawer or garden shed. Store the seeds in paper packets in an airtight container or in airtight jars, labeled with the plant name and harvesting date. Reseal foil packets with tape after opening.

Before sowing, test the viability of seeds by placing 50–100 seeds on moist paper towels in a warm, dark place. Keep them moist and check daily for germination: it should be at least 60 per-cent for viable seeds. If it is low, sow the seeds more thickly than usual.

CROP ROTATION

When planning your vegetable garden, group vegetables into the following categories: alliums (onion family); brassicas (cabbage family); legumes (beans and peas); solanaceous crops (peppers, potatoes, and tomatoes); and umbelliferous crops (carrots, parsnips). Sow vegetables from each group in a different site every 3–4 years (every 1–2 years in a small garden), to avoid a buildup of pests and diseases in the soil. This is especially important with alliums or brassicas.

WHERE TO SOW VEGETABLES

There are two principal ways of growing vegetables: in rows or in beds. Vegetables have traditionally been grown in spaced rows, or "drills," in rectangular plots; this

THE RAISED OR DEEP-BED SYSTEM

A deep bed improves the soil, so that it is possible to sow up to four times as densely as in a conventional bed. Cultivate the ground deeply and dig in organic matter. Mark out the area of the bed: it should be no more than 5ft (1.5m) wide to allow easy access without walking on the soil. Mound the surface, using topsoil from another area, so that the bed is slightly raised.

system is best if a large crop is required. Nowadays the bed system, with vegetables spaced equally in narrow beds lined by paths, is more popular. The benefit of this system is that only the actual bed needs to be dug, manured, and fertilized, not the soil in between. Also, all of the work can be done from the paths, avoiding soil compaction. Raised beds (*see above*) warm up more quickly in spring and give greater yields because crops can be grown closer together.

PREPARING THE SOIL FOR SOWING

Most vegetables prefer a well-drained, moisture-retentive, slightly acidic soil and one that is rich in nutrients, especially for long-term crops. Choose a sheltered but not shaded site. Thoroughly dig the soil in autumn, adding plenty of well-rotted organic matter, such as manure or compost. Do not sow any root crops (except potatoes) on freshly manured ground, because they will produce forked roots.

In spring, loosen up the soil and add fertilizer. Normally, a balanced one of nitrogen, phosphorus, and potassium (potash) is used for vegetables, but certain crops have specific needs, such as lime for brassicas.

Just before sowing, rake over the soil to give a smooth, loose surface, known as a "fine tilth." This allows seeds to be sown at a consistent depth and to obtain the oxygen essential for germination. Heavy, wet soils are cold and lack oxygen: if possible, wait until the soil is workable before sowing or transplanting seedlings. If the soil is wet, stand on a board to avoid compaction. Dry soil is also a problem (*see below*), since water is needed to enter the seeds and moisten the seed embryos for germination.

Most vegetables need soil at a minimum of 45°F (7°C), to germinate. Some, such as corn and squash, require higher temperatures, while others, such as cabbage or lettuce, will not germinate if the temperature is too high. Some will bolt, or go to seed, if sown at the wrong time of year (*see* A–Z of Vegetables, *pp.292–309*).

SOWING SEEDS IN STANDARD DRILLS

1 Mark out a row with a string line and pegs, or with a stake. Use the corner of a hoe to draw out a small, even drill in the soil to the depth required for the seeds.

2 Stand on a board to avoid compacting the soil. Sprinkle the seeds thinly and evenly along the drill. Cover the seeds with soil without dislodging them. Water in.

SOWING IN DRY OR WET SOIL

DRY CONDITIONS *When the soil is very dry, water the base of the drill first, then sow the seeds and cover over with dry soil.*

WET CONDITIONS *If the soil drains slowly or is very heavy, sprinkle a layer of sand in the drill before sowing the seeds.*

SOWING SEEDS IN A WIDE DRILL

1 Take a hoe and drag it toward you, applying a light and even pressure. Mark out parallel drills 6–9in (15–23cm) wide at the required depth for the seeds.

2 Space large seeds, or trickle-sow smaller seeds, along each drill. Make sure that the required distance is left between the seeds, depending upon their size.

3 Carefully cover the seeds with soil. Use the hoe or a rake, or draw the soil over gently with your foot. Take care not to dislodge the seeds. Water in well.

4 Protect the seeds from birds or foraging animals if necessary by pegging wire netting over the row. Remove the netting before the seedlings grow through the mesh.

FLUID-SOWING PREGERMINATED SEEDS

1 Pregerminate the seeds on moist absorbent paper. As soon as they have swelled and have begun to sprout, wash the seeds carefully into a fine-meshed sieve under gently running water.

2 Mix up some wallpaper paste (without fungicide) in a jar. Use about 8fl oz (250ml) of paste for 100 seeds. Tap the seeds into the jar and stir gently to distribute them evenly through the paste.

3 Draw out a drill of the appropriate depth in the seedbed; water it if the soil is dry. Pour the paste into a plastic bag and knot the open end. Snip off one corner to leave a ½in (1cm) hole.

4 Gently squeeze a line of paste and seeds into the drill. Label the drill, then carefully draw the soil over the seeds with the back of a rake to cover them. Finish by lightly raking over the soil surface.

Fluid-sowing pregerminated seeds

Crops such as beets, carrots, and parsnips need a higher temperature for germination than their seedlings need for growth. In colder climates, this may affect the yields of spring sowings. To obtain a reliable germination rate, seeds can be pregerminated, or chitted, and then fluid-sown. First the seeds are scattered on damp paper towels in a saucer or seed tray indoors at 70°F (21°C). They usually germinate within 24–48 hours, depending on the crop.

The seeds can then be mixed with a clear gel, such as water-based glue or wallpaper paste, before sowing in drills (*see above*). Do not use wallpaper paste containing fungicide, which may kill the seeds. Sow when the seed roots are no longer than ⅕in (5mm), or they may be damaged during sowing. Gel helps keep the seeds moist until they root, but the soil should still be watered if needed in the first 2–3 weeks. The seedlings develop more quickly with this method.

SPACE-SOWING AT STATIONS

Draw out drills at appropriate spacings for the crop (here peas). To mark the intervals at which the seeds should be sown, draw more drills at right angles to the first set. Sow 2–3 seeds at each intersection, or "station." Water in and label.

Space-sowing at stations

This method of sowing has become popular because it reduces the amount of thinning necessary, makes more economical use of seeds, and avoids the need to transplant crops that may suffer a check in growth if root disturbance occurs at the seedling stage.

To station-sow, drills are made at the correct spacing and depth for the crop. The "stations" at which to sow the seeds are measured out, either by drawing out more drills (*see below left*) or by making shallow holes along each original drill.

Broadcast-sowing

Some crops, such as carrots or radish, may be broadcast-sown over a well-prepared seedbed (*see p.32*), rather than into drills. This method makes efficient use of space and may be used for early sowings into a cold frame or a plastic-film tunnel (*see p.39*) in colder climates.

Because the crop will be difficult to weed, it is preferable to broadcast-sow outdoors onto a stale seedbed, where weed seeds in the soil have been allowed to germinate and then hoed off before sowing a crop (*see p.32*).

If the seeds are very small, they can first be mixed with some fine sand to ensure even distribution. Once sown (*see right*), the seeds should not be covered too deeply; if they are too far down in the soil, they may rot before they have a chance to germinate.

Thinning seedlings

Seedlings must be thinned at an early stage before they become crowded and compete for light and moisture. Thin in two or three stages, taking out the weaker or damaged seedlings each time so that the leaves of the remainder gradually have more room to grow. At the last thinning, the seedlings should be left at the spacing recommended for mature plants (*see* A–Z of Vegetables, *pp.292–309*). This method avoids any gaps opening up if some seedlings die off in the meantime.

Seedlings of crops such as cabbages, lettuces, or onions may be lifted for transplanting. Firm the soil again by giving the seedbed a good watering.

Multiple-sowing techniques

Seeds of two or more crops may be sown together to maximize use of the available ground (*see facing page*). A fast-growing crop is generally sown between a slower-growing crop so that

BROADCAST-SOWING

1 Prepare and water the seedbed, then, when the surface has dried off, rake it to create a fine tilth. Broadcast the seeds by scattering them thinly and evenly from your hand, or a packet, over the surface.

2 Cover over the seeds by lightly drawing the rake over the soil at right angles to the original direction of raking. Use a watering can with a fine rose to water the seedbed thoroughly. Label the seedbed.

THINNING SMALL SEEDLINGS

Thin small seedlings by nipping them out at the base of the stem between finger and thumb, or use scissors. This avoids disturbing the roots of the other seedlings. Thin enough to leave a little clear space between the seedlings that remain.

one crop can be harvested before the slower crop begins to fill in the space.

There are two methods of multiple-sowing. Intercropping involves sowing two crops in alternate drills; when intersowing, two crops are sown in the same drill. Intercropping can also be employed to combine a tall-growing crop with a trailing or root vegetable, so that the growth of each crop does not compete with the other. For instance, you can sow corn with squashes or plant potato tubers with brassica seedlings and cut down the potatoes as the brassicas mature. Intercropping is also ideal for deep beds (*see p.283*). Peas may be sown down the middle with potatoes or corn on either side, or onions, shallots, or brassicas may be sown with leeks, roots, and greens along the sides where the soil is more moist.

Sowing in containers

Sow in a seed tray, small pot (*see below left*), or pan, depending on how many plants will be required. Generally, a 3½in (9cm) pot or a 5–6in (13–15cm) pan is sufficient for most vegetable crops.

To prepare the container, fill loosely with seed soil mix (*see p.34*), tap the container on the bench, and level off any excess with a straight piece of wood or cardboard. Firm the surface with a presser board or an empty pot to within ¾in (2cm) of the rim. Water if needed, then broadcast-sow the seeds or sow singly on the surface. Sieve a little moist soil mix over the seeds and give a final press. Cover with glass or a plastic bag or place in a closed case, ventilating daily to remove excess condensation.

Keep the seedlings in good light once germinated. As soon as the seedlings produce 1–2 seed leaves, they should be transplanted singly (*see below, center*) to avoid overcrowding and any damage to the seedling roots. Prepare 2–3in (5–8cm) pots or cells, as before, with potting mix. Make a hole in each pot or cell and carefully insert a seedling, firm in, and water.

Sowing in cell packs

Seeds can be sown directly into cells (*see below*). This eliminates the need for transplanting and allows plants to grow unhindered. It is especially good for plants that are set back by root disturbance. A good-sized cell allows seedlings to develop strong roots, even if conditions are not suitable for planting out at the optimum time. Pelleted seeds can be sown one seed per cell; other seeds are sown 2–3 per cell and thinned.

MULTIPLE-SOWING TECHNIQUES

▲ INTERCROPPING *Thinly sow rows of quick-growing vegetables (here of lettuce) between drills with seeds sown at stations of a slower crop (here of broccoli). When the seedlings have two leaves, thin out to allow healthy growth.*

► INTERSOWING *Station-sow* (see facing page) *a slow crop such as parsnips. Sow seeds of a faster-maturing crop such as radish* (inset) *thinly between stations. Lift the fill-in crop with care to avoid disturbing the main crop's roots.*

BROADCAST-SOWING IN POTS

1 *For seeds that germinate erratically, or if only a few plants are needed, sow in a 3½in (9cm) pot of seed soil mix, scattering the seeds thinly and evenly. Cover to their own depth of mix, water, and label.*

2 *When the seedlings (here cabbages) have two seed leaves, transplant them into cells of soil mix. Discard much smaller ones and any that show signs of cold damage or disease. Water and label the seedlings.*

SOWING IN CELL PACKS

Fill cell packs with seed soil mix and firm lightly. Make holes about ¼in (5mm) deep in each cell. Sow several seeds in each hole, lightly cover with mix, label, then water. Thin the seedlings when they appear to leave the strongest in each cell.

MULTIBLOCK-SOWING

1 *Fill a cell tray with moist potting mix. Make a shallow depression in each cell with your finger. Sow 3–4 seeds in each cell and lightly cover with mix. Water, label, then put the tray in a light, warm place.*

2 *The seeds should germinate within 5–7 days. Do not thin the seedlings. When they have one or two true leaves, plant out seedlings in their plugs, at the correct distance for the crop (here turnips).*

3 *Leave the unthinned seedlings to develop as clusters of vegetables. Despite being crowded, the plants should produce attractive "baby" vegetables.*

Multiblock-sowing

In this method of sowing (*see above*), 3–5 seeds are allowed to germinate and grow as a group. The benefit of this method is that many plants may be grown in a small space. It is suitable for root, bulb, and stem vegetables such as onions, turnips, beets, and leeks, rather than leafy crops such as lettuces.

Transplanting from a seedbed

Water the seedbed if it is dry, then lift out the seedlings gently with a trowel, retaining as much root and soil on them as possible. Never handle the stems. Tease the seedlings apart and discard any that are diseased: look out for wire stem (a shriveled, brown stem beneath the soil surface), root rots, and clubroot; also discard weak, small seedlings.

Plant healthy specimens in moist soil, preferably in the evening, when showers are expected. Make a hole just large enough for the roots, then position the seedling so that its lowest leaves are just above soil level. Planting too high exposes the stalk, which may snap off in the wind; planting too deep can allow diseases to develop. Firm in each seedling so that there are no air pockets around the roots, then water in well.

Transplanting container-sown plants

Before transplanting in colder climates, ensure the seedlings are hardened off well by placing them in a cold frame, gradually increasing the ventilation over a period of 7–10 days. Alternatively, place in a sheltered site outside during the day for increasingly longer periods.

Water seedlings well before lifting them. Each should come out with a good, clean root ball. Some cell packs are reusable, with holes at the base, so use a piece of wood or stake to push out the plugs. Plant out as above and firm in, just covering each root ball to prevent it from drying out, and water in well.

GROWING VEGETABLES IN CONTAINERS

Most vegetables can grow successfully in containers, either outdoors or protected in a greenhouse. Exceptions are vegetables that need a lot of space, such as squash, larger brassicas, rhubarb, and corn.

Outdoor containers are ideal for those with tiny gardens or as a way of avoiding soil-borne diseases. In colder climates, early crops may be produced under glass, or plants may be started inside and moved outside to grow. It is also possible to extend the season by bringing plants in containers under cover in autumn.

Suitable containers include grow bags, terracotta or plastic pots, barrels and windowboxes, and even hanging baskets. The containers must be a minimum of 10in (25cm) or up to 3ft (90cm) in diameter and up to 2ft (60cm) deep. Make sure that the containers are out of full sun for part of the day, in a sheltered site. Do not place them too close together, or the plants will produce more leaf than crop.

Good drainage is vital: make drainage holes in the base. Use good garden soil with added peat and well-rotted manure or compost, and add a suitable fertilizer. Crops may be sown direct, or the seedlings may be transplanted into the containers. Once it is planted, mulch each container with composted bark, well-rotted manure, compost, or gravel to help retain moisture. Water up to three times daily in hot weather; apply a liquid fertilizer regularly.

▲ Grow bags *Crops such as tomatoes (as here), eggplants, and cucumbers may be raised in grow bags, particularly where soil-borne diseases are prevalent.*

► Climbing crops *Climbing crops such as runner beans or cucumbers should be grown in large containers of soil-based mix to allow for vigorous root development.*

Culinary herbs

Few things may be more delightful than going into the garden and picking some fresh herbs for use in the kitchen. Culinary herbs generally are short-lived plants, so they must be propagated regularly. In most cases, this is easy to do. Cultivars, especially variegated ones, do not come true from seeds, while other herbs may not set seeds, especially in colder climates; these herbs may be increased from cuttings, division, or layering, depending on the type of plant material. The only way to grow annual and biennial herbs is from seeds. Most herbs prefer a free-draining soil that is reasonably fertile, but not too rich, in full sun. For details on specific culinary herbs, see the A–Z of Culinary Herbs (*pp.290–91*).

Taking cuttings

Cuttings may be taken from the first, soft shoots at the start of the growing season, when they have the highest rooting potential, or from semi-ripened shoots later in the season; some shoots root best if taken with a heel. Cuttings may also be taken from the creeping roots or rhizomes of certain herbs.

Softwood cuttings

Taking softwood stem-tip cuttings from the new growth is suitable for many perennial herbs, such as lemon balm, mint, oregano, rosemary, sage, and thyme, and this is especially useful if the plant is not large enough to supply root cuttings (*see p.288*). Taking cuttings often spurs a plant into new growth and helps keep it bushy.

In spring or early summer, prepare some containers (pots, seed trays, or cell packs) with a free-draining rooting medium, such as one of equal parts fine bark and peat. A free-draining mix is essential because the cuttings are at risk of rot before they root.

Collect the cuttings material in small batches in the morning, when they are less likely to become dehydrated (*see below*). Use a sharp knife, not scissors, which tend to pinch and seal the stem and hinder the rooting process. Place the shoots immediately in the shade in a plastic bag or bucket of water, because even a slight loss of moisture will hinder the cuttings' ability to form roots.

Prepare the cuttings as shown below, leaving the top leaves to feed the cutting as it roots. Do not tear off the leaves, because any damage can admit disease – carefully cut them off with a knife.

Make a hole in the rooting medium for each cutting. Never allow the leaves to touch the medium or be covered with it, because they will rot and may encourage fungal growth that can spread up the stem and to other cuttings. Overcrowding the container also increases the risk of fungal disease.

Do not insert cuttings of different species in the same container because they quite often take different periods of time to root. Dip difficult-to-root cuttings in hormone rooting compound just before inserting them.

Keep the cuttings out of direct sun in hot weather – bright shade is best for the first week. In cool climates, the best place is a greenhouse. Cover the container with a plastic bag (*see below*) or a cut-off plastic bottle (*see p.39*). To stop excess moisture from dripping onto the cuttings, turn the plastic bag inside out every few days when condensation builds up. If fungal growth appears on a cutting, pick it out at once.

Softwood cuttings of easily rooted herbs, such as lemon balm, marjoram, mint, and tarragon, will root in water, as for perennial cuttings (*see p.156*).

Heel cuttings
In spring, select a new shoot (here of purple sage) not more than 4in (10cm) long. Grasp it near the base and gently pull it away from the main stem so that it retains a small sliver of bark (the "heel"). Trim the heel of the cutting and remove its lower leaves (see inset).

Heel cuttings

Take these from short new shoots (*see above*). The growth hormones that assist the rooting process are concentrated in the "heel" of old wood. When pulling away the shoot, avoid tearing bark from the shoot, since this may expose it to infection. Treat as for softwood cuttings.

Taking softwood cuttings of herbs

1 In spring, take 4in (10cm) cuttings (here of golden lemon balm) from healthy, nonflowering shoots of the new growth, cutting just above a node. To prevent the leaves from losing moisture, place the cuttings in water.

2 Fill a pot with equal parts moist bark and peat. Trim the base of each cutting just below a node, then strip off all but the top two or three leaves. Insert the cuttings in the medium so that the leaves are just above the surface.

3 Firm in gently and water. Allow the pot to drain, then label it. Tent the pot with a clear plastic bag supported on stakes to prevent contact with the leaves. Keep the cuttings in a lightly shaded position at about 68°F (20°C).

4 When well rooted (usually after about four weeks), knock out the new plants and gently tease them apart. Try to keep the medium around the roots intact. Pot each cutting individually in a pot ½in (1cm) larger than the root ball.

TAKING ROOT CUTTINGS OF HORSERADISH

1 In spring, lift a healthy plant, taking care not to damage the roots. Cut off one or two lengths of root, 6–12in (15–30cm) long.

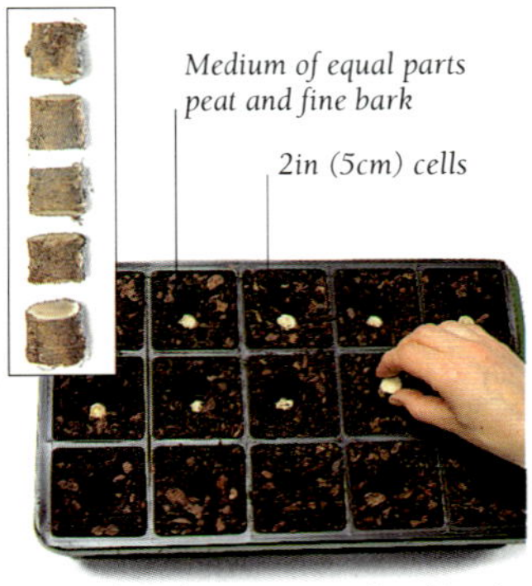

2 Slice the roots into ½in (1cm) sections (see inset). Insert each cutting 1–2½in (2.5–6cm) deep in a prepared cell tray.

3 When the cuttings have good root systems, transplant to their final positions. Hold by the leaves and plant at the same depth.

TRIMMING OTHER ROOT CUTTINGS

To distinguish the ends when taking root cuttings, make a straight cut near the crown and an angled cut near the root tip.

TAKING CUTTINGS OF MINT RHIZOMES

1 Treat rhizomes of herbs such as mint as root cuttings. Lift the plant and select rhizomes that have plenty of growth buds. Divide them into 1½–3in (4–8cm) sections.

2 Make holes in a prepared pot about 1in (2.5cm) apart. Insert the cuttings (see inset) vertically and cover with ¼in (5mm) of medium. Firm and water.

3 Place the cuttings in a warm, bright area. As growth starts, water with a liquid fertilizer. When they have rooted (see inset), knock them out of the pot and tease apart.

4 Pot the cuttings singly into a bark and peat mix. Water in, label, and leave in a warm, bright place until well established and ready for planting out.

Semi-ripe cuttings of herbs

Herbs such as hyssop or rosemary may be rooted from cuttings taken from new shoots that are semi-ripe, that is, no longer soft but firm and starting to turn brown. Prepare them as for softwood cuttings (*see p.287*). Tender herbs such as bay root more successfully if provided with bottom heat of 64°F (18°C) and high humidity – a heated closed case is ideal. The cuttings will be in the same medium for longer than softwood cuttings, so use a very free-draining mix of equal parts peat, fine grit or perlite, and fine bark.

Spray the cuttings every morning and afternoon for the first week. Never spray at night, because the lower temperatures may encourage rot or powdery mildew on the wet leaves. Rooting medium is low in nutrients, so give a foliar feed once a week when the cuttings show signs of rooting, usually in 4–8 weeks.

As for all cuttings, do not test for rooting by tugging, because this may disturb the cutting at a crucial time. Instead, check for new roots showing at the base of the container; alternatively, wait for new shoots to appear.

In colder climates, once they are rooted, harden off the cuttings. Bring them, in stages over 2–3 weeks, into sunny, airy conditions, then pot singly in soil-based potting mix (*see p.34*). Label and water well. When the cuttings are growing well, 4–5 weeks later, pinch out the growing tips to make them bush out and become stronger. Allow the new plants to establish and thoroughly root down in the pots before planting out.

Root cuttings of herbs

This method is suitable for herbs with thonglike or creeping roots, such as horseradish, or rhizomes, such as mint. Take the root cuttings in spring or autumn. First prepare a container with some rooting medium of one part fine bark and one part peat and firm to just below the rim. Water well and allow to drain while preparing the cuttings.

Lift the parent plant and remove some healthy roots. For most herbs, including mint (*see above*), they should be of average thickness. Most cuttings are prepared by dividing the roots into 1½–3in (4–8cm) sections, each with an angled cut at the base (*see box above*).

Rhizome cuttings should have at least one growth bud. Insert them vertically with the bud toward the top, 1–2½in (2.5–6cm) apart. Horseradish roots do not have visible buds but root readily whichever way up they are, so they can simply be sliced into small sections (*see above*). Water the cuttings, then label and date them: this is important with root cuttings, which cannot be identified until they have grown on.

Keep the cuttings in a bright place at 50°F (10°C) or above, such as under the greenhouse bench or on a windowsill, but not in direct sunlight. Do not water until new roots or topgrowth appears (2–3 weeks), then apply a liquid feed. Root cuttings often produce shoots before roots, so check for good root growth before potting the cuttings.

In colder climates, slowly harden off the cuttings once they are rooted by putting them outside during the day and into a cold greenhouse at night. Pot them in a soil-based potting mix once they are weaned, and water well. Omit this stage if the cuttings were rooted in cell packs. Treat the cuttings thereafter as for semi-ripe cuttings.

Division

Perennial herbs lend themselves to being divided, once the plant is well established. It is a simple method of propagating a few plants at a time. Division restricts the spread of the plant and keeps it healthy and vigorous, thus producing lots of new growth that can be used in the kitchen; it also prevents shrubby herbs from becoming too woody. This technique is good for fennel, French tarragon, lemon balm, lovage, mint, oregano, and thyme.

Herbs should be divided either after flowering in late summer or in early spring. The best time is when growth is minimal, and in warm, mild weather to avoid cold damage. It is important not to allow the roots to dry out, so the new divisions should be replanted as soon as possible. Before dividing the plant, therefore, dig over the planting site, make sure it is free of weeds, and add a handful of general-purpose fertilizer.

When you lift the plant (*see below*), remove all the roots, because any piece left in the ground may produce another plant. This is particularly important with invasive plants such as horseradish or mint. Wash the roots to make it easier to disentangle them and divide the plant (*see below*). Small or herbaceous plants may be pulled apart, but larger or woody clumps will need to be cut into pieces, using a clean, sharp knife or pruners. Make sure that each section has a good root system, and discard any old, woody, or very congested sections.

Replant the divisions immediately (*see below*). Water thoroughly, even in damp weather. Keep the plants weed-free and well watered until established.

Separating herb suckers

Woody herbs such as bay sometimes send out offshoots, or suckers, from the roots. These should be removed in spring, because they will spoil the shape of the plant. If they have roots, the suckers can be potted and grown on.

To detach a suckering shoot, scrape back the soil to expose the base of the plant and carefully pull off the long suckering root where it joins the parent plant. Cut back its main root to just below the fibrous, feeding roots. If there are several shoots on the sucker, divide the main root so that each shoot has its own roots. Cut back the topgrowth by about half, then pot each sucker in soil-based potting mix, and allow to root in high humidity at 59°F (15°C).

Rooted suckers may be planted outdoors in warm climates. In colder climates, grow on under cover or in a sheltered spot and keep frost-free for the first winter before planting out.

Layering

If an herb has flexible shoots growing close to the ground, they can be simple layered. This is a reliable method for bay, sage, thyme, winter savory, and trailing forms of rosemary. It helps to cut back low branches of the parent plant during winter to induce formation of vigorous shoots for layering. Prepare the soil around the plant where the shoots are to be layered during winter or early spring by mixing in peat or compost and fine grit to aid drainage.

Layer young, ripe shoots in summer. Each shoot to be layered is laid in a trench in the prepared soil and pinned down (*see p.290*). The trench is then filled in and firmed well. Keep the soil moist until the stem is well rooted; usually this takes 2–3 months and is accompanied by new growth on the shoots. In autumn, uncover the soil between the rooted layer and the parent plant and sever the shoot. Allow the layer to grow on. Pinch out the growing tip from the layer 3–4 weeks later and lift if the roots are well advanced and showing lots of new growth. Otherwise, leave it for another year.

Plant out each layer in prepared soil. Label, water, and allow to establish. In some climates, it will be necessary to protect the young (*continued on p.290*)

DIVISION OF HERBS

1 In late summer, after flowering, choose a vigorous, mature plant (here thyme). Lift the plant with a garden fork, taking care not to damage the roots.

2 Shake off as much loose soil as possible and remove any dead leaves or stems. Wash the roots clean in a bucket of water or with a garden hose.

3 If the parent plant has plenty of topgrowth, trim it back with pruners to about 4in (10cm) to minimize moisture loss through the leaves.

4 Divide the plant into smaller pieces, each with a good root system and strong topgrowth. Cut with clean, sharp pruners or pull apart by hand.

5 Before replanting, dust any cut surfaces with fungicide. Prepare a planting site and replant the divisions at the same depth as before, spacing them sufficiently far apart to allow for growth. Firm, label, and water thoroughly.

SIMPLE LAYERING HERBS

1 *Select a young, healthy, low-growing shoot (here of rosemary). Strip the leaves from about 20in (50cm) of the stem, starting 4in (10cm) from the tip.*

2 *Lower the shoot to the ground and mark its position on the soil. Dig a trench sloping away from the plant that is 4–6in (10–15cm) deep at the far end.*

3 *Lay the stripped stem along the base of the trench. Scratch the bark a little at the point where it bends. Pin the stem against the side of the trench with wire staples.*

4 *Fill the trench with soil, firm in, and label. Water and keep the soil moist. The stem should produce roots at the point where it bends* (see inset) *after 3–4 weeks.*

(*continued from p.289*) layers of tender herbs, such as bay, against cold and drying winds with fleece or straw. For this reason, it helps in cold climates to pot young layers as soon as they have rooted in equal parts peat, fine grit or perlite, and fine bark, and overwinter them in a cool greenhouse before planting out in spring.

MOUND LAYERING HERBS

This technique is best used on specimens of perennial herbs that are past their best, such as rosemary, sage, lavender, and winter savory, and is especially good for thymes, which can become woody.

In the spring, mix some soil with equal parts of peat and sand, then pile it over the plant (*see below*). If any soil is washed away by rain, replace it. By late summer, roots should have formed along many of the stems. The rooted layers can be removed and potted or planted out as for standard layers (*see above*). Dispose of the old plant.

MOUND LAYERING

In spring, to encourage the stems to root, mound 3–5in (8–13cm) of sandy soil over the crown of the plant (here thyme), so that just the tips of the shoots are visible. Keep the mound watered. In late summer or autumn, remove the soil and cut off the rooted layers (see inset).

SOWING SEEDS

Seeds of annual and biennial herbs, such as angelica, basil, borage, caraway, chervil, cilantro, dill, sweet marjoram, and parsley, may be sown in containers under cover or outdoors or in seedbeds, depending on the climate. Perennial herbs can be raised from seeds, but vegetative propagation results in mature plants more quickly. Many culinary herbs are species and, if grown apart from other forms, come true from home-gathered seeds.

GATHERING SEEDS FROM HERBS

Gather the seeds for sowing as soon as they ripen in the summer or autumn. Bear in mind that certain herbs may cross-pollinate. When different cultivars of lavender, marjoram, mint, and thyme are grown near each other, the chances of the plants naturally hybridizing are high, and the seedlings will vary in appearance and flavor. Closely related species may also interbreed if they flower at the same time; dill and fennel are known to cross, resulting in an herb with an indeterminate flavor.

Seeds should be gathered as soon as the color of the seed pod changes. The seeds ripen very fast, usually to a pale brown color, so watch them carefully. To test if a seedpod is ripe, tap it gently. If a few seeds scatter, it is time to gather them. Cut off the seedheads on their stalks and dry them to extract the seeds.

Tie the stalks in small bundles: keep them loose so that air can circulate between them. Hang the bunches to dry thoroughly for up to two weeks in a warm, but airy, dark place; do not use an artificial source of heat – it may kill some seeds. Place a large piece of paper or a sheet under the seedheads to gather the seeds as they fall (*see facing page*). Alternatively, the seedheads may be enclosed in paper bags (not plastic ones, which will make the seedheads "sweat") or in muslin (*see facing page*) before hanging them up. Store dry seeds as for vegetable seeds (*see p.282*).

SOWING HERB SEEDS

Sow herb seeds as for vegetable seeds (*see pp.282–6*). Most herbs germinate at about 55°F (13°C). In colder regions, sow tender herbs, such as basil and cilantro, in containers under cover in early spring or outdoors in late spring.

A–Z OF CULINARY HERBS

ANGELICA *ANGELICA ARCHANGELICA* (syn. *A. officinalis*) Seeds viable for three months; sow in autumn outdoors; if they germinate and die back in winter, they will regrow in spring.

ANISE HYSSOP *AGASTACHE FOENICULUM* (syn. *A. anisata*) Softwood cuttings in summer. Divide in spring. Seeds in spring or autumn.

BASIL *OCIMUM BASILICUM* Sow seeds under cover at 64°F (18°C) in late spring or outdoors at 59°F (15°C) in early summer; seedlings taprooted and prone to damping off; needs warm, sheltered site.

BAY *LAURUS NOBILIS* Semi-ripe cuttings in late summer or early autumn; root in high humidity. Divide suckers in spring. Simple layer in spring. Surface-sow seeds in autumn under cover with bottom heat of 64°F (18°C); keep just moist; germination can take 10–20 days or 6–12 months.

BEE BALM, BERGAMOT *MONARDA DIDYMA* Softwood cuttings in early summer. Root cuttings in spring. Divide in early spring. Seeds with bottom heat of 64°F (18°C) in spring or outdoors after frosts.

BORAGE *BORAGO OFFICINALIS* Sow seeds outdoors in early to late spring, 2in (5cm) deep; taprooted.

CARAWAY *CARUM CARVI* Sow seeds in early autumn in cells or pots; for root crop, sow in drills and thin to 8in (20cm); bolts if transplanted late; dislikes root disturbance.

CHERVIL *ANTHRISCUS CEREFOLIUM* Sow seeds

If the seeds are very fine (such as oregano seeds), use a piece of cardboard folded in half. Put a small amount of seeds in the fold and gently tap the cardboard to sow evenly. When sowing dark seeds outdoors, pour a little sand into the bottom of the drill (*see p.283*) before sowing. This makes it easy to see the seeds and avoids sowing too thickly.

Herbs from the carrot family, such as caraway, chervil, dill, or parsley, as well as basil and borage, have long taproots; transplanting sets them back. Sow the seeds direct outdoors or singly in pots or cells to avoid disturbing them.

Seeds of most herbs germinate in a few weeks. With herbs that are slow to germinate, such as bay, chives, fennel, parsley and sage, provide bottom heat of 64°F (18°C) in cool climates. Otherwise, sow outdoors when the soil temperature is above 50°F (10°C), and all risk of frost is passed. Keep the soil moist.

Some herb seedlings, for example basil, oregano, and thyme, are prone to damping off (*see p.46*). Keep the soil mix just moist, watering from the bottom and never at night.

Seeds of herbs used in quantity, such as basil or parsley, are best sown in successive batches every 3–4 weeks.

▲ SELF-SOWN SEEDLINGS
Many herbs (here Chinese chives) self-sow in favorable conditions. Lift them when they are large enough to handle, then transplant.

◄ GATHERING SEEDS
Ripening seedheads are best hung on their stalks upside down in a warm, dry, airy place. Lay paper on the floor below or enclose the seedheads in cloth to catch the seeds as they fall.

at 50°F (10°C) in early to late spring; taprooted (*see above*). Prefers semi-shade.
CHIVES *ALLIUM SCHOENOPRASUM* Divide bulb clumps in spring or autumn (*see p.254*); plant in clumps of 6–10, 6in (15cm) apart. Sow 10–15 seeds per 1¼in (3cm) cell in spring with bottom heat of 64°F (18°C).
CILANTRO *CORIANDRUM SATIVUM* Sow seeds in early or late spring; dislikes excess moisture or humidity; thin to 2in (5cm) apart for leaf crop (cilantro) or 9in (23cm) apart for seed crop. Try 'Morocco' for a seed crop.
DILL *ANETHUM GRAVEOLENS* Sow seeds in early spring or outdoors in late spring, shallowly in poor soil, thin to 8in (20cm); seeds viable for three years; taprooted.
FENNEL *FOENICULUM VULGARE* Divide every 2–3 years in autumn. Sow seeds in early spring in pots or cells, cover with perlite; bottom heat of 59–70°F (15–21°C) helps; sow outdoors in late spring and thin to 20in (50cm).
HORSERADISH *ARMORACIA RUSTICANA* (syn. *Cochlearia armoracia*) Root cuttings in early spring. Divide clumps in spring or autumn. Can be invasive.
HYSSOP *HYSSOPUS OFFICINALIS* Softwood or heel cuttings in late spring or after flowering. Sow seeds in spring with bottom heat of 64°F (18°C) or outdoors after frosts.
JUNIPER *JUNIPERUS COMMUNIS* Take softwood cuttings in spring or semi-ripe heel cuttings in summer or autumn. Sow seeds outdoors in spring or autumn; germinates in four weeks or in a year.
LEMON BALM *MELISSA OFFICINALIS* Take softwood cuttings in late spring or early summer. Divide in spring or autumn. Seeds in spring with minimum watering.
LEMON VERBENA *ALOYSIA TRIPHYLLA* Take softwood cuttings in late spring or semi-ripe cuttings in summer.
LOVAGE *LEVISTICUM OFFICINALE* Divide in autumn or spring. Sow seeds outdoors in autumn or in spring under cover with bottom heat of 59°F (15°C). Space 2ft (60cm) apart.
MINTS *MENTHA SPECIES* Take softwood cuttings in summer. Take rhizome cuttings in spring. Divide in spring. Invasive.
MYRTLE *MYRTUS COMMUNIS* Take softwood cuttings in late spring or semi-ripe cuttings in summer.
OREGANO, MARJORAM *ORIGANUM VULGARE* Take softwood cuttings in summer. Divide in spring or after flowering. Surface-sow seeds in spring thinly; germination often erratic.
PARSLEY *PETROSELINUM CRISPUM* Sow annual seeds in early spring with bottom heat of 64°F (18°C), or in late spring 1in (2.5cm) deep in rich soil at 59°F (15°C); keep moist; germination is slow.

BORAGO OFFICINALIS

ROSEMARY *ROSMARINUS OFFICINALIS* Semi-ripe cuttings in late summer. Heel cuttings in spring. Simple or mound layer in summer.
SAGE *SALVIA OFFICINALIS* Take heel or 6in (15cm) softwood cuttings in spring. Simple layer in summer after flowering. Mound layer in spring. Sow seeds of species only in early spring, covered with perlite; bottom heat of 59°F (15°C) is useful.
SORREL *RUMEX ACETOSA* Divide in autumn. Seeds in spring or outdoors in midspring.
SWEET CICELY *MYRRHIS ODORATA* Take root cuttings in spring or autumn. Divide in autumn. Sow seeds outdoors in autumn or winter; slow to germinate.
SWEET MARJORAM *ORIGANUM MAJORANA* Softwood cuttings and division, as for marjoram, in warm climates. In colder climates, sow as annual in spring.
TARRAGON *ARTEMISIA DRACUNCULUS* Softwood cuttings in summer. Take cuttings from underground runners in spring after frosts. Divide mature plants every 2–3 years in spring. French tarragon rarely produces ripe seeds in cold climates, but Russian tarragon (subsp. *dracunculoides*) seeds freely.
THYMES *THYMUS SPECIES* Take 2–3in (5–8cm) softwood cuttings in late spring or summer. Take 2in (5cm) heel cuttings in late spring. Simple layer in early autumn or mound layer in spring. Surface-sow seeds of *T. vulgaris* only, in spring with bottom heat of 68°F (20°C) or outdoors in late spring or early summer at 59°F (15°C).

A–Z OF VEGETABLES

INDEX TO MAIN ENTRIES

For other, less common vegetable crops, see the sidebar list on p.309.

ABELMOSCHUS OKRA

SEEDS in spring

Okra (*Abelmoschus esculentus*), one of the podded vegetables in this tender genus, is an annual. Soak bought or home-gathered seeds for 24 hours before sowing to aid germination. In warmer regions, sow seeds thinly in drills 2ft (60cm) apart when the soil reaches a temperature of 61–64°F (16–18°C). Thin the seedlings to 8in (20cm) apart.

In colder areas, sow seeds in pots; germinate under mist (*see p.44*) with bottom heat of 68°F (20°C) and 70 per-cent humidity. Plant out under cover, preferably in low-nitrogen soil, in late spring to early summer, 16in (40cm) apart and at the same temperature and humidity. Harvest pods in 8–11 weeks.

SOWING OKRA SEEDS IN POTS
Sow three seeds to a 3½in (9cm) pot. When the seedlings have their seed leaves, gently pull out the most leggy or any weak seedlings and leave the sturdiest one to grow on.

ALLIUM ONIONS, SCALLIONS, SHALLOTS, LEEKS, GARLIC

Bulb onions

SEEDS from spring to summer
SETS from late winter to spring
CLOVES from winter to spring

The vegetable alliums include bulb onions, scallions, shallots, leeks, and garlic. Mostly cool-season annuals, they grow best at 55–75°F (12–24°C); the bulbs need full sun in late summer to early autumn to ripen. They also like a rich soil. Crop rotation is important, because they suffer from soil-borne diseases such as white rot and neck rot.

BULB ONIONS AND SCALLIONS

Bulb onions (*Allium cepa*) can be raised from seeds, but sets (small, immature bulbs) are often more successful because they are less disease-prone, tolerate poor soil, and may be started before onion maggots are a threat. Some sets are heat-treated to prevent bolting. Plant sets (*see below*) in loose soil: if it is too firm, the roots will push the sets out of the ground.

Onions need a long growing season, so they should be sown early. Sow seeds thinly in drills in spring or under cover in seed trays or cells from late winter to early spring. They can also be sown in

PLANTING ONION SETS

1 As soon as soil conditions allow, make shallow drills, 10in (25cm) apart. Push the sets gently into the soil. Space them 4in (10cm) apart, or 2in (5cm) if they are very small or if small onions are required.

2 Draw the soil gently over the sets and firm so that the tips are just visible. Trim off any dead foliage or stems so that birds do not pull them out. There is no need to water them in unless the soil is extremely dry.

SOWING ONION SEEDS

Sow onion seeds thinly in drills, and thin according to the desired size of the crop: the closer the spacing, the smaller the mature bulb. Here, seedlings were thinned to 1in (2.5cm), 2in (5cm), and 4in (10cm) intervals.

ONION SEEDS AND SETS

	BULB ONIONS	SCALLIONS	SHALLOTS	LEEKS	GARLIC
METHOD AND TIMING	Seeds: late winter to early spring, or late summer to overwinter Sets: late winter to early spring or autumn Heat-treated sets: early or late spring	Seeds: early spring to summer; late summer for overwintering Sets: late winter to early spring	Seeds: early spring or late summer Sets: autumn to early spring	Seeds under cover, singly or multiblocks: mid- to late winter; transplant early summer Seeds outdoors: early to midspring	Cloves: singly in cells in autumn or spring; transplant spring
SPACING OF SEEDS OR SETS	Seeds: sow thinly; thin to desired spacing (*see facing page*) Small sets: 2in (5cm) Large sets: 4in (10cm)	1in (2.5cm)	Seeds and sets: 6in (15cm)	Multiblock seedlings: 9in (23cm) Single seedlings: 4–6in (10–15cm)	7in (18cm)
SPACING OF ROWS	Seeds and sets: 10in (25cm)	8–12in (20–30cm)	Seeds and sets: 8–12in (20–30cm)	12in (30cm)	7in (18cm)
SOWING OR PLANTING DEPTH	Seeds: ½in (1cm) Sets: 1–1½in (2.5–4cm)	½in (1cm)	Seeds and sets: ½in (1cm)	Seeds: ½in (1cm) Seedlings: 6–8in (15–20cm)	1in (2.5cm)
TIME UNTIL HARVEST	Seeds: up to 42 weeks Sets: 12–18 weeks	2–10 weeks; over winter 30–35 weeks	Seeds: 42 weeks Sets: 16 weeks	16–20 weeks; can be left to stand over winter	16–36 weeks

multiblocks, six seeds to a cell (*see p.286*). For successive crops, sow every two weeks. Destroy infested plants or dust drills with an insecticide to control onion maggots. To gather seeds, leave a few vigorous plants to flower in autumn or the following spring.

Scallions are cultivars of bulb onions that are harvested as young plants. Sow as for bulb onions, or plant sets and harvest in a few weeks.

SHALLOTS

Shallots (*Allium cepa* Aggregatum Group) are raised from sets in the same way as bulb onions and suffer from the same pests and diseases. Remove loose skins or leaves before planting the sets to avoid birds pulling them out. If you have healthy stock, save your own sets to store over winter: they should be ¾in (2cm) in diameter. Seeds may also be available; sow them as for bulb onions.

LEEKS

Leeks (*Allium porrum*) are biennials grown as annuals, needing a rich, loose soil high in nitrogen and a long growing season. Sow seeds in drills as for bulb onions or in cells (*see below*) at 50–59°F (10–15°C). For large leeks with well-blanched stems, transplant 8in (20cm) tall seedlings into deep holes (*see below*) or trenches. Leeks are prone to thrips damage. To gather the seeds, leave a few healthy plants to flower in the spring.

GARLIC

These biennials (*Allium sativum*) need a long growing season and a period of cold at 32–50°F (0–10°C). They do not like soils that are heavy, very cold, or high in nitrogen. For best results, buy seed cloves suited to your area and start them in cells (*see left*). Plant temperature-tolerant cultivars in spring.

PLANTING GARLIC CLOVES

PREPARING GARLIC CLOVES *Pry apart the bulb into cloves with your thumbs. Clean off loose tunics and discard any cloves that show signs of disease, such as rot. Each clove should retain a piece of basal plate* (see inset).

PLANTING GARLIC IN CELLS *In autumn, plant garlic cloves singly in cells, 1in (2.5cm) deep with basal plates downward. Cover with soil mix. Keep cold over winter. Transplant in spring when they start to sprout.*

TRANSPLANTING LEEK SEEDLINGS

MULTIBLOCKS *Sow seeds in cells, four to a cell. Transplant each clump of seedlings into a seedbed. Space the clumps 9in (23cm) apart, in rows that are 12in (30cm) apart.*

SINGLE LEEK SEEDLINGS *For well-blanched leeks, make holes 6–8in (15–20cm) deep and 4–6in (10–15cm) apart and insert a seedling in each one so that the roots are in contact with the soil at the bottom. Water in and allow the soil to fall in naturally.*

SCALLION SEEDLINGS

Scallions are best sown thinly. If they are sown densely, thin to 1in (2.5cm) apart to grow on, and use the thinnings as salad vegetables.

APIUM CELERY, CELERIAC

SEEDS in spring (celery) (celeriac)

Celery (*Apium graveolens*) and celeriac (*Apium graveolens* var. *rapaceum*) are both biennial stem vegetables and temperate crops that can survive light frosts. They prefer a deep, rich, moist soil and a growing temperature of 59–70°F (15–21°C).

CELERY

The seeds need light and a minimum of 59°C (15°C) to germinate and should be treated with a fungicide to counteract fungal leaf spots. For trench celery, prepare a trench 15in (38cm) wide and 12in (30cm) deep and work in manure or compost. In warmer climates, sow shallowly outdoors – trench celery in single rows to facilitate hilling up, or self-blanching types in a block (*see below*). Celery seeds may also be fluid-sown (*see p.284*). Thin out seedlings with 4–6 true leaves to 15in (38cm) apart for trench celery or 9in (23cm) apart for self-blanching. In colder regions, sow indoors: under mist (*see p.44*) is best. Do not sow too early; seedlings may bolt if the temperature falls below 50°F (10°C). If sown in trays, transplant the seedlings when each has one true leaf into to 2–3in (5–8cm) cells. Once they have 4–6 true leaves they may be transplanted outdoors if all risk of frost is past, in late spring or early summer. Protect with fleece if necessary.

SELF-BLANCHING CELERY SEEDLINGS
Plant out celery seedlings in a rich soil in late spring or early summer. Plant self-blanching celery in blocks 9in (23cm) square to encourage the stems to blanch naturally.

CELERIAC SEEDLINGS IN A CELL PACK
Sow celeriac in seed trays or cells at a minimum temperature of 59°F (15°C). Thin to one seedling per cell and harden off. Transplant when the seedlings are 3–4in (8–10 cm) tall and have six or seven leaves.

CELERIAC

Celeriac has a bulblike swollen stem and requires the same conditions as celery but can survive 14°F (-10°C) if protected by straw. It needs a six-month growing season for the stem to develop. Sow the seeds in cells (*see above*) or in trays as for celery. When they are 3in (8cm) tall, harden off (*see p.286*) the seedlings and transplant outdoors. Space them 12–15in (30–38cm) apart and take care not to bury the crowns.

ARACHIS PEANUT

SEEDS in early spring

Peanuts are tender tropical annuals that require a growing temperature of 68–86°F (20–30°C) with 80 percent humidity, and a sandy, free-draining soil low in nitrogen. Fertilized flowers produce shoots that penetrate the soil; the fruits then develop into peanuts. Rain or watering during flowering will impede the pollination process and reduce the crop.

In warmer areas, sow seeds singly outdoors 2in (5cm) deep, in drills (*see p.283*) 3ft (90cm) apart, with a minimum soil temperature of 61°F (16°C). Alternatively, station-sow (*see p.284*) 6in (15cm) apart. Thin seedlings to 12in (30cm).

In colder climates, sow indoors in 3½in (9cm) pots or in cells to germinate at 68°F (20°C). Leave the containers in a sunny spot and cover with a plastic bag or place in a closed case to maintain the humidity. Transplant the seedlings into a greenhouse bed when the seedlings are 4–6in (10–15cm) tall, spacing as for outdoors. Begin hilling up when the seedlings are 6in (15cm) to obtain a crop in 16–24 weeks.

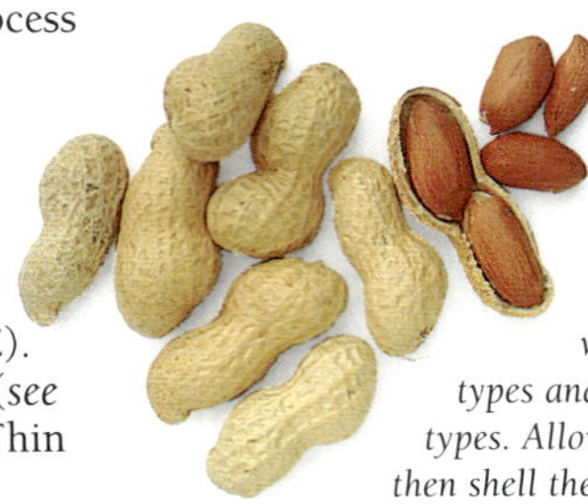

GATHERING PEANUTS
Harvest the pods 16–20 weeks after sowing for upright types and 3–4 weeks later for prostrate types. Allow the seeds to dry in the pods, then shell them and store in a dry place.

ASPARAGUS

Asparagus spears

SEEDS in spring
DIVISION in late winter or early spring

Asparagus (*Asparagus officinalis*) is perennial, with separate male and female plants. It may be divided, but male, F1 hybrid seeds produce very robust plants. Asparagus grows best at 61–75°F (16–24°C) and needs cold winters to induce a dormant period for the plant to crop well in spring. The soil should be low in nitrogen, weed-free, free-draining, and not in a frost pocket. If necessary, grow asparagus in a raised bed (*see p.283*) to improve drainage, and add lime to acidic soils.

SEEDS

Sow seeds 1in (2.5cm) deep and 3in (8cm) apart in rows 12in (30cm) apart (*see p.283*). Transplant the largest as for crowns (*see below*) to their permanent positions in the following spring. Alternatively, sow in cells in early spring.

DIVISION OF AN ASPARAGUS

1 *In late winter or early spring, when the buds are just developing and before the new root growth begins in earnest, carefully lift the crown with a fork. Shake off any excess soil.*

3 *To prevent rot from setting in, cut away any damaged, diseased, or old growth from each section with a sharp knife. Take great care not to damage or cut into the buds. Dig a trench 12in (30cm) wide and 8in (20cm) deep.*

at 55–61°F (13–16°C); transplant as for crowns (*see below*) in early summer. Allow plants to build up vigor, then begin to harvest after two years.

DIVISION

Asparagus beds last 20 years if left undisturbed. When lifted, crowns will suffer a check in growth and cropping but, if needed, crowns of three years or more may be divided (*see below*). With mature plants, take divisions from the edges in early spring before new growth appears, and discard the woody center.

With all division, take care not to damage the fleshy roots, and never allow the crowns to dry out. Always replant divided crowns in a new site to avoid soil-borne diseases such as root rot. Placing the crowns on a ridge of soil provides extra drainage, helps prevent rot, and ensures better contact with the soil. Mulch after replanting to retain moisture. In warmer climates, cover the bud tips with 2in (5cm) of loose soil to prevent drying out. Divided crowns should provide a crop in two years.

CROWN

2 *Pry apart the crown with your thumbs into sections, each with at least one good bud. If necessary, cut through the crown with a sharp knife before gently teasing apart the roots.*

4 *Work in 3in (8cm) well-rotted manure and top with 2in (5cm) of soil. Make a 4in (10cm) high ridge along the center of the trench. Space the crowns on it, 12in (30cm) apart. Cover with soil so that only the bud tips are visible.*

ATRIPLEX ORACH, MOUNTAIN SPINACH

SEEDS from early spring to late summer

Orach (*Atriplex hortensis*) is a fast-growing leafy annual that self-sows freely. A deep, rich, moisture-retentive soil gives best results. Orach grows best at a temperature of 61–64°F (16–18°C). It bolts and self-sows in hot weather.

SEEDS

Fertile seeds are enclosed in papery bracts; those without bracts are infertile. Cut off seeded stalks for drying (*see p.282*). Orach does not transplant well so is best sown direct outdoors from early spring. Make successive sowings every 2–3 weeks during the growing season for a continuous crop. Sow seeds thinly in drills (*see p.283*) 2ft (60cm) apart. Thin the seedlings to 15in (38cm) apart. Orach is attacked by slugs and snails; control them (*see p.47*) when the seedlings are small and vulnerable. Water copiously in summer, especially in dry conditions. Harvest the young leaves after seven weeks.

BETA BEET, CHARD

SEEDS in spring

This small group of vegetables, derived from *Beta vulgaris*, includes the leafy vegetables known variously as Swiss chard, seakale beet, spinach beet, and silver beet, and beets (*Beta vulgaris* subsp. *vulgaris*), grown for their swollen roots. They are all biennials, but beets are grown as annuals.

LEAF BEETS AND CHARD

Chard is a "cut and come again" leafy vegetable that comes in white-, yellow-, and red-stemmed cultivars. It is hardy to 7°F (-14°C) and grows best at 61–64°F (16–18°C). It is bolt-resistant in the first year if sown after midspring and will withstand hot weather if it is well watered.

Sow the seeds in midspring in drills (*see p.283*) 15in (38cm) apart. Thin the seedlings to 6in (15cm) or up to 12in (30cm) if larger plants are required. Sow in early autumn for an early spring crop; these crops tend to go to seed in mid- to late spring, depending on the temperature: the cooler it is, the slower they are to bolt.

BEETS

Beets grow best in cool, even temperatures, ideally around 16°C (61°F). Most cultivars have multigerm seeds (*see right*). There are also some monogerm cultivars, which have single seeds.

Sow the seeds outdoors when the soil temperature is at least 45°F (7°C) after washing them (*see right*). Space the drills 12in (30cm) apart, and thin the seedlings to 3–4in (7–10cm) apart. For earlier crops in colder climates, sow in early spring under cloches or in the greenhouse in cells (*see p.285*), and plant out the seedlings when they are 2in (5cm) tall. For a continuous crop, sow seeds at three-week intervals until midsummer. Beets should be ready to harvest in 7–13 weeks.

▲ CHARD
The leaf and stem color varies greatly with the cultivar (here 'Rhubarb Chard'). Chards and other leaf beets can serve a double purpose as vegetables and also as an ornamental crop grown in a border.

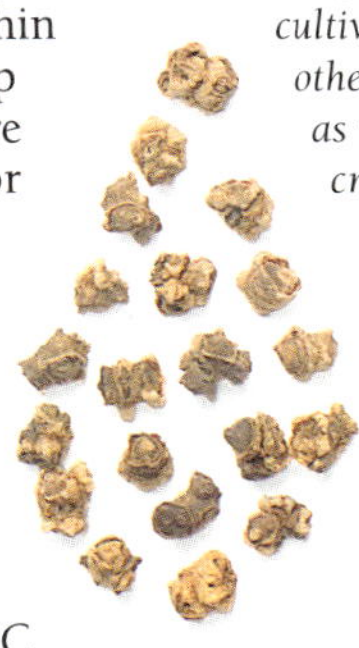

◄ BEET SEEDS
Beet seeds are usually multigerm; each is really a cluster of seeds and produces a clump of seedlings. Thin each to one seedling for a regular crop or leave unthinned to form baby beets, as for multiblock sowing.

▲ PREPARING BEET SEEDS
To encourage rapid germination, place the multigerm beet seeds in a sieve and rinse them thoroughly under cold running water before sowing. This removes the chemicals that inhibit germination. Sow the seeds immediately.

BRASSICA CABBAGE FAMILY

Purple-headed cauliflower

SEEDS (rutabaga)

The brassica family includes a wide range of biennial vegetables; some are grown as annuals or biennials for the shoots or flowerheads, others as annuals for the leaves and roots. Most are cool-season crops of varying hardiness, with many cultivars for different seasons. They perform badly and usually bolt quickly when temperatures exceed 77°F (25°C). In mild zones they can be grown almost all year, but in hot climates only during cooler weather. Stored seeds remain viable for several years but need to be grown in isolation to come true.

Leafy brassicas prefer a firm soil and need high levels of nitrogen, but freshly manured soil causes lush, disease-prone growth. Crop rotation (*see p.282*) is vital to avoid a buildup of clubroot. If this is a problem, lime the soil and sow seeds in cells to give the plants a healthy start. Leafy brassicas may be sown with root crops or catch crops such as annual herbs or lettuces (*see p.285*).

BRUSSELS SPROUTS

Cultivars (*Brassica oleracea* Gemmifera Group) are sown from early to late spring, depending on whether they mature in late autumn, midwinter, or early spring, or in summer in warmer climates. Early types are less hardy, but late crops survive 14°F (-10°C). Sow in cells (*see p.285*) or a seedbed (*see p.283*), under cover for earliest sowings. Transplant dwarf cultivars 18in (45cm), and tall ones 2ft (60cm), apart in early summer. Keep new plants moist until established and control downy mildew (*see p.47*). Harvest in 20 weeks.

CABBAGE

Cabbages (*Brassica oleracea* Capitata Group) prefer 59–68°F (15–20°C), but the hardiest withstand 14°F (-10°C) for a short time. It is vital to sow cultivars at the correct time for the expected crop (*see chart below*). Sow in cells (*see p.285*) or a seedbed or direct (*see p.283*) if conditions permit. Transplant when seedlings are 2–3in (5–8cm) tall at the appropriate spacings (*see chart below*). Use treated seeds to protect against clubroot or flea beetle. Protect seedlings from cabbage root maggot, if needed, with collars (*see facing page*). Keep young plants watered during dry spells and spray if necessary.

BROCCOLI

This (*Brassica oleracea* Italica Group) is a cool-season crop and prefers an average temperature below 59°F (15°C), but cold may damage buds and young flowerheads. It does not transplant well: sow 2–3 seeds at stations (*see p.284*) or in cells (*see p.285*) and transplant deeply. Spacing depends on the size of head required (*see chart, facing page*); closer spacing produces smaller heads.

CAULIFLOWER

Success with cauliflowers (*Brassica oleracea* Botrytis Group) depends on sowing at the correct time and avoiding checks in growth, such as from dry soil or transplanting. It is vital to choose the correct cultivar for the cropping season (*see chart, facing page*). In warmer regions, sow main crops from midsummer to autumn. Seeds germinate best at 70°F (21°C). Sow direct in spring or early summer for baby vegetables, in rows 9in (23cm) apart and thin to 4in (10cm) apart. Control downy mildew (*see p.47*), especially on early sowings.

PLANTING DEPTH *Plant brassica seedlings to cover most of the stalk, so that the lowest leaves are just above the soil. The mature plant may otherwise need staking, since the topgrowth could be too heavy for a leggy stalk to support.*

CHINESE CABBAGE

If sown in spring, Chinese cabbage (*Brassica rapa* var. *pekinensis*) is likely to bolt unless kept at 68–77°F (20–25°C) for the first three weeks. Most cultivars withstand only light frosts. It is safer to delay sowing until early summer in colder climates. Sow in rows (*see p.283*) 18in (45cm) apart and thin plants to 12in (30cm). Chinese cabbage is very prone to clubroot. Harvest after 8–10 weeks.

SOWING SPROUTS

1 Line a saucer about 5in (13cm) in diameter with paper towels. Add water to soak the paper, then drain off any excess. Scatter the seeds thickly over the paper. Label and leave in a cool, bright place at a maximum temperature of 59°F (15°C) to germinate. Cover loosely with a clear plastic bag to retain moisture.

2 The seeds should root into the paper. Check daily to ensure that the paper is moist, and water as necessary, gently pouring water against the side of the saucer to avoid disturbing the seedling roots. Allow to absorb, then pour off any excess after one hour. The seedlings should be ready to harvest in 7–10 days (see above).

SOWING CABBAGE SEEDS

WHEN HARVESTED	SPRING	EARLY SUMMER	SUMMER	AUTUMN	WINTER (FOR STORAGE)	WINTER (TO USE FRESH)
TYPE OF CABBAGE	Small, pointed or round heads or loose, leafy greens	Large, mainly round, heads	Large, round heads	Large, round heads (includes red cabbage)	Smooth, white-leaved heads	Blue-green and Savoy
WHEN TO SOW	Late summer to early autumn	Late winter to early spring	Early to mid-spring	Late spring to early summer	Spring	Late spring to early summer
SPACING OF PLANTS	9in (23cm)	15in (38cm)	15in (38cm)	15in (38cm)	18in (45cm)	18in (45cm)
SPACING OF ROWS	12in (30cm)	15in (38cm)	15in (38cm)	15in (38cm)	18in (45cm)	18in (45cm)

SOWING SEEDS OF CAULIFLOWER AND BROCCOLI

	CAULIFLOWER (TO HARVEST IN DIFFERENT SEASONS)				BROCCOLI	SPROUTING BROCCOLI
	WINTER (FROST-FREE AREAS)	WINTER	EARLY SUMMER	SUMMER & AUTUMN		
WHEN AND WHERE TO SOW	Late spring in seedbed	Early summer in seedbed	Autumn in cold frame Midwinter in warm green-house	Early cultivars: spring under cover Others: late spring in seedbed	Autumn or spring to summer in cells or at stations. Protect from frost if needed	Spring in cells or seedbed
WHEN TO TRANSPLANT	Midsummer	Midsummer	Midspring	Early summer	Early autumn	Early to midsummer
SPACING OF PLANTS	28in (70cm)	24in (60cm)	24in (60cm)	24in (60cm)	12–18in (30–45cm)	24in (60cm)
SPACING OF ROWS	28in (70cm)	18in (45cm)	18in (45cm)	18in (45cm)	6–12in (15–30cm)	12in (30cm)
TIME UNTIL HARVEST	40 weeks	40 weeks	16–33 weeks	16 weeks	11–14 weeks	50 weeks

MUSTARD AND SPROUTS

Sow mustard sprouts (*Brassica hirta* and *B. napus*) on paper towels (*facing page*) or in seed trays under cover at any time for salad crop. From spring to early autumn, sow mustard in wide drills or broadcast (*pp.283–4*) for a seed crop.

KALE, CURLY KALE, BORECOLE

Some kales (*Brassica oleracea* Acephala Group) survive 5°F (-15°C). Sow summer-cropping kales in early spring, and autumn or winter crops in late spring. Purple kale is best for late sowings. Sow in cells (*see p.285*) or a seedbed (*p.283*). Transplant seedlings 12–30in (30–75cm) apart in 18–30in (45–75cm) rows, depending on the cultivar. Sow dwarf cultivars, 12–16in (30–40cm), in containers (*see p.286*). Multiblock sow for "baby" kales (*p.286*).

KOHLRABI

A cool-season crop, kohlrabi (*Brassica oleracea* Gongylodes Group) grows best at 64–77°F (18–25°C). Young plants bolt below 50°F (10°C). In milder climates, sow from spring to late summer; in hotter climates, sow in spring and autumn. Purple types are best for late sowings. Sow direct in rows (*see p.283*) 12in (30cm) apart, thinning seedlings to 10in (25cm) apart. In colder climates, sow under cover in spring in gentle heat and transplant seedlings when they are 2in (5cm) tall and protect with cloches or fleece (*see p.39*) if necessary. For baby vegetables, sow in multiblocks (*p.286*).

BOK CHOI

In spring to autumn, sow bok choi (*Brassica rapa* var. *chinensis*) direct (*see p.283*) or in cells (*see p.285*), to germinate at 59–68°F (15–20°C). Most cultivars tolerate cold down to 23°F (-5°C). Thin the seedlings to 4–18in (10–45cm) apart, depending on the cultivar. Choose bolt-resistant cultivars for spring sowings and cold-resistant ones for later sowings.

TRANSPLANTING BRASSICA SEEDLINGS

CONTROLLING WEEDS *A good method of controlling weeds around young brassica seedlings is to cover the plot with biodegradable brown paper. Cut slits at the required spacings and plant the seedlings through the slits.*

COLLARS FOR SEEDLINGS *To prevent cabbage root maggots from laying eggs at the bases of seedlings, cut 6in (15cm) squares of carpet padding. Make a slit into the center of each. Fit each collar so it lies flat at the base of the stem.*

BABY TURNIPS *Turnips are best harvested young. Sow the seeds in multiblocks for large numbers of small turnips (here white turnips). Harvest when the roots are the size of a golf ball, after 5–6 weeks. Make successive sowings every three weeks in the growing season.*

SPROUTING BROCCOLI

With a long growing season, sprouting broccoli (*Brassica oleracea* Italica Group) needs a fertile soil. Sow seeds in spring (*see chart above*) to harvest in the following spring. In milder climates, sow in late summer to autumn or winter. Transplant 3–4in (7–18cm) seedlings deep for stability (*see facing page*) and stake on exposed sites. Purple cultivars are more prolific and hardier, down to 10°F (-12°C), than green ones.

RUTABAGA

Rutabaga (*Brassica napus* Napobrassica Group) is the hardiest root crop and prefers light, low-nitrogen soil. Sow seeds outdoors at 50–59°F (10–15°C) from late spring to early summer, in rows 15in (38cm) apart (*see p.283*), thinning in stages to 9in (23cm) apart. As well as flea beetles (use dressed seeds), cabbage root maggot can be a problem in many areas: use collars (*see left*). Harvest in 26 weeks.

TURNIP

A temperate crop growing best at about 68°F (20°C), turnips (*Brassica rapa* Rapifera Group) tolerate light frosts. Sow seeds under cover in late winter to early spring for early crops, thinning to 4in (10cm) apart, then successively sow until early summer. Sow main crops outdoors in late summer and thin to 6in (15cm) apart. Harvest early autumn.

CAPSICUM SWEET PEPPERS, CHILI PEPPERS

Sweet peppers

SEEDS in spring

Sweet, or bell, peppers (*Capsicum annuum* Grossum Group) and the hotter chili peppers (Longum Group) are annual fruiting vegetables. Being tropical or subtropical, they require a minimum growing temperature of 70°F (21°C) and 70 percent humidity, but fewer fruits set at temperatures above 86°F (30°C). Chili peppers are more tolerant of heat.

Peppers are self-pollinating but are aided by insect pollinators. If grown in isolation, at a distance of about 500ft (150m) from other types, they should come fairly true from home-gathered seeds. In hybrid seedlings, the hot pepper gene is dominant, so a sweet pepper crossed with a hot pepper results in a seedling that is a little more fiery. Dry the ripe peppers to ensure the seeds are ripe before extracting them (*see right*). Store seeds in a cool, dry place.

If growing peppers outdoors, sow seeds in pots in midspring, transplant, and plant 18–20in (45–50cm) apart in early summer, or when warm enough. If growing peppers under cover, sow seeds in containers (*see p.285*) at 70°F (21°C) in early spring. Transplant the seedlings singly into 2½–3½in (6–9cm) pots when they have 2–4 leaves. At 3–4in (8–10cm), plant them 18–20in (45–50cm) apart in a greenhouse bed or in grow bags, or pot into 8in (20cm) pots. Harvest in 12–14 weeks. As they ripen, fruits change to red, yellow, or purple; some are best used green.

EXTRACTING PEPPER SEEDS

1 To extract seeds (here of chili peppers) remove shoots with ripe fruits that have no discoloration. Hang in a bright, airy place to dry, with trays underneath to catch any seeds.

2 After 3–5 weeks, the dried peppers will start to shrivel and the seeds will be fully ripe. Wear gloves to protect the skin from stinging chili juice; do not touch your face. Cut open each pepper lengthwise. Scrape out the seeds.

CHENOPODIUM GOOD KING HENRY

SEEDS from late spring to early summer
DIVISION in spring

Good King Henry (*Chenopodium bonus-henricus*) is a perennial leafy vegetable that crops for 12–20 years. It goes to seed quickly so is best grown in part shade to slow it down. Sow in rows 18in (45cm) apart (*see p.283*). Thin seedlings (*see p.285*) to 12–15in (30–38cm) apart. Pick flower shoots as early as possible.

To divide mature plants, dig up the roots. Take well-rooted clumps from the outside of the plant, which is usually more vigorous, and discard the old, woody crown. Replant the divisions 12in (30cm) apart in 18in (45cm) rows.

CICHORIUM CHICORY, ENDIVE, RADICCHIO

SEEDS from spring to midwinter

This genus includes the leafy vegetables chicory (*Cichorium intybus*) and endive (*C. endivia*). All are grown as annuals and prefer a fertile, free-draining soil that is low in nitrogen.

CHICORY AND BELGIAN ENDIVE

Sow chicory as for lettuce (*see p.303*). The sowing times depend on the type of chicory – sow Belgian types in spring or early summer for forcing; red types (radicchio) in early to midsummer; and sugar loaf types in summer. Sugar loaf cultivars will tolerate light frosts. Chicory takes 8–10 weeks to mature. Lift mature Belgian endive in autumn for forcing in pots.

ENDIVE

Endive is a cool-season crop, preferring a temperature of 50–68°F (10–20°C). It survives some cold, but hardier types, such as broad-leaved escaroles, will survive 14°F (-10°C). If sown early and exposed to temperatures below 41°F (5°C), endive is liable to bolt. Sow seeds as for lettuce (*see p.303*) from early summer onward to harvest in 7–13 weeks. Endive is a useful vegetable for intercropping with brassicas (*see pp.296–7*) and other long-term crops.

CURLY ENDIVE
Endives with curled leaves are less prone to bolt in hot weather than broad-leaved escaroles.

CITRULLUS WATERMELON

SEEDS from mid-spring to early summer

Watermelons (*Citrullus lanatus*) are tropical annuals that require growing temperatures of 77–86°F (25–30°C). They need fertile, sandy loam enriched with well-rotted manure and a general-purpose fertilizer.

In hotter climates, sow seeds direct, two per station (*see p.284*) and 3ft (90cm) apart. Thin later to the best seedling at each station. To assist the formation of fruits, transfer pollen from male to female flowers – female flowers have a swelling, the budding fruit, at the base. Harvest 11–14 weeks later.

In cooler climates, sow two seeds per 2½–3½in (6–9cm) pot (*see p.285*); they should germinate at 72–77°F (22–25°C). Select the best seedlings, thin to one per pot, then harden off (*see p.286*) when 4–6in (10–15cm) tall. Transplant into a sunny, sheltered spot after all danger of frost has passed, 3ft (90cm) apart. Plant each seedling on a slight mound and, if necessary, protect with fleece or a cloche (*see p.39*) until well established. Remove any covers at flowering time to reduce humidity and encourage pollination.

Watermelons do not cross with other cucurbits; seeds should come fairly true if parents are grown 1000ft (400m) from other cultivars. Collect the seeds as for melons (*see p.300*); they remain viable for up to five years.

COLOCASIA Cocoyam, Taro

DIVISION in spring
CUTTINGS in spring

Cocoyams (*Colocasia esculenta*, syn. *C. antiquorum*) are tropical perennials with edible tubers that require growing temperatures of 70–81°F (21–27°C) with humidity of over 75 percent. They need a rich, very moist soil with high nitrogen. Seeds are rarely available, so propagation is usually from existing tubers or cuttings. Large tubers may be cut into sections, provided each portion has a healthy dormant bud. In warmer climates, plant tubers or portions of tuber 18in (45cm) apart at 2–3 times their depth, with 3ft (90cm) between rows. In colder areas, root in 8–12in (20–30cm) pots of rooting medium in greenhouse beds or grow bags under cover; damp down regularly to keep humid. If conditions permit, transplant rooted tubers to a sheltered, sunny site.

Alternatively, force tubers into growth in late winter (*see below*) and take basal stem cuttings from the new shoots. Root the cuttings in the same conditions as for tubers. Harvest in 16–24 weeks.

TAKING BASAL STEM CUTTINGS OF COCOYAM

1 In late winter, two-thirds bury healthy tubers in a box of moist peat. Keep in a bright place at a minimum of 70°F (21°C) in 75 percent humidity until shoots appear.

2 When shoots are 4–5in (10–12cm) tall, cut out each one with a small piece of tuber at the base. Plant out 18in (45cm) apart in rows 3ft (90cm) apart at 70°F (21°C) or insert in 10in (25cm) pots.

CRAMBE Seakale

SEEDS in spring
CUTTINGS from late autumn to early winter

The stem vegetable (*Crambe maritima*) in this genus is a perennial. It needs a deep and rich, slightly acidic sandy soil. The seeds have corky coats that will inhibit germination; scrape off these coverings with your nails. Sow thinly in drills (*see* p.283) or outdoors in seed trays. Seeds germinate at 45–50°F (7–10°C) slowly and unevenly. Transplant 3–4in (8–10cm) tall seedlings.

Generally, root cuttings, or "thongs," are more successful (*see below*). Take them from healthy, three-year-old plants. Lift the parent plant without damaging the roots, then clean off the excess soil. To avoid inserting cuttings upside down, make a slanting cut at the bottom of each root. Overwinter them in a frost-free place before planting out in early spring. Harvest young stems in the second or third year. For a succession of crops, take cuttings every third year.

TAKING ROOT CUTTINGS OF SEAKALE

1 Select roots about the thickness of a pencil. Using a clean, sharp knife, make an angled cut at the bottom of each one. Remove these from the rootstock, cutting straight across near the top of the root. Discard the old crown.

2 Cut the roots into 3–6in (8–15cm) sections, cutting the top of each one with a straight cut and the base with an angled cut. Tie the cuttings into bundles of five or six with raffia or twine, matching up straight and angled ends.

3 Fill a 6–8in (15–20cm) deep box with 4–5in (10–13cm) of sharp sand. Insert the bundles angled ends down and not touching. Completely cover with more sand. Water and leave in a frost-free, shady place until spring.

OVERGROWN CUTTING

GOOD CUTTING

4 Carefully lift the cuttings when the buds are just beginning to break (see left) in early spring. If they are allowed to grow on (see far left), the buds will waste energy that is needed to produce roots.

5 With thumb and forefinger, rub off all but the strongest bud from the top of each cutting (see inset). Plant out the cuttings 15in (38cm) apart in a prepared bed so that the buds are 1in (2.5cm) below the surface.

CUCUMIS Cucumber, Melon

SEEDS in spring

Cucumbers and gherkins (*Cucumis sativus*) and melons (*C. melo*) are all tender, annual climbers grown for their fruit crops.

Cucumber and gherkin

These plants grow best at 64–86°F (18–30°C) and are damaged below 50°F (10°C). European or greenhouse cultivars that fruit without pollination need a nighttime minimum of 68°F (20°C). Soil should be moisture-retentive, free-draining, and high in nitrogen and organic matter. Seeds germinate at 68°F (20°C) and seedlings transplant badly, so direct-sow in warm climates. Sow each seed ¾in (2cm) deep on a mound to keep the roots warm and well-drained. Space climbing types 18in (45cm) apart and bush types 30in (75cm) apart.

In colder climates, sow seeds in pots or cells (*see above*) and plant outdoors when risk of frost has passed, or at the same spacings in beds under cover. Protect new plants from wind and cold (*see pp.38–39*). Harvest cucumbers 12 weeks after sowing; gherkins are ready when they are 3in (8cm) long.

Melon

The various types of melon need a fertile soil with a high organic and nitrogen content and a growing temperature of about 77°F (25°C). Sow the seeds as for cucumbers, but spaced 3ft (90cm) apart in rows 3–5ft (90cm–1.5m) apart. They usually germinate at 64°F (18°C). In colder climates, sow two seeds per 3in (8cm) pot and thin out the weaker seedling. Harvest in 12–20 weeks. Seeds can be gathered from healthy fruit.

SOWING CUCUMBER SEEDS

1 Sow seeds singly on their sides in 3in (8cm) pots, half filled with seed soil mix. Keep at 64–70°F (18–21°C). In seven days, when each seedling has grown above the pot rim, fill in with more mix, then water.

2 A few weeks after sowing, dig a hole 12in (30cm) deep and wide and fill with well-rotted manure. Cover with a mound about 6in (15cm) high of manured soil to help drainage; plant the seedling on top. Firm, label, and water.

EXTRACTING MELON SEEDS

1 Pick melons when ripe. Label and leave them in a cool, dry place until almost rotten to allow the seeds to continue ripening.

2 Scoop out the seeds into a sieve and rinse off the pulp under running water. If the pulp is left on the seeds, it will inhibit germination.

3 Spread out the seeds to dry on paper towels in a warm, airy place for 7–10 days. Store in a cool, dry place for spring sowing.

CUCURBITA Pumpkin, Squash, Zucchini

Zucchini flower

SEEDS from early to late spring

Cucurbits are all tender, annual, fruiting vegetables. They include summer squashes and zucchini, also called courgettes, (*Cucurbita pepo*), and winter squashes and pumpkins (*C. pepo, maxima, C. moschata*). They require the same soil as cucumbers (*see above*), but pumpkins and winter squashes prefer medium to high nitrogen levels.

Generally, cucurbits are raised from seeds in the same way as for cucumbers. Sow 2–3 seeds to a 2in (5cm) pot and thin to the sturdiest seedling before transplanting into mounded soil (*see above*). Or, in late spring, sow 2–3 seeds at stations (*see p.284*) at the spacings given in the chart (*see right*). Sow seeds about 1in (2.5cm) deep. Pumpkin seeds germinate more quickly if soaked overnight before sowing. Protect young plants from cold if necessary (*see pp.38–39*). Mulch after sowing or planting out to keep moist. Cucurbits are good for intercropping (*see p.285*) with tall crops such as corn.

Cucurbits will cross-pollinate with others of the same species. To keep the seeds true to type (*see right*), tie the ends of one female and several male flower buds the evening before they open, to prevent insect pollination. The next day, brush the stamens of the male flowers over the stigma of the female. Seal the female flower until it withers, then label the resulting fruit clearly. The seeds remain viable for 5–10 years.

Gathering pumpkin or squash seeds
Leave ripe pumpkins or squashes for at least three weeks in a sunny, airy place at about 70°F (21°C) to allow the seeds to mature. When a fruit starts to soften, cut it in half and flick out the seeds with a knife. If needed, wash off any flesh, then dry on paper towels before storing.

CYNARA CARDOON, GLOBE ARTICHOKE

Globe artichoke

SEEDS in early spring (cardoon)
DIVISION in spring (globe artichokes)

Cardoons (*Cynara cardunculus*), grown for their stems, and globe artichokes (*Cynara scolymus*), grown for the immature flowerheads, are perennials; they need an open site with fertile, moist soil, plenty of well-rotted manure or compost, and a growing temperature of 55–64°F (13–18°C).

CARDOON

Cardoons are best raised from seeds. Sow seeds singly under cover in pots (*see p.285*) in early spring to germinate at 50–59°F (10–15°C). If using home-gathered seeds (*see below left*), do not try to separate the seeds from the plumes before sowing them; just spread them over the soil mix. Transplant the seedlings when 10in (25cm) tall. Harden off (*see p.286*) in cold climates. Plant out in late spring 15in (38cm) apart in 18in (45cm) wide trenches. Space the rows 4ft (1.2m) apart to allow room to hill up the stems as they grow. Harvest the stems in the following year.

EXTRACTING CARDOON SEEDS

Hang the prickly flowerheads in a paper bag in a warm, dry place. When they are completely dry, crush them firmly, using a hammer. Pick out the plumes that bear the seeds. Store in a cool, dry place until spring. Sow with the plumes.

GLOBE ARTICHOKE

They are best divided because seeds do not come true to type and seedlings may be difficult to overwinter. There are two ways to divide an established plant.

If lettuce root aphid is a problem, taking offsets avoids transmitting them. Take rooted offsets (*see right*) from the edges of the plant because they are most vigorous, and leave the parent plant undisturbed. Replant the offsets to grow on, even those with little or no roots. Water them in if conditions are dry. In colder areas, protect offsets with fleece until they are established and with straw, mulch, or leaves in the first winter.

Established plants may also be lifted and divided like herbaceous perennials. Using a knife, two hand forks, or a spade, split the plant into 3–4 pieces, each with at least two strong shoots and some good roots. Discard the old, woody crown. Trim the leaves on the divisions to 5in (13cm) to reduce moisture loss and replant as for offsets in a well-prepared bed. Treat as offsets until established. The first flowerheads may be cut in late summer of the first year.

GLOBE ARTICHOKE OFFSETS

1 In spring, select a healthy sideshoot with 2–3 leaves and cut it away from the woody crown of the parent plant. Take care to preserve any roots. To avoid the risk of rot, trim off the old stalks to just above the young leaves.

2 Space the offsets at least 2ft (60cm) apart, with 30in (75cm) between rows. If the offset has few roots (see inset), bury the stem just deep enough to keep it upright. Water and label.

SOWING CUCURBITA SEEDS

GERMINATION TEMPERATURE	Summer squash and zucchini: 59°F (15°C) Pumpkins and winter squash: 68°F (20°C)
SPACING OF SEEDLINGS	Bush cultivars: 3ft (90cm) apart each way Trailing cultivars: 4–6ft (1.2–2m) Pumpkins and winter squash: 6–10ft (2–3m)
IDEAL GROWING TEMPERATURE	Summer squash and zucchini: 64–81°F (18–27°C) Pumpkins and winter squash: 64–86°F (18–30°C)
TIME UNTIL HARVEST	Summer squash and zucchini: 7–8 weeks or when about 4in (10cm) long Pumpkins and winter squash: 12–20 weeks

DAUCUS CARROT

Carrot

SEEDS from spring to late summer

Carrots (*Daucus carota*) are biennial root crops, grown as annuals on light, fertile, low-nitrogen soil. Begin to sow (*see pp.283–5*) when soil temperatures are above 45°F (7°C), under cover in colder areas. Sow seeds ½–¾in (1–2cm) deep, broadcast or in rows 6in (15cm) apart. Fluid-sow or use primed seeds for more even germination. Thin to 1½–3in (4–8cm), depending on the required size. Round-rooted carrots may be multiblock sown (*see p.286*). Protect the crop from carrot rust flies with a 3ft (90cm) fine mesh barrier or sow in early summer, after the flies are active. Carrots take 9–12 weeks to mature.

MULTIBLOCK CARROT SEEDLINGS
Plant out clumps of seedlings when they are 1in (2.5cm) tall. Using a planting board to measure accurately, plant clumps 9in (23cm) apart, in staggered rows 9in (23cm) apart.

FOENICULUM Florence fennel

Florence fennel

Seeds from spring to late summer

This annual vegetable (*Foeniculum vulgare* var. *dulce*) is fairly hardy and withstands light frost. It grows best in a fertile, low-nitrogen, moist soil at 50–61°F (10–16°C). The seeds germinate at about 59°F (15°C). Sow older cultivars after the longest day of the year in colder climates; otherwise, they will bolt. Florence fennel also bolts if checked or left to stand. Station-sow (*see p.284*) seeds 12in (30cm) apart each way and thin to single seedlings. Sow bolt-resistant cultivars in cells (*see p.285*) under cover in spring; harden off and plant out in early summer. In warm areas, sow direct in spring for summer crops, and in late summer for autumn crops. On light soils, lightly hill up to avoid wind-rock. Harvest after 15 weeks.

HELIANTHUS Jerusalem artichoke

Division in autumn

This perennial tuberous vegetable (*Helianthus tuberosus*) is very vigorous. It grows best in temperate climates in a range of soils, and it can become invasive if left in place.

Lift a plant in autumn to select healthy tubers. Overwinter them in a box of peat to prevent drying out. Divide large tubers (*see right*) and plant in spring as soon as the soil is workable. Choose the site carefully, since the plants can grow to 10ft (3m) tall. Water in very dry conditions.

Mature tubers may be lifted 16–20 weeks after planting as required: they do not store well and keep best in the soil.

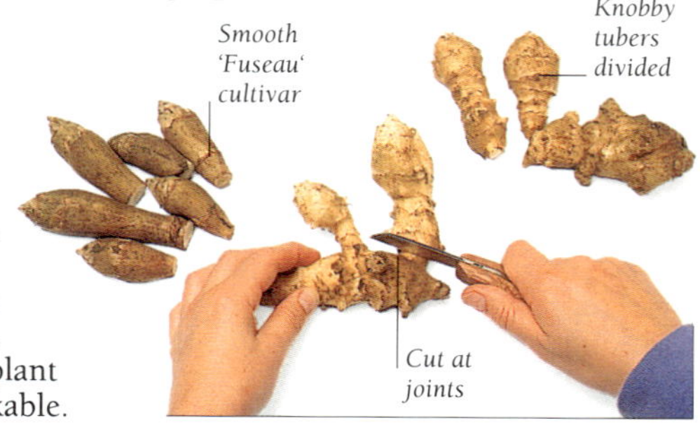

Dividing Jerusalem artichoke tubers
Seed tubers larger than a hen's egg may be cut into pieces, each with several buds (see above). *Smaller tubers may be planted whole. Plant the tubers, buds uppermost, 4–6in (10–15cm) deep, in rows 12in (30cm) apart. Label and water in.*

LABLAB Hyacinth bean

Hyacinth bean

Seeds in spring
Cuttings in spring

The hyacinth bean (*Lablab purpureus*) is a tender, short-lived tropical perennial, grown as an annual crop in climates with frost. It grows best at 64–86°F (18–30°C) with 70 percent humidity and tolerates most soils.

Seeds

In warmer climates, sow the seeds direct in rows (*see p.283*). Space climbing cultivars 12–18in (30–45cm) apart along rows 30–36in (75–100cm) apart; and dwarf types 12–16in (30–40cm) apart in rows 18–24in (45–60cm) apart. In colder regions, sow seeds under cover (*see p.285*) in 2–3½in (5–9cm) pots at 68°F (20°C) with 70 percent humidity. When the seedlings are 4–6in (10–15cm) tall, harden off and transplant as above in a sheltered sunny site, or 20–24in (50–60cm) apart in grow bags or a greenhouse bed. Start harvesting in 9 weeks.

Cuttings

Take 8–10in (20–25cm) softwood stem cuttings and root under mist as for sweet potatoes (*see below*). Treat rooted cuttings as seedlings (*see above*).

IPOMOEA Sweet potato

Seeds in spring
Tubers in spring
Cuttings in spring

The tropical sweet potato (*Ipomoea batatus*) is grown as an annual crop and needs a highly fertile, sandy soil with a high nitrogen level and a growing temperature of 75–79°F (24–26°C). In warm climates, it is best grown from tubers or cuttings; in cooler regions, seeds are the best option, but tuber yields are smaller.

Seeds

Sow seeds in 8–10in (20–25cm) pots to germinate at 75°F (24°C). In warm, humid climates, plant out seedlings when they are 4–6in (10–15cm) tall. In colder areas, grow on under cover at 77–82°F (25–28°C) with 70 percent humidity. Keep well ventilated. Harvest the tubers 20 weeks after sowing.

Tubers

Seed tubers must be "cured" before storing overwinter. Lift the tubers in autumn and allow to dry in the sun for 4–7 days at 82–86°F (28–30°C) and in humidity of 85–90 percent. Cover them at night if there is a risk of frost. They can then be stored in shallow trays at 50–59°F (10–15°C) for several months.

In warm, humid climates, plant seed tubers at the start of the rainy season. In colder climates, plant them in spring after frost. Make raised ridges 30in (75cm) apart, then insert tubers 2–3in (5–8cm) deep and 10–12in (25–30cm) apart. Protect from winds if needed. Harvest new tubers in 12–20 weeks.

Cuttings ("Slips")

Prepare stem cuttings as shown below. In warm, humid areas, insert to half their length in ridges as for tubers (*see left*). In colder areas, root them in pots of soilless rooting medium under cover in the same conditions as for seedlings (*see far left*). Transplant rooted cuttings into a greenhouse border or grow bags. Harvest tubers in 12–20 weeks.

TAKING SWEET POTATO STEM CUTTINGS

1 *Select young, healthy, vigorous shoots on a mature plant and cut them off just above a leaf joint. Place the shoots in a plastic bag to reduce moisture loss. Prepare the cuttings immediately: if they wilt, they will not root.*

2 *Remove lower leaves. Trim each shoot below a leaf joint. Insert three or four 8–10in (20–25cm) long cuttings to one 6in (15cm) pot.*

LACTUCA Lettuce

SEEDS at any time

Lettuce (*Lactuca sativa*) requires a growing temperature of 50–68°F (10–20°C) and rich, moisture-retentive soil. The seeds do not germinate above 77°F (25°C). Lettuces may be raised from seeds over a long period, but it is vital to choose a cultivar to suit the seasons of sowing and harvesting. Only some cultivars are suitable for warm climates; others tend to bolt at high temperatures in midsummer. Rotate crops every two years to avoid a build-up of fungal disease. Lettuces are good catch crops for intercropping (*see p.285*).

Sow seeds direct from early spring to early autumn at stations (*see p.284*) 12in (30cm) apart, or 6in (15cm) apart for small cultivars. Fluid-sow for more even germination (*see p.284*). Sowing in cells (*see p.285*) makes best use of space and avoids checks in growth when transplanting. For successive crops, sow a batch every 10–14 days. Transplant into moist soil when seedlings have 5–6 leaves, and shade in hot weather until established. Begin to pick looseleaf lettuces in seven weeks; butterhead, cos, and iceberg types in 11–12 weeks.

Hardy cultivars for overwintering outdoors can be sown direct or under cloches in late summer and early autumn to harvest in late spring to early summer; they can also be sown in mid- to late winter in cells under cover and planted out in early spring.

LEPIDIUM Cress

SEEDS in spring, late summer or in autumn

Cress (*Lepidium sativum*) is a cool-season annual crop that quickly goes to seed in hot weather if not sown in shade at 59–68°F (15–20°C). Sow (*see pp.283–4*) broadcast or in rows 6in (15cm) apart. Cress is good for intercropping (*see p.285*) and can be sown as for sprouts (*see p.296*) on paper towels for a crop in ten days.

MUSTARD AND CRESS
Sow cress seeds three days before an equal quantity of mustard (see p.297) seeds on moist paper towels. Keep moist until the seedlings are ready to harvest.

LYCOPERSICON Tomato

Tomato

SEEDS in spring
GRAFTING in spring

Perennial in the tropics, this tender fruiting vegetable (*Lycopersicon esculentum*) is grown as an annual crop in colder climates. They need a rich, moist soil, sun, and temperatures of 70–75°F (21–24°C). Apart from F1 hybrids, tomatoes come true to type, so it is worth saving seeds. Older cultivars that are prone to diseases such as Verticillium and tomato mosaic may be grafted to increase their resistance.

SEEDS

Seeds germinate at around 59°F (15°C). In hot climates, sow outdoors in rows 24in (60cm) apart (*see p.283*). Thin tall cultivars to 15–18in (38–45cm) apart; bush types to 18–24in (45–60cm). Seeds may also be fluid sown (*see p.284*). In most areas, sow under cover in cells or trays of soilless seed mix (*see p.285*) or rockwool. Transplant seedlings when 3in (8cm) tall, singly into 3½in (9cm) pots. Plant outdoors after frost, when nighttime temperatures remain above 45°F (7°C). Harvest from 7–8 weeks onward.

If saving seeds, allow the fruits to ripen just beyond the eating stage. Cut open and squeeze the pulp and seeds into a bowl. Label and leave undisturbed in a warm place for 2–3 days. A thick skin should form, and the gel that coats the seeds will ferment. After 3–4 days (no longer), scoop the skin off the top and rinse the seeds thoroughly in a sieve under running water. Spread out on paper towels to dry. Seeds can be stored in a cool, dry place for up to four years.

GRAFTING

Use virus-free F1 hybrids as rootstocks for grafting (*see below*). Stagger sowing seeds of the scion and stock if necessary, so that they germinate at the same time.

APPROACH GRAFTING TOMATO CULTIVARS

1 Sow the rootstock 4–5 days before the scion. Remove it from the pot when it is 6in (15cm) tall. Make a ¾in (2cm) downward cut, 3in (8cm) from the stem base. Make an upward cut of the same length on the scion (see inset).

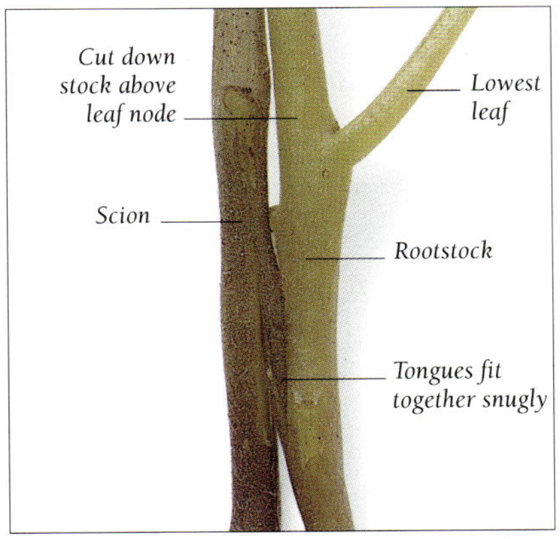

2 Fit the tongues of the scion and stock plant together. Bind the graft firmly with grafting or transparent adhesive tape, so that the cuts are completely covered. Cut down the stock, making an angled cut just above the lowest leaf.

3 Pot the grafted plant in a 4in (10cm) pot in soilless potting mix. Grow on in high humidity at a minimum of 59–64°F (15–18°C). After 2–3 weeks, the graft should callus over. Remove the tape carefully.

4 Knock the plant out of its pot. Carefully cut through the base of the scion, making an angled cut just below the graft union. Gently pull away the severed roots, then replant the grafted plant into its final position.

MESEMBRYANTHEMUM

ICEPLANT

Iceplant

SEEDS in early spring

This tender perennial (*Mesembryanthemum crystallinum*) is grown as an annual. It needs sun and light, free-draining soil. In colder areas, sow seeds indoors in trays or pots (*see p.285*) and transplant into cells when large enough to handle. Harden off and plant out 12in (30cm) apart in early summer, under cloches if needed. In warm regions, sow direct in rows 12in (30cm) apart, and thin seedlings to the same spacing. Harvest in four weeks.

OXALIS OCA

TUBERS in spring

These plants (*Oxalis tuberosa*) are tender perennials, growing best in 70 percent humidity at about 68–72°F (20–22°C). In hot climates, plant the seed tubers as for potatoes (*see p.307*), but 20in (50cm) apart. In colder climates, start the tubers into growth under cover in 8in (20cm) pots in early spring and transplant in late spring when shoots are 6in (15cm) tall. Keep the young plants warm under cloches or plastic film (*see p.39*). Harvest in 6–8 months; mature tubers will be smaller in colder areas.

PASTINACA PARSNIP

SEEDS in early or in late spring

Parsnips (*Pastinaca sativa*) are a cool-season annual crop and grow best in a deep, light soil. The seeds must be fresh to germinate; pregerminated or primed seeds (*see p.282*) germinate more evenly. Seeds germinate very slowly if soil temperature is below 45°F (12°C).

Sow seeds direct in early spring for crops in autumn to early winter, or sow in late spring for overwintering crops. Sowing in late spring avoids the first generation of carrot rust fly and gives tender roots. Sow in autumn and winter also in warm climates. Station-sow (*see p.284*) seeds ¾in (2cm) deep and 4in (10cm) apart, with 12in (30cm) between rows. If broadcast-sown in wide drills, thin to 3in (8cm) apart for smaller roots, 4in (10cm) for larger roots.

Parsnips may be intersown with a faster-maturing crop, such as radishes (*see facing page*). Sow three parsnip seeds at 4in (10cm) intervals and radish seeds between them spaced about 1in (2.5cm) apart. Parsnips should be ready to harvest from 16 weeks after sowing.

PHASEOLUS BEAN

Scarlet runner bean

SEEDS from spring to midsummer

These legumes or podded vegetables include the runner bean (*Phaseolus coccineus*), the green bean (*Phaseolus vulgaris*), and the Lima bean (*P. lunatus*). They are all temperate-season, tender crops grown as annuals. Very high temperatures with high humidity prevent the flowers from setting and therefore reduce the crop. Legumes are greedy feeders; a few months before sowing, prepare the soil with plenty of well-rotted compost to supply the deep roots. Cold and wet soil can cause seeds to fail to germinate or seedlings to emerge blind. To avoid this, sow in containers (*see p.285*) or pregerminate seeds (*see right*).

Beans may be collected for use as seeds (*see p.282*), except from F1 hybrids, when the pods turn yellow. When dwarf cultivars yellow, uproot an entire plant and hang to dry. Discard any shriveled seeds. Seeds last 3–4 years.

RUNNER BEAN

These beans need 100 frost-free days to mature and a sheltered site to encourage pollinating insects. Sow outdoors under a tepee or row of stakes, two seeds per stake, when the soil is warm enough (*see chart, below*). For early crops in cold areas, sow singly in cells or pots in midspring and transplant after all risk of frosts has passed.

PREGERMINATING GREEN BEANS
Spread the beans out on moist paper towels in a saucer and keep damp at a minimum temperature of 54°F (12°C). Sow the beans as soon as shoots appear, before they turn green.

GREEN, KIDNEY, OR HARICOT BEAN

These are self-pollinating and need a light, rich soil. Pregerminate the beans if necessary (*see above*). Sow climbing cultivars (pole beans) as for runner beans. Sow dwarf types in staggered rows. Successive sowings can be made up to midsummer (*see chart, below*).

LIMA OR BUTTER BEAN

These tropical plants prefer a sandy soil low in nitrogen. In subtropical or warm-temperate areas, grow in the open (*see chart, below*) in full sun, providing shade until the plants are established. In cooler climates, sow in pots as for *Lablab* (*see p.302*). Small-seeded cultivars will grow only after the start of summer, when daylight lasts less than 12 hours.

SOWING BEAN SEEDS

	RUNNER BEAN	GREEN, KIDNEY, OR HARICOT BEAN	LIMA OR BUTTER BEAN
WHEN TO SOW	Midspring to early summer	Midspring to midsummer	Spring
GERMINATION/ SOIL TEMPERATURE	54°F (12°C)	54°F (12°C)	64°F (18°C)
SPACING OF SEEDS OR SEEDLINGS	6in (15cm)	Climbing types: 2½–4in (6–10cm) Dwarf types: 9in (23cm)	Climbing types: 12–18in (30–45cm) Dwarf types: 12–16in (30–40cm)
SPACING OF ROWS	Double rows at 2ft (60cm)	Climbing types: double rows at 60cm (24in) Dwarf types: single rows at 9in (23cm)	Climbing types: 30–36in (75–100cm) Dwarf types: 18–24in (45–60cm)
SOWING DEPTH	2in (5cm)	1½–2in (4–5cm)	1in (2.5cm)
GROWING TEMPERATURE	57–84°F (14–29°C)	61–86°F (16–30°C)	64–86°F (18–30°C)
TIME UNTIL HARVEST	13–17 weeks	7–13 weeks	12–16 weeks

PISUM Pea, Snow pea, Sugar pea

Pea

SEEDS from spring to early summer or in autumn

Peas (*Pisum sativum*) are cool-season annual crops. They grow best at 55–64°F (13–18°C) in moisture-retentive, free-draining soil but suffer excessively in cold, wet, or dry soil. Dress the soil with potassium sulfate before sowing, and rotate the crops (*see p.282*).

Seeds need a soil temperature of 50°F (10°C) to germinate but stay dormant in high summer temperatures. Sow in succession every ten days, or sow more than one cultivar for staggered crops. Wrinkled seeds are hardiest so are best for autumn sowing. Before sowing, soak seeds overnight to aid germination. Sow two rows of seeds 2in (5cm) deep in a wide drill or broadcast in single drills (*p.283*). Sow snow or sugar peas also in deep beds, 2–3in (5–8cm) apart.

To protect seeds from mice, sow in guttering (*see right*); guard seeds against birds with netting (*see p.45*).

Peas may be harvested after 10–12 weeks. Seeds come true to type so are worth saving (*see p.282*). Choose strong plants and allow the pods to mature. The seeds are ripe when the peas rattle in the pod. They remain viable for three years.

SOWING PEA SEEDS IN GUTTERING

1 Take a length of plastic guttering that is 3½–6ft (1.1–2m) long. Fill with soilless seed mix up to ½in (1cm) from the rim. Sow pea seeds in a double row, about 2in (5cm) apart. Water them to settle the soil mix.

2 Cover the seeds up to the rim with more soil mix. Water again to settle the mix. Label. Leave in a sheltered place such as on a sunny windowsill to germinate. The temperature should be above 50°F (10°C).

3 When the seedlings are 3–4in (8–10cm) tall and their roots are well developed, they can be transplanted. Draw out a shallow trench to the same depth and length as the guttering, then gently push sections of the seedlings, no more than 18in (45cm) at a time, into the trench. Firm in.

RAPHANUS Radish

SEEDS in spring to late summer

Annual and biennial radishes (*Raphanus sativus*) are annual root crops. They prefer a light, rich soil with low nitrogen levels and should be rotated regularly. Large winter cultivars such as 'Black Spanish Winter' and the Oriental radishes tolerate cold. Each type is sown differently (*see chart, below*).

Seeds of small radishes are usually sown direct, in batches, at ten-day intervals. Broadcast-sow (*see p.284*) very thinly or sow in drills (*see p.283*). Small, round types may be used for intersowing (*see p.285*) with long-term crops such as parsnips. Most large winter or Oriental types bolt if sown before midsummer in colder climates. Selected cultivars of small, round types may be sown earlier or later than usual, under cover if necessary.

Dust seeds with an appropriate insecticide against cabbage root maggot and flea beetle and repeat as needed; flea beetle is a particular threat in dry weather. Radishes may be grown for seed crops. Summer radishes produce small, hot, edible seedpods.

DUSTING RADISH SEEDLINGS
Dust seedlings with an insecticide at the two-leaf stage to protect against flea beetle, or fertilize to keep foliage vigorous.

SOWING RADISH SEEDS

	SMALL, ROUND	SMALL, LONG	LARGE, WINTER	ORIENTAL (DAIKON)	SEED CROPS
SIZE OF RADISH	1in (2.5cm) diameter	3in (8cm) long	1lb (500g) or more in weight	2in (5cm) diameter; 8in (20cm) long	
WHEN TO SOW	Spring to late summer	Spring to late summer	Summer	Mid- to late summer	Spring to late summer
SPACING OF PLANTS	1in (2.5cm)	1in (2.5cm)	6in (15cm)	4in (10cm)	6in (15cm)
SPACING OF ROWS	6in (15cm)	6in (15cm)	12in (30cm)	12in (30cm)	12in (30cm)
SOWING DEPTH	½in (1cm)	½in (1cm)	¾in (2cm)	¾in (2cm)	½in (1cm)
TIME UNTIL HARVEST	Main crop: 3–4 weeks Early or late crops: 6–8 weeks	3–4 weeks	10–12 weeks	7–8 weeks	8–10 weeks, or when pods are crisp and green

RHEUM RHUBARB

SEEDS in spring
DIVISION from autumn to early spring

The edible rhubarb (*Rheum* x *hybridum*, syn. *R.* x *cultorum*) is a perennial. It does not thrive in high temperatures and needs soil enriched with well-rotted manure or compost and a period of winter cold to bring it out of dormancy. Seedlings vary, so rhubarb is best increased by division. A few stems may be harvested in the first year from divisions or in the second year from seedlings.

Sow seeds in a seedbed (*see p.283*), 1in (2.5cm) deep, 12in (30cm) apart. Thin to 6in (15cm) apart. In autumn or the following spring, transplant the best. Sow also in early summer in warm areas.

Divide crowns once they are 3–4 years old, preferably in late autumn. Take pieces of the rootstock, or "sets," at least 4in (10cm) in diameter (*see right*).

DIVIDING RHUBARB
Lift or expose the crown. Using a spade, cut through it carefully, ensuring there is at least one main bud on each piece. Replant into well-manured soil, 3ft (90cm) apart each way. Fill in around each root so that the bud is just above the surface. Firm around the bud, then mulch.

RORIPPA WATERCRESS

SEEDS in early autumn
CUTTINGS in spring

Rooted cuttings of this annual (*Rorippa nasturtium-aquaticum*, syn. *Nasturtium officinale*) may be grown in water (*see below*) or in trays of gravel watered daily. Sow seeds on 2in (5cm) of peat or capillary matting (*see right*); keep moist at 64–70°F (18–21°C) until germination, then circulate the water water daily with a pump or by hand. Harvest 4in (10cm) stems in 8–14 weeks.

SOWING WATERCRESS SEEDS

Stir pregerminated seeds into fresh wallpaper paste. Line a seed tray with moist capillary matting. Spread the paste. Cover with glass.

TAKING WATERCRESS CUTTINGS

1 Cut 2in (5cm) from the stems of healthy plants, cutting just below a leaf joint. Trim off lower leaves from the bottom two-thirds of each cutting. Place the cuttings in a jar filled with water. Allow to root in a bright place out of direct sunlight, at about 61°F (16°C) for a week or so.

2 When the cuttings have developed good root growth, drop them into a calm part of an unpolluted running stream to grow on.

SCORZONERA

SEEDS in spring or in late summer

Scozonera hispanica is a perennial usually grown as an annual. It needs a deep, light, fertile soil with low nitrogen levels. It grows best in temperatures of around 61°F (16°C).

Use fresh seeds, because they do not store well. Plants flower in the second year and produce seeds in daisylike heads. Seeds need a soil temperature of at least 45°F (7°C) to germinate. Sow in spring in 8in (20cm) rows (*see p.283*); thin to 4in (10cm) apart. Harvest roots after at least four months, in autumn. Alternatively, sow in late summer for a harvest in the following autumn.

SOLANUM

EGGPLANT, POTATO

Eggplant fruit and flower

SEEDS in spring (eggplant)
TUBERS in spring (potato)

This genus includes both the eggplant (*Solanum melongena*), grown for its fruit, and the tuberous potato (*S. tuberosum*). Both require a deep, free-draining, fertile soil.

EGGPLANT

These tender perennials are grown as annuals in cold climates. They grow best in soil with medium nitrogen and in temperatures of 77–86°F (25–30°C) and 75 percent humidity; growth is checked below 68°F (20°C). For the best rate of germination, soak seeds in warm water for 24 hours. Sow thinly in trays or pots (*see p.285*) and transplant into 3½in (9cm) pots as soon as the seedlings are large enough to handle. Harden off if needed (*see p.286*) and plant out when 3–4in (8–10cm) tall. In warm climates, plant in full sun 24–30in (60–75cm) apart each way, but protect from winds and low temperatures, which may stunt growth and cause bud drop.

In cold climates, transplant into beds under cover at the same spacing as above or into 8in (20cm) pots of soil-based mix or grow bags. To save seeds, leave the fruits until ready to drop off the plant, then hang up until the color dulls, to allow the seeds to ripen. Slice in half, pick out the seeds, and dry.

POTATO

These perennials are tender and grow best at 61–64°F (16–18°C). They need soil enriched with organic material;

SPROUTING SEED POTATOES

To sprout seed potatoes, place in a box or tray in a single layer, "eyes" uppermost. Store in a light, cool place until ¾in (2cm) green sprouts appear (usually six weeks). In a warm, dark place, the tubers produce pale, weak sprouts (see inset).

PLANTING SEED POTATOES

	FIRST EARLY CROP	SECOND EARLY CROP	MAIN CROP
WHEN TO PLANT	Early spring	Midspring	Late spring
SPACING OF TUBERS AND ROWS	12in (30cm) in rows 18in (45cm) apart	15in (38cm) in rows 27in (68cm) apart	15in (38cm) in rows 30in (75cm) apart
TIME UNTIL HARVEST	100–110 days	110–120 days	125–140 days

early crops prefer medium nitrogen levels, main crops need high nitrogen. Rotate crops (*see p.282*) to avoid buildup of soil-borne diseases: early crops are best rotated every three years and main crops every five years.

Use only certified virus-free seed tubers, which are grown free of aphids to avoid the spread of viruses. If growing potatoes for seed tubers, be sure to protect them from aphids.

In colder regions with a shorter growing season, seed potatoes are often sprouted under cover (*see facing page*) to start them into growth before planting. The more sprouts there are on a tuber, the higher the yield will be. For large early potatoes, rub off all but three sprouts. Discard any that look unhealthy.

If needed, cover earlies with fleece or plastic film (*see p.39*) to protect against light frosts. Plant main crop potatoes when the soil temperature is above 45°F (7°C) and all risk of frost is past. Potatoes may be intercropped (*see p.285*) with leafy brassicas or in a deep bed with peas or beans.

Seed tubers may be planted in various ways: in a trench, raised bed, or through black plastic to avoid the necessity to hill up the growing shoots (*see below*). If space is limited or conditions are unsuitable, early potatoes can also be grown in deep containers (*see below*) outdoors or in a warm greenhouse.

Problems that may affect the tubers include slugs, wireworms (*see p.47*), potato cyst nematodes, blight, ring rot, common potato scab, bacterial rot (destroy at once), internal rust spot, and potato spraing. Many cultivars are available with varying degrees of resistance to disease.

PLANTING SEED POTATOES IN A BED

IN A TRENCH *Using a spade, make a drill that is 3–6in (8–15cm) deep. Set the tubers in the drill at the correct spacing (see chart, above), with the sprouts uppermost. Cover and mound up slightly. Begin hilling up around the new shoots when they are about 6in (15cm) tall.*

ON A DEEP BED *Prepare a raised bed (see p.283). Lay the tubers on the soil, 4in (10cm) apart, noting their positions. Cover them with 6–8in (15–20cm) of well-rotted compost. Top with black plastic and weigh down. Make slits above each tuber for the shoots to grow through.*

UNDER BLACK PLASTIC *Prepare a nursery bed and cover it with black plastic, anchoring it by burying the edges. Make cross-shaped cuts in the plastic 12in (30cm) apart each way. Plant a seed tuber through each slit, 4–5in (10–12cm) deep, with its sprouted end uppermost.*

PLANTING SEED POTATOES IN A CONTAINER

1 *Fill a 12in (30cm) pot with soil-based potting mix or soil to one-third of its depth, and mix in a small handful of general-purpose fertilizer. Place a sprouted tuber in the center, with the sprouted end uppermost.*

2 *Cover the tuber with about 2in (5cm) more potting mix or soil, and grow on in a frost-free greenhouse. When the new shoots are 6in (15cm) tall, begin to hill them up in stages, half-burying the shoots each time.*

3 *When the shoots have been hilled up to the rim of the pot, water and allow to grow on. Knock out the pot to harvest the potatoes when the flowers open or when the top foliage begins to die back.*

SPINACIA Spinach

SEEDS from late winter to midsummer

Spinach (*Spinacia oleracia*) is an annual, leafy crop, growing best at 61–64°F (16–18°C). The seeds are difficult to germinate above 86°F (30°C). Sow them in drills (*see p.283*) at three-week intervals, ¾in (2cm) deep and 2in (5cm) apart, with 12in (30cm) between rows. Thin seedlings to 6in (15cm) for large plants. Use specially bred cultivars for summer sowing to avoid bolting. Give high levels of nitrogen and water. Begin harvesting in 6–8 weeks. Sow seeds of hardier cultivars in early autumn for cutting in early spring.

STACHYS Chinese artichoke

TUBERS in late winter

The tuberous vegetable, *Stachys affinis*, is a perennial. The tubers need a long growing season of 5–7 months, so plant early in the season. Collect large, fresh tubers and divide as for Jerusalem artichokes (*see p.302*). Plant the tubers upright in light soil, about 3in (8cm) deep and 12in (30cm) apart.

TETRAGONIA New Zealand spinach

SEEDS in mid- or in late spring

The seeds of this perennial (*Tetragonia tetragonioides*, syn. *T. expansa*) have very hard coats; soak overnight before sowing. Sow seeds in drills 18in (45cm) apart (*see p.283*) after all risk of frost is past; thin to 18in (45cm) apart. Sow in midspring in warm climates or under cover in cells (*see p.285*) to plant out in late spring or early summer. In warm climates, cuttings are possible.

TRAGOPOGON Salsify

Salsify flowers

SEEDS from early to late spring

Tragopogon porrifolius, also known as vegetable oyster plant, is a biennial grown as an annual root crop. The roots grow best in the same conditions and soil as scorzonera (*see p.306*). Raised beds are ideal. Always use fresh seeds; viability quickly declines. Sow seeds in drills (*see p.283*) 12in (30cm) apart, ½in (1cm) deep. Thin seedlings to 4in (10cm) apart. Roots mature in four months; they may be left longer in the soil until needed. Leave roots over winter for a spring crop of flower buds.

VICIA Broad or Fava bean

Broad beans

SEEDS in autumn, early spring, or late winter

Broad beans (*Vicia faba*) are an annual crop, growing best below 60°F (15°C). Some cultivars are quite hardy, tolerating 14°F (–10°C) on free-draining, well-manured soil. Broad beans require low nitrogen levels and should be rotated every three years.

Seeds germinate at low temperatures. Sow them in autumn or early spring (*see below*). In cold regions, sow seeds in containers (*see p.285*) under cover in late winter and transplant in spring. If needed, protect seedlings from frost (*see p.39*) and mice and birds (*see p.45*).

Harvest beans from early sowings in 12–16 weeks and from winter sowings in 28–35 weeks. If saving seeds, grow the parent plants in a block and save seeds from plants in the center to reduce variability. Hang up to dry (*see p.282*). Seeds stored in a cool, airtight place may last for up to ten years.

SOWING BROAD BEANS

Sow broad beans 4in (10cm) apart, in rows 6in (15cm) apart. Make 2in (5cm) deep holes, and drop a bean into each. Cover with soil, water in, and label.

ZEA Corn

Sweet corn cob

SEEDS in spring

Corn (*Zea mays*) is an annual that needs fertile, free-draining soil with medium nitrogen levels. It is important to grow only one type to avoid cross-pollination, which impairs the flavor, particularly of the supersweet types. Corn requires full sun and growing temperatures of 61–95°F (16–35°C) for 70–110 days to mature.

Seeds germinate at 50°F (10°C). Sow in an open site to assist pollination, which is by the wind. Pollination is also improved by growing the plants in blocks: station-sow 2–3 seeds (*see p.284*) at stations 14in (35cm) apart. Thin the seedlings to one per station.

BOTTLE CLOCHES FOR CORN

In colder climates, protect corn seedlings with bottle cloches. Cut the bottoms off the bottles. Place one over each seedling. Remove before the plants reach the tops of the bottles.

VIGNA Mung beans, Bean sprouts

SEEDS at any time

Presoak the seeds for 48 hours before sowing. They must be kept moist without being waterlogged, which leads to rot. One method is to sow them onto moist capillary matting, paper towels, or blotting paper as shown right. Keep the seeds at a temperature of 70°F (21°C). The sprouts should be ready to eat after 7–10 days. Alternatively, keep the beans in a jar (*see far right*) at the same temperature and soak two times a day by pouring water through the muslin, then draining off the water.

SOWING BEAN SPROUTS

Line a seed tray with damp paper towels. Sow thickly with presoaked seeds. Cover with plastic wrap to keep moist. Ventilate occasionally.

In cold regions, sow seeds of early cultivars in a sheltered site. Another option is to sow singly in cells under cover *(see p.285)*, but transplant the seedlings quickly, within two weeks, to avoid a check in growth.

Problems include corn rootworm, European corn borer, armyworm, cutworms, spotted cucumber beetle, asparagus beetles, and various smuts. Raccoons may tear down the entire plant to obtain the ears.

Corn may be grown as an intercrop *(see p.285)*, for example with squashes, as shown *(below, left)*. For baby ears, space early cultivars 6in (15cm) apart. If saving the seeds of open-pollinated heirloom cultivars, grow an isolated block of at least 100 plants for seeds that are true to type.

CORN PLANTED IN A BLOCK
Male and female flowers are borne on the same plant. The male flowers, produced in tassels at the top of the plant (see above) *release pollen when the wind blows. The pollen adheres to the silky strands of the female flowers* (see inset), *under which ears form. Sow corn in blocks to obtain a good rate of pollination and crop.*

SPROUTING BEANS IN A JAR

Soak beans in 1in (2.5cm) of cold water in a jar overnight (see inset). *Seal with muslin; drain off the water. Leave in a warm, dark place. Rinse twice daily until sprouted.*

OTHER VEGETABLES

AFRICAN OR INDIAN SPINACH *AMARANTHUS CRUENTUS* In colder areas, sow under cover in early summer or in cells at 72°F (22°C) and 70 percent humidity. Transplant 15–20in (38–50cm) apart; protect until established. In warmer climates, sow in drills 12in (30cm) apart; thin seedlings to 4–6in (10–15cm).

ARUGULA, SALAD ROCKET *ERUCA SATIVA* Sow seeds in succession from late winter to early summer at 46–50°F (8–10°C), then from late summer to midautumn. In colder areas, protect early and late sowings under cover.

ASPARAGUS PEA *LOTUS TETRAGONOLOBUS* (syn. *TETRAGONOLOBUS PURPUREUS*) Seeds in mid- to late spring at 50–59°F (10–15°C) in cells or 10in (25cm) apart in 15in (38cm) rows.

CAPE GOOSEBERRY, STRAWBERRY TOMATO *PHYSALIS PERUVIANA* Sow seeds as for tomato (*see p.303*); transplant under cover in colder climates to ensure ripe fruits.

CEYLON, INDIAN, OR VINE SPINACH *BASELLA ALBA* In warmer climates, sow seeds direct in spring at 77–86°F (25–30°C), 16–20in (40–50cm) apart. In colder climates, sow in trays or 2½in (6cm) pots; transplant seedlings into 8in (20cm) pots, grow bag, or indoor bed.

CHICK PEA, *CICER ARIETINUM* Sow three seeds at stations 10in (25cm) apart in late spring at 50–59°F (10–15°C); do not thin. Sow under cover if needed. Dry plants for seeds (*see p.282*) before first frost.

CHINESE BROCCOLI *BRASSICA RAPA* VAR. *ALBOGLABRA* Sow seeds direct or in cells in late spring to early autumn as for broccoli (*see p.296*); crops best from mid- to late summer sowings.

CHOP SUEY GREENS *CHRYSANTHEMUM CORONARIUM* Sow seeds thinly in rows 9in (23cm) apart at 50–59°F (10–15°C) from early spring to early summer. Bolts in heat; sow again in late summer to early autumn.

CORN SALAD, LAMB'S LETTUCE *VALERIANELLA LOCUSTA* Sow seeds in cells in late spring at 50–59°F (10–15°C) or direct, 15in (38cm) apart from mid- to late summer.

DANDELION *TARAXACUM OFFICINALE* Sow seeds in spring at 50–59°F (10–15°C) in rows 14in (35cm) apart; thin to 2in (5cm) apart.

EVENING PRIMROSE *OENOTHERA BIENNIS* Sow seeds thinly as for parsnip (*see p.304*).

GROUND CHERRY *PHYSALIS PRUINOSA* Sow seeds direct as for tomato (*see p.303*), but 4in (10cm) apart in rows 15in (38cm) apart.

HAMBURG PARSLEY *PETROSELINUM CRISPUM* VAR. *TUBEROSUM* Sow as for parsnip (*see p.304*).

HOT PEPPER *CAPSICUM FRUTESCENS* Sow seeds at 64–70°F (18–21°C) from early to midspring; transplant to 2ft (60cm) apart from late spring to early summer.

JICAMA *PACHYRHIZUS TUBEROSUS* Seeds in trays in spring at 59°F (15°C); transplant into pots; plant out in early summer. In warm areas, treat tubers as for potatoes (*p.307*).

LAND CRESS *BARBAREA VERNA* Sow seeds at 50–59°F (10–15°C) in mid- or late summer for autumn to spring crops; sow from midspring to early summer for summer crop (tends to bolt). Space rows 8in (20cm) apart; thin to 6in (15cm) apart.

MIZUNA GREENS *BRASSICA JUNCEA* VAR. *JAPONICA* Sow seeds in cells in late spring at 59°F (15°C) or direct; space 4in (10cm) apart for small heads, 18in (45cm) apart for large heads. Good intercrop (*see p.285*).

MUSTARD GREENS *BRASSICA JUNCEA* Sow seeds direct or in cells at 59°F (15°C) mid- to late summer for autumn or winter crop, in early autumn under cover for late winter to spring crop. Thin to 12in (30cm) apart.

PORTUGAL CABBAGE *BRASSICA OLERACEA* TRONCHUDA GROUP Sow in late spring at 50–59°F (10–15°C), 3–4 seeds at stations 2ft (60cm) apart in rows 30in (75cm) apart; thin to one per station.

RAMPION *CAMPANULA RAPUNCULUS* Sow fine seeds in early summer in sand along drills 9in (23cm) apart at 50–59°F (10–15°C); thin to 4in (10cm) apart.

SKIRRET *SIUM SISARUM* Sow seeds as for salsify (*see p.308*) in early spring or early autumn. Lift and divide tubers in early spring; replant 12in (30cm) apart.

SORREL *RUMEX SCUTATUS* Sow seeds in spring or autumn at 50°F (10°C), in cells or in rows 12in (30cm) apart; thin to 10–12in (25–30cm) apart. Self-sows readily.

SOYBEAN *GLYCINE MAX* Sow seeds in mid- to late spring at 54°F (12°C), 3in (8cm) apart in double rows 15in (38cm) apart. Space double rows 30in (75cm) apart. Long-term crop.

SUMMER PURSLANE *PORTULACA OLERACEA* Sow at 50–54°F (10–12°C) thinly in 6in (15cm) rows in summer. In colder areas, sow in trays, transplant into cells, plant out after frosts.

TEXEL GREENS *BRASSICA CARINATA* Sow direct at 50–59°F (10–15°C) every 2–3 weeks from early spring to early autumn, in rows 12in (30cm) apart; thin to 1in (2.5cm). For small leaves, broadcast-sow in wide drills (*p.283*); do not thin. Sow under cloches if needed.

TOMATILLO *PHYSALIS IXOCARPA* Sow seeds as for tomatoes (*p.303*).

WELSH ONION *ALLIUM FISTULOSUM* Seeds in spring or late summer in rows 9in (23cm) apart at 50–59°F (10–15°C); thin to 8in (20cm). Divide every 3–4 years as for chives (*see p.291*).

WINTER PURSLANE *MONTIA PERFOLIATA* Sow in spring or late summer and autumn at 50°F (10°C), in trays, broadcast or in 6–9in (15–23cm) rows.

ARUGULA

GLOSSARY

The glossary explains horticultural terms that occur in this book, as applicable to plant propagation. Fuller definitions may be found throughout the text.

ACIDIC (of soil) With a pH value below 7.
ADVENTITIOUS BUD Latent or dormant bud on the stem or root, often invisible until stimulated into growth.
AERATION Opening up of soil/soil mix structure to allow free circulation of air.
ALKALINE (of soil) With a pH value above 7.
ANGIOSPERM Flowering plant that bears ovules, later seeds, enclosed in ovaries (*see also* Gymnosperm).
APOMIXIS (*adj.* apomictic) Asexual production of ripe seeds. Offspring are *clones*, genetically identical to parent.
AUXIN Synthetic or naturally occurring substances in plants controlling shoot growth, root formation, and other physiological processes.
AXILLARY BUD Bud borne in the angle between a leaf and a stem, between a main stem and a sideshoot, or between a stem and a bract.
BISEXUAL (hermaphrodite) Refers to flower that bears male and female reproductive organs.
BLEEDING The oozing of sap through a cut or wound.
BREAK To produce new growth, often when a shoot emerges from a bud.
CALLUS Protective tissue formed by the *cambium* to aid healing around a wound, particularly in woody plants.
CAMBIUM Layer of growth tissue capable of producing new cells to increase the girth and length of stems and roots.
CAPPING A crust forming on the surface of soil or soil mix caused by heavy rain or watering or by compaction.
CHITIN An extract from crustacean and insect exoskeletons, used in soil mixes.
CHLOROPHYLL Green pigment that enables plants to capture energy from sunlight and so manufacture food (*see also* Photosynthesis).
CHROMOSOME String of genes contained within a cell nucleus, responsible for transmitting hereditary characteristics.
CLEISTOGAMIC Type of self-pollinating, often insignificant, flower that remains closed.
CLONE A genetically identical group of plants derived from one individual by vegetative propagation or *apomixis*.
COTYLEDON (Seed leaf) First leaf or pair of leaves produced by a seed, frequently different from the true leaves.
CROSS To interbreed (*see also* Hybrid).
CROWN 1.Upper part of rootstock from which shoots arise, at or just below soil level. 2.Branched part of tree above the trunk. 3.Entire rootstock, as in asparagus and rhubarb.
DICOTYLEDON *Angiosperm* with two seed leaves, net-veined leaves, often a cambium layer, and floral parts in fours or fives (*see also* Monocotyledon).
DIOECIOUS With male and female flowers on separate plants; both male and female plants are needed for fruits.
DORMANCY (*adj.* dormant) Temporary cessation of growth, and slowing down of other functions, in plants in unfavorable conditions.
DRILL Narrow, straight furrow in the soil, in which seeds are sown.
EPICORMIC SHOOTS Shoots that develop from latent or *adventitious buds* under the bark of a tree or shrub, usually close to pruning cuts or wounds.
ETIOLATED Describes a plant that has unusually elongated, often pale, shoots as a result of low light levels.
EXTENSION GROWTH New growth made during one season.
EYE 1.A *dormant* or latent growth bud that is visible at a node. 2.The center of a flower.
GREX Collective term applied to all the progeny of an artificial cross from known parents of different *taxa*. Mainly used for orchids and rhododendrons.
GYMNOSPERM Tree or shrub, usually evergreen, that bears naked seeds in cones rather than enclosed in ovaries, such as conifers (*see also* Angiosperm).
HEAD BACK To cut back the main branches of a tree or shrub by at least one half of their length.
HYBRID The offspring of genetically different parents, usually of distinct species (interspecific hybrid). F1 hybrids are uniform, vigorous offspring, resulting from crossing two genetically pure parents.
INFLORESCENCE A group of flowers borne on a single axis (stem).
INTERGENERIC HYBRID *Hybrid* from two different, but usually closely related, genera.
LATEX Milky white *sap* or fluid that bleeds from some plants when stem is cut or wounded; may be irritant.
LINE OUT To insert cuttings or to transplant seedlings or new plants in rows in a nursery bed.
MAIDEN A tree in its first year.
MERISTEM Tip of a shoot or root in which cells divide to produce leaf, flower, stem, or root tissue; may be used in micropropagation.
MONOCARPIC Refers to plants that flower and produce seeds once, then die.
MONOCOTYLEDON *Angiosperm* with a single seed leaf, parallel-veined leaves, no cambium layer, and floral parts usually in threes (*see also* Dicotyledon).
MONOECIOUS With separate male and female flowers on the same plant.
MONOPODIAL With a stem or rhizome growing indefinitely from a terminal bud, not usually forming sideshoots.
MOTHER PLANT *See* Parent plant.
NODE Point on a stem or root, often swollen, from which shoots, leaves, leaf buds, or flowers arise.
PARENT PLANT Plant that provides seeds or vegetative material for propagation.
PETIOLE Leaf stalk, connecting the leaf to a stem or branch.
pH Measure of acidity or alkalinity, used for soils or soil mixes (*see* Acidic, Alkaline). Neutral soil has a pH of 7.
PHLOEM Part of tissue within the stem that transports nutrients around the plant (*see also* Vascular bundle).
PHOTOSYNTHESIS Complex series of chemical reactions in green plants and some bacteria, in which energy from sunlight is absorbed by *chlorophyll* and carbon dioxide and water are converted into sugars and oxygen.
PITH (of stems) The soft plant tissue at the center of a stem.
SAP Plant fluid contained in the cells and *vascular bundle*.
SELF-FERTILE Refers to a plant that produces viable seeds when fertilized with its own pollen.
SELF-STERILE Refers to a plant that needs pollen from another individual of the species, but not a *clone*, to produce viable seeds.
SPORT (mutation) Natural or induced genetic change, often evident as a flower or shoot of a different color from the *parent plant*.
STIPULE Leaflike or bractlike structure borne, usually in pairs, at the point where a *petiole* arises from a stem.
STOCK PLANT A plant used to produce propagation material, whether seeds or vegetative material.
SYMPODIAL Form of growth in which the terminal bud dies or ends in an *inflorescence*, and growth continues from the lateral buds.
TAXON (pl. TAXA) A group of living organisms, applied to groups of plants that share distinct, defined characters.
TRANSPIRATION Evaporation of water from the leaves and stems of plants.
TURGID Refers to a plant when its cells are fully charged with water.
XYLEM Woody tissue in plants that transports water and supports the stem.
VASCULAR BUNDLE Conductive tissue, including the *cambium*, *phloem*, and *xylem*, that enables sap to pass around the plant.

INDEX

Page numbers in *italics* refer to illustrations

C

T

ACKNOWLEDGMENTS

ADDITIONAL EDITORIAL ASSISTANCE
Louise Abbott, Claire Calman, Alison Copland, Nigel Rowlands, Alexa Stace; thanks also to Polly Boyd, Candida Frith-Macdonald, Linden Hawthorne, Anna Hayman, Irene Lyford, Lesley Malkin, Andrew Mikolajski, Geoff Stebbins, Sarah Wilde

ADDITIONAL DESIGN ASSISTANCE
Ursula Dawson

PICTURE RESEARCH
Angela Anderson

JACKET DESIGN
Nathalie Godwin

INDEX
Dorothy Frame

PHOTOGRAPHY
Peter Anderson

ADDITIONAL PHOTOGRAPHY
Andy Crawford and Tim Sandall

The publishers would also like to thank the following for their kind permission to reproduce their photographs: AKG photo 12t; Peter Anderson 230; Heather Angel: 260cl; A-Z Botanical Collection Ltd: Matt Johnston 10bl, Lino Pastorelli 11tl, Pallava Bagla 16bl; The Bridgeman Art Library: Giraudon, Valley of the Nobles, Thebes 12b; British Museum 13tl; Bruce Colman Limited: Dr Eckart Pott 10br; John Cullum, Writtle College: 15 cl & c; Environmental Images: Pete Fryer 45cr; Mary Evans Picture Library 13b; Mike Harridge 173tl; The Garden Picture Library: Vaughan Fleming 46c, Michael Howes 46bl; David A. Hastilow: 13tr; Holt Studios International: Nigel Cattlin 15tcl, 15tr, 46cr, Bob Gibbons 308cr; Andrew Lawson: 146, 204br; John Mattock 115cr & inset; NHPA: Laurie Campbell 20cl, R. Sorensen & J. Olsen 36t; Clive Nichols 214; Oxford Scientific Films: Kathie Atkinson 20t, C. Prescott-Allen 279tc, Merlin D. Tuttle 16bc; Sue Phillips 173tc; David Ridgway 10tr; RHS Wisley: A. J. Halstead 46br, 71br; Science Photo Library: Claude Nuridsany & Marie Perennou 178bl, Philippe Plailly 14tr; Sinclair Stammers 15tl, 15br; Rosenfeld Images Ltd 15tcr; Harry Smith Collection: 19cl, 46cl, 225c, 261cr, 270c; H. D. Tindall 299 tr; Two Wests & Elliott: 44bc & br; Woodfall Wild Images: John Robinson 19t

PROPS AND LOCATION PHOTOGRAPHY
Seeds from Chiltern Seeds; Colegrave Seeds; Mr Fothergill's Seeds; Unwins Seeds. Pruners by Felco; other tools by kind permission of Spear & Jackson. Other items courtesy of Ron Ansell; Rupert Bowlby; Erin Gardena; Matthew Greenfield, Growth Technology, Taunton; John McLaughlan Horticulture; Neill Tools Ltd; Christopher Pietrzak; Two Wests & Elliott; Windrush Mill

Thanks to Brian and Janet Arm of Redleaf Nursery, Martin Gibbons at the Palm Centre, Terry Hewitt of Holly Gate Cactus Nursery and R. Harkness & Co. Ltd for providing plants and locations for photography

PHOTOGRAPHIC MODELS
Principal model: Clare Shedden
Thanks also to: Peter Anderson, Jim Arbury, Bernard Boardman, Rosminah Brown, David Cooke, Charles Day, Jim England, Claire Gosling, David Hide, Steve Josland, Rod Leeds, John Mattock, Greg Mullins, Nigel Rothwell, Cecilia Whitefield, Robert Woodman

DK Publishing would also like to thank:
In the United States, Miles Anderson of Miles' To Go, Tucson; in Australia, Frances Hutchison for much invaluable advice; in the UK, Bill Heritage for advice on water garden plants; Dr. Roger Turner of the British Society of Plant Breeders Ltd; Rosminah Brown, Greg Mullins, Greg Redwood and Nigel Rothwell at the Royal Botanic Gardens, Kew

All the staff of the Royal Horticultural Society for their time and assistance, in particular:
At Vincent Square, Susanne Mitchell, Barbara Haynes and Karen Wilson
At Wisley, Jim Gardiner, David Hide and Jim England for making the photography possible and for their invaluable guidance; Jim Arbury, Marion Cox, Alan Robinson for expert advice; and the ever-patient staff in the garden, in Glass, Propagation and the Plant Centre, including John Batty, Bernard Boardman, Andy Collins, Graham Cuerden, Charles Day, Sally Ann Edge, Anne Eve, Claire Gosling, Andrew Hart, Richard Head, Lucinda Lachelin, Rupert Lambert, Jon-Paul Nicholson, Ashley Ramsbottom, Gill Skilton, Annie Ward and Sam Veal

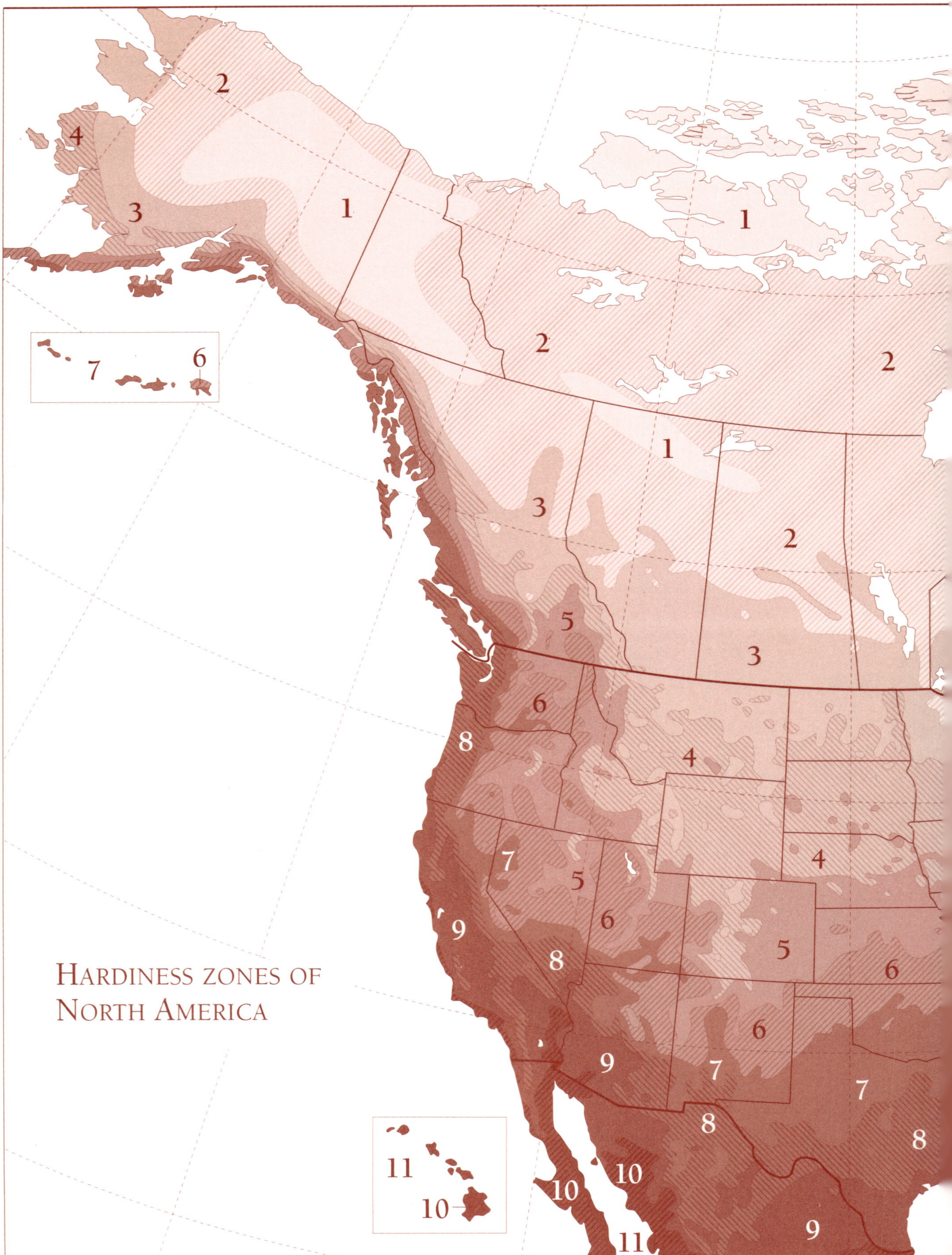
HARDINESS ZONES OF
NORTH AMERICA
1
2
3
4
5
6
7
8
9
10
11